[2.1]	x^n	the nth power of x, or x
	$P(x)$, $D(y)$, etc.	P of x, D of y, etc.
[2.8]	$a^{1/n}$	the nth real root of a for $a \in R$, or the positive one if there are two
[2.9]	$\sqrt[n]{a}$	the nth real root of a for $a \in R$, or the positive one if there are two
[4.1]	(x, y)	the ordered pair of numbers whose first component is x and whose second component is y
	$A \times B$	the Cartesian product of A and B
	$R \times R$, or R^2	the Cartesian product of R and R
[4.2]	f, g, h, F, etc.	names of functions
	$f(x)$	f of x, or value of f at x
	f^{-1}	the inverse function of f
[4.3]	d	distance between two points
	m	the slope of a line
[4.7]	(x, y, z)	the ordered triple of numbers whose first component is x, second component is y, and third component is z
	$(R \times R) \times R$, or R^3	the Cartesian product of $(R \times R)$ and R
[6.2]	$\log_b x$	the logarithm to the base b of x
[6.3]	$\text{antilog}_b x$	the antilogarithm to the base of b of x
[6.4]	e	an irrational number, approximately equal to 2.7182818
[7.1]	$\cos x$	element in the range of the cosine function
	$\sin x$	element in the range of the sine function
[7.2]	$\bar{s}$ or $\bar{x}$	length of reference arc corresponding to arc of length s or x
[7.6]	$\tan x$	element in the range of the tangent function
	$\sec x$	element in the range of the secant function
	$\csc x$	element in the range of the cosecant function
	$\cot x$	element in the range of the cotangent function

(continued inside back cover)

MODERN COLLEGE ALGEBRA
AND TRIGONOMETRY

EDWIN F. BECKENBACH

University of California, Los Angeles

IRVING DROOYAN

Los Angeles Pierce College

Wadsworth Publishing Company, Inc.

Belmont, California

MODERN COLLEGE ALGEBRA AND TRIGONOMETRY

Modern College Algebra and Trigonometry by
Beckenbach and Drooyan

L. C. Cat. Card No.: 67-25821

Printed in the United States of America

THIRD PRINTING: JULY 1969

PREFACE

This book is a modified revision of the authors' *Integrated College Algebra and Trigonometry*. It is designed for students who have completed from one and one-half to two years of high school algebra and a course in high school geometry, or equivalent courses offered at the college level, but who require additional preparation in mathematics prior to undertaking the study of calculus or courses in a field such as business. For those students who, for some extended period of time, have not taken a mathematics course, or for those students who are weak in fundamental skills, an extensive amount of review of such skills is provided in early chapters of this text.

The topics covered in this book as well as the spirit in which they are presented reflect the recommendations of various mathematics curriculum study groups. In particular, all of those topics recommended by the Committee on the Undergraduate Program of the Mathematical Association of America for the Level 0 Course are covered herein. The organization of the material permits considerable flexibility in the kind of course for which the book can be used. Specific suggestions in this regard appear in the Teachers' Manual, available from the publisher.

Structure plays a heavy role in the development, and is used to advantage in introducing matrices, complex numbers, and vectors. Beginning with the set of real numbers in Chapter 1, the student learns that this set constitutes a complete ordered field. In Chapter 10, on matrices, he is introduced to the notion of a vector space. Fields and vector spaces appear again in Chapter 12, on complex numbers and vectors.

Chapters following Chapter 3 center around the function concept. Starting with constant, linear, and quadratic algebraic functions in Chapter 4, the study of the properties of various kinds of functions proceeds through polynomial, rational, exponential, and logarithmic functions, with heavy emphasis given to sketching graphs of these functions. The traditional topics of plane analytic geometry are covered in Chapters 4, 5, and 6 in sufficient depth that students who have successfully used this text can proceed directly to the study of calculus. The periodic circular and trigonometric functions become an integral part of the presentation, starting with Chapter 7. Chapters 7, 8, and 9 are concerned entirely with circular and trigonometric functions. Chapter 11, on linear systems, includes a section on transformations of the plane; Chapter 12, on complex numbers, includes sections on the trigonometric form for a complex number and De Moivre's theorem.

Chapters 10 through 14 are essentially independent of each other, and any or all may be omitted for a briefer course. Furthermore, some of the problems occurring at the ends of various exercise sets throughout the book ask for proofs omitted from the text. Assignment or nonassignment of these problems can be used to offer courses of varying degrees of rigor.

The functional use of a second color in the text makes it possible to highlight key procedures in routine manipulations; it also permits stress to be laid on basic concepts. Color is used in graphs to focus attention on the parts of the figure under discussion. Marginal annotations direct the reader's attention to important ideas. Exercises are provided in each section, and the answers to the odd-numbered problems, including graphs, are given at the end of the book. A solutions manual, with detailed solutions of all problems, is available to the instructor.

The authors wish to express their appreciation to Professor William Wooton, our co-author in *Essentials of College Algebra*, for his permission to use material from that text. We would also like to thank Professors Don E. Edmonson of the University of Texas, Frank Gentry of the University of New Mexico, Robert Herrera of Los Angeles City College, James Jackson of the College of San Mateo, Gerald Rogers of the University of Arizona, and Robert J. Wisner of New Mexico State University for their helpful suggestions during the preparation of other manuscripts from which this text was developed. Our special thanks go to Professor Jackson and to Professor Tyrus Buquoi of Los Angeles Pierce College for assistance in the preparation of the present text. We also express our appreciation to Mrs. Doris Wooton and Mrs. Gertrude Drooyan for typing the manuscript and to Mrs. Alice Beckenbach for critically reading it.

Edwin F. Beckenbach
Irving Drooyan

CONTENTS

5 POLYNOMIAL AND RATIONAL FUNCTIONS

6 EXPONENTIAL AND LOGARITHMIC FUNCTIONS

7 CIRCULAR FUNCTIONS

8 TRIGONOMETRIC FUNCTIONS

9 INVERSE FUNCTIONS AND CONDITIONAL EQUATIONS

10 MATRICES AND DETERMINANTS

11 LINEAR SYSTEMS

12 COMPLEX NUMBERS AND VECTORS

13 SEQUENCES AND SERIES

14 PROBABILITY

APPENDIX

1 PROPERTIES OF REAL NUMBERS

1.1 DEFINITIONS AND SYMBOLS

A **set** is simply a collection of some kind. It may be a collection of people, colors, numbers, or anything else. In algebra, we are interested in sets of numbers of various sorts and in their relations to sets of points or lines in a plane or in space. Any one of the collection of things in a set is called a **member** or **element** of the set, and is said to be **contained in** or **included in** (or, sometimes, just **in**) the set. For example, the counting numbers 1, 2, 3, $\cdots$ (where the ellipsis, $\cdots$; indicate that the sequence continues indefinitely) are the elements of the set we call the set of **natural numbers.**

Sets are usually designated by means of capital letters, A, B, C, etc. They are identified by means of **braces** { }, with the members either listed or described.

Set notation For example, the elements might be listed as in {1, 2, 3}, or described as in {first three natural numbers}. The expression "{1, 2, 3}" is read "the set whose elements are one, two, and three"; "{first three natural numbers}" is read "the set whose elements are the first three natural numbers."

Using the undefined notion of set membership, we can be more specific about some other terms we shall be using.

DEFINITION 1.1 *Two sets A and B are **equal**, A = B, if and only if they have the same members—that is, if and only if every member of each is a member of the other.*

Thus, if A denotes {1, 2, 3}, B denotes {3, 2, 1}, C denotes {2, 3, 4}, and D denotes {natural numbers between 1 and 5}, then $A = B$ and $C = D$. The phrase "if and only if" used in this definition is simply the mathematician's

"If and only if" way of making two statements at once. Definition 1.1 means: "Two sets are equal if they have the same members. Two sets are equal only if they have the same members." The second of these statements is logically equivalent to: "Two sets have the same members if they are equal."

DEFINITION 1.2 *If the elements of a set A can be paired with the elements of a set B in such fashion that each element of A is paired with one and only one element of B, and conversely, then such a pairing is called a* **one-to-one correspondence** *between A and B.*

For example, if $A = \{a, b, c\}$ and $B = \{1, 2, 3\}$, then the sets A and B can be put into one-to-one correspondence in six different ways, two of which are shown:

$$\{a, b, c\} \qquad \{a, b, c\}$$
$$\updownarrow \updownarrow \updownarrow \qquad \updownarrow \updownarrow \updownarrow$$
$$\{1, 2, 3\} \qquad \{2, 1, 3\}$$

DEFINITION 1.3 *Two sets are* **equivalent** *if and only if a one-to-one correspondence exists between them.*

The symbol $\sim$ is used to denote equivalence. Thus, $A \sim B$ is read "A is equivalent to B." Intuitively, equivalent sets are sets that contain the same number of members. Clearly, if two sets are equal, they are equivalent, but the converse is not necessarily true—equality of sets requires that the members be identical, not merely that the sets be in one-to-one correspondence.

| Equivalence symbol |

DEFINITION 1.4 *If every member of a set A is a member of a set B, then A is a* **subset** *of B. If, in addition, B contains at least one member not in A, then A is a* **proper subset** *of B.*

| Subset symbols |

The symbol $\subseteq$ (read "is a subset of" or "is contained in") will be used to denote the subset relationship, and the symbol $\subset$ (read "is a proper subset of" or "is properly contained in") will be used for proper subsets Thus

$$\{1, 2, 3\} \subseteq \{1, 2, 3, 4\}$$

and

$$\{1, 2, 3\} \subseteq \{1, 2, 3\}$$

both make valid usage of $\subseteq$, but $\subset$ is valid only for the first of these pairs of sets. That is, we have

$$\{1, 2, 3\} \subset \{1, 2, 3, 4\} \quad \text{but not} \quad \{1, 2, 3\} \subset \{1, 2, 3\}.$$

Of course, by definition, every set is a subset of itself.

The set that contains no elements is called the **empty set** or **null set**, and is denoted by the symbol $\varnothing$ (read "the empty set" or "the null set"); $\varnothing$ is a subset of every set, and is a proper subset of every set except itself. If a set S is the null set or is equivalent to the set $\{1, 2, 3, \cdots, n\}$ for some fixed natural number n, then S is said to be **finite**. A set that is not finite is called an **infinite set**. For example, the set of *all* natural numbers, $\{1, 2, 3, \cdots\}$, is an infinite set.

DEFINITION 1.5 *Two sets A and B are* **disjoint** *if and only if A and B contain no member in common.*

For example, if $A = \{1, 2, 3\}$ and $B = \{5, 6, 7\}$, then A and B are disjoint.

| Set-member-ship notation | The symbol $\in$ (read "is a member of" or "is an element of") is used to denote membership in a set. Thus, |

$$2 \in \{1, 2, 3\}.$$

Note that we write

$$\{2\} \subset \{1, 2, 3\} \quad \text{and} \quad 2 \in \{1, 2, 3\},$$

but not

$$\{2\} \in \{1, 2, 3\} \quad \text{or} \quad 2 \subset \{1, 2, 3\},$$

since $\{2\}$ is a *subset*, whereas 2 is an *element*, of $\{1, 2, 3\}$.

When discussing an individual but unspecified element of a set containing more than one member, we usually denote the element by a lower-case italic letter (for example, a, d, s, x), or sometimes by a letter from the Greek alphabet: α (alpha), β (beta), γ (gamma), and so on. When symbols are used in this way, they are called **variables**.

DEFINITION 1.6 *A* **variable** *is a symbol representing an unspecified element of a given set containing more than one element.*

If the given set, called the **replacement set** of the variable, is a set of numbers, then the variable represents a number. Thus

$$x \in A$$

means that the variable x represents an (unspecified) element of the set A.

A symbol used to denote the member of a set containing only one member is called a **constant**.

When discussing sets, it is often helpful to have in mind some general set from which the elements of all of the sets under consideration are drawn. For example, if we wish to talk about sets of college students, we may want to consider all college students in this country, or all students in general; or, taking a larger view, we may want to consider students as a special kind of human being—say, all those human beings who are consciously striving to increase their knowledge. Thus, we can draw sets of college students from any one of a number of different general sets. Such a general set is called the **universe of discourse** or the **universal set**, and we shall usually denote it by the capital letter U. It follows that any set in a particular discussion is a subset of U for that discussion.

| Negation symbol | The slant bar, /, drawn through certain symbols for relations, is used to indicate negation. Thus $\neq$ is read "is not equal to," $\not\subset$ is read "is not a subset of," and $\notin$ is read "is not an element of." For example, |

$$\{1, 2\} \neq \{1, 2, 3\}, \quad \{1, 2, 3\} \not\subset \{1, 2\}, \quad 3 \notin \{1, 2\}.$$

Another symbolism useful in discussing sets is illustrated by

$$\{x \mid x \in A \quad \text{and} \quad x \notin B\}$$

(read "the set of all x such that x is a member of A and is not a member of B"). This symbolism, called **set-builder notation**, will be used extensively in this book. What it does is to specify a variable (in this case, x) and, at the same time, to state a condition on the variable (in this case, that x is contained in the set A and is not contained in the set B).

EXERCISE 1.1

Designate each of the following sets by using braces and listing the members.

Example.   {natural numbers between 8 and 12}

Solution.   {9, 10, 11}

1. {natural numbers between 3 and 10}

2. {natural numbers between 20 and 27}

3. {days in the week}   4. {months in the year}

5. {digits in your age in years}   6. {digits in your home address}

Designate each of the following sets by using set-builder notation.

Example.   {even natural numbers}

Solution. $\{x \mid x = 2n, n$ a natural number$\}$ $n = 0\}$

7. {odd natural numbers} $\{2n+1 \mid n \in U$ or $n = 0\}$ 8. {rational numbers}

9. {solutions of $2^x = 5$}   10. {solutions of $x^x = 5$}

11. {elements not in set A} $x \mid x \notin A$ 12. {elements in set B} $x \mid x \in B$

Let $a \in A$, but otherwise let a be unspecified. In each of the following, state whether or not a is a constant.

13. $A = \{6, 7, 8, 9\}$ 14. $A = \{6\}$ 15. $A = \{$natural numbers$\}$

16. $A = \{$natural numbers between 2 and 4$\}$

In Problems 17–20, replace the colored comma with either $=$ or $\neq$.

17. {natural numbers less than 3}, {1, 2}

18. {4}, {7}   19. $\varnothing$, {0}   20. {5, 7, 9}, {7, 9, 5}

In Problems 21–24, replace the colored comma with either $\in$ or $\notin$.

21. 3, {2, 3, 4}   22. 5 $\{x \mid x$ is an even natural number$\}$

23. {2}, {2, 3, 4}   24. $\varnothing$, {2, 3, 4}

In Problems 25–28, replace the colored comma with either $\subset$ or $\not\subset$.

25. 5, {4, 5, 6} $\subset$ 26. {5, 4, 6}, {4, 5, 6} $\subset$

27. $\varnothing$, {4, 5, 6} $\not\subset$ 28. {3, 4}, {4, 5, 6} $\not\subset$

29. Let $U = \{5, 6, 7\}$. List the subsets of U that contain

    a. three members   b. two members

    c. one member   d. no members

30. Let $U = \{1, 2, 3, 4\}$. List the subsets of U that contain

    a. four members   b. three members   c. two members

    d. one member   e. no members   f. 2 and one other member

31. Let $U = \{1, 2, 3, 4, 5, 6, 7, 8, 9\}$, $A = \{1, 2, 3, 4\}$, $B = \{4, 5, 6, 7\}$, and $C = \{6, 7\}$. Replace the comma in each of the following with either $\subset$ or $\not\subset$.

    a. A, U b. C, A c. A, B d. C, B

32. Let $U = \{\text{natural numbers}\}$, $A = \{\text{even natural numbers}\}$, $B = \{\text{odd natural numbers}\}$, $C = \{x \mid x \text{ is a natural number between 1 and 10}\}$, and $D = \{x \mid x \text{ is a natural number less than 9}\}$. Which of the following are true? $A = \{$

    a. $A \sim D$ F   b. $C = D$ F   c. $C \subset D$ F

    d. $A \sim B$ T   e. $A = B$ F   f. $D \subset C$ F

    g. $A \sim U$ T
    (2,1)(4,2)(6,3) (8,4)   h. A and B are disjoint. T   i. $A \subset U$ T

    j. $C \sim D$ k. $C \subset A$ l. C and B are disjoint.

$\sim$ equvivilant $A = \{2n \mid n \in U\}$

1.2 OPERATIONS ON SETS $B = \{2n+1 \mid n \in U \text{ or } n = 0\}$

    Ideas involving universal sets, subsets thereof, and certain operations on sets can be depicted by means of plane geometric figures called **Venn diagrams.** Figure 1.1 is such a diagram, representing a universe having as its elements all points of the rectangle and its interior, and having a number of subsets of the universe denoted by circles and their interiors. In this figure, sets A, B, and C are disjoint, D is a subset of C, and E is neither a subset of C nor disjoint from C.

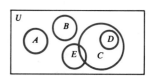

    There are several mathematically important operations on the subsets of a given universe U. A **binary**

Figure 1.1

operation on the subsets of U is a rule that assigns to each pair A and B of subsets of U, taken in a definite order (A first and B second), a third subset C of U. One such operation is defined as follows.

DEFINITION 1.7 *The **union** of two subsets A and B of U is the set of all elements of U that belong either to A or to B or to both.*

| **Set-union symbol** | The symbol $\cup$ is used to denote the union of sets. Thus $A \cup B$ (read "the union of A and B" or, sometimes, "A cup B") is |

the set of all elements that are in either A or B or both.

Example. If $A = \{1, 2, 3, 4, 5\}$ and $B = \{2, 3, 4, 5, 6\}$, then

$$A \cup B = \{1, 2, 3, 4, 5, 6\}.$$

Notice that each element in $A \cup B$ is listed only once in this example, since repetition would be redundant. Figure 1.2 is a Venn diagram in which the shaded region depicts $A \cup B$.

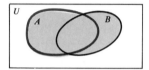
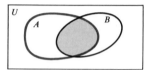

Figure 1.2   **Figure 1.3**

A second binary set operation of interest is defined as follows.

DEFINITION 1.8 *The **intersection** of two subsets A and B of U is the set of all elements of U that belong to both A and B.*

| **Set-intersection symbol** | The symbol $\cap$ is used to denote intersection. Thus $A \cap B$ (read "the intersection of A and B" or, sometimes, "A cap B") |

denotes the set of all elements of U that are in both A and B.

Example. If $A = \{1, 2, 3, 4, 5)$ and $B = \{2, 3, 4, 5, 6\}$, then

$$A \cap B = \{2, 3, 4, 5\}.$$

Figure 1.3 is a Venn diagram in which the shaded region depicts $A \cap B$.

Both operations, union and intersection, are binary operations, because they are applied to two sets in relation to each other. The following operation on sets, however, applies to only one set in relation to U.

DEFINITION 1.9 *The **complement** of a set A in U is the set of all elements of U that do not belong to A.*

The symbol A' (or, sometimes, $\bar{A}$, $\sim A$, or $\tilde{A}$) denotes the complement of A in U.

Example. If $U = \{1, 2, 3, 4, 5\}$ and $A = \{2, 4\}$, then

$$A' = \{1, 3, 5\}.$$

The shaded part of the Venn diagram in Figure 1.4 represents A'.

Figure 1.4

EXERCISE 1.2

Let $U = \{1, 2, 3, 4, 5, 6, 7, 8, 9, 10\}$, $A = \{2, 4, 6, 8, 10\}$, $B = \{1, 2, 3, 4, 5\}$,   and
$C = \{1, 3, 5, 7, 9\}$. List the members of each of the following.

1. $A' = C$	2. B' $\{6, 7, 8, 9, 10\}$	3. $C' = A$	4. $A \cap B$ $\{2, 4\}$
5. $A \cup B$	6. $A \cup C$	7. $A \cap C$	8. $A' \cap B'$
9. $A' \cup C'$	10. $(A \cap B)'$	11. $A' \cup C$	12. $C' \cap B$

For the each of the Problems 13–24, copy the Venn diagram shown here on a sheet of
paper. Shade the part of the diagram corresponding to each of the following.

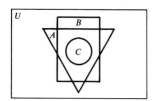

13. $A \cap B$	14. $C \cap A$	15. $C \cap B$
16. $A \cap C'$	17. $B \cap C'$	18. $B' \cup A'$
19. $B' \cap A'$	20. $B' \cap A$	21. $A' \cap B$
22. $(C \cap B)'$	23. $(C' \cap A)'$	24. $(A' \cap B)'$

Using Venn diagrams if necessary, complete each of the following.

25. $(A')' =$	26. $A \cap A' =$	27. $A \cap U =$	28. $A \cup A' =$
29. $A \cup U =$	30. $A \cap \varnothing =$	31. $A \cup \varnothing =$	32. $A \cap A =$
33. $\varnothing' \cap \varnothing =$	34. $A \cup A =$	35. $\varnothing \cup \varnothing =$	36. $U \cap U =$

37. Under what conditions would each of the following be true?

a. $A \cup B = \varnothing$	b. $A \cup \varnothing = \varnothing$	c. $A \cap U = U$
d. $A \cup B = A$	e. $A \cup \varnothing = U$	f. $A' \cap U = U$
g. $A \cap B = A$	h. $A' \cup \varnothing = \varnothing$	i. $A \cup B = A \cap B$

1.3 THE FIELD POSTULATES

**Sets of
numbers**   Some sets of numbers with which you should already be at
least somewhat familiar are the following:

1. The set N of **natural numbers**, whose elements are the counting, or natural,
   numbers:

$$N = \{1, 2, 3, \cdots\}.$$

2. The set J of **integers**, whose elements are the positive and negative whole
   numbers and zero:

$$J = \{\cdots, -2, -1, 0, 1, 2, \cdots\}.$$

3. The set Q of **rational numbers**, whose elements are all those numbers that can be represented as the quotient of two integers $\dfrac{a}{b}$ or a/b, where b is not 0. Among the elements of Q are such numbers as $-3/4$, $18/27$, $3/1$, and $-6/1$. In symbols,

$$Q = \left\{ x \,\middle|\, x = \frac{a}{b}, \, a \in J, \, b \in J, \, b \neq 0 \right\}.$$

Equivalently, rational numbers are numbers with terminating or repeating decimal representations.

4. The set H of **irrational numbers**, whose elements are the numbers with decimal representations that are nonterminating and nonrepeating. Among the elements of this set are such numbers as $\sqrt{2}$, π, and $-\sqrt{7}$. An irrational number cannot be represented in the form a/b, where a and b are integers. In symbols,

$$H = \{\text{irrational numbers}\}.$$

5. The set R of **real numbers**, which is the union of the set of all rational numbers and the set of all irrational numbers:

$$R = \{x \,|\, x \in (Q \cup H)\}.$$

6. The set I of **imaginary numbers**, whose members can be represented in the form $x + yi$, where x and y are real numbers, $y \neq 0$, and $i = \sqrt{-1}$:

$$I = \{x + yi \,|\, x \in R, \, y \in R, \, y \neq 0, \quad i = \sqrt{-1}\}.$$

If $x = 0$, then the imaginary number $x + yi$ is written yi, with $y \in R$, $y \neq 0$. Such a number is called a **pure imaginary number**.

7. The set C of **complex numbers**, whose members can be represented in the form $x + yi$, where x and y are real numbers, and $i = \sqrt{-1}$:

$$C = \{x + yi \,|\, x \in R, \, y \in R, \quad i = \sqrt{-1}\}.$$

Conceptually, as will be pointed out in Chapter 12, the complex number $x + 0i$ can be distinguished from the real number x, just as the rational number $a/1$ can be distinguished from the integer a. Nevertheless, for practical purposes, it is useful and convenient to identify $x + 0i$ with x, and $a/1$ with a. What is more important from the point of view of algebraic structure, of course, is the fact that this identification is entirely consistent; thus, for example, we have

$$(3 + 0i) + (4 + 0i) = 7 + 0i,$$

just as we have

$$3 + 4 = 7.$$

Relations between sets of numbers With this familiar identification, the foregoing sets of numbers are related as indicated in Figure 1.5.

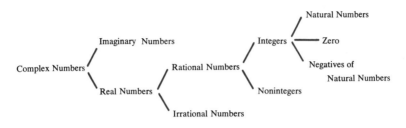

Figure 1.5

We can characterize each of the foregoing sets by stating properties that we assume them to have. In mathematics, when we make formal assumptions about members of a set or about their properties, we call the assumptions **axioms** or **postulates**. The words **property**, **law**, and **principle** are sometimes used in referring to assumptions, although these words may also be applied to certain consequences thereof.

The first assumptions to be considered here have to do with *equality*. An **equality**, or an "is equal to" assertion, is simply a mathematical statement that two symbols or words, or two groups of symbols or words, are names for the same thing.

Equality postulates We postulate that, for any members a, b, and c of any set S, the equality $(=)$ relationship satisfies the following laws:

E-1 $a = a$.   *Reflexive law for equality.*

E-2 If $a = b$, then $b = a$.   *Symmetric law for equality.*

E-3 If $a = b$ and $b = c$, then $a = c$.   *Transitive law for equality.*

E-4 If $a = b$, then a may be replaced by b *Substitution law for equality.*
and b by a in any mathematical state-
ment without altering the truth or
falsity of the statement.†

These axioms serve to clarify how we shall be using symbols, and to warn that we must not change the meaning of a symbol in the middle of a discussion or use the same symbol for two different things in the same context.

Other axioms, somewhat different conceptually, are used to characterize mathematical systems. They are assumptions made about the behavior of elements of sets under binary operations.

† We have adopted a very powerful postulate in E-4, one that subsumes E-1, E-2, and E-3 as special cases. By wording E-4 as we have, we can eliminate a great deal of fussiness in later arguments, and, because E-1, E-2, and E-3 are fundamental properties of the equality relation, we have elected to retain them as postulates.

DEFINITION 1.10 *A **binary operation** in a set A is a rule that assigns to any pair of elements of A, taken in a definite order, another element of A.*

Since the set R of real numbers is the set of greatest interest to us at the moment, let us list some of the properties we assume real numbers to possess under the binary operations of addition and multiplication, for which we

Addition and multiplication postulates

shall use the familiar symbols $+$ and $\times$, respectively.

We postulate eleven basic laws for the elements a, b, and c of the set R of real numbers in relation to addition and multi-plication. These are listed on page 11.

Use of parentheses

Parentheses are used in stating some of the relations (and hereafter) to indicate that symbols within parentheses are to be viewed as representing a single entity.

Postulates F-1 and F-6 assert that the sum and product of any two real numbers are always real numbers, and that each sum and each product of real numbers is unique. When the performance of an operation on two elements of some set always results in another element of the same set, we say that the set is **closed** with respect to that operation.

To give meaning to expressions $a + b + c$, $a \times b \times c$, $a + b + c + d$, and so on, let us make the following agreement.

DEFINITION 1.11 *If a, b, c, d, $\cdots \in R$, then*

$$a + b + c = (a + b) + c, \quad a + b + c + d = (a + b + c) + d, \quad \cdots,$$

and

$$a \times b \times c = (a \times b) \times c, \quad a \times b \times c \times d = (a \times b \times c) \times d, \quad \cdots.$$

Postulates F-2 and F-7 assert, however, that three real addends in a sum or three real factors in a product may be associated in either of two ways without altering the result. Thus, combining Definition 1.11 with Postulates F-2 and F-7, we have, for example,

$$2 + 3 + 4 = (2 + 3) + 4 = 2 + (3 + 4)$$

and

$$2 \times 3 \times 4 = (2 \times 3) \times 4 = 2 \times (3 \times 4).$$

Postulates F-3, F-4, F-9, and F-11 are "existence axioms"; they assert the existence of certain elements in the set that behave in specified ways under addition and multiplication.

Postulates F-5 and F-10 state that the order in which we add or multiply two real numbers does not affect the sum or product. Thus,

$$2 + 4 = 4 + 2 \quad \text{and} \quad 2 \times 4 = 4 \times 2.$$

Postulate F-8 relates the operations of addition and multiplication.

FIELD PROPERTIES OF THE SET R OF REAL NUMBERS

Let a, b, c be arbitrary elements of R.

F-1 $a + b$ is a unique element of R.   *Closure law for addition.*

F-2 $(a + b) + c = a + (b + c)$.   *Associative law for addition.*

F-3   There exists an element $0 \in R$ (called   *Additive-identity law.*
the **identity element for addition**) with
the property $a + 0 = a$ and $0 + a = a$
for each $a \in R$.

F-4   For each element $a \in R$, there exists   *Additive-inverse law.*
an element $^-a \in R$ (called the **additive
inverse** or **negative** of a) with the
property

$$a + (^-a) = 0 \quad \text{and} \quad (^-a) + a = 0.\dagger$$

F-5 $a + b = b + a$.   *Commutative law for addition.*

F-6 $a \times b$ is a unique element of R.   *Closure law for multiplication.*

F-7 $(a \times b) \times c = a \times (b \times c)$.   *Associative law for multiplication.*

F-8 $a \times (b + c) = a \times b + a \times c$ and   *Distributive law.*
$(b + c) \times a = b \times a + c \times a$.

F-9   There exists an element $1 \in R$ (called   *Multiplicative-identity law.*
the **identity element for multiplication**),
$1 \neq 0$, with the property $a \times 1 = a$ and
$1 \times a = a$ for each element $a \in R$.

F-10 $a \times b = b \times a$.   *Commutative law for multiplication.*

F-11 For each element $a \in R$, $a \neq 0$, there   *Multiplicative-inverse law.*
exists an element $a^{-1} \in R$ (called the
multiplicative inverse or **reciprocal**
of a) with the property

$$a \times (a^{-1}) = 1 \text{ and } (a^{-1}) \times a = 1.$$

† See page 12 for an alternative symbol for ^-a.

If, for a given set F and a given pair of binary operations (denoted $+$ and

Field postulates

$\times$ but not necessarily ordinary addition and multiplication) in F, the Postulates F-1 through F-11 (with R replaced by F throughout) are satisfied by the elements of F, then F is called a **field** under these operations. Thus, we speak of the **field R of real numbers**.

In terms of the operations of addition and multiplication, let us now define two new operations on real numbers.

DEFINITION 1.12 *The **difference** of elements $a \in R$ and $b \in R$, denoted by $a - b$, is given by*

$$a - b = a + (^-b).$$

The operation of finding a difference is called **subtraction**. This definition explains why we ordinarily write $-b$ for ^-b (the negative of b).

DEFINITION 1.13 *The **quotient** of elements $a \in R$ and $b \in R$, $b \neq 0$, denoted by $\dfrac{a}{b}$, a/b, or $a \div b$, is given by*

$$\frac{a}{b} = a \times (b^{-1}).$$

The operation of finding a quotient is called **division**. In particular, for $a = 1$ we have, by the substitution law for equality,

$$\frac{1}{b} = 1 \times b^{-1},$$

and, by the multiplicative-identity law,

$$1 \times b^{-1} = b^{-1},$$

whence, by the transitive law for equality,

$$\frac{1}{b} = b^{-1}.$$

Additive and multiplicative inverse notation

In all that follows, *we shall ordinarily write $-a$ for the additive inverse of a, and any of b^{-1}, $\dfrac{1}{b}$, $1/b$, or $1 \div b$ for the multiplic-ative inverse of b.* We shall also follow the customary practice of writing ab or $a \cdot b$ for $a \times b$.

EXERCISE 1.3

Let $N = \{$natural numbers$\}$, $J = \{$integers$\}$, $Q = \{$rational numbers$\}$, $H = \{$irrational numbers$\}$, $R = \{$real numbers$\}$, $I = \{$imaginary numbers$\}$, and $C = \{$complex numbers$\}$. State whether each statement is true or false.

1. $-5 \in N$ 2. $0 \in Q$ 3. $\sqrt{3} \in R$

4. $\pi \in C$ 5. $-3 \in R$ 6. $-7 \in H$

7. $\{-1, 1\} \subset N$ 8. $\{-1, 1\} \subset J$ 9. $\{-1, 1\} \subset Q$

10. $\{-1, 1\} \subset H$ 11. $\{-1, 1\} \subset R$ 12. $\{-1, 1\} \subset C$

Represent each set, listing members if finite, and using ellipses, $\cdots$, if infinite.

Examples.

a. {natural numbers between 5 and 9}   b. {integers greater than 3}

Solutions.

a. $\{6, 7, 8\}$ b. $\{4, 5, 6, \cdots\}$

13. {first five natural numbers}   14. {integers between -4 and 5}

15. {natural numbers less than 7}   16. {integers greater than -5}

17. {integers between -10 and -5}   18. {nonnegative integers}

Use set-builder notation, $\{x \mid \text{condition on } x\}$, to represent each set.

Example. {natural numbers greater than 12}

Solution. $\{x \mid x \subset N \text{ and } x \text{ is greater than } 12\}$

19. {natural numbers}   20. {integers}

21. {real numbers}   22. {integers less than -6}

23. {real numbers between -4 and 3}   24. {nonnegative real numbers}

25. Let $A = \{4, -2, 2/5, \sqrt{-7}, 0, -3/4, \sqrt{2}, \sqrt{7}, \sqrt{-1}\}$. Designate each of the following sets by using braces and listing the members.

     a. {natural numbers in A}   b. {integers in A}

     c. {rational numbers in A}   d. {real numbers in A}

26. Let $B = \{-6, 3, \sqrt{5}, -3/4, \sqrt{-2}, 0, 5, -1, \sqrt{3}\}$. Designate each of the following sets by using braces and listing the members.

     a. {natural numbers in B}   b. {integers in B}

     c. {irrational numbers in B}   d. {real numbers in B}

Each variable in Problems 27–50 denotes a real number. Each of the statements 27–32 is an application of one of the Postulates E-1 through E-4. Justify each statement by citing the appropriate postulate. (There may be more than one correct justification.)

Example. If $3 = a$, then $a = 3$.

Solution. Symmetric law of equality

27. If $a + 3 = b$ and $b = 7$, then $a + 3 = 7$.   28. If $x = 5$ and $y = x + 2$, then $y = 5 + 2$.

29. If $2 + y = 6$, then $6 = 2 + y$.   30. If $a = 2c$ and $c = 6$, then $a = 2 \cdot 6$.

31. If $y = 7 + x$ and $7 + x = z$, then $y = z$.   32. $x + 8 = x + 8$.

Each of the statements 33–50 is an application of one of the Postulates F-1 through F-11. Justify each statement by citing the appropriate postulate. All variables denote elements of the set R of real numbers.

Example. $2(3 + 1) = 2 \cdot 3 + 2 \cdot 1$

Solution.   Distributive law

33. ab is a real number.

34. $7 + 0 = 7$

35. $(2 \cdot 3) \cdot 4 = 2 \cdot (3 \cdot 4)$

36. $(5 + 4) + 1 = (4 + 5) + 1$ commut

37. $3 + (-3) = 0$

38. $5 + (-2) = (-2) + 5$

39. $a\left(\dfrac{1}{a}\right) = \left(\dfrac{1}{a}\right)a \quad (a \neq 0)$

40. $\dfrac{1}{c}(a + b) = \dfrac{1}{c} \cdot a + \dfrac{1}{c} \cdot b \quad (c \neq 0)$

41. $(a + b) + c = c + (a + b)$

42. $(a + b) + c = (b + a) + c$

43. $a + (b + c)d = a + bd + cd$ dist

44. $a + (b + c)d + = a + d(b + c)$

45. $a + (b + c)d = (b + c)d + a$

46. $(a + b) + [-(a + b)] = 0$

47. $a(b + c) = (b + c)a$

48. $a[b + (c + d)] = ab + a(c + d)$

49. $ab + a(c + d) = ab + ac + ad$

50. $ab + ac = ba + ac$ comm

Which of the sets in Problems 51–58 are closed under the stated operation?

51. {even natural numbers}, addition

52. {odd natural numbers}, addition

53. {odd natural numbers}, multiplication

54. {even natural numbers}, multiplication

55. {0, 1}, multiplication

56. {0, 1}, addition

57. {natural numbers}, division

58. {natural numbers}, subtraction

1.4   FIELD PROPERTIES

The field postulates together with the postulates for equality imply other properties of the real numbers. Such implications are generally stated as **theorems**. A theorem is simply an assertion of a fact that follows logically from the postulates (or axioms) and other theorems. It usually consists of two parts: an "if" part, called the **hypothesis**, and a "then" part, called the **conclusion**. Proving a theorem consists of showing that the conclusion is a logical consequence of the hypothesis and the axioms in our system. Proofs are sometimes displayed in a distinctive two-column format, one column containing a chain of assertions, and the other containing a reason for each assertion.

Proofs

It is interesting to note that the theorems of this section are consequences of the equality postulates and the field postulates, and nothing more. Accordingly, with appropriate changes in wording they are valid in *any* field, not just the field R of real numbers.

Addition law for equality   First, consider the following result, which reaffirms the uniqueness of the sum of two real numbers.

THEOREM 1.1   *If* $a, b, c \in R$ *and if* $a = b$, *then*

$$a + c = b + c \quad and \quad c + a = c + b.$$

Proof.

Statement	*Reason*
1. $a, b, c \in R$ and $a = b$.	1. Hypothesis.
2. $a + c \in R$ and $c + a \in R$.	2. Closure law for addition.
3. $a + c = a + c$.	3, 3′. Reflexive law for equality.
3′. $c + a = c + a$.	
4. $a + c = b + c$.	4, 4′. Substitution in (3) from (1)
4′. $c + a = c + b$.	and (3′) from (1), by substitution law for equality.

Thus, if the hypothesis "$a, b, c \in R$ and $a = b$" is true, then the conclusion "$a + c = b + c$ and $c + a = c + b$" follows logically. Both equations,

$$a + c = b + c \quad and \quad c + a = c + b,$$

were included in the conclusion of Theorem 1.1, because applications to further results are sometimes immediate from one form and sometimes from the other.

Multiplication law for equality   A theorem closely analogous to Theorem 1.1 can be stated as follows.

THEOREM 1.2   *If* $a, b, c \in R$, *and if* $a = b$, *then*

$$ac = bc \quad and \quad ca = cb.$$

The proof of Theorem 1.2 exactly parallels that of Theorem 1.1, and is left as an exercise.

Uniqueness of the additive inverse   The next theorem is an assertion that the additive inverse of a real number is unique—that is, that a given real number has only one additive inverse.

THEOREM 1.3   *If* $a, b \in R$, *and if* $a + b = 0$, *then*

$$b = -a \quad and \quad a = -b.$$

Proof.

Statement	Reason
1. $a, b \in R$ and $a + b = 0$.	1. Hypothesis.
2. $(-a) + (a + b) = (-a) + 0$.	2. Theorem 1.1.
3. $(-a) + (a + b) = [(-a) + a] + b$.	3. Associative law for addition.
4. $[(-a) + a] + b = (-a) + 0$.	4. Substitution from (3) to (2).
5. $(-a) + a = 0$.	5. Additive-inverse law.
6. $0 + b = (-a) + 0$.	6. Substitution from (5) to (4).
7. $0 + b = b$.	7. Additive-identity law.
8. $b = (-a) + 0$.	8. Substitution from (7) to (6).
9. $(-a) + 0 = -a$.	9. Additive-identity law.
10. $b = -a$.	10. Substitution from (9) to (8).

This concludes the first part of the proof. Now, to show that $a = -b$, you can just replace Step 2 by

$$(a + b) + (-b) = 0 + (-b),$$

and a similar argument applies. Notice that in this proof there are many steps involving substitution or transitivity. In actual practice, these steps are frequently omitted, and the proof for the first part of Theorem 1.3, when condensed, would appear as follows:

Statement	Reasons
1. $a, b \in R$ and $a + b = 0$.	1. Hypothesis.
2. $(-a) + (a + b) = (-a) + 0$.	2. Theorem 1.1.
3. $[(-a) + a] + b = (-a) + 0$.	3. Associative law for addition.
4. $0 + b = (-a) + 0$.	4. Additive-inverse law.
5. $b = -a$.	5. Additive-identity law.

In the last step, for example, we did not state that $0 + b = b$ and $(-a) + 0 = -a$ and then argue that $b = -a$ by the substitution law; this amount of detail now

Degree of rigor seems superfluous. The degree of rigorous detail desirable in proofs of this kind is purely relative. If a line of argument is clear and valid, most reasonable persons will not insist on the dotting of all i's and the crossing of all t's. What is important is that you be able to see and understand the argument.

Cancellation law for addition A result analogous to Theorem 1.3 holds for the multiplicative inverse and is left as an exercise.

For the following theorem, we give another example of a condensed proof.

THEOREM 1.4 *If $a, b, c \in R$, and $a + c = b + c$, then $a = b$.*

Proof.

Statement	*Reason*
1. $a + c = b + c$.	1. Hypothesis.
2. $a + c + (-c) = b + c + (-c)$.	2. Theorem 1.1.
3. $a + 0 = b + 0$.	3. Additive-inverse law.
4. $a = b$.	4. Additive-identity law.

Cancellation law for multiplication The following theorem is similar to Theorem 1.4.

THEOREM 1.5 *If $a, b, c \in R$, $c \neq 0$, and $ac = bc$, then $a = b$.*

Zero as a factor The proof of this theorem and the proofs of the following two theorems about the additive-identity element 0 as a factor in a product are also left as exercises.

THEOREM 1.6 *For every $a \in R$, $a \cdot 0 = 0$.*

THEOREM 1.7 *If $a, b \in R$, and $a \cdot b = 0$, then either $a = 0$, or $b = 0$, or both.*

Combining Theorems 1.6 and 1.7, we see that for $a, b \in R$ we have $ab = 0$ *if and only if* at least one of the factors is 0.

Laws of signs The following theorem concerns the familiar "laws of signs" for operating with real numbers.

THEOREM 1.8 *If $a, b \in R$, then*

$$\text{I} \quad -(-a) = a,$$

$$\text{II} \quad (-a) + (-b) = -(a + b),$$

$$\text{III} \quad (-a)(b) = -(ab),$$

$$\text{IV} \quad (-a)(-b) = ab,$$

$$\text{V} \quad \frac{-a}{b} = \frac{a}{-b} = -\frac{a}{b} \quad (b \neq 0),$$

$$\text{VI} \quad \frac{-a}{-b} = \frac{a}{b} \quad (b \neq 0).$$

The proof of part I is presented without the reasons being specifically listed. You should make sure, however, that you can supply a reason for each step.

Proof of 1.8-I.

$$a + (-a) = 0,$$

$$[a + (-a)] + [-(-a)] = 0 + [-(-a)],$$

$$a + [(-a) + (-(-a))] = 0 + [-(-a)],$$

$$a + 0 = 0 + [-(-a)],$$

$$a = -(-a),$$

$$-(-a) = a.$$

Properties of quotients   The proofs of the remaining parts of Theorem 1.8 are left as exercises, as are the proofs of Theorems 1.9 to 1.11, which are concerned with the familiar properties of quotients.

THEOREM 1.9 *If $a, b, c \in R$, then*

$$\frac{a}{b} = \frac{c}{d} \quad (b, d \neq 0)$$

if and only if $ad = bc$.

Fundamental principle of fractions   As a direct consequence of this characterization of equal quotients, we have a theorem that is sometimes referred to as the *fundamental principle of fractions*.

THEOREM 1.10 *If $a, b, c \in R$ then*

$$\frac{ac}{bc} = \frac{a}{b} \quad (b, c \neq 0).$$

Next, let us group a number of assertions about quotients into a single theorem.

THEOREM 1.11 *If $a, b, c, d \in R$, then*

$$\text{I} \quad \frac{1}{a} \cdot \frac{1}{b} = \frac{1}{ab} \quad (a, b \neq 0),$$

$$\text{II} \quad \frac{a}{b} \cdot \frac{c}{d} = \frac{ac}{bd} \quad (b, d \neq 0),$$

$$\text{III} \quad \frac{a}{c} + \frac{b}{c} = \frac{a+b}{c} \quad (c \neq 0),$$

$$\text{IV} \quad \frac{a}{b} + \frac{c}{d} = \frac{ad+bc}{bd} \quad (b, d \neq 0),$$

$$\text{V} \quad \frac{a}{b} - \frac{c}{d} = \frac{ad-bc}{bd} \quad (b, d \neq 0),$$

$$\text{VI} \quad \frac{1}{\frac{a}{b}} = \frac{b}{a} \quad (a, b \neq 0),$$

$$\text{VII} \quad \frac{\frac{a}{b}}{\frac{c}{d}} = \frac{ad}{bc} \quad (b, c, d \neq 0).$$

EXERCISE 1.4

In Problems 1–20, each statement is justifiable by one part of Theorems 1.1–1.11. Cite an appropriate justification. All variables denote elements of the set R of real numbers.

Example. If $p + q + 3 = 4 + 3$, then $p + q = 4$.

Solution. Theorem 1.4

1. If $x = 3$, then $x + 9 = 3 + 9$.

2. $-2 - q = -(2 + q)$

3. $\dfrac{-2}{5} = -\dfrac{2}{5}$

4. $\dfrac{4(x + y)}{6} = \dfrac{2(x + y)}{3}$

5. $\dfrac{x}{3} + \dfrac{y + z}{3} = \dfrac{x + y + z}{3}$

6. $\dfrac{p}{3} \cdot \dfrac{q}{4} = \dfrac{pq}{12}$

7. If $4p = 0$, then $p = 0$.

8. $(-5)(-6) = 5 \cdot 6$

9. If $3x = 2y$, then $\dfrac{3}{2} = \dfrac{y}{x}$.

10. $\dfrac{-x}{-3} = \dfrac{x}{3}$

11. $\dfrac{\frac{2}{5}}{\frac{3}{7}} = \dfrac{2 \cdot 7}{5 \cdot 3}$

12. $\dfrac{\frac{1}{2}}{\frac{3}{3}} = \dfrac{3}{2}$

13. $(-3)(p) = -(3p)$

14. $x - (-y) = x + y$

15. $\dfrac{x}{3} + \dfrac{y}{2} = \dfrac{2x + 3y}{3 \cdot 2}$

16. $\dfrac{x}{-3} = -\dfrac{x}{3}$

17. If $p + q = 7$, then $4(p + q) = 4 \cdot 7$.

18. If $(r + s) + 7 = 0$, then $r + s = -7$.

19. If $6(x - y) = 3z$, then $2(x - y) = z$.

20. $\dfrac{x + 1}{4} - \dfrac{y + 3}{3} = \dfrac{3(x + 1) - 4(y + 3)}{4 \cdot 3}$

Prove each of the following, using the statement-reason format. All variables denote elements of the set R of real numbers.

21. If $a = b$, then $ac = bc$ and $ca = cb$.

22. $\dfrac{1}{a}$ $(a \neq 0)$ is unique; that is, if $a \cdot b = 1$, then $b = \dfrac{1}{a}$.

23. 0 is unique; that is, if $a + b = a$, then $b = 0$.

24. 1 is unique; that is, if $a \neq 0$ and $a \cdot b = a$, then $b = 1$.

25. If $ac = bc$ and $c \neq 0$, then $a = b$.

                                                        $0 + 0 = 0$

                                         $a \cdot (0 + 0) = 0$ # Rule 24

26. If $a \in R$, then $a \cdot 0 = 0$.

27. If $a \cdot b = 0$, then either $a = 0$ or $b = 0$ or both.

28. $(-a) + (-b) = -(a + b)$ 29. $(-a)(b) = -(ab)$

30. $(-a)(-b) = ab$ 31. $\dfrac{-a}{b} = \dfrac{a}{-b} = -\dfrac{a}{b}$ $(b \neq 0)$

32. $\dfrac{-a}{-b} = \dfrac{a}{b}$ $(b \neq 0)$ 33. $\dfrac{a}{b} = \dfrac{c}{d}$ $(b, d \neq 0)$ if and only if $ad = bc$.

34. $\dfrac{ac}{bc} = \dfrac{a}{b}$ $(b, c \neq 0)$ 35. $\dfrac{1}{a} \cdot \dfrac{1}{b} = \dfrac{1}{ab}$ $(a, b \neq 0)$

36. $\dfrac{a}{b} \cdot \dfrac{c}{d} = \dfrac{ac}{bd}$ $(b, d \neq 0)$ 37. $\dfrac{a}{c} + \dfrac{b}{c} = \dfrac{a + b}{c}$ $(c \neq 0)$

38. $\dfrac{a}{b} + \dfrac{c}{d} = \dfrac{ad + bc}{bd}$ $(b, d \neq 0)$ 39. $\dfrac{a}{b} - \dfrac{c}{d} = \dfrac{ad - bc}{bd}$ $(b, d \neq 0)$

40. $\dfrac{\frac{1}{a}}{\frac{a}{b}} = \dfrac{b}{a}$ $(a, b \neq 0)$ 41. $\dfrac{\frac{a}{b}}{\frac{c}{d}} = \dfrac{ad}{bc}$ $(b, c, d \neq 0)$

42. $\dfrac{a}{b} = q$, if and only if $a = bq$ $(b \neq 0)$.

43. Derive the second equation,

$$(b + c)a = ba + ca,$$

in Field Postulate F-8 from the other postulates and the first equation,

$$a(b + c) = ab + ac.$$

1.5   ORDER AND COMPLETENESS

     Let us now assume the possibility of establishing the existence of a one-to-one correspondence between the real numbers and the points on a geometric line (for each real number there corresponds one and only one point on the line, and vice versa). To illustrate this, we imagine the line scaled in convenient units, with the positive direction (from 0 toward 1) denoted by an arrowhead. The line is then called a **number line**, the real number corresponding to a point on the line is called the **coordinate** of the point, and the point is called the **graph** of the number.

Numbers and the number line

Sets of numbers can be graphed by means of this correspondence. For example, to give a number-line representation of {1, 3, 5}, we simply draw a graph of the number line and indicate the required points with solid dots, as shown in Figure 1.6.

Figure 1.6

A horizontal number-line graph directed to the right can be used to illustrate the separation of the real numbers into three disjoint subsets: {negative real numbers}, {0}, {positive real numbers}. The point associated with 0 is called the **origin**. The set of numbers whose elements are associated with the points on the right-hand side of the origin belong to the set R_+ of **positive real numbers**, and the set whose elements are associated with the points on the other side belong to the set R_- of

Two uses of "negative"

negative real numbers. Notice that the word "negative" has now been used in two ways. In one case, we refer to the *negative of a number*, as in Postulate F-4, whereas in the other we refer to a *negative number*, which is the negative of a positive number.

It is possible to categorize the set of positive real numbers without recourse to geometric considerations, though of course we shall continue

Order postulates

to find it convenient to refer also to the number line. With this in mind, let us state two more postulates that apply to real numbers.

O-1   If a is a real number, then exactly one   *Trichotomy law.*
of the following is true: a is positive, a
is zero, or $-a$ is positive.

O-2   If a and b are positive real numbers,   *Closure law for positive numbers.*
then $a + b$ is positive and ab is positive.

The first of these postulates asserts that every real number belongs either to the set R_+, the set {0}, or the set R_-, but to only one of them. The second asserts that the set R_+ of positive real numbers is closed with respect to the binary operations of addition and multiplication.

Since the set R of real numbers satisfies Postulates O-1 and O-2 as well as Postulates F-1 through F-11, we say that R is an **ordered field**. Similarly, the set Q of rational numbers is an ordered field. But as we shall see in Chapter 12, the set C of complex numbers is not an ordered field even though it is a field.

Products of positive and negative numbers

By Postulate O-2, if a and b are positive real numbers, then ab is a positive real number. This fact, together with Parts III and IV of Theorem 1.8, is sufficient to establish that the product of a positive real number and a negative real number is a negative real number, while the product of two negative real numbers is a positive real number. Formally, we have the following.

THEOREM 1.12 *The product of a positive real number and a negative real number is a negative real number.*

THEOREM 1.13 *The product of two negative real numbers is a positive real number.*

Theorem 1.13 and Postulate O-2, together, imply the following.

THEOREM 1.14 *If $a \in R$, $a \neq 0$, then $a \cdot a$ is a positive real number.*

The addition of a positive real number d to a real number a can be visualized on a number-line graph as the process of locating the point corresponding to a on the line, and then moving along the line d units to the right to arrive at the point corresponding to $a + d$ (Figure 1.7). With this idea in mind, we define what is meant by "less than."

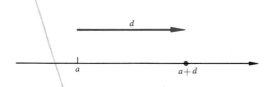

Figure 1.7

DEFINITION 1.14 *If $a, b \in R$, then a is **less than** b if and only if there exists a positive real number d such that $a + d = b$.*

Since d is positive, this definition implies that of any two real numbers, a and b, if the graph of a lies to the left of the graph of b, then a is less

Less-than and greater-than symbols

than b. The inequality symbol $<$ is used to denote the phrase "is less than," and $a < b$ is read "a is less than b." The inequality symbol $>$ means "is greater than." The statements $a < b$ and $b > a$ are taken as equivalent.

Now let us consider some important basic relationships resulting from our definition of "less than" and "greater than." First we restate Postulates O-1 and O-2 for real numbers a and b.

O-1′   If $a \in R$, then exactly one of the following is true: $a > 0$, $a = 0$, or $-a > 0$.

O-2′   If $a, b \in R$, and $a > 0$ and $b > 0$, then $a + b > 0$ and $ab > 0$.

Similarly, Theorems 1.12 and 1.13 can be stated thus:

THEOREM 1.12′ *If $a, b \in R$, and $a > 0$ and $b < 0$, then $ab < 0$.*

THEOREM 1.13′ *If $a, b \in R$, and $a < 0$ and $b < 0$, then $ab > 0$.*

We introduce the symbols $\leq$ and $\geq$ (read "is less than or equal to" and "is greater than or equal to," respectively) in giving a more precise formulation to Theorem 1.14.

THEOREM 1.14′   *If $a \in R$, then $a \cdot a \geq 0$, with the sign of equality holding if and only if $a = 0$.*

Thus we have

$$(2)(2) = 4 > 0, \quad (-3)(-3) = 9 > 0, \quad \text{but} \quad (0)(0) = 0.$$

The simple relation $a \cdot a \geq 0$ is probably the most useful and famous of all inequalities.

Definition 1.14 and the field postulates have the following implications, which we shall not prove.

THEOREM 1.15   *For any $a, b, c \in R$:*

    I   *If $a < b$ and $b < c$, then $a < c$.*

    II   *If $a < b$, then $a + c < b + c$.*

    III   *If $a < b$ and $c > 0$, then $ac < bc$.*

    IV   *If $a < b$ and $c < 0$, then $ac > bc$.*

Transitivity for inequalities   As you can see, Theorem 1.15-I is comparable to the transitive law for equality. That is, we can say that "less than" is a transitive relationship.

Opposites   The graphs of the numbers a and $-a$ on a number-line graph lie the same distance from the origin, but on opposite sides of it. If we wish to refer to the *distance* of the graph of a number from the origin, and not to the side of the origin on which it is located, then we use the term **absolute value**. Thus, the absolute value of a and the absolute value of $-a$ are the same nonnegative number. The symbol $|a|$ is used to denote the absolute value of a. We formalize the definition as follows:

DEFINITION 1.15   *If $a \in R$, then the **absolute value** of a is*

$$|a| = \begin{cases} a, & \text{if } a \geq 0, \\ -a, & \text{if } a < 0. \end{cases}$$

For example, $|-3| = -(-3) = 3, \quad |7| = 7, \quad \text{and} \quad |0| = 0.$

Continued inequalities   We often write two inequalities expressing a transitive relationship together. Thus $a < b$ and $b < c$ are written together as $a < b < c$. Similarly, $0 < x$ and $x \leq 1$ are written together as $0 < x \leq 1$.

The set of real numbers has one further property that is of fundamental importance, and one that is needed to establish the existence of irrational real numbers. Before stating the property, let us introduce some terminology.

DEFINITION 1.16 *If S is a nonempty subset of the set R of real numbers, and if b is a real number such that for every $x \in S$ we have $b \geq x$, then b is an **upper bound** of S. If $b \leq x$ for every $x \in S$, then b is a **lower bound** of S.*

For example, if $S = \{1, 3, 4\}$, then 6 and 4 are upper bounds of S, and -7 is a lower bound of S.

If a subset S of the set R of real numbers has an upper bound, it is said to be **bounded above**; otherwise it is **unbounded above**. Similarly, if it has a lower bound it is said to be **bounded below**, and otherwise it is **unbounded below**. For example, the set $N = \{1, 2, 3, \cdots\}$ of natural numbers is bounded below but unbounded above.

DEFINITION 1.17 *If b is an upper bound for a nonempty set S of real numbers and if no real number $b' < b$ is an upper bound for S, then b is the **least upper bound** for S. If b is a lower bound for S, and if no real number $b' > b$ is a lower bound for S, then b is the **greatest lower bound** for S.*

If a set has a least upper bound or a greatest lower bound, these bounds may or may not be in the set. For example, consider the set of real numbers $S = \{x \mid 0 < x \leq 1\}$. Since for every $x \in S$, we have $0 < x$ and $1 \geq x$, 0 is a lower and 1 an upper bound for S. Moreover, it is intuitively evident that there exists no real number b such that for every $x \in S$ we have either $0 < b \leq x$ or $x \leq b < 1$. Thus, 0 is the greatest lower bound and 1 the least upper bound for S. In this example, the least upper bound is a member of S, while the greatest lower bound is not a member of S.

Completeness postulate   With these definitions, we are prepared to state the following postulate.

O-3 Every nonempty subset of the set R of real numbers that is bounded above has a least upper bound.   *Postulate of completeness.*

This postulate assures us, for example, that there is a real number, denoted by $\sqrt{2}$, which is the least upper bound of $\{x \mid x \in R \text{ and } x^2 \leq 2\}$.

Thus the set R of real numbers is a **complete ordered field**. The set Q of rational numbers is an ordered field, but not a complete ordered field.

Characterization of the real-number field   We have now come to the end of our list of postulates for the real-number system R. It can be shown that *any* complete ordered field R' can be put in one-to-one correspondence with R in such a way that the results of its two operations are consistent with the results of the operations of addition and multiplication, respectively, in R. For example, if we have

$$
\begin{array}{ccccccc}
R & + & \times & 1 & 2 & 3 & \\
& \updownarrow & \updownarrow & \updownarrow & \updownarrow & \updownarrow & \text{etc.,}\\
R' & + & \times & 1 & 2 & 3 &
\end{array}
$$

then $1+2=3$, $1\times2=2$, etc. We call such a relation-preserving one-to-one correspondence an **isomorphism**. Thus *any complete ordered field R' is isomorphic with R.*

EXERCISE 1.5

In Problems 1–8, for $x, y \in R$, justify each statement by citing one part of Theorem 1.15.

Example.   If $2 < 3x$, then $-4 > -6x$.

Solution.   Part IV. Each member of $2 < 3x$ is multiplied by -2 to yield $-4 > -6x$.

1. If $x < 3$, and $y < x$, then $y < 3$.   2. If $x + 1 < 0$, then $x < -1$.

3. If $y < 8$, then $3y < 24$.   4. If $y < 4$, then $y + 2 < 6$.

5. If $x < 7$, then $x - 2 < 5$.   6. If $x < 9$, then $-2x > -18$.

7. If $-6x < 12$, then $x > -2$.   8. If $x - 3 < 5$, then $x < 8$.

In Problems 9–18, express each statement by means of symbols.

Examples.

a. 5 is not greater than 7.   b. x is between 5 and 8.

Solutions.

a. $5 \not> 7$, or $5 \leq 7$ b. $5 < x < 8$

9. 7 is greater than 3. $>$ 10. 2 is less than 5. $<$

11. -4 is less than -3. $<$ 12. -4 is greater than -7.

13. x is between 1 and -1, inclusive.   14. x is negative.

15. x is positive.   16. x is nonpositive.

17. x is nonnegative.   18. $|2x|$ is less than or equal to 8.

In Problems 19–24, replace the comma with an appropriate order symbol to form a true statement.

19. $-2 \overset{<}{,} 5$ 20. $3 \overset{<}{,} 4$ 21. $-7 \overset{<}{,} -1$

22. $|-3|, |-5|$ 23. $|-3|, |3|$ 24. $|-x|, 0$ $(x \in R)$

In Problems 25–30, for $x, y \in R$, write an equivalent relation without using the negation symbol, $/$.

25. $2 \not> 5$ $<$ 26. $-1 \not< -2$ $>$ 27. $7 \not> 8$ $<$

28. $|x| \not> 3$ $\geq$ 29. $|x| \not> 3$ 30. $x \not> |y|$

31. What is the greatest lower bound of $\{x \mid x \in R \text{ and } x > 0\}$?

32. What is the least upper bound of $\{x \mid x \in R \text{ and } |x| < 1\}$?

33. What is the least upper bound of $\{x \mid x \in R \text{ and } x^2 < 7\}$?

34. What is the greatest lower bound of $\{x \mid x \in R_+ \text{ and } x^2 > 9\}$?

2 ALGEBRAIC EXPRESSIONS

2.1 DEFINITIONS; SUMS OF POLYNOMIALS

Any grouping of constants and variables generated by applying a finite number of the elementary operations—addition, subtraction, multiplication, division, or the extraction of roots—is called an **algebraic expression**. For example,

$$\frac{3x^2 + \sqrt{2x - 1}}{3} \quad \text{and} \quad xy + 3x^2z - \sqrt[5]{z}$$

are algebraic expressions.

If two algebraic expressions have equal values for all value(s) of the variable(s) for which both expressions are defined, then we say that on the set of these values of the variable(s) the expressions are equivalent.

Equivalence of algebraic expressions

You should recall that an expression of the form x^n is called a **power** of x, where x is the **base** of the power and n is the **exponent** of the power.

DEFINITION 2.1 *If $n \in N$ (i.e., $n \in \{natural\ numbers\}$) and $x \in R$, then*

$$x^n = \underbrace{x \cdot x \cdot x \cdots x.}_{n\ factors}$$

In any algebraic expression of the form $A + B + C + \cdots$, where A, B, C, $\cdots$ are algebraic expressions, A, B, C, $\cdots$ are called **terms** of the expression. For example, in $x + (y + 3)$ the terms are x and $(y + 3)$, but in $x + y + 3$ the terms are x, y, and 3. If an algebraic expression contains no variable in a denominator and contains only nonnegative integral powers of a variable, then the expression is a **polynomial**. For example,

$$5x, \quad \frac{3x^2}{2} - \frac{7x}{2}, \quad 0, \quad 2x^2 - 3x + 4, \quad \text{and} \quad \frac{y}{4} - \frac{\sqrt{7}}{4}$$

are polynomials, whereas

$$\frac{3}{x}, \quad 3 + \sqrt{x}, \quad \text{and} \quad \frac{2x-1}{2x+1}$$

are algebraic expressions, but not polynomials, in the variable x.

Polynomials consisting of one, two, or three terms are also called **monomials, binomials,** and **trinomials,** respectively. Thus $3x^2y$ is a monomial, $x + 4x^2$ is a binomial, and $x + y + z$ is a trinomial.

The **degree** of a monomial is given by the exponent of the variable in the monomial. Thus, 5 is of degree zero, $2x$ is of first degree, and $3x^4$ is of fourth degree; but no degree is assigned to the special monomial 0. If a monomial contains more than one variable, its degree is given by the sum of the exponents on the variables; $3x^2y^3z$ is of sixth degree in x, y, and z. It can also be described as being of second degree in x, third degree in y, fifth degree in x and y, and so on. The **degree of a polynomial** is the same as the degree of its term of greatest degree. Since no degree is assigned to the monomial 0, no degree is assigned to the zero polynomial 0, either.

Polynomial terms viewed as being added   Because $a - b$ is defined to be $a + (-b)$, we shall view the signs in any polynomial as signs denoting positive or negative coefficients, and the operation involved to be addition. Thus

$$3x - 5x + 4x = (3x) + (-5x) + (4x),$$

and its terms are $3x$, $-5x$, and $4x$.

Also, as regards multiplication and division, since

$$\frac{a}{b} = a\left(\frac{1}{b}\right),$$

Numerical coefficients   we can view division by a constant as multiplication by its reciprocal (multiplicative inverse), and, for example, write

$$\frac{3x^2}{4} + \frac{x}{2} \quad \text{as} \quad \frac{3}{4}x^2 + \frac{1}{2}x.$$

Addition and multiplication in polynomials   Accordingly, since a polynomial can be considered to involve only the operations of addition and multiplication, and since the set R of real numbers is closed with respect to these operations, it follows that, for any specific real value of x, a polynomial with real coefficients represents a real number. Therefore, the postulates for the real numbers are applicable to the terms in such polynomials and to the polynomials themselves.

Simplification of polynomials   By applying the commutative, associative, and distributive laws in various ways, we can frequently rewrite polynomials and their sums in what might be termed "simpler" form.

Example. $2x^2 + 3x + 5 + 2x + 6x^2 + 7 = 2x^2 + 6x^2 + 3x + 2x + 5 + 7$

$$= (2 + 6)x^2 + (3 + 2)x + (5 + 7)$$

$$= 8x^2 + 5x + 12$$

Here we have reduced the number of terms from six to three.

Representation of polynomials We shall often be concerned with polynomials in one variable. A polynomial of degree n, $n \geq 0$, in x can be represented—when its terms are rearranged, if need be—by an expression of the form

$$a_0 x^n + a_1 x^{n-1} + a_2 x^{n-2} + \cdots + a_{n-1}x + a_n \quad (a_0 \neq 0),$$

where it is understood that the a's are the (constant) coefficients of the powers of x in the polynomial.

The term $a_0 x^n$ is called the **leading term**, and the coefficient a_0 is called the **leading coefficient**, in the polynomial. It is often convenient to have the leading term of the form x^n. In this case (that is, when $a_0 = 1$), the polynomial is said to be **monic**.

If the coefficients in a polynomial are real numbers, then the polynomial is called a **polynomial over the real-number field**, or simply a **polynomial over R**. If the variable x is restricted to represent only real numbers, then the polynomial is said to be a **polynomial in the real variable x**. If *both* the coefficients and the variable are restricted to real values, we say that the polynomial is a **real polynomial**.

Polynomials are frequently represented by symbols such as

Symbols for polynomials $$P(x), \ D(y), \ \text{and} \ Q(z)$$

(read "P of x," "D of y," and "Q of z"), where the symbol in the parentheses designates the variable. Thus, we might write

$$P(x) = 2x^3 - 3x + 2,$$

$$D(y) = y^6 - 2y^2 + 3y - 2,$$

$$Q(z) = 8z^4 + 3z^3 - 2z^2 + z - 1.$$

Value of a polynomial for a given value of x The notation $P(x)$ can be used to denote values of the polynomial for specific values of x. Thus, $P(2)$ means the value of the polynomial $P(x)$ when x is replaced by 2. For example, if

$$P(x) = x^2 - 2x + 1,$$

then

$$P(2) = 2^2 - 2(2) + 1 = 1$$

and

$$P(-4) = (-4)^2 - 2(-4) + 1 = 25.$$

In some applications, the notation $P(x)|_a^b$ denotes $P(b) - P(a)$. Thus if

$$P(x) = \frac{x^2}{2} - 4x,$$

$$P(x)|_2^3 = P(3) - P(2) = \left[\frac{3^2}{2} - 4(3)\right] - \left[\frac{2^2}{2} - 4(2)\right] = -\frac{3}{2}.$$

EXERCISE 2.1

In Problems 1–6, give the degree of each polynomial. If the expression is not a polynomial, so state.

Example. $x^3y^2 + y^4 + x$.

Solution.   Fifth degree in x and y; fourth degree in y; third degree in x.

1. $y^3 + 6y + 4$ 2. $x^2 - x$ 3. $x^3y - xy^2 + x^2$

4. $4 - \dfrac{2}{x^2}$ 5. $\dfrac{x^2 + 3}{x^3}$ 6. $x^4 - x^3y^2 - y^3$

Example.   If $P(x) = 2x^2 - x + 3$, find $P(3)$, $P(-3)$, $P(0)$, $P(a)$.

Solution. $P(3) = 2(3)^2 - (3) + 3 = 18$

$P(-3) = 2(-3)^2 - (-3) + 3 = 24$

$P(0) = 2(0)^2 - (0) + 3 = 3$

$P(a) = 2a^2 - a + 3$

7. If $P(x) = x^3 - 3x^2 + x + 1$, find $P(2)$, $P(0)$, $P(x)|_0^2$, $P(x)|_{-2}^2$.

8. If $P(x) = 2x^3 + x^2 - 3x + 4$, find $P(3)$, $P(-3)$, $P(0)$, $P(x)|_{-3}^0$, $P(x)|_0^3$.

9. If $P(x) = x^{12}$, find $P(1)$, $P(-1)$, $P(0)$, $P(x)|_0^1$, $P(x)|_{-1}^1$.

10. If $P(x) = x^{13}$, find $P(1)$, $P(-1)$, $P(0)$, $P(x)|_0^1$, $P(x)|_{-1}^1$.

Example.   If $P(x) = x - 4$ and $Q(x) = x + 2$, find $P(Q(2))$ and $P(Q(x))$.

Solution. $Q(2) = 2 + 2 = 4$, so $P(Q(2)) = P(4) = 4 - 4 = 0$;

$P(Q(x)) = (x + 2) - 4 = x - 2$

11. If $P(x) = x + 2$ and $Q(x) = x - 3$, find $P(Q(2))$, $Q(P(2))$, $P(x) - Q(x)$.

12. If $P(x) = 2x + 1$ and $Q(x) = \dfrac{1}{2}(x - 1)$, find $P(Q(x))$, $Q(P(x))$, $(P(2))^2$.

13. If $P(x) = x^2 + 3$ and $Q(x) = 6$, find $P(Q(2))$, $Q(P(2))$, $P(Q(0))$.

14. If $P(x) = 2x^2 - 3x$ and $Q(x) = x^2 + 1$, find $P(Q(0))$, $Q(P(0))$, $P(Q(1)) - Q(P(-2))$.

In Problems 15–18, express as a polynomial a. $P(x) + Q(x)$ and b. $P(x) - Q(x)$.

15. $P(x) = 3x - 2$, $Q(x) = 3 - x$

16. $P(x) = x^2 + 3x - 2$, $Q(x) = 2x^2 + x - 2$

17. $P(x) = x^2 - 2x + 3$, $Q(x) = 2x^2 - 2x - 1$

18. $P(x) = 2x^3 - 3x^2 + x - 1$, $Q(x) = x^3 + 3x - 2$

In Problems 19–24, given that $P(x) = 2x^2 - 3x + 2$, $Q(x) = 3 - 2x + x^2$, and $S(x) = -2x^2 + 3x - 5$, write each expression as an equivalent polynomial.

19. $P(x) + Q(x)$ $2x^2 - 3x + 2$ $+ x^2 - 2x \quad 3$ $3x^2 - 5x + 5$

20. $P(x) + [Q(x) - S(x)]$

21. $P(x) - [Q(x) + S(x)]$

22. $P(x) - [Q(x) - S(x)]$

23. $[Q(x) - P(x)] - S(x)$

24. $S(x) - [-P(x) - Q(x)]$

25. If $P(x)$ is of degree n and $Q(x)$ is of degree $n - 2$, what is the degree of $P(x) + Q(x)$? Of $P(x) - Q(x)$?

26. If $P(x)$ and $Q(x)$ are polynomials, with $P(0) = 4$ and $Q(0) = 3$, what is the value of $P(x) + Q(x)$ for $x = 0$? Of $P(x) - Q(x)$ for $x = 0$?

2.2 PRODUCTS OF POLYNOMIALS

By Definition 2.1, for $x \in R$ and $n \in N$, we have

$$x^n = \underbrace{x \cdot x \cdot x \cdots x.}_{n \text{ factors}}$$

Now, consider the product $x^m \cdot x^n$, where m and n are natural numbers.

Since

$$x^m = x \cdot x \cdot x \cdots x \quad (m \text{ factors})$$

and

$$x^n = x \cdot x \cdot x \cdots x \quad (n \text{ factors}),$$

it follows that

$$x^m \cdot x^n = \underbrace{(x \cdot x \cdot x \cdots x)}_{m \text{ factors}} \underbrace{(x \cdot x \cdot x \cdots x)}_{n \text{ factors}}$$

$$= \underbrace{x \cdot x \cdot x \cdots x.}_{(m + n) \text{ factors}}$$

In the same way, we have

$$(x^m)^n = \underbrace{(x \cdot x \cdot x \cdots x)}_{m \text{ factors}} \underbrace{(x \cdot x \cdot x \cdots x)}_{m \text{ factors}} \cdots \underbrace{(x \cdot x \cdot x \cdots x)}_{m \text{ factors}} = x^{mn}$$

$$\underbrace{}_{n \text{ factors}}$$

and, for $y \in R$,

$$(xy)^n = \underbrace{(xy)(xy)(xy) \cdots (xy)}_{n \text{ factors}} = \underbrace{(x \cdot x \cdot x \cdots x)}_{n \text{ factors}} \underbrace{(y \cdot y \cdot y \cdots y)}_{n \text{ factors}} = x^n y^n.$$

Products of powers

We state the above results formally:

THEOREM 2.1 *If $x, y \in R$ and $m, n \in N$, then*

$$\text{I} \quad x^m x^n = x^{m+n},$$

$$\text{II} \quad (x^m)^n = x^{mn},$$

$$\text{III} \quad (xy)^n = x^n y^n.$$

Examples.

a. $x^2 x^3 = x^5$ b. $(x^3)^5 = x^{15}$ c. $(xy)^4 = x^4 y^4$

Product of monomials

We can use the commutative and associative laws and Theorem 2.1 to rewrite an expression for the product of any two monomials.

Examples.

a. $(3x^2 y)(2xy^2) = 6x^3 y^3$ b. $(-xy^3)(4xyz)(2yz) = -8x^2 y^5 z^2$

The **generalized distributive law**,

$$a(b_1 + b_2 + \cdots + b_n) = ab_1 + ab_2 + \cdots + ab_n,$$

can be applied to write as a polynomial the product of a monomial and a polynomial containing more than one term.

Example. $3x(x + y + z) = 3x^2 + 3xy + 3xz$

In its complete form, the generalized distributive law requires mathematical induction for its proof, but its validity as applied in our example here—or in any similar example—can readily be verified; thus we have

$$3x(x + y + z) = 3x[(x + y) + z] = 3x(x + y) + 3xz$$

$$= 3x^2 + 3xy + 3xz.$$

The distributive law can be applied successively to the product of polynomials containing more than one term.

Example.

$$(3x + 2y)(x - y) = 3x(x - y) + 2y(x - y)$$
$$= 3x^2 - 3xy + 2xy - 2y^2$$
$$= 3x^2 - xy - 2y^2$$

Standard binomial products

The following binomial products are types so frequently encountered that you should learn to recognize them on sight:

$$(x + a)(x + b) = x^2 + (a + b)x + ab,$$
$$(x + a)^2 = x^2 + 2ax + a^2,$$
$$(x + a)(x - a) = x^2 - a^2.$$

EXERCISE 2.2

Write each product in polynomial form in which constants and powers of each variable in each term are combined.

Examples.

a. $(-2x^2)(3xy)(y^2)$

b. $a^n \cdot a^{n+1}$

Solutions.

a. $-6x^3y^3$

b. $a^{n+(n+1)}$
   a^{2n+1}

1. $(-3x^2)(-2xy)(-y^3)$ $-6x^3y^4$

2. $(a^3)(-2ab^2)(-b^3)$ $2a^4b^5$

3. $a^{n+1} \cdot a^{n-1}$ a^{2n}

4. $y^{2n-1} \cdot y^{n+2}$

Examples.

a. $2(x^2 - x - 1)$

b. $(x - 3)(x + 5)$

Solutions.

a. $2x^2 - 2x - 2$

b. $x^2 + 5x - 3x - 15$
   $x^2 + 2x - 15$

5. $abc(a - b + 2c)$

6. $-ab(2a - b + 3c)$

7. $(x + 2)(x + 5)$

8. $(x - 3)(x + 2)$

9. $(x - 2y)^2$

10. $(2x - y)^2$

11. $(5x + 1)(2x + 3)$

12. $(2x + 3)(x - 5)$

13. $(3a + 2b)(3a - 2b)$

14. $(5x - y)(5x + y)$

15. $(x + 4)(x^2 + 2x - 1)$ 16. $(x - 2)(x^2 - x + 3)$

17. $2(x + 1)(x + 3)$ 18. $3(x - 1)(x + 2)$

19. $-(2a - b)(c - 3d)$ 20. $-(3a - b)(c + 3d)$

21. $a(a - b)(a^2 + ab + b^2)$ 22. $b(a + b)(a^2 - ab + b^2)$

23. $2\{a - [a - 2(a + 1) + 1] + 1\}$ 24. $-\{4 - [3 - 2(a - 1) + a] + a\}$

25. $2x\{x + 3[2(2x - 1) - x + 1] + 5\}$ 26. $-x\{4 - 2[1 - 2(x + 3)] - x\}$

27. If $P(x) = x^2 - 3x + 7$, find $P(x - 1)$, $P(2 - x)$.

28. If $P(x) = x^2 + 2x + 1$, find $P(x + h)$, $P(x - h)$.

29. If $P(x) = x^2 - 3x$, find $[P(-x)]^2$, $[P(a^2)]^2 - P(a^2)$, $[P(2x) - P(x)]^2$.

30. If $P(x) = 3 - x^2$, find $[P(3)]^2$, $[P(3)]^2 - P(3^2)$, $P(x + b) - P(x)$.

31. Simplify the difference $(a + b)^2 - (a^2 + b^2)$. What are the conditions on a and b for $a^2 + b^2$ to be greater than $(a + b)^2$? For $a^2 + b^2$ to be less than $(a + b)^2$?

2.3 FACTORING POLYNOMIALS

What do we mean when we say that we have *factored* an integer or a polynomial? It is true, for example, that

$$2 = 4\left(\frac{1}{2}\right),$$

Factors in a domain	but we would not ordinarily say that 4 and $\frac{1}{2}$ are factors of 2. On the other hand, since

$$10 = (2)(5),$$

we do say that 2 and 5 are factors of 10 in the domain J of integers.

Now consider the polynomial

$$2x^2 - 10.$$

As we shall presently see, in the domain of polynomials in x having *integral* coefficients—that is, coefficients that are integers—its complete factorization is given by

$$2x^2 - 10 = 2(x^2 - 5);$$

but in the domain of polynomials in x having real numbers as coefficients, its complete factorization is

$$2x^2 - 10 = 2(x - \sqrt{5})(x + \sqrt{5}).$$

Thus the result depends in part on the domain in which we consider that the factorization is being performed. The choice of order of factors is arbitrary;

the arrangement that seems most "natural" should be used, although this arrangement is admittedly not always easy to determine. For instance, the forms

Order of factors and terms

$2(x - \sqrt{5})(x + \sqrt{5})$ and $2(x + \sqrt{5})(x - \sqrt{5})$ are equivalent, but it is difficult to affirm one as more "natural" than the other. Ordinarily, however, we write monomial factors first, and order the terms within a factor according to descending degree of the variable.

We say that a polynomial having integral coefficients is **prime** if it is not the product of two polynomials having integral coefficients with no common integral factor other than 1 or -1. For example, in the polynomial

$$2x^2 + x - 3,$$

the coefficients 2, 1, and -3 have no common integral factor other than 1 or -1, but the polynomial is not prime; instead, it is the product of two prime polynomials, namely,

$$2x^2 + x - 3 = (2x + 3)(x - 1).$$

We say that a polynomial other than 0 or 1 with integral coefficients is **completely factored** if it is written equivalently as a product of prime polynomials. One very common type of factoring is that involving quadratic (second-degree) binomials or trinomials with integral coefficients. From Section 2.2, we recall that

Factors of quadratics

$$(x + a)(x + b) = x^2 + (a + b)x + ab, \tag{1}$$

$$(x + a)^2 = x^2 + 2ax + a^2, \tag{2}$$

$$(x + a)(x - a) = x^2 - a^2. \tag{3}$$

These three forms are those most commonly encountered in the chapters that follow. In this section, we are interested in viewing these relationships from right to left—that is, from polynomial to factored form.

There are a few other polynomials that occur frequently enough to justify a study of their factorization. In particular, the forms

$$(a + b)(x + y) = ax + ay + bx + by, \tag{4}$$

$$(x + a)(x^2 - ax + a^2) = x^3 + a^3, \tag{5}$$

$$(x - a)(x^2 + ax + a^2) = x^3 - a^3 \tag{6}$$

are often encountered in one or another part of mathematics. We are again interested in viewing these relationships from right to left.

Factors by grouping

Expressions such as the right-hand member of form (4) are factorable by grouping. For example, to factor

$$3x^2y + 2y + 3xy^2 + 2x,$$

we write it in the form

$$3x^2y + 2x + 3xy^2 + 2y$$

and factor the common monomial x from the first group of two terms and y from the second group of two terms, obtaining

$$x(3xy + 2) + y(3xy + 2).$$

If now we factor the common binomial $(3xy + 2)$ from each term, we have

$$(3xy + 2)(x + y),$$

in which both factors are prime.

The application of forms (5) and (6) is direct.

Example. $$8a^3 + b^3 = (2a)^3 + b^3$$
$$= (2a + b)[(2a)^2 - 2ab + b^2]$$
$$= (2a + b)(4a^2 - 2ab + b^2)$$

EXERCISE 2.3

Factor completely in the domain of polynomials with integer coefficients. (Assume that all variables in exponents represent natural numbers.)

Examples.

a. $18x^2y - 24xy^2 + 6xy$ b. $x^{2n} + x^n$ c. $4a^3 - 5a^2 + a$

Solutions.

a. $(2)(3)xy(3x - 4y + 1)$ b. $x^n(x^n + 1)$ c. $a(4a^2 - 5a + 1)$
$a(4a - 1)(a - 1)$

1. $9x^5y - 3x^4y + 6x^3y$ 2. $x^2y^2z^2 + 2xyz - xz$

3. $x^{3n} + x^n$ 4. $x^{4n} - x^{2n}$

5. $x^{n+2} - x^{n+1} + 2x^n$ 6. $x^{n-2} - 3x^{n-1} + x^n$

7. $x^2 - 8x + 12$ 8. $6 - a - a^2$

9. $x^2 - 25$ 10. $4x^2 + 12x + 9$

11. $3x^2 + 12x + 12$ 12. $x^4y^2 - x^2y^2$

Examples.

a. $by - ay + bx - ax$ b. $8x^3 - y^3$

Solutions.

a. $y(b - a) + x(b - a)$ b. $(2x)^3 - y^3$
$(b - a)(y + x)$ $(2x - y)(4x^2 + 2xy + y^2)$

13. $y^4 + 3y^2 + 2$ 14. $x^4 - 5x^2 + 4$

15. $2a^4 - a^2 - 1$

16. $3z^4 - 11z^2 - 4$

17. $x^4 - (y - 2x)^4$

18. $ax^2 + x + ax + 1$

19. $x^2 + ax + xy + ay$

20. $3x + y - 6x^2 - 2xy$

21. $a^3 + 2ab^2 - 4b^3 - 2a^2b$

22. $6x^3 - 4x^2 + 3x - 2$

23. $y^3 - 27x^3$

24. $8 + x^3y^3$

25. $x^3 + (x - y)^3$

26. $(x + y)^3 - z^3$

Examples.

a. $a^{2n} - 9$

b. $x^{4n} - 3x^{2n} - 4$

Solutions.

a. $(a^n - 3)(a^n + 3)$

b. $(x^{2n} - 4)(x^{2n} + 1)$
$(x^n - 2)(x^n + 2)(x^{2n} + 1)$

27. $a^{2n} - 4$

28. $x^{2n} - y^{2n}$

29. $x^{4n} - y^{4n}$

30. $x^{4n} - 2x^{2n} + 1$

31. $3x^{4n} - 10x^{2n} + 3$

32. $6y^{2n} + 30y^n - 900$

33. $2y^{2n} - 12y^n - 1440$

34. $2x^{2n} - 23x^ny^n - 39y^{2n}$

35. Show that $ac - ad + bd - bc$ can be factored both as $(a - b)(c - d)$ and as $(b - a)(d - c)$.

36. Show that $a^2 - b^2 - c^2 + 2bc$ can be factored as $(a - b + c)(a + b - c)$.

37. Consider the polynomial $x^4 + x^2y^2 + 25y^4$. If $9x^2y^2$ is both added to and subtracted from this expression (thus producing an equivalent expression), we have

$$x^4 + x^2y^2 + 25y^4 + 9x^2y^2 - 9x^2y^2,$$

$$(x^4 + 10x^2y^2 + 25y^4) - 9x^2y^2,$$

$$(x^2 + 5y^2)^2 - 9x^2y^2,$$

$$[(x^2 + 5y^2) - 3xy][(x^2 + 5y^2) + 3xy],$$

$$(x^2 - 3xy + 5y^2)(x^2 + 3xy + 5y^2).$$

By adding and subtracting an appropriate monomial, factor $x^4 + x^2y^2 + y^4$.

38. Use the method of Problem 37 to factor $x^4 - 3x^2y^2 + y^4$.

2.4 QUOTIENTS OF POLYNOMIALS

It is easy to show that the set of integers is not closed with respect to division; 2/3, 1/5, 8/9, and $-3/4$ are all examples of noninteger quotients of integers. Similarly, we can see that the set of polynomials is not closed with respect to division, because $1/x$ is a counterexample. That is, $1/x$ is the quotient of the polynomials 1 and x, but is not, itself, a polynomial. In Exercise 1.4, Problem 42, you were asked to show that if a, b, and q are real numbers, with $b \neq 0$, then

$$\frac{a}{b} = q \quad \text{if and only if} \quad a = bq.$$

When we observe that the closure laws guarantee the applicability of the real-number axioms to real polynomials, this problem suffices to validate the following theorem.

THEOREM 2.2 *If A, D, and Q are real polynomials, then for values of the variables for which D $\neq$ 0,*

$$\frac{A}{D} = Q \quad \text{if and only if} \quad A = DQ.$$

If a polynomial Q exists such that $A = DQ$, $D \neq 0$, then A is said to be **exactly divisible** by D. If A is not exactly divisible by D, then the quotient A/D cannot be written equivalently as a polynomial.

Let us examine some ways in which we can rewrite quotients of polynomials, even if the resulting expressions are not always, themselves, polynomials. We begin with the simplest case, that in which A and D are monomials and their quotient is a polynomial. Consider

$$\frac{x^m}{x^n} \quad (x \in R, \ x \neq 0, \ m,n \in N, \ \text{and} \ m > n).$$

We have

$$\frac{x^m}{x^n} = x^m \cdot \frac{1}{x^n} = (x^{m-n} \cdot x^n) \cdot \frac{1}{x^n} = x^{m-n} \cdot \left(x^n \cdot \frac{1}{x^n} \right) = x^{m-n} \cdot 1,$$

from which we obtain

$$\frac{x^m}{x^n} = x^{m-n}.$$

| Quotient of powers |

This establishes the first part of the following result. Proof of the second part is similar to the proof of Theorem 2.1-III and will be omitted.

THEOREM 2.3 *If x, y $\in$ R, x $\neq$ 0, m, n $\in$ N, and m > n, then*

$$\text{I} \quad \frac{x^m}{x^n} = x^{m-n},$$

$$\text{II} \quad \left(\frac{y}{x} \right)^n = \frac{y^n}{x^n}.$$

The theorem enables us, for example, to write

$$\frac{12a^5b^3}{4a^2b^2} = \frac{12}{4} \cdot a^{5-2}b^{3-2} = 3a^3b \quad (a, b \neq 0).$$

Note that a and b are not permitted to take the value 0, because if they were, $3a^3b$ would represent a real number, 0, although $(12a^5b^3)/(4a^2b^2)$ would not be defined.

Quotient of polynomials

Theorem 1.11-III (together with the closure laws) permits us to rewrite quotients of polynomials of the form $(A + B)/C$, $C \neq 0$, in the form $A/C + B/C$, and then to do such further rewriting as seems indicated. For example,

$$\frac{2x^3 + 4x^2 + 8x}{2x} = \frac{2x^3}{2x} + \frac{4x^2}{2x} + \frac{8x}{2x},$$

and, by an application of Theorem 2.3-I, the right-hand member can then be denoted by the expression

$$x^2 + 2x + \frac{8x}{2x} \quad (x \neq 0).$$

Though Theorem 2.3 is not applicable to the variable factors in expressions such as $8x/2x$, by Theorem 1.11-II and the fact that $x/x = 1$ for $x \neq 0$, we can write

$$\frac{8x}{2x} = \frac{8}{2} \cdot \frac{x}{x} = \frac{8}{2} \cdot 1 = 4,$$

for every $x \neq 0$. Thus,

$$\frac{2x^3 + 4x^2 + 8x}{2x} = x^2 + 2x + 4 \quad (x \neq 0).$$

As mentioned at the start of this section, however, quotients of polynomials cannot always be represented by polynomials. For example, we have

$$\frac{2x^3 + 4x + 1}{x} = \frac{2x^3}{x} + \frac{4x}{x} + \frac{1}{x}$$

$$= 2x^2 + 4 + \frac{1}{x} \quad (x \neq 0),$$

where the resulting expression is not a polynomial.

If the divisor of a quotient contains more than one term, the familiar **long-division algorithm** involving successive subtractions can be used to rewrite the quotient. For example, the computation

$$
\begin{array}{r}
x - 3 \\
x^2 + 2x - 1 \overline{\smash{\big)}\ x^3 - x^2 - 7x + 3} \\
\underline{x^3 + 2x^2 - x} \\
-3x^2 - 6x + 3 \\
\underline{-3x^2 - 6x + 3} \\
0
\end{array}
$$

shows that, for $x^2 + 2x - 1 \neq 0$,

$$\frac{x^3 - x^2 - 7x + 3}{x^2 + 2x - 1} = x - 3.$$

It is most convenient to arrange the dividend and the divisor in descending powers of the variable before using the division algorithm, and to leave an appropriate space for any missing terms (terms with coefficient 0) in the dividend.

When the divisor is not a factor of the dividend, the division process will produce a nonzero remainder. For example, from

$$
\begin{array}{r}
x^3 - 3x^2 + 10x - 28 \\
x + 3 \,\overline{\smash{\big)}\, x^4 \qquad\quad + x^2 + 2x - 1} \\
\underline{x^4 + 3x^3} \\
-3x^3 + x^2 \\
\underline{-3x^3 - 9x^2} \\
10x^2 + 2x \\
\underline{10x^2 + 30x} \\
-28x - 1 \\
\underline{-28x - 84} \\
83 \quad \text{(remainder)}
\end{array}
$$

we see that

$$\frac{x^4 + x^2 + 2x - 1}{x + 3} = x^3 - 3x^2 + 10x - 28 + \frac{83}{x + 3} \qquad (x \neq -3).$$

Observe in the foregoing example that a space is left in the dividend for a term involving x^3, even though the dividend contains no such term.

If the divisor is of the form $x + c$, the process of dividing one polynomial by another can be simplified by a process called **synthetic division**. Consider the foregoing example. If we omit writing the variables and write only the coefficients of the terms, and use zero for the coefficient of any missing power, we have

$$
\begin{array}{r}
1 - 3 + 10 - 28 \\
1 + 3 \,\overline{\smash{\big)}\, 1 + 0 + 1 \ +2 \ -1} \\
\underline{1 + 3} \\
-3 + (1) \\
\underline{-3 - 9} \\
10 + (2) \\
\underline{-10 + 30} \\
-28 - (1) \\
\underline{-28 - 84} \\
83 \quad \text{(remainder)}.
\end{array}
$$

Now, observe that the numerals shown in color are repetitions of the numerals written immediately above and are also repetitions of the coefficients of the associated variable in the quotient; the numbers in parentheses, ( ), are repetitions of the coefficients of the dividend. Therefore, the whole process can be written in compact form as

$$
\begin{array}{rrrrrr}
(1) & 3\,\rule[-1ex]{0.5pt}{3ex}\,1 & 0 & 1 & 2 & -1 \\
(2) & & 3 & -9 & 30 & -84 \\
(3) & 1 & -3 & 10 & -28 & 83 \quad \text{(remainder: 83)}
\end{array}
$$

where the repetitions are omitted and where 1, the coefficient of x in the divisor, has also been omitted.

The entries in line (3), which are the coefficients of the variables in the quotient

Synthetic-division process

and the remainder, have been obtained by *subtracting* the detached **coefficients** in line (2) from the detached coefficients of terms of the same degree in line (1). We could obtain the same result by replacing 3 with -3 in the divisor and *adding* instead of subtracting at each step, and this is what is done in the *synthetic-division* process. The final form then appears as

$$
\begin{array}{rrrrrr}
(1) & -3\,\rule[-1ex]{0.5pt}{3ex}\,1 & 0 & 1 & 2 & -1 \\
(2) & & -3 & 9 & -30 & 84 \\
(3) & 1 & -3 & 10 & -28 & 83 \quad \text{(remainder: 83).}
\end{array}
$$

Comparing the results of using synthetic division with those obtained by the same process using long division, we observe that the entries in line (3) are the coefficients of the polynomial $x^3 - 3x^2 + 10x - 28$, and that there is a remainder of 83.

Example. Write $\dfrac{3x^3 - 4x - 1}{x - 2}$ in the form $Q + \dfrac{r}{D}$, where r is a constant.

Solution. Using synthetic division, we first write

$$
2\,\rule[-1ex]{0.5pt}{3ex}\;\; 3 \quad 0 \quad -4 \quad -1,
$$

where 0 has been inserted in the position that would be occupied by the coefficient of a second-degree term if such a term were present in the dividend. Our divisor, $x - 2$, is indicated by the negative of -2, or 2. Continuing the synthetic division, we write,

$$
\begin{array}{rrrrr}
(1) & 2\,\rule[-1ex]{0.5pt}{3ex}\,3 & 0 & -4 & -1 \\
(2) & & 6 & 12 & 16 \\
(3) & 3 & 6 & 8 & 15 \quad \text{(remainder: 15).}
\end{array}
$$

This process employs these steps:

1. 3 is "brought down" from line (1) to line (3).
2. 6, the product of 2 and 3, is written in the next position on line (2).
3. 6, the sum of 0 and 6, is written on line (3).
4. 12, the product of 2 and 6, is written in the next position on line (2).
5. 8, the sum of -4 and 12, is written on line (3).
6. 16, the product of 2 and 8, is written in the next position on line (2).
7. 15, the sum of -1 and 16, is written on line (3).

We can use the first three entries on line (3) as coefficients to write a polynomial of degree one less than the degree of the dividend. This polynomial is the quotient lacking the remainder. The last number is the remainder. Thus, for $x - 2 \neq 0$, the quotient when $3x^3 - 4x - 1$ is divided by $x - 2$ is $3x^2 + 6x + 8$, with a remainder of 15; that is,

$$\frac{3x^3 - 4x - 1}{x - 2} = 3x^2 + 6x + 8 + \frac{15}{x - 2} \quad (x \neq 2).$$

The foregoing example illustrates a theorem that we shall state without proof.

THEOREM 2.4 *If $P(x)$ is a real polynomial of degree $n \geq 1$, and c is any real number, then there exist a unique real polynomial $Q(x)$ of degree $n - 1$, and a unique real number r, such that*

$$P(x) = (x - c)Q(x) + r.$$

Although this theorem does not directly involve the quotient $\dfrac{P(x)}{x - c}$, it does assure us that, for $x \neq c$,

$$\frac{P(x)}{x - c} = Q(x) + \frac{r}{x - c}.$$

Now consider the following important result.

THEOREM 2.5 *If $P(x)$ is a real polynomial, then for every real number c there exists a unique polynomial $Q(x)$ such that*

$$P(x) = (x - c)Q(x) + P(c).$$

Proof. From Theorem 2.4, we know that, for every real number c, there exists a real polynomial $Q(x)$ and a real number r such that

$$P(x) = (x - c)Q(x) + r.$$

Since this is true for all $x \in R$, it must be true for $x = c$. Thus we have

$$P(c) = (c - c)Q(c) + r$$
$$= 0 \cdot Q(c) + r$$
$$= r,$$

and the theorem is proved.

This theorem is called the **remainder theorem** because it asserts that the remainder, when $P(x)$ is divided by $x - c$, is the value of P at c, that is, $P(c)$. Since synthetic division offers a quick means of obtaining this remainder, we can usually find values $P(c)$ more rapidly by synthetic division than by direct substitution.

Example.   If $P(x) = x^3 - x^2 + 3$, find $P(3)$ by the remainder theorem.

Solution.   Synthetically dividing $x^3 - x^2 + 3$ by $x - 3$, we have

$$
\begin{array}{r|rrrr}
3 & 1 & -1 & 0 & 3 \\
  &   & 3 & 6 & 18 \\
\hline
  & 1 & 2 & 6 & 21
\end{array}
$$

and, by inspection, $r = P(3) = 21$.

EXERCISE 2.4

Write each quotient as a polynomial. (Assume that all variables in exponents represent natural numbers.)

Examples.

a. $\dfrac{6x^2y^3}{2xy}$

b. $\dfrac{x^{2n+3}}{x^{n+1}}$

c. $\dfrac{2y^3 - 6y^2 + y}{y}$

Solutions.

a. $\dfrac{6}{2} \cdot x^{2-1}y^{3-1}$

$3xy^2 \quad (x, y \neq 0)$

b. $x^{2n+3-(n+1)}$

$x^{n+2} \quad (x \neq 0)$

c. $\dfrac{2y^3}{y} - \dfrac{6y^2}{y} + \dfrac{y}{y}$

$2y^2 - 6y + 1 \quad (y \neq 0)$

1. $\dfrac{8a^3y^5}{2a^2y^3}$ $4ay^2$

2. $\dfrac{38a^3b^5}{19ab^3}$

3. $\dfrac{x^{2n+2}}{x^{n-1}}$ x^{n+1}

4. $\dfrac{a^{2n+3}}{a^{n-4}}$

5. $\dfrac{x^{2n}y^{n+1}}{x^ny}$

6. $\dfrac{r^{2n}s^{n+5}}{r^{n-1}s^{n+3}}$

7. $\dfrac{8a^2 + 4a + 4}{2}$

8. $\dfrac{12x^3 - 8x^2 + 36x}{4x}$

9. $\dfrac{x^3 - 4x^2 - 3x}{x}$

10. $\dfrac{8a^2x^2 - 4ax^2 + ax}{ax}$

Write each quotient, P/D, in the form $Q + R/D$, where the degree of R is less than the degree of D.

Examples.

a. $\dfrac{2y^3 - 6y^2 + 2y - 4}{y}$

b. $\dfrac{y^3 + y^2 - 5y + 2}{y^2 - 2y}$

Solutions.

a. $\dfrac{2y^3}{y} - \dfrac{6y^2}{y} + \dfrac{2y}{y} - \dfrac{4}{y}$

$2y^2 - 6y + 2 - \dfrac{4}{y} \quad (y \neq 0)$

b.
$$\begin{array}{r} y + 3 \\ y^2 - 2y\,\overline{)\,y^3 + y^2 - 5y + 2} \\ \underline{y^3 - 2y^2} \\ 3y^2 - 5y \\ \underline{3y^2 - 6y} \\ y + 2 \end{array}$$

$y + 3 + \dfrac{y+2}{y^2 - 2y} \quad (y \neq 0, 2)$

11. $\dfrac{15x^3y - 10x^2y + 3y}{5xy}$ $3x^2 - 2x + \tfrac{3}{5t}$

12. $\dfrac{38a^{2n} - 19a^n + 3}{19a^n}$

13. $\dfrac{4y^3 + 12y + 5}{2y + 1}$ 14. $\dfrac{2x^4 + 13x^3 - 7}{2x - 1}$

15. $\dfrac{4y^5 - 4y^2 - 5y + 1}{2y^2 + y + 1}$ 16. $\dfrac{2x^3 - 3x^2 - 15x - 1}{x^2 + 5}$

Use synthetic division to write each quotient $P(x)/D(x)$ in the form $Q(x) + r/D(x)$, where $Q(x)$ is a polynomial and r is a constant.

Examples.

a. $\dfrac{2x^4 + x^3 - 1}{x + 2}$ b. $\dfrac{x^3 - 1}{x - 1}$

Solutions.

a. $\underline{-2}\big|$ 2   1   0   0 -1 b. $1\big|$ 1   0   0 -1

               -4 6 -12 24   1   1   1

         2   -3 6 -12 23   1   1   1   0

$2x^3 - 3x^2 + 6x - 12 + \dfrac{23}{x + 2}$ $(x \ne -2)$ $x^2 + x + 1$ $(x \ne 1)$

17. $\dfrac{x^4 - 3x^3 + 2x^2 - 1}{x - 2}$ 18. $\dfrac{x^4 + 2x^2 - 3x + 5}{x - 3}$ 19. $\dfrac{2x^3 + x - 5}{x + 1}$

20. $\dfrac{3x^3 + x^2 - 7}{x + 2}$ 21. $\dfrac{2x^4 - x + 6}{x - 5}$ 22. $\dfrac{3x^4 - x^2 + 1}{x - 4}$

23. $\dfrac{x^3 + 4x^2 + x - 2}{x + 2}$ 24. $\dfrac{x^3 - 7x^2 - x + 3}{x + 3}$ 25. $\dfrac{x^6 + x^4 - x}{x - 1}$

26. $\dfrac{x^6 + 3x^3 - 2x - 1}{x - 2}$ 27. $\dfrac{x^5 - 1}{x - 1}$ 28. $\dfrac{x^5 + 1}{x + 1}$

29. $\dfrac{x^6 - 1}{x - 1}$ 30. $\dfrac{x^6 + 1}{x + 1}$

Use synthetic division in Problems 31-36.

31. $P(x) = x^3 + 2x^2 + x - 1$; find $P(1)$, $P(2)$, and $P(3)$.

32. $P(x) = x^3 - 3x^2 - x + 3$; find $P(1)$, $P(2)$, and $P(3)$.

33. $P(x) = 2x^4 - 3x^3 + x + 2$; find $P(-2)$, $P(2)$, and $P(4)$.

34. $P(x) = 3x^4 + 3x^2 - x + 3$; find $P(-2)$, $P(2)$, and $P(4)$.

35. $P(x) = 3x^5 - x^3 + 2x^2 - 1$; find $P(-3)$, $P(2)$, and $P(3)$.

36. $P(x) = 2x^6 - x^4 + 3x^3 + 1$; find $P(-3,)$ $P(2)$, and $P(3)$.

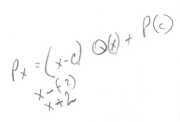

37. Use synthetic division to show that the first three terms in the expansion of the quotient

$$\frac{x^n - 1}{x - 1} \quad (x \neq 1, n \in N)$$

are $x^{n-1} + x^{n-2} + x^{n-3}$, and then argue that the quotient is $x^{n-1} + x^{n-2} + x^{n-3} + \cdots + x + 1$ and the remainder is 0.

2.5 EQUIVALENT RATIONAL EXPRESSIONS

A fraction is an expression denoting a quotient. If the numerator (dividend) and the denominator (divisor) are polynomials, then the fraction is said to be a **rational expression**. Trivially, any polynomial can be considered as being a rational expression, since it is the quotient of itself and 1. For each replacement of the variable(s) for which the numerator and denominator of a fraction represent real numbers and for which the denominator is not zero, a rational expression represents a real number. Of course, for any value(s) of the variable(s) for which the denominator vanishes (is equal to zero), the fraction does not represent a real number and is said to be undefined.

Since it is true that, for each replacement of the variable(s) for which its denominator is not zero, a rational expression represents a real number, some theorems for rational expressions follow directly from Theorems 1.10 and 1.11 and the laws of closure.

THEOREM 2.6 *If A, B, C, and D represent polynomials, then for values of the variables for which the denominators do not vanish,*

$$\text{I} \quad \frac{A}{B} = \frac{C}{D} \text{ if and only if } AD = BC,$$

$$\text{II} \quad -\frac{A}{B} = \frac{-A}{B} = \frac{A}{-B} = -\frac{-A}{-B},$$

$$\text{III} \quad \frac{A}{B} = \frac{-A}{-B} = -\frac{-A}{B} = -\frac{A}{-B},$$

$$\text{IV} \quad \frac{AC}{BC} = \frac{A}{B} \quad (\textit{fundamental principle of fractions}).$$

A fraction is said to be in **lowest terms** when the numerator and denominator do not contain certain prescribed types of factors in common. The arithmetic fraction a/b, where a and b are integers and $b \neq 0$, is in lowest terms provided a

and b are relatively prime—that is, provided they contain no common positive integral factors other than 1. If the numerator and denominator of a fraction are polynomials with integral coefficients, then the fraction is said to be in lowest terms if the numerator and denominator cannot be expressed as products of polynomials having integral coefficients with a common factor other than ± 1.

To express a given fraction in lowest terms (called **reducing** the fraction), we can factor the numerator and denominator and apply the fundamental principle of fractions.

Example.
$$\frac{y}{y^2} = \frac{1 \cdot y}{y \cdot y} = \frac{1}{y} \quad (y \neq 0)$$

Diagonal lines are sometimes used to abbreviate the procedure in the example. We may write

$$\frac{y}{y^2} = \frac{\overset{1}{\cancel{y}}}{\underset{y}{\cancel{y^2}}} = \frac{1}{y} \quad (y \neq 0),$$

using the diagonal lines instead of writing $\dfrac{1 \cdot y}{y \cdot y}$. Reducing a fraction to lowest terms should be accomplished mentally whenever convenient.

Reduction of rational expressions   To reduce fractions with polynomial numerators and denominators, you should, when possible, write them in factored form. Common factors are then evident by inspection.

Example.
$$\frac{2x^2 + x - 15}{2x + 6} = \frac{(2x - 5)(x + 3)}{2(x + 3)}$$

$$= \frac{2x - 5}{2} \quad (x \neq -3)$$

We can also change fractions to equivalent fractions in higher terms by applying the fundamental principle in the form

$$\frac{A}{B} = \frac{AC}{BC} \quad (B, C \neq 0).$$

We might want to do this, for instance, in order to express two given fractions A/B and D/C as equivalent fractions with the same denominator BC.

In general, to change a fraction A/B to an equivalent fraction with BC as denominator, we can determine the factor C by inspection, and then can multiply the numerator and the denominator of the original fraction by this factor.

EXERCISE 2.5

Reduce to lowest terms where possible. Specify restrictions on the variable(s) for which the reduction is not valid.

Examples.

a. $\dfrac{a-b}{b^2-a^2}$

b. $\dfrac{a+b}{b}$

Solutions.

a. $\dfrac{-(b-a)}{(b-a)(b+a)}$

$\dfrac{-1}{b+a}$ $(b \neq a, -a)$

b. Expression is in lowest terms $(b \neq 0)$.

1. $\dfrac{a^2bc}{ab^2c}$ $\dfrac{a}{b}$

2. $\dfrac{24x^4y^2z}{16x^3y^2z}$

3. $\dfrac{2x+2y}{x+y}$

4. $\dfrac{x^2+x}{x+1}$

5. $\dfrac{a-b}{b-a}$

6. $\dfrac{x^2-xy}{y-x}$

7. $\dfrac{x^2-1}{1-x}$

8. $\dfrac{x^2-16}{4-x}$

9. $\dfrac{2x^3-4y^2-3x}{2x}$

10. $\dfrac{8a^2x^2-4ax^2+ax}{2ax}$

11. $\dfrac{y^2+5y-14}{y-2}$

12. $\dfrac{x^2+5x+6}{x+3}$

13. $\dfrac{4y^2+8y-5}{1-2y}$

14. $\dfrac{2x^2+13x-7}{1-2x}$

15. $\dfrac{x^3-y^3}{x^2-y^2}$

16. $\dfrac{x^4-y^4}{x^2+y^2}$

17. $\dfrac{y^4-16}{y^4-y^2-12}$

18. $\dfrac{a^3-a^2+b^2+b^3}{3a^2+6ab+3b^2}$

19. $\dfrac{x^2-2xy+y^2+x-y}{y^2-x^2}$

20. $\dfrac{8x^2-8xy-x^3-y^3+8y^2}{x^4+x^2y^2+y^4}$

Express each of the given fractions as an equivalent fraction with the given denominator. Specify values for the variable for which the fractions are not equivalent.

21. $\dfrac{3}{4}; \dfrac{}{12}$

22. $\dfrac{1}{5}; \dfrac{}{10}$

23. $\dfrac{b}{a}; \dfrac{}{a^2b}$

24. $\dfrac{b}{2a}; \dfrac{}{6a^3b^2}$

25. $\dfrac{3}{y+2}; \dfrac{}{y^2 - y - 6}$

26. $\dfrac{2}{x+3}; \dfrac{}{x^2 + x - 6}$

27. $\dfrac{3}{a+3}; \dfrac{}{a^3 + 27}$

28. $\dfrac{-2}{x^2 + y^2}; \dfrac{}{x^4 - y^4}$

29. Is the value of the fraction $\dfrac{x(1-x)}{x^2 - 3x + 2}$ equal to that of $\dfrac{x}{2-x}$ for all values of x? If not, for what value(s) of x does the equality fail to hold?

30. Write three equivalent forms of the fraction $\dfrac{1}{a-b}$ $(a \neq b)$ by changing the sign or signs of the numerator, denominator, or fraction itself.

31. What are the conditions on a and b for the fraction $\dfrac{-1}{a-b}$ $(a \neq b)$ to represent a positive number? A negative number?

32. Is the fraction $\dfrac{x-2}{1+x^2}$ defined for all values of $x \in R$? For what value(s) of x does the fraction equal zero?

2.6 SUMS OF RATIONAL EXPRESSIONS

Since rational expressions represent real numbers for each replacement of the variable(s) for which the denominators are not zero, the following theorem is a direct consequence of Theorem 1.11-III and the laws of closure.

THEOREM 2.7 *If A, B, and C are polynomials, then for values of the variables for which $C \neq 0$,*

$$\frac{A}{C} + \frac{B}{C} = \frac{A+B}{C}.$$

This principle, of course, extends to the sum of any number of fractions.

If the fractions in a sum have unlike denominators, we can replace the fractions with equivalent fractions having common denominators and then write the sum as a single fraction.

Example.

$$\frac{3x^2 - 5x}{2} + \frac{x^2 + 2}{3} = \frac{(3x^2 - 5x)(3)}{2(3)} + \frac{(x^2 + 2)(2)}{(3)(2)}$$

$$= \frac{(9x^2 - 15x) + (2x^2 + 4)}{6}$$

$$= \frac{11x^2 - 15x + 4}{6}$$

Differences can be viewed as sums and then expressed as a single fraction by an application of Theorem 2.7.

In rewriting fractions in a sum so that they share a common denominator, any such denominator may be used. If the **least common multiple** of the denominators (called the **least common denominator**) is used, however, the resulting fraction will be in simpler form than if any other common denominator is employed. The least

Least common multiple of polynomials

common multiple of two or more natural numbers is the least natural number that is exactly divisible by each of the given numbers.

The notion of a least common multiple among several polynomial expressions is, in general, meaningless without further specification of what is desired. We can, however, define the least common multiple of a set of polynomials with integral coefficients to be the polynomial of lowest degree with integral coefficients yielding a polynomial quotient upon division by each of the given polynomials, and to be, among all such polynomials, the one having the least possible positive leading coefficient.

Very often, the least common multiple of a set of natural numbers or polynomials can be determined by inspection. When inspection fails us, however, we can find the least common multiple of a set of polynomials with integer coefficients as follows:

1. Express each polynomial in completely factored form.

2. Write as factors of a product each *different* factor occurring in any of the polynomials, including each factor the greatest number of times it occurs in any one of the given polynomials.

Example. Find the least common multiple of 12, 15, and 18.

Solution.   12   15   18

$2\cdot 2\cdot 3$ $3\cdot 5$ $3\cdot 3\cdot 2$

The least common multiple is $2^2\cdot 3^2\cdot 5$, or 180.

Example. Find the least common multiple of x^2, $x^2 - 9$, and $x^3 - x^2 - 6x$.

Solution. x^2 $x^2 - 9$ $x^3 - x^2 - 6x$

$x\cdot x$ $(x - 3)(x + 3)$ $x(x - 3)(x + 2)$

The least common multiple is $x^2(x + 2)(x + 3)(x - 3)$.

Now, to simplify sums of fractions having different denominators, we can

Addition of rational expressions

ascertain the least common denominator of the fractions, determine the factor necessary to express each of the fractions as a fraction having this common denominator, write the fractions accordingly, and then express the sum as a single fraction.

Example.   Write $\dfrac{3}{x} + \dfrac{2}{x^2} + \dfrac{3}{xy}$ as a single fraction.

Solution.   The least common denominator of the fractions is x^2y.

$$\frac{3}{x} + \frac{2}{x^2} + \frac{3}{xy} = \frac{3(xy)}{x(xy)} + \frac{2(y)}{x^2(y)} + \frac{3(x)}{xy(x)}$$

$$= \frac{3xy}{x^2y} + \frac{2y}{x^2y} + \frac{3x}{x^2y}$$

$$= \frac{3xy + 2y + 3x}{x^2y} \qquad (x, y \neq 0)$$

EXERCISE 2.6

Write each sum or difference as a single fraction in lowest terms. Assume that no variable in a denominator takes a value for which the denominator vanishes.

1. $\dfrac{x-1}{2y} + \dfrac{x}{2y}$

2. $\dfrac{y+1}{x} + \dfrac{y-1}{x}$

3. $\dfrac{2a-b}{a} - \dfrac{a-b}{a}$

4. $\dfrac{3a-1}{b} - \dfrac{2-a}{b}$

5. $\dfrac{a+2}{3} - \dfrac{a-3}{9}$

6. $\dfrac{a-2}{9} - \dfrac{a+1}{3}$

7. $\dfrac{2}{a+b} + \dfrac{1}{2a+2b}$

8. $\dfrac{7}{5x-10} + \dfrac{5}{3x-6}$

9. $\dfrac{2}{3-x} - \dfrac{1}{x-3}$

10. $\dfrac{7}{y-3} + \dfrac{3}{3-y}$

11. $\dfrac{a+1}{a+2} - \dfrac{a+2}{a+3}$

12. $\dfrac{5x-y}{3x+y} - \dfrac{6x-5y}{2x-y}$

13. $\dfrac{x+2y}{2x-y} - \dfrac{2x+y}{x-2y}$

14. $\dfrac{x-2y}{x+y} - \dfrac{2x-y}{x-y}$

15. $\dfrac{y}{y^2-16} - \dfrac{y+1}{y^2-5y+4} + \dfrac{1}{y+4}$

16. $\dfrac{1}{b^2-1} - \dfrac{1}{b^2+2b+1} + \dfrac{1}{b+1}$

17. $x + \dfrac{1}{x-1} - \dfrac{1}{(x-1)^2}$

18. $y - \dfrac{2y}{y^2-1} + \dfrac{3}{y+1}$

19. $x - 1 + \dfrac{3}{2x-1} - \dfrac{x}{4x^2-1}$

20. $2y - 3 - \dfrac{1}{y^2+2y+1} + \dfrac{3}{y+1}$

21. $\dfrac{y+3}{3y^2+7y+4} - \dfrac{y-7}{3y^2+13y+12}$

22. $\dfrac{a+b}{a^2+2ab-3b^2} - \dfrac{a-2b}{a^2-b^2} + \dfrac{2a+b}{a^2+4ab+3b^2}$

23. $\dfrac{xy}{(z-x)(x-y)} + \dfrac{yz}{(z-y)(x-z)} + \dfrac{xz}{(y-x)(y-z)}$

24. $\dfrac{1}{(a-b)(b-c)} + \dfrac{1}{(b-c)(c-a)} + \dfrac{1}{(c-a)(a-b)}$

2.7 PRODUCTS AND QUOTIENTS OF RATIONAL EXPRESSIONS

By Parts II and VII of Theorem 1.11 and the laws of closure, we have the following result.

THEOREM 2.8 *If A, B, C, and D are real polynomials, then for values of the variables for which the denominators do not vanish,*

$$\text{I} \quad \frac{A}{B} \cdot \frac{C}{D} = \frac{AC}{BD},$$

$$\text{II} \quad \frac{A}{B} \div \frac{C}{D} = \frac{AD}{BC}.$$

Simplification of products and quotients   We can use Theorem 2.8 to rewrite a product or quotient of fractions as a single fraction in lowest terms.

Example.
$$\frac{x^2-2x+1}{x^2+2x-3} \cdot \frac{x^2+3x}{x^2+2x} = \frac{(x-1)(x-1)}{(x+3)(x-1)} \cdot \frac{x(x+3)}{x(x+2)}$$

$$= \frac{(x-1)[(x-1)(x+3)x]}{(x+2)[(x-1)(x+3)x]}$$

$$= \frac{x-1}{x+2} \quad (x \neq -3, -2, 0, 1)$$

Since the factors of the numerator and denominator of the product of two fractions are just the factors of the numerators and denominators, respectively, of the fractions, we can divide common factors out of the numerators and denominators before writing the product as a single fraction. Thus, in the example above, we could write

$$\frac{x^2-2x+1}{x^2+2x-3} \cdot \frac{x^2+3x}{x^2+2x} = \frac{\overset{1}{\cancel{(x-1)}}(x-1)}{\cancel{(x+3)}(\cancel{x-1})} \cdot \frac{\overset{1}{\cancel{x}}\overset{1}{\cancel{(x+3)}}}{\cancel{x}(x+2)}$$

$$= \frac{x-1}{x+2} \quad (x \neq -3, -2, 0, 1).$$

Example.
$$\frac{x^3-8}{x^3+8} \div \frac{(x+1)(x^2+2x+4)}{(x-1)(x^2-2x+4)} = \frac{x^3-8}{x^3+8} \cdot \frac{(x-1)(x^2-2x+4)}{(x+1)(x^2+2x+4)}$$

$$= \frac{(x-2)\cancel{(x^2+2x+4)}^{\,1} \; (x-1)\cancel{(x^2-2x+4)}^{\,1}}{(x+2)\cancel{(x^2-2x+4)}_{\,1} \; (x+1)\cancel{(x^2+2x+4)}_{\,1}}$$

$$= \frac{(x-2)(x-1)}{(x+2)(x+1)} \quad (x \neq -2, -1, 1)$$

When the quotient of two fractions is given in the form of a **complex fraction** (a fraction containing a fraction in either the numerator or the denominator or both), we have a choice of procedures available to us for writing the quotient in the form of a simple (not complex) fraction.

Example. Write $\dfrac{x+\frac{3}{4}}{x-\frac{1}{2}}$ as a simple fraction in lowest terms.

Solution 1. We can apply the fundamental principle of fractions to multiply numerator and denominator by the least common denominator of the simple fractions involved. Thus, we have

$$\frac{\left(x+\frac{3}{4}\right)4}{\left(x-\frac{1}{2}\right)4} = \frac{4x+3}{4x-2} \quad \left(x \neq \frac{1}{2}\right).$$

Solution 2. Alternatively, we can rewrite the complex fraction as follows.

$$\frac{x+\frac{3}{4}}{x-\frac{1}{2}} = \frac{\frac{4x+3}{4}}{\frac{2x-1}{2}}$$

$$= \frac{4x+3}{4} \cdot \frac{2}{2x-1}$$

$$= \frac{4x+3}{\cancel{4}_{2}} \cdot \frac{\cancel{2}^{1}}{2x-1} = \frac{4x+3}{4x-2} \quad \left(x \neq \frac{1}{2}\right)$$

In the event you have more complicated expressions involving complex fractions, you can rewrite the expression by attacking small parts of it at a time.

EXERCISE 2.7

Write each product or quotient as a single fraction in lowest terms.

1. $\dfrac{-12a^2b}{5c} \cdot \dfrac{10b^2c}{24a^3b}$

2. $\dfrac{a^2}{xy} \cdot \dfrac{3x^3y}{4a}$

3. $\dfrac{xy}{a^2b} \div \dfrac{x^3y^2}{ab}$

4. $\dfrac{24a^3b}{-6xy^2} \div \dfrac{3a^2b}{12x}$

5. $\dfrac{x^2-x-20}{x^2+7x+12} \cdot \dfrac{2x^2+6x}{x^2-25}$

6. $\dfrac{4x^2+8x+3}{2x^2-5x+3} \cdot \dfrac{6x^2-9x}{1-4x^2}$

7. $\dfrac{25a^2b^2-16}{4ab+1} \div \dfrac{5ab+4}{16a^2b^2+16ab+3}$

8. $\dfrac{a^2-25}{a^2-16} \div \dfrac{a^2+2a-15}{a^2+a-12}$

9. $\dfrac{x^2-y^2}{x^2} \cdot \dfrac{x^2-xy+y^2}{x^2} \div \dfrac{x^3+y^3}{x^4}$

10. $\dfrac{a^3-b^3}{ab} \cdot \dfrac{a^2b}{a^2-b^2} \div \dfrac{ab^2}{a+b}$

11. $\left(1+\dfrac{1}{x}\right) \cdot \left(1-\dfrac{1}{x}\right)$

12. $\left(x-\dfrac{1}{x}\right) \div \left(x+\dfrac{1}{x}\right)$

13. $\left[\dfrac{3}{x-1} - \dfrac{2}{x+1}\right] \cdot \dfrac{x-1}{x}$

14. $\left[\dfrac{x}{x^2-9} + \dfrac{2}{x-3}\right] \cdot \dfrac{x-1}{x}$

15. $\left[\dfrac{2y}{2y-1} - \dfrac{3}{y}\right] \div \dfrac{3}{2y^2-y}$

16. $\left[\dfrac{y}{y^2-1} - \dfrac{y}{y^2-2y+1}\right] \div \dfrac{y}{y-1}$

17. $\dfrac{\dfrac{2}{a}+\dfrac{3}{2a}}{5+\dfrac{1}{a}}$

18. $\dfrac{1+\dfrac{1}{x}}{1-\dfrac{1}{x}}$

Example. Write $\dfrac{1}{x+\dfrac{1}{x+\dfrac{1}{x}}}$ as a simple fraction in lowest terms.

Solution. We can begin by simplifying the lower right-hand expression, $\dfrac{1}{x+\dfrac{1}{x}}$.
We have

$$\frac{1}{x+\dfrac{1}{x}} = \frac{(1)x}{\left(x+\dfrac{1}{x}\right)x} = \frac{x}{x^2+1}.$$

Thus,

$$\frac{1}{x+\dfrac{1}{x+\dfrac{1}{x}}} = \frac{1}{x+\dfrac{x}{x^2+1}}.$$

From this point, we can apply either of the methods shown in the example on page 52 to the right-hand member above. Using the first method, we have

$$\frac{1}{x+\dfrac{1}{x+\dfrac{1}{x}}} = \frac{1(x^2+1)}{\left(x+\dfrac{x}{x^2+1}\right)(x^2+1)} = \frac{x^2+1}{x^3+x+x} = \frac{x^2+1}{x^3+2x} \quad (x \neq 0).$$

$\uparrow$

$x(x^2+1) = x^3+x$

$\dfrac{x}{x^2+1} \quad \dfrac{x^{2+1}}{1} = x$

19. $a - \dfrac{a}{a + \dfrac{1}{4}}$

20. $x - \dfrac{x}{1 - \dfrac{x}{1 - x}}$

21. $1 - \dfrac{1}{1 - \dfrac{1}{y - 2}}$

22. $2y + \dfrac{3}{3 - \dfrac{2y}{y - 1}}$

23. $\dfrac{1 + \dfrac{1}{1 - \dfrac{a}{b}}}{1 - \dfrac{3}{1 - \dfrac{a}{b}}}$

24. $\dfrac{1 - \dfrac{1}{\dfrac{a}{b} + 2}}{1 + \dfrac{3}{\dfrac{a}{2b} + 1}}$

2.8   ROOTS AND EXPONENTS

Thus far, powers of real numbers have been defined for natural-number exponents, and some simple properties of products and quotients of powers have been examined. Powers with integral and rational exponents can now be defined in a manner consistent with these properties.

Reason for defining a^0 to be 1

Thus, by Theorem 2.3-I, for $a \in R$, $a \neq 0$, and m, $n \in N$, $m > n$, we have

$$\frac{a^m}{a^n} = a^{m-n}. \tag{1}$$

If (1) is to hold also for $m = n$, then we must have

$$\frac{a^n}{a^n} = a^{n-n} = a^0.$$

Since $a^n/a^n = 1$, we therefore make the following definition.

DEFINITION 2.2   *If $a \in R$, $a \neq 0$, then*

$$a^0 = 1.$$

In the same way, if (1) is also to hold for $m = 0$, then we must have

Reason for defining a^{-n} to be $1/a^n$

$$\frac{a^0}{a^n} = a^{0-n} = a^{-n}.$$

Since $a^0 = 1$, we therefore make the following definition.

DEFINITION 2.3   *If $a \in R$, $a \neq 0$, and $n \in N$, then*

$$a^{-n} = \frac{1}{a^n}.$$

Next, by Theorem 2.1-II, for $a \in R$, and m, $n \in N$, we have

$$(a^m)^n = a^{mn}. \tag{2}$$

If (2) is to hold for $m = 1/n$, and $a^{1/n}$ is a real number, then we must have

$$(a^{1/n})^n = a^{(1/n)(n)} = a^{n/n} = a^1 = a,$$

so that the nth power of $a^{1/n}$ must be a. A number having a as its nth power is called an **nth root** of a. In particular, for $n = 2$ or 3, respectively, an nth root is called a **square root** or a **cube root**.

Number of nth roots of a if n is odd	For n odd, each $a \in R$ has just one real nth root. Thus $(-2)^3 = -8$ and $2^3 = 8$, so that -2 is the real cube root of -8, and 2 is the real cube root of 8.
n even, $a > 0$	For n even and $a > 0$, a has two real nth roots. Thus $(-2)^4 = 16$ and $2^4 = 16$, so that -2 and 2 are both fourth roots of 16.
n even, $a < 0$	For n even and $a < 0$, a has no real nth root. Thus -1 has no real square root since the square of each real number is nonnegative.
$a = 0$	If $a = 0$, then a has exactly one nth root, namely 0.

We therefore make the following definition.

DEFINITION 2.4 *If $a \in R$, $n \in N$, then $a^{1/n}$ is the real number, if one exists, and is the positive one if two exist, such that*

$$(a^{1/n})^n = a.$$

Examples. $\frac{1}{2} = Sq\ Root$

a. $25^{1/2} = 5$,   b. $-25^{1/2} = -5$,

c. $(-25)^{1/2}$ is not a real number.   d. $27^{1/3} = 3$,

e. $-27^{1/3} = -3$,   f. $(-27)^{1/3} = -3$

Order of taking power and root	To generalize from rational exponents of the form $1/n$, for $n \in N$, to rational exponents of the form m/n, for $m \in J$, $n \in N$, we need the results expressed in the following two theorems.

THEOREM 2.9 *If $a^{1/n} \in R$, $m \in J$,   and $n \in N$,   then*

$$(a^{1/n})^m = (a^m)^{1/n}.$$

Proof. Since $n \in N$, we can write

$$\underbrace{(a^{1/n})^m \cdot (a^{1/n})^m \cdot (a^{1/n})^m \cdots (a^{1/n})^m}_{n\ \text{factors}} = [(a^{1/n})^m]^n$$

$$= (a^{1/n})^{mn}$$
$$= (a^{1/n})^{nm}$$
$$= [(a^{1/n})^n]^m$$
$$= a^m.$$

Thus, since $[(a^{1/n})^m]^n = a^m$, $(a^{1/n})^m$ is an nth root of a^m, and by Definition 2.4 this root is denoted by $(a^m)^{1/n}$. Hence $(a^{1/n})^m = (a^m)^{1/n}$.

Observe that Theorem 2.9 requires that $a^{1/n}$ be a real number. This requirement is not satisfied if n is even and a is negative. If, for instance, $a = -3$, $m = 2$, and $n = 2$, then $(a^{1/n})^m = [(-3)^{1/2}]^2$ is not a real number because $(-3)^{1/2}$ is not a real number, whereas $(a^m)^{1/n} = [(-3)^2]^{1/2} = 9^{1/2} = 3$.

THEOREM 2.10   *If $a^{1/(np)} \in R$, $m \in J$, $n \in N$, and $p \in N$, then*

$$(a^{1/(np)})^{mp} = (a^{1/n})^m.$$

The proof is similar to that of Theorem 2.9 and will be omitted except for the hint that each member of the equation is the same npth root of a^{mp}.

Theorems 2.9 and 2.10 show that, if $a^{1/(np)}$ is a real number, then $a^{m/n}$ can be considered equally well as $(a^{1/n})^m$, $(a^m)^{1/n}$, $(a^{1/(np)})^{mp}$, or $(a^{mp})^{1/(np)}$. For example,

$$(16^{1/2})^3 = 4^3 = 64, \qquad (16^3)^{1/2} = 4096^{1/2} = 64,$$
$$(16^{1/4})^6 = 2^6 = 64, \qquad (16^6)^{1/4} = 16{,}777{,}216^{1/4} = 64.$$

We choose the following definition.

DEFINITION 2.5   *If $a^{1/n} \in R$, $m \in J$, and $n \in N$, then*

$$a^{m/n} = (a^{1/n})^m.$$

Observe that requiring $n \in N$ does not alter the fact that m/n can represent every rational number, since all that is done is to restrict the denominator of the fraction representing the rational number to be positive, which is always possible in light of Theorem 1.8-V and VI.

Powers with rational exponents have the same fundamental properties as powers with natural-number exponents, as long as the powers are real

Properties of rational powers

numbers. Recall from Theorems 2.1 and 2.3 that powers with natural-number exponents exhibit the properties set forth in the following theorem for powers with rational exponents. We state this theorem without proof.

THEOREM 2.11   *If a^m, a^n, $b^n \in R$, $a, b \neq 0$, and $m, n \in Q$, then*

     I $a^m \cdot a^n = a^{m+n}$,

     II $(a^m)^n = a^{mn}$,

     III $(ab)^n = a^n b^n$,

     IV $\dfrac{a^m}{a^n} = a^{m-n}$,

     V $\left(\dfrac{a}{b}\right)^n = \dfrac{a^n}{b^n}.$

KNOW

Let us look at a few examples of applications of this theorem.

Examples.

a. $\dfrac{x^{2/3}}{x^{1/3}} = x^{2/3 - 1/3} = x^{1/3} \quad (x \neq 0)$

b. $\left(\dfrac{a^3 b^6}{c^{12}}\right)^{2/3} = \dfrac{(a^3)^{2/3}(b^6)^{2/3}}{(c^{12})^{2/3}} = \dfrac{a^2 b^4}{c^8} \quad (c \neq 0)$

c. $(a^6)^{1/2} = (|a|^6)^{1/2} = |a|^3$

Observe that in the last example it was necessary to use absolute-value notation. For example, with $a = -2$ we have

$$(a^6)^{1/2} = [(-2)^6]^{1/2} = 64^{1/2} = 8 = |a|^3,$$

whereas

$$a^3 = (-2)^3 = -8 = -|a|^3 \neq |a|^3.$$

EXERCISE 2.8

Write each of the following as a power with exponent 1.

Examples.   a. $64^{1/2}$

b. $\left(\dfrac{8}{27}\right)^{-2/3}$

Solutions.   a. 8

b. $\left[\left(\dfrac{8}{27}\right)^{1/3}\right]^{-2} = \left(\dfrac{2}{3}\right)^{-2} = \dfrac{9}{4}$

$\left[(81)^{\frac{1}{4}}\right]^{-3}$

1. $(32)^{1/5}$ 2. $(-27)^{1/3}$ 3. $(81)^{-3/4}$ 4. $(81)^{-1/2}$

5. $\left(\dfrac{1}{8}\right)^{-5/3}$ 6. $\left(\dfrac{1}{8}\right)^{5/3}$ 7. $\left(\dfrac{4}{9}\right)^{3/2}$ 8. $\left(\dfrac{4}{9}\right)^{-3/2}$

Write each of the following as a product or quotient of powers in which each variable occurs but once, and all exponents are positive. Assume all variable bases are positive and all variable exponents are natural numbers.

Examples.   a. $\dfrac{(x^{1/2}y^2)^2}{(x^{2/3}y)^3}$

b. $(y^{2n} \cdot y^{n/2})^4$

Solutions.   a. $\dfrac{xy^4}{x^2 y^3} = \dfrac{y}{x}$

b. $y^{8n} \cdot y^{2n} = y^{10n}$

9. $x^{1/3} \cdot x^{5/3}$ 10. $x^{4/3} \cdot x^{1/2}$ 11. $a^{2/3} \cdot a^{3/4}$ 12. $x^{1/2} \cdot x^{5/6}$

13. $\dfrac{x^{5/6}}{x^{4/3}}$ 14. $\dfrac{x^{1/2}}{x^{1/3}}$ 15. $\dfrac{x^{-2/5}}{x^{2/3}}$ 16. $\left(\dfrac{a^6}{c^3}\right)^{-2/3}$

17. $\left(\dfrac{y^4}{x^2}\right)^{1/2}$ 18. $\left(\dfrac{16}{ab^2}\right)^{1/4}$ 19. $\left(\dfrac{x^5 y^8}{y^{13}}\right)^{1/4}$ 20. $\left(\dfrac{125x^3 y^4}{27x^{-6}y}\right)^{1/3}$

21. $(x^2)^{n/2} \cdot (y^{2n})^{2/n}$ 22. $(x^{n/2})^2 \cdot (y^n)^{5/n}$ 23. $\dfrac{x^{2n}}{x^{n/2}}$ 24. $\left(\dfrac{a^n}{b}\right)^{1/2} \cdot \left(\dfrac{b}{a^{2n}}\right)^{3/2}$

25. $\dfrac{x^{3n}y^{2m-1}}{(x^n y^m)^{1/2}}$ 26. $\left(\dfrac{m^{2a^2}}{n^{4a}}\right)^{1/a}$

 Apply the distributive law to write each product as a sum.

27. $x^{1/3} \cdot (x^{2/3} - x^{1/3})$ $\ x^{\frac{3}{3}} - x^{\frac{2}{3}}$ 28. $y^{2/3} \cdot (y^{2/3} + y^{1/3})$ $\ y^{\frac{4}{3}} + y$

29. $(x^{1/2} - y^{-1/2})^2$ 30. $(x^{1/2} + y^{1/2})(x^{1/2} - y^{1/2})$

31. $(x + y)^{1/2} \cdot [(x + y)^{1/2} - (x + y)]$ 32. $(a - b)^{2/3} \cdot [(a - b)^{-1/3} + (a - b)]$

33. $(x^{1/3} + y^{1/3})(x^{2/3} - x^{1/3} \cdot y^{1/3} + y^{2/3})$ 34. $(a^{1/3} - b^{1/3})(a^{2/3} + a^{1/3} \cdot b^{1/3} + b^{2/3})$

Factor as indicated.

Examples.   a. $y^{-1/2} + y^{1/2} = y^{-1/2}(?)$ b. $(x + y)^{1/2} + (x + y)^{3/2} = (x + y)^{1/2}(?)$

Solutions.   a. $y^{-1/2}(1 + y)$ b. $(x + y)^{1/2}(1 + x + y)$

35. $x^{3/2} + x = x(?)$ $\left(x^{\frac{1}{2}} + 1\right)$ 36. $y - y^{2/3} = y^{1/3}(?)$

37. $x^{-3/2} + x^{-1/2} = x^{-1/2}(?)$ $\left(x + 1\right)$ 38. $z^{1/2} + z^{-1/3} = z^{1/6}(?)$

39. $(x + 1)^{1/2} - (x + 1)^{-1/2} = (x + 1)^{-1/2}(?)$

40. $(y + 2)^{1/5} - (y + 2)^{-4/5} = (y + 2)^{-4/5}(?)$

41. $x^{2n} + x^{n/2} = x^{n/2}(?)$ 42. $y^{n+1} + y^{2n} = y(?)$

43. $x - y = (x^{1/2} - y^{1/2})(?)$ $\left(x^{\frac{1}{2}} + y^{\frac{1}{2}}\right)$ 44. $x + y = (x^{1/3} + y^{1/3})(?)$

In the previous problems, the variables were restricted to represent positive numbers. In Problems 45–50, consider variable bases to denote *any* element of the set of real numbers and simplify.

Examples.   a. $[(-3)^2]^{1/2}$ b. $[u^2(u + 5)]^{1/2}$

Solutions.   a. $|-3| = 3$ b. $|u|(u + 5)^{1/2}$

45. $[(-5)^2]^{1/2}$ 46. $[(-3)^{12}]^{1/4}$ 47. $[4x^2]^{1/2}$

48. $[x^2(x - 1)]^{1/2}$ 49. $\dfrac{2}{[x^2(x + 1)]^{1/2}}$ 50. $\left[\dfrac{9}{x^6(x^2 + 1)}\right]^{1/2}$

2.9 RADICAL EXPRESSIONS

Powers of real numbers with rational numbers for exponents are frequently denoted by symbols involving the use of the radical sign, $\sqrt{\ }$.

DEFINITION 2.6 *If $a^{1/n} \in R$, and $n \in N$, then*

$$\sqrt[n]{a} = a^{1/n}.$$

Naturally, the radical expression on the left is not defined if the power on the right is not. In the symbolism $\sqrt[n]{a}$, a is called the **radicand** and n the **index** of the radical, and the expression is called a **radical expression of order n.** If no index is shown with a radical expression, as, for example, in the case $\sqrt{a}$, then the index 2 is understood to apply. The symbol $\sqrt{a}$ denotes the nonnegative square root of

Alternative representation of $|x|$

a, where, of course, a cannot be negative. The symbol $\sqrt{x^2}$, where $x \in R$, therefore provides us with an alternative means of writing $|x|$. That is, $\sqrt{x^2} = |x|$.

An immediate consequence of the foregoing definition and the theorems pertaining to exponents in Section 2.8 is the following.

THEOREM 2.12 *For real values of a and b for which all the radical expressions in the equation denote real numbers,*

> I   A. $\sqrt[n]{a^n} = a$ *(n an odd natural number)*,
>
> B. $\sqrt[n]{a^n} = |a|$ *(n an even natural number)*,
>
> II $\sqrt[n]{a^m} = (\sqrt[n]{a})^m$ *(n ∈ N, m ∈ J)*,
>
> III $\sqrt[n]{a} \cdot \sqrt[n]{b} = \sqrt[n]{ab}$ *(n ∈ N)*,
>
> IV $\dfrac{\sqrt[n]{a}}{\sqrt[n]{b}} = \sqrt[n]{\dfrac{a}{b}}$ *(b ≠ 0, n ∈ N)*,
>
> V $\sqrt[m]{\sqrt[n]{a}} = \sqrt[mn]{a}$ *(m, n ∈ N)*,
>
> VI $\sqrt[cn]{a^{cm}} = \sqrt[n]{a^m}$ *(n, c ∈ N, m ∈ J)*.

It might be noted in III and IV that if $a < 0$, $b < 0$, and n is even, then the radicals in the left-hand member are not defined, even though the radical in the right-hand member is.

The several parts of this theorem can be used to rewrite radical expressions in various ways, and, in particular, to write them in what is called "simplest" form. A radical expression is said to be in **simplest form** if

  a. the radicand contains no polynomial factor raised to a power equal to or greater than the index of the radical,
  b. the radicand contains no fractions,
  c. no radical expressions are contained in denominators of fractions, and
  d. the index of the radical and the power in the radicand have no common factor other than 1 in N.

Examples.   a. $\sqrt[3]{24x^3y^2} = \sqrt[3]{8x^3}\sqrt[3]{3y^2} = 2x\sqrt[3]{3y^2}$

b. $\sqrt[6]{49x^2} = \sqrt[3\cdot2]{7^2x^2} = \sqrt[3]{7x}$ $(x \geq 0)$

c. $\dfrac{\sqrt[3]{4a^2}}{\sqrt[3]{b}} = \dfrac{\sqrt[3]{4a^2}\sqrt[3]{b^2}}{\sqrt[3]{b}\sqrt[3]{b^2}} = \dfrac{\sqrt[3]{4a^2b^2}}{\sqrt[3]{b^3}} = \dfrac{\sqrt[3]{4a^2b^2}}{b}$ $(b \neq 0)$

The process employed in simplifying the expression in part c in the foregoing example is called "rationalizing the denominator," because the result is a fraction with denominator free of radicals. This does not exclude the possibility that the denominator is an irrational number.

Sums and products of radical expressions   Since we have defined our radical expressions so that they represent real numbers, the properties of the real numbers can be applied. For example, the distributive law permits us to express certain sums as products and certain products as sums.

Examples.

a. $2\sqrt{5} + 4\sqrt{5} = (2 + 4)\ \sqrt{5} = 6\sqrt{5}$

b. $(\sqrt{x} + 2)(\sqrt{x} - 1) = \sqrt{x}(\sqrt{x} - 1) + 2(\sqrt{x} - 1) = x - \sqrt{x} + 2\sqrt{x} - 2 = x + \sqrt{x} - 2$

The distributive law also provides us with a means of rationalizing denominators of fractions in which radicals occur in one or both of two terms. To accomplish this, we first recall that

$$(a - b)(a + b) = a^2 - b^2,$$

where the expression in the right-hand member contains no linear term. Each of the two factors of a product exhibiting this property is said to be the **conjugate** of the other. Now consider a fraction of the form

$$\frac{a}{b + \sqrt{c}},$$

Rationalization of binomial denominators   where c is positive and $b \neq -\sqrt{c}$. If we multiply the numerator and denominator of this fraction by the conjugate of the denominator, then the denominator of the resulting fraction will contain no term involving $\sqrt{c}$, and hence will be free of radicals. That is,

$$\frac{a}{b + \sqrt{c}} = \frac{a(b - \sqrt{c})}{(b + \sqrt{c})(b - \sqrt{c})} = \frac{ab - a\sqrt{c}}{b^2 - c} \quad (b^2 \neq c),$$

where the denominator has been rationalized. This process is equally applicable to radical fractions of the form

$$\frac{a}{\sqrt{b}+\sqrt{c}},$$

since

$$\frac{a}{\sqrt{b}+\sqrt{c}}=\frac{a(\sqrt{b}-\sqrt{c})}{(\sqrt{b}+\sqrt{c})(\sqrt{b}-\sqrt{c})}=\frac{a\sqrt{b}-a\sqrt{c}}{b-c}.$$

It should be noted, though, that it is not *always* preferable, in working with fractions, to have their denominators rationalized. Sometimes, in fact, it is desirable to rationalize the numerator. Thus, for example,

$$\frac{\sqrt{b}+\sqrt{c}}{a}=\frac{(\sqrt{b}+\sqrt{c})(\sqrt{b}-\sqrt{c})}{a(\sqrt{b}-\sqrt{c})}=\frac{b-c}{a(\sqrt{b}-\sqrt{c})}.$$

EXERCISE 2.9

Write in radical form. Assume that all variables represent positive real numbers and that all radicands are positive except where specifically indicated to the contrary.

Examples.　a. $5^{1/2}$　　　　b. $xy^{2/3}$　　　　c. $(x-y^2)^{-1/2}$

Solutions.　a. $\sqrt{5}$　　　　b. $x\sqrt[3]{y^2}$　　　　c. $\dfrac{1}{\sqrt{x-y^2}}$

1. $a^{2/3}$　　　2. $x^{3/2}$　　　3. $3x^{1/3}$　　　4. $-6xy^{1/2}$

5. $-6(xy)^{2/3}$　　6. $x^{1/5}y^{3/5}$　　7. $(x-y)^{4/7}$　　8. $(24-3x)^{-3/4}$

Write an equivalent expression, using positive fractional exponents in lowest terms.

Examples.　a. $\sqrt{2^3}$　　　　b. $7\sqrt[3]{a^2}$　　　　c. $\dfrac{1}{\sqrt{a-b}}$

Solutions.　a. $2^{3/2}$　　　　b. $7a^{2/3}$　　　　c. $\dfrac{1}{(a-b)^{1/2}}$

9. $\sqrt[3]{x^2}$　　　10. $\sqrt[5]{xy}$　　　11. $\sqrt[5]{2xy^2}$　　12. $a\sqrt[5]{x^2y^3}$

13. $-3\sqrt[4]{a^3b}$　　14. $7\sqrt[7]{x^5}$　　15. $3\sqrt[3]{x^2-y}$　　16. $-a\sqrt[5]{x^4-y^4}$

Find the root indicated.

Examples.　a. $\sqrt[5]{-32}$　　　b. $\sqrt[3]{x^6y^3}$　　　c. $\sqrt{x^2y^6}$

Solutions.　a. -2　　　　b. x^2y　　　　c. xy^3

17. $\sqrt{144}$　　　18. $-\sqrt{169}$　　　19. $\sqrt[3]{-27}$　　　20. $-\sqrt[6]{64}$

21. $\sqrt{x^4y^2}$　　22. $\sqrt[3]{8y^6}$　　23. $\sqrt{\dfrac{4}{9}x^6y^{10}}$　　24. $\sqrt[3]{\dfrac{-8x^3}{125}}$

Write in simplest form.

Examples.   a. $\sqrt{300}$ b. $\sqrt[3]{2x^7y^3}$ c. $\sqrt{2xy}\sqrt{8x}$

Solutions.   a. $\sqrt{100}\sqrt{3}$ b. $\sqrt[3]{6^6y^3}\sqrt[3]{2x}$ c. $\sqrt{16x^2}\sqrt{y}$

           $10\sqrt{3}$ $x^2y\sqrt[3]{2x}$ $4x\sqrt{y}$

25. $\sqrt{4x^5}$ 26. $\sqrt{16y^3}$ 27. $\sqrt[3]{3x^5y^5}$

28. $\sqrt[3]{-8x^6}$ 29. $\sqrt[4]{9}\sqrt[4]{27}$ 30. $\sqrt[3]{a^4}\sqrt[3]{a^7}$

Rationalize the denominator of each of the following.

Examples.

a. $\sqrt{\dfrac{3x}{7y}}$ b. $3\sqrt{\dfrac{2}{y}}$ c. $\dfrac{\sqrt{6a}\sqrt{5a}}{\sqrt{15}}$

Solutions.

a. $\dfrac{\sqrt{3x}}{\sqrt{7y}}\cdot\dfrac{\sqrt{7y}}{\sqrt{7y}}$ b. $\dfrac{\sqrt[3]{2}\sqrt[3]{y^2}}{\sqrt[3]{y}\sqrt[3]{y^2}}$ c. $\sqrt{\dfrac{30a^2}{15}}$

   $\dfrac{\sqrt{21xy}}{7y}$ $\dfrac{\sqrt[3]{2y^2}}{y}$ $a\sqrt{2}$

31. $\dfrac{\sqrt{6x}}{\sqrt{2xy}}$ 32. $\dfrac{\sqrt[3]{a^5b^3}}{\sqrt[3]{ab}}$ 33. $\dfrac{\sqrt[3]{2a^2b^3}}{\sqrt[3]{a^2b^2}}$ 34. $\dfrac{\sqrt[3]{42x^3}}{\sqrt[3]{\frac{1}{8}x^2}}$

35. $\dfrac{\sqrt{x}\sqrt{xy^3}}{\sqrt{y}}$ 36. $\dfrac{\sqrt[4]{ab}\sqrt[4]{ab^4}}{\sqrt[4]{b}}$ 37. $\dfrac{\sqrt[3]{ab}\sqrt[3]{b^2}}{\sqrt[3]{a}}$ 38. $\dfrac{\sqrt[3]{4ab^2}\sqrt[3]{2a}}{\sqrt[3]{16a^5b^3}}$

Rationalize the numerator of each of the following.

39. $\dfrac{\sqrt{7}}{7}$ 40. $\dfrac{\sqrt{6a^3}}{\sqrt{8a}}$ 41. $\dfrac{\sqrt[3]{96xy^2}}{\sqrt[3]{12x^2y}}$ 42. $\dfrac{\sqrt[6]{4x^{14}}}{\sqrt[6]{32x^2}}$

Reduce the order of each radical.

Examples.

a. $\sqrt[4]{5^2}$ b. $\sqrt[12]{81}$ c. $\sqrt[4]{x^2y^2}$

Solutions.

a. $\sqrt[4/2]{5^{2/2}}$ b. $\sqrt[12/4]{3^{4/4}}$ c. $\sqrt[4/2]{x^{2/2}y^{2/2}}$

   $\sqrt{5}$ $\sqrt[3]{3}$ $\sqrt{xy}$

43. $\sqrt[6]{81}$ 44. $\sqrt[10]{32}$ 45. $\sqrt[4]{16x^2}$ 46. $\sqrt[9]{8a^3}$

47. $\sqrt[6]{8x^3}$ 48. $\sqrt[6]{125z^3}$ 49. $\sqrt[6]{(x-1)^2}$ 50. $\sqrt[12]{(x-2y)^4}$

Write each of the following using fractional exponents, and then as a radical in simplest form.

Examples.

a. $\sqrt{\sqrt{6}}$ b. $\sqrt{\sqrt[3]{128}}$ c. $\sqrt{\sqrt[3]{xy^2}\sqrt[4]{xy^3}}$

Solutions.

a. $(6^{1/2})^{1/2}$ b. $[(128)^{1/3}]^{1/2}$ c. $([xy^2(xy^3)^{1/4}]^{1/3})^{1/2}$

   $6^{1/4}$ $(2^7)^{1/6}$ $x^{1/6}y^{2/6}x^{1/24}y^{3/24}$

   $\sqrt[4]{6}$ $2\sqrt[6]{2}$ $x^{5/24}y^{11/24}$

                                                                          $\sqrt[24]{x^5y^{11}}$

51. $\sqrt{\sqrt{8}}$ 52. $\sqrt{4\sqrt{16}}$ 53. $\sqrt[3]{2\sqrt{8a^4b^6}}$

54. $\sqrt[5]{9\sqrt{27x^3y}}$ 55. $\sqrt[3]{2\sqrt[3]{2\sqrt{2}}}$ 56. $\sqrt{\sqrt[3]{ab^2}\sqrt[4]{a^3b^2}}$

Write each sum as a product.

Examples.

a. $4\sqrt{2}+3\sqrt{2}-\sqrt{2}$ b. $2\sqrt{3}+4\sqrt{12}$

Solutions.

a. $(4+3-1)\sqrt{2}$ b. $2\sqrt{3}+4\cdot2\sqrt{3}$
   $6\sqrt{2}$ $10\sqrt{3}$

57. $\sqrt{3}+2\sqrt{3}$ 58. $3\sqrt{5}-6\sqrt{5}$ 59. $\sqrt{8}-\sqrt{50}-\sqrt{2}$

60. $\sqrt{50}+2\sqrt{32}-\sqrt{2}$ 61. $3\sqrt[3]{16}-\sqrt[3]{2}$ 62. $\sqrt[3]{54}+2\sqrt[3]{128}$

Multiply factors and write all radicals in the result in simplest form.

Examples.

a. $\sqrt{x}(\sqrt{2x}-\sqrt{x})$ b. $(\sqrt{x}-2\sqrt{y})(2\sqrt{x}+\sqrt{y})$

Solutions.

a. $x\sqrt{2}-x$ b. $2x-2y-3\sqrt{xy}$

63. $\sqrt{2}(3+\sqrt{3})$ 64. $\sqrt{6}(3+\sqrt{6})$ 65. $(3+\sqrt{5})(2-\sqrt{5})$

66. $(5-\sqrt{3})(5+\sqrt{3})$ 67. $(\sqrt{x}-2\sqrt{3})(\sqrt{x}+\sqrt{3})$ 68. $(2-\sqrt[3]{4})(2+\sqrt[3]{4})$

Rationalize denominators.

Examples.

a. $\dfrac{3}{\sqrt{2}-1}$ b. $\dfrac{1}{\sqrt{x}-\sqrt{y}}$

Solutions.

a. $\dfrac{3}{(\sqrt{2}-1)}\dfrac{(\sqrt{2}+1))}{(\sqrt{2}+1))}$ b. $\dfrac{1}{(\sqrt{x}-\sqrt{y})}\dfrac{(\sqrt{x}+\sqrt{y})}{(\sqrt{x}+\sqrt{y})}$

$\dfrac{3\sqrt{2}+3}{2-1}$ $\dfrac{\sqrt{x}+\sqrt{y}}{x-y}$

$3\sqrt{2}+3$

69. $\dfrac{-4}{1+\sqrt{3}}$ 70. $\dfrac{1}{2-\sqrt{2}}$ 71. $\dfrac{x}{\sqrt{x}-3}$

72. $\dfrac{\sqrt{x}}{\sqrt{x}-\sqrt{y}}$ 73. $\dfrac{4\sqrt{2}-\sqrt{5}}{4\sqrt{2}+\sqrt{5}}$ 74. $\dfrac{4\sqrt{a}-\sqrt{3a+1}}{\sqrt{a}+\sqrt{3a+1}}$

Rationalize numerators.

75. $\dfrac{1-\sqrt{2}}{2}$ 76. $\dfrac{1-\sqrt{x+a}}{\sqrt{x+a}}$

77. Find the value of y^2-3y+1, for $y=3-\sqrt{2}$.

78. Find the value of $3x^2-4x-2$, for $x=\dfrac{2-\sqrt{10}}{3}$.

Rationalize denominators.

79. $\dfrac{1}{\sqrt[3]{a}-\sqrt[3]{b}}$ *Hint:* Multiply numerator and denominator by $\sqrt[3]{a^2}+\sqrt[3]{ab}+\sqrt[3]{b^2}$.

80. $\dfrac{1}{\sqrt[3]{a^2}-\sqrt[3]{ab}+\sqrt[3]{b^2}}$

In the previous problems, the variables were restricted to represent positive numbers. In Problems 81–84, consider variable bases to denote any element of the set of real numbers and simplify.

81. $\sqrt{4x^2}$ 82. $\sqrt{9x^2y^4}$ 83. $\sqrt{9(x^3-x^2)}$ 84. $\sqrt{18(x^6-x^7)}$

3 EQUATIONS AND INEQUALITIES IN ONE VARIABLE

3.1 EQUIVALENT EQUATIONS; FIRST-DEGREE EQUATIONS

We come now to one of the more important tasks in the study of elementary algebra—that of solving equations and inequalities over an ordered field—in particular, over the ordered field R of real numbers. In this chapter, we shall review a few of the procedures involved.

Equations and inequalities involving variables and constants are called **sentences**, while those involving only constants are called **statements.** Sentences can be classified as either **conditional sentences** or **identities**. An identity is a sentence that is true for every value in the replacement set of any variable or variables involved, while a conditional sentence is false for at least one value in the replacement set. For example, $x + 2 = 3$ is a conditional sentence for $x \in R$, while $x(x + 2) = x^2 + 2x$ is an identity over R.

If we replace the variable x in $P(x) = Q(x)$ with an element from its replacement set U and the resulting statement is true, then the element is a **root**, or **solution**, of the equation and is said to **satisfy** the equation. The subset of U consisting of all solutions of an equation is called the **solution set** of the equation in U. If two equations have the same solution set in U, then they are said to be **equivalent**.

Solution of an equation by solving an equivalent equation

To solve an equation over a given set, we usually determine the members of the solution set by inspection, or else we generate a sequence of equivalent equations until we arrive at one with an obvious solution set. The following theorem is frequently used in generating equivalent equations over the set of real numbers.

THEOREM 3.1 *If $P(x)$, $Q(x)$, and $R(x)$ are expressions, then for all values of x for which $P(x)$, $Q(x)$, and $R(x)$ are real numbers,*

$$P(x) = Q(x)$$

is equivalent to each of the following:

I $P(x) + R(x) = Q(x) + R(x)$,

II $P(x) \cdot R(x) = Q(x) \cdot R(x)$ *for $x \in \{x \mid R(x) \neq 0\}$.*

Proof of 3.1-I. Let r denote any solution of $P(x) = Q(x)$. By definition,

$$P(r) = Q(r).$$

Moreover, the theorem assumes that $P(r)$, $Q(r)$, and $R(r)$ are real numbers. Then, applying Theorem 1.1, we have

$$P(r) + R(r) = Q(r) + R(r).$$

But this shows that r is a solution of

$$P(x) + R(x) = Q(x) + R(x).$$

Since each step in the argument is reversible, Part I of the theorem is proved. The proof of Part II proceeds in a similar way.

Any application of Theorem 3.1 is called an **elementary transformation**.
The equation

$$ax + b = 0, \tag{1}$$

where $a, b \in R$ and $a \neq 0$, is a **first-degree** or **linear** equation over R. Any equation that can be reduced to this form by elementary transformations, therefore, is

Solution of a linear equation

equivalent to a first-degree equation. We can show that such an equation has one and only one solution in R. By Theorem 3.1-I, (1) is equivalent to

$$ax = -b, \tag{2}$$

and, by Theorem 3.1-II, (2) is equivalent to

$$x = -\frac{b}{a}, \tag{3}$$

which, of course, has the unique solution $-b/a$. Since (1), (2), and (3) are equivalent, (1) therefore has the unique solution $-b/a$.

An equation containing more than one variable, or containing symbols such as a, b, and c, representing constants, can often be solved for one of the symbols in terms of the remaining symbols by applying elementary transformations until the desired symbol is obtained by itself as one member of an equation.

Example. Solve $cx = c - x$, for x.

Solution. We generate the following sequence of equivalent equations.

$$cx + x = c$$

$$x(c + 1) = c$$

$$x = \frac{c}{c+1} \quad (c \neq -1)$$

(handwritten annotations in left margin:)
$0 \cdot x + b = 0$
$b \neq 0$ no solutions
$b = 0$ every x is a solution

Equations can be used to express quantitative relationships in word problems

Word problems symbolically. In the following set of exercises, you will encounter a few such problems that lead to linear equations.

EXERCISE 3.1

Solve. Consider R to be the replacement set of the variable.

1. $-3[x - (2x + 3) - 2x] = -9$
   $-3x + 6x - 9 + 6x = -9 \quad x = -2$

2. $4 - (x - 3)(x + 2) = 10 - x^2$

3. $6 + 3x - x^2 = 4 - (x - 2)(x + 3)$

4. $\dfrac{y}{2} + \dfrac{y}{3} - \dfrac{y}{4} = 7$

5. $\dfrac{2x - 1}{5} = \dfrac{x + 1}{2}$

6. $\dfrac{3}{5} = \dfrac{x}{x + 2}$

7. $\dfrac{2}{x - 9} = \dfrac{9}{x + 12} = 2(x+12) = 9(x-9)$
   $(2x + 24 = 9x + 81)$
   $-7x = 105$
   $x = 15$

8. $\dfrac{x}{x - 2} = \dfrac{2}{x - 2} + 7$

9. $\dfrac{5}{x - 3} = \dfrac{x + 2}{x - 3} + 3$

10. $\dfrac{2}{y + 1} + \dfrac{1}{3y + 3} = \dfrac{1}{6}$

11. $\dfrac{y}{y + 2} - \dfrac{3}{y - 2} = \dfrac{y^2 + 8}{y^2 - 4} \quad -14$

12. $\dfrac{4}{2x - 3} + \dfrac{4x}{4x^2 - 9} = \dfrac{1}{2x + 3}$

Solve. Assume that all constants are real numbers and that the replacement set of all variables is R. Leave the results in the form of an equation equivalent to the given equation. State any restrictions on the constants and variables.

13. $v = k + gt$, for k

14. $v = k + gt$, for t

15. $A = \dfrac{h}{2}(b + c)$, for c

16. $S = \dfrac{a}{1 - r}$, for r

17. $l = a + (n - 1)d$, for n

18. $\dfrac{1}{r} = \dfrac{1}{r_1} + \dfrac{1}{r_2}$, for r

19. $x^2 y' - 3x - 2y^3 y' = 1$, for y'

20. $2xy' - 3y' + x^2 = 0$, for y'

21. $x_1 x_2 - 2x_1 x_3 = x_4$, for x_1

22. $3x_1 x_3 + x_1 x_2 = x_4$, for x_1

23. $\dfrac{y - y_1}{x - x_1} = 6$, for y

24. $\dfrac{y - y_1}{x - x_1} = 2$, for x

25. For what value of k does the equation $2x - 3 = \dfrac{4 + x}{k}$ have as its solution set $\{-1\}$?

26. Find a value of k in $3x - 1 = k$ so that the equation is equivalent to $2x + 5 = 1$.

27. When the length of each side of a square is increased by five inches, the area is increased by 85 square inches. Find the length of a side of the original square.

28. How much pure alcohol should be added to 12 ounces of a 45% solution to obtain a 60% solution?

If a side of a square is increased
by 5 the area is increased by 85
$$(x+5)^2 = x^2 + 85$$

29. A sum of $2000 is invested at simple interest, part at 3% and the remainder at 4%. Find the amount invested at each rate if the yearly income from the two investments is $66.

30. An airplane travels 1260 miles in the same time that an automobile travels 420 miles. If the rate of the airplane is 120 miles per hour greater than the rate of the automobile, find the rate of each.

31. Two cars start together and travel in the same direction, one going twice as fast as the other. At the end of three hours, they are 96 miles apart. How fast is each traveling? $2x - x = \dfrac{96}{3}$

32. Clerk A can process 50 applications in four hours, and clerk B can process 50 applications in eight hours. How long will it take both clerks working together to process 100 applications?

3.2 SECOND-DEGREE EQUATIONS

The equation

$$ax^2 + bx + c = 0 \quad (a \neq 0)$$

is a **second-degree** or **quadratic** equation. Any equation that can be reduced to this form by elementary transformations is, therefore, equivalent to a quadratic equation. We shall designate the form shown as the **standard form** for such equations.

Theorem 3.2 is of value to us in finding solutions of quadratic equations.

THEOREM 3.2   *If $P(x)$ and $Q(x)$ are expressions, then for all values of r for which $P(r)$ and $Q(r)$ are real numbers, r is a solution of $P(x) \cdot Q(x) = 0$ if and only if $P(r) = 0$, $Q(r) = 0$, or both.*

The proof of Theorem 3.2 follows directly from Theorems 1.6 and 1.7.

Example.   Find the solution set in R of $x^2 + 2x - 15 = 0$.

Solution.   Since $x^2 + 2x - 15 = (x + 5)(x - 3)$ is an identity over R, we have $(x + 5)(x - 3) = 0$. But, by Theorem 3.2, $(x + 5)(x - 3) = 0$ is true if and only if $x + 5 = 0$ or $x - 3 = 0$, and we can see by inspection that the solutions to these equations are -5 and 3. Hence, the solution set we seek is $\{-5, 3\}$.

Number of solutions of a quadratic equation   In general, the solution set of a quadratic equation *over the real numbers* may contain two, one, or no real numbers as elements. The equation in the foregoing example has two real solutions. Now, consider the equation

$$x^2 - 2x + 1 = 0.$$

Since $x^2 - 2x + 1 = 0$ is equivalent to

$$(x - 1)^2 = 0,$$

and since the only value of x for which $(x - 1)^2 = 0$ is 1, this is the only member of the solution set of $x^2 - 2x + 1 = 0$.

Before exhibiting an example of a quadratic equation over the real numbers in the real variable x having an empty solution set, let us consider the special case of a quadratic equation, $x^2 - a = 0$, where $a > 0$. Since $x^2 - a = 0$ is equivalent to $x^2 = a$, and since $x^2 = a$ implies that x must be a square root of a, we have as the solution set for $x^2 - a = 0$, $\{\sqrt{a}, -\sqrt{a}\}$. It is now easy to exhibit a quadratic equation having no real solutions, for example, $x^2 + 1 = 0$. Since, by Theorem 1.14', there exists no number $x \in R$ such that its square is negative, the solution set in R for the given equation is $\emptyset$. In Chapter 12 when we turn our attention to the set C of complex numbers, you will see that *every* quadratic equation over this set has a nonempty solution set in C.

Quadratic equations of the form

$$(x - a)^2 = b,$$

where, for now, $b \geq 0$, can be solved by observing that $x - a$ must be one of the square roots of b. That is, if $(x - a)^2 = b$, then either

$$x - a = \sqrt{b} \quad \text{or} \quad x - a = -\sqrt{b},$$

and conversely. Thus it is evident that the solution set of $(x - a)^2 = b$ $(b \geq 0)$ is

$$\{a + \sqrt{b}, a - \sqrt{b}\}.$$

General solution of a quadratic equation

Being able to find solution sets for quadratic equations of the form $(x - a)^2 = b$ enables us to find the solution set of any quadratic equation. Let us first consider the general quadratic equation in standard form

$$ax^2 + bx + c = 0 \quad (a \neq 0), \quad a, b, c \in R,$$

for the special case in which $a = 1$, that is,

$$x^2 + bx + c = 0. \tag{4}$$

We can write the equation in the equivalent form

$$(x - p)^2 = q,$$

which we can solve as above. We begin the process by adding $-c$ to each member of (4), which yields

$$x^2 + bx \qquad\qquad = -c. \tag{5}$$

If we then add $(b/2)^2$ to each member of (5), we obtain

$$x^2 + bx + \left(\frac{b}{2}\right)^2 = -c + \left(\frac{b}{2}\right)^2, \tag{6}$$

in which the left-hand member is equal to $(x + b/2)^2$, and we have

$$\left(x + \frac{b}{2}\right)^2 = -c + \frac{b^2}{4}. \tag{7}$$

Since we have performed only elementary transformations, (7) is equivalent to (5), and we can solve (7) by the method of the preceding section, provided that

$$-c + \frac{b^2}{4} \geq 0.$$

The technique used to obtain equations (6) and (7) is called **completing the square**. We can determine the term necessary to complete the square in (5) by dividing the coefficient b of the first-degree term by the number 2 and squaring the result. The expression obtained, $x^2 + bx + (b/2)^2$, is called a **perfect square** and may be written in the form $(x + b/2)^2$.

Because the general quadratic equation

$$ax^2 + bx + c = 0 \quad (a \neq 0)$$

can be written equivalently in the form

$$x^2 + \frac{b}{a}x + \frac{c}{a} = 0,$$

the foregoing process can be applied to obtain the **quadratic formula**

$$x = \frac{-b \pm \sqrt{b^2 - 4ac}}{2a},$$

where the roots of the general quadratic equation are expressed in terms of the coefficients. The symbol $\pm$ (read "plus or minus") is used to condense the writing of the two equations

$$x = \frac{-b + \sqrt{b^2 - 4ac}}{2a} \quad \text{and} \quad x = \frac{-b - \sqrt{b^2 - 4ac}}{2a}$$

into a single equation. We need only substitute the coefficients a, b, and c of a given quadratic equation in the formula to find the solution set for the equation.

Methods for solving quadratic equations

We now have the following methods available to solve quadratic equations:

1. Factoring when convenient and using Theorem 3.2.
2. Extracting roots when the member containing the variable is a perfect square. We complete the square if necessary.
3. Applying the quadratic formula, which is simply the end product of completing the square in the general case.

An examination of the quadratic formula,

$$x = \frac{-b \pm \sqrt{b^2 - 4ac}}{2a},$$

suffices to show that if $ax^2 + bx + c = 0$ is to have a nonempty solution set in the

Determination of number of real solutions of a quadratic equation over R

set of real numbers, then $\sqrt{b^2 - 4ac}$ must be real. This in turn implies that only those quadratic equations for which $b^2 - 4ac \geq 0$ will have real solutions. The number represented by $b^2 - 4ac$ is called the **discriminant** of the quadratic equation $ax^2 + bx + c = 0$. It yields the following information about the solution set of the equation for $a, b, c \in R$.

1. If $b^2 - 4ac = 0$, then there is precisely one real solution.
2. If $b^2 - 4ac < 0$, then there are no real solutions.
3. If $b^2 - 4ac > 0$, then there are two real solutions.

Solutions of applied problems

In some cases, the mathematical model we obtain for a physical situation is a quadratic equation that has two real solutions. It may be that one but not both of the solutions to the equation fits the physical situation. For example, if we were asked to find two consecutive *natural numbers* of which the product is 72, we would write the equation

$$x(x + 1) = 72$$

as our model. Solving this equation, we have

$$x^2 + x - 72 = 0,$$

$$(x + 9)(x - 8) = 0,$$

with solution set $\{8, -9\}$. Since -9 is not a natural number, we must reject it as a possible solution of our original problem; the solution 8, however, leads to the consecutive natural numbers 8 and 9. For additional examples, observe that we would not accept -6 feet as the height of a man, or $27/4$ for the number of persons in a room.

A quadratic equation used as a model for a physical situation may have two, one, or no meaningful solutions—meaningful, that is, in a physical sense. Answers to word problems should always be checked against the universal set of meaningful numbers for the original problem.

EXERCISE 3.2

Solve by factoring.

Example. $x^2 + x = 30$

Solution.   Write an equivalent equation in standard form, and factor the left-hand member.

$$x^2 + x - 30 = 0$$

$$(x + 6)(x - 5) = 0 \qquad \textit{(Solution continued overleaf.)}$$

Determine solutions by inspection, or set each factor equal to zero and solve each linear equation.

$$x + 6 = 0 \qquad x - 5 = 0$$

$$x = -6 \qquad x = 5$$

The solution set is $\{-6, 5\}$.

1. $x^2 + 2x = 0$ $x(x+2) = 0$

                $0 \quad -2$

2. $x^2 - x = 5x$

3. $x^2 + 5x - 14 = 0$

4. $3x^2 - 6x = -3$

5. $x(2x - 3) = -1$

6. $(x - 2)(x + 1) = 4$

7. $3 = \dfrac{10}{x^2} - \dfrac{7}{x}$ $-\frac{10}{3}$

8. $\dfrac{2}{x - 3} - \dfrac{6}{x - 8} = -1$

Solve for x by the extraction of roots.

Example. $(x + 3)^2 = 7$

Solution. Set $x + 3$ equal to each square root of 7.

$$x + 3 = \sqrt{7} \qquad x + 3 = -\sqrt{7}$$

$$x = -3 + \sqrt{7} \qquad x = -3 - \sqrt{7}$$

The solution set is $\{-3 + \sqrt{7}, -3 - \sqrt{7}\}$.

9. $x^2 = 4$ $2, -2$

10. $9x^2 - 100 = 0$

11. $x^2 = 5$ $\sqrt{5}, -\sqrt{5}$

12. $(x - 1)^2 = 4$

13. $(x - 6)^2 = 5$

14. $(x - a)^2 = 4$

Solve by completing the square.

Example. $2x^2 + x - 1 = 0$

Solution. Write an equivalent equation with the constant term as the right-hand member and the coefficient of x^2 equal to 1.

$$x^2 + \frac{1}{2}x \quad = \frac{1}{2}$$

Add the square of one-half of the coefficient of the first-degree term to each member.

$$x^2 + \frac{1}{2}x + \frac{1}{16} = \frac{1}{2} + \frac{1}{16}$$

Rewrite the left-hand member as the square of an expression.

$$\left(x + \frac{1}{4}\right)^2 = \frac{9}{16}$$

Set $x + \dfrac{1}{4}$ equal to each square root of $\dfrac{9}{16}$.

$$x + \frac{1}{4} = \frac{3}{4} \qquad x + \frac{1}{4} = -\frac{3}{4}$$

$$x = \frac{1}{2} \qquad x = -1$$

The solution set is $\left\{ \dfrac{1}{2}, -1 \right\}$.

(handwritten)
$x^2 + 4x \;\; -12$
$(x+2)^2 \;=\; 12 + \dfrac{4^2}{4}$
$x+2 = \sqrt{16} = \pm 4$

$x + 2 = +4$
$x = 2$

$x + 2 = -4$
$x = -6$

15. $x^2 + 4x - 12 = 0$

16. $x^2 - 2x + 1 = 0$

17. $x^2 + 9x + 20 = 0$

18. $x^2 - 2x - 1 = 0$

19. $2x^2 = 2 - 3x$

20. $2x^2 + 4x = -1$

(handwritten)
$x^2 + 9x = -20$
$\left(x + \dfrac{9}{2}\right)^2 = -20 + \left(\dfrac{9}{2}\right)^2$
$\left(x + \dfrac{9}{2}\right)^2 = -20 + \dfrac{81}{4}$
$x + \dfrac{9}{2} = \pm \sqrt{\dfrac{1}{4}}$
$x = -\dfrac{1}{2} - \dfrac{9}{2} = -5$
$x = +\dfrac{1}{2} - \dfrac{9}{2} = -4$

Reduce each of the following equations to equivalent equations of the form

$$(x - h)^2 + (y - k)^2 = r^2$$

by completing the squares in x and y.

Example. $x^2 + y^2 - 4x + 6y = 5$

Solution.   Write an equivalent equation in the form

$$[x^2 - 4x + (\;\;)] + [y^2 + 6y + (\;\;)] = 5 + (\;\;) + (\;\;).$$

Complete the squares in x and y.

$$[x^2 - 4x + 4] + [y^2 + 6y + 9] = 5 + 4 + 9$$

$$(x - 2)^2 + (y + 3)^2 = 18, \quad \text{or} \quad (x - 2)^2 + [y - (-3)]^2 = (\sqrt{18})^2$$

21. $x^2 + y^2 - 4x - 4y - 17 = 0$

22. $x^2 + y^2 + 6x - 6y + 18 = 0$

23. $x^2 + y^2 + 6x - 2y + 6 = 0$

24. $x^2 + y^2 - 2x + 4y + 2 = 0$

25. $4x^2 + 4y^2 - 4x + 8y = 11$

26. $16x^2 + 16y^2 - 8x + 16y = 59$

Solve for x, using the quadratic formula.

(handwritten)
$x^2 - 4x + 4 \quad y^2 - 4y + 4 = +17 + 4 + 4 = 25$
$(x+2)^2 + (y+2)^2 = 5^2$

Example. $\dfrac{x^2}{4} + \dfrac{x}{4} = 3$

(handwritten)
$x^2 + 6x + 9 + y^2 - 2y + 1 = -6 + 9 + 1$
$(x+3)^2 + (y+1)^2 = 2^2$

Solution.   Write an equivalent equation in standard form.

$$x^2 + x - 12 = 0$$

Substitute 1 for a, 1 for b, and -12 for c in the quadratic formula, and simplify.

$$x = \frac{-1 \pm \sqrt{1 + 48}}{2} = \frac{-1 \pm 7}{2}$$

The solution set is $\{3, -4\}$.

(handwritten)
$4x^2 - 4x + 1 + 4y^2 + 8y + 4 = 11$
$(2x - 1)^2 + (2y + 2)^2 = 4^2$

27. $x^2 - 3x + 2 = 0$ 28. $x^2 + 4x + 4 = 0$

29. $2x^2 = 7x - 6$ 30. $3x^2 = 5x - 1$

31. $\dfrac{x^2}{3} = \dfrac{1}{2}x + \dfrac{3}{2}$ 32. $\dfrac{x^2 - 3}{2} + \dfrac{x}{4} = 1$

33. $x^2 - 2\sqrt{5}x + 5 = 0$ 34. $x^2 + 2\sqrt{2}x + 2 = 0$

35. $2x^2 - \sqrt{3}x - 3 = 0$ 36. $2x^2 + \sqrt{7}x - 7 = 0$

37. $x^2 - kx - 2k^2 = 0$ 38. $2x^2 - kx + 3 = 0$

39. $ax^2 - x + c = 0$ 40. $x^2 + 2x + c + 3 = 0$

41. Determine k so that the roots of $kx^2 + 4x + 1 = 0$ will be equal. *Hint:* Use the discriminant.

42. Determine k so that $x^2 - kx + 9 = 0$ will have just one real root.

43. Determine k so that the roots $x^2 + 2x + k + 3 = 0$ will be two real numbers.

44. Determine k so that the roots of $x^2 + 9x + k = 2$ will be two real numbers.

45. Find two consecutive natural numbers such that the sum of their squares is 85.

46. Two airplanes with lines of flight at right angles to each other pass each other (at slightly different altitudes) at noon. One is flying at 140 miles per hour and one at 180 miles per hour. How far apart are they at 12:30 PM?

47. A box without a top is to be made from a square piece of tin by cutting a two-inch square from each corner and folding up the sides. If the box is to hold 128 cubic inches, what should be the length of each side of the original square?

48. Suppose a ball thrown upward reaches a height h in feet given by the equation $h = 32t - 8t^2$, where t is the time in seconds after the throw. How long will it take the ball to reach a height of 24 feet on its way up? How long after the throw will the ball return to the ground?

49. The distance s a body falls in a vacuum is given by $s = v_0 t + \frac{1}{2}gt^2$, where s is measured in feet, t is measured in seconds, v_0 is the initial velocity in feet per second, and g is the constant of acceleration due to gravity (approximately 32 ft/sec/sec). How long will it take a body to fall 150 feet if v_0 is 20 feet per second? If the body starts from rest?

50. A man sailed a boat across a lake and back in two and a half hours. If his rate returning was two miles per hour less than his rate going, and if the distance each way was six miles, find his rate each way.

3.3 EQUATIONS INVOLVING RADICALS

Equality of like powers   In order to find solution sets for equations containing radical expressions, we shall need the following result.

THEOREM 3.3 *If $U(x)$ and $V(x)$ are expressions in x, then the solution set of $U(x) = V(x)$ is a subset of the solution set of $[U(x)]^n = [V(x)]^n$, for each natural number n.*

This theorem, which simply asserts that products of equal numbers are equal numbers, permits us to raise both members of an equation to the same natural-number power with the assurance that we do not lose any solutions of the original equation in the process. On the other hand, it does not assert that the resulting equation will be equivalent to the original equation, and indeed it will not always be. The equation $[U(x)]^n = [V(x)]^n$ may have additional solutions (called **extraneous solutions**) that are not solutions of $U(x) = V(x)$. Thus, if $a = b$, then $a^4 = b^4$, but the converse does not necessarily hold. That is, a^4 and b^4 may be equal, but $a \neq b$. For example, $(3)^4 = (-3)^4$, but $3 \neq -3$. The solution set of the equation $x^4 = 81$, obtained from $x = 3$ by raising each member to the fourth power,

| Necessity of checking solutions | contains -3 as an extraneous real solution, since -3 does not satisfy the original equation even though it does satisfy $x^4 = 81$. Because the result of applying the foregoing process is not always an equivalent equation, each solution obtained |

through its use *must* be substituted for the variable in the original equation to check its validity. Substitution of the second equation in this theorem for the first is not an elementary transformation.

Example. Find the solution set of $\sqrt[3]{x-1} = -1$.

Solution. If we raise each member of $\sqrt[3]{x-1} = -1$ to the third power, we obtain

$$(\sqrt[3]{x-1})^3 = (-1)^3,$$

$$x - 1 = -1,$$

which is equivalent to

$$x = 0.$$

Since $\sqrt[3]{0-1} = -1$, 0 is a solution of the original equation. Moreover, 0 is the only real solution, since Theorem 3.3 guarantees that the solution set of $\sqrt[3]{x-1} = -1$ is a subset of the solution set of $x = 0$.

Example. Find the solution set of $\sqrt{x+2} + 4 = x$.

Solution. We first write the equivalent equation,

$$\sqrt{x+2} = x - 4,$$

and then apply Theorem 3.3. We obtain

$$(\sqrt{x+2})^2 = (x-4)^2,$$

$$x + 2 = x^2 - 8x + 16. \quad \textit{(Solution continued overleaf.)}$$

This last equation is equivalent to

$$x^2 - 9x + 14 = 0,$$

$$(x - 2)(x - 7) = 0,$$

which clearly has solutions 2 and 7. Upon replacing x with 2 in the original equation, however, we obtain

$$\sqrt{2 + 2} + 4 = 2,$$

or

$$3 + 4 \overset{?}{=} 6 = 2,$$

which is false. Hence, 2 is not a solution of the original equation; it is an extraneous root. On the other hand, 7 does satisfy the original equation, so the solution set we seek is {7}.

It is sometimes necessary to apply Theorem 3.3 more than once in solving certain equations, such as those in Problems 7–10 of Exercise 3.3.

Substitution of variables   Some equations that are not polynomial equations can nevertheless be solved through the solutions of related polynomial equations.

Example.   Find the solution set of $y + 2\sqrt{y} - 8 = 0$.

Solution.   If we set $p = \sqrt{y}$ and substitute in the given equation, we have

$$p^2 + 2p - 8 = 0,$$

$$(p + 4)(p - 2) = 0,$$

which has -4 and 2 as solutions. Since $-4 < 0$, we must reject it as a source for solutions because $p = \sqrt{y}$, and $\sqrt{y}$ is always nonnegative. The other value, $p = 2$, leads to $\sqrt{y} = 2$ and hence $y = 4$. The solution set we seek is {4}.

The technique of substituting one variable for another—or, more generally, a variable for an expression—is not limited to cases involving radicals, but is useful in any situation in which an equation is polynomial in form.

EXERCISE   3.3

Solve and check. If there is no solution, so state.

1. $\sqrt{x} = 8$ 2. $\sqrt{y + 8} = 1$

3. $\sqrt[3]{2 - y} = 3$ 4. $\sqrt[5]{7 - x} = 2$

5. $2x - 3 = \sqrt{7x - 3}$ 6. $\sqrt{x + 3}\sqrt{x - 9} = 8$

7. $\sqrt{y + 4} = \sqrt{y + 20} - 2$ 8. $\sqrt{x} + \sqrt{2} = \sqrt{x + 2}$

9. $\sqrt{5 + \sqrt{x}} = \sqrt{x} - 1$ 10. $\sqrt{13 + \sqrt{x}} = \sqrt{x} + 1$

11. $(5 + x)^{1/2} + x^{1/2} = 5$ 12. $(y + 7)^{1/2} + (y + 4)^{1/2} = 3$

13. $(y^2 - 3y + 5)^{1/2} - (y + 2)^{1/2} = 0$ 14. $(z - 3)^{1/2} + (z + 5)^{1/2} = 4$

Solve. Leave the results in the form of an equation. Assume denominators not zero.

15. $r = \sqrt{\dfrac{A}{\pi}}$, for A 16. $t = \sqrt{\dfrac{2v}{g}}$, for g

17. $x\sqrt{xy} = 1$, for y 18. $P = \pi\sqrt{\dfrac{l}{g}}$, for g

19. $x = \sqrt{a^2 - y^2}$, for y 20. $y = \dfrac{1}{\sqrt{1 - x}}$, for x

Solve for x, y, or z.

Example. $x^4 - 10x^2 + 9 = 0$

Solution. Set $p = x^2$ and solve for p.

$$p^2 - 10p + 9 = 0$$
$$(p - 9)(p - 1) = 0$$
$$p - 9 \quad \text{or} \quad p = 1$$

Set each value of $p = x^2$ and solve for x.

$$x^2 = 9 \qquad\qquad x^2 = 1$$
$$x = 3 \text{ or } -3 \qquad x = 1 \text{ or } -1$$

The solution set is $\{3, -3, 1, -1\}$.

21. $x - 2\sqrt{x} - 15 = 0$ 22. $x^4 - 5x^2 + 4 = 0$

23. $2x^4 + 17x^2 - 9 = 0$ 24. $z^4 - 2z^2 - 24 = 0$

25. $(y^2 + 5y)^2 - 8y(y + 5) - 84 = 0$ 26. $y^2 - 5 - 5\sqrt{y^2 - 5} + 6 = 0$

27. $y^{2/3} - 2y^{1/3} - 8 = 0$ 28. $z^{2/3} - 2z^{1/3} - 35 = 0$

29. $y^{-2} - y^{-1} - 12 = 0$ 30. $z^{-2} + 9z^{-1} - 10 = 0$

3.4 SOLUTION OF INEQUALITIES

Sentences such as

$$x + 3 \geq 10 \qquad\qquad (1)$$

and

$$\frac{-2y - 3}{3} < 5 \qquad\qquad (2)$$

are called **inequalities**. For appropriate values of the variable, one member of an inequality represents a real number that is less than ($<$), less than or equal to ($\leq$), greater than or equal to ($\geq$), or greater than ($>$) the real number represented by the other member.

Any element of the replacement set of the variable for which an inequality is valid is called a **solution,** and the set of all solutions of an inequality is called the **solution set** of the inequality. Inequalities that are true for every element in the replacement set of the variable—such as $x^2 + 1 > 0$, $x \in R$—are called **absolute** or **unconditional inequalities.** Inequalities that are not true for every element of the replacement set are called **conditional inequalities**—for example, (1) and (2) above.

Solution of inequalities by solving equivalent inequalities

As in the case with equations, we shall solve a given inequality by generating a series of **equivalent inequalities** (inequalities having the same solution set) until we arrive at one of which the solution set is obvious. To do this, we shall need the following theorem applicable to inequalities.

THEOREM 3.4   *If $P(x)$, $Q(x)$, and $R(x)$ are expressions, then for all values of x for which $P(x)$, $Q(x)$, and $R(x)$ are real numbers,*

$$P(x) < Q(x)$$

is equivalent to each of the following:

     I $P(x) + R(x) < Q(x) + R(x)$,

     II $P(x) \cdot R(x) < Q(x) \cdot R(x)$ *for* $x \in \{x \mid R(x) > 0\}$,

     III $P(x) \cdot R(x) > Q(x) \cdot R(x)$ *for* $x \in \{x \mid R(x) < 0\}$.

Similarly, the sentence

$$P(x) \leq Q(x)$$

is equivalent to sentences of the form I–III, *with* $<$ *(or* $>$*) replaced by* $\leq$ *(or* $\geq$*) under the same conditions, $R(x) > 0$ and $R(x) < 0$, as above.*

We shall here restrict our attention to a proof of III.

Proof of III. Let r denote any solution of $P(x) < Q(x)$, for which $R(r) < 0$. Then, by definition,

$$P(r) < Q(r)$$

is true for the real numbers $P(r)$ and $Q(r)$. Since $R(r)$ is a negative real number, Theorem 1.15-IV yields

$$P(r) \cdot R(r) > Q(r) \cdot R(r).$$

This shows that r is a solution of $P(x) \cdot R(x) > Q(x) \cdot R(x)$. Conversely, if r is any such solution, for which $R(r) < 0$, then $1/[R(r)] < 0$, and Theorem 1.15-IV gives

$$\frac{1}{R(r)} \cdot P(r) \cdot R(r) < \frac{1}{R(r)} \cdot Q(r) \cdot R(r),$$

from which we have

$$P(r) < Q(r).$$

This shows that r is a solution of $P(x) < Q(x)$. Thus since any solution of $P(x) < Q(x)$ is a solution of $P(x) \cdot R(x) > Q(x) \cdot R(x)$ provided $R(x) < 0$, and conversely, these sentences are equivalent. The proofs of the other parts of the theorem are similar.

Note that Theorem 3.4 does not permit multiplying by zero, and variables in multipliers are restricted from values for which the expression vanishes. The result of applying any part of this theorem is an elementary transformation.

Solution of a linear inequality   Theorem 3.4 can be applied to solve inequalities in the same way that the theorems of equality are applied to solve equations.

Example.   Solve $\dfrac{x-3}{4} < \dfrac{2}{3}$.

Solution.   Multiplying each member by 12 gives

$$3(x-3) < 8,$$

or

$$3x - 9 < 8.$$

Adding 9 to each member gives

$$3x < 17.$$

Finally, multiplying each member by $\dfrac{1}{3}$, we obtain

$$x < \frac{17}{3},$$

and the solution set is

$$S = \left\{ x \mid x < \frac{17}{3} \right\}.$$

Graphical representation of inequality solution set   The solution set in the foregoing example can be pictured on a number-line graph as shown in Figure 3.1. The heavy line indicates points with coordinates in the solution set.

Figure 3.1

Inequalities sometimes appear in a form such as

$$-6 < 3x \le 15, \tag{3}$$

where an expression is bracketed between two inequality symbols. As indicated in Chapter 1, this means $-6 < 3x$ *and* $3x \le 15$. The solution set of such an inequality is obtained in the same manner as the solution set of any other inequality. In (3) above, each expression may be multiplied by 1/3 to obtain

$$-2 < x \le 5.$$

The solution set,

$$S = \{x \mid -2 < x \le 5\},$$

is shown on the number-line graph in Figure 3.2. Note that the open dot at the left-hand endpoint of the interval indicates that -2 *is not* a member of the solution set, whereas the solid dot at the other end indicates that 5 *is* a member of the solution set.

Figure 3.2

Solution of a quadratic inequality   Quadratic inequalities offer somewhat different problems. For example, consider the inequality

$$x^2 + 4x < 5.$$

To determine values of x for which this condition holds, we might first rewrite the sentence equivalently as

$$x^2 + 4x - 5 < 0,$$

$$(x + 5)(x - 1) < 0.$$

It is clear here that only those values of x for which the factors $x + 5$ and $x - 1$ are opposite in sign will be in the solution set, which can be determined analytically by noting that $(x + 5)(x - 1) < 0$ implies that either

$$x + 5 < 0 \quad \text{and} \quad x - 1 > 0$$

or

$$x + 5 > 0 \quad \text{and} \quad x - 1 < 0.$$

Each of these two cases can be considered separately.

First, $x + 5 < 0$ and $x - 1 > 0$ imply $x < -5$ and $x > 1$, conditions which are not satisfied by any values of x. But $x + 5 > 0$ and $x - 1 < 0$ imply $x > -5$ and $x < 1$, which lead to the solution set,

$$S = \{x \mid -5 < x < 1\}.$$

An alternative set notation for this solution set is

$$S = \{x \mid x > -5\} \cap \{x \mid x < 1\}.$$

Use of sign graphs in solving an inequality   One relatively easy way to visualize the solution set of a quadratic inequality is to indicate on a number line the signs associated with each factor for number replacements for the variable. Figure 3.3 shows such an arrangement, or **sign graph**,

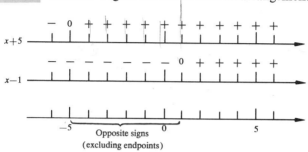

Figure 3.3

for the example above. This picture is constructed by first showing on the top number line the places where $x + 5$ is positive ($x > -5$) and the places where it is negative ($x < -5$), and then showing on a second line those places where $x - 1$ is positive ($x > 1$) and those where it is negative ($x < 1$). The bottom line can then be marked by observing those parts of the first two lines where the signs are alike and those parts where the signs are opposite. Since it is desired that the product $(x + 5)(x - 1)$ be negative, the third line shows clearly that this occurs where $-5 < x < 1$, so that the solution set of the inequality is $\{x \mid -5 < x < 1\}$.

Multiplication of an inequality by a variable   Inequalities involving fractions have to be approached with care if any fraction contains a variable in the denominator. If Theorem 3.4 is invoked to multiply each member by an expression containing the variable, we have to be careful either to distinguish between those values of the variable for which the expression denotes a positive and negative number, respectively, or else make sure that the expression by which we multiply is always positive. Problems 17–22 in the exercise involve such inequalities.

EXERCISE 3.4

Solve and represent the solution set on a line graph.

1. $x + 7 > 8$

2. $x - 5 \leq 7$

3. $3x - 2 > 1 + 2x$

4. $2x + 3 \leq x - 1$

5. $\dfrac{2x - 3}{2} \leq 5$

6. $\dfrac{3x + 4}{3} > 12$

Graph each of the following sets and rewrite in simpler set notation.

Example. $\{x \mid x + 2 \geq 0\} \cap \{x \mid x - 3 < 1\}$

Solution.   Solve each inequality and graph. Indicate the region where the graphs overlap.

7. $\{x \mid x - 2 < 3\} \cap \{x \mid x + 4 > 2\}$

8. $\left\{ x \left| \dfrac{1 + x}{2} \leq 3 \right. \right\} \cap \{x \mid x \leq 6\}$

9. $\{x \mid 2x - 1 > 5\} \cap \left\{ x \left| \dfrac{x - 1}{3} \geq 4 \right. \right\}$

10. $\{x \mid x > 2\} \cap \left\{ x \left| \dfrac{2x + 5}{2} < 0 \right. \right\}$

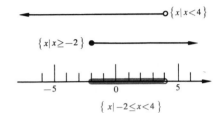

Find the solution set of each inequality.

11. $(x + 1)(x - 2) > 0$

12. $(x + 2)(x + 5) < 0$

13. $x^2 - 3x - 4 > 0$

14. $x^2 - 5x - 6 \geq 0$

15. $x^2 < 5$

16. $4x^2 + 1 < 0$

Example. $\dfrac{x}{x - 2} \geq 5$

Solution.   We can approach this directly by means of a sign graph. We first rewrite the given inequality equivalently as

$$\frac{x}{x - 2} - 5 \geq 0,$$

from which we obtain

$$\frac{-4x + 10}{x - 2} \geq 0.$$

For this to be valid, $x - 2$ must not be 0, and the numerator and denominator must be

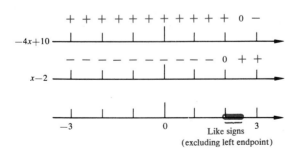

of like sign. The sign graph shows that the quotient $(-4x + 10)/(x - 2)$ is positive or zero for x between 2 and 5/2, including 5/2 but excluding 2, a value of x for which the denominator is 0. The desired solution set is therefore $\{x \mid 2 < x \leq 5/2\}$, with graph as shown on the last line of the sign graph.

17. $\dfrac{2}{x} \leq 4$ 18. $\dfrac{3}{x-6} > 8$

19. $\dfrac{x}{x+2} > 4$ 20. $\dfrac{x+2}{x-2} \geq 6$

21. $\dfrac{2}{x-2} \geq \dfrac{4}{x}$ 22. $\dfrac{3}{4x+1} > \dfrac{2}{x-5}$

23. $x(x-2)(x+3) > 0$ 24. $x^3 - 4x \leq 0$

3.5   SENTENCES INVOLVING ABSOLUTE VALUES

In Section 1.5, we defined the absolute value of a real number by

$$|x| = \begin{cases} x, & \text{if } x \geq 0, \\ -x, & \text{if } x < 0. \end{cases}$$

The absolute value of a difference

More generally, then, the expression $|x - a|$ satisfies

$$|x - a| = \begin{cases} x - a, & \text{if } x - a \geq 0, \text{ or, equivalently, if } x \geq a, \\ -(x - a), & \text{if } x - a < 0, \text{ or, equivalently, if } x < a, \end{cases}$$

and can be interpreted on a number line as denoting the distance the graph of x is located from the graph of a, as shown in Figure 3.4.

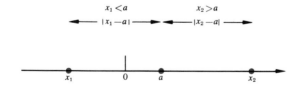

Figure 3.4

Example.   Find the solution set of $|x - 3| = 5$.

Solution 1.   This can be solved by inspection. Since $x - 3$ represents the distance the graph of x is located from the graph of 3, and since by the equation this distance is 5, the two solutions of the equation are $3 + 5$, or 8, and $3 - 5$, or -2. Thus, the solution set is $\{-2, 8\}$.

Solution 2. By definition, $|x - 3| = 5$ implies that

$$x - 3 = 5$$

or else

$$-(x - 3) = 5.$$

The equation $x - 3 = 5$ is equivalent to $x = 8$, and $-(x - 3) = 5$ is equivalent to $x = -2$. Hence the solution set is given by

$$S - \{x \mid x = 8\} \cup \{x \mid x = -2\} = \{-2, 8\}.$$

Inequalities involving abso- lute values   Inequalities involving absolute-value notation require some additional discussion. For example, consider the inequality

$$|x + 1| > 3.$$

By definition, this inequality is equivalent to

$$x + 1 > 3 \quad \text{for} \quad x + 1 \geq 0$$

and

$$-(x + 1) > 3 \quad \text{for} \quad x + 1 < 0,$$

so that the solution set is given by

$$S = \{x \mid x > 2 \text{ or } x < -4\}. \tag{1}$$

Alternatively, we could also write

$$S = \{x \mid x > 2\} \cup \{x \mid x < -4\},$$

where the union gives a precise meaning to the word "or" used in (1). The graph of the solution set is shown in Figure 3.5.

Figure 3.5

EXERCISE 3.5

Solve.

Example. $|x + 5| = 8$

Solution. Determine the solution set by considering $|x + 5|$ as $|x - (-5)|$, or else write the equation as two first-degree equations and solve each of them.

$$x + 5 = 8 \qquad -(x + 5) = 8$$

$$x = 3 \qquad\qquad x = -13$$

The solution set is $\{3, -13\}$.

1. $|x| = 6$

2. $|x| = 3$

3. $|x - 1| = 4$

4. $|x - 6| = 3$

5. $\left| x - \dfrac{2}{3} \right| = \dfrac{1}{3}$

6. $\left| x - \dfrac{3}{4} \right| = \dfrac{1}{2}$

Solve and graph each solution set on a number line.

7. $|x| < 2$

8. $|x - 1| > 2$

9. $|x + 3| \geq 4$

10. $|x + 1| \leq 8$

11. $|2x - 5| \geq 3$

12. $|2x + 4| < -1$

Replace each of the following inequalities with a single inequality involving an absolute value symbol.

Example. $-3 < x < 7$.

Solution.   Since the average of 7 and -3 is $[7 + (-3)]/2 = 4/2 = 2$, the values of x are centered about 2. Subtracting 2 from each member, we have:

$$-5 < x - 2 < 5,$$
$$|x - 2| < 5.$$

13. $1 < x < 3$

14. $-5 \leq x \leq 9$

15. $-9 \leq x \leq -7$

16. $5 < x < 13$

17. $-7 \leq 2x \leq 12$

18. $-5 < 3x < 10$

19. A student must have an average of at least 80%, but less than 90%, on five tests in a course to receive a B. His grades on the first four tests were 98%, 76%, 86%, and 92%. What grade on the fifth test would give him a B in the course?

20. Fahrenheit and Centigrade temperatures are related by $C = \dfrac{5}{9}(F - 32)$. Within what range must the temperature be in Fahrenheit degrees for the temperature in Centigrade degrees to lie between $-10°$ and $20°$, inclusive?

In Problems 21–26, consider $a, b \in R$.

21. Show that $|-a| = |a|$. *Hint:* Consider two possible cases, a nonnegative and a negative.

22. Show that $|a - b| = |b - a|$. *Hint:* Consider two possible cases, $a - b \geq 0$ and $a - b < 0$.

23. Show that $|a^2| = |a|^2 = a^2$.

24. Show that $|ab| = |a| \cdot |b|$. *Hint:* Consider four possible cases, with a nonnegative and negative, and b nonnegative and negative.

25. Show that $\left| \dfrac{a}{b} \right| = \dfrac{|a|}{|b|}$ $(b \neq 0)$.

26. Show that $|a - b| \leq |a| + |b|$. *Hint:* Consider four cases.

4 RELATIONS AND FUNCTIONS

4.1 CARTESIAN PRODUCTS

When the order in which the numbers of a number pair are to be considered is specified, the pair is called an **ordered pair**, and the pair is denoted by a symbol such as (3, 2), (2, 3), (-1, 5), or (0, 3). Each of the two numbers in an ordered pair is called a **component** of the ordered pair, the first and second being called the **first component** and the **second component**, respectively.

Having established what is meant by an ordered pair, we are ready to define a set operation involving such pairs.

DEFINITION 4.1 *The **Cartesian product** of two sets A and B, denoted by $A \times B$, is the set of all ordered pairs (x, y) such that $x \in A$ and $y \in B$.*

Example. If $A = \{1, 2, 3\}$ and $B = \{5, 6\}$, then

$$A \times B = \{(1, 5), (1, 6), (2, 5), (2, 6), (3, 5), (3, 6)\}$$

and

$$B \times A = \{(5, 1), (5, 2), (5, 3), (6, 1), (6, 2), (6, 3)\}.$$

In this book, we are particularly interested in the case in which $A = B$, or, more specifically, in the Cartesian product $U \times U$, where U is the universe of discourse. We shall call $U \times U$ the **Cartesian set** of U.

Example. If $U = \{1, 2, 3\}$, then

$$U \times U = \{(1, 1), (1, 2), (1, 3), (2, 1), (2, 2), (2, 3), (3, 1), (3, 2), (3, 3)\}.$$

The most important Cartesian set with which we shall be concerned is that formed from the set R of real numbers. The product $R \times R$, which is often denoted by R^2, is the set of all possible ordered pairs of real numbers. The fact that each member

> $R \times R$, or R^2, and the geometric plane

of R^2 corresponds to a point in the geometric plane, and the coordinates of each point in the geometric plane are the components of a member of R^2, is the basis for all plane graphing. The correspondence between points in the plane and ordered pairs of real numbers is usually established through a **Cartesian** (or **rectangular**) **coordinate system**, as shown in Figure 4.1.

> **Equations in two variables**

Equations in two variables, such as

$$3x + 2y = 12, \quad x^2 y + 3x = y^5, \quad \text{and} \quad \sqrt{xy} = y^2 - 5,$$

with $x, y \in R$, have, as solutions, ordered pairs of numbers. For example, if the components of $(2, 3)$ are substituted for the variables x and y, in that order, in the equation

$$3x + 2y = 12,$$

the result is

$$3(2) + 2(3) = 12,$$

which is true. On the other hand, if y is replaced with 2 and x with 3, we have

$$3(3) + 2(2) = 12,$$

which is false. The same pair of numbers can yield a true statement and a false statement, depending on

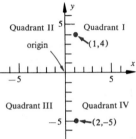

Figure 4.1

the order in which the replacements are made. In this book, the first component is a value for the **abscissa** x, and the second component a value for the **ordinate** y.

> **Solutions of an equation in two variables**

We can find ordered pairs that satisfy a given equation in two variables by assigning values to one variable and determining the associated values for the other. Thus, for

$$y = x - 1,$$

we can obtain solutions by replacing x with, say, 1, 2, and 3 in turn. This gives us $(1, 0)$, $(2, 1)$, and $(3, 2)$ as solutions.

We shall be interested primarily in discussing solutions of equations in R^2. Since many open sentences in two variables will select an infinite number of ordered pairs from this set, we shall use the set-builder notation

$$\{(x, y) \mid \text{condition on } x \text{ and } y\}$$

to represent the solution sets of these equations.

EXERCISE 4.1

Determine each Cartesian product, $A \times B$.

1. $A = \{1\}, B = \{-1, -2\}$ 2. $A = \{-1, -2\}, B = \{1\}$

3. $A = \{-1, 0, 1\}, B = \{0, 1\}$ 4. $A = \{5, 10\}, B = \{1, 2, 3, 4\}$

5. $A = \{a, b\}, B = \{c, d\}$ 6. $A = \{a, b, c\}, B = \{x\}$

In each Problem 7–12, supply the missing components so that the ordered pairs

a. $(0, \quad)$ b. $(1, \quad)$ c. $(2, \quad)$ d. $(-3, \quad)$ e. $\left(\dfrac{2}{3}, \quad\right)$

are solutions of the given equation.

7. $2x + y = 6$ 8. $y = 9 - x^2$ 9. $y = \dfrac{3x}{x^2 - 2}$

10. $y = 0$ 11. $y = \sqrt{3x + 11}$ 12. $y = |x - 1|$

13. If $A = \{1, 2, 3, \cdots, n\}$ and $B = \{1, 2, 3, \cdots, m\}, n < m$, how many members has

    a. $A \times B$?   b. $B \times A$?

    c. $(A \times B) \cup (B \times A)$?   d. $(A \times B) \cap (B \times A)$?

14. Let $A = \{1, 2, 3, \cdots, n\}$, $B = \{1, 2, 3, \cdots, m\}$, and $n < m$.

    a. How many members of $A \times B$ are of the form (a, a)?

    b. Is it possible to find values for n and m such that $A \times B$ has 13 members? If so, give a pair of such values.

    c. How many members (a, b) of $A \times A$ satisfy the condition that $a < b$? $a \le b$?

15. In Chapter 14, we shall use *deleted* Cartesian sets. A **deleted Cartesian set** is a Cartesian set exclusive of its members with equal first and second components. Let $U = \{1, 2, 3, 4\}$.

    a. List the deleted Cartesian set of U.

    b. How many members has the deleted Cartesian set of U?

    c. How many members are in the deleted Cartesian set of U if $U = \{1, 2, 3, \cdots, n\}$?

16. Let $A \subset U$ and $B \subseteq U$.

    a. Is it possible that $(A \times B) \subseteq (U \times U)$?

    b. Is it necessary that $(A \times B) \subseteq (U \times U)$?

    c. Is it possible that $(A \times B) \subset (U \times U)$?

    d. Is it necessary that $(A \times B) \subset (U \times U)$?

    e. Is it possible that $(A \times B) = (U \times U)$?

4.2 SUBSETS OF CARTESIAN SETS

Any sentence in two variables, x and y, expresses a relationship that might or might not hold between ordered pairs of elements in the replacement sets of the two variables, and this relationship precisely determines the solution set of the sentence in two variables. For $x, y \in U$, this solution set is always a subset of $U \times U$. The relationship specified by the sentence is thus most specifically identified with a subset of ordered pairs of some universe of discourse U. This leads us to the following.

DEFINITION 4.2 *Any subset S of $U \times U$ is a **relation** in U.*

The relation is said to be in U because the components of the ordered pairs in the relation are elements of U. Alternatively, we frequently refer to the relationship as being in $U \times U$.

The set of all first components in the ordered pairs in a relation is called the **domain** of the relation, and the set of all second components is called the **range** of the relation.

Example. Let U be the set R of real numbers, and let

$$S = \left\{ (x, y) \mid y = \frac{1}{x - 2} \right\}.$$

What is the domain of S? The range?

Solution. Since for every real number x except 2, $1/(x - 2)$ is a real number, the domain of S consists of all real numbers except 2. That is, the domain of S is $\{x \mid x \in R, x \neq 2\}$. To determine the range of S, we solve the equation $y = 1/(x - 2)$ explicitly for x to obtain $x = (1 + 2y)/y$. Now, since for each real number y except 0, $(1 + 2y)/y$ is real, the range of S is $\{y \mid y \in R, y \neq 0\}$.

There is a special kind of relation that is important in mathematics. This special kind of relation is called a *function*.

DEFINITION 4.3 *A **function** is a relation in which no two ordered pairs have the same first component and different second components.*

Graphical characterization of a function   A function, therefore, associates each element in its domain with one and only one element in its range. In a graphical sense, this implies that no two of the ordered pairs in a function graph into points on the same vertical line.

As you should recall from your earlier study of algebra, graphs on R^2, that is, on $R \times R$, are often continuous lines and curves. Figure 4.2 shows three such graphs.

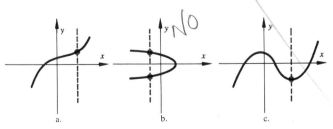

a.   b.   c.

Figure 4.2

Imagine a vertical line moving across each of these from left to right. If the vertical line at any position cuts the graph of the relation in more than one point, then the relation is not a function. Thus, although Figures 4.2-a and 4.2-c show the graphs of relations that are functions, Figure 4.2-b shows the graph of a relation that is not a function, because the vertical line shown in the figure cuts the graph in two places. This means that for the particular value of x involved, the relation associates two distinct values for y.

Algebraic characterization of a function

When a relation is defined by an equation, one way in which we can test whether or not the relation is a function is to solve the equation explicitly for the variable y representing an element in the range, and see whether or not more than one value of y is associated with any single value of x.

Example.   Is the relation $\{(x, y) \mid y^2 = 1 + x^2\}$ in R^2 a function?

Solution.   Since $y^2 = 1 + x^2$ implies either $y = \sqrt{1 + x^2}$ or $y = -\sqrt{1 + x^2}$, the assignment of a real value to x will result in two different values for y, and hence the relation is not a function.

Notation such as that introduced in Chapter 2 for polynomials, namely $P(x)$, is widely used in discussing functions. In general, functions are denoted by single symbols; for example, f, g, h, and F might be so used. The symbol for a function can be used in conjunction with the variable representing an element in the domain to represent the associated element in the range. Thus $f(x)$, read "f of x" or "the value of f at x," is the element in the range of f associated with the element x in the domain.

Function notation

Suppose

$$f = \{(x, y) \mid y = x + 3\}.$$

The alternative notation

$$f = \{(x, f(x)) \mid f(x) = x + 3\}$$

can be used, where $f(x)$ plays the same role as y.

Since in almost all cases in this book we shall be interested in functions of which the domains and ranges are sets of real numbers (such functions are called **real-valued functions** of a real variable), in any place where a function is discussed and the domain is not specified, we shall understand that the domain is *the set of all real numbers for which a real number exists in the range*.

By Definition 4.3, a function is a set of ordered pairs (x, y) such that no two have the same first component and different second components. When the components of every ordered pair in a function f are interchanged, another set of ordered pairs results, a set of ordered pairs which may or may not be a function. For example, if

$$(1, 5), (2, 5), \text{ and } (3, 6)$$

are ordered pairs in f, then

$$(5, 1), (5, 2), \text{ and } (6, 3)$$

will be members of the relation formed by interchanging the components of these ordered pairs. Clearly these latter pairs cannot be members of a function since two of them, (5, 1) and (5, 2), have the same first component and different second components. If, however, a function f is *one-to-one*—that is, if no two ordered pairs in f have the same second components (same values for y)—then the relation obtained by interchanging the first and second components of every pair in the function will also be a function. This function is called the *inverse function* of f. The notation f^{-1} (read "f inverse") is frequently used to denote the inverse function of f.

Test for inverse function

DEFINITION 4.4 *If the function f is such that no two of its ordered pairs with different first components have the same second component, then the **inverse function** f^{-1} is the set of ordered pairs obtained from f by interchanging the first and second components of each ordered pair in f.*

It is evident from this definition that the domain and range of f^{-1} are just the range and domain, respectively, of f. If $y = f(x)$ defines a function f, and if f is one-to-one, then an interchange of the variables x and y yields the equation $x = f(y)$, which defines the inverse of f. For example, the inverse of the function defined by

$$y = 3x + 2$$

is defined by

$$x = 3y + 2,$$

or, when y is expressed in terms of x, by

$$y = \frac{1}{3}x - \frac{2}{3}.$$

EXERCISE 4.2

Specify the domain that would yield real numbers y for elements in the range of the relation defined by each equation.

Examples.

a. $y = \sqrt{16 - x^2}$

b. $y = \dfrac{1}{x(x + 2)}$

Solutions.

a. For what values of x is
$16 - x^2 \geq 0$?
The domain is
$\{x \mid -4 \leq x \leq 4\}$.

b. For what values of x is
$x(x + 2) \neq 0$?
The domain is
$\{x \mid x \neq 0, -2\}$.

domain is $\{x \mid x \in R\}$

1. $y = x + 7$

2. $y = 2x - 3$ *(domain $\{x \mid x \in R\}$)*

3. $y = x^2$

4. $y = \dfrac{1}{x}$

5. $y = \dfrac{1}{x - 2}$ $x \neq 2$ *domain $\{x \mid x \in R, x \neq 2\}$*

6. $y = \dfrac{1}{x^2 + 1}$

7. $y = \sqrt{x}$

8. $y = \sqrt{4 - x}$

9. $y = \sqrt{4 - x^2}$

10. $y = \sqrt{x^2 - 9}$

11. $\dfrac{4}{x(x - 1)}$ $= y$ $x \neq 0, \; x \neq 1$

12. $y = \dfrac{x}{(x - 1)(x + 2)}$ $x \neq -2, \; x \neq 1$

State whether or not the given equation defines a function.

Examples.

  a. $x^2 y = 3$ b. $x^2 + y^2 = 36$

Solutions.   Solve explicitly for y.

  a. $y = \dfrac{3}{x^2}$ b. $y = \pm \sqrt{36 - x^2}$

Yes. There is only one value of y associated with each value of x ($x \neq 0$).   No. There are two values of y associated with values of x satisfying $|x| < 6$.

13. $x + y = 3$ 14. $y = -x^2$ 15. $y = \sqrt{x^2 - 5}$

16. $y = \sqrt{16 - x^2}$ $16 - x^2 \neq 0$ $16 - x^2 \geq 0$ 17. $x^2 + y^2 = 16$ 18. $y = \pm \sqrt{x^2}$

19. $y^2 = x^3$ $16 \geq x^2$ $4 \geq x$ 20. $y = ax^n$

If $f(x) = x + 2$, find the given element in the range. $x^2 + y^2 = r^2 \Rightarrow y^2 = $ *circle*

Example. $f(3)$

Solution.   Substitute 3 for x.

$$f(3) = (3) + 2 = 5$$

The element is 5.

21. $f(0)$ 22. $f(1)$ 23. $f(-3)$ 24. $f(a)$

If $g(x) = x^2 - 2x + 1$, find the given element in the range.

25. $g(-2)$ 26. $g(0)$ 27. $g(a + 1)$ 28. $g(a - 1)$

If $f(x) = x + 2$ defines a function, find the element in the domain of f associated with the given element in the range.

Example. $f(x) = 5$

Solution.   Replacing $f(x)$ with $x + 2$, we have

$$x + 2 = 5,$$

$$x = 3.$$

The element is 3.

29. $f(x) = 3$ 30. $f(x) = -2$ 31. $f(x) = a$ 32. $f(x) = a + 2$

If $g(x) = x^2 - 1$, find all elements in the domain of g associated with the given element in the range.

33. $g(x) = 0$ 34. $g(x) = 3$ 35. $g(x) - 8$ 36. $g(x) - 5$

37. Suppose $f(x) = x + 2$ and $g(x) = x - 2$. Find each of the following.

  a. $f(0)$ b. $g(2)$ c. $f(g(2))$ d. $f(g(x))$

38. If $f(x) = x^2 - x + 1$, find each of the following.

  a. $f(x + h) - f(x)$ b. $\dfrac{f(x + h) - f(x)}{h}$

39. Consider $\{(x, f(x)) \mid f(x) = x^2\}$. Does $f(a) + f(b) = f(a + b)$?

40. Any function satisfying the condition that $f(-x) = f(x)$ for all x in the domain is called an **even function**. Any function satisfying the condition that $f(-x) = -f(x)$ for all x in the domain is called an **odd function**. Which of the following functions are even and which are odd?

  a. $\{(x f(x)) \mid f(x) = x^2\}$ b. $\{(x, f(x)) \mid f(x) = x^3\}$

  c. $\{(x, f(x)) \mid f(x) = x^4 - x^2\}$ d. $\{(x, f(x)) \mid f(x) = x^3 - x\}$

Each of the following equations defines a function. Write an equation defining the inverse relation and state whether or not the inverse relation is a function.

41. $y = x + 2$ 42. $y = 3x - 1$ 43. $2x - 3y = 6$

44. $x + 4y = 0$ 45. $y = x^2 - 3$ 46. $x^2 - 2y = 4$

4.3 LINEAR FUNCTIONS

A **first-degree equation** or **linear equation** in x and y is an equation that can be written equivalently in the form

$$Ax + By + C = 0 \quad (A \text{ and } B \text{ not both } 0). \tag{1}$$

We shall call (1) the **standard form** for a linear equation. The graph of any such equation (technically, of its solution set) in R^2 is a straight line,

> **The graph of a first-degree equation**

although we do not prove this here, and hence functions defined by such equations are called **linear functions.** For $B \neq 0$, such an equation defines a function having as its domain the set of real numbers x. Since any two distinct points determine a straight line, it is evident that we need find only two solutions of such an equation to determine its graph, that is, the graph of the solution set of the equation. In practice, the two solutions easiest to find are usually those whose first and second components, respectively, are zero, that is, the solutions $(0, y)$ and $(x, 0)$. The x-coordinate of the point at which the graph crosses the x-axis is called the **x-intercept**, and the y-coordinate of the point at which the graph crosses the y-axis is called the **y-intercept**. As an example, consider the function

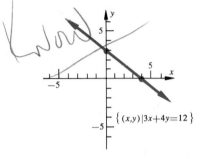

Figure 4.3

$$f = \{(x, y) \mid 3x + 4y = 12\}. \qquad (2)$$

If $y = 0$, we have $x = 4$, and the x-intercept is 4. If $x = 0$, then $y = 3$, and the y-intercept is 3. Thus the graph of (2) appears as in Figure 4.3.

If the graph intersects both axes at or near the origin, the intercepts either do not represent two separate points, or the points are too close together to be of much use in drawing the graph. It is then necessary to plot at least one other point at a distance far enough removed from the origin to establish the line with pictorial accuracy.

There are two special cases of linear equations worth noting. First, an equation such as

$$y - 4 = 0$$

may be considered an equation in two variables,

$$0x + y = 4.$$

For each x, this equation assigns $y = 4$. That is, any ordered pair of the form $(x, 4)$ is a solution of the equation. For instance,

Equations of horizontal lines

$$(1, 4), (2, 4), (3, 4),$$

are all solutions of the equation. If we graph these points and connect them with a straight line, we have Figure 4.4-a.

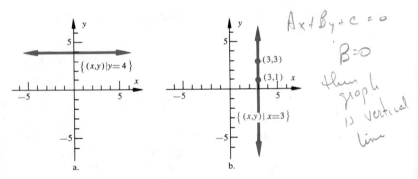

Figure 4.4

Since the equation

$$y - 4 = 0$$

assigns to each x the same value for y, the function defined by this equation is called a **constant function**.

The other special case of the linear equation is of the type

$$x - 3 = 0,$$

which may be looked upon as

$$x + 0y = 3.$$

Here, only one value is permissible for x, namely 3, whereas any value may be assigned to y. That is, any ordered pair of the form $(3, y)$ is a solution of this equation. If we choose two solutions, say $(3, 1)$ and $(3, 3)$, and complete the graph, we have Figure 4.4-b. It is clear that this equation does not define a function (Why?), and accounts for

Equations of vertical lines

our restriction $B \neq 0$ on the standard form of a first-degree equation in two variables, $Ax + By + C = 0$, in order that this equation should define a function.

Any two distinct points in the plane are the endpoints of a line segment. Two fundamental properties of a line segment are its **length** and its **inclination** with respect to the x-axis.

Figure 4.5 shows the line segment joining two points, $P_1 (x_1, y_1)$ and $P_2 (x_2 y_2)$. If a line parallel to the x-axis is constructed through P_1, and a line parallel to the

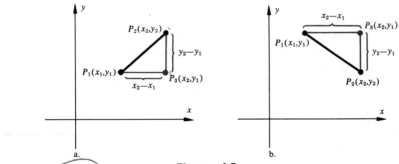

Figure 4.5

Distance between two points

y-axis through P_2, then these lines will intersect at a point P_3 with coordinates (x_2, y_1). The distance from P_1 to P_3 is then $|x_2 - x_1|$, and the distance from P_2 to P_3 is $|y_2 - y_1|$. The Pythagorean theorem applied to these distances yields the length d of the line segment joining P_1 and P_2, namely,

$$d = \sqrt{|x_2 - x_1|^2 + |y_2 - y_1|^2}.$$

Since $|x_2 - x_1|^2 = (x_2 - x_1)^2$ and $|y_2 - y_1|^2 = (y_2 - y_1)^2$, we accordingly have

$$d = \sqrt{(x_2 - x_1)^2 + (y_2 - y_1)^2}.$$

This is known as the **distance formula**.

Slope of a line segment

The inclination of the line segment joining P_1 and P_2 is measured by forming the ratio of the differences $y_2 - y_1$ and $x_2 - x_1$, and is called the **slope** m of the line segment. Thus

$$m = \frac{y_2 - y_1}{x_2 - x_1} \quad (x_2 - x_1 \neq 0).$$

For the segment in Figure 4.5a the slope is positive, while for the one in Figure 4.5-b the slope is negative. If a line segment is parallel to the

Positive, negative, and zero slope

x-axis, then $y_2 - y_1 = 0$ and the line segment has slope 0; but if it is parallel to the y-axis, then $x_2 - x_1 = 0$ and its slope is not defined; see Figure 4.6.

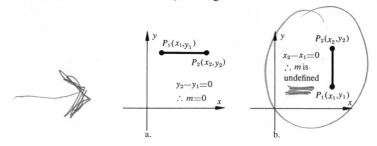

Figure 4.6

It can be shown (by similar triangles, say) that the slopes of any two line segments contained in the same line are equal, and hence we can say that

Slope of a line

the slope of a line is equal to the slope of any of its segments.

Using the slope concept, we can rewrite the defining equation for a linear function in other useful forms. Consider a line having slope m and passing through a given point (x_1, y_1), as shown in Figure 4.7. If we choose *any other* point on the line and assign to it the coordinates (x, y), it is evident that the slope of the line is given by

$$\frac{y - y_1}{x - x_1} = m,$$

from which

$$y - y_1 = m(x - x_1). \tag{3}$$

Note that (3) is satisfied also by $(x, y) = (x_1, y_1)$. Since now x and y are the coordinates of *any* point on the line, (3) is an equation of the line passing through (x_1, y_1) with slope m. This is called the **point-slope form** for a linear equation.

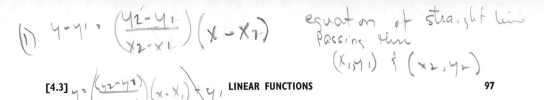

(handwritten top) ① $y - y_1 = \left(\dfrac{y_2 - y_1}{x_2 - x_1}\right)(x - x_1)$ equation of straight line passing thru (x_1, y_1) & (x_2, y_2)

(handwritten) $y = \left(\dfrac{y_2 - y_1}{x_2 - x_1}\right)(x - x_1) + y_1$

Now consider the equation of the line with slope m passing through a given point on the y-axis having coordinates $(0, b)$, as shown in Figure 4.8. Substituting $(0, b)$ in the point-slope form of a linear equation,

(handwritten) straight line formula also

② $$y - y_1 = m(x - x_1),$$

we obtain

$$y - b = m(x - 0),$$

from which

(handwritten) slope-intercept form

(handwritten) (now)

③ $$y = mx + b. \tag{4}$$

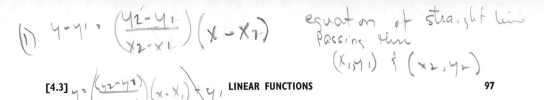

Figure 4.7   **Figure 4.8**

Equation (4) is called the **slope-intercept form** for a linear equation. Any linear equation in standard form can be written equivalently in the slope-intercept form by solving for y in terms of x if $B \neq 0$. For example,

$$2x + 3y - 6 = 0$$

(handwritten) $\dfrac{x}{a} + \dfrac{y}{b} = 1$ straight line that passes thru x at a and thru y at b.

can be written equivalently as

$$y = -\frac{2}{3}x + 2.$$

The slope of the line, $-2/3$, and the y-intercept, 2, can now be read directly from the last form of the equation.

EXERCISE 4.3

Find the distance between each of the given pairs of points, and find the slope of the line segment joining them.

Example. $(3, -5), (2, 4)$

Solution. Consider $(3, -5)$ as P_1 and $(2, 4)$ as P_2.

$$d = \sqrt{(x_2 - x_1)^2 + (y_2 - y_1)^2}$$

$$m = \frac{y_2 - y_1}{x_2 - x_1}$$

$$= \sqrt{(2 - 3)^2 + [4 - (-5)]^2} = \sqrt{1 + 81}$$

$$= \frac{4 - (-5)}{2 - 3} = \frac{9}{-1}$$

Distance, $\sqrt{82}$; slope, -9.

1. $(1, 1), (4, 5)$ 2. $(-1, 1), (5, 9)$ 3. $(-3, 2), (2, 14)$

4. $(-4, -3), (1, 9)$ 5. $(2, 1), (1, 0)$ 6. $(-3, 2), (0, 0)$

Find the length of the sides of the triangle having vertices as given.

7. $(10, 1), (3, 1), (5, 9)$ 8. $(0, 6), (9, -6), (-3, 0)$

9. $(5, 6), (11, -2), (-10, -2)$ 10. $(-1, 5), (8, -7), (4, 1)$

Find the equation, in standard form, of the line through each of the given points and having the given slope. Sketch the graph of the equation.

Example. $(3, -5), m = -2$

Solution.   Substitute given values in the point-slope form of the linear equation.

$$y - y_1 = m(x - x_1)$$
$$y - (-5) = -2(x - 3)$$
$$y + 5 = -2x + 6$$
$$2x + y - 1 = 0$$

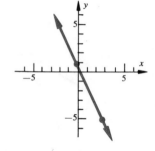

11. $(-3, -2), m = \dfrac{1}{2}$ 12. $(0, 0), m = 3$ 13. $(-1, 0), m = 1$

14. $(2, -3), m = 0$ 15. $(-4, 2), m = 0$ 16. $(-1, -2),$ parallel to y-axis

Write each of the equations in slope-intercept form; specify the slope and the y-intercept of the line. Sketch the graph of the equation.

Example. $2x - 3y = 5$

Solution.   Solving explicitly for y, we obtain

$$y = \frac{2}{3}x - \frac{5}{3}.$$

Compare with the general slope-intercept form

$$y = mx + b.$$

Slope, $\dfrac{2}{3}$; y-intercept, $-\dfrac{5}{3}$.

17. $3x + 2y = 1$ 18. $3x - y = 7$ 19. $x - 3y = 2$

20. $2x - 3y = 0$ 21. $8x - 3y = 0$ 22. $-x = 2y - 5$

23. Write the equation, in standard form, of the line with the same slope as $x - 2y = 5$ and passing through the origin. Sketch the graph of this equation.

24. Write the equation, in standard form, of the line through $(0, 5)$ with the same slope as $2y - 3x = 5$. Sketch the graph of this equation.

25. Show that, for $x_2 \neq x_1$,

$$y - y_1 = M(x - x_1)$$

$$y - y_1 = \left(\frac{y_2 - y_1}{x_2 - x_1}\right)(x - x_1)$$

is an equation of the line joining the points (x_1, y_1) and (x_2, y_2). This is the **two-point form** of the linear equation.

26. Using the general equation in Problem 25, find the equation of the lines through the given points.

Leave $y = Mx + c$

a. $(2, 1)$ and $(-1, 3)$ b. $(3, 0)$ and $(5, 0)$

c. $(-2, 1)$ and $(3, -2)$ d. $(-1, -1)$ and $(1, 1)$

27. Consider the linear function

$$F = \{(x, y) \mid y = F(x)\}.$$

If $(2, 3)$ and $(-1, 4)$ are known to be in F, find $F(x)$ in terms of x.

28. Show that if a and b are nonzero numbers denoting the x- and y-intercepts of a straight line, then $\dfrac{x}{a} + \dfrac{y}{b} = 1$ is an equation for the line. This is called the **intercept form** of the equation.

29. Using the general equation in Problem 28, find the equation of the lines having the given intercepts.

a. x-intercept 3, y-intercept -1 b. x-intercept -2, y-intercept 2

30. Show that the triangle with vertices $(0, 6)$, $(9, -6)$, and $(-3, 0)$ is a right triangle. *Hint:* Use the converse of the Pythagorean theorem; that is, if $c^2 = a^2 + b^2$, then the triangle is a right triangle. $d = \sqrt{(x_1 - x_1)^2 + (y^2 - y_1)^2}$

$15 = \sqrt{(9 - 0)^2 + (-6 - 6)^2}$ $(-3 - 9)^2 (0 - 6)^2$

31. Show by similar triangles that the coordinates of the midpoint of the line segment joining the points $P_1(x_1, y_1)$ and $P_2(x_2, y_2)$ are given by

$$x = \frac{x_1 + x_2}{2} \quad \text{and} \quad y = \frac{y_1 + y_2}{2}.$$

32. Using the results of Problem 31, find the coordinates of the midpoint of the line segment joining the points whose coordinates are given.

a. $(2, 4)$ and $(6, 8)$ b. $(-4, 6)$ and $(6, -10)$

33. Given that $Ax + By + C = 0$ $(A \neq 0)$ defines a linear function f, find an equation defining f^{-1}.

34. Graph $f = \{(x, y) \mid y = 4 - 2x\}$, and also graph f^{-1} using the same set of axes. How are the graphs related to the graph of $y = x$?

4.4 QUADRATIC FUNCTIONS

Consider the quadratic equation in two variables,

$$y = x^2 - 4. \tag{1}$$

As with linear equations in two variables, solutions of this equation must be ordered pairs (x, y). We need replacements for both x and y in order to obtain a statement we can adjudge to be true or false. As before, such ordered pairs can be found by arbitrarily assigning values to x and computing related values for y. For instance, assigning the value -3 to x in Equation (1), we obtain

$$y = (-3)^2 - 4,$$

$$y = 5,$$

and $(-3, 5)$ is a solution. Similarly, we find that

$$(-2, 0), (-1, -3), (0, -4), (1, -3), (2, 0), \text{ and } (3, 5)$$

are also solutions of (1). Plotting the corresponding points on the plane, we have the graph in Figure 4.9-a. Clearly, these points do not lie on a straight line, and we may reasonably inquire whether the graph of the solution set of (1),

> **Graph of a quadratic function**

$$S = \{(x, y) \mid y = x^2 - 4\},$$

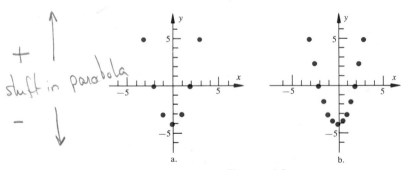

Figure 4.9

forms any kind of a meaningful pattern on the plane. By plotting additional solutions of (1)—solutions with x-components between those already found—we may be able to obtain a clearer picture. Thus we find the solutions

$$\left(\frac{-5}{2}, \frac{9}{4}\right), \left(\frac{-3}{2}, \frac{-7}{4}\right), \left(\frac{-1}{2}, \frac{-15}{4}\right), \left(\frac{1}{2}, \frac{-15}{4}\right), \left(\frac{3}{2}, \frac{-7}{4}\right), \left(\frac{5}{2}, \frac{9}{4}\right),$$

(handwritten:) Equation of circle   (2,3)   radius 4 $(x-2)^2 + (y-3)^2 = 16$

and by plotting these points in addition to those found earlier, we have the graph in Figure 4.9-b. It now appears reasonable to connect these points in sequence, say from left to right, by a smooth curve as in Figure 4.10, and to assume that the resulting curve is a good approximation to the graph of (1). (You should realize, of course, that regardless of how many individual points are plotted, we have no absolute assurance that the smooth curve is a good approximation to the true graph; more information is needed—for example, in this case, that for $|x_2| > |x_1|$ we have correspondingly $y_2 > y_1$.) This curve is an example of a **parabola**.

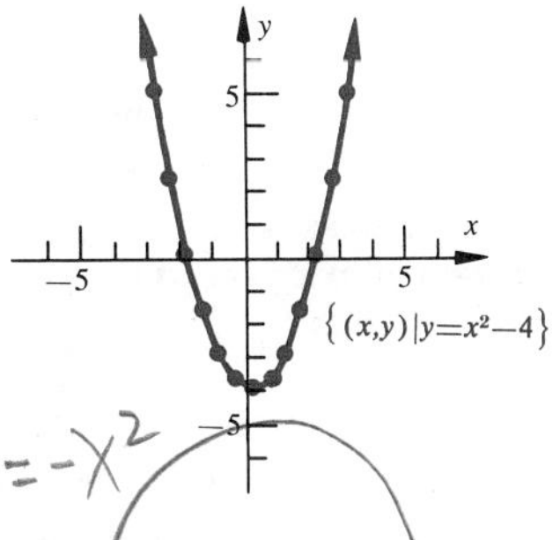

More generally, the graph of the solution set of any quadratic equation of the form

(handwritten: know)
$$y = ax^2 + bx + c, \qquad (2)$$

(handwritten: $y = -x^2$)

{(x,y)|y=x²−4}

Figure 4.10

where a, b, and c are real and $a \neq 0$, is a parabola.

Since for each x an equation of the form (2) will determine only one y, such an equation defines a function having as domain the entire set of real numbers and as range some subset of the reals. For example, we observe from the graph in Figure 4.10 that the range of the function defined by (1) is the set of real numbers

$$\{y \mid y \geq -4\}.$$

The lowest or highest point on a parabola

To show that there is a lowest (or else a highest) point on the graph of (2), we can proceed as follows by completing the square:

(handwritten:)
if constant > 1
parabola is narrow

if constant < 1
parabola is wide

$a > 0$ minimum ∪

$a < 0$ maximum ∩

$$y = ax^2 + bx + c \quad (a \neq 0)$$

$$= a\left(x^2 + \frac{b}{a}x + \frac{c}{a}\right)$$

$$= a\left(x^2 + \frac{b}{a}x + \frac{b^2}{4a^2} - \frac{b^2}{4a^2} + \frac{c}{a}\right)$$

$$= a\left(x^2 + \frac{b}{a}x + \frac{b^2}{4a^2}\right) - \frac{b^2 - 4ac}{4a}$$

$$= a\left(x + \frac{b}{2a}\right)^2 - \frac{b^2 - 4ac}{4a}. \qquad (3)$$

(handwritten:) $y = x^2$ $= f(x)$ $f(x) = f(-x)$

Now if $a > 0$, then the first term on the right is 0 at $x = -b/2a$, and otherwise this term is positive; hence the lowest point on the graph is

$$\left(\frac{-b}{2a}, -\frac{b^2 - 4ac}{4a}\right). \qquad (4)$$

Similarly, if $a < 0$, then the first term on the right in (3) is negative except at $x = -b/2a$, and accordingly (4) gives the highest point on the graph in this case.

Consider the graph of the function

$$S = \{(x, f(x)) \mid f(x) = ax^2 + bx + c\}, \tag{5}$$

for $a \neq 0$, and the solution set of the equation

$$ax^2 + bx + c = 0. \tag{6}$$

Any value of x for which $f(x) = 0$ in (5) will be a solution of (6). Since any point on the x-axis has y-coordinate zero [i.e., $f(x) = 0$], the x-intercepts of the graph of (2) are the real solutions of (6). Values of x for which $f(x) = 0$ are called the **zeros of the function**. Thus we have three different names for the same set of values:

Roots, zeros, and x-intercepts

1. The *elements of the solution set* of the equation $ax^2 + bx + c = 0$. These are called the *solutions* or *roots* of the equation.
2. The *zeros of the function* defined by $f(x) = ax^2 + bx + c$.
3. The *x-intercepts* of the graph of the equation $y = ax^2 + bx + c$.

EXERCISE 4.4

Graph. (First obtain the x-intercepts and the maximum or minimum point analytically, and then sketch the rest of the curve.)

Example. $\{(x, y) \mid y = x^2 - 7x + 6\}$

Solution. Since the solution set of $x^2 - 7x + 6 = 0$ is $\{1, 6\}$, the x-intercepts are 1 and 6. By completing the square in the right-hand member of

$$y = x^2 - 7x + 6,$$

we obtain

$$y = \left(x^2 - 7x + \frac{49}{4}\right) - \frac{49}{4} + 6,$$

or

$$y = \left(x - \frac{7}{2}\right)^2 - \frac{25}{4}.$$

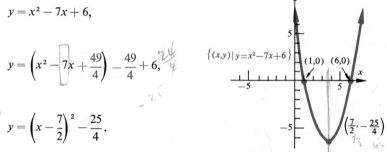

For $x = 7/2$, y has a minimum value $-25/4$. Therefore, the minimum point is at $(7/2, -25/4)$. Find several other solutions and complete the graph.

1. $\{(x, y) \mid y = x^2 - 5x + 4\}$ 2. $\{(x, g(x)) \mid g(x) = x^2 - 3x + 2\}$

3. $\{(x, y) \mid y = x^2 - 6x - 7\}$ 4. $\{(x, y) \mid y = x^2 - 3x + 2\}$

5. $\{(x, f(x)) \mid f(x) = -x^2 + 5x - 4\}$ 6. $\{(x, f(x)) \mid f(x) = -x^2 - 8x + 9\}$

7. $\{(x, g(x)) \mid g(x) = \frac{1}{2}x^2 + 2\}$ 8. $\{(x, y) \mid y = -\frac{1}{2}x^2 - 2x\}$

9. Graph $\{(x, f(x))\,|\,f(x) = x^2 + 1\}$. Represent $f(0)$ and $f(4)$ by drawing line segments from $(0, 0)$ to $(0, f(0))$ and from $(4, 0)$ to $(4, f(4))$.

10. Graph $\{(x, g(x))\,|\,g(x) = x^2 + 1\}$. Represent $f(-3)$ and $f(2)$ by drawing line segments from $(-3, 0)$ to $(-3, f(-3))$ and from $(2, 0)$ to $(2, f(2))$.

Solve Problems 11 and 12 by completing the square.

11. Find two numbers having sum 8 and product as great as possible.

12. Find the maximum possible area of a rectangle with perimeter 100 inches.

13. Graph the relation $\{(x, y)\,|\,x = y^2\}$.
   a. What kind of a curve is the graph?
   b. Is the given relation a function? Why or why not?

14. Graph the relation $\{(x, y)\,|\,x = y^2 - 2y\}$.
   a. What kind of a curve is the graph?
   b. Is the given relation a function? Why or why not?

Graph each of the following relations.

15. $\{(x, y)\,|\,x = y^2 - 4\}$

16. $\{(x, y)\,|\,x = y^2 - 2y - 3\}$

17. $\{(x, y)\,|\,x = y^2 - 4y + 4\}$

18. $\{(x, y)\,|\,x = 2y^2 + 3y - 2\}$

4.5 CONIC SECTIONS

In Section 4.4, we discussed quadratic equations of the form

$$y = ax^2 + bx + c \quad (a \neq 0), \tag{1}$$

whose graphs are parabolas, opening upward if $a > 0$ and downward if $a < 0$. Similarly, an equation of the form

$$x = ay^2 + by + c \quad (a \neq 0) \tag{2}$$

also has a graph that is a parabola, opening to the right if $a > 0$ and to the left if $a < 0$.

In addition to (1) and (2), above, there are other types of second-degree equations in two variables. Their graphs are referred to as **conic sections** or **conics** because such curves result from the intersection of a plane and a right circular cone, as shown in Figure 4.11 on page 104, or of a plane and a right circular cylinder.

The graphs of relations defined by equations of the form

$$Ax^2 + By^2 = C \quad (A^2 + B^2 \neq 0) \tag{3}$$

Classification of central conics

are symmetric *with respect to the origin*. That is, if the point with coordinates (x_1, y_1) is on the graph, then so is the point with coordinates $(-x_1, -y_1)$. For this reason, their graphs are called **central conics**. There exist the following possibilities:

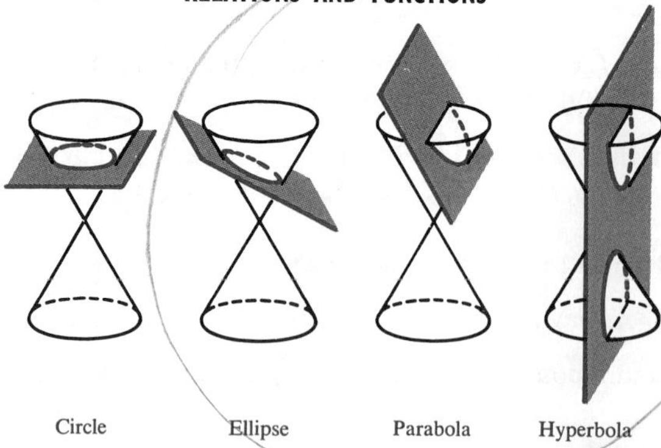

Circle   Ellipse   Parabola   Hyperbola

Figure 4.11

The graph is

(a) a circle if $A = B$ and A, B, and C have like signs;

(b) an ellipse if $A \neq B$ and A, B, and C have like signs;

(c) a hyperbola if A and B are opposite in sign and $C \neq 0$;

(d) two distinct lines through the origin if A and B are opposite in sign and $C = 0$ (see Problems 13 and 14, Exercise 4.5);

(e) two distinct parallel lines if one of A and $B = 0$ and the other has the same sign as C;

(f) two coincident parallel lines (one line) through the origin if one of A and $B = 0$ and also $C = 0$;

(g) a point if A and B are both ≥ 0 or both ≤ 0 and $C = 0$;

(h) the null set, $\varnothing$, if A and B are both ≥ 0 and $C < 0$, or if A and B are both ≤ 0 and $C > 0$.

Graph of a central conic   After we recognize the general form of a central conic, the location of a few points should suffice to sketch the complete graph. The intercepts, for instance, are always easy to identify. Consider the relation

$$\{(x, y) \mid 4y^2 = 8 - x^2\}. \tag{4}$$

By comparing the defining equation in standard form, $x^2 + 4y^2 = 8$, with (b), we note immediately that its graph is an ellipse. If $y = 0$, then $x = \pm\sqrt{8}$; if $x = 0$, then $y = \pm\sqrt{2}$. We can accordingly sketch the graph of (4) as in Figure 4.12. As another example, consider the relation

$$\{(x, y) \mid x^2 - y^2 = 3\}. \tag{5}$$

By comparing the defining equation with (c), we see that its graph is a hyperbola. If $y = 0$, then $x = \pm\sqrt{3}$, and if $x = 0$, then y^2 would have to be negative, an impossibility in the field of real numbers (see Theorem 1.14). Thus the graph does not cross the y-axis. By assigning a few other arbitrary values to one of the variables, say x, e.g., $(4, \ )$ and $(-4, \ )$, we can find additional ordered pairs

$$(4, \sqrt{13}), (4, -\sqrt{13}), (-4, \sqrt{13}), (-4, -\sqrt{13})$$

$2x^2 + 3y^2 = 4$ ellipse
$2x^2 + 2y^2 = 4$ circle

satisfying (5). The graph can then be sketched as shown in Figure 4.13. The formulas developed in Problems 13 and 14 in the following exercise can often be used to help sketch the graph of a hyperbola.

Parabola has function

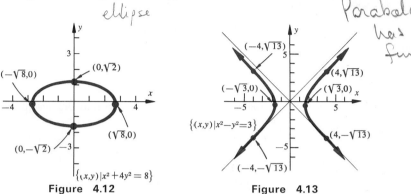

ellipse

Figure 4.12

Figure 4.13

EXERCISE 4.5

Name and sketch the graph of each of the following relations.

1. $\{(x, y)\,|\,x^2 + y^2 = 49\}$

2. $\{(x, y)\,|\,x^2 + 9y = 0\}$ parabola

3. $\{(x, y)\,|\,x^2 + 2y^2 = 8\}$ ellipse

4. $\{(x, y)\,|\,x^2 = 2y^2 + 8\}$ hyperbola

5. $\{(x, y)\,|\,x^2 - 9y^2 = 0\}$ (d)

6. $\{(x, y)\,|\,y = 4 - 2x^2\}$

7. $\{(x, y)\,|\,4x^2 + 4y^2 = 1\}$ (a)

8. $\{(x, y)\,|\,3x^2 - 12 = -4y^2\}$ $3x^2 + 4y^2 = 12$ ellipse

why 9. $\{(x, y)\,|\,y - 4 = 3x - x^2\}$ ∩

10. $\{(x, y)\,|\,y = x^2 - 3x + 12\}$

11. On a single set of axes, sketch the family of four curves that are graphs of the function defined by $y = x^2 + k$ $(k = -2, 0, 2, 4)$. What effect does varying k have on the graph?

12. Graph $\{(x, y)\,|\,x^2 + y^2 = 25\}$ and $\{(x, y)\,|\,4x^2 + y^2 = 36\}$ on the same set of axes. What is the significance of the coordinates of the points of intersection, $\{(x, y)\,|\,x^2 + y^2 = 25\} \cap \{(x, y)\,|\,4x^2 + y^2 = 36\}$?

13. Graph $\{(x, y)\,|\,4x^2 - y^2 = 0\}$. Generalize from the result and discuss the graph of any relation of the form $\{(x, y)\,|\,Ax^2 - By^2 = 0\ (A, B > 0)\}$. See rule c

14. By solving $Ax^2 - By^2 = C$ $(A, B, C > 0)$ for y, obtain the expression

$$y = \pm\sqrt{\frac{A}{B}}\,|x|\left(\sqrt{1 - \frac{C}{Ax^2}}\right)$$

and argue that the graph of $Ax^2 - By^2 = C$ approaches the graphs of

$$y = \pm\sqrt{\frac{A}{B}}\,|x|$$

as $|x|$ increases. *Note:* These lines are called the *asymptotes* of the hyperbola.

4.6 GRAPHS OF INEQUALITIES

A sentence of the form

$$Ax + By + C \leq 0,$$

or

$$Ax + By + C < 0,$$

A and B not both 0, is an inequality of the first degree and defines the relation

$$\{(x, y) \mid Ax + By + C \leq 0\},$$

or

$$\{(x, y) \mid Ax + By + C < 0\},$$

respectively. Such relations in R^2 can be represented on the plane, but the graph will be a region of the plane (a half-plane) rather than a straight line. For example, consider the relation

Graph of a linear inequality

$$S = \{(x, y) \mid 2x + y - 3 < 0\}. \tag{1}$$

When the defining inequality is rewritten in the equivalent form

$$y < -2x + 3, \tag{2}$$

we see that solutions (x, y) are such that for each x, y is less than $-2x + 3$. The graph of the equation

$$y = -2x + 3 \tag{3}$$

is simply a straight line, as illustrated in Figure 4.14-a. To graph the relation S, we need only observe that any point below this line has a y-coordinate that satisfies (2), and consequently the solution set of (2), which is S, corresponds to the entire

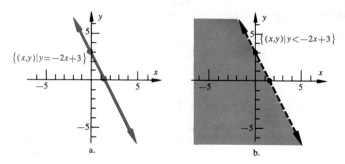

Figure 4.14

region below the line. The region is indicated on the graph with shading, as in Figure 4.14-b. That the line itself is not in the graph is indicated by means of a broken line. Had the defining inequality been

The boundary line of a graph

$$2x + y - 3 \leq 0,$$

the line would have been a part of the graph and would have been shown as a solid line.

To determine which half-plane to shade in constructing graphs of first-degree relations, we select any point in either half-plane and find out whether or not the coordinates of the point satisfy the defining sentence. If so, then the half-plane containing the selected point is shaded; if not, the opposite half-plane is shaded.

Determination of the half plane

A very convenient point to use in this process is the origin. Thus, in the foregoing example, the replacement of x and y in $2x + y - 3 < 0$ by 0 results in $2(0) + 0 - 3 < 0$, which is true, and hence the half-plane containing the origin is shaded.

Inequalities do not ordinarily define functions, according to the definition in Section 4.2, because it usually is not true that each element of the domain is associated with a unique element in the range. As an exception, though, consider the inequality $|x - y| \leq 0$, which is equivalent to the equation $x - y = 0$.

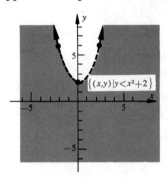

Figure 4.15

Relations of the form

$$\{(x, y) \mid y < ax^2 + bx + c\} \tag{4}$$

or

$$\{(x, y) \mid y > ax^2 + bx + c\} \tag{5}$$

can be graphed in the same manner as that by which we graph relations defined by linear inequalities in two variables. We first graph the relation defined by the equation having the same members as the defining inequality and then shade an appropriate region as required. For instance, to graph

Graph of a quadratic inequality

$$\{(x, y) \mid y < x^2 + 2\}, \tag{6}$$

we first graph

$$\{(x, y) \mid y = x^2 + 2\} \tag{7}$$

and then shade the area below the curve, as shown in Figure 4.15. Since the graph of (7) is not part of the graph of (6), a broken curve is used.

Shade good part

EXERCISE 4.6

Graph the relation.

Example. $\{(x, y) \mid 2x + y \geq 4\}$

Solution. Graph the equality $2x + y = 4$.

Substitute 0 for x and y and determine that $2(0) + (0) \geq 4$ is false, so the origin is not in the graph.

Shade the region above the graph of $2x + y = 4$.

The line is included in the graph.

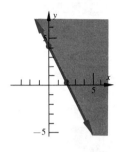

1. $\{(x, y) \mid y < x\}$
2. $\{(x, y) \mid y > x\}$
3. $\{(x, y) \mid y \leq x + 2\}$
4. $\{(x, y) \mid y \geq x - 2\}$
5. $\{(x, y) \mid x + y < 5\}$
6. $\{(x, y) \mid 2x + y < 2\}$
7. $\{(x, y) \mid 3 \geq 2x - 2y\}$
8. $\{(x, y) \mid 0 \geq x + y\}$
9. $\{(x, y) \mid x > 0\}$
10. $\{(x, y) \mid y < 0\}$
11. $\{(x, y) \mid x < 0\}$
12. $\{(x, y) \mid x < -2\}$
13. $\{(x, y) \mid -1 < x < 5\}$
14. $\{(x, y) \mid 0 \leq y \leq 1\}$
15. $\{(x, y) \mid |x| < 3\}$
16. $\{(x, y) \mid |y| > 1\}$

Example. $\{(x, y) \mid y \geq x^2 + 2x\}$

Solution. Graph $\{(x, y) \mid y = x^2 + 2x\}$.

Shade the region above the graph of $y = x^2 + 2x$.

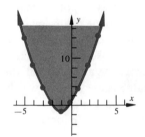

17. $\{(x, y) \mid y > x^2\}$
18. $\{(x, y) \mid y < x^2\}$
19. $\{(x, y) \mid y \geq x^2 + 3\}$
20. $\{(x, y) \mid y \leq x^2 + 3\}$
21. $\{(x, y) \mid y < 3x^2 + 2x\}$

22. $\{(x, y) \mid y > 3x^2 + 2x\}$

23. $\{(x, y) \mid y \leq x^2 + 3x + 2\}$

24. $\{(x, y) \mid y \geq x^2 + 3x + 2\}$

25. $\{(x, y) \mid y \geq 2x^2 - 5x + 2\}$

26. $\{(x, y) \mid y \leq 2x^2 - 5x + 2\}$

27. $\{(x, y) \mid |x| + |y| \leq 1\}$

28. $\{(x, y) \mid |x| + |y| \geq 1\}$

Hint: Consider the graphs in each quadrant separately: $x, y \geq 0$; $x \leq 0$, $y \geq 0$; $x, y \leq 0$; and $x \geq 0$, $y \leq 0$.

29. $\{(x, y) \mid x + |x| = y\}$

30. $\{(x, y) \mid x - |x| = y\}$

4.7 EQUATIONS IN THREE VARIABLES

omit

If each ordered pair of real numbers (x, y) is itself paired with a real number z, the pairing can be represented by the ordered triple (x, y, z) The universe for the set of all such ordered triples is sometimes represented by the symbol R^3. This denotes the Cartesian product of $R \times R$, or R^2, with R, that is, $(R \times R) \times R$, or $R^2 \times R$.

An equation in three variables, such as

$$x^2 + 2y^2 - 3z - 4 = 0, \tag{1}$$

has **ordered triples** of real numbers as solutions, just as an equation in two variables has ordered pairs of real numbers as solutions. For example, $(1, 0, -1)$ is a solution of (1) because if x, y, and z are replaced with $1, 0$, and -1, respectively, the result is

$$1^2 + 2(0)^2 - 3(-1) - 4 = 0,$$
$$1 + 0 + 3 - 4 = 0,$$
$$0 = 0,$$

which is a true statement. On the other hand, $(1, 1, 1)$ is not a solution of (1) because

$$1^2 + 2(1)^2 - 3(1) - 4 \neq 0.$$

Example.   Find a second solution in R^3 of (1) above.

Solution.   Select any arbitrary real-number replacements for *any two* variables, say 2 for x and 1 for y, and determine the value of the third variable, in this case z. Thus,

$$2^2 + 2(1)^2 - 3z - 4 = 0,$$
$$z = \frac{2}{3},$$

and a solution is $\left(2, 1, \dfrac{2}{3}\right)$.

Example.   Find the solution of (1) above with first and second components zero.

Solution.   Substituting 0 for x and 0 for y, we have

$$0 + 0 - 3z - 4 = 0,$$
$$z = -\frac{4}{3},$$

and the solution is $\left(0, 0, -\dfrac{4}{3}\right)$.

A solution in R^3 of an equation such as $x = 3$ is any ordered triple of the form $(3, y, z)$, where y and z may be any real numbers, just as a solution in R^2 is any ordered pair of the form $(3, y)$, where y may be any real number. Similarly, solutions in R^3 of an equation such as $y = 4$ are of the form $(x, 4, z)$, and solutions in R^3 of an equation such as $z = 5$ are of the form $(x, y, 5)$. Furthermore, solutions in R^3 of an equation such as $x^2 + y^2 = 25$ are ordered triples (x, y, z) such that $x^2 + y^2 = 25$ and z is any real number.

Each member of R^3 can be paired with a point in space by using an extension of a standard Cartesian coordinate system of the plane. If each of three mutually perpendicular lines in space intersecting at a point is scaled (or coordinatized) with origin at the point of intersection, each line then becomes an **axis** of a three-dimensional coordinate system, as suggested by Figure 4.16. The planes determined by the axes

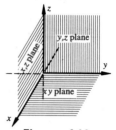

Figure 4.16

R^3 **and geometric space** taken in pairs are called **coordinate planes**, and we identify them by using the letters associated with the two axes they contain; that is, we refer to them as the xy-plane, the xz-plane, and the yz-plane.

By associating each component of an ordered triple (x, y, z) with the directed (perpendicular) distance from a coordinate plane to a point in space, a one-to-one correspondence can be established between R^3 and the set of all

Cartesian coordinates for points in space points in space. One way to visualize the pairing of an ordered triple (x, y, z) with its graph in space is suggested by Figure 4.17. The rectangular prism with one vertex at the origin, as shown, will have the point paired with (x, y, z) as vertex opposite the origin. For example, the graphs of $(2, 3, 5)$, $(3, 4, -2)$, and $(1, -5, 2)$ are shown in Figure 4.18. Of course it is not necessary to sketch the entire rectangular prism in order to locate a point.

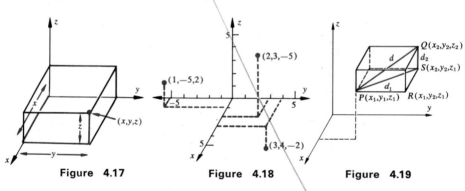

Figure 4.17   Figure 4.18   Figure 4.19

The coordinate planes separate space into eight regions called **octants**. The region in which all the coordinates of each point are positive numbers is called the **first octant**. The remaining octants are not ordinarily assigned numbers.

The formula for the distance between two points in a plane (see page 96) has a natural extension to three dimensions. Figure 4.19 shows points $P(x_1, y_1, z_1)$ and $Q(x_2, y_2, z_2)$ as opposite vertices of a rectangular prism with faces *parallel* to the coordinate planes. Vertices R and S in the bottom face are also

Distance between points in space shown, together with their coordinates. Since P, R, and S are coplanar points in a plane parallel to the xy-plane, the distance from P to S is given by

$$d_1 = \sqrt{(x_2 - x_1)^2 + (y_2 - y_1)^2}.$$

Then, because P, Q, and S are coplanar points in a plane parallel to the z-axis, we have

$$d_2 = |z_2 - z_1|.$$

From the Pythagorean theorem, we obtain

$$d^2 = d_1^2 + d_2^2,$$

$$d^2 = (x_2 - x_1)^2 + (y_2 - y_1)^2 + (z_2 - z_1)^2,$$

from which

$$d = \sqrt{(x_2 - x_1)^2 + (y_2 - y_1)^2 + (z_2 - z_1)^2}.$$

This is known as the **distance formula** in R^3.

Example. Find the distance from $(6, 3, -6)$ to $(10, 0, 6)$.

Solution. Setting $(x_2, y_2, z_2) = (6, 3, -6)$ and $(x_1, y_1, z_1) = (10, 0, 6)$, we have

$$d = \sqrt{(6 - 10)^2 + (3 - 0)^2 + (-6 - 6)^2}$$

$$= \sqrt{(-4)^2 + 3^2 + (-12)^2}$$

$$= \sqrt{16 + 9 + 144} = \sqrt{169} = 13.$$

EXERCISE 4.7

Find the solution(s) with the given components of each equation in R^3.

Example. $x^2 + 2y^2 - z^2 = 4; \ (0, 3, ?)$

Solution.   Substituting 0 for x and 3 for y yields

$$(0)^2 + 2(3)^2 - z^2 = 4,$$

$$-z^2 = -14,$$

$$z = \sqrt{14} \text{ or } -\sqrt{14}.$$

Hence, the solutions are $(0, 3, \sqrt{14})$ and $(0, 3, -\sqrt{14})$.

1. $x - y + z = 2$;   a. $(2, 1, ?)$,   b. $(-1, ?, 3)$,   c. $(?, 2, -2)$

2. $x^2 - 3y - z = 4$;   a. $(1, -1, ?)$,   b. $(4, ?, 2)$,   c. $(?, -2, 0)$

3. $x^2 + 2y^2 + z = 0$;   a. $(4, 0, ?)$,   b. $(0, ?, -4)$,   c. $(?, 0, 5)$

4. $3x^2 - y^2 + 2z^2 = 2$;   a. $(0, -1, ?)$,   b. $(2, ?, 0)$,   c. $(?, 3, 0)$

5. $z = 4x^2 + y^2$;   a. $(-1, 2, ?)$,   b. $(3, ?, -2)$,   c. $(?, 4, 1)$

6. $z = x^2 - 2y^2$;   a. $(2, 0, ?)$,   b. $(-1, ?, 0)$,   c. $(0, 3, ?)$

Find the solutions of each equation in R^3 where the
   a. first and second components are zero,
   b. first and third components are zero, and
   c. second and third components are zero.

Example. $x^2 + 3y - z = 4$

Solution.

a. $(0)^2 + 3(0) - z = 4$; hence $z = -4$, and $(0, 0, -4)$ is a solution.

b. $(0)^2 + 3y - (0) = 4$; hence $y = \dfrac{4}{3}$, and $\left(0, \dfrac{4}{3}, 0\right)$ is a solution.

c. $x^2 + 3(0) - (0) = 4$; hence $x = 2$ or $x = -2$, and $(2, 0, 0)$ and $(-2, 0, 0)$ are solutions.

   7. $x + 2y + 3z = 6$ 8. $x - 3y + 4z = 12$
   9. $2x^2 + y^2 + z^2 = 4$ 10. $x^2 + 3y^2 - z = 12$
   11. $x^2 - y - z^2 = 9$ 12. $4x^2 - 2y^2 - z = 8$
   13. $z = 4x^2 - y^2$ 14. $z = x^2 + 2y^2$

Specify the *form* of a solution for each equation in R^3 with the given component.

Example. $x^2 + y = 4$, where $x = 3$

Solution.   Substituting 3 for x, we have

$$(3)^2 + y = 4,$$
$$y = -5.$$

Hence, a solution in R^3 is of the form $(3, -5, z)$, where z can be any real number.

   15. $x^2 - y = 6$, where $x = 2$ 16. $y^2 + 3z = 12$, where $y = 3$
   17. $x^2 - z^2 = 9$, where $z = 2$ 18. $x^2 + y^2 = 4$, where $x = 0$
   19. $y = 3$ 20. $z = -4$ 21. $x = -2$ 22. $y = 0$

Graph each set of ordered triples.

Example. $\{(4, 5, 2), (2, -6, 3), (0, 0, 4)\}$

Solution.   The graph is shown at the right.

   23. $\{(0, 0, 2), (3, 0, 0), (0, 4, 0)\}$

   24. $\{(0, 0, -2), (-3, 0, 0), (0, -5, 0)\}$

   25. $\{(2, 3, 0), (3, 0, 4), (0, 2, 5)\}$

   26. $\{(-3, 1, 0), (4, 0, -2), (0, -3, 1)\}$

   27. $\{(4, 3, 4), (7, 6, 1), (1, 5, 3)\}$

   28. $\{(3, 3, 6), (2, -3, 3), (2, 4, -3)\}$

   29. $\{(-5, 3, 1), (-5, -4, 2), (1, 2, -6)\}$

   30. $\{(5, 5, 5), (5, 5, -5), (5, -5, -5)\}$

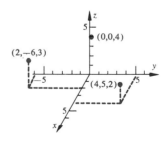

Find the distance between the points with given coordinates.

Example. $(2, -1, 4)$ and $(-3, 4, 5)$

Solution.   From the distance formula in R^3, we have

$$d = \sqrt{(x_2 - x_1)^2 + (y_2 - y_1)^2 + (z_2 - z_1)^2}$$

$$= \sqrt{(-3 - 2)^2 + [4 - (-1)]^2 + (5 - 4)^2}$$

$$= \sqrt{25 + 25 + 1} = \sqrt{51}.$$

31. $(4, 2, -1)$ and $(5, -1, 2)$ 32. $(3, -3, 0)$ and $(0, 2, -1)$

33. $(3, 3, -5)$ and $(1, 4, -2)$ 34. $(-6, 1, 3)$ and $(-4, 4, 2)$

35. $(0, -2, 4)$ and $(-3, 1, 2)$ 36. $(-5, 4, 6)$ and $(2, -7, -2)$

4.8 GRAPHS OF FUNCTIONS OF TWO VARIABLES

If the equation $x^2 + y^2 - z - 4 = 0$
is solved for z in terms of x and y, we have

$$z = x^2 + y^2 - 4.$$

In this form, the equation quite apparently serves
to pair every ordered pair (x, y) of real numbers
with exactly one real number z. Such a pairing
constitutes a function, with domain the set R^2,
or $R \times R$. Since $x^2 \geq 0$ and $y^2 \geq 0$ for all
$x, y \in R$, the range of the function is the set of
real numbers

$$\{z \mid z \geq -4\}.$$

In set notation, we can represent the function as

$$\{((x, y), z) \mid z = x^2 + y^2 - 4\}.$$

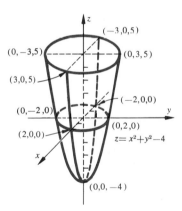

Figure   4.20

Graph of an equation in three variables

Just as the solution set of an equation in two variables in R^2
has a graph that is generally a curve in the plane, the graph of
the solution set of an equation in three variables in R^3 is
generally a surface in space. For example, Figure 4.20 shows
part of the graph of the solution set of

$$z = x^2 + y^2 - 4.$$

Because pictures of surfaces such as this are difficult to draw, we shall focus our
attention mainly on **sections of surfaces**, which are the curves formed where a
surface intersects a plane. In particular, we shall examine sections in planes parallel
to the coordinate planes and in the coordinate planes themselves.

In the universe R^3, equations of the form

$$x = k, \quad y = k, \quad \text{and} \quad z = k,$$

where k is a constant, determine planes parallel to coordinate planes, as shown in Figures 4.21-a, b, and c. This is simply a reflection of the fact that ordered triples of the form

$$(k, y, z), \quad (x, k, z), \quad \text{and} \quad (x, y, k)$$

have graphs located at a fixed distance $|k|$ on one side or the other of one of the coordinate planes, with the side depending on the sign of k.

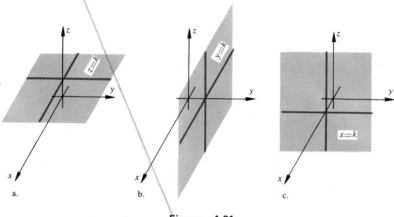

a.   b.   c.

Figure 4.21

We can use planes of this kind to help sketch surfaces in space by sketching sections of the surface determined by the planes. In many cases, sections parallel to a particular one of the coordinate planes will offer a better picture than sections parallel to either of the other coordinate planes. This suggests

that some care should be given to selecting the most appropriate planes to use. Of course, in sketching any surface the first thing to do is to draw the sections in the coordinate planes. These particular sections are called **traces**. To identify the traces of a surface, we look at the equation of the surface when *each of the variables has, in turn, the value* 0. For example, consider the equation

$$2x^2 + 2y^2 + z^2 = 72. \tag{1}$$

To find an equation for the trace in the xy-plane, we set z equal to 0. Thus this trace has equation $2x^2 + 2y^2 = 72$, with graph a circle, as shown in Figure 4.22-a.

To find the trace in the yz-plane, we set x equal to 0. This trace has equation $2y^2 + z^2 = 72$, with graph an ellipse, as shown in Figure 4.22-b.

To find the trace in the xz-plane, we set y equal to 0. This trace has equation $2x^2 + z^2 = 72$, with graph an ellipse, as shown in Figure 4.22-c.

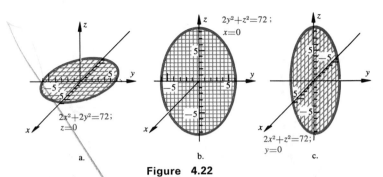

a.   b.   c.

Figure 4.22

Now several additional sections for the surface associated with (1) will suggest the appearance of the entire surface. Rewriting (1) equivalently as

$$2x^2 + 2y^2 = 72 - z^2,$$

we observe that for values $|z| < \sqrt{72}$, the equation has the form

$$x^2 + y^2 = k, \quad k > 0,$$

the graph of which is a circle for all such k. This means that sections which are graphs of such equations can aid us in completing the sketch of the entire surface. First, let us take z equal to 2 and 6, for example, in turn and obtain the resulting equations and their respective sections as shown in Figure 4.23-a. Similar sections can be obtained below the xy-plane for z equal to -2 and -6.

Using all the information available from the traces in the coordinate planes and the sections obtained for selected values of z, we can sketch the entire surface, as shown in Figure 4.23-b.

Because $2x^2 + 2y^2 + z^2 = 72$ pairs each ordered pair in $\{(x, y) \mid 2x^2 + 2y^2 < 72\}$ with *more than one value* z, the set of ordered triples determined by the equation $2x^2 + 2y^2 + z^2 = 72$ is not a function. By solving for z, however, we have

$$z = \sqrt{72 - 2x^2 - 2y^2} \quad \text{or} \quad z = -\sqrt{72 - 2x^2 - 2y^2},$$

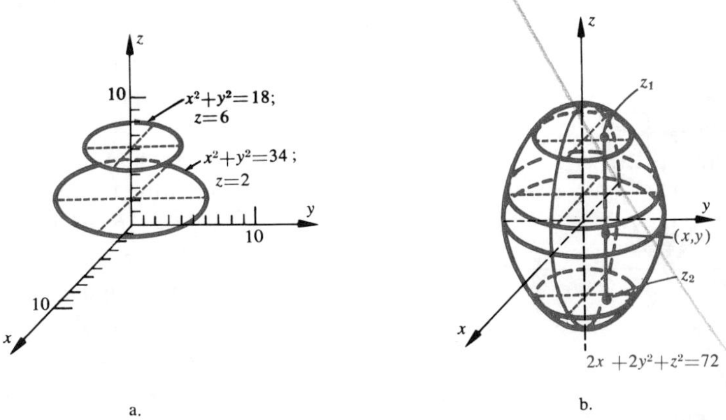

a.

b.

Figure 4.23

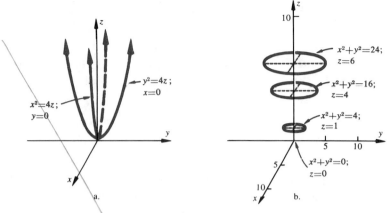

Figure 4.24

and either of these equations defines a function with domain

$$\{(x, y) \mid 2x^2 + 2y^2 < 72\}$$

and with range either

$$\{z \mid 0 \leq z \leq \sqrt{72}\} \quad \text{or} \quad \{z \mid -\sqrt{72} \leq z \leq 0\}.$$

Now consider, as a second example, the graph of

$$x^2 + y^2 = 4z.$$

We can first sketch the traces of the surface in the coordinate planes, as shown in Figure 4.24-a. Notice that the trace in the xy-plane, with equation $x^2 + y^2 = 0$, is the point at the origin. By inspection, we observe that the sections that will best delineate the surface are those parallel to (and above) the xy-plane. For $z < 0$, we have $x^2 + y^2 < 0$, which has no solutions with real-number components. We can therefore let $z = 1$, $z = 4$, and $z = 6$, for example, in turn and sketch the associated sections.

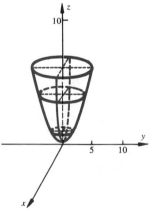

Figure 4.25

The equation of the section in the plane $z = 1$ is $x^2 + y^2 = 4$, the equation for the section in the plane $z = 4$ is $x^2 + y^2 = 16$, and the equation for the section in the plane $z = 6$ is $x^2 + y^2 = 24$. The sections are shown in Figure 4.24-b.

Using all the information obtained from the traces in the coordinate planes and sections in the planes corresponding to $z = 1$, $z = 4$, and $z = 6$, we complete the graph of the entire surface, as shown in Figure 4.25.

EXERCISE 4.8

Graph each set of ordered triples or each equation in R^3.

Example. $\{(x, y, z) \mid z = 3\}$

Solution.   The graph is shown at the right.

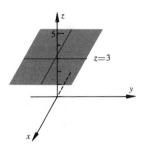

1. $\{(x, y, z) \mid x = 3\}$

2. $\{(x, y, z) \mid y = 4\}$

3. $\{(x, y, z) \mid z = 5\}$

4. $\{(x, y, z) \mid x = -2\}$

5. $y = -6$

6. $z = -3$ 7. $x = 5$ 8. $y = 0$

Graph the trace on the specified coordinate plane for each equation if such trace exists.

Example. $4x^2 - y^2 - z^2 = -16$; xy-plane

Solution.   On the xy-plane, $z = 0$.

For $z = 0$,

$$4x^2 - y^2 = -16, \qquad y^2 - 4x^2 = 16.$$

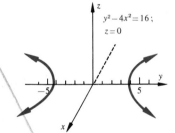

9. $3x + 2y + 4z = 12$; xy-plane

10. $x - 4y + 2z = 8$; yz-plane

11. $x^2 + 2y^2 + 4z^2 = 16$; xz-plane   12. $x^2 + y + 2z^2 = 4$; yz-plane

13. $4x^2 - y^2 + z = 36$; xy-plane   14. $x^2 + 3y^2 - z^2 = 16$; xz-plane

15. $-4x^2 + y^2 + 2z^2 = -4$; yz-plane   16. $-x + y - 6z^2 = 12$; xz-plane

Graph the section of each surface on the specified plane if such section exists.

Example. $y = x^2 + z^2$; $y = 4$

Solution.   The graph is shown at the right.

For $y = 4$,

$$x^2 + z^2 = 4.$$

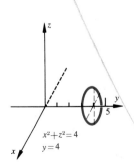

17. $4x + 2y + 3z = 13$; $z = 3$

18. $x + 3y + 2z = -6$; $y = -4$

19. $x^2 + y^2 + z^2 = 25$; $x = 3$

20. $x^2 + 4y^2 - 2z^2 = 16$; $z = 3$

21. $x - 4y^2 + z^2 = 0$; $y = 1$ 22. $3x^2 + y^2 - z = 4$; $x = 2$

23. $4x^2 - 9y^2 - 2z^2 = 28$; $z = 2$ 24. $2x^2 + y - z^2 = -12$; $y = -4$

Using appropriate traces and sections, graph each equation in R^3.

25. $x^2 + y^2 + z^2 = 9$ 26. $2x^2 + 4y^2 + z^2 = 16$

27. $3x - y + 3z = 6$ 28. $2x + y + z = 4$

29. $x^2 + 9y^2 + 9z^2 = 36$ 30. $x^2 - 2y^2 + z^2 = 16$

31. $x^2 - y + z^2 = 0$ 32. $4x^2 + 2y^2 - z = 8$

The graph in R^3 of a first-degree equation, of the form $ax + by + cz = d$, is a plane. Find the intercepts of the graph of each equation on the coordinate axes and show the graph in one octant.

Example. $3x - y + 2z = 6$

Solution.   The ordered triples corresponding to the points of intersection of the plane and the coordinate axes are shown in the figure.

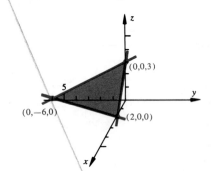

33. $x + 3y + 2z = 6$ 34. $x + 4y + 2z = 8$

35. $2x + 4y + 3z = 12$ 36. $3x + y + 2z = 6$

37. $3x - y + 3z = 6$ 38. $2x - 2y + z = 4$

39. $2x + y - 2z = 8$ 40. $-3x + 2y + z = 6$

Graph.

41. $\{(x, y, z) | 2x + y = 6\}$ 42. $\{(x, y, z) | x^2 + y^2 = 25\}$

43. $\{(x, y, z) | 4y^2 + z^2 = 16\}$ 44. $\{(x, y, z) | 4x^2 - y = 0\}$

Graph the solution set in R^3 of each equation.

45. $x + 3y = 6$ 46. $x^2 + z^2 = 16$

47. $y^2 + z = 4$ 48. $x^2 - 4y^2 = 16$

POLYNOMIAL AND
5 RATIONAL
FUNCTIONS

5.1 POLYNOMIAL FUNCTIONS

In Section 4.3, we graphed linear functions

$$\{(x, f(x)) \mid f(x) = a_0 x + a_1 \quad (a_0 \neq 0)\},$$

and in Section 4.4, we graphed quadratic functions

$$\{(x, f(x)) \mid f(x) = a_0 x^2 + a_1 x + a_2 \quad (a_0 \neq 0)\}.$$

We can graph any real polynomial function

$$\{(x, P(x)) \mid P(x) = a_0 x^n + a_1 x^{n-1} + \cdots + a_n \quad (a_0 \neq 0)\}$$

by similar methods—that is, by combining the plotting of points with a considera-

Graphs of polynomial functions

tion of certain general properties of the defining equations. In the case of the general polynomial equation, we shall lean more heavily on the use of plotted points. There is one fact about polynomials, however, that can be useful. This involves *turning points*, or local maximum and minimum values of y. Thus, for example, in Figure 5.1-a there is one local maximum as well as one local minimum, or a total

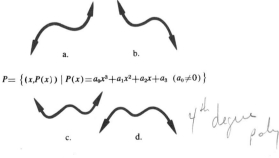

a.   b.

$$P = \left\{(x, P(x)) \mid P(x) = a_0 x^3 + a_1 x^2 + a_2 x + a_3 \ (a_0 \neq 0)\right\}$$

c.   d. 4th degree poly

$$P = \left\{(x, P(x)) \mid P(x) = a_0 x^4 + a_1 x^3 + a_2 x^2 + a_3 x + a_4 \ (a_0 \neq 0)\right\}$$

Figure 5.1

corrolary - an odd degree polynomial | even degree polynomial
has at least one real root | may not have any real
| roots

120   POLYNOMIAL AND RATIONAL FUNCTIONS   [5.1]

of two turning points, and in Figure 5.1-c one local maximum and two local minima, for a total of the three turning points. In general, we have the following.

THEOREM 5.1 *If* $P(x) = a_0 x^n + a_1 x^{n-1} + \cdots + a_n$ *is a real polynomial equation of degree n, then the graph of*

$$\{(x, P(x)) \mid P(x) = a_0 x^n + a_1 x^{n-1} + \cdots + a_n \ (a_0 \neq 0)\}$$

is a smooth curve that has at most $n - 1$ *turning points.*

The proof of this theorem involves ideas we shall not discusss herein, and is omitted. In accordance with this theorem, the graphs of third- and fourth-degree polynomial functions might appear as in Figure 5.1-a, b, and c, d, respectively.

To ascertain whether the graph of a polynomial function ultimately goes up to the right, taking the general form (a) or (c) rather than (b) or (d), we can examine the leading coefficient, a_0, of the right-hand member of the defining equation; if $a_0 > 0$, then we can look for a form similar to (a) or (c), whereas if $a_0 < 0$, we can expect something similar to (b) or (d). The graph ultimately goes up or down to the right according as $a_0 > 0$ or $a_0 < 0$. If $a_0 > 0$, then it ultimately goes down to the left as in (a) and (d), or up to the left as in (b) and (c), according as n is odd or even, and vice versa if $a_0 < 0$.

General form of a polynomial graph

For the actual graphing process, we can obtain ordered pairs $(x, f(x))$ for any polynomial function either by direct substitution or by using the remainder theorem.

Example.   Graph $\{(x, P(x)) \mid P(x) = 2x^3 + 13x^2 + 6x\}$.

Solution.   Since P is defined by a cubic polynomial with positive leading coefficient, we expect a graph having a form similar to Figure 5.1-a. Now, to find points $(x, P(x))$ lying on the graph, we shall use the process of synthetic division and find $P(x)$ by the remainder theorem. Since we know nothing about where to look for turning points, let us start with $x = 0$. By inspection, $P(0) = 0$, so that the graph includes the origin. For $x = 1$, we have

n even
(a₀ > 0)
x → ∞
P(x) → ∞
P(x) → ∞

$$\begin{array}{r|rrrr} 1 & 2 & 13 & 6 & 0 \\ & & 2 & 15 & 21 \\ \hline & 2 & 15 & 21 & 21 \end{array}$$

and $P(1) = 21$, so that $(1, 21)$ is on the graph. For $x = 2$, we have

(a₀ < 0)

$$\begin{array}{r|rrrr} 2 & 2 & 13 & 6 & 0 \\ & & 4 & 34 & 80 \\ \hline & 2 & 17 & 40 & 80 \end{array}$$

and $(2, 80)$ is on the graph. Since the signs involved at each step in the last row of the division process here are positive, it is evident that for values $x > 2$, $P(x)$ is positive and

(handwritten top margin) roots – zeros cross X axis

(handwritten) theorem If $P(a) > 0$ and $P(b) < 0$ then at some point c
between a, b $P(c) = 0$

will grow increasingly large; consequently, let us turn our attention to negative values
of x. For $x = -1$, we have

$$\begin{array}{r|rrrr} -1 & 2 & 13 & 6 & 0 \\ & & -2 & -11 & 5 \\ \hline & 2 & 11 & -5 & 5 \end{array}$$

and $(-1, 5)$ is on the graph. Similarly we find that the following points lie on the graph
of P:

$$(-2, 24), (-3, 45), (-4, 56), (-5, 45), \text{ and } (-6, 0).$$

The graphs of the nine ordered pairs are shown in Figure 5.2-a. These points make the

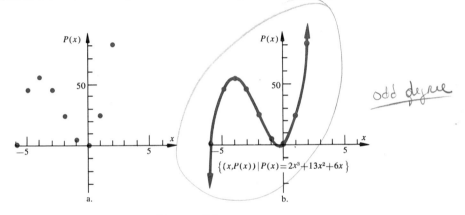

(handwritten) odd degree

$$\{(x, P(x)) \mid P(x) = 2x^3 + 13x^2 + 6x\}$$

a.   b.

Figure 5.2

general appearance of the graph clear, and there remains only the question of whether
there is a zero for the function between -1 and 0. If to x we assign values $-3/4, -1/4$,
and $-1/2$, we obtain the additional pairs $(-3/4, 63/32), (-1/4, -23/32)$, and $(-1/2, 0)$.
For $-1/2 < x < 0$, we have $P(x) < 0$, and the graph can be sketched as in Figure 5.2-b.

EXERCISE 5.1

Graph. Include approximations to all turning points.

1. $\{(x, P(x)) \mid P(x) = x^3 - 4x^2 + 3x\}$

2. $\{(x, P(x)) \mid P(x) = x^3 - 2x^2 + 1\}$

3. $\{(x, P(x)) \mid P(x) = 2x^3 + 9x^2 + 7x - 6\}$

4. $\{(x, P(x)) \mid P(x) = 3x^3 + 2x^2 - x + 1\}$

5. $\{(x, P(x)) \mid P(x) = x^4\}$

6. $\{(x, P(x)) \mid P(x) = -x^4 + x\}$

7. $\{(x, P(x)) \mid P(x) = x^4 - x^3 - 2x^2 + 3x - 3\}$

8. $\{(x, P(x)) \mid P(x) = x^4 - 4x^3 - 4x + 12\}$

(handwritten right margin)
n odd $a_n > 0$ (+)
$x \to \infty$ $P(x) \to \infty$
$x \to -\infty$ $P(x) \to -\infty$

$a_n < 0$ (−)
$x \to \infty$ $P(x) \to -\infty$
$x \to -\infty$ $P(x) \to \infty$

a polynomial of degree n has at most n roots

5.2 REAL ZEROS OF POLYNOMIAL FUNCTIONS

In Section 5.1, we graphed polynomial functions by plotting a number of points and using the degree of the polynomial involved to help us deduce a basic pattern for the curve. We also implicitly assumed the following theorem on continuity in the process. The proof of this theorem is omitted.

Continuity

THEOREM 5.2 If $P(x) = a_0 x^n + a_1 x^{n-1} + \cdots + a_n$, $a_i \in R$, and if k is a real number between $P(x_1)$ and $P(x_2)$, then there exists at least one $c \in R$ between x_1 and x_2 such that $P(c) = k$.

Essentially, since $P(x)$ must assume all values between any two of its values, this result shows that the graph of P must be a continuous curve. This continuity property of the values of a polynomial, together with the theorems given without proof below, enables us to deduce some facts about real zeros of a polynomial function without having to graph the function.

To begin with, a polynomial function of degree $n \geq 1$ over R can have at most n real zeros, and may have none. In Chapter 12, you will find that, with an agreement on how to count zeros, every such function has exactly n complex zeros (zeros that are complex numbers, real or imaginary) and that when imaginary zeros (zeros that are imaginary complex numbers) exist for a polynomial over R, there are always an even number of them.

Number of zeros

Turning now to real zeros only, let us agree that a **variation in sign** occurs in a polynomial with real coefficients if, as the polynomial is viewed from left to right, successive coefficients are opposite in sign. For example, in the polynomial

$$P(x) = 3x^5 - 2x^4 - 2x^2 + x - 1,$$

there are three variations in sign, and in

$$P(-x) = -3x^5 - 2x^4 - 2x^2 - x - 1,$$

there are no variations in sign. We then have the following result, which is called **Descartes' Rule of Signs**.

THEOREM 5.3 If $P(x)$ is a polynomial over the field R of real numbers, then the number of positive real zeros of $P(x)$ is either equal to the number of variations in sign occurring in the coefficients of $P(x)$, or else is less than this number by an even natural number. Moreover, the number of negative real zeros of $P(x)$ is either equal to the number of variations in sign occurring in $P(-x)$, or else is less than this number by an even natural number.

know

Example. Find an upper bound on the number of real positive zeros and real negative zeros of

$$\{(x, P(x)) \mid P(x) = 3x^4 + 3x^3 - 2x^2 + x + 1\}.$$

Solution. Since $P(x) = 3x^4 + 3x^3 - 2x^2 + x + 1$ has but two variations in sign, $P(x)$ can have no more than two positive real zeros. Since

$$P(-x) = 3(-x)^4 + 3(-x)^3 - 2(-x)^2 + (-x) + 1 = 3x^4 - 3x^3 - 2x^2 - x + 1$$

has two variations in sign, $P(x)$ can have at most two negative real zeros.

changes odd degree terms

Bounds on sets of zeros   The following theorem is sometimes helpful in isolating real zeros of a polynomial function with real coefficients.

THEOREM 5.4 *Let $P(x)$ be a polynomial over the field R of real numbers.*

I   *If $c_1 \geq 0$, and the coefficients of the terms in $Q(x)$ and the term $P(c_1)$ are all of the same sign in the right-hand member of*   *upper bond*

$$P(x) = (x - c_1)Q(x) + P(c_1),$$

then $P(x)$ can have no zero greater than c_1.

II   *If $c_2 \leq 0$, and the coefficients of the terms in $Q(x)$ and the term $P(c_2)$ alternate in sign (zero suitably denoted by $+0$ or -0) in the right-hand member of*

$$P(x) = (x - c_2)Q(x) + P(c_2), \quad lower$$

then $P(x)$ can have no zero less than c_2.

lower

    This theorem permits us to place upper and lower bounds on the set of zeros of the polynomial function

$$P = \{(x, P(x)) \mid P(x) = a_0 x^n + \cdots + a_n\},$$

that is, on the members of the solution set of $P(x) = 0$.

Example. Show that 2 and -2 are upper and lower bounds, respectively, for the set of zeros of

$$\{(x, P(x)) \mid P(x) = 18x^3 - 12x^2 - 11x + 10\}.$$

Solution. To find $Q(x)$, we use synthetic division to divide $P(x)$ by $(x - 2)$:

$$
\begin{array}{r|rrrr}
2 & 18 & -12 & -11 & 10 \\
  &   & 36 & 48 & 74 \\
\hline
  & 18 & 24 & 37 & 84
\end{array}
\qquad \text{all same}
$$

Since $Q(x) = 18x^2 + 24x + 37$ and $P(2) = 84 > 0$, from Theorem 5.4-I it follows that 2 is an upper bound for the set of zeros of P. Next dividing $P(x)$ by $(x + 2)$, we have

$$
\begin{array}{r|rrrr}
-2 & 18 & -12 & -11 & 10 \\
   &   & -36 & 96 & -170 \\
\hline
   & 18 & -48 & 85 & -160
\end{array}
\qquad \text{alternate}
$$

Since $Q(x) = 18x^2 - 48x + 85$ and $P(-2) = -160$, it follows from Theorem 5.4-II that -2 is a lower bound for the set of zeros of P.

Example. Find the least nonnegative integer and the greatest nonpositive integer that are, by Theorem 5.4, upper and lower bounds, respectively, for the set of zeros of

$$\{(x, P(x))\mid P(x) = x^4 - x^3 - 10x^2 - 2x + 12\}.$$

Solution. We shall first seek an upper bound by dividing $P(x)$ successively by $(x - 1)$, $(x - 2)$, and so on. Each row after the first in the following array is the bottom row in the synthetic division involved.

	1	−1	−10	−2	12
1	1	0	−10	−12	0
2	1	1	−8	−18	−24
3	1	2	−4	−14	−30
4	1	3	2	6	36

Since the numbers in the last row are all positive, 4 is an upper bound. Next, we divide by $(x + 1)$, $(x + 2)$, and so on, in search of a lower bound.

	1	−1	−10	−2	12
−1	1	−2	−8	6	6
−2	1	−3	−4	6	0
−3	1	−4	2	−8	36

Since the signs in the row following -3 alternate, -3 is a lower bound. Had the numbers in the row been 1, 0, 2, -8, 36, then the sign " $-$ " could arbitrarily have been assigned to 0 to give the desired pattern of alternating signs.

To narrow the search for real zeros of a polynomial function still further, we have the **location theorem**, which follows directly from Theorem 5.2.

THEOREM 5.5 *Let $P(x)$ be a polynomial over the field R of real numbers. If $x_1, x_2 \in R$, with $x_1 < x_2$, and if $P(x_1)$ and $P(x_2)$ are opposite in sign, then there exists at least one $c \in R$, $x_1 < c < x_2$, such that $P(c) = 0$.*

This theorem expresses the fact that if the graphs of $(x_1, P(x_1))$ and $(x_2, P(x_2))$ are on opposite sides of the x-axis, then the graph of $y = P(x)$ must cross the x-axis at some (at least one) point with abscissa c between x_1 and x_2.

Example. Verify that $\{(x, f(x))\mid f(x) = 2x^3 - 3x^2 + 4x - 6\}$ has a zero between 1 and 2.

Solution. We can apply synthetic division to find $f(1)$ and $f(2)$.

	2	−3	4	−6
1	2	−1	3	−3
2	2	1	6	6

Since $f(1) = -3$ and $f(2) = 6$, Theorem 5.5 assures us that f has a zero between 1 and 2.

EXERCISE 5.2

Use Theorem 5.3 to find bounds on the number of positive zeros and the number of negative zeros of the function defined by each equation.

1. $P(x) = x^4 - 2x^3 + 2x + 1$ 2, 7

2. $R(x) = 3x^4 + 3x^3 + 2x^2 - x + 1$

3. $Q(x) = 2x^5 + 3x^3 + 2x + 1$ 0,

4. $P(x) = 4x^5 - 2x^3 - 3x - 2$

5. $S(x) = 3x^4 + 1$

6. $Q(x) = 2x^5 - 1$

Find the least nonnegative integer and the greatest nonpositive integer that are, by Theorem 5.4, an upper bound and a lower bound, respectively, for the set of real zeros of the function defined by each equation.

7. $P(x) = x^3 + 2x^2 - 7x - 8$

8. $Q(x) = x^3 - 8x + 5$

9. $Q(x) = x^4 - 2x^3 - 7x^2 + 10x + 10$

10. $R(x) = x^3 - 4x^2 - 4x + 12$

11. $S(x) = x^5 - 3x^3 + 24$

12. $R(x) = x^5 - 3x^4 - 1$

13. $P(x) = 2x^5 + x^4 - 2x - 1$

14. $G(x) = 2x^5 - 2x^2 + x - 2$

Use Theorem 5.5 to verify each statement in Problems 15–20.

15. $\{(x, f(x)) \mid f(x) = x^3 - 3x + 1\}$ has a zero between 0 and 1.

16. $\{(x, f(x)) \mid f(x) = 2x^3 + 7x^2 + 2x - 6\}$ has a zero between -2 and -1.

17. $\{(x, g(x)) \mid g(x) = x^4 - 2x^2 + 12x - 17\}$ has a zero between -3 and -2.

18. $\{(x, g(x)) \mid g(x) = 2x^4 + 3x^3 - 14x^2 - 15x + 9\}$ has a zero between -2 and -1.

19. $\{(x, P(x)) \mid P(x) = 2x^2 + 4x - 4\}$ has one zero between -3 and -2, and one between 0 and 1.

20. $\{(x, P(x)) \mid P(x) = x^3 - x^2 - 2x + 1\}$ has one zero between -2 and -1, one between 0 and 1, and one between 1 and 2.

Use information from Theorems 5.1 to 5.5 and sketch the graph of the function given in each specified problem.

21. Problem 15 above

22. Problem 16

23. Problem 17

24. Problem 18

25. Problem 19

26. Problem 20

5.3 RATIONAL ZEROS OF POLYNOMIAL FUNCTIONS

If all the coefficients of the defining equation

$$P(x) = a_0 x^n + a_1 x^{n-1} + \cdots + a_n \quad (a_0 \neq 0)$$

Possible rational zeros of a polynomial function P are integers, then we can identify all possible rational zeros of P by means of the following.

THEOREM 5.6   *If the rational number in lowest terms p/q is a solution of*

$$P(x) = a_0 x^n + a_1 x^{n-1} + \cdots + a_n = 0,$$

where $a_i \in J$ ($a_0 \neq 0$), then p is an integral factor of a_n and q is an integral factor of a_0.

Proof.   Since p/q is a solution of $P(x) = 0$, we have

$$a_0 \left(\frac{p}{q}\right)^n + a_1 \left(\frac{p}{q}\right)^{n-1} + \cdots + a_n = 0,$$

and we can multiply each member here by q^n to obtain

$$a_0 p^n + a_1 p^{n-1} q + \cdots + a_n q^n = 0.$$

Adding $-a_n q^n$ to each member and factoring p from each term in the left-hand member of the resulting equation, we have

$$p(a_0 p^{n-1} + a_1 p^{n-2} + \cdots + a_{n-1}) = -a_n q^n.$$

Since the set of integers is closed under addition and multiplication, the expression in parentheses in the left-hand member here represents an integer, say r, so that we have

$$pr = -a_n q^n,$$

where pr is an integer having p as a factor. Hence, p is a factor of $-a_n q^n$. But p and q^n have no factor in common, because, by hypothesis, p/q is in lowest terms; hence p must be a factor of a_n. In a similar manner, by writing the equation

$$a_0 p^n + a_1 p^{n-1} q + \cdots + a_n q^n = 0$$

in the form

$$-a_0 p^n = a_1 p^{n-1} q + \cdots + a_n q^n,$$

we can factor q from each term in the right-hand member and show that q must be a factor of a_0.

Example.   List all possible rational zeros of

$$\{(x, P(x)) \mid P(x) = 2x^3 - 4x^2 + 3x + 9\}.$$

Solution.   Rational zeros p/q must, by Theorem 5.6, be such that p is an integral factor of 9 and q is an integral factor of 2. Hence

$$p \in \{-9, -3, -1, 1, 3, 9\}, \qquad q \in \{-2, -1, 1, 2\},$$

and the set of possible rational zeros of P is

$$\left\{ -9, -\frac{9}{2}, -3, -\frac{3}{2}, -1, -\frac{1}{2}, \frac{1}{2}, 1, \frac{3}{2}, 3, \frac{9}{2}, 9 \right\}.$$

Handwritten at top:

$2x^3 - 4x^2 + x - 6$

$\frac{p}{q}$ root $\Rightarrow$ q = $\pm 1, \pm 2$

p : $\pm 1, \pm 2, \pm 3, \pm 6$

$\frac{p}{q} = \pm \frac{1}{2}, \pm \frac{3}{2}$

It is important to observe that Theorem 5.6 does not assure us that a polynomial function with integral coefficients indeed has a rational zero; it

Test for rational zeros

simply enables us to identify possibilities for rational zeros. These can then be checked by synthetic division. The identification of the zeros of P in the previous example is left as an exercise.

As a special case of Theorem 5.6, it is evident that if a function P is defined by

$$P(x) = x^n + a_1 x^{n-1} + \cdots + a_n,$$

in which $a_i \in J$ and the coefficient of x^n is 1, then any rational zero of P must be an integer, and, moreover, must be an integral factor of a_n.

Example. Find all rational zeros of

$$\{(x, P(x)) \mid P(x) = x^3 - 4x^2 + x + 6\}.$$

Solution. The only possible rational zeros of P are $-6, -3, -2, -1, 1, 2, 3,$ and 6. Using synthetic division, we set up the following array.

	1	-4	1	6
-6	1	-10	61	-360
-3	1	-7	22	-60
-2	1	-6	13	-20
-1	1	-5	6	0

We can cease our trials with -1, since, by the remainder theorem, -1 is a zero of P, and the remaining zeros can be obtained from the depressed equation $x^2 - 5x + 6 = 0$ by writing this as $(x - 2)(x - 3) = 0$ and observing that 2 and 3 are also zeros. Had the trial process begun with -1, 2, or 3, rather than -6, a single trial would have rendered the rational zeros immediately evident.

Handwritten: q = 1st digit　p = last digit

EXERCISE 5.3

Find all integral zeros of each function.

1. $\{(x, f(x)) \mid f(x) = 3x^3 - 13x^2 + 6x - 8\}$

2. $\{(x, f(x)) \mid f(x) = x^4 - x^2 - 4x + 4\}$

3. $\{(x, f(x)) \mid f(x) = x^4 + x^3 + 2x - 4\}$

4. $\{(x, f(x)) \mid f(x) = 5x^3 + 11x^2 - 2x - 8\}$

5. $\{(x, P(x)) \mid P(x) = 2x^4 - 3x^3 - 8x^2 - 5x - 3\}$

6. $\{(x, P(x)) \mid P(x) = 3x^4 - 40x^3 + 130x^2 - 120x + 27\}$

Find all rational zeros of each function.

7. $\{(x, f(x)) \mid f(x) = 2x^3 + 3x^2 - 14x - 21\}$

8. $\{(x, f(x)) \mid f(x) = 3x^4 - 11x^3 + 9x^2 + 13x - 10\}$

9. $\{(x, P(x)) \mid P(x) = 4x^4 - 13x^3 - 7x^2 + 41x - 14\}$

Handwritten notes on right side:

$x^3 - 4y^2 + x + 6$

3	1	-4	1	6
		3	-3	-6
	1	-1	-2	0

$x^2 - x - 2 = 0$

$x^2 - x - 2$

$(x - 2)(x + 1)$

$(x + 2)$ (-1)

10. $\{(x, P(x))\mid P(x) = 2x^3 - 4x^2 + 3x + 9\}$

11. $\{(x, Q(x))\mid Q(x) = 2x^3 - 7x^2 + 10x - 6\}$

12. $\{(x, Q(x))\mid Q(x) = x^3 + 3x^2 - 4x - 12\}$

Use information from Theorems 5.1 to 5.6 and sketch the graph of the function given in each specified problem.

13. Problem 1 above   14. Problem 2

16. Problem 4   15. Problem 3

17. Problem 5   18. Problem 6

5.4 IRRATIONAL ZEROS OF POLYNOMIAL FUNCTIONS

Theorem 5.5 can often be used to isolate some real zeros of polynomial functions on intervals of the domain. Once we have isolated such zeros,

Linear interpolation various means exist for obtaining closer approximations to them, in particular to zeros that are irrational. We shall be concerned with only one such means herein—namely, linear interpolation.

Consider the function

$$P = \{(x, P(x)) \mid P(x) = x^3 - 3x^2 - 2x + 5\}.$$

By means of synthetic division and the remainder theorem, we can establish that $(1, 1)$ and $(2, -3)$ are in the function, and hence, by the location theorem, there is at least one zero between 1 and 2. Actually, since $P(x)$ is positive for x large and

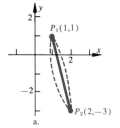

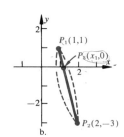

a.   b.

Figure 5.3

positive, and $P(x)$ is negative for x large in absolute value and negative, we can see that one of the remaining two roots must be greater than 2

Isolation of a zero and the other must be less than 1, and therefore that there is exactly one zero between 1 and 2. Since the only rational zero for P would have to be an integer (the leading coefficient is 1), any zeros between 1 and 2 must be irrational. Figure 5.3-a shows the two points P_1 (1, 1), and P_2 (2, -3), and a line segment joining them.

The dashed lines show possibilities for the graph of P on the interval $1 < x < 2$; but since we are uncertain of the curvature, we cannot be sure on which side of the line segment the graph actually lies. In either case, however, the point where the segment intersects the x-axis clearly is close (in some sense) to the point where the graph of P intersects this axis. In Figure 5.3-b we show the same segment, this time with an additional detail. If we can find a value for the coordinate of the x-intercept of the line segment P_1P_2, then we will have a first approximation to a zero for P. Since the slope of P_1P_3 is the same as the slope for P_1P_2, we have

$$\frac{0 - 1}{x_1 - 1} = \frac{-3 - 1}{2 - 1},$$

from which

$$x_1 = \frac{5}{4}.$$

To find $P(5/4)$, we divide $P(x)$ synthetically by 1.25, as follows.

$$
\begin{array}{r|rrrr}
1.25 & 1 & -3 & -2 & 5 \\
     &   & 1.25 & -2.1875 & -5.234375 \\
\hline
     & 1 & -1.75 & -4.1875 & -0.234375
\end{array}
$$

Thus, $P(5/4) \approx -0.2344$. Figure 5.4-a shows our present situation, from which it is clear that the graph of P crosses the x-axis to the left of P_3, so that, at least insofar as this point is concerned, the graph of P is concave upward on this interval. We can now repeat the linear-interpolation process, using P_1 and P_4, to obtain another approximation to the zero for P. Figure 5.4-b shows the necessary detail. Again, since the slope of P_1P_4 is the same as the slope of P_1P_5, we have

$$\frac{0 - 1}{x_2 - 1} = \frac{-0.2344 - 1}{1.25 - 1},$$

from which

$$x_2 \approx 1.2025.$$

Thus, a second approximation to the desired zero of P is 1.2025. This process can be continued as long as necessary to obtain any desired degree of accuracy. To three decimal places, the zero sought here is 1.202.

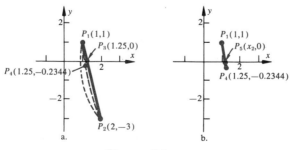

Figure   5.4

EXERCISE 5.4

Find to one decimal place the indicated real zero(s) of the function.

1. $\{(x, P(x))\mid P(x) = x^3 - 3x + 1\}$; between 1 and 2

2. $\{(x, P(x))\mid P(x) = 2x^3 - x^2 + 3x + 1\}$; between 0 and -1

3. $\{(x, P(x))\mid P(x) = x^3 - 2x - 5\}$; between 2 and 3

4. $\{(x, P(x))\mid P(x) = x^3 + 2x^2 - 1\}$; between 0 and 1

5. $\{(x, P(x))\mid P(x) = x^3 + 3x^2 - 6x - 3\}$; the greatest positive

6. $\{(x, P(x))\mid P(x) = 2x^3 - 5x^2 - x + 5\}$; the least positive

7. $\{(x, P(x))\mid P(x) = x^3 + x - 1\}$; all

8. $\{(x, P(x))\mid P(x) = x^4 - 4x^3 - 4x + 12\}$; all

9. Find to two decimal places an approximation for $\sqrt[3]{5}$. *Hint:* Consider the equation $x^3 - 5 = 0$.

10. Find to two decimal places an approximation for $\sqrt[5]{2}$.

5.5   RATIONAL FUNCTIONS

A function defined by an equation of the form

$$y = \frac{P(x)}{Q(x)}, \tag{1}$$

where $P(x)$ and $Q(x)$ are polynomials in x, and $Q(x)$ is not the zero polynomial, is called a **rational function.** Rational functions with real coefficients (that is, rational functions over R) are of importance in the calculus and provide some interesting problems with respect to their graphs. We shall consider them only briefly here.

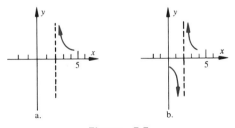

a.   b.

Figure 5.5

Since $P(x)/Q(x)$ is not defined for values of x for which $Q(x) = 0$, it is evident that we shall not be able to find points in $R \times R$ having such x-coordinates. We

**Graph
near vertical
asymptotes**

can, however, consider the graph for values of x as close as we please to a value, say x_0, for which $Q(x_0) = 0$, but still with $x \neq x_0$. This consideration is usually described by saying that x "approaches" x_0, "grows close" to x_0, etc., and

correspondingly that $Q(x)$ approaches 0. Thus, the closer $Q(x)$ approaches 0, if $P(x)$ does not approach 0 at the same time, then the larger $|y|$ becomes in (1). For example, Figure 5.5-a shows the behavior of

$$\left\{ (x, y) \mid y = \frac{2}{x - 2} \right\}, \qquad (2)$$

*straight line to which
a curve gets close*

as x approaches 2 from the right. In situations such as this, the vertical line that the curve approaches is called a **vertical asymptote**.

THEOREM 5.7 *The graph of the rational function over R defined by $y = P(x)/Q(x)$ has a vertical asymptote at $x = a$ for each value a at which $Q(x)$ vanishes and $P(x)$ does not vanish.*

In Figure 5.5-a we see the behavior of the function (2) as x approaches 2 from the right. We are also interested in its behavior as x approaches 2 from the left. Figure 5.5-b illustrates this. As long as $x > 2$, we have $x - 2 > 0$ and $2/(x - 2) > 0$; but if $x < 2$, then we have $x - 2 < 0$ and $2/(x - 2) < 0$.

**Horizontal
asymptotes**

The graphs of some rational functions have **horizontal asymptotes**, which can, in general, be identified by using the following theorem.

*R not defined where denominator
has roots (zeros)*

THEOREM 5.8 *The graph of the rational function over R defined by*

$$y = \frac{a_0 x^n + a_1 x^{n-1} + \cdots + a_n}{b_0 x^m + b_1 x^{m-1} + \cdots + b_m},$$

$$\frac{2x^3 + \frac{1}{2}x - 1}{x^4 + \sqrt{2}x^2 - \sqrt{3}}$$

where $a_0, b_0 \neq 0$ and n, m are nonnegative integers, has

I *a horizontal asymptote at $y = 0$ if $n < m$,*

II *a horizontal asymptote at $y = a_0/b_0$ if $n = m$,*

III *no horizontal asymptotes if $n > m$.*

Though we shall not give a rigorous proof of this theorem here, we can certainly make the results plausible. If $n < m$, we can divide the numerator and denominator of the right-hand member of

$$y = \frac{a_0 x^n + a_1 x^{n-1} + \cdots + a_n}{b_0 x^m + b_1 x^{m-1} + \cdots + b_m}$$

by x^m to obtain, for $x \neq 0$,

$$y = \frac{\dfrac{a_0}{x^{m-n}} + \dfrac{a_1}{x^{m-n+1}} + \cdots + \dfrac{a_n}{x^m}}{b_0 + \dfrac{b_1}{x} + \cdots + \dfrac{b_m}{x^m}}.$$

Now, as $|x|$ grows larger and larger, each term containing an x in its denominator grows closer and closer to 0, and we find the expression on the right approaching $0/b_0$, so that y approaches 0. But if, as y grows close to 0, $|x|$ is increasing without bound, then y is approaching the line $y = 0$ asymptotically, and actually must approach 0 from one of the four directions shown in Figure 5.6-a. A similar argument shows that if $n = m$, then, as $|x|$ increases without bound, y approaches the line $y = a_0/b_0$ from one of the directions shown in Figure 5.6-b. If $n > m$, then as $|x|$ becomes larger and larger, so does $|y|$.

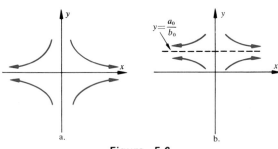

$n > m$

oblique

a.   b.

Figure 5.6

In particular, if $n = m + 1$, that is, if the numerator is of degree one greater than the denominator, we can argue that though the graph has no horizontal asymptote,

Oblique asymptotes   it does have an **oblique asymptote**. We shall illustrate a special case only, but the technique involved is quite general.

Example. Find all asymptotes for the graph of $\left\{(x, y) \mid y = \dfrac{x^2 - 4}{x - 1}\right\}$.

Solution. First we note that, by Theorem 5.7, there is a vertical asymptote at $x = 1$ and that, by Theorem 5.8, there are no horizontal asymptotes. If, however, we rewrite $y = (x^2 - 4)/(x - 1)$ by dividing $x^2 - 4$ by $x - 1$, we obtain $y = x + 1 - 3/(x - 1)$. Now as $|x|$ grows larger and larger, $3/(x - 1)$ grows smaller and smaller, and the graph of $y = (x^2 - 4)/(x - 1)$ approaches the graph of $y = x + 1$. Hence, the graph of $y = x + 1$, which is an oblique line, is an asymptote to the curve.

Helpful items for graphing   Identifying asymptotes is one aid to the graphing of a rational function over R. Other helpful items are the following:

1. The zeros of the function, because these give us the x-intercepts.

2. The domain and range, because these let us know where we can expect to find parts of the graph and where we cannot.

IF numerator is 0 graph will
cross x axis
if not never

3. Some specific points on the graph, because these give us guidelines in sketching.

Example.   Graph $\left\{(x, y)\,|\, y = \dfrac{x-1}{x-2}\right\}$.

Solution.   We can begin by observing that the numerator of the right-hand member will be equal to 0 when x is equal to 1. Therefore, when $x = 1$, we have $y = 0$, and 1 is

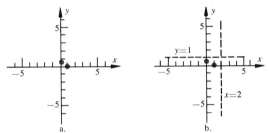

Figure   5.7

an x-intercept. Also, when $x = 0$, we have $y = \dfrac{1}{2}$, so that $\dfrac{1}{2}$ is a y-intercept. Thus we can begin our graph as shown in Figure 5.7-a. By inspection, $y = (x - 1)/(x - 2)$ is defined for all real x except $x = 2$, so that $\{x\,|\,x \neq 2\}$ is the domain. Similarly, if we solve the defining equation for x in terms of y, we have $x = (2y - 1)/(y - 1)$, which is defined for all values of y except 1. Hence $\{y\,|\,y \neq 1\}$ is the range of the function. From the defining equation and Theorem 5.7, we see that there is a vertical asymptote at $x = 2$ and a horizontal asymptote at $y = 1$. We can then add this information to our graph, as indicated in Figure 5.7-b. Next we call our powers of observation into play. That the vertical asymptote, for example, is approached downward instead of upward from the left can be confirmed by observing that if x is just less than 2, say $2 - p$, $0 < p < 1/10$, then the denominator $x - 2$ in the expression for y is $2 - p - 2 = -p$, which is barely negative, whereas the numerator $x - 1 = 2 - p - 1 = 1 - p$ is definitely positive; hence y is negative and $|y|$ large. The graph appears in Figure 5.8-a. To find the curve when

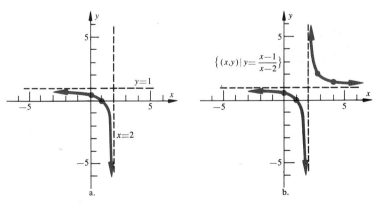

Figure   5.8

$x > 2$, that is, to the right of the vertical asymptote, we simply find one or two points associated with such values of x. For example, we might choose 3 and 4. If $x = 3$, then $y = (3 - 1)/(3 - 2) = 2$, and $(3, 2)$ is on the curve. If $x = 4$, then $y = (4 - 1)/(4 - 2) = 3/2$, and $(4, 3/2)$ is on the curve. Again, the knowledge that $x = 2$ and $y = 1$ are asymptotes, together with the location of the points $(3, 2)$ and $(4, 3/2)$, leads us to the complete graph of $\{(x, y) \mid y = (x - 1)/(x - 2)\}$, as shown in Figure 5.8-b.

Example. Graph $\left\{(x, y) \mid y = \dfrac{x^2 - 4}{x - 1}\right\}$.

Solution. This is the same function we investigated in the example on page 132, where we found the vertical asymptote $x = 1$ and the oblique asymptote $y = x + 1$.

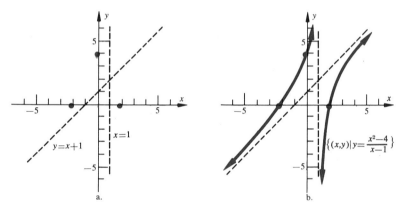

Figure 5.9

By inspection, if $x = 0$, then $y = 4$, and if $y = 0$, then $x = 2$ or $x = -2$, so that there is a y-intercept at 4, as well as x-intercepts at 2 and -2. We therefore have the situation shown in Figure 5.9-a. Without any further information, we have strong reason to suspect that the graph will appear as shown in Figure 5.9-b. The plotting of a few check points, say $(-1, 3/2)$, $(1/2, 15/2)$, $(3/2, -7/2)$, and $(3, 5/2)$, would tend to confirm our conjecture.

EXERCISE 5.5

Determine the vertical asymptotes of the graph of each function.

Example. $\{(x, y) \mid x^2 y - 4y = 1\}$

Solution. Express y explicitly in terms of x by means of an equivalent equation.

$$y(x^2 - 4) = 1$$

$$y = \frac{1}{x^2 - 4}$$

The denominator $x^2 - 4$ vanishes for $x = 2, -2$. Therefore, by Theorem 5.7, there are vertical asymptotes at $x = 2, -2$.

$x^2 - x - 6$

1. $\left\{(x, y)\mid y = \dfrac{1}{x-3}\right\}$

2. $\left\{(x, y)\mid y = \dfrac{1}{x+4}\right\}$

3. $\left\{(x, y)\mid y = \dfrac{4}{(x+2)(x-3)}\right\}$ $-2 \quad +3$

4. $\left\{(x, y)\mid y = \dfrac{8}{(x-1)(x+3)}\right\}$

5. $\left\{(x, y)\mid y = \dfrac{2x-1}{x^2+5x+4}\right\}$

6. $\left\{(x, y)\mid y = \dfrac{x+3}{2x^2-5x-3}\right\}$ $\dfrac{-b \pm \sqrt{b^2 - 4ac}}{2a}$

7. $\{(x, y)\mid xy + y = 4\}$

8. $\{(x, y)\mid x^2 y + xy = 3\}$

Graph.

9. $\left\{(x, y)\mid y = \dfrac{1}{x}\right\}$

10. $\left\{(x, y)\mid y = \dfrac{1}{x+4}\right\}$

11. $\left\{(x, y)\mid y = \dfrac{1}{x-3}\right\}$

12. $\left\{(x, y)\mid y = \dfrac{1}{x-6}\right\}$

13. $\left\{(x, y)\mid y = \dfrac{4}{(x+2)(x-3)}\right\}$

14. $\left\{(x, y)\mid y = \dfrac{8}{(x-1)(x+3)}\right\}$

15. $\left\{(x, y)\mid y = \dfrac{2}{(x-3)^2}\right\}$

16. $\left\{(x, y)\mid y = \dfrac{1}{(x+4)^2}\right\}$

Determine any vertical, horizontal, or oblique asymptotes of the graphs of each of the following.

Example. $\left\{(x, y)\mid y = \dfrac{6x^2 + 1}{2x^2 + 5x - 3}\right\}$

Solution. The defining equation can be written equivalently as

$$y = \frac{6x^2 + 1}{(2x - 1)(x + 3)}.$$
$$\tfrac{1}{2} \qquad -3$$

By Theorem 5.7, there are vertical asymptotes at $x = 1/2$ and $x = -3$. By Theorem 5.8-II, there is a horizontal asymptote at $y = 6/2$, or 3.

17. $\left\{(x, y)\mid y = \dfrac{x}{x^2-4}\right\}$ $(x+2)(x-2)$ horz at o vert

18. $\left\{(x, y)\mid y = \dfrac{3x+6}{x^2+3x+2}\right\}$ horz at $y=0$ vert $-1, -2$

19. $\left\{(x, y)\mid y = \dfrac{x^2-9}{x-4}\right\}$ vert at 4 obley at $x+y$

20. $\left\{(x, y)\mid y = \dfrac{x^3-27}{x^2-1}\right\}$

21. $\left\{(x, y)\mid y = \dfrac{x^2-3x+2}{x^2-3x-4}\right\}$ horiz at 1 vert at $4, -1$

22. $\left\{(x, y)\mid y = \dfrac{x^2}{x^2-x-6}\right\}$

Graph. Use information concerning the zeros of each function, and any vertical, horizontal, and oblique asymptotes.

23. $\left\{(x, y) \mid y = \dfrac{x}{x - 2}\right\}$ ·2

24. $\left\{(x, y) \mid y = \dfrac{x - 1}{x + 3}\right\}$

25. $\left\{(x, y) \mid y = \dfrac{2x - 4}{x^2 - 9}\right\}$ ⁺³ ˣ⁻³

26. $\left\{(x, y) \mid y = \dfrac{3x}{x^2 - 5x + 4}\right\}$

27. $\left\{(x, y) \mid y = \dfrac{x^2 - 4}{x^3}\right\}$ 0

28. $\left\{(x, y) \mid y = \dfrac{x - 2}{x^2}\right\}$

29. $\left\{(x, y) \mid y = \dfrac{x^2 - 4x + 4}{x - 1}\right\}$

30. $\left\{(x, y) \mid y = \dfrac{x^2 + 4}{x - 2}\right\}$

31. $\left\{(x, y) \mid y = \dfrac{x + 1}{x(x^2 - 4)}\right\}$

32. $\left\{(x, y) \mid y = \dfrac{x^2 + x - 2}{x(x^2 - 9)}\right\}$

$y = b^x = 0$

$y = b^0$

Domain = all reals
Range = $y > 0$

never negative #

EXPONENTIAL AND
6 LOGARITHMIC
FUNCTIONS

6.1 EXPONENTIAL FUNCTIONS

Powers of the form b^x, where $b \in R$, $b > 0$, and x denotes a *rational number*, were discussed in Chapter 2. These can be used to define functions. Notice that the base b is here restricted to positive real numbers to ensure that b^x be real for all rational numbers x.

If, now, we are to define a function over R using b^x, we must also be able to interpret powers with *irrational exponents*, such as

$$b^{\sqrt{2}}, \quad b^{-\sqrt{3}}, \quad \text{and} \quad b^{\pi},$$

to be real numbers. The following two theorems, the first one of which is presented without proof, will be useful in doing this.

THEOREM 6.1 *Let $x \in Q$, i.e., $x \in \{$rational numbers$\}$, and let $x > 0$. Then*

$$b^x > 1 \text{ if } b > 1, \quad b^x = 1 \text{ if } b = 1, \quad \text{and} \quad 0 < b^x < 1 \text{ if } 0 < b < 1.$$

THEOREM 6.2 *Let $x, y \in Q$, and let $x > y$. Then*

$$b^x > b^y \text{ if } b > 1, \quad b^x = b^y \text{ if } b = 1, \quad \text{and} \quad b^x < b^y \text{ if } 0 < b < 1.$$

Theorem 6.2 follows directly from Theorem 6.1. For example, if $b > 1$, then by Theorem 6.1, since $x - y > 0$, we have

$$\frac{b^x}{b^y} = b^{x-y} > 1,$$

from which

$$b^x > b^y.$$

You should recall that irrational numbers can be approximated by rational numbers to as great a degree of accuracy as desired. For example, $\sqrt{2} \approx 1.4$, or

$f(x) = b^x$

domain = all real numbers
range = all positive numbers

$\sqrt{2} \approx 1.414$, etc. Since b^x $(b > 0)$ is defined for rational x, by Theorem 6.2 we can write the sequence of inequalities

$$2^1 < 2^2,$$

$$2^{1 \cdot 4} < 2^{1 \cdot 5},$$

$$2^{1 \cdot 41} < 2^{1 \cdot 42},$$

$$2^{1 \cdot 414} < 2^{1 \cdot 415},$$

and so on.

As a result of Theorem 6.2, we can be sure that if $b > 1$, then b^x increases as x increases; and if $0 < b < 1$, then b^x decreases as x increases. This process can be continued indefinitely, and it seems plausible and is actually true, though we shall not prove it, that in the above sequence the difference between the number on the left and that on the right can be made as small as we please by going far enough in the sequence. This being the case, the completeness property O-3 of the real numbers guarantees that there is just one number, which

Definition of powers with real-number exponents

we denote by $2^{\sqrt{2}}$, that lies between the number on the left and the number on the right no matter how long this process of approximation is continued. Since we can produce the same type of argument for any irrational exponent x, we shall assume that b^x $(b > 0)$ is defined in this way for all real values of x and that the laws of exponents for rational exponents are valid for such powers.

Thus Theorem 2.11, pertaining to powers with rational-number exponents, when appropriately reworded, is also applicable to powers with real-number exponents.

Since for each real x there is one and only one number b^x, the equation

$$f(x) = b^x \quad (b > 0) \tag{1}$$

defines a function. Because $1^x = 1$ for all $x \in R$, (1) defines a constant function if $b = 1$. If $b \neq 1$, we say that (1) defines an **exponential function**.

Exponential functions can perhaps be visualized most clearly by considering their graphs. We illustrate two typical examples, in which $0 < b < 1$ and $b > 1$, respectively. Assigning values to x in the equations

$$f(x) = \left(\frac{1}{2}\right)^x \quad \text{and} \quad f(x) = 2^x,$$

we find some ordered pairs in each solution set and sketch the graphs of $\{(x, f(x)) \mid f(x) = (1/2)^x\}$ and $\{(x, f(x)) \mid f(x) = 2^x\}$, shown in Figures 6.1-a and 6.1-b, respectively.

Notice that in accordance with Theorem 6.2, the graph of the function determined

Increasing and decreasing functions

by $f(x) = (1/2)^x$ goes *down* to the right, and the graph of the function determined by $f(x) = 2^x$ goes *up* to the right. For this reason, we say that the former function is a *decreasing* function and that the latter is an *increasing* function. In either case, the domain is the set of real numbers, and the range is the set of positive real numbers.

(handwritten annotations):

w/neg # you invert answer $(\frac{1}{2})^{-1}$

$b^{-4} = (\frac{1}{b})^4$ $b^{-y} = \frac{1}{b^x}$

$(\frac{1}{2})$ all above t axis

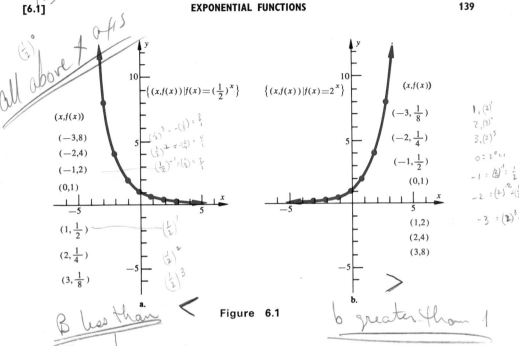

Figure 6.1

(handwritten): B less than a.   b greater than 1 b.

(handwritten right side):
1, $(2)^1$
2, $(2)^2$
3, $(2)^3$
$0 : 2^0 = 1$
$-1 : (2)^{-1} = \frac{1}{2}$
$-2 : (2)^{-2} = (\frac{1}{2})^2 = \frac{1}{4}$
$-3 : (2)^{-3} = (\frac{1}{2})^3 = \frac{1}{8}$

EXERCISE 6.1

Find the second component of each of the ordered pairs that makes the pair a solution of the corresponding equation.

1. $y = 3^x$; $(0, 1)$, $(1, 3)$, $(2, 9)$

2. $y = -2^x$; $(0, -1)$, $(1, -2)$, $(2, -4)$

3. $y = -5^x$; $(0, -1)$, $(1, -5)$, $(2; 25)$

4. $y = 4^x$; $(0, 1)$, $(1, 4)$, $(2, 16)$

5. $y = \left(\frac{1}{2}\right)^x$; $(-3, 8)$, $(0, 1)$, $(3, \frac{1}{8})$

6. $y = \left(\frac{1}{3}\right)^x$; $(-3, 27)$, $(0, 1)$, $(3, \frac{1}{27})$

7. $y = 10^x$; $(-2, \frac{1}{100})$, $(1, 10)$, $(0, 1)$

8. $y = 10^{-x}$; $(0, 1)$, $(1, \frac{1}{10})$, $(2, \frac{1}{100})$

Graph each function.

9. $\{(x, y) \mid y = 4^x\}$

10. $\{(x, y) \mid y = 5^x\}$

11. $\{(x, y) \mid y = 10^x\}$

12. $\{(x, y) \mid y = 10^{-x}\}$

13. $\{(x, y) \mid y = 2^{-x}\}$

14. $\{(x, y) \mid y = 3^{-x}\}$

15. $\left\{(x, y) \mid y = \left(\frac{1}{3}\right)^x\right\}$

16. $\left\{(x, y) \mid y = \left(\frac{1}{4}\right)^x\right\}$

17. $\left\{(x, y) \mid y = \left(\frac{1}{2}\right)^{-x}\right\}$

18. $\left\{(x, y) \mid y = \left(\frac{1}{3}\right)^{-x}\right\}$

19. Graph $\{(x, f(x)) \mid f(x) = 1^x\}$. Is this an exponential function? Name the function.

20. Graph $F = \{(x, y) \mid y = 10^x, x > 0\}$ and $F^{-1} = \{(x, y) \mid x = 10^y, x > 0\}$ on the same set of axes.

21. Solve for x by inspection.

     a. $10^x = \dfrac{1}{100}$ b. $\left(\dfrac{1}{2}\right)^x = 16$ c. $16^x = 8$

22. Determine an integer n such that $n < x < n + 1$.

     a. $3^x = 16.2$ b. $4^x = 87.1$ c. $10^x = 0.016$

6.2 LOGARITHMIC FUNCTIONS

In the exponential function

$$\{(x, y) \mid y = b^x \ (b > 0, b \neq 1)\}, \tag{1}$$

illustrated in Figure 6.1 for $b = 1/2$ and $b = 2$, there is only one x associated with each y. Thus by Definition 4.4 we have the inverse function

Inverse of an exponential function

$$\{(x, y) \mid x = b^y \ (b > 0, b \neq 1, x > 0)\}. \tag{2}$$

Observe that the restriction $x > 0$ is made in order that y be a real number, because there is no real number y for which b^y is not positive.

The graphs of functions of this form can be illustrated by the example

$$\{(x, y) \mid x = 10^y \ (x > 0)\}.$$

We consider x the variable denoting an element in the domain and, in the defining equation, assign arbitrary values for x, say,

$$(0.01, \quad), (0.1, \quad), (1, \quad), (10, \quad), (100, \quad),$$

to obtain the ordered pairs

$$(0.01, -2), (0.1, -1), (1, 0), (10, 1), (100, 2).$$

These can be graphed and connected with a smooth curve as shown in Figure 6.2.

It is always useful to be able to express the variable denoting an element in the range explicitly in terms of the variable denoting an element in the domain. To do this in an equation such as that defining the function (2), we use the notation

$$y = \log_b x \quad (x > 0, b > 0, b \neq 1). \tag{3}$$

Here, $\log_b x$ is read "the logarithm to the base b of x." Functions defined by such equations are called **logarithmic functions**.

Properties of logarithmic functions

From the graph in Figure 6.2, we generalize from $\log_{10} x$ to $\log_b x$, and observe that a logarithmic function has the following properties:

Properties

Know

1. The domain is the set of positive real numbers, and the range is the set of all real numbers.
2. If $b > 1$, then $\log_b x < 0$ for $0 < x < 1$, $\log_b x = 0$ for $x = 1$, and $\log_b x > 0$ for $x > 1$.
3. If $0 < b < 1$, then $\log_b x > 0$ for $0 < x < 1$, $\log_b x = 0$ for $x = 1$, and $\log_b x < 0$ for $x > 1$. The graph of a logarithmic function for $0 < b < 1$ is illustrated in Figure 6.3.

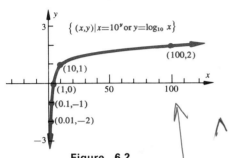

Figure 6.2   Figure 6.3

It should be recognized that the equations appearing in (2) and (3) are different equations determining the same función, in the same way that

Logarithmic and exponential statements

$x = y + 4$ and $y = x - 4$ determine the same function, and we may use whichever equation suits our purpose. Thus, exponential statements may be written in logarithmic form, and logarithmic statements may be written in exponential form.

Examples.

a. $5^2 = 25$ can be written as $\log_5 25 = 2$.

$\log_5 x = 2$
$5^2 = x \cdot 25$

b. $8^{1/3} = 2$ can be written as $\log_8 2 = \frac{1}{3}$.

c. $3^{-2} = \frac{1}{9}$ can be written as $\log_3 \frac{1}{9} = -2$.

Examples.

a. $\log_{10} 100 = 2$ can be written as $10^2 = 100$.

b. $\log_3 81 = 4$ can be written as $3^4 = 81$.

c. $\log_2 \frac{1}{2} = -1$ can be written as $2^{-1} = \frac{1}{2}$.

The logarithmic function associates with each number x the exponent y such that the power b^y is equal to x. In other words, we can think of $\log_b x$ as an exponent on b. Thus

$$b^{\log_b x} = x.$$

Laws of logarithms

Since a logarithm is an exponent, the following theorem follows directly from the properties of powers with real-number exponents.

$\log_b (y^0) = -\log by$

$\log 1$ is always 0

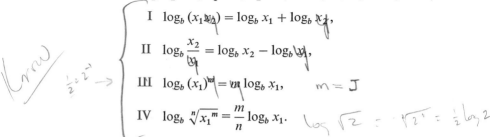

THEOREM 6.3   *If $x_1, x_2 \in R$, $x_1 > 0$, $x_2 > 0$, $b > 0$, $b \neq 1$, $m \in J$, $n \in N$, then*

$$\text{I} \quad \log_b (x_1 x_2) = \log_b x_1 + \log_b x_2,$$

$$\text{II} \quad \log_b \frac{x_2}{x_1} = \log_b x_2 - \log_b x_1,$$

$$\text{III} \quad \log_b (x_1)^m = m \log_b x_1, \qquad m = J$$

$$\text{IV} \quad \log_b \sqrt[n]{x_1^m} = \frac{m}{n} \log_b x_1. \qquad \log \sqrt{2} = \sqrt{2^1} = \tfrac{1}{2} \log 2$$

The validity of I can be shown as follows: Since

$$x_1 = b^{\log_b x_1} \text{ and } x_2 = b^{\log_b x_2},$$

it follows that

$$x_1 x_2 = b^{\log_b x_1} \cdot b^{\log_b x_2}$$
$$= b^{\log_b x_1 + \log_b x_2},$$

and, by the definition of a logarithm,

$$\log_b (x_1 x_2) = \log_b x_1 + \log_b x_2.$$

The validity of II, III, and IV can be established in a similar manner. A more general result than Theorem 6.3-III, and one that also follows from properties of powers with real number exponents, is that for every $k \in R$,

$$\text{V} \quad \log_b (x_1)^k = k \log_b x_1.$$

We shall refer to this result as Theorem 6.3-V.

EXERCISE 6.2

Express in logarithmic notation.

1. $4^2 = 16$
2. $5^3 = 125$
3. $3^3 = 27$
4. $8^2 = 64$
5. $\left(\frac{1}{2}\right)^2 = \frac{1}{4}$
6. $\left(\frac{1}{3}\right)^2 = \frac{1}{9}$
7. $8^{-1/3} = \frac{1}{2}$
8. $64^{-1/6} = \frac{1}{2}$
9. $10^2 = 100$
10. $10^0 = 1$
11. $10^{-1} = 0.1$
12. $10^{-2} = 0.01$

Express in exponential notation.

13. $\log_2 64 = 6$
14. $\log_5 25 = 2$
15. $\log_3 9 = 2$
16. $\log_{16} 256 = 2$
17. $\log_{1/3} 9 = -2$
18. $\log_{1/2} 8 = -3$
19. $\log_{10} 1000 = 3$
20. $\log_{10} 1 = 0$
21. $\log_{10} (0.01) = -2$

Find the value of each of the following.

22. $\log_5 5$ ~ 1

23. $\log_7 49$ = 2

24. $\log_2 32$ = 5

25. $\log_4 64$ = 3

26. $\log_5 \sqrt{5}$ = $\frac{1}{2}$

27. $\log_3 \sqrt{3}$ = $\frac{1}{2}$

28. $\log_3 \frac{1}{3}$ = −1

29. $\log_5 \frac{1}{5}$ = −1

30. $\log_3 3$ = 1

31. $\log_2 2$ = 1

32. $\log_{10} 10$ = 1

33. $\log_{10} 100$ = 2

34. $\log_{10} 1$ ~ 0

35. $\log_{10} 0.1$

36. $\log_{10} 0.01$

Solve for x, y, or b.

Examples.

a. $\log_2 x = 3$

b. $\log_b 2 = \frac{1}{2}$

Solutions. Determine the solution by inspection or by writing in exponential form.

a. $2^3 = x$
$x = 8$

b. $b^{1/2} = 2$
$(b^{1/2})^2 = (2)^2$
$b = 4$

37. $\log_3 9 = y$ ✓

38. $\log_5 125 = y$ 3

39. $\log_b 8 = 3$ ✓

40. $\log_b 625 = 4$ = 5

41. $\log_4 3x = 3$ 64

42. $\log_{1/2} x = -5$

43. $\log_2 \frac{1}{8} = y$ −3

44. $\log_5 5 = y$

45. $\log_b 10 = \frac{1}{2}$

46. $\log_b 0.1 = -1$

47. $\log_2 x = 2$

48. $\log_{10} x = -3$

49. Show that $\log_b 1 = 0$ for $b > 0$.

50. Show that $\log_b b = 1$ for $b > 0$.

51. Show that $\log_b b^x = x$ for $b > 0$.

52. Graph $y = \log_2 x$. By examining the graph, what can you assert about $\log_2 a$ and $\log_2 b$ if $a < b$?

Express as the sum or difference of simpler logarithmic quantities.

Example. $\log_b (xy/z)^{1/2}$

Solution. By Theorem 6.3-V,

$$\log_b \left(\frac{xy}{z}\right)^{1/2} = \frac{1}{2} \log_b \left(\frac{xy}{z}\right).$$

By Theorems 6.3-I and II,

$$\frac{1}{2} \log_b \left(\frac{xy}{z}\right) = \frac{1}{2} [\log_b x + \log_b y - \log_b z].$$

53. $\log_b (xy)$

54. $\log_b (xyz)$

55. $\log_b \left(\frac{x}{y}\right)$

56. $\log_b \left(\dfrac{xy}{z} \right)$ 57. $\log_b x^5$ 58. $\log_b x^{1/2}$

59. $\log_b \sqrt[3]{x}$ 60. $\log_b \sqrt[3]{x^2}$ 61. $\log_b \sqrt{\dfrac{x}{z}}$

62. $\log_b \sqrt{xy}$ 63. $\log_{10} \sqrt[3]{\dfrac{xy^2}{z}}$ 64. $\log_{10} \sqrt[5]{\dfrac{x^2 y}{z^3}}$

65. $\log_{10} \left(2\pi \sqrt{\dfrac{l}{g}} \right)$ 66. $\log_{10} \sqrt{s(s-a)(s-b)(s-c)}$

Express as a single logarithm with coefficient 1.

Example. $\dfrac{1}{2}(\log_b x - \log_b y)$

Solution. By Theorems 6.3-II and V,

$$\frac{1}{2}(\log_b x - \log_b y) = \frac{1}{2}\log_b \left(\frac{x}{y}\right) = \log_b \left(\frac{x}{y}\right)^{1/2}.$$

67. $\log_b x + \log_b y$ 68. $\log_b x - \log_b y$

69. $2\log_b x + 3\log_b y$ $\log_b x^2 y^3$ 70. $\dfrac{1}{4}\log_b x - \dfrac{3}{4}\log_b y$

71. $3\log_b x + \log_b y - 2\log_b z$ 72. $\dfrac{1}{3}(\log_b x + \log_b y - 2\log_b z)$

73. $\log_{10}(x-2) + \log_{10} x - 2\log_{10} z$ 74. $\dfrac{1}{2}(\log_{10} x - 3\log_{10} y - 5\log_{10} z)$

75. Show that $\dfrac{1}{4}\log_{10} 8 + \dfrac{1}{4}\log_{10} 2 = \log_{10} 2$.

76. Show that $4\log_{10} 3 - 2\log_{10} 3 + 1 = \log_{10} 90$.

77. Show that $10^{2 \log_{10} x} = x^2$.

78. Show that $a^{2 \log_a 3} + b^{3 \log_b 2} = 17$.

79. Show that $\log_{10}[\log_3 (\log_5 125)] = 0$.

80. Using the definition of a logarithm ($\log_b x$ is a number such that $b^{\log_b x} = x$) and the laws of exponents, prove Theorem 6.3-II.

6.3 LOGARITHMS TO THE BASE 10

There are two logarithmic functions of special interest in mathematics; one is defined by

$$y = \log_{10} x, \tag{1}$$

and the other by

$$y = \log_e x, \tag{2}$$

where e is an irrational number with decimal approximation 2.7182818 to eight digits. Because these functions possess similar properties, and because we are more familiar with the number 10, we shall, for the present, confine our attention to (1).

Values for $\log_{10} x$ are called **logarithms to the base 10** or **common logarithms**. From the definition of $\log_{10} x$,

$$10^{\log_{10} x} = x \quad (x > 0); \tag{3}$$

that is, $\log_{10} x$ is the exponent that must be placed on 10 so that the resulting power is x. The problem with which we are concerned in this section is that of finding $\log_{10} x$ for each positive x. First, $\log_{10} x$ can easily be

Determination of $\log_{10} x$

determined for all values of x that are *integral* powers of 10:

$$\log_{10} 10 \quad = \log_{10} 10^1 = 1,$$

$$\log_{10} 100 \quad = \log_{10} 10^2 = 2,$$

etc., and similarly

$$\log_{10} 1 \quad = \log_{10} 10^0 \quad = 0,$$

$$\log_{10} 0.1 \quad = \log_{10} 10^{-1} = -1,$$

$$\log_{10} 0.01 \quad = \log_{10} 10^{-2} = -2,$$

$$\log_{10} 0.001 = \log_{10} 10^{-3} = -3.$$

A table of logarithms is used to find $\log_{10} x$ for $1 \leq x \leq 10$ (see page 365). Consider the excerpt from this table shown in Figure 6.4. Each number in the column headed by x represents the first two significant digits of x, while each number in the row opposite x contains the third significant digit of x. The digits located at the intersection of a row and a column form the logarithm of x. For

x	0	1	2	3	4	5	6	7	8	9
3.8	.5798	.5809	.5821	.5832	.5843	.5855	.5866	.5877	.5888	.5899
3.9	.5911	.5922	.5933	.5944	.5955	.5966	.5977	.5988	.5999	.6010
4.0	.6021	.6031	.6042	.6053	.6064	.6075	.6085	.6096	.6107	.6117
4.1	.6128	.6138	.6149	.6160	.6170	.6180	.6191	.6201	.6212	.6222
4.2	.6232	.6243	.6253	.6263	.6274	.6284	.6294	.6304	.6314	.6325
4.3	.6335	.6345	.6355	.6365	.6375	.6385	.6395	.6405	.6415.	.6425
4.4	.6435	.6444	.6454	.6464	.6474	.6484	.6493	.6503	.6513	.6522
4.5	.6532	.6542	.6551	.6561	.6571	.6580	.6590	.6599	.6609	.6618
4.6	.6628	.6637	.6646	.6656	.6665	.6675	.6684	.6693	.6702	.6712

Figure 6.4

example, to find $\log_{10} 4.25$, we look at the intersection of the row opposite 4.2 under x and the column headed by 5. Thus, we see that

$$\log_{10} 4.25 = 0.6284.$$

The equality sign is used here in an inexact sense; $\log_{10} 4.25 \approx 0.6284$ is more proper, because $\log_{10} 4.25$ is irrational and cannot be precisely represented by a rational number. We shall follow customary usage, however, writing $=$ instead of $\approx$, and leave the intent to the context.

Now suppose we wish to find $\log_{10} x$ for values of x outside the range of the table—that is, for $0 < x < 1$ or $x > 10$. This can be done quite readily by first representing the number in scientific notation—

Characteristic and mantissa

that is, as the product of a number between 1 and 10 and a power of 10—and applying Theorem 6.3-I. For example,

$$\log_{10} 42.5 = \log_{10} (4.25 \times 10^1) = \log_{10} 4.25 + \log_{10} 10^1$$
$$= 0.6284 + 1 = 1.6284,$$

$$\log_{10} 425 = \log_{10} (4.25 \times 10^2) = \log_{10} 4.25 + \log_{10} 10^2$$
$$= 0.6284 + 2 = 2.6284.$$

Observe that the decimal portion of the logarithm is always 0.6284, and the integral portion is just the exponent on 10 when the number is written in scientific notation.

This process can be reduced to a mechanical one by considering $\log_{10} x$ to consist of two parts, an integral part (called the **characteristic**) and a nonnegative decimal fraction part (called the **mantissa**). Thus the table of values for $\log_{10} x$ for $1 < x < 10$ can be looked upon as a table of mantissas for $\log_{10} x$ for all $x > 0$.

For example, to find $\log_{10} 43700$, we first write

$$\log_{10} 43700 = \log_{10} (4.37 \times 10^4).$$

Upon examining the table of logarithms, we find that $\log_{10} 4.37 = 0.6405$, so that

$$\log_{10} 43700 = 4.6405,$$

where we have prefixed the characteristic 4.

Now consider an example of the form $\log_{10} x$ for $0 < x < 1$. To find $\log_{10} 0.00402$, we first write

$$\log_{10} 0.00402 = \log_{10} (4.02 \times 10^{-3}).$$

Examining the table, we find that $\log_{10} 4.02$ is 0.6042. Upon adding 0.6042 to the characteristic -3, we obtain

$$\log_{10} 0.00402 = -2.3958,$$

where the decimal portion of the logarithm is no longer 0.6042 as it is in the case of all numbers $x > 1$ for which the first three significant digits of x are 402. To circumvent this situation, it is customary to write the logarithm in a form in which the decimal part is positive. In the foregoing example, we write

$$\log_{10} 0.00402 = 0.6042 - 3$$
$$= 0.6042 + (7 - 10)$$
$$= 7.6042 - 10,$$

and the fractional part is positive. The logarithm

$$6.6042 - 9$$

is an equally valid representation, but $7.6042 - 10$, in which a multiple of 10 is subtracted, is customary in most cases.

Determination of antilog$_{10}$ x
It is possible to reverse the process described in this section and, being given $\log_{10} x$, to find x. In this event, x is referred to as the **antilogarithm** (antilog$_{10}$) of $\log_{10} x$. For example, antilog$_{10}$ 1.6395 can be obtained by locating the mantissa, 0.6395, in the body of the log$_{10}$ tables and observing that the associated antilog$_{10}$ is 4.36. Thus

$$\text{antilog}_{10}\ 1.6395 = 4.36 \times 10^1 = 43.6.$$

If we seek the common logarithm of a number that is not an entry in the table (for example, $\log_{10} 3712$), or if we seek x when $\log_{10} x$ is not an entry in the table, it is customary to use a procedure called **linear interpolation**.

A table of common logarithms is a set of ordered pairs. For each number x there is an associated number $\log_{10} x$, and we have $(x, \log_{10} x)$ displayed in convenient tabular form. Because of space limitations, only three digits for the number x and four for the number $\log_{10} x$ appear in Table 1 (pages 365 and 366). By means of linear interpolation, however, the table can be used to find approximations to logarithms for four-digit numbers.

Let us examine geometrically the concepts involved. A portion of the graph of

$$y = \log_{10} x$$

is shown in Figure 6.5. The curvature is exaggerated to illustrate the principle involved. We propose to use the line segment joining the points

Linear interpolation
P_1 and P_2 as an approximation to the curve passing through the points. If a large graph of $y = \log_{10} x$ were available, the value of, say, $\log_{10} 4.257$ could be found by using the value of the ordinate (RT) to the curve for $x = 4.257$. Since there is no way to accomplish this with a table of values only, we shall instead use the value of the ordinate (RS) to the line segment as an approximation to the ordinate of the curve.

This can be accomplished directly from the set of numbers available in the table of logarithms. Consider Figure 6.6, where $P_2 P_3$

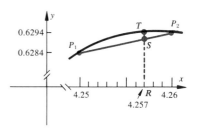

Figure 6.5

and $P_4 P_5$ are perpendicular to $P_1 P_3$. From geometry, we have $\Delta P_1 P_4 P_5 \sim$ $\Delta P_1 P_2 P_3$, where the lengths of the corresponding sides are proportional, and hence

$$\frac{x}{X} = \frac{y}{Y}. \tag{4}$$

If we know any three of these numbers, the fourth can be determined. For the purpose of interpolation, we assume all of our numbers now have four-digit numerals; that is, we consider 4.250 instead of 4.25, and 4.260 instead of 4.26. We note that the point corresponding to 4.257 is located just 7/10 of the distance between the points corresponding to 4.250 and 4.260, respectively, and the value $Y(0.0010)$ is just the difference between the logarithms 0.6284 and 0.6294. It follows from (4) that

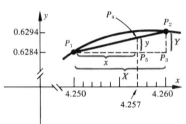

$$\frac{7}{10} = \frac{y}{0.0010},$$

from which

$$y = \frac{7}{10}(0.0010) = 0.0007.$$

Figure 6.6

We now add 0.0007 to 0.6284 and thus obtain a good approximation to the required logarithm. That is,

$$\log_{10} 4.257 = 0.6291.$$

An example in Exercise 6.3 shows a convenient arrangement for the calculations involved in the example presented here. The antilogarithm of a number can be found by a similar procedure. With practice, however, it is possible to interpolate mentally in both cases.

A table of logarithms to the base 10, together with the various parts of Theorem 6.3, facilitates certain computations involving products, quotients, powers, and roots, and also enables us to solve exponential equations in one variable in which the variable occurs in an exponent.

Before illustrating the use of Theorem 6.3, let us make two observations:

L-1   If $M = N$ ($M, N > 0$), then $\log_b M = \log_b N$.

L-2   If $\log_b M = \log_b N$, then $M = N$.

These assertions should seem plausible, because the values of the variables in logarithmic functions are in one-to-one correspondence.

Example. Compute $\dfrac{(8.21)^{1/2}(2.17)^{2/3}}{(3.14)^3}$.

handwritten: $\log \sqrt{x} = \frac{1}{2} \log x$
$\sqrt{9} = \frac{1}{2} \log 9 = \frac{1}{2} .954$
$= .477$
$= 3$

Solution.   Setting

$$N = \frac{(8.21)^{1/2}(2.17)^{2/3}}{(3.14)^3},$$

and using L-1, we obtain

$$\log_{10} N = \log_{10} \frac{(8.21)^{1/2}(2.17)^{2/3}}{(3.14)^3}$$

$$= \log_{10} (8.21)^{1/2} + \log_{10} (2.17)^{2/3} - \log_{10} (3.14)^3$$

$$= \frac{1}{2} \log_{10} 8.21 + \frac{2}{3} \log_{10} 2.17 - 3 \log_{10} 3.14.$$

The table provides values for the logarithms involved here, and the remainder of the computation to find $\log_{10} N$ is routine.

EXERCISE 6.3

Find each logarithm.

Examples.

a. $\log_{10} 16.8$

b. $\log_{10} 0.043$ *handwritten:* -2

Solutions.   Represent the number in scientific notation.

a. $\log_{10} (1.68 \times 10^1)$

b. $\log_{10} (4.3 \times 10^{-2})$

Determine the mantissa from the table.

handwritten: $.6335 - 2 (8-10)$
$.2335 + (-10)$
$8 - .6335$

0.2253

0.6335

Add the characteristic as determined by the exponent on the base 10.

1.2253   *handwritten:* 10^{+x} 10^{-x}

8.6335 − 10

1. $\log_{10} 6.73$

2. $\log_{10} 891$

3. $\log_{10} 0.813$

4. $\log_{10} 0.00214$

5. $\log_{10} (2.48 \times 10^2)$

6. $\log_{10} (5.39 \times 10^{-3})$

Find each antilogarithm.

Example.   antilog$_{10}$ 2.7364

Solution.   Locate the mantissa in the body of the table of mantissas and determine the associated antilog$_{10}$ (a number between 1 and 10); write the characteristic as an exponent on the base 10.

$$5.45 \times 10^2 = 545$$

7. antilog$_{10}$ 0.6128

8. antilog$_{10}$ 0.2504

9. antilog$_{10}$ 0.5647

10. antilog$_{10}$ 3.9258

11. antilog$_{10}$ (8.8075 − 10)   *handwritten:* $.06\sqrt{2}$

12. antilog$_{10}$ (3.9722 − 5)

Find each logarithm; interpolate as required.

Example. $\log_{10} 4.257$

Solution. Interpolate mentally or use the following procedure.

$$
\begin{array}{cc}
x & \log_{10} x
\end{array}
$$

$$
10\left\{7\left\{\begin{array}{c|c}
4.250 & 0.6284 \\
4.257 & ? \\
4.260 & 0.6294
\end{array}\right\}y\right\}0.0010
$$

Set up a proportion and solve for y.

$$
\frac{7}{10} = \frac{y}{0.0010}
$$

$$
y = 0.0007
$$

Add 0.0007, the value of y, to 0.6284.

$$
\log_{10} 4.257 = 0.6284 + 0.0007 = 0.6291
$$

13. $\log_{10} 4.213$ 14. $\log_{10} 8.184$ 15. $\log_{10} 1522$

16. $\log_{10} 203.4$ 17. $\log_{10} 0.5123$ 18. $\log_{10} 0.008351$

Find each antilogarithm, interpolating as required.

Example. $\text{antilog}_{10} 0.6446$

Solution. Interpolate mentally or use the following procedure.

$$
\begin{array}{cc}
x & \text{antilog}_{10} x
\end{array}
$$

$$
0.0010\left\{0.0002\left\{\begin{array}{c|c}
0.6444 & 4.410 \\
0.6446 & ? \\
0.6454 & 4.420
\end{array}\right\}y\right\}0.010
$$

Set up a proportion and solve for y.

$$
\frac{0.0002}{0.0010} = \frac{y}{0.010}
$$

$$
y = 0.002
$$

Add 0.002, the value of y, to 4.410.

$$
\text{antilog}_{10} 0.6446 = 4.410 + 0.002 = 4.412
$$

19. $\text{antilog}_{10} 0.5085$ 20. $\text{antilog}_{10} 0.8087$

21. $\text{antilog}_{10} 1.0220$ 22. $\text{antilog}_{10} 3.0759$

23. $\text{antilog}_{10} (8.7055 - 10)$ 24. $\text{antilog}_{10} (9.8742 - 10)$

Compute by means of logarithms.

Example. $\dfrac{(23.4)(0.681)}{4.13}$

Solution. Let $P = \dfrac{(23.4)(0.681)}{4.13}$.

Then

$$\log_{10} P = \log_{10} 23.4 + \log_{10} 0.681 - \log_{10} 4.13$$
$$= (1.3692) + (9.8331 - 10) - (0.6160)$$
$$= 0.5863,$$

and $P = \text{antilog}_{10}\ 0.5863 = 3.857$.

25. $(2.32)(1.73)$ 26. $\dfrac{3.15}{1.37}$ 27. $(2.3)^5$

28. $\sqrt[3]{8.12}$ 29. $(0.0128)^5$ 30. $\sqrt[5]{0.0471}$

31. $\dfrac{(0.421)^2(84.3)}{\sqrt{21.7}}$ 32. $\dfrac{(6.49)^2\sqrt[3]{8.21}}{17.9}$

Solve. Leave solutions in logarithmic form using the base 10.

Example. $3^{x-2} = 16$.

Solution. By Property L-1,

$$\log_{10} 3^{x-2} = \log_{10} 16.$$

By Theorem 6.3-V,

$$(x - 2)\log_{10} 3 = \log_{10} 16,$$

from which

$$x - 2 = \frac{\log_{10} 16}{\log_{10} 3},$$

$$x = \frac{\log_{10} 16}{\log_{10} 3} + 2.$$

The solution set is $\left\{\dfrac{\log_{10} 16}{\log_{10} 3} + 2\right\}$.

33. $3^{x+1} = 8$ 34. $2^{x-1} = 9$ 35. $3^{x+2} = 10$

36. $4^{x^2} = 15$ 37. $8^{x^2} = 21$ 38. $3^{-x} = 10$

Solve. Leave the results in the form of an equation equivalent to the given equation.

39. $y = x^n$, for n 40. $y = Cx^{-n}$, for n

41. $y = e^{kt}$, for t 42. $y = Ce^{-kt}$, for t

43. Find an approximate value for $2^{\sqrt{2}}$ to two decimal places.

44. Find an approximate value for 2^{π} to two decimal places.

45. The period T of a simple pendulum is given by the formula $T = 2\pi\sqrt{L/g}$, where T is in seconds, L is the length of the pendulum in feet, and $g \approx 32$ ft/sec². Find the period of a pendulum 1 foot long.

46. The area A of a triangle in terms of the lengths of its sides is given by the formula $A = \sqrt{s(s-a)(s-b)(s-c)}$, where a, b, and c are the lengths of the sides of the triangle and s equals one-half of the perimeter. Find the area of a triangle in which the lengths of the three sides are 2.314 inches, 4.217 inches, and 5.618 inches.

6.4 LOGARITHMS TO BASES OTHER THAN 10

The number e ($e \approx 2.718218$) mentioned in Section 6.3 is of great mathematical interest and importance. It is possible to determine $\log_e x$ provided we have a table of $\log_{10} x$. Indeed, given a table of $\log_b x$, we can always find $\log_a x$ for any $a > 0$, $a \neq 1$. We can do this as follows.

Since $x > 0$ and $a \neq 1$, we have

$$x = a^{\log_a x}. \tag{1}$$

By applying Property L-1 of Section 6.3, we can equate the logarithms to the base b ($b > 0$, $b \neq 1$) of each member of (1) to obtain

$$\log_b x = \log_b a^{\log_a x}.$$

By Theorem 6.3-V, this yields

$$\log_b x = \log_a x \cdot \log_b a,$$

or

$$\log_a x = \frac{\log_b x}{\log_b a}. \tag{2}$$

Conversion to base e

Equation (2) gives us a means of finding $\log_a x$ when we have a table of logarithms to the base b. In particular, if $a = e$ and $b = 10$, we have

$$\log_e x = \frac{\log_{10} x}{\log_{10} e}. \tag{3}$$

Since $\log_{10} e \approx 0.4343$, (3) can be written

$$\log_e x = \frac{\log_{10} x}{0.4343}, \tag{4}$$

or

$$\log_e x = 2.3026 \log_{10} x, \tag{5}$$

which gives us a direct means of approximating $\log_e x$ when we have a table of logarithms to the base 10.

A table of $\log_e x$ will be found on page 368. We cannot, however, do as we did with a table of $\log_{10} x$—that is, simply list mantissas for logarithms over a certain interval and then manipulate characteristics to take care of all other intervals. Our numeration system is based on 10 and not on e. With the help of logarithms, though, we can use formula (5), above, and the table of $\log_{10} x$ on pages 365 and 366 to find $\log_e x$.

Example.   Find $\log_e 278$.

Solution.   We shall do this in two ways.

1. Since

$$\log_e x = 2.3026 \log_{10} x,$$

we have

$$\log_e 278 = 2.3026 \log_{10} 278$$
$$= 2.3026 (2.4440)$$
$$= 5.63.$$

2. Alternatively, we observe that $278 = 2.8 \times 10^2$. Hence

$$\log_e 278 \approx \log_e (2.8 \times 10^2) = \log_e 2.8 + 2 \log_e 10$$
$$= 1.0296 + 2(2.3026)$$
$$= 1.0296 + 4.6052$$
$$= 5.63.$$

Example.   Find $\log_e 0.278$.

Solution.   We observe that $0.278 = 2.8 \times 10^{-1}$. Hence

$$\log_e 0.278 = \log_e (2.8 \times 10^{-1}) = \log_e 2.8 + \log_e 10^{-1}$$
$$= \log_e 2.8 - \log_e 10$$
$$= 1.0296 - 2.3026$$
$$= -1.2730.$$

As one would expect, the logarithm is negative.

The process used in the preceding example can be reversed to find antilog$_e$ x. If, however, a table for the exponential function $\{(x, y) \mid y = e^x\}$ is available (see Table II on page 367), the antilog$_e$ x can be read directly from this, since antilog$_e$ $x = e^x$.

Examples.

a. antilog$_e$ $3.2 = e^{3.2}$
$= 24.533.$

b. antilog$_e$ $(-3.2) = e^{-3.2}$
$= 0.0408.$

EXERCISE 6.4

Find each logarithm.

Example. $\log_3 7$

Solution.   Use logarithms to base 10 to evaluate.

$$\log_3 7 = \frac{\log_{10} 7}{\log_{10} 3} = \frac{0.8451}{0.4771} = 1.77$$

1. $\log_2 10$ 2. $\log_2 5$ 3. $\log_5 240$ 4. $\log_3 18$

5. $\log_7 8.1$ 6. $\log_5 60$ 7. $\log_{100} 38$ 8. $\log_{100} 240$

Find each logarithm directly from Table III on page 368.

9. $\log_e 3$ 10. $\log_e 8$ 11. $\log_e 17$ 12. $\log_e 98$

13. $\log_e 327$ 14. $\log_e 107$ 15. $\log_e 450$ 16. $\log_e 605$

Find each antilogarithm directly from Table II on page 367.

17. antilog$_e$ 0.50   18. antilog$_e$ 1.5   19. antilog$_e$ 3.4

20. antilog$_e$ 4.5   21. antilog$_e$ 0.231   22. antilog$_e$ 1.43

23. antilog$_e$ −0.15   24. antilog$_e$ −0.95   25. antilog$_e$ −2.5

26. antilog$_e$ −4.2   27. antilog$_e$ −0.255   28. antilog$_e$ −3.65

Solve without using the tables of logarithms.

29. If $\log_2 8 = 3$, find $\log_8 2$.

30. If $\log_4 16 = 2$, find $\log_{16} 4$.

31. If $\log_{10} 3 = 0.4771$, find $\log_3 10$.

32. If $\log_{10} e = 0.4343$, find $\log_e 10$.

33. If $\log_{10} 5 = 0.6990$, find $\log_5 100$.

34. If $\log_{10} 3 = 0.4771$, find $\log_3 100$.

35. Show that $(\log_{10} 4 - \log_{10} 2) \log_2 10 = 1$.

36. Show that $(2 \log_2 3)(\log_9 2 + \log_9 4) = 3$.

37. The amount of a certain radioactive element remaining at any time t is given by $y = y_0 e^{-0.4t}$, where t is measured in seconds and y_0 is the amount present initially. How much of the element would remain after three seconds if 40 grams were present initially?

38. The number of bacteria present in a culture is related to time by the formula $N = N_0 e^{0.04t}$, where N_0 is the amount of bacteria present at time $t = 0$, and t is time in hours. If 10,000 bacteria are present 10 hours after the beginning of the experiment, how many were present when $t = 0$?

7 CIRCULAR FUNCTIONS

7.1 THE CIRCULAR FUNCTIONS COSINE AND SINE

The graphs of some functions display interesting cyclical characteristics. Thus the domain of the function whose graph is shown in Figure 7.1 can clearly be divided into equal successive subintervals in such a way that over each subinterval the function takes on every value in its range; more

Notion of periodicity

importantly, the graph over each subinterval is a repetition of the graph over every other equal subinterval. Functions that display this property are said to be "periodic," and the length of each of the equal subintervals is called a **period** of the function. More formally, we have the following.

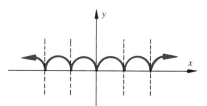

Figure 7.1

DEFINITION 7.1 *If f is a function with domain $D \subseteq R$, such that for some $a \in R$, $a \neq 0$, the values $x + a$ and $x - a$ are in D for each $x \in D$, and*

$$f(x + a) = f(x),$$

*then f is **periodic** with **period** a.*

If there is a smallest positive number a for which the function is periodic, then a is called the **fundamental period** of the function. Of course, if a function is periodic with period a, it is also periodic with period $2a$, $3a$, $-a$, and, in general, ka, $k \in J$, $k \neq 0$; but we are primarily concerned only with the fundamental period, and when we refer to the period of a function we shall ordinarily mean its fundamental period.

Circular and trigonometric functions

The most common periodic functions are the circular functions (defined using arc lengths on a circle) and trigonometric functions (defined using angles). In this chapter, we shall study circular functions.

155

Periodic functions can be defined using the unit circle with equation $x^2 + y^2 = 1$.

The unit circle Consider, intuitively, a point moving steadily in a counterclockwise direction around the circle. At any given time, the moving point occupies a position on the circle; the point, in turn, is associated with an ordered pair (x, y). If the distance along the circle from the point $(1, 0)$ to the point (x, y) is designated by s, then we can associate the real number s with the ordered pair (x, y) (Figure 7.2). We assume, of course, that there is such a thing as a "distance" measured counterclockwise along the circle from $(1, 0)$ to (x, y). The question of how to assign a measure of length to an arc of a curve is not a trivial one, but a discussion of the problems

Arc length on the unit circle involved is more properly a concern of the calculus, and we shall not go into the matter here. We shall assume that every arc of a circle has a length and that there is a one-to-one correspondence between the members of R_+ and the lengths of all arcs of the unit circle measured in a *counterclockwise* direction from the point $(1, 0)$ to points (x, y) on the circle. In particular, the distance once around the unit circle counterclockwise from $(1, 0)$ back to $(1, 0)$ is 2π, twice around is 4π, and so on. This latter statement results from the definition of π as the ratio of the circumference of a circle to its diameter.

Let us agree that values of $s < 0$ denote lengths of arc measured from $(1, 0)$ in a *clockwise* direction to points (x, y) on the circle (Figure 7.3). This extends the one-to-one correspondence of the set of lengths of arcs on the unit circle to the entire set R of real numbers.

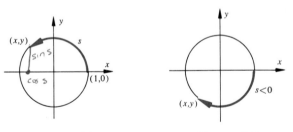

Figure   7.2   Figure   7.3

Especially useful are the associations of the members of R with the members of the set of all first components of the ordered pairs (x, y), and of the members of R with the members of the set of all second components of the ordered pairs. Before making this association, let us first rename these components.

DEFINITION 7.2 *If (x, y) is the point at arc length s from $(1, 0)$ on the unit circle $x^2 + y^2 = 1$, then x is the **cosine** of s, and y is the **sine** of s. We denote this by writing*

$$x = \cos s,$$

$$y = \sin s.$$

That is, we call the first component of the point (x, y) located at arc length s from $(1, 0)$ on the unit circle the cosine of s, and the second component the sine of s, and we denote these by cos s and sin s, respectively. Thus, $(x, y) = (\cos s, \sin s)$.

Having given meaning to the symbolism cos s and sin s, we can now define two new functions.

DEFINITION 7.3 *If $s \in R$, then*

$$\text{I} \quad \text{cosine} = \{(s, x) \mid x = \cos s\},$$

$$\text{II} \quad \text{sine} = \{(s, y) \mid y = \sin s\}.$$

As you can see, the domain of each of these functions is the set R. The range of the

Domain and range of cosine and sine

cosine function is the set of all first components of the ordered pairs corresponding to points on the unit circle, and hence is the set $\{x \mid |x| \le 1\}$. Similarly, the range of the sine function is $\{y \mid |y| \le 1\}$.

Since for $k \in J$,

$$\cos (s + 2k\pi) = \cos s,$$

circumference = 2π
$\cos(s + 2\pi) = \cos s$
$\sin(s + 2\pi) = \sin s$ (1)

and

know

$$\sin (s + 2k\pi) = \sin s,$$ (2)

the functions cosine and sine are periodic, with period 2π.

Fundamental period of cosine and sine

To see that 2π is in fact the *fundamental* period of the cosine function, suppose there were a value a, $0 < a < 2\pi$, such that $\cos (s + a) = \cos s$ for all $s \in R$. In particular, we would then have

$$\cos a = \cos (0 + a)$$

$$= \cos 0$$

$$= 1,$$

an impossibility for $0 < a < 2\pi$, since $(1, 0)$ is the *only* point on the unit circle with first coordinate 1.

The proof that 2π is also the fundamental period of the sine function is left as an exercise.

Values of cosine and sine for multiples of 2π

Some values of cos s and sin s corresponding to special values of s are readily available. Thus we have

$$(\cos 0, \sin 0) = (1, 0),$$

so that

$$\cos 0 = 1 \quad \text{and} \quad \sin 0 = 0.$$

circumf = 2π

Further,

$$(\cos 2\pi, \sin 2\pi) = (1, 0),$$

and in general, for any $k \in J$,

$$(\cos 2k\pi, \sin 2k\pi) = (1, 0),$$

so that

$$\cos 2k\pi = 1 \quad \text{and} \quad \sin 2k\pi = 0$$

for every $k \in J$.

Values for multiples of $\pi/2$

Figure 7.4 shows the coordinates of three other points on the unit circle with which we can associate specific values of s. Since the arc of a circle included in a quadrant is one-fourth of the circumference of the circle, that is, $\frac{1}{4} \cdot 2\pi$, we know immediately that

$$\cos \frac{\pi}{2} = 0, \qquad \sin \frac{\pi}{2} = 1, \qquad (3)$$

$$\cos \pi = -1, \qquad \sin \pi = 0, \qquad (4)$$

$$\cos \frac{3\pi}{2} = 0, \qquad \sin \frac{3\pi}{2} = -1. \qquad (5)$$

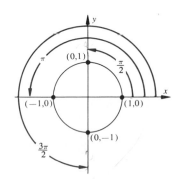

Figure 7.4

2π

$\frac{1}{4}$ "

Example. Find $\cos \frac{7\pi}{2}$.

Solution. Expressing $7\pi/2$ as the sum of an integral multiple of 2π and a number between 0 and 2π, we have $7\pi/2 = 3\pi/2 + 2\pi$. From (1), we obtain

$$\cos \left(\frac{3\pi}{2} + 2\pi \right) = \cos \frac{3\pi}{2},$$

and from (5),

$$\cos \frac{7\pi}{2} = \cos \frac{3\pi}{2} = 0.$$

Notice that in finding values for $\cos s$ and $\sin s$ we are finding *coordinates of points* on the unit circle.

We can find other special values for $(\cos s, \sin s)$ by using the geometry of the unit circle and the distance formula,

$$d^2 = (x_2 - x_1)^2 + (y_2 - y_1)^2.$$

First consider $s = \pi/4$. Figure 7.5 shows the unit circle and the designated value for s. Since (x, y) bisects the arc from $(1, 0)$ to $(0, 1)$, it follows from geometric considerations that $x = y$. Because $x^2 + y^2 = 1$, we have

$$x^2 + x^2 = 1,$$

$$2x^2 = 1,$$

$$x^2 = \frac{1}{2},$$

and

$$x = \frac{1}{\sqrt{2}} \quad \text{or} \quad x = -\frac{1}{\sqrt{2}}.$$

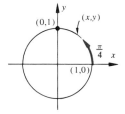

Figure 7.5

Now, both x and y are positive in the first quadrant, so the desired value for x is $1/\sqrt{2}$. Since $x = y$, y is also equal to $1/\sqrt{2}$, and hence we have

$$\cos \frac{\pi}{4} = \frac{1}{\sqrt{2}} \quad \text{and} \quad \sin \frac{\pi}{4} = \frac{1}{\sqrt{2}}.$$

Values for $\cos s$ and $\sin s$ for s equal to $3\pi/4$, $5\pi/4$, and $7\pi/4$ can be found using geometric symmetry. These are listed in Table 7.1 on page 160.

Next, consider $s = \pi/6$, as pictured in Figure 7.6. If the ordered pair corresponding to $s = \pi/6$ is given by (x, y), then the ordered pair corresponding to $s = -\pi/6$ is given by $(x, -y)$. Now the arc from $(x, -y)$ to (x, y) is of length $\pi/6 + \pi/6 = \pi/3$, and so is the arc from (x, y) to $(0, 1)$. Because, in a circle, equal arcs subtend equal chords, the distance from $(0, 1)$ to (x, y) is the same as the distance from (x, y) to $(x, -y)$. Using the distance formula, we therefore have

$$(x - 0)^2 + (y - 1)^2 = (x - x)^2 + (-y - y)^2,$$

or

$$x^2 + y^2 - 2y + 1 = 4y^2.$$

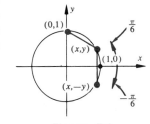

Figure 7.6

Since $x^2 + y^2 = 1$, we can substitute 1 for $x^2 + y^2$ in this equation and obtain

$$1 - 2y + 1 = 4y^2,$$

$$4y^2 + 2y - 2 = 0,$$

$$2(2y - 1)(y + 1) = 0,$$

so that

$$y = \frac{1}{2} \quad \text{or} \quad y = -1.$$

Know

TABLE 7.1

s	$\cos s$	$\sin s$	s	$\cos s$	$\sin s$
0	1	0	π	-1	0
$\dfrac{\pi}{6}$	$\dfrac{\sqrt{3}}{2}$	$\dfrac{1}{2}$	$\dfrac{7\pi}{6}$	$-\dfrac{\sqrt{3}}{2}$	$-\dfrac{1}{2}$
$\dfrac{\pi}{4}$	$\dfrac{1}{\sqrt{2}}$	$\dfrac{1}{\sqrt{2}}$	$\dfrac{5\pi}{4}$	$-\dfrac{1}{\sqrt{2}}$	$-\dfrac{1}{\sqrt{2}}$
$\dfrac{\pi}{3}$	$\dfrac{1}{2}$	$\dfrac{\sqrt{3}}{2}$	$\dfrac{4\pi}{3}$	$-\dfrac{1}{2}$	$-\dfrac{\sqrt{3}}{2}$
$\dfrac{\pi}{2}$	0	1	$\dfrac{3\pi}{2}$	0	-1
$\dfrac{2\pi}{3}$	$-\dfrac{1}{2}$	$\dfrac{\sqrt{3}}{2}$	$\dfrac{5\pi}{3}$	$\dfrac{1}{2}$	$-\dfrac{\sqrt{3}}{2}$
$\dfrac{3\pi}{4}$	$-\dfrac{1}{\sqrt{2}}$	$\dfrac{1}{\sqrt{2}}$	$\dfrac{7\pi}{4}$	$\dfrac{1}{\sqrt{2}}$	$-\dfrac{1}{\sqrt{2}}$
$\dfrac{5\pi}{6}$	$-\dfrac{\sqrt{3}}{2}$	$\dfrac{1}{2}$	$\dfrac{11\pi}{6}$	$\dfrac{\sqrt{3}}{2}$	$-\dfrac{1}{2}$
π	-1	0	2π	1	0

Because (x, y) is in the first quadrant, we must select the value $1/2$ as the y-coordinate. Next, we use $x^2 + y^2 = 1$ to find a value for x. Thus

$$x^2 + \left(\frac{1}{2}\right)^2 = 1,$$

from which

$$x = \pm\frac{\sqrt{3}}{2}.$$

Because (x, y) is in the first quadrant, we have $x = \sqrt{3}/2$, and it follows that

$$\cos\frac{\pi}{6} = \frac{\sqrt{3}}{2} \quad \text{and} \quad \sin\frac{\pi}{6} = \frac{1}{2}. \tag{6}$$

With this information, values for $\cos s$ and $\sin s$ for s equal to $5\pi/6$, $7\pi/6$, and

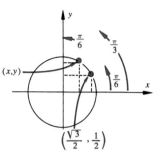

$11\pi/6$ can be obtained using geometric symmetry. (These values are also listed in Table 7.1.) From (6), we can quickly find values for $\cos(\pi/3)$ and $\sin(\pi/3)$ by symmetry. Figure 7.7 shows the point (x, y) associated with s equal to $\pi/3$; clearly, the abscissa of (x, y) is the ordinate of $(\sqrt{3}/2, 1/2)$, and the ordinate of (x, y) is the abscissa of $(\sqrt{3}/2, 1/2)$. Hence

$$\cos\frac{\pi}{3} = \frac{1}{2} \quad \text{and} \quad \sin\frac{\pi}{3} = \frac{\sqrt{3}}{2}.$$

Figure 7.7

Again, values for $\cos s$ and $\sin s$ for s equal to $2\pi/3$, $4\pi/3$, and $5\pi/3$ can be obtained from geometric considerations and are listed in Table 7.1.

Signs of co-sine and sine   Table 7.2 summarizes in a convenient and useful form the sign associated with $x = \cos s$ and $y = \sin s$ in each quadrant.

TABLE 7.2

Quadrant II	↑	Quadrant I
x or $\cos s < 0$		x or $\cos s > 0$
y or $\sin s > 0$		y or $\sin s > 0$
Quadrant III		Quadrant IV
x or $\cos s < 0$		x or $\cos s > 0$
y or $\sin s < 0$		y or $\sin s < 0$

Table 7.1, in conjunction with Equations (1) and (2), can be used to find values of $\cos s$ and $\sin s$ for values of s differing by $2k\pi$, $k \in J$, from those listed in the table.

Example.   Find $\cos\dfrac{9\pi}{2}$ and $\sin\dfrac{9\pi}{2}$.

Solution.   We first observe that $9\pi/2 = 4\pi + \pi/2$. Then

$$\cos\frac{9\pi}{2} = \cos\left(4\pi + \frac{\pi}{2}\right) = \cos\frac{\pi}{2} = 0,$$

and

$$\sin\frac{9\pi}{2} = \sin\left(4\pi + \frac{\pi}{2}\right) = \sin\frac{\pi}{2} = 1.$$

Values of cosine and sine in terms of each other   By Definition 7.2, $x = \cos s$ and $y = \sin s$ are subject to the condition that $x^2 + y^2 = 1$. Hence we have the following basic identity relating $\cos s$ and $\sin s$.

THEOREM 7.1   *For every $s \in R$,*

$$\cos^2 s + \sin^2 s = 1. \tag{7}$$

Note that for convenience we write $\cos^2 s$ for $(\cos s)^2$ and $\sin^2 s$ for $(\sin s)^2$. Now Theorem 7.1 can be used to write

$$\sin s = \begin{cases} \sqrt{1 - \cos^2 s} & \text{in Quadrants I and II,} \quad (8a) \\ -\sqrt{1 - \cos^2 s} & \text{in Quadrants III and IV,} \quad (8b) \end{cases}$$

and

$$\cos s = \begin{cases} \sqrt{1 - \sin^2 s} & \text{in Quadrants I and IV,} \quad (9a) \\ -\sqrt{1 - \sin^2 s} & \text{in Quadrants II and III.} \quad (9b) \end{cases}$$

Therefore, if either $\sin s$ or $\cos s$ is known, and we can determine the quadrant in which the terminal point of the arc of length s lies, then we can find the value for the other.

Example. If $\cos s = -3/5$ and $\pi < s < 3\pi/2$, find $\sin s$.

Solution. Using (8b), we have

$$\sin s = -\sqrt{1 - \cos^2 s} = -\sqrt{1 - \left(\frac{3}{5}\right)^2} = -\sqrt{\frac{16}{25}} = -\frac{4}{5}.$$

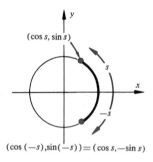

(cos s, sin s)

(cos (−s), sin(−s)) = (cos s, −sin s)

Figure 7.8

Values of cos (−s) and sin (−s)

Because the circle is symmetric to the horizontal axis, it follows that if $(\cos s, \sin s) = (x, y)$, then $(\cos (-s), \sin (-s)) = (x, -y)$.

We thus have the following theorem, which is illustrated in Figure 7.8 for the case $0 < s < \pi/2$.

THEOREM 7.2 *For every* $s \in R$,

$$\text{I} \quad \cos (-s) = \cos s, \qquad (10)$$

$$\text{II} \quad \sin (-s) = -\sin s. \qquad (11)$$

Any function f with domain $D \subseteq R$, such that

$$f(-s) = f(s)$$

for every $s \in D$, is called an **even function**. On the other hand, if

$$f(-s) = -f(s)$$

for every $s \in D$, then f is called an **odd function**. Hence, cosine is an even function and sine is an odd function.

EXERCISE 7.1

In Problems 1–16, use relationships (1) and (2), page 157, Theorem 7.2, and Table 7.1, as appropriate, to find each given function value.

$\tan s = \dfrac{\sin s}{\cos s}$

I	II	III	IV
all	sin	tan	cos

Pos

Example. $\sin\dfrac{11\pi}{4}$

Solution. $\sin\left(2\pi+\dfrac{3\pi}{4}\right)=\sin\dfrac{3\pi}{4}=\dfrac{1}{\sqrt{2}}$

1. $\cos\dfrac{9\pi}{4}$ 2. $\sin\dfrac{9\pi}{4}$ 3. $\cos\left(-\dfrac{8\pi}{3}\right)$ 4. $\sin\left(-\dfrac{5\pi}{3}\right)$

5. $\sin\dfrac{15\pi}{6}$ 6. $\cos\dfrac{15\pi}{6}$ 7. $\sin\left(-\dfrac{11\pi}{2}\right)$ 8. $\cos\left(-\dfrac{11\pi}{2}\right)$

9. $\sin 8\pi$ 10. $\cos 12\pi$ 11. $\sin(-5\pi)$ 12. $\cos(-7\pi)$

13. $\cos\left(-\dfrac{7\pi}{4}\right)$ 14. $\sin\left(-\dfrac{9\pi}{4}\right)$ 15. $\cos\left(\pi-\dfrac{5\pi}{3}\right)$ 16. $\sin\left(2\pi-\dfrac{7\pi}{6}\right)$

17. If $\sin s=\dfrac{1}{3}$ and $\cos s>0$, find $\cos s$. $\sqrt{1-\left(\frac{1}{3}\right)^2}\;=\;1-\left(\frac{1}{9}\right)\sqrt{\frac{8}{9}}$

18. If $\sin s=-\dfrac{2}{3}$ and $\cos s<0$, find $\cos s$.

19. If $\cos s=\dfrac{5}{13}$ and $\sin s<\cos s$, find $\sin s$.

20. If $\cos s=\dfrac{12}{13}$ and $\sin s>0$, find $\sin s$.

21. If $\cos s=-\dfrac{1}{4}$ and $\sin s>0$, find $\sin s$. $\sqrt{1-\left(\frac{1}{4}\right)^2}\;=\;1-\frac{1}{16}\;\frac{15}{16}$

22. If $\cos s=-\dfrac{1}{4}$ and $\sin s<0$, find $\sin s$.

In Problems 23–28, assume $0\le s<2\pi$ and give the value of s for which both conditions are true. Use Table 7.1 as necessary.

23. $\sin s=1/\sqrt{2}$ and $\cos s>0$ 24. $\cos s=1/\sqrt{2}$ and $\sin s<0$

25. $\cos s=-\sqrt{3}/2$ and $\sin s>0$ 26. $\sin s=-1/2$ and $\cos s<0$

27. $\sin s=\sqrt{3}/2$ and $\cos s<0$ 28. $\cos s=-1/\sqrt{2}$ and $\sin s>0$

29. Over what subinterval of $0\le s\le\pi$ is it true that $\sin s>\cos s$? *Hint:* Use Table 7.1.

30. Over what subinterval of $0\le s\le\pi/2$ is it true that $\sin s<\cos s$?

In Problems 31–34, use the symmetry of the circle and other geometric considerations to make a conjecture about the relationship between the given pairs for $0<s<\pi/2$.

31. $\cos(\pi-s)$ and $\cos s$ 32. $\sin(\pi+s)$ and $\sin s$

33. $\sin\left(\dfrac{\pi}{2}+s\right)$ and $\cos s$ 34. $\cos\left(\dfrac{3\pi}{2}-s\right)$ and $\sin s$

35. On a pair of Cartesian axes, let the horizontal axis be the s-axis and the vertical axis be the x-axis. Use values from Table 7.1 to locate corresponding points of the cosine function for the interval $0 \le s \le 2\pi$, and connect these points with a smooth curve going from left to right.

36. In Problem 35, let the vertical axis be the y-axis, and similarly graph the sine function over the interval $0 \le s \le 2\pi$.

37. Prove that the sine function is periodic, with fundamental period 2π.

38. Prove that $f = \{(s, y) \mid y = \cos s + \sin s\}$ is periodic with period 2π.

7.2 SUM, DIFFERENCE, AND REDUCTION FORMULAS FOR THE COSINE FUNCTION

Figure 7.9 shows selected points on the unit circle together with their coordinates. Since the arc length from $(1, 0)$ to $(\cos (s_1 + s_2), \sin (s_1 + s_2))$ is $s_1 + s_2$, and from $(\cos s_1, -\sin s_1)$ to $(\cos s_2, \sin s_2)$ the arc length is also $s_1 + s_2$, the respective chords have equal lengths. Using the distance formula to express this fact, and substituting from Theorem 7.2, we have

> **Values of $\cos (s_1+s_2)$ and $\cos (s_1-s_2)$**

$$\sqrt{[\cos (s_1 + s_2) - 1]^2 + [\sin (s_1 + s_2) - 0]^2}$$
$$= \sqrt{(\cos s_2 - \cos s_1)^2 + [\sin s_2 - (-\sin s_1)]^2},$$

or, squaring both members,

$$[\cos (s_1 + s_2) - 1]^2 + \sin^2 (s_1 + s_2)$$
$$= (\cos s_2 - \cos s_1)^2 + (\sin s_2 + \sin s_1)^2.$$

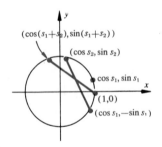

Figure 7.9

If we now perform the operations indicated, we have

$$\cos^2 (s_1 + s_2) - 2 \cos (s_1 + s_2) + 1 + \sin^2 (s_1 + s_2)$$
$$= \cos^2 s_2 - 2 \cos s_1 \cos s_2 + \cos^2 s_1 + \sin^2 s_2 + 2 \sin s_1 \sin s_2 + \sin^2 s_1.$$

Regrouping terms, we obtain

$$[\cos^2 (s_1 + s_2) + \sin^2 (s_1 + s_2)] - 2 \cos (s_1 + s_2) + 1$$
$$= (\cos^2 s_2 + \sin^2 s_2) + (\cos^2 s_1 + \sin^2 s_1) \mid 2 \cos s_1 \cos s_2 + 2 \sin s_1 \sin s_2,$$

and since $\cos^2 s + \sin^2 s = 1$, it follows that

$$1 - 2 \cos (s_1 + s_2) + 1 = 1 + 1 - 2 \cos s_1 \cos s_2 + 2 \sin s_1 \sin s_2.$$

This simplifies to the following result.

THEOREM 7.3 *For each $s_1, s_2 \in R$,*

$$\cos (s_1 + s_2) = \cos s_1 \cos s_2 - \sin s_1 \sin s_2. \tag{1}$$

By replacing s_2 with $-s_2$ in the sum formula (1), and using formulas (6) and (7) in Theorem 7.2, we obtain the following companion result.

THEOREM 7.4   *For each* $s_1, s_2 \in R$,   *cosine*

$$\cos (s_1 - s_2) = \cos s_1 \cos s_2 + \sin s_1 \sin s_2. \qquad (2)$$

addition

Reduction formulas for cosine

The extremely important relationships (1) and (2) are called, respectively, the **sum formula** and the **difference formula** for the cosine function. These are used in proving the following results.

THEOREM 7.5   *For each* $s \in R$,

I $\cos (\pi - s) = -\cos s,$
    Cos s, cosc + Sos, Sins~

II $\cos (\pi + s) = -\cos s,$
     Cos s, Cos s₂ - Sins; Sins₂

III $\cos \left(\dfrac{\pi}{2} - s\right) = \sin s,$

IV $\cos \left(\dfrac{\pi}{2} + s\right) = -\sin s,$

V $\cos \left(\dfrac{3\pi}{2} - s\right) = -\sin s,$

VI $\cos \left(\dfrac{3\pi}{2} + s\right) = \sin s,$

VII $\cos (2\pi - s) = \cos s.$

We shall prove only Part I here and leave the remainder as exercises.

Proof of 7.5-I. In relationship (2), replace s_1 with π and s_2 with s to obtain

$$\cos (\pi - s) = \cos \pi \cos s + \sin \pi \sin s.$$

From Table 7.1, $\cos \pi = -1$ and $\sin \pi = 0$, so that this equation becomes

$$\cos (\pi - s) = (-1)(\cos s) + 0 \sin s = -\cos s,$$

and the proof is complete.

The formulas in Theorem 7.5 are called **reduction formulas** for the cosine function. Geometric interpretations of I, II, and VII are shown in Figure 7.10. In each case, it is apparent that if s is the length of an arc terminating in Quadrants II, III, or IV, then the arc can be visualized either as the sum or as the difference of two arcs, one of measure $n\pi$, $n \in J$, and the other measuring $\bar{s}$, where $0 < \bar{s} < \pi/2$. We refer to the arc measuring $\bar{s}$ as the **reference arc** for s. For example, the reference arc of an arc measuring $5\pi/4$ is one measuring $\pi/4$, because $5\pi/4 = \pi + \pi/4$, while the reference arc for an arc measuring $-8\pi/3$ measures $\pi/3$ because $-8\pi/3 = -3\pi + \pi/3$.

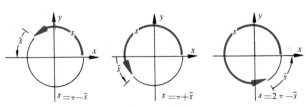

Figure   7.10

In Section 7.1, we found function values (elements in the range) for the cosine function for selected elements in the domain by using the distance formula and certain geometric considerations. It is necessary, however, that we be able to find—or, more precisely, to approximate—a function value for any given real number. To do this, we use tables that provide such approximations to the desired number of decimal places. The means by which the tables are constructed will not concern us at present.

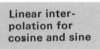

Use of tables for cosine

Because the circular functions are periodic and reduction formulas are available, we need tables only over the interval $0 \leq s \leq \pi/2$. Table V in the Appendix gives approximate function values at intervals of 0.01 for the cosine function and other circular functions to be discussed in the following sections.

Examples.

a. $\cos 0.73 \approx 0.7452$ b. $\cos 1.29 \approx 0.2771$

Notice that in Table V the letter x is used to represent an element in the domain. This is customary in many tables. In this usage, of course, x can be thought of as representing an arc length along the unit circle, just as s did.*

Use of reduction formulas

An appropriate reduction formula enables us to approximate function values of x outside the interval $0 \leq x \leq \pi/2$. In such cases, note that $\pi/2 \approx 1.57$, $\pi \approx 3.14$, $3\pi/2 \approx 4.71$, and $2\pi \approx 6.28$. Also note that $\bar{x}$ is used in the same way as $\bar{s}$.

Example.   Find $\cos 3.03$.

Solution.   Since $1.57 < 3.03 < 3.14$, we can use the reduction formula

$$\cos x = -\cos (\pi - x).$$

Thus,

$$\cos 3.03 \approx -\cos (3.14 - 3.03)$$

$$\approx -\cos 0.11$$

$$\approx -0.9940.$$

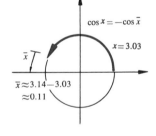

A sketch of the unit circle, including the reference arc, helps interpret the effect of the reduction formula.

Linear interpolation for cosine and sine

To find approximations to function values for numbers with four-digit numerals, we can use the method of linear interpolation explained in Section 6.3 for tables of logarithms.

Table V can also be used to find elements in the domain of the cosine function for specified elements in the range. For the

---

* In fact, because x is ordinarily the variable used to represent an element in the domain of a function, we shall hereafter use x for this purpose. Thus we shall hereafter be using x where we heretofore used s.

time being, we shall restrict our attention to finding such elements only in the interval $\{x \mid 0 \le x \le \pi/2\}$.

Example.   Approximate the member of $\{x \mid 0 < x < 1.57\}$ for which $\cos x = 0.9664$.

Solution.   From Table V, we see that x is approximately equal to 0.26.

EXERCISE   7.2

Use Table V in the Appendix to find approximations for each of the following. Use linear interpolation as required.

1. cos 0.59   2. cos 0.47   3. cos 1.32

4. cos 1.01   5. cos 0.21   6. cos 0.86

7. cos 0.39   8. cos 1.43   9. cos 0.235

10. cos 1.216   11. cos 1.042   12. cos 0.695

13. $\cos \dfrac{2\pi}{5}$ *Hint:* First express the rational multiple of π in decimal form ($\pi \approx 3.142$) and then use Table V.

14. $\cos \dfrac{\pi}{9}$ 15. $\cos \dfrac{2\pi}{7}$ 16. $\cos \dfrac{\pi}{5}$

Use the fact that the cosine function is periodic, along with the reduction formulas, to find an approximate value for each of the following.

Example.   cos 2

Solution.   Since $\pi \approx 3.14$ and $\pi/2 \approx 1.57$, an arc of length 2 terminates in the second quadrant. We have $\pi - 2 \approx 1.14$, so that $\bar{x} \approx 1.14$ is the length of the reference arc. Using Theorem 7.5-I, then, we obtain

$$\cos 2 = -\cos(\pi - 2)$$

$$\approx -\cos(3.14 - 2)$$

$$= -\cos 1.14$$

$$\approx -0.4176,$$

which is the function value we seek.

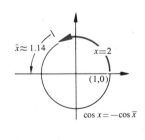

$\cos x = -\cos \bar{x}$

17. cos 2.01   18. cos 4.52   19. cos 5.21

20. cos 2.24   21. cos 1.93   22. cos 5.83

23. cos (−0.47)   24. cos (−1.82)   25. cos 8.41

26. cos 10.32   27. cos (−9.52)   28. cos (−12.61)

Approximate the element x in the domain of the function, $0 \le x \le 1.57$, for the specified element in the range.

29. $\cos x = 0.9664$ 30. $\cos x = 0.2579$ 31. $\cos x = 0.7038$

32. $\cos x = 0.1304$ 33. $\cos x = 0.8600$ 34. $\cos x = 0.2921$

35. Prove Theorem 7.4.

Prove each of the following parts of Theorem 7.5.

36. Part II   37. Part III   38. Part IV

39. Part V   40. Part VI   41. Part VII

42. Prove that $\cos (x - \pi/2) = \sin x$.

43. Prove that $\cos (x - \pi) = - \cos x$.

44. Prove that $\cos (x - 3\pi/2) = - \sin x$.

45. Prove that $\sin (\pi/2 - x) = \cos x$. *Hint:* Substitute $\pi/2 - x$ for s on page 165, Part III, Theorem 7.5.

7.3 SUM, DIFFERENCE, AND REDUCTION FORMULAS FOR THE SINE FUNCTION

From Part III, Theorem 7.5, we have

$$\cos \left(\frac{\pi}{2} - s \right) = \sin s.$$

If now we set $s = x_1 + x_2$, then we obtain

$$\cos \left[\frac{\pi}{2} - (x_1 + x_2) \right] = \sin (x_1 + x_2).$$

This can be rewritten as

$$\cos \left[\left(\frac{\pi}{2} - x_1 \right) - x_2 \right] = \sin (x_1 + x_2),$$

and if the left-hand member is expanded by means of Theorem 7.4, we find that

$$\cos \left(\frac{\pi}{2} - x_1 \right) \cos x_2 + \sin \left(\frac{\pi}{2} - x_1 \right) \sin x_2 = \sin (x_1 + x_2).$$

Values of $\sin (x_1+x_2)$ **and** $\sin (x_1-x_2)$ | By Part III, Theorem 7.5, we have $\cos (\pi/2 - x_1) = \sin x_1$, and from Problem 45, above, we have $\sin (\pi/2 - x_1) = \cos x_1$, so that

$$\cos \left(\frac{\pi}{2} - x_1 \right) \cos x_2 + \sin \left(\frac{\pi}{2} - x_1 \right) \sin x_2 = \sin x_1 \cos x_2 + \cos x_1 \sin x_2,$$

which establishes the following result.

THEOREM 7.6 *If $x_1, x_2 \in R$, then*

$$\sin(x_1 + x_2) = \sin x_1 \cos x_2 + \cos x_1 \sin x_2. \tag{1}$$

By replacing x_2 with $-x_2$ in Theorem 7.6, we obtain a formula for $\sin(x_1 - x_2)$.

THEOREM 7.7 *If $x_1, x_2 \in R$, then*

$$\sin(x_1 - x_2) = \sin x_1 \cos x_2 - \cos x_1 \sin x_2.$$

addition for sine

These relationships are called, respectively, the **sum formula** and the **difference**

Reduction formulas for sine **formula** for the sine function, and can be used in the same way as the sum and difference formulas for the cosine function to establish the following reduction formulas.

THEOREM 7.8 *For each $x \in R$,*

I $\sin(\pi - x) = \sin x$,

V $\sin\left(\dfrac{3\pi}{2} - x\right) = -\cos x$,

II $\sin(\pi + x) = -\sin x$,

VI $\sin\left(\dfrac{3\pi}{2} + x\right) = -\cos x$,

III $\sin\left(\dfrac{\pi}{2} - x\right) = \cos x$,

VII $\sin(2\pi - x) = -\sin x$.

IV $\sin\left(\dfrac{\pi}{2} + x\right) = \cos x$,

Use of tables for sine   Table V in the Appendix also gives approximate function values for the sine function in the interval $0 \le x \le \pi/2$. An appropriate reduction formula can be used to approximate function values of x outside this interval.

Example.   Find $\sin 4.24$.

Solution.   Since we have $\pi \approx 3.14$ and $3\pi/2 \approx 4.71$, an arc of length 4.24 terminates in the third quadrant. The length of the reference arc $\bar{x} \approx 4.24 - 3.14 \approx 1.10$. Using Part II of Theorem 7.8, we obtain

$$\sin 4.24 \approx \sin(3.14 + 1.10)$$

$$= -\sin 1.10$$

$$\approx -0.8912,$$

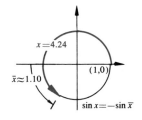

which is the function value we seek.

EXERCISE 7.3

Use Table V in the Appendix to find approximations for each of the following. Use linear interpolation as required.

1. sin 0.31	2. sin 1.36	3. sin 1.21
4. sin 0.72	5. sin 1.01	6. sin 0.29
7. sin 0.86	8. sin 1.50	9. sin 1.362
10. sin 1.042	11. sin 0.754	12. sin 0.479

13. $\sin \dfrac{3\pi}{7}$ (Use $\pi \approx 3.142$.)

14. $\sin \dfrac{\pi}{7}$ 15. $\sin \dfrac{3\pi}{5}$ 16. $\sin \dfrac{2\pi}{9}$

Use the fact that the sine function is periodic, along with the reduction formulas, to find an approximate value for each of the following.

17. sin 2.21	18. sin 3.68	19. sin 5.47
20. sin 2.35	21. sin 1.87	22. sin 5.72
23. sin (−0.31)	24. sin (−1.92)	25. sin 7.61
26. sin 12.24	27. sin (−9.61)	28. sin (−15.32)

Approximate the element x $(0 \le x \le 1.57)$ in the domain of the function for the specified element in the range.

29. sin $x = 0.9975$	30. sin $x = 0.5396$	31. sin $x = 0.8573$
32. sin $x = 0.2280$	33. sin $x = 0.4000$	34. sin $x = 0.9230$

35. Prove Theorem 7.7.

Prove each of the following parts of Theorem 7.8.

36. Part I	37. Part II	38. Part III	39. Part IV
40. Part V	41. Part VI	42. Part VII	

43. Prove that $\sin (x - \pi) = -\sin x$.

44. Prove that $\sin (x - \pi/2) = -\cos x$.

45. Prove that $\cos (\pi/2 - x) = \sin (\pi - x)$.

46. Prove that $\cos (\pi + x) = -\sin (\pi/2 + x)$.

47. Prove that $\cos (3\pi/2 + x) = -\sin (\pi + x)$.

48. Prove that $\cos (\pi - x) = -\sin (\pi/2 + x)$.

7.4 GRAPHS OF SINE AND COSINE FUNCTIONS

We have been using the variables s and x as real numbers associated with arc length on a unit circle. Figure 7.11 illustrates how such arc lengths, in turn, can be associated with line segments on the x-axis of a rectangular coordinate system. Here x is the measure of the line segment on the x-axis that can be thought of as obtained by "unwinding" the arc that has the same measure.

"Unwinding" arcs from the unit circle

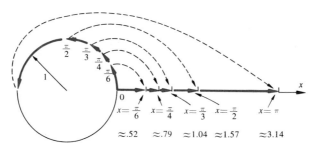

Figure 7.11

The periodic nature of the cosine and sine functions can be seen clearly by graphing these functions on a rectangular coordinate system in R^2, where values for s or x (elements in the domain) are associated with points on the horizontal axis.

Although we have Table V available to find values for $\cos x$ and $\sin x$ for many values of x, the special values for 0, $\pi/6$, $\pi/4$, etc., in Table 7.1, page 160, will suffice for our purposes. Because the graphs of the cosine function and the sine function are called *sine waves*, we shall look first at the graph

Graph of sine

of $\{(x, f(x)) \mid f(x) = \sin x\}$, or in more convenient notation, $\{(x, y) \mid y = \sin x\}$. Graphing some familiar ordered pairs in this function over the interval $0 \le x \le 2\pi$, we have Figure 7.12. Assuming that sine

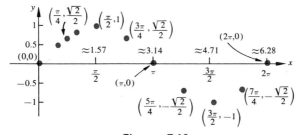

Figure 7.12

is a continuous function, that is, that its graph contains no breaks or gaps (you will prove in calculus that this is true), and that it increases as x increases from 0 to $\pi/2$, then decreases from $\pi/2$ to π, etc., we can join these points with a smooth

Sine starts at 0°
0.1
Cosine "

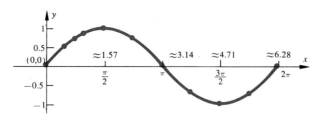

Figure 7.13

curve to produce Figure 7.13. Then, because $\sin (x + 2\pi) = \sin x$, this pattern repeats itself over intervals of length 2π in both directions. Thus we have the pattern shown in Figure 7.14 for the graph of the sine function. Units on the horizontal axis representing integers (short marks) and integral multiples of $\pi/2$ (long marks) are shown.

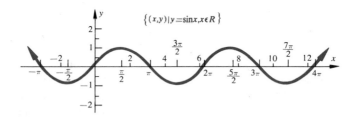

Figure 7.14

The range of the function, $\{y \mid -1 \leq y \leq 1\}$, is clearly evident from the graph. Furthermore, the zeros of the function, πn, where $n = 0, \pm 1,$

Range and zeros of sine

$\pm 2, \pm 3, \cdots$, namely the values of x associated with the points at which the curve crosses the x-axis, are also evident from the graph.

Graphs with this characteristic form are called **sine waves** (as remarked earlier) or **sinusoids**. The portion of the graph over any fundamental period of the function is called a **cycle** of the sine wave. Half the difference of the maximum and minimum ordinates on such a curve is called the **amplitude** of the wave. Thus, for the graph of $y = \sin x$, the amplitude of the wave is $\frac{1}{2}[1 - (-1)] = 1$.

The graph of the cosine function can be obtained in the same manner as the graph of the sine function. From Table 7.1 on page 160, or

Graph of cosine from memory, we obtain the coordinates of several points on the graph, as shown in Figure 7.15. By connecting these points with a smooth curve, we obtain the graph of $\{(x, y) \mid y = \cos x\}$ over one period of the function. Duplicating this pattern over several more periods, we have a representative portion of the entire graph of the cosine function (Figure 7.16).

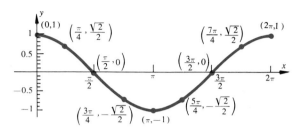

Figure   7.15

Range and zeros of cosine

Notice that the graph of the cosine function is a sinusoid, with amplitude 1. Furthermore, the zeros of the function, $\pi/2 + n\pi$, where $n = 0, \pm1, \pm2, \pm3, \cdots$, and the range $\{y \mid -1 \le y \le 1\}$ are also evident from the graph.

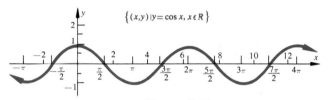

Figure   7.16

Functions defined by equations of the form

$$y = A \sin (Bx + C) \quad \text{and} \quad y = A \cos (Bx + C),$$

where A, B, and C are constants, and A and B are not 0, always have sine waves for graphs. With variations in the numbers A, B, and C, the graphs are variously situated with respect to the origin, and have a variety of amplitudes and periods. To analyze such graphs, let us consider the effect of A on the graphs of the functions defined by $y = A \sin x$ and $y = A \cos x$.

Graphs of $y = A \sin x$ and $y = A \cos x$

For each value of x, each ordinate to the graph of $y = A \sin x$ is A times the ordinate to the graph of $y = \sin x$. Therefore, the amplitude of the graph of $y = A \sin x$ is $|A|$ times the amplitude of the graph of $y = \sin x$. Of course, the graph of $y = A \cos x$ is a similar modification of the graph of $y = \cos x$.

Example. Graph $y = 3 \sin x$, $-\pi \le x \le 4\pi$.

Solution. It may be helpful first to sketch $y = \sin x$, $0 \le x \le 2\pi$, as a reference. Then, since the amplitude of $y = 3 \sin x$ is 3, we can sketch the desired graph on the same coordinate system over the interval $0 \le x \le 2\pi$ by making each ordinate 3 times the corresponding ordinate of the graph of $y = \sin x$. We can then extend this cycle to include the entire interval $-\pi \le x \le 4\pi$, as shown in the figure on page 174.

If like $\sin 3x$ put $\dfrac{\pi}{2}$ π $\dfrac{3\pi}{2}$ 2π *over 3*

$\dfrac{\pi}{2;}\dfrac{\pi}{3}\,\dfrac{\pi}{6}$ $\dfrac{\pi}{3}$ $\dfrac{\pi}{2}$ $\dfrac{2\pi}{3}$

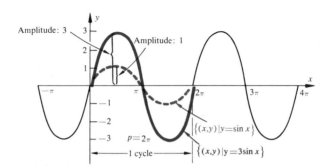

In this figure, the first cycle is sketched with a heavier line for emphasis. Note also that, in this and some of the succeeding figures, different unit lengths are used on the x- and y-axes. For $y = 3\sin x$, the fundamental period p is the same as for $y = \sin x$, namely $p = 2\pi$.

Next let us examine the way the graph of $y = \sin Bx$, $B \neq 0$, differs from the graph of $y = \sin x$. Note first that $\sin Bx$ has values between -1 and 1 inclusive, as has $\sin x$. Also, $\sin (Bx + 2\pi) = \sin Bx$, just as $\sin (x + 2\pi) = \sin x$. If we factor B from $Bx + 2\pi$, however, we have $B(x + 2\pi/B)$, and hence the function defined by $y = \sin Bx$ is periodic with period $2\pi/|B|$.

Graphs of
$y = \sin Bx$ and
$y = \cos Bx$

We use $|B|$ instead of B to ensure a positive number for the period. It can be shown, although it is not done here, that $2\pi/|B|$ is the fundamental period p of the function. Hence the graph of $y = \sin Bx$ is a sine wave with amplitude 1; it completes one cycle over the interval $0 \le x \le 2\pi/|B|$.

Example. Graph $y = \cos 2x$, $\dfrac{-3\pi}{2} \le x \le 2\pi$.

Solution. Let us first sketch a cycle of $y = \cos x$, $0 \le x \le 2\pi$, as a reference. Since $p = 2\pi/|B| = 2\pi/2 = \pi$, we next sketch a cycle of the graph of $y = \cos 2x$ over the interval $0 \le x \le \pi$ on the same coordinate system, and extend the cycle obtained over the interval $-3\pi/2 \le x \le 2\pi$.

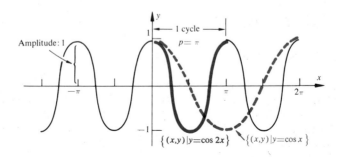

Period = 2π over |b|

Example.   Graph $y = -4 \sin \frac{1}{2}x,\ -2\pi \leq x \leq 4\pi$.

Solution.   We first sketch the graph of $y = \sin x$ as a reference. Since $A = -4$, each ordinate of the graph of $y = -4 \sin x/2$ is the negative of the ordinate of the graph of $y = 4 \sin x/2$. Since $p = 2\pi/|B| = 2\pi/(1/2) = 4\pi$, there is one cycle in the interval $0 \leq x \leq 4\pi$. Hence, we sketch one cycle, and extend it over the interval $-2\pi \leq x \leq 4\pi$.

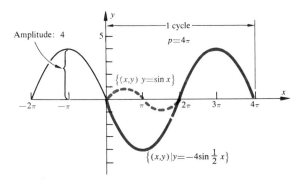

Finally, let us look at the difference between the graph of $y = \sin(x + C)$ and that of $y = \sin x$, where $C > 0$. For $x = -C$, we have

Graphs of
$y = \sin(x+C)$
and
$y = \cos(x+C)$

$\sin(x + C) = \sin 0 = 0$. Similarly, for any real number x_1, the ordinate of $\sin(x + C)$ at $x_1 - C$ will be the same as the ordinate of $\sin x$ at x_1. Hence, the graph of $y = \sin(x + C)$ is said to **lead** the graph of $y = \sin x$ by C. The number C,

itself, is called the **phase shift** of the wave. If $C < 0$, then the graph of $y = \sin(x + C)$ is shifted $|C|$ units to the right of the graph of $y = \sin x$ and is said to **lag** the graph of $y = \sin x$.

Graphs of
$y = A \sin(B+C)$
and
$y = A \cos(B+C)$

We use all of the foregoing information about the effect of A, B, and C on the graph of $y = A \sin(Bx + C)$, or of $y = A \cos(Bx + C)$, to help sketch the graph of such an equation.

Example.   Sketch the graph of $y = 3 \sin\left(2x + \frac{\pi}{3}\right)$.

Solution.   First, let us rewrite the equation by factoring 2 from the expression in parentheses:

$$y = 3 \sin 2\left(x + \frac{\pi}{6}\right). \quad \text{changes } \downarrow \text{ scale}$$

By inspecting this equation, we note the following about the graph:
1. It is a sine wave.
2. It has amplitude 3.
3. It has period $2\pi/2 = \pi$.
4. It leads the graph of $y = 3 \sin 2x$ by $\pi/6$.

With these facts, we can quickly sketch the graph, as shown on page 176.

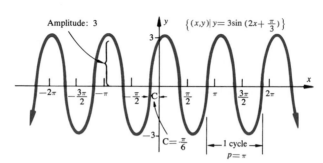

Example. Sketch the graph of $y = \dfrac{1}{2}\sin\dfrac{\pi x}{2}$.

Solution. By inspection, we note that the graph:

   1. Is a sine wave.

   2. Has amplitude 1/2.

   3. Has period $2\pi/(\pi/2) = 4$.

Since the period is 4, we use integers as elements of the domain in sketching the graph.

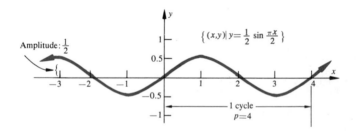

EXERCISE 7.4

Sketch the graphs of the following equations over the interval $-2\pi \le x \le 2\pi$.

1. $y = 2 \sin x$ 2. $y = 3 \cos x$ 3. $y = \dfrac{1}{2}\cos x$

4. $y = \dfrac{1}{3}\cos x$ 5. $y = -4 \sin x$ 6. $y = -\dfrac{1}{2}\cos x$

7. $y = \sin 2x$ 8. $y = \cos 3x$ 9. $y = \cos \dfrac{1}{3}x$

10. $y = \cos \dfrac{1}{2}x$ 11. $y = -3 \sin 2x$ 12. $y = -\dfrac{1}{2}\sin 3x$

13. $y = \sin (x + \pi)$ 14. $y = \cos \left(x - \dfrac{\pi}{2}\right)$ 15. $y = 2 \cos \left(x - \dfrac{\pi}{4}\right)$

16. $y = 3 \sin \left(x + \dfrac{\pi}{6}\right)$ 17. $y = 3 \sin 2\left(x - \dfrac{\pi}{3}\right)$ 18. $y = 2 \cos 3\left(x + \dfrac{\pi}{4}\right)$

19. $y = 2 \sin \pi x$ 20. $y = -3 \cos \dfrac{\pi}{2} x$ 21. $y = -\dfrac{1}{2} \cos \dfrac{\pi}{3} x$

22. $y = \dfrac{1}{4} \sin \dfrac{\pi}{4} x$

From the respective graph, determine the zeros (over the specified domain) of the function defined by the equation in the given problem.

23. Problem 7   24. Problem 8   25. Problem 9

26. Problem 10   27. Problem 19   28. Problem 20

Example. Sketch the graph of $y = \sin x + 2 \cos x$ over the interval $0 \le x \le 2\pi$.

Solution. First, sketch the graphs of $y = \sin x$ and $y = 2 \cos x$ on the same coordinate system over the given interval. The ordinate of the graph of $y = \sin x + 2 \cos x$ at each point x on the x-axis is the *algebraic* sum of the corresponding ordinates of $y = \sin x$ and $y = 2 \cos x$. Thus for $x = \pi/6$,

$$\sin x = 0.5, \quad 2 \cos x = 2\sqrt{3}/2 \approx 1.7, \quad \text{and} \quad \sin x + 2 \cos x \approx 2.2.$$

Now the ordinate can be approximated graphically by adding the directed line segments from the x-axis to the respective curves at $x = \pi/6$. If this is done for a few selected values of x, we obtain a good approximation for the curve.

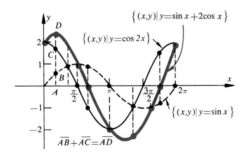

Sketch the graph of each of the following over the interval $-2\pi \le x \le 2\pi$.

29. $y = \sin x + \cos x$ 30. $y = 3 \sin x + \cos x$ 31. $y = \sin 2x + \dfrac{1}{2} \cos x$

32. $y = \sin 3x + 2 \cos \dfrac{1}{2} x$ 33. $y = \sin x - 2 \cos x$ 34. $y = 3 \cos x - \sin 2x$

35. $y = 3 \sin x + 1$ 36. $y = 4 \sin 2x - 3$ 37. $y = x + \cos x$

38. $y = 2x - \cos x$

7.5 ADDITIONAL PROPERTIES OF THE COSINE AND SINE FUNCTIONS

Formulas for cos 2x and sin 2x

The sum and difference formulas for cosine and sine developed in Sections 7.2 and 7.3 can be used to generate still other relationships between values of these functions.

THEOREM 7.9 *If $x \in R$, then*

$$\text{I} \quad \cos 2x = \cos^2 x - \sin^2 x, \tag{1}$$

$$\text{II} \quad \sin 2x = 2 \sin x \cos x. \tag{2}$$

Proof. Let $x_1 = x_2 = x$ in Equation (1) on page 164. Then

$$\cos (x + x) = \cos x \cos x - \sin x \sin x,$$

$$\cos 2x = \cos^2 x - \sin^2 x.$$

Let $x_1 = x_2 = x$ in Equation (1) on page 169. Then

$$\sin (x + x) = \sin x \cos x + \cos x \sin x,$$

$$\sin 2x = 2 \sin x \cos x,$$

as was to be shown.

Formulas for cos x/2 and sin x/2

Alternative forms of the equation for $\cos 2x$ can be obtained by using the relationship $\cos^2 x + \sin^2 x = 1$ to obtain $\cos^2 x = 1 - \sin^2 x$ and $\sin^2 x = 1 - \cos^2 x$, and then replacing the appropriate term in the right-hand member of (1). The results are the formulas:

$$\cos 2x = 1 - 2 \sin^2 x, \tag{3}$$

$$\cos 2x = 2 \cos^2 x - 1. \tag{4}$$

Relationships (3) and (4) lead directly to the following formulas:

THEOREM 7.10 *If $x \in R$, then*

$$\text{I} \quad \cos \frac{x}{2} = \begin{cases} \sqrt{\dfrac{1 + \cos x}{2}} & \text{when } \dfrac{x}{2} \text{ terminates in Quadrant I or IV,} \quad (5) \\[3mm] -\sqrt{\dfrac{1 + \cos x}{2}} & \text{when } \dfrac{x}{2} \text{ terminates in Quadrant II or III;} \quad (5') \end{cases}$$

$$\text{II} \quad \sin \frac{x}{2} = \begin{cases} \sqrt{\dfrac{1 - \cos x}{2}} & \text{when } \dfrac{x}{2} \text{ terminates in Quadrant I or II,} \quad (6) \\[3mm] -\sqrt{\dfrac{1 - \cos x}{2}} & \text{when } \dfrac{x}{2} \text{ terminates in Quadrant III or IV.} \quad (6') \end{cases}$$

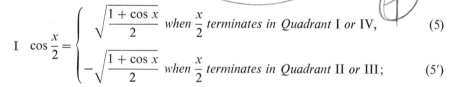

Proof. We shall prove only the formula for $\sin (x/2)$ here and leave the proof of the formula for $\cos (x/2)$ as an exercise. If we replace x in (3) with $x/2$, we have

$$\cos 2\left(\frac{x}{2}\right) = 1 - 2 \sin^2 \frac{x}{2},$$

from which

$$\cos x = 1 - 2 \sin^2 \frac{x}{2},$$

$$\sin^2 \frac{x}{2} = \frac{1 - \cos x}{2},$$

and

$$\sin \frac{x}{2} = \pm \sqrt{\frac{1 - \cos x}{2}}.$$

Now, because $\sin (x/2) > 0$ for $x/2$ in Quadrant I or II, we take the positive square root in these quadrants; and for a similar reason in the remaining quadrants we take the negative square root. Thus our proof is complete.

Example. Find $\sin \frac{\pi}{12}$.

Solution. Since $\frac{\pi}{12} = \frac{1}{2} \left(\frac{\pi}{6} \right)$, from (6) we have

$$\sin \frac{\pi}{12} = \sin \frac{1}{2} \left(\frac{\pi}{6} \right)$$

$$= \sqrt{\frac{1 - \cos (\pi/6)}{2}}$$

$$= \sqrt{\frac{1 - \sqrt{3}/2}{2}} = \sqrt{\frac{2 - \sqrt{3}}{4}} = \frac{1}{2} \sqrt{2 - \sqrt{3}}.$$

EXERCISE 7.5

Use Formulas 1–6 to find values for each of the following.

1. $\sin \dfrac{\pi}{8}$ 2. $\sin \left(-\dfrac{\pi}{8} \right)$ 3. $\cos \dfrac{\pi}{8}$

4. $\cos \left(-\dfrac{\pi}{8} \right)$ 5. $\cos \dfrac{\pi}{12}$ 6. $\cos \left(-\dfrac{\pi}{12} \right)$

Example. Given that $\sin x = 0.2$, and $\pi/2 < x < \pi$, use Formulas 1–6, as appropriate, to find an approximation for $\sin 2x$.

Solution. Since $\sin x = 0.2$ and x terminates in Quadrant II,

$$\cos x = -\sqrt{1 - \sin^2 x} = -\sqrt{1 - 0.04} = -\sqrt{0.96} \approx -0.98.$$

From (2) we have

$$\sin 2x = 2 \sin x \cos x \approx 2(0.2)(-0.98) \approx -0.39.$$

7. Given that $\cos x = 0.7$ and $3\pi/2 < x < 2\pi$, find an approximation for:

  a. $\sin x$ b. $\cos 2x$ c. $\sin 2x$ d. $\cos \dfrac{x}{2}$ e. $\sin \dfrac{x}{2}$

$\sin x = \sqrt{1 - \cos^2 x}$

8. Given that $\cos x = -0.6$ and $\sin x > 0$, find an approximation for:

  a. $\sin x$ b. $\cos 2x$ c. $\sin 2x$ d. $\cos \dfrac{x}{2}$ e. $\sin \dfrac{x}{2}$

9. Given that $\sin x = -0.3$ and $\pi < x < 3\pi/2$, find an approximation for:

  a. $\cos x$ b. $\cos 2x$ c. $\sin 2x$ d. $\cos \dfrac{x}{2}$ e. $\sin \dfrac{x}{2}$

10. Given that $\cos x = 0.4$ and $\sin x < 0$, find an approximation for:

  a. $\sin x$ b. $\cos 2x$ c. $\sin 2x$ d. $\cos \dfrac{x}{2}$ e. $\sin \dfrac{x}{2}$

By means of the formulas in this section, evaluate each of the Exercises 11 to 14 mentally.

11. $2 \sin \dfrac{\pi}{12} \cos \dfrac{\pi}{12}$ 12. $\cos^2 \dfrac{\pi}{12} - \sin^2 \dfrac{\pi}{12}$

13. $2 \cos^2 \dfrac{5\pi}{12} - 1$ 14. $1 - 2 \sin^2 \dfrac{5\pi}{12}$

15. Show that $\sin 2x$ is periodic with fundamental period π.

16. Show that $\cos 2x$ is periodic with fundamental period π.

17. Show that $\sin (x/2)$ is periodic with fundamental period 4π.

18. Show that $\cos (x/2)$ is periodic with fundamental period 4π.

19. Express $\sin^2 x$ in terms of $\cos 2x$. *Hint*: Use Formula (3).

20. Express $\cos^2 x$ in terms of $\cos 2x$.

21. Show that for all $x \in R$, $\cos 3x = 4 \cos^3 x - 3 \cos x$.

22. Show that for all $x \in R$, $\sin 3x = 3 \sin x - 4 \sin^3 x$.

23. Prove Theorem 7.10-I.

7.6 OTHER CIRCULAR FUNCTIONS

The functions sine and cosine can be used to define other periodic functions. First, however, let us give names to some ratios of sine and cosine function values.

DEFINITION 7.4 *Let $x \in R$.*

  I   *The **tangent** of x is denoted by* $\tan x$, *and*

$$\tan x = \frac{\sin x}{\cos x} \qquad \left(x \neq \frac{\pi}{2} + k\pi, k \in J \right).$$

undefined when

II *The **secant** of x is denoted by* sec *x, and*

$$\sec x = \frac{1}{\cos x} \qquad \left(x \neq \frac{\pi}{2} + k\pi, \, k \in J \right).$$

III *The **cosecant** of x is denoted by* csc *x, and*

$$\csc x = \frac{1}{\sin x} \qquad (x \neq k\pi, \, k \in J).$$

IV *The **cotangent** of x is denoted by* cot *x, and*

$$\cot x = \frac{\cos x}{\sin x} \qquad (x \neq k\pi, \, k \in J).$$

Example. If $\sin x = 3/5$ and $\pi/2 \leq x \leq \pi$, find $\cos x$, $\tan x$, $\sec x$, $\csc x$, and $\cot x$.

Solution. By Equation 9b on page 162, for $\pi/2 \leq x \leq \pi$,

$$\cos x = -\sqrt{1 - \sin^2 x}.$$

Then, since $\sin x = \frac{3}{5}$,

$$\cos x = -\sqrt{1 - \left(\frac{3}{5}\right)^2} = -\frac{4}{5}.$$

By Definition 7.4,

$$\tan x = \frac{\sin x}{\cos x} = \frac{3/5}{-4/5} = -\frac{3}{4}, \qquad \sec x = \frac{1}{\cos x} = \frac{1}{-4/5} = -\frac{5}{4},$$

$$\cot x = \frac{\cos x}{\sin x} = \frac{-4/5}{3/5} = -\frac{4}{3}, \qquad \csc x = \frac{1}{\sin x} = \frac{1}{3/5} = \frac{5}{3}.$$

Now, let us take the ratios in Definition 7.4 one at a time and examine the function associated with each.

DEFINITION 7.5 *If $x \in R$, and $x \neq (\pi/2) + k\pi$, $k \in J$, then*

$$\text{tangent} = \{(x, y) \,|\, y = \tan x\}.$$

Domain and range of tangent

Because $\tan x = \sin x/\cos x$, the domain of the tangent function is R, with the exception of the real numbers x for which $\cos x = 0$, that is, with the exception of the real numbers of the form $(\pi/2) + k\pi$, $k \in J$. The range of the tangent function is R.

Since the sine and cosine functions have period 2π, so has the tangent function. We note, however, that

$$\tan x = \frac{\sin x}{\cos x} = \frac{-\sin (x + \pi)}{-\cos (x + \pi)} = \tan (x + \pi),$$

Fundamental period of tangent

so that this function actually has period π also. The proof that this function has no smaller positive period, and therefore that π is its fundamental period, is left as an exercise.

DEFINITION 7.6 *If $x \in R$, and $x \neq k\pi$, $k \in J$, then*

$$\text{cotangent} = \{(x, y) \mid y = \cot x\}.$$

Since $\cot x = \cos x / \sin x$, the domain of the cotangent function is R, excepting those

Cotangent

real numbers for which $\sin x = 0$, that is, all real numbers except those of the form $k\pi$, where $k \in J$. The range of cotangent is R, and, like the tangent function, contangent has fundamental period π.

DEFINITION 7.7 *If $x \in R$, and $x \neq \pi/2 + k\pi$, $k \in J$, then*

$$\text{secant} = \{(x, y) \mid y = \sec x\}.$$

Since $\sec x$ is the reciprocal of $\cos x$, the domain of the secant function is R, except

Secant

for those values of x for which $\cos x = 0$, namely, $x = \pi/2 + k\pi$, $k \in J$. Because $|\cos x| \leq 1$ for all $x \in R$, $\sec x$ is never less than 1 in absolute value; the range of the secant function is $\{y \mid |y| \geq 1\}$. Since the cosine function has fundamental period 2π, the secant function has fundamental period 2π.

DEFINITION 7.8 *If $x \in R$, and $x \neq k\pi$, $k \in J$, then*

$$\text{cosecant} = \{(x, y) \mid y = \csc x\}.$$

Since $\csc x$ is the reciprocal of $\sin x$, the domain of the cosecant function contains

Cosecant

all real numbers except those for which $\sin x = 0$; that is, the domain is all of R except the numbers $k\pi$, $k \in J$. The cosecant function has range $\{y \mid |y| \geq 1\}$ and fundamental period 2π.

Other formulas for tangent

Each of the above functions has its associated sum, difference, and reduction formulas, comparable to and derived from those of sine and cosine.

THEOREM 7.11 *If $x_1, x_2 \in R$ and x_1, x_2 and $x_1 + x_2 \neq \pi/2 + k\pi$, $k \in J$, then*

$$\tan (x_1 + x_2) = \frac{\tan x_1 + \tan x_2}{1 - \tan x_1 \tan x_2}.$$

Proof. By definition, for $x_1 + x_2 \in R$, $x_1 + x_2 \neq \pi/2 + k\pi$, $k \in J$,

$$\tan (x_1 + x_2) = \frac{\sin (x_1 + x_2)}{\cos (x_1 + x_2)}.$$

By Theorems 7.6 and 7.3, we therefore have

$$\tan (x_1 + x_2) = \frac{\sin x_1 \cos x_2 + \cos x_1 \sin x_2}{\cos x_1 \cos x_2 - \sin x_1 \sin x_2}.$$

Dividing numerator and denominator of the right-hand member by $\cos x_1 \cos x_2$, for $x_1, x_2 \in R$, and $x_1, x_2 \neq \pi/2 + k\pi$, $k \in J$, we find

$$\tan (x_1 + x_2) = \frac{\dfrac{\sin x_1 \cos x_2}{\cos x_1 \cos x_2} + \dfrac{\cos x_1 \sin x_2}{\cos x_1 \cos x_2}}{\dfrac{\cos x_1 \cos x_2}{\cos x_1 \cos x_2} - \dfrac{\sin x_1 \sin x_2}{\cos x_1 \cos x_2}}.$$

After simplifying each term in the right-hand member, from Definition 7.4-I we obtain

$$\tan (x_1 + x_2) = \frac{\tan x_1 + \tan x_2}{1 - \tan x_1 \tan x_2},$$

as was to be shown.

Also, by substituting $x_1 - x_2$ for x in the definition of $\tan x$, we can establish a difference formula for tangents in a similar way.

THEOREM 7.12   *If $x_1, x_2 \in R$ and x_1, x_2 and $x_1 - x_2 \neq \pi/2 + k\pi$, $k, \in J$ then*

$$\tan (x_1 - x_2) = \frac{\tan x_1 - \tan x_2}{1 + \tan x_1 \tan x_2}.$$

Formulas for $\tan 2x$ and $\tan x/2$ also follow immediately from formulas we have already developed.

THEOREM 7.13   *If $x \in R$, $x \neq \pi/4 + k\pi/2$, $k \in J$, then*

$$\tan 2x = \frac{2 \tan x}{1 - \tan^2 x}.$$

Proof.   Replacing x_1 and x_2 by x in Theorem 7.11, we obtain

$$\tan (x + x) = \frac{\tan x + \tan x}{1 - \tan x \tan x},$$

$$\tan 2x = \frac{2 \tan x}{1 - \tan^2 x}.$$

THEOREM 7.14   *If $x \in R$ and $x \neq k\pi$, $k \in J$, then*

$$\text{I} \quad \tan \frac{x}{2} = \frac{1 - \cos x}{\sin x},$$

$$\text{II} \quad \tan \frac{x}{2} = \frac{\sin x}{1 + \cos x}.$$

Proof of 7.14-I.   By Definition 7.4,

$$\tan \frac{x}{2} = \frac{\sin \dfrac{x}{2}}{\cos \dfrac{x}{2}},$$

from which, by multiplying numerator and denominator by $2 \sin \dfrac{x}{2}$, we have

$$\tan \frac{x}{2} = \frac{2 \sin^2 \dfrac{x}{2}}{2 \sin \dfrac{x}{2} \cos \dfrac{x}{2}}.$$

Therefore, by Theorems 7.9 and 7.10,

$$\tan \frac{x}{2} = \frac{1 - \cos x}{\sin x},$$

as desired.

The proof of Part II is left as an exercise.

Reciprocal relationships for cotangent, secant, and cosecant	Relationships similar to those developed for tangent in Theorems 7.11 through 7.14 can be derived for cotangent, secant, and cosecant. For practical purposes, however, the reduction formulas for cosine, sine, and tangent are the only ones necessary in view of the fact that

$$\sec x = \frac{1}{\cos x}, \quad \csc x = \frac{1}{\sin x}, \quad \text{and} \quad \cot x = \frac{1}{\tan x}.$$

The circular functions defined by $y = \tan x$, $y = \cot x$, $y = \sec x$, and $y = \csc x$ do not have sine waves for graphs in R^2, although each of these graphs does display periodic properties and all have certain other distinctive features.

To graph $y = \tan x$, we first recall that its fundamental period is π rather than 2π. Next, from Table V, page 370 (or, more directly, from the results of Problems 1 and 2, Exercise 7.6), we can locate the points shown in Figure 7.17 over the interval $0 \leq x \leq \pi$. Because $\tan x$ is undefined for $x = \pi/2$, and $|\tan x|$ increases indefinitely as x approaches $\pi/2$, we expect no point on the graph corresponding to $x = \pi/2$. The line $x = \pi/2$ is an asymptote to the curve.

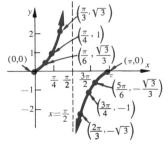

Figure 7.17

Assuming, as in the case of $y = \sin x$ and $y = \cos x$, that tangent is a continuous function wherever it is defined, and that $\tan x$ increases as x increases from 0

Graph of tangent

to $\pi/2$, and from $\pi/2$ to π, we can connect the points in Figure 7.17 with a smooth curve to obtain the graph over one period of the function. Repeating this pattern for a number of periods gives us the characteristic shape of the graph of the tangent function over its entire domain. Observe that the asymptotes to the curve in Figure 7.18 are the

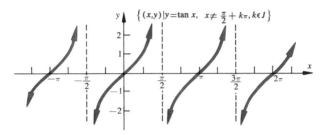

Figure   7.18

graphs of $x = \pi/2 + k\pi$, the zeros of the function defined by $y = \tan x$ are the real numbers $k\pi$, $k \in J$, and the range of tangent is R.

Graphs of reciprocal circular functions

We can sketch the graphs of the other circular functions in a similar way, that is, by using Table V (or the results of Problems 1 and 2, Exercise 7.6), plotting some points over $0 < x < 2\pi$, and joining the points with a curve. These are shown in Figure 7.19 along with the graphs of their respective reciprocal functions.

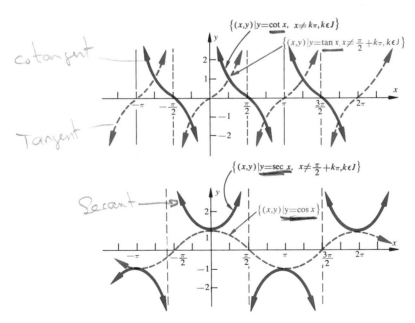

Figure   7.19 (*concluded overleaf*)

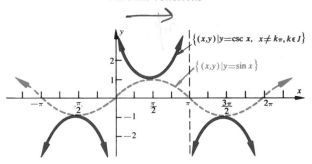

Figure   7.19 (*continued*)

EXERCISE   7.6

1. Use Definition 7.4 and the left-hand side of Table 7.1 on page 160 to construct a similar table for tan x, sec x, csc x, and cot x for $0 \leq x \leq \pi$.

2. Use Definition 7.4 and the right-hand side of Table 7.1 on page 160 to construct a similar table for tan x, sec x, csc x, and cot x for $\pi \leq x \leq 2\pi$.

Using the definitions and theorems stated in this section, find values for the other five of the six circular functions if one function value and the quadrant are as given.

Example. $\tan x = \dfrac{4}{3}$; x terminates in Quadrant III.

Solution.   From Definition 7.4, $\tan x = \dfrac{\sin x}{\cos x}$, so $\dfrac{\sin x}{\cos x} = \dfrac{4}{3}$. Since, in Quadrant III, $\cos x = -\sqrt{1 - \sin^2 x}$, we have

$$\frac{\sin x}{-\sqrt{1 - \sin^2 x}} = \frac{4}{3},$$

or

$$3 \sin x = -4\sqrt{1 - \sin^2 x}.$$

Squaring each member and simplifying, we find that

$$9 \sin^2 x = 16(1 - \sin^2 x),$$
$$25 \sin^2 x = 16,$$
$$\sin^2 x = \frac{16}{25}.$$

It follows that either $\sin x = 4/5$ or $\sin x = -(4/5)$. Since x terminates in Quadrant III, we have $\sin x = -(4/5)$. Using $\sin^2 x + \cos^2 x = 1$, we find that

$$\frac{16}{25} + \cos^2 x = 1,$$

from which either

$$\cos x = \frac{3}{5} \quad \text{or} \quad \cos x = -\frac{3}{5}.$$

In Quadrant III, $\cos x < 0$, and hence $\cos x = -(3/5)$. From these results, and using Definition 7.4, we find

$$\sin x = -\frac{4}{5}, \quad \cos x = -\frac{3}{5}, \quad \sec x = -\frac{5}{3}, \quad \csc x = -\frac{5}{4}, \quad \text{and} \quad \cot x = \frac{3}{4}.$$

3. $\tan x = 5/12$; x terminates in Quadrant I. $\quad \frac{5}{12} = \frac{\sin x}{\sqrt{1-\sin^2 x}} = \quad \frac{25}{144} = \frac{\sin^2 x}{1-1}$

4. $\tan x = 8/15$; x terminates in Quadrant III.

5. $\sin x = -8/17$; x terminates in Quadrant III.

6. $\sec x = -5/3$; x terminates in Quadrant III.

7. $\cot x = -3$; x terminates in Quadrant IV.

8. $\csc x = -17/15$; x terminates in Quadrant IV.

Prove each of the following. In each case, state restrictions on x or function values of x.

9. $\tan\left(\frac{\pi}{2} + x\right) = -\cot x$

10. $\tan(\pi - x) = -\tan x$

11. $\tan(\pi + x) = \tan x$

12. $\tan\left(\frac{3\pi}{2} - x\right) = \cot x$

13. $\tan\left(\frac{3\pi}{2} + x\right) = -\cot x$

14. $\tan(2\pi - x) = -\tan x$

15. $\cot(x_1 + x_2) = \dfrac{\cot x_1 \cot x_2 - 1}{\cot x_1 + \cot x_2}$

16. $\cot(x_1 - x_2) = \dfrac{\cot x_1 \cot x_2 + 1}{\cot x_2 - \cot x_1}$

17. $\cot 2x = \dfrac{\cot^2 x - 1}{2 \cot x}$

18. $\sec(x_1 + x_2) = \dfrac{\sec x_1 \sec x_2}{1 - \tan x_1 \tan x_2}$

19. $\sec 2x = \dfrac{\sec^2 x}{2 - \sec^2 x}$

20. $\csc 2x = \dfrac{\csc x}{2 \cos x}$

Use the fact that the circular functions are periodic, along with the reduction formulas (Problems 9–14 above) and Table V in the Appendix, to obtain an approximation for each function value.

Example. $\tan 3.31$

Solution. $\tan 3.31 \approx \tan(3.31 - 3.14)$

$$\approx \tan 0.17$$

$$\approx 0.1717$$

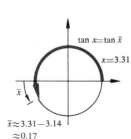

tan x=tan $\bar{x}$

x=3.31

$\bar{x}$

$\bar{x}\approx 3.31 - 3.14$

≈ 0.17

21. $\tan 4.52$ 22. $\tan 5.61$

23. $\tan(-2.30)$ 24. $\tan 8.30$

25. $\tan 12.50$ 26. $\tan(-27.30)$

Approximate the element x, $0 \le x \le 1.57$, in the domain of the function, for the specified element in the range. Interpolate as required.

27. $\tan x = 1.459$ 28. $\cot x = 0.6563$ 29. $\sec x = 2.448$

30. $\csc x = 1.010$ 31. $\cot x = 0.0208$ 32. $\tan x = 0.5000$

Graph each of the following over the interval $-2\pi \le x \le 2\pi$.

33. $y = \csc 2x$ 34. $y = \sec 2x$ 35. $y = \cot 2x$

36. $y = 2 \tan x$ 37. $y = -\tan x$ 38. $y = \cot \frac{1}{2} x$

39. $y = \sec \frac{x}{2}$ 40. $y = \frac{1}{2} \cot 2x$

41. Show graphically that $\tan x = \cot \left(\frac{\pi}{2} - x \right)$.

42. Show graphically that $\cot x = \tan \left(\frac{\pi}{2} - x \right)$.

7.7   IDENTITIES

The fact that all of the circular functions are defined either in terms of the unit circle or in terms of other circular functions suggests that these functions are interrelated in a number of ways. These relationships are called **identities**, since they are true for every permissible replacement of any variables involved. Thus, sine and cosine are related by the identity

$$\sin^2 x + \cos^2 x = 1,$$

as we observed earlier. Also, the definitions of tan, cot, sec, and csc are identities. Thus, the defining relations,

$$\tan x = \frac{\sin x}{\cos x}, \qquad \sec x = \frac{1}{\cos x},$$

$$\cot x = \frac{\cos x}{\sin x}, \qquad \csc x = \frac{1}{\sin x},$$

Proofs of identities

are true for all real numbers x for which the denominators in the right-hand members are not zero. These can be used to prove still other identities.

Example.   Show that $\tan^2 x + 1 = \sec^2 x$ is an identity.

Solution.   We can "prove an identity" by showing that the given equation is equivalent to a true statement or to another equation known to be an identity. Since, for every real number x such that $x \ne \pi/2 + k\pi$, $k \in J$, we have

$$\tan x = \frac{\sin x}{\cos x} \qquad \text{and} \qquad \sec x = \frac{1}{\cos x},$$

we can substitute appropriately in the given equation and obtain

$$\frac{\sin^2 x}{\cos^2 x} + 1 = \frac{1}{\cos^2 x}$$

Because $\cos^2 x \neq 0$ for any x for which $\tan x$ and $\sec x$ are defined, we can multiply each member here by $\cos^2 x$ to obtain the equivalent equation, for all such x,

$$\sin^2 x + \cos^2 x = 1.$$

This is a known identity, and hence the given equation is also an identity.

When we prove an identity, we are actually proving a theorem. Thus, the foregoing example could be stated:

THEOREM 7.15 *For each $x \in R$, $x \neq \pi/2 + k\pi$, $k \in J$,*

$$\tan^2 x + 1 = \sec^2 x.$$

Except for special cases, however, we shall present such relationships simply as exercises.

In proving identities, it is sometimes more convenient to restrict manipulations to one member of the given equation, and sometimes more convenient to work with both members. In Example 1, both members were multiplied by $\cos^2 x$ to prove the identity. The following example restricts the transformations to the left-hand member.

Example. Show that

$$\frac{\sin x}{1 - \cos x} - \cot x = \frac{1}{\sin x} \tag{1}$$

is an identity.

Solution. In proving identities, it is often helpful to rewrite a given equation in terms of $\sin x$ and $\cos x$ only. Doing this here, we have

$$\frac{\sin x}{1 - \cos x} - \frac{\cos x}{\sin x} = \frac{1}{\sin x}.$$

Writing the left-hand member as a single fraction, we have

$$\frac{\sin^2 x - (1 - \cos x) \cos x}{(1 - \cos x) \sin x} = \frac{1}{\sin x},$$

from which

$$\frac{\sin^2 x - \cos x + \cos^2 x}{(1 - \cos x) \sin x} = \frac{1}{\sin x},$$

$$\frac{(\sin^2 x + \cos^2 x) - \cos x}{(1 - \cos x) \sin x} = \frac{1}{\sin x},$$

$$\frac{1 - \cos x}{(1 - \cos x) \sin x} = \frac{1}{\sin x}.$$

Since $1 - \cos x$ is restricted from 0 in (1) above, we can rewrite the left-hand member here and arrive at the equivalent equation

$$\frac{1}{\sin x} = \frac{1}{\sin x},$$

which is clearly an identity, and the demonstration is complete.

The sum and difference formulas, as well as the formulas derived from these, are often involved in identities.

Example.   Show that $\dfrac{\sin 2x}{1 + \cos 2x} = \tan x$ is an identity.

Solution.   Replacing sin $2x$ and cos $2x$ in the given equation with $2 \sin x \cos x$ and $2 \cos^2 x - 1$, we have

$$\frac{2 \sin x \cos x}{1 + (2 \cos^2 x - 1)} = \tan x,$$

$$\frac{2 \sin x \cos x}{2 \cos^2 x} = \tan x,$$

$$\frac{\sin x \cos x}{\cos^2 x} = \tan x.$$

With the restriction that $\cos x \neq 0$, the left-hand member of this equation can be written $\dfrac{\sin x}{\cos x}$, and we have

$$\frac{\sin x}{\cos x} = \tan x,$$

which is true by definition.

For convenience, let us list again the various identities presented earlier as definitions and theorems. While no restrictions are given for variables here, it is important to keep such restrictions in mind when using any identity.

Summary of Identities

1. $\sin^2 x + \cos^2 x = 1$

2. $\cos (-x) = \cos x$

3. $\sin (-x) = -\sin x$

4. $\cos (x_1 + x_2)$

$$= \cos x_1 \cos x_2 - \sin x_1 \sin x_2$$

5. $\cos (x_1 - x_2)$

$$= \cos x_1 \cos x_2 + \sin x_1 \sin x_2$$

6. $\sin (x_1 + x_2)$

$$= \sin x_1 \cos x_2 + \cos x_1 \sin x_2$$

7. $\sin(x_1 - x_2)$

$= \sin x_1 \cos x_2 - \cos x_1 \sin x_2$

8. a. $\cos 2x = \cos^2 x - \sin^2 x$

b. $\cos 2x = 2 \cos^2 x - 1$

c. $\cos 2x = 1 - 2 \sin^2 x$

9. $\sin 2x = 2 \sin x \cos x$

10. $\cos \dfrac{x}{2} = \pm \sqrt{\dfrac{1 + \cos x}{2}}$

11. $\sin \dfrac{x}{2} = \pm \sqrt{\dfrac{1 - \cos x}{2}}$

12. $\tan x = \dfrac{\sin x}{\cos x}$

13. $\tan(-x) = -\tan x$

14. $\sec x = \dfrac{1}{\cos x}$

15. $\csc x = \dfrac{1}{\sin x}$

16. $\cot x = \dfrac{1}{\tan x}$

17. $\cot x = \dfrac{\cos x}{\sin x}$

18. $\tan(x_1 + x_2) = \dfrac{\tan x_1 + \tan x_2}{1 - \tan x_1 \tan x_2}$

19. $\tan(x_1 - x_2) = \dfrac{\tan x_1 - \tan x_2}{1 + \tan x_1 \tan x_2}$

20. $\tan 2x = \dfrac{2 \tan x}{1 - \tan^2 x}$

21. $\tan \dfrac{x}{2} = \dfrac{1 - \cos x}{\sin x}$

22. $\tan \dfrac{x}{2} = \dfrac{\sin x}{1 + \cos x}$

EXERCISE 7.7

Each of the following may be written as a circular function of kx, or $k(x_1 \pm x_2)$, where k is a positive integer, with one or at most two steps. Write the answer directly. Assume that x, x_1, and x_2 take on no value for which a denominator vanishes.

Examples.   a. $\cos(-x)$ b. $2 \sin x \cos x$ c. $2 \cos^2 4x - 1$

Solutions.   a. $\cos x$ b. $\sin 2x$ c. $\cos 2(4x)$

$\cos 8x$

1. $\tan(-x)$

2. $-\sin(-x)$

3. $\dfrac{1}{\cot x}$

4. $1 - 2 \sin^2 x$

5. $\dfrac{\tan x_1 + \tan x_2}{1 - \tan x_1 \tan x_2}$

6. $\dfrac{2 \tan x}{1 - \tan^2 x}$

7. $\cos^2 x - \sin^2 x$

8. $\cos^2 3x - \sin^2 3x$

9. $\sin x_1 \cos x_2 - \cos x_1 \sin x_2$

10. $\sin 5x \cos 3x + \cos 5x \sin 3x$.

11. $\dfrac{2 \tan 3x}{1 - \tan^2 3x}$

12. $\tan^2 x + 1$

13. $1 - \cos^2 x$ 14. $1 - \sec^2 x$

15. $\cos (x_1 + x_2) \cos (x_1 - x_2) - \sin (x_1 + x_2) \sin (x_1 - x_2)$

16. $\sin (x_1 - x_2) \cos (x_1 + x_2) + \cos (x_1 - x_2) \sin (x_1 + x_2)$

Transform each first expression and show that it is identical to the second expression. (Assume suitable restrictions on x in each case.)

17. $\cos x \tan x$; $\sin x$ 18. $\sin x \sec x$; $\tan x$

19. $\sin^2 x \cot^2 x$; $\cos^2 x$ 20. $\dfrac{\cos^2 x}{\cot^2 x}$; $\sin^2 x$

21. $\cos^2 x (1 + \tan^2 x)$; 1 22. $(\csc^2 x - 1) \sin^2 x$; $\cos^2 x$

23. $\sec x \csc x - \cot x$; $\tan x$ 24. $(1 - \cos^2 x)(1 + \cot^2 x)$; 1

25. $\dfrac{\sin x \sec x}{\tan x}$; 1 26. $\cos x \tan x \csc x$; 1

27. $(\sec^2 x - 1)(\csc^2 x - 1)$; 1 28. $\dfrac{\cos x - \sin x}{\cos x}$; $1 - \tan x$

29. $\dfrac{1}{1 + \sin x} + \dfrac{1}{1 - \sin x}$; $2 \sec^2 x$ $\dfrac{2}{1-\sin^2 x} = \dfrac{2}{\cos^2 x} = 2\left(\dfrac{1}{\cos x}\right)^2 = 2\sec^2 x$ 30. $\dfrac{1 + \tan^2 x}{\csc^2 x}$; $\tan^2 x$

Verify that formulas 31–46 are identities.

31. $\sin x \cot x = \cos x$ 32. $\tan x \csc x = \sec x$

33. $\sec x - \cos x = \sin x \tan x$ 34. $\sec x - \sin x \tan x = \cos x$

35. $\dfrac{1 + \tan^2 x}{\tan^2 x} = \csc^2 x$ 36. $\dfrac{\sin^2 x}{1 - \cos x} = \dfrac{1 + \sec x}{\sec x}$

37. $\tan^2 x - \sin^2 x = \sin^2 x \tan^2 x$ 38. $\cot^2 x + \sec^2 x = \tan^2 x + \csc^2 x$

39. $\tan x + \sec x = \dfrac{1}{\sec x - \tan x}$ 40. $\dfrac{\sec x + \csc x}{1 + \tan x} = \csc x$

41. $\sin 2x = \dfrac{2 \tan x}{1 + \tan^2 x}$ 42. $\dfrac{2}{\sin 2x} = \tan x + \cot x$

43. $\cot x - \cot 2x = \csc 2x$ 44. $\dfrac{2}{1 + \cos 2x} = \sec^2 x$

45. $\dfrac{1 + \cos 2x}{\sin 2x} = \cot x$ 46. $\cos 2x = \dfrac{1 - \tan^2 x}{1 + \tan^2 x}$

47. Express $\sin^2 x$ and $\cos^2 x$ in terms of $\cos 2x$.

48. Show that $\sin x_1 \cos x_2 = \frac{1}{2}[\sin (x_1 + x_2) + \sin (x_1 - x_2)]$.

49. Show that $\cos x_1 \cos x_2 = \frac{1}{2}[\cos (x_1 + x_2) + \cos (x_1 - x_2)]$.

50. Show that $\sin x_1 \sin x_2 = \frac{1}{2}[\cos (x_1 - x_2) - \cos (x_1 + x_2)]$.

8 TRIGONOMETRIC FUNCTIONS

8.1 ANGLES AND THEIR MEASURE

In studying geometry, we learn that an angle is the union of two rays with a common endpoint (Figure 8.1-a), and that an angle can be designated by naming a point on each ray together with the common endpoint of the rays, or else by simply assigning a single symbol, say α, to the angle. The common endpoint of the rays is called the **vertex** of the angle, and the rays are called the **sides** of the angle.

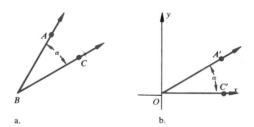

Figure 8.1

Now each angle in the plane is congruent ($\cong$) to an angle with one side along the positive x-axis, and with vertex at the origin (Figure 8.1-b). Such an angle is said to be in **standard position**. The side $\overrightarrow{OC'}$ of $\angle A'OC'$ in Figure 8.1-b is called the **initial side** of the angle, the side $\overrightarrow{OA'}$ is called the **terminal side**, and the angle can be visualized as being formed by a rotation from the initial side $\overrightarrow{OC'}$ into the terminal side $\overrightarrow{OA'}$. In trigonometry, the *amount of rotation* is considered along with the angle itself. If the terminal side of an angle in standard position lies in a given quadrant, we say that the angle is *in* that quadrant.

A measure is assigned to an angle by means of a circle with center at the vertex of the angle. For convenience, we shall restrict this discussion to the set of angles in standard position, although the process described is perfectly general. If the

Angle measurement

circumference of the circle, of radius $r > 0$, is divided into p arcs of equal length, then each of the arcs will have length $2\pi r/p$. Starting at the point $(r, 0)$, we can scale the circumference of the circle in both the counterclockwise and clockwise directions from this point, in terms of this arc length as a unit. In doing this, it is customary to assign *negative* numbers in the *clockwise* direction, and *positive* numbers in the *counterclockwise* direction. As an example, consider the circle in Figure 8.2, where the circumference is divided into 16 equal parts and the arc length of each part is $2\pi r/16$. The terminal side of any angle α in standard position intercepts the circumference at a point, and one of the scale numbers (arc lengths) assigned to that point becomes the measure of the angle, depending on the amount of rotation involved.

Note that although angles such as α_1, a_2, and α_3 in Figure 8.3 have the same initial side and the same terminal side, their measures are different because the amounts of rotation involved are different. Such angles are called **coterminal**.

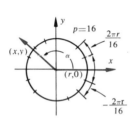

Figure 8.2

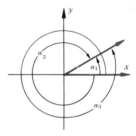

Figure 8.3

Recall from geometry that the lengths of arc intercepted by a given central angle on concentric circles are proportional to the circumferences of the circles. *It follows that the measure assigned to an angle in terms of a given unit is independent of the radius of the measuring circle.*

The two most commonly encountered units of angle measure are the **degree** and the **radian**. In degree measure, the circumference of the circle is divided into 360 arcs of equal length, and hence the unit arc is of length

$$\frac{2\pi r}{360} = \frac{\pi}{180} r,$$

where r is the radius of the circle. For this measure, we use the notation $m°(\alpha)$.

In radian measure, the circumference is divided into 2π arcs of equal length, and hence the length of the unit arc is

$$\frac{2\pi r}{2\pi} = r.$$

For this measure we use the notation $m^R(\alpha)$. Thus, in radian measure, the length of the unit arc is the length of the radius of the circle, and the circumference contains just 2π of these units. In particular, if the unit circle is used as the basis

Mil 1000th of circumference

for $m^R(\alpha)$, then the length of the unit arc is 1. For this reason, the unit circle is customarily used as a reference for the measure of an angle in radians.

Comparison of degree and radian measure Because the measures of a given angle in different units are proportional to the circumference of the measuring circle in these same units, we have

$$\frac{m^\circ(\alpha)}{360} = \frac{m^R(\alpha)}{2\pi},$$

use this one

so that

$$m^\circ(\alpha) = \frac{180}{\pi} m^R(\alpha) \qquad (1)$$

Know

and

$$m^R(\alpha) = \frac{\pi}{180} m^\circ(\alpha). \qquad (2)$$

Equations (1) and (2) are conversion formulas for expressing the relationships between degrees and radians.

Note that m° and m^R are functions, each with the set of all angles as domain and R as range. Several conventions regarding the use of symbolism for angles and their measure are customarily made in mathematics. For one thing, to express a relation such as $m^\circ(\alpha) = 40$ or $m^R(\beta) = \pi/4$, we usually write $\alpha = 40^\circ$ or $\beta = (\pi/4)^R$. Thus, for example, if α, β, and γ are the angles of a triangle, then

Symbolism for angles and their measure

$$m^R(\alpha) + m^R(\beta) + m^R(\gamma) = \pi,$$

and this equation is generally abbreviated

$$\alpha + \beta + \gamma = \pi^R.$$

This notation is consistent with the fact that if α and β are two angles, and $\alpha + \beta$ denotes their sum, then

$$m^R(\alpha + \beta) = m^R(\alpha) + m^R(\beta).$$

Here the **sum** $\alpha + \beta$ is construed to be the result of taking the terminal side of α as the initial side of β, with the same point for vertex, and then viewing $\alpha + \beta$ as the angle with initial side that of α and terminal side that of β, as in Figure 8.4.

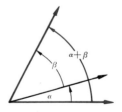

Figure 8.4

Following another convention, we sometimes write, for example,

$$m^\circ(\alpha) = 60^\circ \quad \text{or} \quad m^R(\alpha) = \frac{\pi^R}{3}.$$

Here, the appearance of the degree or radian symbol in the right-hand member of the equation should be interpreted as a clarifying redundancy, rather than as an indication that the functions $m°$ and m^R are being considered as having denominate-number ranges.

Example. Find the degree measure, to the nearest tenth of a degree, of the angle whose radian measure is given.

   a. $\dfrac{\pi^R}{3}$ b. 0.62^R

Solution.

   a. $\dfrac{\pi^R}{3} = \left(\dfrac{180}{\pi} \cdot \dfrac{\pi}{3}\right)° = 60°$ b. $0.62^R = \left(\dfrac{180}{\pi} \cdot 0.62\right)° = \dfrac{111.6°}{\pi} \approx 35.5°$

Example. Find the radian measure, to the nearest hundredth of a radian, of the angle whose degree measure is given.

   a. $30°$ b. $300°$

Solution.

   a. $30° = \left(\dfrac{\pi}{180} \cdot 30\right)^R = \dfrac{\pi^R}{6} \approx 0.52^R$ b. $300° = \left(\dfrac{\pi}{180} \cdot 300\right)^R = \dfrac{5\pi^R}{3} \approx 5.24^R$

Note that, in these examples, the number of units in one measure does not equal the number of units in another measure; e.g., $30 \neq \pi/6$. But an angle whose measure is $30°$ is congruent to an angle whose measure is $(\pi/6)^R$, and we express this fact by writing $30° = (\pi/6)^R$. This is analogous to 36 inches = 3 feet, 6 feet = 2 yards, etc., when indicating lengths of line segments in different units.

If the measure of an angle is given in radians, then the length s of the intercepted arc of a circle with given radius r can be found directly. That is,

$$s = r \cdot m^R(\alpha). \qquad (3)$$

If the measure of an angle is given in degrees, it can first be changed to radian measure and then the length of the intercepted arc can be found directly.

EXERCISE 8.1

Find the degree measure of the angle whose radian measure is as given.

   1. a. 0^R b. $\dfrac{\pi^R}{2}$ c. π^R d. $\dfrac{3\pi^R}{2}$ e. $2\pi^R$

2. By filling in the blank spaces, complete the following table, which compares the radian measure and degree measure of angles that are of frequent occurrence.

$m°(α)$	$m^R(α)$	$m°(α)$	$m^R(α)$
30°	$\frac{\pi}{6}$	210°	$\frac{7\pi}{6}$
45°	$\frac{\pi}{4}$	225°	$\frac{5\pi^R}{4}$
60°	$\frac{\pi^R}{3}$	240°	$\frac{4\pi^R}{3}$
120°	$\frac{2\pi}{3}$	300°	$\frac{5\pi^R}{3}$
135°	$\frac{3\pi}{4}$	315°	$\frac{7\pi}{4}$
150°	$\frac{5\pi^R}{6}$	330°	$\frac{11\pi}{6}$

$\frac{3\pi}{2} = 270°$

Find the degree measure, to the nearest tenth of a degree, of the angle whose radian measure is as given.

3. $\frac{2\pi^R}{9}$ 4. $\frac{3\pi^R}{5}$ 5. $\frac{7\pi^R}{5}$ 6. $\frac{5\pi^R}{8}$

7. 0.30^R 8. 1.25^R 9. 3.62^R 10. 9.14^R

Find the radian measure, to the nearest hundredth of a radian, of the angle whose degree measure is as given.

11. 20° .35   12. 50°   13. 130° 2.27   14. 310°

15. 420°   16. 580°   17. 750° 13.09   18. 800°

19. What is the degree measure, to the nearest hundredth of a degree, of an angle whose radian measure is 1^R?

20. What is the radian measure, to the nearest thousandth of a radian, of an angle whose degree measure is 1°?

Find all angles $α$ satisfying $-360° \leq α \leq 720°$ that are coterminal with the angle whose measure is given. Write a representation for the measures of *all* angles coterminal with the angle.

Examples. a. 24°   b. $-184°$

Solutions. a. $24° + 360° = 384°$ b. $-184° + 360° = 176°$
$\qquad\qquad\quad 24° - 360° = -336°$ $\qquad -184° + 720° = 536°$
$\qquad\qquad\quad 24° + 360°k, \quad k \in J$ $\qquad -184° + 360°k, \quad k \in J$

21. $30°$ 22. $-150°$ 23. $-240°$ 24. $190°$

25. $420°$ 26. $683°$ 27. $-330°$ 28. $-271°$

On a circle with given radius, find the length of the arc intercepted by the angle whose measure is as given.

Example. $r = 3''$; $m°(\alpha) = 120$

Solution. The measure of the angle is first changed to radian measure. Thus

$$m^R(\alpha) = \left(\frac{\pi}{180} \cdot 120\right)^R = \frac{2\pi^R}{3}.$$

Then, by Equation (3),

$$s = r \cdot m^R(\alpha) = 3 \cdot \frac{2\pi}{3} = 2\pi \approx 6.28.$$

Therefore, the desired arc length is approximately $6.28''$.

29. $r = 4''$; $\dfrac{\pi^R}{6}$ 30. $r = 5.2''$; π^R 31. $r = 1.2'$; $0.60^{R'}$

32. $r = 3.6'$; 1^R 33. $r = 2''$; $135°$ 34. $r = 4.3''$; $180°$

8.2 FUNCTIONS OF ANGLES

Historically, interest in the circular functions arose from the study of angles and triangles. In defining the circular functions, we used the notion of arc length on a unit circle to associate a real number [the arc length from the point $(1, 0)$ to a point on the circle] with another real number, the first or second coordinate of the point. Thus we defined functions with real numbers *both* for domain and for range.

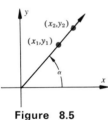

Figure 8.5

Now, consider any angle α in standard position, and let (x_1, y_1) and (x_2, y_2) be any two distinct points (except the origin) in its terminal side or ray (Figure 8.5). We can show that the following equalities of ratios hold:

$$\frac{x_1}{y_1} = \frac{x_2}{y_2} \quad (y_1, y_2 \neq 0), \qquad \frac{x_1}{\sqrt{x_1^2 + y_1^2}} = \frac{x_2}{\sqrt{x_2^2 + y_2^2}}, \quad \text{and} \quad \frac{y_1}{\sqrt{x_1^2 + y_1^2}} = \frac{y_2}{\sqrt{x_2^2 + y_2^2}}.$$

The proofs of these are left as exercises.

Although the figure shows the terminal side of α in the first quadrant, the ratios are equal for coordinates of points on the terminal side of an angle in any quadrant. Because these ratios do not depend on the choice of a point in the terminal side of α, we can use them to define some new functions, each with *the set of angles in standard position* as domain, and with sets of real numbers as ranges.

Geometric ratios in the coordinate plane

Traditionally, six such assignments are made, and the names given the resulting functions are those we have used to name the circular functions.

DEFINITION 8.1 *If α is an angle in standard position, and if $(x, y) \neq (0, 0)$ is any point on the terminal side of α, then*

$$\text{cosine} = \left\{ (\alpha, \cos \alpha) \mid \cos \alpha = \frac{x}{\sqrt{x^2 + y^2}} \right\},$$

II $$\text{sine} = \left\{ (\alpha, \sin \alpha) \mid \sin \alpha = \frac{y}{\sqrt{x^2 + y^2}} \right\},$$

III $$\text{tangent} = \left\{ (\alpha, \tan \alpha) \mid \tan \alpha = \frac{y}{x}, \quad x \neq 0 \right\},$$

IV $$\text{cotangent} = \left\{ (\alpha, \cot \alpha) \mid \cot \alpha = \frac{x}{y}, \quad y \neq 0 \right\},$$

V $$\text{secant} = \left\{ (\alpha, \sec \alpha) \mid \sec \alpha = \frac{\sqrt{x^2 + y^2}}{x}, \quad x \neq 0 \right\},$$

VI $$\text{cosecant} = \left\{ (\alpha, \csc \alpha) \mid \csc \alpha = \frac{\sqrt{x^2 + y^2}}{y}, \quad y \neq 0 \right\}.$$

These functions are called **trigonometric**. Observe that in each place where the expression $\sqrt{x^2 + y^2}$ occurs, the *positive* root is used.

Example. Find the element in the range for each of the six trigonometric functions of α, if the terminal side of α contains the point $(-3, 5)$.

Solution. By Definition 8.1,

$$\cos \alpha = \frac{x}{\sqrt{x^2 + y^2}}$$
$$= \frac{-3}{\sqrt{9 + 25}} = -\frac{3}{\sqrt{34}},$$

$$\sin \alpha = \frac{y}{\sqrt{x^2 + y^2}}$$
$$= \frac{5}{\sqrt{9 + 25}} = \frac{5}{\sqrt{34}},$$

$$\tan \alpha = \frac{y}{x} = \frac{5}{-3} = -\frac{5}{3},$$

$$\sec \alpha = \frac{\sqrt{x^2 + y^2}}{x}$$
$$= \frac{\sqrt{9 + 25}}{-3} = -\frac{\sqrt{34}}{3},$$

$$\csc \alpha = \frac{\sqrt{x^2 + y^2}}{y}$$
$$= \frac{\sqrt{9 + 25}}{5} = \frac{\sqrt{34}}{5},$$

$$\cot \alpha = \frac{x}{y} = \frac{-3}{5} = -\frac{3}{5}.$$

Because every angle in the plane is congruent to an angle in standard position, the definitions of the trigonometric functions can be extended to assign the

Angles not in standard position

same numbers to every angle congruent to a given angle α. Thus, while these functions are defined in terms of angles in standard position, they can be viewed as applying to the set of all angles in the plane. Moreover, since congruent angles have the same measure, we can identify angles in the domain of each function with a particular unit of measure. Thus, we write

$$\sin 30° \quad \text{and} \quad \sin \frac{\pi^R}{6}$$

as abbreviations for "the sine of an angle whose measure is 30 degrees" and "the sine of an angle whose measure is $\pi/6$ radians," respectively.

Relationship between circular and trigonometric functions

The fact that the circular functions are defined using the unit circle, together with the fact that the unit circle can be used to assign measures to angles, makes it reasonable to expect a very close relationship to exist between the circular and trigonometric functions. Such is indeed the case.

Since the trigonometric functions of an angle α have been defined in terms of the coordinates of *any* point other than the origin on the terminal side of α, we can arbitrarily choose the point $P(\cos x, \sin x)$ where the terminal side of the angle intersects the unit circle. Thus,

$$\cos \alpha = \frac{\cos x}{1} = \cos x,$$

and similarly,

$$\sin \alpha = \frac{\sin x}{1} = \sin x$$

(Figure 8.6). From this, we see that the elements in the ranges of the trigonometric functions are equal to the corresponding elements in the ranges of the analogous circular functions. Thus, if we denote any one of the six trigonometric functions by T, and the circular functions of the same name by C, then

$$T(\alpha) = C(x), \tag{1}$$

where x is the length of the arc intercepted by α on the unit circle. Notice that elements x in the domain of C are *real numbers*, while elements α in the domain of T are *angles*. The elements in the range of each function are real numbers.

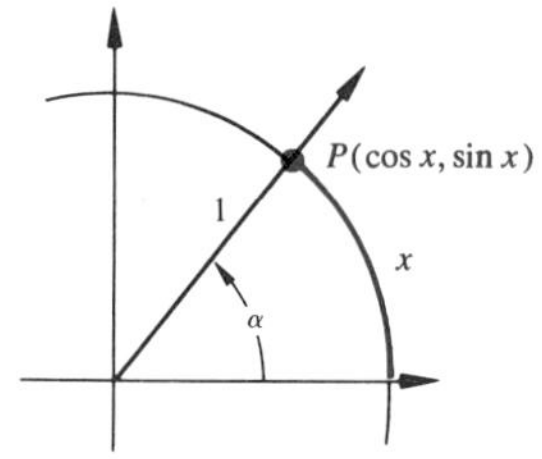

In Section 8.1 we agreed to name an angle by its measure. In particular, if

$P(\cos x, \sin x)$

Figure 8.6

$m^R(\alpha) = x$, then we write $\alpha = x^R$, and if $m°(\alpha) = t$, then we write $\alpha = t°$. Thus by replacing α by x^R in (1), we obtain

$$T(x^R) = C(x)$$

and

$$T(t°) = C(x).$$

For example,

$$\cos \frac{\pi^R}{3} = \cos \frac{\pi}{3}$$

and

$$\cos 60° = \cos \frac{\pi}{3},$$

where in each equation the left-hand member is an element in the range of the *trigonometric* function and the right-hand member is an element in the range of the analogous *circular* function.

Tables for trigonometric functions

Using relationship (1), we obtain the entries of Table 8.1 directly from Table 7.1, page 160, the results of Problems 1 and 2, Exercise 7.6, and the relationship between degree and radian measures of angles. These are left for you to verify.

TABLE 8.1

$m°(\alpha)$	$m^R(\alpha)$	$\sin \alpha$	$\csc \alpha$	$\cos \alpha$	$\sec \alpha$	$\tan \alpha$	$\cot \alpha$
$0°$	0^R	0	not defined	1	1	0	not defined
$30°$	$\dfrac{\pi^R}{6}$	$\dfrac{1}{2}$	2	$\dfrac{\sqrt{3}}{2}$	$\dfrac{2}{\sqrt{3}}$	$\dfrac{1}{\sqrt{3}}$	$\sqrt{3}$
$45°$	$\dfrac{\pi^R}{4}$	$\dfrac{1}{\sqrt{2}}$	$\sqrt{2}$	$\dfrac{1}{\sqrt{2}}$	$\sqrt{2}$	1	1
$60°$	$\dfrac{\pi^R}{3}$	$\dfrac{\sqrt{3}}{2}$	$\dfrac{2}{\sqrt{3}}$	$\dfrac{1}{2}$	2	$\sqrt{3}$	$\dfrac{1}{\sqrt{3}}$
$90°$	$\dfrac{\pi^R}{2}$	1	1	0	not defined	not defined	0
$180°$	π^R	0	not defined	-1	-1	0	not defined
$270°$	$\dfrac{3\pi^R}{2}$	-1	-1	0	not defined	not defined	0

Since, as observed on page 195,

Sum and difference formulas for trigonometric functions

$$m^R(\alpha + \beta) = m^R(\alpha) + m^R(\beta)$$

for any angles α and β, all of the sum and difference formulas are immediately valid for sums and differences of angles. Thus, for any angles α and β,

$$\cos(\alpha + \beta) = \cos\alpha\cos\beta - \sin\alpha\sin\beta$$
$$\cos(\alpha - \beta) = \cos\alpha\cos\beta + \sin\alpha\sin\beta$$
$$\sin(\alpha + \beta) = \sin\alpha\cos\beta + \cos\alpha\sin\beta$$
$$\sin(\alpha - \beta) = \sin\alpha\cos\beta - \cos\alpha\sin\beta.$$

If half of an angle is interpreted to mean an angle formed by the initial side of the angle together with the bisector of the angle (Figure 8.7), then it is also true that

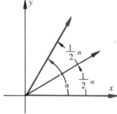

$$m^R(\tfrac{1}{2}\alpha) = \tfrac{1}{2}m^R(\alpha),$$

and the formulas developed in Sections 7.5 and 7.6 are also valid for the trigonometric functions.

In summary, the correspondence between the values of the circular functions and those of the trigonometric functions,

Figure 8.7

$$T(\alpha) = C(x), \tag{1}$$

renders all of the relationships thus far studied for circular functions equally applicable to the trigonometric functions. Because the elements

Other formulas for trigonometric functions

in the domains of the trigonometric functions are angles, an identity such as

$$\sin 2\alpha = 2\sin\alpha\cos\alpha$$

is sometimes called a **double-angle formula**, while an identity such as

$$\sin\frac{\alpha}{2} = \pm\sqrt{\frac{1 - \cos\alpha}{2}}$$

is called a **half-angle formula**.

Trigonometric function values for $\sin\alpha$, $\cos\alpha$, and so on that are not listed in Table 8.1 can be obtained from Table V in the Appendix if $m^R(\alpha)$ is known.

Tables for trigonometric functions

Table VI in the Appendix gives trigonometric function values of angles with given degree measure. The table is graduated in intervals of 10 minutes (10′), one minute being equal to one-sixtieth of a degree. We can interpolate as necessary to find, to four significant figures, values between those listed in the table. Observe that the table reads from top to bottom for $0° \le \alpha \le 45°$, where the function values are identified at the top of the page, and from bottom to top for $45° \le \alpha \le 90°$, where the function values are identified at the bottom of the page.

Example.   Find tan 149°.

Solution.   From the reduction formula

$$\tan \alpha = -\tan (180° - \alpha),$$

we have

$$\tan 149° = -\tan (180° - 149°)$$
$$= -\tan 31°.$$

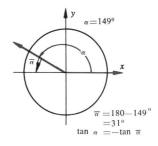

From Table VI in the appendix, we find that
tan 31° ≈ 0.6009. Thus

$$\tan 149° \approx -0.6009.$$

Observe that in the preceding example we again used the symbol ≈ because the function values obtained from the table are approximations to irrational numbers.

EXERCISE 8.2

Use Table V or Table VI, as appropriate, to find values for each of the following. Give values to four significant figures.

1. sin 32°   2. cos 49°   3. tan 33°   4. cot 51°

5. sec 17°   6. csc 84°   7. cos 0.63^R 8. sin 0.42^R

9. cot 1.42^R 10. tan 1.03^R 11. csc $\dfrac{5\pi^R}{9}$ 12. sec $\dfrac{5\pi^R}{12}$

Use the appropriate formulas and the trigonometric function values for 90°, 180°, and 270° to prove each of the following reduction formulas.

Example. $\sin (180° + \theta) = -\sin \theta.$

Solution.   Since $\sin (\alpha + \beta) = \sin \alpha \cos \beta + \cos \alpha \sin \beta,$
$$\sin (180° + \theta) = \sin 180° \cos \theta + \cos 180° \sin \theta$$
$$= (0) \cos \theta + (-1) \sin \theta$$
$$= -\sin \theta.$$

13. $\sin (90° - \theta) = \cos \theta$ 14. $\cos (90° - \theta) = \sin \theta$

15. $\sin (180° - \theta) = \sin \theta$ 16. $\cos (180° + \theta) = -\cos \theta$

17. $\sin (270° + \theta) = -\cos \theta$ 18. $\cos (270° - \theta) = -\sin \theta$

19. $\tan (180° - \theta) = -\tan \theta$ 20. $\tan (270° + \theta) = -\cot \theta$

21. Use the difference formulas and $\sin 360° = 0$ and $\cos 360° = 1$ to show that
    $\sin (360° - \theta) = -\sin \theta.$ $d = \sqrt{(x_2 - x_1)^2 + (y_2 - y_1)^2}$

22. Show that $\cos (360° - \theta) = \cos \theta$ and $\tan (360° - \theta) = -\tan \theta.$

Use Table 8.1 and reduction formulas to find the value of each of the following.

23. sin 150°   24. cos 135°   25. tan 330°

26. cot 120°   27. cos 225°   28. tan 150°

29. sin 330°   30. cos 240°   31. sin (−30°)

32. tan (−60°)   33. sin (−240°)   34. cos (−135°)

35. tan (−300°)   36. tan (−750°)

Use Table V and Table VI, as appropriate, to find function values to four significant figures for each of the following.

37. sin 132°   38. cos 153°   39. tan 320°

40. sin 312°   41. cos (−130°)   42. tan (−605°)

43. sin 2.07^R 44. cos 3.51^R 45. tan 4.21^R

46. tan 6.00^R 47. cos $(−1.63^R)$ 48. sin $(−12.32^R)$

Determine in which quadrant the terminal side of each angle lies.

Example. sin α > 0, cos α < 0.

Solution. Since sin α > 0, the terminal side of α lies in Quadrant I or II; since cos α < 0, the terminal side of α lies in Quadrant II or III. Therefore, the terminal side of α lies in Quadrant II, the intersection of {I, II} and {II, III}.

49. sin α < 0, cos α > 0   50. cos α > 0, tan α < 0

51. sec α > 0, sin α > 0   52. tan α < 0, sin α > 0

53. sec α > 0, csc α < 0   54. cot α > 0, sin α < 0

Prove each of the following identities.

55. $\tan (90° − \theta) = \cot \theta$ 56. $\cot (90° − \theta) = \tan \theta$

57. $\csc (90° − \theta) = \sec \theta$ 58. $\sec (90° − \theta) = \csc \theta$

59. $(1 − \cos^2 \theta)\sec^2 \theta = \tan^2 \theta$ 60. $(\csc \theta − \sec \theta) \sin \theta = 1 − \tan \theta$

61. $\dfrac{1 + \cot \theta}{\csc \theta} = \dfrac{1 + \tan \theta}{\sec \theta}$

62. $(\tan \theta + \cot \theta)(\sec \theta − \cos \theta) = \sec \theta \tan \theta$

63. $\tan (\theta + 45°) = \dfrac{1 + \tan \theta}{1 − \tan \theta}$ 64. $\tan \theta = \dfrac{\sin 2\theta}{1 + \cos 2\theta}$

65. $\cos^4 \theta − \sin^4 \theta = \cos 2\theta$ 66. $\dfrac{\sin 2\theta}{\sin \theta} + \dfrac{\cos 2\theta + 1}{\cos \theta} = 4 \cos \theta$

67. Show (geometrically) that if (x_1, y_1) and (x_2, y_2) are the coordinates of any two points (except the origin) on the terminal side (ray) of an angle in the first quadrant, then the following equalities of ratios hold:

$$\frac{x_1}{y_1} = \frac{x_2}{y_2} \ (y_1, y_2 \neq 0), \quad \frac{x_1}{\sqrt{x_1^2 + y_1^2}} = \frac{x_2}{\sqrt{x_2^2 + y_2^2}}, \quad \text{and} \quad \frac{y_1}{\sqrt{x_1^2 + y_1^2}} = \frac{y_2}{\sqrt{x_2^2 + y_2^2}}.$$

68. Under the same conditions as in Problem 67, explain how the equalities of these ratios hold for the coordinates of two points on the terminal side of an angle whose terminal side is located in the second, third, and fourth quadrants.

8.3 RIGHT TRIANGLES

An examination of Figure 8.8-a makes it evident that, in the first quadrant, any point (x, y) on the terminal side of an angle α determines a right triangle with sides measuring x and y, and with hypotenuse of length $\sqrt{x^2 + y^2}$. Therefore, as special

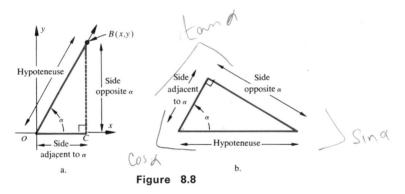

Figure 8.8

cases of trigonometric function values, we can consider the following **trigonometric ratios** of the sides of a right triangle:

$$\sin \alpha = \frac{\text{length of side opposite } \alpha}{\text{length of hypotenuse}},$$

$$\cos \alpha = \frac{\text{length of side adjacent to } \alpha}{\text{length of hypotenuse}},$$

$$\tan \alpha = \frac{\text{length of side opposite } \alpha}{\text{length of side adjacent to } \alpha}.$$

Similar statements can be made about $\csc \alpha$, $\sec \alpha$, and $\cot \alpha$. It is not necessary that the right triangle be oriented in such a way that α is in standard position. The above relations involving ratios of the lengths of the sides of a right triangle are equally applicable to a right triangle in any position, as suggested in Figure 8.8-b.

$$\sin\left(\frac{\pi}{2}-q\right) = \frac{x}{d} = \cos q$$
$$\cos\left(\frac{\pi}{2}-q\right) = \frac{y}{d} = \sin q$$

If we are given some parts of a triangle, that is, the measures of some angles and
Solution of a triangle the lengths of some sides, and asked to find the remaining measures, we are asked to **solve** the triangle. In general, we shall give solutions to the nearest tenth of a unit for lengths and to the nearest 10′ for the degree measures of angles.

Example. If one angle of a right triangle measures 47° and the side adjacent to this angle has length 24, solve the triangle and determine its area.

Solution. We first make a sketch illustrating the situation. Generally the hypotenuse is labeled c, the legs a and b, and the angles opposite a, b, and c are labeled α, β, and γ, respectively, or A, B, and C, respectively. In the present case, we note first that

$$\beta = 90° - \alpha = 90° - 47° = 43°.$$

Next we have

$$\tan 47° = \frac{a}{b} = \frac{a}{24}, \quad \text{or} \quad a = 24 \tan 47°,$$

and

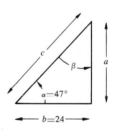

$$\sec 47° = \frac{c}{b} = \frac{c}{24}, \quad \text{or} \quad c = 24 \sec 47°.$$

From Table VI in the Appendix, $\tan 47° \approx 1.072$, and $\sec 47° \approx 1.466$, so that

$$a \approx 24(1.072) \approx 25.7,$$
$$c \approx 24(1.466) \approx 35.2.$$

The area, which is equal to half the product of the length of the base by the length of the altitude, is given by

$$\mathscr{A} = \frac{1}{2} ab \approx \frac{1}{2}(25.7)(24) = 308.4.$$

Note that the ratio selected in each case in the foregoing example was one in
Choice of ratios which the length of the remaining side and the length of the hypotenuse appeared in the numerator. With such a selection of ratios, the operation in the computation is multiplication rather than division.

Use of logarithms in solving triangles Logarithms can be used to perform the computations in the above example and in many of the problems that follow. Handbooks are available with the logarithms of the trigonometric ratios to various degrees of accuracy if you wish to use them, although devices such as the slide rule, desk calculator, and computer have largely replaced logarithms for such computations.

Right triangles play a useful role in finding one trigonometric function value, given another.

$\cos \theta = \frac{1}{3}$

$\tan \alpha = \sqrt{8}$

$\sin \alpha \frac{\sqrt{8}}{3}$

$1^2 + \sqrt{8}^2 = 3^2$

$\sqrt{8} = \sqrt{8}$

$\sin = \frac{\text{len't op side}}{\text{length of hyp}}$

Example. If $\tan \alpha = 2/3$ and α is in Quadrant I, find $\sin \alpha$.

Solution. Sketch a right triangle and label the sides so that $\tan \alpha$ is as given. By the Pythagorean theorem, the hypotenuse of the triangle has length $\sqrt{2^2 + 3^2} = \sqrt{13}$, so that $\sin \alpha = 2/\sqrt{13}$.

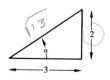

Note in this example that once the length of the hypotenuse is determined, *all* of the values for trigonometric functions of α are available by inspection.

Right triangles are helpful also in quadrants other than the first if care is taken to assign *directed distances* as lengths to the sides, while viewing the length of the hypotenuse as always positive. This is simply a variation on our procedures for finding function values using reduction formulas or using reference angles.

Example. If $\cot \alpha = \frac{3}{7}$, and $\sin \alpha < 0$, find $\cos \alpha$.

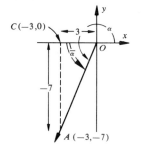

Solution. Since $\cot \alpha > 0$ while $\sin \alpha < 0$, α can only lie in Quadrant III. Make a sketch, and show a perpendicular line segment from the point $A(-3, -7)$ on the terminal side of α to the point $C(-3, 0)$ on the x-axis. The point $(-3, -7)$ was selected because, in the triangle OAC,

$$\cot \bar{\alpha} = \frac{\text{length of side adjacent to } \alpha}{\text{length of side opposite } \alpha},$$

and $|\cot \bar{\alpha}| = |\cot \alpha|$. By the Pythagorean theorem,

$$\text{length of } \overline{OA} = l(\overline{OA}) = \sqrt{(-3)^2 + (-7)^2} = \sqrt{9 + 49} = \sqrt{58}.$$

By inspection, then, $\cos \alpha = \frac{-3}{\sqrt{58}}$.

EXERCISE 8.3

Solve each of the following right triangles ABC, and determine its area. Consider $C = 90°$. In all problems in this exercise set, give lengths to the nearest tenth of a unit and angle measures to the nearest 10'.

1. $a = 6, b = 8$ 2. $c = 24, A = 32°$

3. $b = 120, B = 54°$ 4. $a = 3.5, B = 48°$

5. $c = 16, A = 22°$ 6. $a = 5, c = 16$

7. In the right triangle ABC, find a if $\sin A = \frac{4}{5}$ and $c = 20$.

8. In the right triangle ABC, find b if $\tan A = \frac{3}{4}$ and $a = 12$.

9. Find the other trigonometric function values of θ when $\sin \theta = -\dfrac{1}{2}$ and the terminal side of θ is in the third quadrant.

10. Find the other trigonometric function values of θ when $\tan \theta = -\dfrac{7}{24}$ and the terminal side of θ is in the fourth quadrant.

11. Find the length of the base of an isosceles triangle if the length of one of the equal sides is 12 inches and the measure of one of the equal angles is $40°$.

12. Find the perimeter of a regular pentagon inscribed in a circle of radius 8 inches.

In each case, sketch the angle θ and an appropriate right triangle, and find the other trigonometric function values.

13. $\sin \theta = \dfrac{3}{5}$ 　　　　　 14. $\cos \theta = -\dfrac{12}{13}$ 　　　　　 15. $\tan \theta = \dfrac{5}{12}$

16. $\cot \theta = \dfrac{4}{3}$ 　　　　　 17. $\sec \theta = -2$ 　　　　　 18. $\csc \theta = 3$

19. Find the value of $\dfrac{\sin \theta + 2 \cos \theta - \tan \theta}{1 - \cot \theta + \sec \theta}$ if $\tan \theta = 1$ and the terminal side of θ is in the third quadrant.

20. Find the value of $\dfrac{\csc^2 \theta + \sin \theta - 1}{2 - \tan^2 \theta + \cot^2 \theta}$ if $\sin \theta = \dfrac{1}{2}$ and the terminal side of θ is in the second quadrant.

In Problems 21 and 22, given the information pertaining to the figure, find the length of the line segment denoted by x.

21. Given:
$$l(\overline{BA}) = 25,$$
$$\alpha = 16°,$$
$$\beta = 12°,$$
BC is a straight line.

22. Given:
$$l(\overline{AB}) = 350,$$
$$\alpha = 21°,$$
$$\beta = 8°,$$
BD is a straight line.

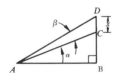

23. Find the area of a parallelogram if two of its adjacent sides are 22 and 28 inches in length and the measure of the included angle is $40°$.

24. In a circle, the length of the radius is 10 inches and the length of a chord is 12 inches. Find the measure of the angle made by two lines tangent to the circle at the ends of the chord.

25. A rectangle is 80 feet long and 64 feet wide. Find the measures of the angles between a diagonal and the sides.

26. The sides of an isosceles triangle have lengths, 6, 6, and 8. Find a measure for each angle in the triangle.

27. The angle of elevation (the angle between the line of sight and the horizontal) from a point 200 feet from the base of a building to the base of a flagpole on top of the building is 60°. The angle of elevation from the same spot to the top of the flagpole is 65°. How tall is the flagpole?

28. Each of two surveyors is located 200 feet from a flagpole. If the angle between the flagpole and one surveyor, when measured by the other surveyor, is 36°, how far apart are the two surveyors?

29. Show that if s is the length of the side of a regular polygon of n sides, and r is the length of the radius of the inscribed circle, then $r = \tfrac{1}{2}s \cot (180°/n)$.

8.4 THE LAW OF SINES

The fact that the area $\mathscr{A}$ of a triangle is equal to one-half the product of the length of its base and the length of its altitude gives us an immediate expression for its area in terms of the lengths of two sides of the triangle and the measure of the included angle. Thus, from Figure 8.9,

Expressions for the area of a triangle

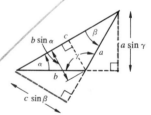

Figure 8.9

$$\mathscr{A} = \tfrac{1}{2}c(b \sin \alpha) = \tfrac{1}{2}bc \sin \alpha,$$
$$\mathscr{A} = \tfrac{1}{2}a(c \sin \beta) = \tfrac{1}{2}ac \sin \beta,$$
$$\mathscr{A} = \tfrac{1}{2}b(a \sin \gamma) = \tfrac{1}{2}ab \sin \gamma.$$

Because each triangle has only one area, we can equate the right-hand members of these equations to obtain

$$\frac{1}{2} bc \sin \alpha = \frac{1}{2} ac \sin \beta = \frac{1}{2} ab \sin \gamma.$$

Multiplying each member here by $2/(abc)$, we obtain the following result, called the **Law of Sines.**

THEOREM 8.1   *If α, β, and γ are the angles of a triangle, and if a is the length of the side opposite α, b is the length of the side opposite β, and c is the length of the side opposite γ, then*

$$\frac{\sin \alpha}{a} = \frac{\sin \beta}{b} = \frac{\sin \gamma}{c}.$$

Use of the law of sines in solving triangles   The law of sines can be used to solve certain triangles. Let us first consider the case in which two angles and one side of a triangle are given.

Example. Solve the triangle for which

$$\alpha = 45°, \quad \beta = 60°, \quad \text{and} \quad a = 10.$$

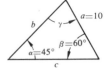

Solution. It is helpful first to make a sketch. Then, from Theorem 8.1, we have

$$\frac{\sin 45°}{10} = \frac{\sin 60°}{b},$$

from which

$$b = \frac{10 \sin 60°}{\sin 45°} = \frac{10 \cdot \dfrac{\sqrt{3}}{2}}{\dfrac{1}{\sqrt{2}}} \approx 12.245 \approx 12.2.$$

Next, we observe that

$$\gamma = 180° - \alpha - \beta = 180° - 45° - 60° = 75°.$$

From Theorem 8.1, we have

$$\frac{\sin 45°}{a} = \frac{\sin 75°}{c}.$$

Then, from Table VI,

$$c = \frac{10 \sin 75°}{\sin 45°} \approx 10 \left(\frac{0.9659}{0.7071} \right) \approx 10(1.36) = 13.6.$$

Thus, we have

$$b \approx 12.2, \quad c \approx 13.6, \quad \text{and} \quad \gamma = 75°.$$

If the lengths of two sides of a triangle, say a and b, and the measure of an angle opposite one of them, say α, are given, and the law of sines is used to solve the triangle, we may encounter ambiguity, depending on the value of a in relation to those of b and α. In Figure 8.10, we hold b and α constant and observe the possible situations as a assumes different values.

Ambiguous case

First we determine the length h of the altitude of a triangle with the given measures for the angle α and the adjacent side b. Since $\sin \alpha = h/b$,

$$h = b \sin \alpha.$$

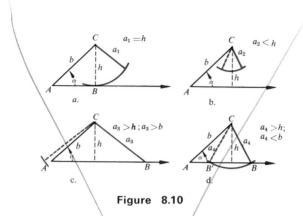

Figure 8.10

Now consider the case (Figure 8.10-a) in which the length a of the given side satisfies the equation

$$a = b \sin \alpha.$$

We have a unique solution—a right triangle. Next consider the case (Figure 8.10-b) in which the length a of the given side satisfies the inequality

$$a < b \sin \alpha.$$

Since a is less than h, the given values are such that no triangle is possible. Next consider the case (Figure 8.10-c) in which the length a of the given side is such that

$$a > b \sin \alpha \quad \text{and} \quad a \geq b.$$

Here we have a unique solution. For the fourth and last possibility (Figure 8.10-d), in which the length a of the given side is such that

$$a > b \sin \alpha \quad \text{and} \quad a < b,$$

we have two triangles possible, $\triangle ABC$ and $\triangle AB'C$.

Of course, if the given angle α is obtuse (Figure 8.11), then any specified lengths of the sides and measures of the angles permit only two possibilities:

1. $a \leq b$, no triangle (as shown in Figure 8.11-a);
2. $a > b$, one oblique triangle (as shown in Figure 8.11-b).

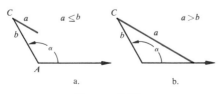

Figure 8.11

Example. Solve the triangle for which $a = 4$, $b = 3$, and $\beta = 45°$.

Solution. We first sketch a figure and observe that this gives rise to the ambiguous case in which we are given the lengths of two sides and the measure of an angle opposite one of them. We first check for the number of possible solutions and observe that $b > a \sin \beta$ and $b < a$. Therefore, there are two triangles with the given measurements. Using Theorem 8.1, we next determine a value for $\sin \alpha$. We have

$$\frac{\sin \alpha}{4} = \frac{\sin 45°}{3},$$

$$\sin \alpha = \frac{4}{3} \cdot \frac{\sqrt{2}}{2} = \frac{2}{3}\sqrt{2} \approx \frac{2}{3}(1.414) \approx 0.9426.$$

Because $\sin \alpha > 0$ in Quadrants I and II, from Table VI we have either

$$\alpha \approx 70° \; 30' \quad \text{or} \quad \alpha' \approx 180° - 70° \; 30' = 109° \; 30'.$$

If $\alpha \approx 70° \; 30'$, then $\gamma \approx 180° - 45° - 70° \; 30' = 64° \; 30'$, and we therefore have

$$\frac{\sin 45°}{3} \approx \frac{\sin 64° \; 30'}{c},$$

so that

$$c \approx 3\left(\frac{0.9026}{0.7071}\right) \approx 3.8.$$

If $\alpha' \approx 109° \; 30'$, then $\gamma' \approx 180° - 45° - 109° \; 30' = 25° \; 30'$, and we have

$$\frac{\sin 45°}{3} \approx \frac{\sin 25° \; 30'}{c},$$

so that

$$c' \approx 3\left(\frac{0.4305}{0.7071}\right) \approx 1.8.$$

Thus, the two solutions for the triangle are

$$\alpha \approx 70° \; 30', \quad \gamma \approx 64° \; 30', \quad c \approx 3.8$$

and

$$\alpha' \approx 109° \; 30', \quad \gamma' \approx 25° \; 30', \quad c' \approx 1.8.$$

EXERCISE 8.4

Solve the following triangles. In all problems in this exercise, give lengths to the nearest tenth and angle measures to the nearest $10'$.

1. $b = 10$, $B = 30°$, $A = 80°$ 2. $a = 64$, $B = 36° \; 10'$, $C = 82° \; 20'$

3. $c = 78.1$, $A = 58° \; 50'$, $C = 63° \; 10'$ 4. $b = 1.02$, $B = 41° \; 10'$, $C = 80° \; 20'$

5. $a = 84.2$, $A = 110°$, $C = 22° \; 20'$ 6. $c = 0.94$, $A = 41° \; 10'$, $B = 96° \; 50'$

Determine the number of triangles that satisfy the conditions in each problem.

Example. $b = 34, c = 12, C = 30°$

Solution. Sketch a figure and determine

$$c < h = b \sin C$$

$$h = b \sin C = 34 \cdot \frac{1}{2} = 17.$$

Since $12 < 17$, we have

$$c < b \sin C,$$

and no triangle exists for the given data.

7. $a = 5.4, b = 7.0, B = 30°$ 8. $b = 4.9, c = 3.2, C = 30°$

9. $a = 31.1, c = 41.3, C = 30°$ 10. $a = 42.3, b = 20.7, B = 30°$

11. $b = 16.2, c = 14.3, C = 20°$ 12. $a = 141, b = 182, B = 20°$

13. $a = 4.6, b = 2.3, B = 30°$ 14. $b = 68.1, c = 41.3, C = 30°$

Solve the following triangles.

15. $a = 4.8, c = 3.9, A = 113°$ 16. $a = 3.2, b = 2.6, B = 54°$

17. $b = 6.21, c = 4.39, B = 42° \ 40'$ 18. $a = 179, b = 212, B = 114° \ 10'$

19. $b = 1.8, c = 1.5, C = 32° \ 30'$ 20. $a = 9.4, b = 8.6, B = 54° \ 20'$

21. $a = 8.4, b = 6.9, B = 62° \ 10'$ 22. $b = 0.42, c = 0.21, B = 31° \ 50'$

23. $a = 13.84, b = 6.92, A = 60°$ 24. $a = 4.72, c = 9.44, A = 30°$

25. $b = 420, c = 610, B = 33° \ 20'$ 26. $a = 5.42, b = 6.82, A = 43° \ 30'$

Find the area $\mathscr{A}$ of each of the following triangles to the nearest tenth of a unit.

Example. $a = 23.1, A = 44°, C = 26°$

Solution. Make a sketch. Since we are given measures for two angles and one side, only one solution is possible. First we have

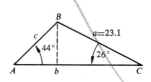

$$B = 180° - 44° - 26° = 110°.$$

From the law of sines,

$$\frac{b}{\sin 110°} = \frac{23.1}{\sin 44°},$$

and

$$b = \frac{23.1 \sin 110°}{\sin 44°}. \quad \textit{(Solution continued overleaf.)}$$

Since $h = 23.1 \sin 26°$,

$$\mathcal{A} = \frac{1}{2}hb = \frac{1}{2}(23.1 \sin 26°) \cdot \left(\frac{23.1 \sin 110°}{\sin 44°}\right) \approx 158.$$

27. $a = 6.4$, $b = 8.2$, $B = 30°$ 28. $c = 4.5$, $A = 24°$, $C = 61°$

29. $b = 4.95$, $A = 16° \; 10'$, $B = 60° \; 30'$ 30. $b = 6.3$, $c = 4.3$, $B = 42° \; 10'$

31. $a = 1.14$, $b = 8.31$, $B = 29°$ 32. $b = 2.16$, $c = 4.32$, $C = 60°$

The law of sines is useful in solving right triangles with the aid of a slide rule. In each of the right triangles in Problems 33–36 $(C = 90°)$, set up an expression of the form

$$\frac{a}{\sin A} = \frac{b}{\sin B} = \frac{c}{\sin 90°}$$

that could be used to solve for the remaining parts of the triangle.

33. $a = 23.1$, $A = 34° \; 20'$ 34. $b = 102$, $A = 62° \; 10'$

35. $b = 0.497$, $B = 41° \; 30'$ 36. $c = 1.05$, $A = 18° \; 50'$

37. Show that, in any triangle ABC, if $\alpha = 2\gamma$, then $\cos \gamma = a/2c$.

38. From a window in a tower, 85 feet above the ground, the angle of elevation to the top of a nearby building measures $34° \; 30'$. From a point on the ground directly below the window, the angle of elevation to the top of the same building measures $50° \; 20'$. Find the height of the building.

39. Two men, 500 feet apart, observe a balloon between them that is in the same vertical plane with the men. The respective angles of elevation of the balloon are observed by the men to measure $80° \; 10'$ and $52° \; 50'$. Find the height of the balloon above the ground.

40. The diagonal of a parallelogram is 60 inches long, and the diagonal makes angles measuring $32°$ and $28°$ with the sides of the parallelogram. Find the lengths of the sides of the parallelogram.

Show that, in any triangle ABC, each of the following is true.

41. $\dfrac{a+b}{b} = \dfrac{\sin \alpha + \sin \beta}{\sin \beta}$ 42. $\dfrac{a-b}{b} = \dfrac{\sin \alpha - \sin \beta}{\sin \beta}$

43. $\dfrac{a-b}{a+b} = \dfrac{\tan \frac{1}{2}(\alpha - \beta)}{\tan \frac{1}{2}(\alpha + \beta)}$ (This is called the Law of Tangents.)

8.5 THE LAW OF COSINES

The x- and y-coordinates of a point on the terminal side of an angle β in standard position, when the point is located b units from the origin, are $b \cos \beta$ and $b \sin \beta$, respectively (Figure 8.12). We can use this fact to derive a very useful formula.

Figure 8.13 shows points $A(x_1, y_1)$ and $B(x_2, y_2)$ lying on the terminal sides of angles α and β, respectively. Now, if $B(x_2, y_2)$ is located b units from the origin, while $A(x_1, y_1)$ is located a units from the origin, then

$$\begin{aligned}
[l(\overline{AB})]^2 &= (x_2 - x_1)^2 + (y_2 - y_1)^2 \\
&= (b \cos \beta - a \cos \alpha)^2 + (b \sin \beta - a \sin \alpha)^2 \\
&= b^2 \cos^2 \beta - 2ab \cos \beta \cos \alpha + a^2 \cos^2 \alpha + b^2 \sin^2 \beta \\
&\qquad - 2ab \sin \alpha \sin \beta + a^2 \sin^2 \alpha \\
&= b^2(\cos^2 \beta + \sin^2 \beta) + a^2(\cos^2 \alpha + \sin^2 \alpha) \\
&\qquad - 2ab(\cos \beta \cos \alpha + \sin \beta \sin \alpha).
\end{aligned}$$

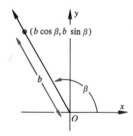

Figure 8.12

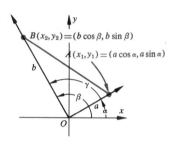

Figure 8.13

A distance formula

Thus, by Formulas 1 and 5 on page 190, we have the following formula for the square of the distance between two points A and B in the plane:

$$[l(\overline{AB})]^2 = a^2 + b^2 - 2ab \cos (\beta - \alpha).$$

Note that $\beta - \alpha$, or γ, is just the angle between the terminal sides of the angles β and α.

In view of the fact that the location of the axes in the plane is purely a matter of convenience, we have established the following theorem, which is known as the **Law of Cosines**.

THEOREM 8.2 *If α, β, and γ are the angles of a triangle, and a, b, and c are the lengths of the sides opposite α, β, and γ, respectively, then*

$$c^2 = a^2 + b^2 - 2ab \cos \gamma, \qquad (1)$$

$$b^2 = a^2 + c^2 - 2ac \cos \beta, \qquad (2)$$

$$a^2 = b^2 + c^2 - 2bc \cos \alpha. \qquad (3)$$

Use of the law of cosines in solving triangles

This theorem has many applications, among them the solution of certain triangles. If we are given the measure of an angle and the lengths of the adjacent sides, we can use the law of cosines to help us find the remaining parts of the triangle.

Example.   Solve the triangle for which

$$\alpha = 100°, \quad b = 10, \quad \text{and} \quad c = 12$$

Solution.   Make a sketch of the triangle and label the sides and angles. We can first find a by using the law of cosines; thus,

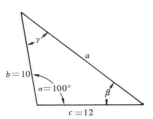

$$a^2 = b^2 + c^2 - 2bc \cos \alpha,$$

$$a^2 = 10^2 + 12^2 - 2(10)(12) \cos 100°,$$

$$a^2 \approx 100 + 144 - 240(-0.1736) = 244 + 41.664 \approx 285.7.$$

From the table of squares in the Appendix, we find that $16^2 = 256$, while $17^2 = 289$; therefore, a is a little less than 17. We shall use 17. Next, to find β, we again use the law of cosines, or now we can use the law of sines because we have the length of a side opposite a given angle. Let us use the law of cosines. Thus, $a^2 \approx 285.7$ (from the earlier computations), $b^2 = 100$, and $c^2 = 144$. From the law of cosines,

$$b^2 = a^2 + c^2 - 2ac \cos \beta,$$

$$\cos \beta = \frac{b^2 - a^2 - c^2}{-2ac},$$

$$\cos \beta \approx \frac{100 - 285.7 - 144}{-2(17)(12)} \approx 0.8.$$

From Table VI in the Appendix, $\beta \approx 36° \, 50'$. Since the sum of the angles of a triangle is 180°, we can find an approximation for γ by noting that

$$\gamma = 180° - \alpha - \beta \approx 180° - 100° - 36° \, 50' = 43° \, 10'.$$

We have, then, for the remaining parts of the triangle,

$$a \approx 17, \quad \beta \approx 36° \, 50', \quad \text{and} \quad \gamma \approx 43° \, 10'.$$

Of course, if greater precision were desired in the preceding example, we could resort to various other means of approximating $\sqrt{285.664}$, and dispense with rounding measures of angles to the nearest 10′.

Since (1), (2), and (3), above, are relationships between three sides and one angle of a triangle, we can, as we did in the preceding example, use any of these forms to solve for the measure of an angle, given the lengths of the three sides.

EXERCISE   8.5

Find the remaining parts of the triangle. In all problems in this exercise, give lengths and areas to the nearest tenth and angle measurements to the nearest 10′.

1. $a = 10; b = 4, \gamma = 30°$ 2. $b = 14.2, c = 7.9, \alpha = 64° \, 10'$

3. $a = 4.9, c = 6.8, \beta = 122° \, 20'$ 4. $a = 241, c = 104, \beta = 148° \, 10'$

5. $b = 14.6, c = 6.21, \alpha = 80° \, 40'$ 6. $b = 9.4, c = 10.2, \alpha = 100° \, 50'$

7. $a = 5$, $b = 8$, $c = 7$ 8. $a = 4.5$, $b = 5.3$, $c = 2.8$

9. Find the greatest angle of the triangle whose sides are 5.1, 4.2, and 4.5.

10. Find the least angle of the triangle whose sides are 29.5, 33.2, and 41.4.

11. Find the area of the triangle in Problem 1, above.

12. Find the area of the triangle in Problem 2, above.

13. Show that $1 + \cos \alpha = \dfrac{(b + c + a)(b + c - a)}{2bc}$.

14. Show that $1 - \cos \alpha = \dfrac{(a - b + c)(a + b - c)}{2bc}$.

15. Show that if $s = \dfrac{a + b + c}{2}$, then $\cos \dfrac{1}{2}\alpha = \sqrt{\dfrac{s(s - a)}{bc}}$. *Hint:* Recall (page 191) that

$\cos \dfrac{1}{2}\alpha = \sqrt{\dfrac{1 + \cos \alpha}{2}}$, and use this information in conjunction with the result from

Problem 13, above.

16. Show that if $s = \dfrac{a + b + c}{2}$, then $\sin \dfrac{1}{2}\alpha = \sqrt{\dfrac{(s - b)(s - c)}{bc}}$. *Hint:* See suggestion in

Problem 15.

In Problems 17 and 18, use the results of either Problem 15 or Problem 16.

17. Find the greatest angle of the triangle whose sides are 6.3, 4.8, and 4.3.

18. Find the least angle of the triangle whose sides are 16.4, 23.4, and 20.1.

19. Use the results of Problems 13 and 14 to show that the area $\mathscr{A}$ of a triangle is given by

$$\mathscr{A} = \sqrt{s(s - a)(s - b)(s - c)},$$

where $s = \dfrac{a + b + c}{2}$. This formula is known as **Hero's formula.**

20. Use the results of Problem 19, above, to find the area of the triangle in
    (a) Problem 7, above;   (b) Problem 8, above.

21. Show that the Pythagorean theorem is a special case of the law of cosines.

22. Find the least angle of the triangle with vertices at the points $(0, 0)$, $(5, -2)$, and $(-7, -3)$.

23. Find the area of the triangle with vertices at the points $(1, 1)$, $(5, 5)$, and $(-2, 6)$. (See Problem 19, above.)

8.6 POLAR COORDINATES

The Cartesian coordinates that we have been using specify the location of a point in the plane by giving the directed distances of the point from a pair of fixed perpendicular lines, the axes. There is an alternative coordinate system that is frequently used in the plane, in which the location of a point is specified in a different manner.

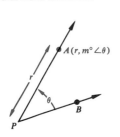

Figure 8.14

In the plane, consider a fixed ray $\overrightarrow{PB}$ and any point A. We can describe the location of A by giving the distance r from P to A and specifying the angle BPA (Figure 8.14), which is customarily designated by θ. By stating the ordered pair $(r, m°(\theta))$ or $(r, m^R(\theta))$, we clearly identify the location of A. We ordinarily write (r, θ) for either of these ordered pairs, where the meaning should be clear from the context. The components of such an ordered pair are called **polar coordinates** of A. The fixed ray PB is called the **polar axis,** and the initial point P of the polar axis is called the **pole** of the system.

The set of polar coordinates for a given point

Notice that while there is a one-to-one correspondence between the set of ordered pairs in a Cartesian coordinate system and the points in the geometric plane, each point in the plane has infinitely many pairs of polar coordinates. In the first place, if (r, θ) are polar coordinates of A, then so are

$$(r, \theta + k360°), k \in J$$

(Figure 8.15-a). In the second place, if we let $-r < 0$ denote the directed distance from P to A along the negative extension of the ray $\overrightarrow{PA'}$ in a direction opposite that

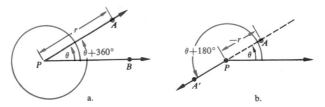

Figure 8.15

of $\overrightarrow{PA}$ (Figure 8.15-b), then we see that also $(-r, \theta + 180°)$, and more generally

$$(-r, \theta + 180° + k360°), k \in J,$$

are polar coordinates of A. The pole P itself is represented by $(0, \theta)$ for any θ whatsoever.

Example. Write four additional sets of polar coordinates for the point having polar coordinates $(3, 30°)$.

Solution. With positive values for r, two more pairs of polar coordinates for $(3, 30°)$ are $(3, 390°)$ and $(3, -330°)$. Using negative values for r, we have $(-3, 210°)$

and $(-3, -150°)$. Figure 8.16 shows these cases. Of course there are infinitely many other possible polar coordinates for the same point.

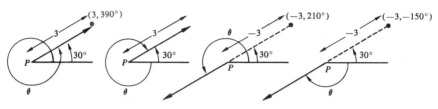

Figure 8.16

Relationships between polar and rectangular coordinates   Cartesian and polar coordinates of a point can be related by means of the trigonometric functions. If the pole P in a polar coordinate system is also the origin O in a Cartesian coordinate system, and if the polar axis coincides with the positive x-axis of the Cartesian system, as shown in Figure 8.17, then the coordinates (x, y) can be expressed in terms of the polar coordinates (r, θ) by the following equations:

$$x = r \cos \theta,$$

$$y = r \sin \theta. \tag{1}$$

Figure 8.17

Conversely, we have

$$r = \pm\sqrt{x^2 + y^2}, \tag{2}$$

$$\cos \theta = \frac{x}{\pm\sqrt{x^2 + y^2}}, \quad \sin \theta = \frac{y}{\pm\sqrt{x^2 + y^2}} \quad [(x, y) \neq (0, 0)].$$

The sets of equations (1) and (2) enable us to find rectangular coordinates for a point with a given pair of polar coordinates, and vice versa.

Example. Find the rectangular coordinates of the point with polar coordinates $(4, 30°)$. Show the graph of the point on a combined polar and rectangular coordinate system.

Solution. Using (1), we obtain

$$x = 4 \cos 30° = 4 \cdot \frac{\sqrt{3}}{2} = 2\sqrt{3},$$

$$y = 4 \sin 30° = 4 \cdot \frac{1}{2} = 2.$$

The rectangular coordinates are $(2\sqrt{3}, 2)$. The graph appears in Figure 8.18, overleaf.

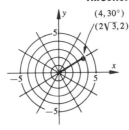

Figure 8.18

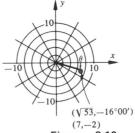

Figure 8.19

Example. Find a pair of polar coordinates for the point with Cartesian coordinates $(7, -2)$. Show the graph of the point on a combined polar and rectangular coordinate system.

Solution. By (2), $r = \pm \sqrt{x^2 + y^2} = \pm\sqrt{49 + 4} = \pm\sqrt{53}$. Choosing the positive sign, and noting that the point $(7, -2)$ is in the fourth quadrant, we have

$$\sin \theta = \frac{-2}{\sqrt{53}},$$

from which

$$\theta \approx -16° \ 00'.$$

A pair of polar coordinates is therefore

$$(\sqrt{53}, \ -16° \ 00'),$$

where the given angle measure is an approximation. The graph appears in Figure 8.19.

| **Equations in polar form and in rectangular form** | Equations (1) can be used to transform Cartesian equations to polar form, and equations (2) can be used to transform polar equations to Cartesian form. |

Example. Transform $x^2 + y^2 - 2x + 3 = 0$ to polar form.

Solution. From (1), we find that $x^2 = r^2 \cos^2 \theta$ and $y^2 = r^2 \sin^2 \theta$. Thus we have

$$r^2 \cos^2 \theta + r^2 \sin^2 \theta - 2r \cos \theta + 3 = 0,$$

from which

$$r^2(\cos^2 \theta + \sin^2 \theta) - 2r \cos \theta + 3 = 0,$$

$$r^2 - 2r \cos \theta + 3 = 0.$$

Example. Transform $r(1 - 2 \cos \theta) = 3$ to Cartesian form.

Solution. Using (2), we have

$$\pm\sqrt{x^2 + y^2} \left[1 - 2 \left(\frac{x}{\pm \sqrt{x^2 + y^2}} \right) \right] = 3,$$

from which

$$\pm\sqrt{x^2 + y^2} - 2x = 3,$$

$$\pm\sqrt{x^2 + y^2} = 2x + 3.$$

Upon squaring each member, we have the equation

$$x^2 + y^2 = 4x^2 + 12x + 9,$$

from which

$$3x^2 - y^2 + 12x + 9 = 0.$$

EXERCISE 8.6

Find four sets of polar coordinates $(-360° < \theta \le 360°)$ for the point with polar coordinates as given.

1. $(6, 485°)$ 2. $(-3, 518°)$ 3. $(-2, -450°)$

4. $(5, 720°)$ 5. $(6, -600°)$ 6. $(3, -395°)$

Find the Cartesian coordinates of a point with polar coordinates as given.

7. $(5, 45°)$ 8. $(-3, 30°)$ 9. $\left(\dfrac{1}{2}, 330°\right)$

10. $\left(\dfrac{3}{4}, 225°\right)$ 11. $(10, -135°)$ 12. $(-6, -240°)$

Find two sets of polar coordinates, one involving an angle of positive measure and one an angle of negative measure, for the point with Cartesian coordinates as given.

13. $(3\sqrt{2}, 3\sqrt{2})$ 14. $\left(-\dfrac{\sqrt{3}}{2}, \dfrac{1}{2}\right)$ 15. $(-1, -\sqrt{3})$

16. $(0, -4)$ 17. $(0, 0)$ 18. $(-6, 0)$

Transform the given equation to an equation in polar form.

19. $x^2 + y^2 = 25$ 20. $x = 3$ 21. $y = -4$

22. $x^2 + y^2 - 4y = 0$ 23. $x^2 + 9y^2 = 9$ 24. $x^2 - 4y^2 = 4$

Transform the given equation to an equation in Cartesian form.

25. $r = 5$ 26. $r = 4 \sin \theta$ 27. $r = 9 \cos \theta$

28. $r \cos \theta = 3$ 29. $r(1 - \cos \theta) = 2$ 30. $r(1 + \sin \theta) = 2$

31. Show by transformation of coordinates that the graph of $r = \sec^2(\theta/2)$ is a parabola.

32. Show by transformation of coordinates that the graph of $r = \csc^2(\theta/2)$ is a parabola.

33. Graph $\{(r, \theta) \mid r = 4 \sin \theta, 0 \le \theta < 360°\}$.

34. Graph $\{(r, \theta) \mid r = 9 \cos \theta, 0 \le \theta < 360°\}$.

9 INVERSE FUNCTIONS AND CONDITIONAL EQUATIONS

9.1 INVERSES OF CIRCULAR FUNCTIONS

Each of the circular functions has an inverse relation, but none of these inverses is a function. We recall from Section 4.2 that the inverse of a

Inverse relations of the circular functions

function is the relation obtained by interchanging the components x and y of each ordered pair in the function. For this reason, the graph of the inverse of a function can be obtained by reflecting the graph of the function in the line with equation $y = x$. Furthermore, the resulting inverse is a function if and only if the function is one-to-one.

Now consider the sine function,

$$\{(x, y) \mid y = \sin x\}, \tag{1}$$

and the inverse of this function,

$$\{(x, y) \mid x = \sin y\}. \tag{2}$$

Both graphs are shown in Figure 9.1, where it is evident that each is the reflection of the other in the line $y = x$. The equation $x = \sin y$ in (2), above, does not define a function, because for each element x_i in its domain there are an unlimited number of elements in its range.

The inverse relation of the sine function is called the **arcsine relation**:

$$\text{arcsine} = \{(x, y) \mid x = \sin y\}.$$

As you can see from Figure 9.1, its domain is $\{x \mid -1 \leq x \leq 1, x \in R\}$ and its range is R.

Each circular and trigonometric function has an inverse relation. Thus we have

$$\text{arccosine} = \{(x, y) \mid x = \cos y\},$$

and

$$\text{arctangent} = \{(x, y) \mid x = \tan y\},$$

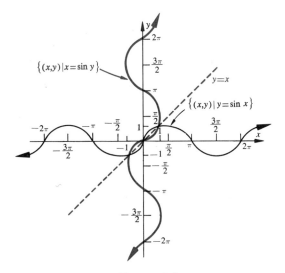

Figure 9.1

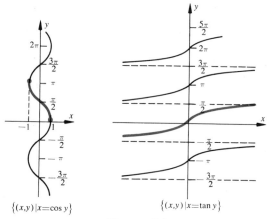

$\{(x,y)\,|\,x{=}\cos y\}$ $\{(x,y)\,|\,x{=}\tan y\}$

Figure 9.2

whose graphs are shown in Figure 9.2. The arccosecant, arcsecant, and arccotangent are less frequently used and their graphs are not shown.

By suitably restricting the *domains* of the circular functions—that is, by suitably restricting the *ranges* of the respective inverse relations—we can define an **inverse function** for each circular and each trigonometric function. As here defined, this is called the **principal-valued** inverse function, and to distinguish it a capital initial letter is often used. Thus for the sine function, we have the

Inverse functions of the circular functions

principal-valued inverse function

$$\text{Arcsine} = \left\{(x, y) \,|\, x = \sin y, \quad -\frac{\pi}{2} \le y \le \frac{\pi}{2}\right\}.$$

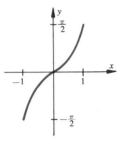

Figure 9.3

The graph of Arcsine is shown in Figure 9.3.

Because there is now a unique element y in the range $\{y \mid -\pi/2 \leq y \leq \pi/2\}$ corresponding to each x in the domain $\{x \mid -1 \leq x \leq 1\}$, we can use inverse-function notation and write

$$y = \text{Arcsin } x$$

to mean

$$x = \sin y \quad \text{and} \quad -\frac{\pi}{2} \leq y \leq \frac{\pi}{2}.$$

Alternatively, we write

$$y = \text{Sin}^{-1} x$$

with this same meaning (but with the understanding, of course, that $\text{Sin}^{-1} x$ does *not* denote $1/\text{Sin } x$).

Notation for the inverse circular functions

The restricted ranges for the inverse functions for the cosine and tangent functions are indicated by heavy lines in Figure 9.2. For all such inverses, we use similar notation; thus, we write either Arccos x or $\text{Cos}^{-1} x$ for the element in the range of the Arccosine function corresponding to the element x in the domain.

DEFINITION 9.1 *The inverse circular functions corresponding to the six circular functions are*

I $\text{Arcsine} = \left\{(x, y) \mid y = \text{Sin}^{-1} x, \quad -\frac{\pi}{2} \leq y \leq \frac{\pi}{2}\right\}$,

II $\text{Arccosine} = \{(x, y) \mid y = \text{Cos}^{-1} x, \quad 0 \leq y \leq \pi\}$,

III $\text{Arctangent} = \left\{(x, y) \mid y = \text{Tan}^{-1} x, \quad -\frac{\pi}{2} < y < \frac{\pi}{2}\right\}$,

IV $\text{Arccotangent} = \{(x, y) \mid y = \text{Cot}^{-1} x, \quad 0 < y < \pi\}$,

V $\text{Arcsecant} = \left\{(x, y) \mid y = \text{Sec}^{-1} x, \quad 0 \leq y \leq \pi, \quad y \neq \frac{\pi}{2}\right\}$,

VI $\text{Arccosecant} = \left\{(x, y) \mid y = \text{Csc}^{-1} x, \quad -\frac{\pi}{2} \leq y \leq \frac{\pi}{2}, \quad y \neq 0\right\}$.

Inverse trigonometric functions

An analogous definition can be made for the inverse trigonometric functions provided that members of the ranges shown are interpreted as radian measures for angles in standard position.

Note that the foregoing restrictions are on the *ranges* of the functions, in distinction from the usual prescription of the *domain* of a function. Although these
particular ranges are the ones customarily chosen, the choices

**Choice of
domains for
inverse
functions**

actually are quite arbitrary. We might just as well, for example,
have restricted the Arccosine function to the range $-\pi \leq y \leq 0$
or to the range $-2\pi \leq y \leq -\pi$. The ranges for the functions
have generally been chosen to involve small values of y, to have
relatively simple graphs, and of course to yield a one-to-one correspondence
between domain and range.

Example.   Find Arctan 0.2236.

Solution.   From Table V in the Appendix, we find 0.2236 in the column headed tan x.
Since this corresponds to tan 0.22, and since $-\pi/2 < 0.22 < \pi/2$, we have

$$\text{Arctan } 0.2236 \approx 0.22.$$

It is helpful to interpret symbolism such as $\cos(\text{Arcsin } \sqrt{3}/4)$ by using triangles.
Since $\sqrt{3}/4$ can be intepreted as the ratio of the length of the side of a triangle
opposite an angle α to the length of the hypotenuse
of the triangle, you can assert that $\alpha = \text{Arcsin } \sqrt{3}/4$ is
the angle pictured in Figure 9.4. From the Pythagorean
relationship, the remaining side of the triangle has
length

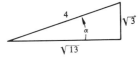

$$\sqrt{4^2 - (\sqrt{3})^2} = \sqrt{16 - 3} = \sqrt{13},$$

Figure 9.4

which is also labeled. Then, since $\text{Arcsin } \sqrt{3}/4 = \alpha$, by inspecting the triangle
sketched you can see that

$$\cos\left(\text{Arcsin } \frac{\sqrt{3}}{4}\right) = \cos\alpha = \frac{\sqrt{13}}{4}.$$

Alternatively, you can interpret $\cos(\text{Arcsin } \sqrt{3}/4)$ by using the unit circle
(Figure 9.5). By definition, the range of the Arcsine function is the interval
from $-\pi/2$ to $\pi/2$. Since $\sqrt{3}/4 > 0$, the terminal endpoint of the arc of length x,
associated with $\text{Arcsin } \sqrt{3}/4$, is in the first quadrant and can be denoted by
$(u, \sqrt{3}/4)$, where

$$u = \cos x = \cos\left(\text{Arcsin } \frac{\sqrt{3}}{4}\right).$$

From the Pythagorean theorem,

$$u^2 + \left(\frac{\sqrt{3}}{4}\right)^2 = 1,$$

$$u^2 + \frac{3}{16} = 1,$$

$$u^2 = \frac{13}{16},$$

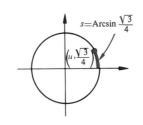

Figure 9.5

so that $u = \sqrt{13}/4$ or $u = -\sqrt{13}/4$. Since the point is in the first quadrant, the positive value must be chosen, and

$$\cos\left(\text{Arcsin } \frac{\sqrt{3}}{4}\right) = \frac{\sqrt{13}}{4}.$$

Consider now a case in which the element in the domain is not specified.

Example.   Write $\sin(\text{Cos}^{-1} x)$ as an equivalent expression without inverse notation.

Solution.   Note that $\text{Cos}^{-1} x$ is a real number, y, such that $\cos y = x$. Notice also that $0 \le \text{Cos}^{-1} x \le \pi$ for each x for which it is defined, and hence $\sin(\text{Cos}^{-1}x) \ge 0$. Therefore, using $\sin^2 y + \cos^2 y = 1$, we have

$$\sin(\text{Cos}^{-1} x) = \sin y = \sqrt{1 - \cos^2 y} = \sqrt{1 - x^2}.$$

Observe that it follows from the definitions of the inverse functions that $\sin(\text{Sin}^{-1} x) = x$, $\cos(\text{Cos}^{-1} x) = x$, etc. For example, if $\text{Sin}^{-1} x$ is a real number y, then

$$x = \sin y = \sin(\text{Sin}^{-1} x).$$

EXERCISE 9.1

Find the value of each of the following if it exists. Express results in terms of rational multiples of π. You may be able to recall these values from memory, or you may wish to use Table 7.1, page 160.

Examples.   a. $\text{Arccos } \dfrac{1}{2}$ b. $\text{Tan}^{-1}(-1)$

Solutions.   a. $\dfrac{\pi}{3}$ b. $-\dfrac{\pi}{4}$

1. $\text{Arcsin } \dfrac{1}{2}$ 2. $\text{Arctan } \sqrt{3}$ 3. $\text{Cot}^{-1} 1$ 4. $\text{Cos}^{-1} \dfrac{1}{\sqrt{2}}$

5. $\text{Cos}^{-1} 2$ 6. $\text{Sec}^{-1} 2$ 7. $\text{Arctan}\left(-\dfrac{1}{\sqrt{3}}\right)$ 8. $\text{Arcsin } \dfrac{\sqrt{3}}{2}$

Use Table V in the Appendix as necessary to find each of the following.

9. $\text{Arctan } 0.1003$ 10. $\text{Arcsec } 1.053$ 11. $\text{Sin}^{-1} 0.3802$

12. $\text{Cos}^{-1} 0.6675$ 13. $\text{Arcsin }(-0.8624)$ 14. $\text{Arccos }(-0.3902)$

15. $\text{Tan}^{-1} 3.467$ 16. $\text{Csc}^{-1} 1.422$

Find the value for each of the the following, if it exists.

Examples.

a. $\mathrm{Cos}^{-1}\,(\tan \pi)$

b. $\sin \dfrac{1}{2}\left(\mathrm{Cos}^{-1}\dfrac{1}{2}\right)$

Solutions.

a. Since $\tan \pi = 0$,

$\mathrm{Cos}^{-1}\,(\tan \pi) = \mathrm{Cos}^{-1}\,0 = \dfrac{\pi}{2}.$

b. Since $\mathrm{Cos}^{-1}\dfrac{1}{2} = \dfrac{\pi}{3},$

$\sin \dfrac{1}{2}\left(\mathrm{Cos}^{-1}\dfrac{1}{2}\right) = \sin \dfrac{1}{2}\left(\dfrac{\pi}{3}\right) = \dfrac{1}{2}.$

17. $\mathrm{Sin}^{-1}\left(\cos \dfrac{\pi}{4}\right)$

18. $\mathrm{Cos}^{-1}\left(\sin \dfrac{\pi}{2}\right)$

19. $\mathrm{Tan}^{-1}\left(\tan \dfrac{\pi}{3}\right)$

20. $\mathrm{Sin}^{-1}\left(\sin \dfrac{3\pi}{2}\right)$

21. $\sin \left(\mathrm{Arccos}\,\dfrac{1}{2}\right)$

22. $\tan \left(\mathrm{Arcsin}\,\dfrac{\sqrt{3}}{2}\right)$

23. $\cos \,(\mathrm{Cot}^{-1}\,(-\sqrt{3}))$

24. $\sin \,(\mathrm{Tan}^{-1}\,(-1))$

25. $\sin \left(2\,\mathrm{Arcsin}\,\dfrac{1}{2}\right)$

26. $\sin \left(2\,\mathrm{Cos}^{-1}\,\dfrac{3}{5}\right)$

27. $\tan \dfrac{1}{2}\left(\mathrm{Arcsin}\,\dfrac{12}{13}\right)$

28. $\cos \dfrac{1}{2}\,(\mathrm{Tan}^{-1}\,0)$

29. $\sin \left(\mathrm{Sin}^{-1}\,\dfrac{1}{2} + \mathrm{Cos}^{-1}\,\dfrac{3}{5}\right)$

30. $\cos \left(\mathrm{Sin}^{-1}\,\dfrac{1}{\sqrt{2}} + \mathrm{Cos}^{-1}\,\dfrac{4}{5}\right)$

31. $\mathrm{Arccos}\,(\sin\,(\mathrm{Arctan}\,(-1)))$

32. $\sin \,(\mathrm{Cos}^{-1}\,(\tan 0))$

Write each of the following without inverse notation.

Example. $\sin \,(\mathrm{Cos}^{-1}\,x + \mathrm{Sin}^{-1}\,y)$

Solution.   From the formula for $\sin \,(x_1 + x_2)$, page 169, we have

$\sin \,(\mathrm{Cos}^{-1}\,x + \mathrm{Sin}^{-1}\,y) = \sin \,(\mathrm{Cos}^{-1}\,x)\,\cos \,(\mathrm{Sin}^{-1}\,y) + \cos \,(\mathrm{Cos}^{-1}\,x)\,\sin \,(\mathrm{Sin}^{-1}\,y).$

Evaluating each factor of each term in the right-hand member, we obtain

$$\sin \,(\mathrm{Cos}^{-1}\,x + \mathrm{Sin}^{-1}\,y) = (\sqrt{1-x^2})(\sqrt{1-y^2}) + xy$$

$$= \sqrt{(1-x^2)(1-y^2)} + xy.$$

33. $\cos \,(\mathrm{Arcsin}\,x)$

34. $\cot \,(\mathrm{Arctan}\,x)$

35. $\tan \,(\mathrm{Sin}^{-1}\,y)$

36. $\sin \,(\mathrm{Tan}^{-1}\,y)$

37. $\cos \left(\dfrac{1}{2}\,\mathrm{Arccos}\,x\right)$

38. $\sin \,(\mathrm{Sin}^{-1}\,x - \mathrm{Sin}^{-1}\,y)$

Solve the following for x in terms of y.

Example. $y = 2 \text{ Arcsin } 3x$.

Solution. We have

$$\frac{y}{2} = \text{Arcsin } 3x,$$

and from the definition of Arcsin, we write the expression as

$$3x = \sin\frac{y}{2}, \quad \text{and then as} \quad x = \frac{1}{3}\sin\frac{y}{2}.$$

39. $y = 3 \text{ Arccos } 2x$ 40. $y = 2 \text{ Sin}^{-1}\left(\dfrac{x}{5}\right)$

41. $y = \dfrac{1}{2}\text{Tan}^{-1}(x + \pi)$ 42. $y = \dfrac{2}{3}\text{Cot}^{-1}(\pi x)$

43. Show that $\text{Arcsin }\dfrac{2}{5} = \text{Arctan }\dfrac{2}{\sqrt{21}}$.   44. Show that $\text{Arccos }\dfrac{1}{3} = \text{Arccot }\dfrac{1}{2\sqrt{2}}$.

45. Is $\text{Arccos }(\cos x) = x$? Why or why not?

46. Is $\text{Arcsin }(\sin x) = x$? Why or why not?

9.2 CONDITIONAL EQUATIONS

In Sections 7.7 and 8.2, we observed that certain equations involving circular or trigonometric function values are *identities*; that is, they are true for all permissible values of any variables involved. In this section, we shall be concerned with *conditional* equations of a similar kind, namely, equations that involve circular or trigonometric function values but that are not satisfied by all permissible values of any variables involved.

Solution of conditional equations
Various procedures exist for solving conditional equations that involve circular or trigometric function values. Of course, the methods applicable to algebraic equations are also valid for such equations, as you will see in the following examples.

Because the circular and trigonometric functions are periodic, we should expect that equations involving $\sin x$, $\tan x$, or other circular or trigonometric function values have infinite solution sets.

Example. Solve $\sin x = -1$ for:

         a. $x \in R$,

         b. $x \in \{\text{angles with measures given in radians}\}$,

         c. $x \in \{\text{angles with measures given in degrees}\}$.

Solution.   By inspection, the solutions are:

a. $\left\{x \mid x = \dfrac{3\pi}{2} + 2k\pi, \quad k \in J\right\}$,

b. $\left\{x \mid x = \left(\dfrac{3\pi}{2} + 2k\pi\right)^R, \quad k \in J\right\}$,

c. $\{x \mid x = (270 + k \cdot 360°), \quad k \in J\}$.

Example.   Specify $\{w \mid \sqrt{3}/2 = \sin w, \ w \in R\}$ in terms of rational multiples of π.

Solution.   Recalling that $(\cos w, \sin w)$ is the point on the unit circle associated with an arc of length w, we can use the unit circle to help us visualize the situation here. Since we know (from Table 7.1 on page 160 or from memory) that $\sqrt{3}/2 = \sin(\pi/3)$, we know that w_1, the first-quadrant value for w, must be $\pi/3$. Using $\pi/3$ as a reference arc, and the fact that $\sin w$ is positive only in the first and second quadrants, we observe that the only other value for w in our set over the interval $0 \leq w < 2\pi$ is $w_2 = 2\pi/3$. Hence,

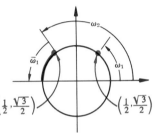

$$\left\{w \mid \dfrac{\sqrt{3}}{2} = \sin w\right\} = \left\{w \mid w = \dfrac{\pi}{3} + 2k\pi, \ k \in J\right\} \cup$$

$$\left\{w \mid w = \dfrac{2\pi}{3} + 2k\pi, \ k \in J\right\}.$$

Use of identities in solving conditional equations

The identities we have developed for the circular and trigonometric functions are useful in solving some equations. We can use these identities to rewrite equations involving more than one function value as equivalent equations involving values of only one function.

Example.   Solve $\sin \alpha = \cos \alpha$ over the interval $0 \leq \alpha \leq \pi/2$.

Solution.   Since $\sin \alpha \neq 0$ when $\cos \alpha = 0$, the equation is not satisfied if $\cos \alpha = 0$. We can accordingly assume that $\cos \alpha \neq 0$, and hence can multiply each member by $1/\cos \alpha$ to obtain

$$\dfrac{\sin \alpha}{\cos \alpha} = 1,$$

or, equivalently,

$$\tan \alpha = 1.$$

Therefore we have as our solution set $\{\pi/4\}$.

Some equations that involve circular or trigonometric function values are not of the first degree. In such cases, an algebraic factorization will sometimes lead to a solution.

Example.   Solve $2 \sin u \cos u - \sin u - 2 \cos u + 1 = 0$ over $0 \leq u \leq 2\pi$.

Solution.   If $\sin u$ is factored from the first two terms of the left-hand member of the given equation, and -1 from the second two terms, the result is

$$(\sin u)(2 \cos u - 1) - 1(2 \cos u - 1) = 0.$$

Then, factoring $2 \cos u - 1$ from each term in the left-hand member, we have

$$(2 \cos u - 1)(\sin u - 1) = 0.$$

Therefore, we seek

$$\{u \mid 2 \cos u - 1 = 0\} \cup \{u \mid \sin u - 1 = 0\}.$$

If $2 \cos u - 1 = 0$, then $\cos u = 1/2$, and if $\sin u - 1 = 0$, then $\sin u = 1$. Thus, the values of u satisfying these equations are of the form

$$\frac{\pi}{3} + 2k\pi, \quad \frac{5\pi}{3} + 2k\pi, \quad \text{or} \quad \frac{\pi}{2} + 2k\pi, \quad k \in J.$$

Over the interval $0 \leq u \leq 2\pi$, then, we have the solution set $\{\pi/3, 5\pi/3, \pi/2\}$.

EXERCISE 9.2

Specify the given set in terms of rational multiples of π.

Example. $\{w \mid \tan w = -1\}$.

Solution. $\{w \mid \tan w = -1\} = \left\{ w \,\middle|\, w = \dfrac{3\pi}{4} + k\pi \right\}$,   where $k \in J$.

1. $\left\{ p \,\middle|\, \sin p = \dfrac{1}{2} \right\}$ 2. $\{q \mid 1 = \cot q\}$ 3. $\{y \mid 2 = \cos y\}$

4. $\{y \mid \tan y = \sqrt{3}\,\}$ 5. $\left\{ r \,\middle|\, \cos r = \dfrac{1}{\sqrt{2}} \right\}$ 6. $\{s \mid 2 = \sec s\}$

7. $\left\{ x \,\middle|\, -\dfrac{\sqrt{3}}{2} = \sin x \right\}$ 8. $\left\{ x \,\middle|\, \cos x = -\dfrac{\sqrt{3}}{2} \right\}$

In all the following problems in this exercise, use Table V or VI as necessary, and give results to the nearest reading in the table. In Problems 9–20, find the solution set of each equation for

a. $x \in R$,   b. x an angle whose measure is given in (1) radians, and (2) degrees.

9. $\cos x = \dfrac{1}{2}$ 10. $\sin x = \dfrac{\sqrt{2}}{2}$ 11. $\tan x = \sqrt{3}$

12. $\cot x = -1$ 13. $\sec x - \sqrt{2} = 0$ 14. $\csc x + 1 = 0$

15. $4 \sin x - 1 = 0$ 16. $2 \tan x + 3 = 0$ 17. $3 \cot x - 1 = 0$

18. $3 \cos x + 1 = 0$ 19. $2 \sec x - 5 = 0$ 20. $3 \csc x + 8 = 0$

In Problems 21–26, find the solution set of each equation over R.

21. $\sin x - \sqrt{3} \cos x = 0$ 22. $3 \sin x + \cos x = 0$

23. $\tan^2 x - 1 = 0$ 24. $2 \sin^2 x - 1 = 0$

25. $\sin^2 x - \cos^2 x = 1$ 26. $\sin x + \cos x \tan x = 3$

In Problems 27–32, find the solution set of each equation for θ a member of the set of angles such that $0° \leq \theta \leq 360°$.

27. $(2 \sin \theta - 1)(2 \sin^2 \theta - 1) = 0$ 28. $(\tan \theta - 1)(2 \cos \theta + 1) = 0$

29. $2 \sin \theta \cos \theta + \sin \theta = 0$ 30. $\tan \theta \sin \theta - \tan \theta = 0$

31. $2 \sin \theta \cos \theta + 2 \sin \theta - \cos \theta - 1 = 0$ *Hint:* First factor by grouping.

32. $2 \sin \theta \tan \theta + \tan \theta - 2 \sin \theta - 1 = 0$

In Problems 33–40 find the solution set of each equation for α a member of the set of angles such that $0^R \leq \alpha \leq 2\pi^R$.

Example. $\tan^2 \alpha + \sec \alpha - 1 = 0$.

Solution.   Since $\tan^2 \alpha = \sec^2 \alpha - 1$, the given equation can be written equivalently as

$$\sec^2 \alpha - 1 + \sec \alpha - 1 = 0,$$
$$\sec^2 \alpha + \sec \alpha - 2 = 0,$$
$$(\sec \alpha + 2)(\sec \alpha - 1) = 0.$$

Now observe that the solution set is

$$\{\alpha \,|\, \sec \alpha + 2 = 0\} \cup \{\alpha \,|\, \sec \alpha - 1 = 0\}$$

over the interval $0^R \leq \alpha \leq 2\pi^R$. If $\sec \alpha + 2 = 0$, then $\sec \alpha = -2$, and if $\sec \alpha - 1 = 0$, then $\sec \alpha = 1$. Over the interval $0^R \leq \alpha \leq 2\pi^R$ the required solution set is

$$\left(\frac{2\pi^R}{3}, \frac{4\pi^R}{3}\right) \cup \{0^R, 2\pi^R\} = \left(0^R, \frac{2\pi^R}{3}, \frac{4\pi^R}{3}, 2\pi^R\right).$$

33. $\tan^2 \alpha - 2 \tan \alpha + 1 = 0$ 34. $4 \sin^2 \alpha - 4 \sin \alpha + 1 = 0$

35. $\cos^2 \alpha + \cos \alpha = 2$ 36. $\cot^2 \alpha = 5 \cot \alpha - 4$

37. $\sec^2 \alpha + 3 \tan \alpha - 11 = 0$ 38. $\tan^2 \alpha + 4 = 2 \sec^2 \alpha$

39. $\sin^2 \alpha + \sin \alpha - 1 = 0$ *Hint:*   Use the quadratic formula.

40. $\tan^2 \alpha = \tan \alpha + 3$

41. Approximate a solution of $\dfrac{1}{2} x - \sin x = 0$, $x \in R$, $x \neq 0$, by graphical methods. *Hint:*

    Graph $y_1 = \dfrac{1}{2} x$ and $y_2 = \sin x$ on the same coordinate system and determine a value

    of x for which $y_1 = y_2$.

42. Approximate a solution of $\cos x = x^2$, $x \in R$, by graphical methods.

43. Approximate a solution of $x + \sin x = 2$, $x \in R$, by graphical methods.

9.3 CONDITIONAL EQUATIONS FOR MULTIPLES

Equations that contain circular or trigonometric function values such as $\sin 2x$, $\cos 3\alpha$, etc., need further consideration.

Example.   Solve $\sqrt{2} \cos 3\alpha = 1$ over the interval $0° \leq \alpha \leq 360°$.

Solution.   The equation can be written equivalently as

$$\cos 3\alpha = \frac{1}{\sqrt{2}}.$$

Therefore, we have

$$3\alpha = 45° + k \cdot 360° \quad \text{or} \quad 3\alpha = 315° + k \cdot 360°,$$

from which

$$\alpha = 15° + k \cdot 120° \quad \text{or} \quad \alpha = 105° + k \cdot 120°, \quad k \in J.$$

Because we want solutions over the interval $0° \leq \alpha \leq 360°$, we consider 0, 1, 2 as replacements for k and obtain the solution set

$$\{15°, 135°, 255°, 105°, 225°, 345°\}.$$

A judicious selection of one or more of the identities encountered earlier can frequently help you solve certain kinds of equations. The following examples illustrate two such cases.

Example.   Solve $\sin \alpha \cos \alpha = 1/4$ over the interval $0^R \leq \alpha \leq 2\pi^R$.

Solution.   Multiplying each member of the given equation by 2, we obtain the equivalent equation

$$2 \sin \alpha \cos \alpha = \frac{1}{2}.$$

Since $2 \sin \alpha \cos \alpha = \sin 2\alpha$ for every α in the desired interval, this latter equation is equivalent to

$$\sin 2\alpha = \frac{1}{2}.$$

Therefore, we have

$$2\alpha = \left(\frac{\pi}{6} + 2k\pi\right)^R \quad \text{or} \quad 2\alpha = \left(\frac{5\pi}{6} + 2k\pi\right)^R, \quad k \in J,$$

so that

$$\alpha = \left(\frac{\pi}{12} + k\pi\right)^R \quad \text{or} \quad \alpha = \left(\frac{5\pi}{12} + k\pi\right)^R, \quad k \in J.$$

Because we want the solutions over the interval $0^R \le \alpha \le 2\pi^R$, we consider 0 and 1 as replacements for k and obtain

$$\left\{ \frac{\pi}{12}^R, \frac{13\pi^R}{12}, \frac{5\pi^R}{12}, \frac{17\pi^R}{12} \right\}.$$

Example. Solve $\cos 2x = \sin x$, $x \in R$.

Solution. Since $\cos 2x = 1 - 2 \sin^2 x$, the equation $\cos^2 x = \sin x$ can be written equivalently as

$$1 - 2 \sin^2 x = \sin x,$$

$$2 \sin^2 x + \sin x - 1 = 0,$$

$$(2 \sin x - 1)(\sin x + 1) = 0,$$

from which

$$\sin x = \frac{1}{2} \quad \text{or} \quad \sin x = -1.$$

Then as solution set we have

$$\left\{ x \mid x = \frac{\pi}{6} + 2\pi k \right\} \cup \left\{ x \mid x = \frac{5\pi}{6} + 2\pi k \right\} \cup \left\{ x \mid x = \frac{3\pi}{2} + 2\pi k \right\}, \quad k \in J.$$

EXERCISE 9.3

In all problems in this exercise, use Table V or VI as necessary. In Problems 1–12, solve each equation over the interval $0° \le \theta \le 360°$.

1. $\cos 2\theta = \dfrac{\sqrt{2}}{2}$

2. $\tan 2\theta = \sqrt{3}$

3. $\sin \dfrac{1}{2} \theta = \dfrac{1}{2}$

4. $\cot \dfrac{1}{3} \theta = -1$

5. $\tan 3\theta = 0$

6. $\sin 4\theta = 1$

7. $\sin \theta \cos \theta = \dfrac{1}{2}$

8. $\cos^2 \theta - \sin^2 \theta = -1$

9. $\cos 2\theta + \sin 2\theta = 0$

10. $\sin \theta \cos \theta = \dfrac{\cos 2\theta}{2}$

11. $2 \cos^2 2\theta + \cos 2\theta - 1 = 0$

12. $\tan^2 2\theta + 2 \tan 2\theta + 1 = 0$

In Problems 13–22, solve each equation over R.

13. $\sin 2x - \cos x = 0$

14. $\cos 2x = \cos^2 x - 1$

15. $\cos 2x = \cos x - 1$

16. $\sin x = \sin 2x$

17. $\cos 2x \cdot \sin x + \sin x = 0$ 18. $\sin 2x \cdot \cos x - \sin x = 0$

19. $\sin 4x - 2 \sin 2x = 0$ *Hint:* $\sin 4x = \sin 2(2x)$.

20. $\sin 3x + 4 \sin^2 x = 0$ *Hint:* $\sin 3x = \sin (x + 2x)$.

21. $\sin 2x + 2 \sin x - \cos x - 1 = 0$

22. $\sin 2x + \sin x + 2 \cos x + 1 = 0$

10 MATRICES AND DETERMINANTS

10.1 MATRIX ADDITION

A **matrix** is a rectangular array of real numbers (or other suitable entities), which are called **entries**, or **elements**, of the matrix. In this book, we shall consider only real numbers as entries. A matrix is customarily displayed in a pair of brackets or parentheses (we shall use brackets). Thus

$$\begin{bmatrix} 1 & 2 & 3 \\ 4 & 5 & 6 \end{bmatrix} \quad \text{and} \quad \begin{bmatrix} 2 \\ 1 \end{bmatrix}$$

are matrices. The **order** or **dimension** of a matrix is the ordered pair having as first component the number of (horizontal) **rows** and as second component the number of (vertical) **columns** in the matrix. Thus,

$$\begin{bmatrix} 1 & 2 & 3 \\ 4 & 5 & 6 \end{bmatrix}, \quad \begin{bmatrix} 1 \\ 2 \\ 3 \end{bmatrix}, \quad \text{and} \quad \begin{bmatrix} a_1 & a_2 & a_3 & a_4 \\ b_1 & b_2 & b_3 & b_4 \\ c_1 & c_2 & c_3 & c_4 \\ d_1 & d_2 & d_3 & d_4 \end{bmatrix}$$

are 2×3 (read "two by three"), 3×1 (read "three by one"), and 4×4 (read "four by four") matrices, respectively. Note that the number of *rows* is given first, and then the number of *columns*. A matrix consisting of a single row is called a **row matrix** or a **row vector**, whereas a matrix consisting of a single column is called a **column matrix** or a **column vector**.

Matrix notation   Matrices are frequently denoted by capital letters. Thus, we might want to talk about the matrices A and B, where

$$A = \begin{bmatrix} a_1 & a_2 \\ b_1 & b_2 \end{bmatrix} \quad \text{and} \quad B = [b_1 \quad b_2].$$

To show that A is a 2×2 matrix, we can write $A_{2 \times 2}$. Similarly, $B_{1 \times 2}$ is a matrix with one row and two columns.

To represent the entries of a matrix, either single or double subscript notation is employed. Consider any 3×3 matrix, A. We can represent A by

$$A = \begin{bmatrix} a_1 & a_2 & a_3 \\ b_1 & b_2 & b_3 \\ c_1 & c_2 & c_3 \end{bmatrix},$$

where a different letter is used for each row, and a single subscript denotes the column in which each particular entry is located. Alternatively, we can use a different letter for each column, and let the subscript denote the row. Thus, we can also use the notation

$$A = \begin{bmatrix} a_1 & b_1 & c_1 \\ a_2 & b_2 & c_2 \\ a_3 & b_3 & c_3 \end{bmatrix}.$$

A much more useful convention involves double subscripts, where a single letter, say a, is used to denote an entry in a matrix, and then *two* subscripts are appended, the first subscript telling in which *row* the entry occurs, and the second telling which *column*. Thus, we write

$$A = \begin{bmatrix} a_{11} & a_{12} & a_{13} \\ a_{21} & a_{22} & a_{23} \\ a_{31} & a_{32} & a_{33} \end{bmatrix},$$

where a_{21} is the element in the second *row* and first *column*, a_{33} is the element in the third *row* and third *column*, and, if we wish to generalize, a_{ij} is the element in *i*th *row* and *j*th *column*.

DEFINITION 10.1 *Two matrices, A and B, are **equal** if and only if both matrices are of the same order and $a_{ij} = b_{ij}$ for each i, j.*

Thus,

$$\begin{bmatrix} 2 & 1 \\ 3 & 0 \end{bmatrix} = \begin{bmatrix} \frac{4}{2} & 2-1 \\ \sqrt{9} & 0 \end{bmatrix}, \quad \text{but} \quad \begin{bmatrix} 2 & 1 \\ 3 & 0 \end{bmatrix} \neq \begin{bmatrix} 2 & 3 \\ 1 & 0 \end{bmatrix}.$$

DEFINITION 10.2 *The **transpose** of a matrix A, denoted by A^t, is the matrix in which the rows are the columns of A and the columns are the rows of A.*

Examples. a. $\begin{bmatrix} 2 & 1 \\ 3 & 0 \end{bmatrix}^t = \begin{bmatrix} 2 & 3 \\ 1 & 0 \end{bmatrix}$ b. $\begin{bmatrix} 1 & 2 & 3 \\ 4 & 5 & 6 \end{bmatrix}^t = \begin{bmatrix} 1 & 4 \\ 2 & 5 \\ 3 & 6 \end{bmatrix}$

DEFINITION 10.3 *The **sum** of two matrices of the same order, $A_{m \times n}$ and $B_{m \times n}$, is the matrix $(A + B)_{m \times n}$ in which the entry in the ith row and jth column is $a_{ij} + b_{ij}$, for $i = 1, 2, 3, \cdots, m$ and $j = 1, 2, 3, \cdots, n$.*

Examples. $\begin{bmatrix} 3 & 1 & 2 \\ 2 & 1 & 4 \end{bmatrix} + \begin{bmatrix} 1 & 0 & 2 \\ -1 & 3 & 0 \end{bmatrix} = \begin{bmatrix} 3+1 & 1+0 & 2+2 \\ 2+(-1) & 1+3 & 4+0 \end{bmatrix}$

$$= \begin{bmatrix} 4 & 1 & 4 \\ 1 & 4 & 4 \end{bmatrix}.$$

The sum of two matrices of different order is not defined.

DEFINITION 10.4 *A matrix with each entry equal to 0 is a **zero matrix**.*

Zero matrices are generally denoted by the symbol **0**. This distinguishes a zero matrix from the real number 0. For example,

$$\mathbf{0}_{2 \times 4} = \begin{bmatrix} 0 & 0 & 0 & 0 \\ 0 & 0 & 0 & 0 \end{bmatrix}$$

is the 2 × 4 zero matrix.

DEFINITION 10.5 *The **negative** of the matrix $A_{m \times n}$, denoted by $-A_{m \times n}$, is the matrix formed by replacing each entry in the matrix $A_{m \times n}$ with its additive inverse.*

For example, if

$$A_{3 \times 2} = \begin{bmatrix} 3 & -1 \\ 2 & -2 \\ -4 & 5 \end{bmatrix}, \quad \text{then} \quad -A_{3 \times 2} = \begin{bmatrix} -3 & 1 \\ -2 & 2 \\ 4 & -5 \end{bmatrix}.$$

Properties of sums of matrices

The sum $B_{m \times n} + (-A_{m \times n})$ is called the **difference** of $B_{m \times n}$ and $A_{m \times n}$ and is denoted $B_{m \times n} - A_{m \times n}$.

At this point, we are able to establish the following facts concerning the set of all $m \times n$ matrices with real-number entries, for any given m and n.

THEOREM 10.1 *If A, B, and C are m × n matrices with real-number entries, then:*

I $(A + B)_{m \times n}$ *is a matrix with real-number entries.*   .*Closure law for addition.*

II $(A + B) + C = A + (B + C)$.   *Associative law for addition.*

III   *The matrix $\mathbf{0}_{m \times n}$ has the property that for every matrix $A_{m \times n}$,*   *Additive-identity law.*
$$A + 0 = A \quad \text{and} \quad 0 + A = A.$$

IV   *For every matrix $A_{m \times n}$, the matrix $-A_{m \times n}$ has the property that*   *Additive-inverse law.*
$$A + (-A) = 0 \quad \text{and} \quad (-A) + A = 0.$$

V $A + B = B + A$.   *Commutative law for addition.*

Proof of 10.1-III. Since each entry of the zero matrix is 0, it follows that the entries of $A_{m \times n} + \mathbf{0}_{m \times n}$ are $a_{ij} + 0 = a_{ij}$ and the entries of $\mathbf{0}_{m \times n} + A_{m \times n}$ are $0 + a_{ij} = a_{ij}$, and the theorem is proved.

Example.

$$\begin{bmatrix} a_{11} & a_{12} \\ a_{21} & a_{22} \end{bmatrix} + \begin{bmatrix} 0 & 0 \\ 0 & 0 \end{bmatrix} = \begin{bmatrix} a_{11} & a_{12} \\ a_{21} & a_{22} \end{bmatrix}$$

Proof of 10.1-IV. Let the entries of $A_{m \times n}$ and $-A_{m \times n}$ be a_{ij} and $-a_{ij}$, respectively. Since each entry of $A + (-A)$ is $a_{ij} - a_{ij}$, or 0, we have $A + (-A) = \mathbf{0}$. Similarly, $(-A) + A = \mathbf{0}$, and the theorem is proved.

For example, if

$$A = \begin{bmatrix} 1 & -1 & 2 \\ 3 & -1 & 1 \end{bmatrix},$$

then

$$A + (-A) = \begin{bmatrix} 1 & -1 & 2 \\ 3 & -1 & 1 \end{bmatrix} + \begin{bmatrix} -1 & 1 & -2 \\ -3 & 1 & -1 \end{bmatrix} = \begin{bmatrix} 0 & 0 & 0 \\ 0 & 0 & 0 \end{bmatrix} = \mathbf{0}.$$

The proof of Parts I, II, and V of Theorem 10.1 for the case of 2×2 matrices are left as exercises.

EXERCISE 10.1

State the order and find the transpose of each matrix.

Example.

$$\begin{bmatrix} 2 & 4 \\ 1 & -3 \\ 6 & 0 \end{bmatrix}$$

Solution. 3×2 matrix; $\begin{bmatrix} 2 & 4 \\ 1 & -3 \\ 6 & 0 \end{bmatrix}^t = \begin{bmatrix} 2 & 1 & 6 \\ 4 & -3 & 0 \end{bmatrix}.$

1. $\begin{bmatrix} 6 & -1 \\ 2 & 3 \end{bmatrix}$ 2. $\begin{bmatrix} 4 & 1 \\ 0 & -2 \end{bmatrix}$ 3. $\begin{bmatrix} 2 & -7 & 3 \\ 1 & 4 & 0 \end{bmatrix}$

4. $\begin{bmatrix} -3 & 1 \\ 6 & 0 \\ 0 & 2 \end{bmatrix}$ 5. $\begin{bmatrix} 2 & 3 & -1 \\ 4 & 0 & 1 \\ -2 & 3 & 1 \end{bmatrix}$ 6. $\begin{bmatrix} 4 & -1 & -2 \\ 3 & 0 & 0 \\ 2 & 1 & 1 \end{bmatrix}$

7. $\begin{bmatrix} 4 & -3 & -1 & 0 \\ 2 & 1 & 1 & 6 \end{bmatrix}$ 8. $\begin{bmatrix} -2 & 1 & 3 & 2 \\ 4 & 0 & 0 & -2 \\ -1 & 3 & 2 & 4 \end{bmatrix}$ 9. $[0 \ \ 0 \ \ 0 \ \ 0 \ \ 0]$

Write each sum as a single matrix.

Example. $\begin{bmatrix} 2 & 1 & 4 \\ 3 & -1 & 0 \end{bmatrix} + \begin{bmatrix} 6 & 3 & 0 \\ -2 & 1 & 0 \end{bmatrix}$

Solution. $\begin{bmatrix} 2+6 & 1+3 & 4+0 \\ 3-2 & -1+1 & 0+0 \end{bmatrix} = \begin{bmatrix} 8 & 4 & 4 \\ 1 & 0 & 0 \end{bmatrix}$

10. $\begin{bmatrix} 2 & 3 \\ 1 & 6 \end{bmatrix} + \begin{bmatrix} 1 & -2 \\ 2 & 3 \end{bmatrix}$

11. $\begin{bmatrix} 4 & -1 & 3 \\ 2 & 1 & 0 \end{bmatrix} + \begin{bmatrix} 3 & -1 & 0 \\ 4 & 0 & -2 \end{bmatrix}$

12. $\begin{bmatrix} 3 & 0 & -1 \\ 2 & 1 & 2 \end{bmatrix} + \begin{bmatrix} 6 & -1 & 0 \\ 0 & 2 & 4 \end{bmatrix}$

13. $[1 \quad 3 \quad 5 \quad 7] + [0 \quad -2 \quad 1 \quad 3]$

14. $\begin{bmatrix} 4 \\ 3 \\ -1 \end{bmatrix} + \begin{bmatrix} 6 \\ 0 \\ -2 \end{bmatrix}$

15. $\begin{bmatrix} 2 & 3 \\ 1 & 0 \\ -1 & 2 \end{bmatrix} + \begin{bmatrix} -2 & 0 \\ -3 & 0 \\ 4 & -1 \end{bmatrix}$

16. $\begin{bmatrix} 2 & 3 & 4 \\ -1 & 6 & 2 \\ 1 & 0 & 3 \end{bmatrix} + \begin{bmatrix} 0 & 0 & 0 \\ 0 & 0 & 0 \\ 0 & 0 & 0 \end{bmatrix}$

17. $\begin{bmatrix} 2 & -3 \\ 4 & -1 \\ -2 & 1 \end{bmatrix} + \begin{bmatrix} -2 & 3 \\ -4 & 1 \\ 2 & -1 \end{bmatrix}$

18. Show that $\begin{bmatrix} b_{11} - a_{11} & b_{12} - a_{12} \\ b_{21} - a_{21} & b_{22} - a_{22} \end{bmatrix}$ is a solution of the matrix equation

$X + A = B$, where $A = \begin{bmatrix} a_{11} & a_{12} \\ a_{21} & a_{22} \end{bmatrix}$ and $B = \begin{bmatrix} b_{11} & b_{12} \\ b_{21} & b_{22} \end{bmatrix}$.

19. Use the results of Problem 18 to argue that $X + A = B$ and $X = B - A$ are equivalent matrix equations in the system of 2×2 matrices.

Solve each of the following matrix equations.

20. $X + \begin{bmatrix} 3 & -1 \\ 2 & 1 \end{bmatrix} = \begin{bmatrix} 5 & 1 \\ -3 & 5 \end{bmatrix}$

21. $X - \begin{bmatrix} -1 & 0 \\ 0 & 0 \end{bmatrix} = \begin{bmatrix} 3 & -1 \\ 2 & 1 \end{bmatrix}^t$

22. $X + \begin{bmatrix} 3 & 2 \\ -1 & 4 \end{bmatrix} = \begin{bmatrix} -2 & -2 \\ -1 & 5 \end{bmatrix}$

23. $\begin{bmatrix} 1 & 3 \\ 1 & 0 \end{bmatrix}^t - \begin{bmatrix} 0 & 1 \\ 1 & 0 \end{bmatrix} = \begin{bmatrix} 2 & 2 \\ 1 & 3 \end{bmatrix}^t - X$

24. Prove that $\mathbf{0}_{m \times n}$ is the only additive identity matrix of order $m \times n$.

25. Prove that $-A_{m \times n}$ is the only additive inverse of the matrix $A_{m \times n}$.

26. Prove Theorem 10.1-I.

27. Prove Theorem 10.1-II.

28. Prove Theorem 10.1-V.

10.2 MATRIX MULTIPLICATION

We shall be interested in two kinds of products involving matrices: (1) the product of a matrix and a real number, and (2) the product of two matrices. Let us consider them one at a time.

DEFINITION 10.6 *The* **product** *of a real number c and an m × n matrix A with entries a_{ij} is the matrix cA with corresponding entries ca_{ij}, for i = 1, 2, 3,···, m and j = 1, 2, 3, ···, n.*

Example. $3\begin{bmatrix} 2 & 1 \\ 0 & 5 \end{bmatrix} = \begin{bmatrix} 3 \times 2 & 3 \times 1 \\ 3 \times 0 & 3 \times 5 \end{bmatrix} = \begin{bmatrix} 6 & 3 \\ 0 & 15 \end{bmatrix}.$

Properties of products of matrices and real numbers

The following theorem asserts some simple algebraic laws for the multiplication of matrices by real numbers.

THEOREM 10.2 *If A and B are m × n matrices, and c and d are real numbers, then*

I   *cA is an m × n matrix,*   V $1A = A$,

II $c(dA) = (cd)A$,   VI $(-1)A = -A$,

III $(c + d)A = cA + dA$,   VII $0A = \mathbf{0}$,

IV $c(A + B) = cA + cB$,   VIII $c\mathbf{0} = \mathbf{0}$.

Proof. We shall prove only Part IV, leaving the remaining parts as exercises. Since the elements of $A + B$ are of the form $a_{ij} + b_{ij}$, it follows, by definition, that the elements of $c(A + B)$ are of the form $c(a_{ij} + b_{ij})$. But, since a_{ij}, b_{ij}, and c denote real numbers, $c(a_{ij} + b_{ij}) = ca_{ij} + cb_{ij}$. Now, the elements of cA are of the form ca_{ij}, and those of cB are of the form cb_{ij}, so that the elements of $cA + cB$ are of the form $ca_{ij} + cb_{ij}$, and the theorem is proved.

Mathematical systems satisfying Theorems 10.1 and 10.2 are called **vector spaces** over the field R of real numbers. For example, the set $S_{2 \times 3}$ of 2 × 3 matrices—or more generally the set $S_{m \times n}$ of $m \times n$ matrices, with m and n fixed—is a vector

Vector spaces over fields

space over R. (It is also a vector space over the field Q of rational numbers.) The set of geometric vectors in the plane and the set of geometric vectors in space are likewise vector spaces over R, and, as we shall see in Chapter 12, so is the set of all complex numbers. The properties of these various vector spaces differ in part from one vector space to another, of course; but any result that follows strictly from Theorems 10.1 and 10.2 holds for *all* vector spaces.

Turning now to the product of two matrices, we have the following.

DEFINITION 10.7   *The **product** of the matrices $A_{m \times p}$ and $B_{p \times n}$ is the matrix $(AB)_{m \times n}$ with entries determined as follows: The entry c_{ij} in the ith row and jth column of $(AB)_{m \times n}$ is found by multiplying the first element in the ith row of A by the first element of the jth column of B, to this product adding the product of the second element in the ith row of A with the second element in the jth column of B, to this sum adding the product of the third element in the ith row of A with the third element in the jth column of B, and so on.*

For example, the product of the matrices

$$A_{2 \times 2} = \begin{bmatrix} a_{11} & a_{12} \\ a_{21} & a_{22} \end{bmatrix} \quad \text{and} \quad B_{2 \times 2} = \begin{bmatrix} b_{11} & b_{12} \\ b_{21} & b_{22} \end{bmatrix}$$

is the matrix

$$(AB)_{2 \times 2} = \begin{bmatrix} a_{11}b_{11} + a_{12}b_{21} & a_{11}b_{12} + a_{12}b_{22} \\ a_{21}b_{11} + a_{22}b_{21} & a_{21}b_{12} + a_{22}b_{22} \end{bmatrix}.$$

The following schematic shows how to find the entry in the first row and first column of AB.

$$\begin{bmatrix} a_{11} & a_{12} \\ a_{21} & a_{22} \end{bmatrix} \begin{bmatrix} b_{11} & b_{12} \\ b_{21} & b_{22} \end{bmatrix} = \begin{bmatrix} a_{11}b_{11} + a_{12}b_{21} & \\ & \end{bmatrix}.$$

Example.

If $A = \begin{bmatrix} 1 & 2 \\ -1 & 3 \end{bmatrix}$ and $B = \begin{bmatrix} 2 & 1 \\ 1 & 1 \end{bmatrix}$, find AB and BA.

Solution.

$$AB = \begin{bmatrix} 1 & 2 \\ -1 & 3 \end{bmatrix} \begin{bmatrix} 2 & 1 \\ 1 & 1 \end{bmatrix} = \begin{bmatrix} 2+2 & 1+2 \\ -2+3 & -1+3 \end{bmatrix} = \begin{bmatrix} 4 & 3 \\ 1 & 2 \end{bmatrix},$$

$$BA = \begin{bmatrix} 2 & 1 \\ 1 & 1 \end{bmatrix} \begin{bmatrix} 1 & 2 \\ -1 & 3 \end{bmatrix} = \begin{bmatrix} 2-1 & 4+3 \\ 1-1 & 2+3 \end{bmatrix} = \begin{bmatrix} 1 & 7 \\ 0 & 5 \end{bmatrix}.$$

This example shows very clearly that the multiplication of matrices, in general, is *not commutative*. Thus, when discussing products of matrices,

Right and left multiplication

we must specify the *order* in which the matrices are to be considered as factors. For the product AB, we say that A is right-multiplied by B, and that B is left-multiplied by A.

Note that the definition of the product of two matrices, A and B, requires that the matrix A have the same number of *columns* as B has *rows*; the result, AB, then has the same number of rows as A and the same number of columns as B. Such matrices A and B are said to be **conformable** for multiplication. The fact that two matrices are conformable in the order AB, however, does not mean that they necessarily are conformable in the order BA.

Example.

If $A = \begin{bmatrix} 3 & 1 & 2 \\ 1 & 0 & 1 \end{bmatrix}$ and $B = \begin{bmatrix} 1 & -1 \\ 2 & 1 \\ 3 & 1 \end{bmatrix}$, find AB.

Solution. Since A is a 2×3 matrix, and B is a 3×2 matrix, they are conformable for multiplication. We have

$$AB = \begin{bmatrix} 3 & 1 & 2 \\ 1 & 0 & 1 \end{bmatrix} \begin{bmatrix} 1 & -1 \\ 2 & 1 \\ 3 & 1 \end{bmatrix} = \begin{bmatrix} 3+2+6 & -3+1+2 \\ 1+0+3 & -1+0+1 \end{bmatrix} = \begin{bmatrix} 11 & 0 \\ 4 & 0 \end{bmatrix}.$$

In much of the matrix work in this book, we shall focus our attention on matrices having the same number of rows as columns. For brevity, a matrix of order $n \times n$ is often called a **square matrix of order** n. Although many of the ideas we shall discuss are applicable to matrices of any order, we shall apply the notions only to square matrices. If A is a square matrix, then A^2, A^3, etc., denote $AA, (AA)A$, etc.

THEOREM 10.3   *If A, B, and C are $n \times n$ square matrices, then*

$$(AB)C = A(BC).$$

THEOREM 10.4   *If A, B, and C are $n \times n$ square matrices, then*

$$\text{I} \quad A(B + C) = AB + AC$$

$$\text{II} \quad (B + C)A = BA + CA.$$

The proofs of these theorems involve some complicated symbolism and are omitted here, but you will be asked to show their validity for the case of 2×2 matrices in the exercises. Observe that, because matrix multiplication is not, in general, commutative, we must establish both the left-hand and the right-hand distributive property.

DEFINITION 10.8   *The **principal diagonal** of a square matrix is the ordered set of entries a_{ij}, where $i = j$, extending from the upper left-hand corner to the lower right-hand corner of the matrix.*

For example, the principal diagonal of

$$\begin{bmatrix} 1 & 3 & -1 \\ 5 & 2 & 3 \\ 6 & 4 & 0 \end{bmatrix}$$

consists of 1, 2, and 0, in that order.

DEFINITION 10.9   *A **diagonal matrix** is a square matrix in which all entries not in the principal diagonal are 0.*

Thus,

$$\begin{bmatrix} 4 & 0 \\ 0 & 2 \end{bmatrix} \quad \text{and} \quad \begin{bmatrix} 1 & 0 & 0 \\ 0 & 1 & 0 \\ 0 & 0 & 0 \end{bmatrix}$$

are diagonal matrices.

DEFINITION 10.10 $I_{n \times n}$ *denotes the diagonal matrix having* 1's *for entries on the principal diagonal.*

For example,

$$I_{2 \times 2} = \begin{bmatrix} 1 & 0 \\ 0 & 1 \end{bmatrix} \quad \text{and} \quad I_{4 \times 4} = \begin{bmatrix} 1 & 0 & 0 & 0 \\ 0 & 1 & 0 & 0 \\ 0 & 0 & 1 & 0 \\ 0 & 0 & 0 & 1 \end{bmatrix}$$

The importance of $I_{n \times n}$ to the operation of multiplication of $n \times n$ matrices is apparent in the following result.

THEOREM 10.5 *For each matrix* $A_{n \times n}$, *we have*

$$A_{n \times n} I_{n \times n} = I_{n \times n} A_{n \times n} = A_{n \times n}.$$

Further, if for the matrix $B_{n \times n}$, *we have*

$$A_{n \times n} B_{n \times n} = B_{n \times n} A_{n \times n} = A_{n \times n}$$

for all matrices $A_{n \times n}$, *then*

$$B_{n \times n} = I_{n \times n}.$$

Accordingly, $I_{n \times n}$ is the **identity element** for multiplication in the set of $n \times n$ square matrices, and $I_{n \times n}$ is unique. The proof of this theorem, for the illustrative case $n = 2$, is left as an exercise.

| Properties of products of matrices | We can summarize the properties of multiplication of $n \times n$ matrices by listing them as we did the analogous properties for addition. That is, corresponding to Theorem 10.1, we have the following theorem. |

THEOREM 10.6 *If* $S_{n \times n}$ *is the set of* $n \times n$ *square matrices, for* n *a fixed positive integer, and* $A, B, C \in S_{n \times n}$, *then:*

I $AB \in S_{n \times n}$.   *Closure law for multiplication.*

II $(AB)C = A(BC)$.   *Associative law for multiplication.*

III $A(B + C) = AB + AC$ *and*   *Distributive laws.*
      $(B + C)A = BA + CA$.

IV $AI_{n \times n} = A$ *and* $I_{n \times n} A = A$.   *Multiplicative-identity law.*

Proof. Property I is an immediate consequence of Definition 10.7. Properties II, III, and IV are repetitions of the properties stated in Theorems 10.3, 10.4, and 10.5, respectively.

If you compare the properties for sums and products of $n \times n$ matrices as listed in Theorems 10.1 and 10.6, with those that characterize a field on page 11, you will see that the set is not a field, because two of the field properties do *not* hold in $S_{n \times n}$. As we have already pointed out, the commutative law does not hold for matrix multiplication, and in Section 10.5 we shall see that there are square $n \times n$ matrices other than the zero $n \times n$ matrix that do not have multiplicative inverses.

The set of $n \times n$ matrices not a field

Order of multiplication

The following result relates the order in which matrices can be multiplied by real numbers and by other matrices.

THEOREM 10.7 *If A and B are $n \times n$ square matrices, and a is a real number, then*

$$a(AB) = (aA)B = A(aB).$$

The easy proof for the illustrative case $n = 2$ is left as an exercise.

EXERCISE 10.2

Write each product as a single matrix.

Examples. a. $3 \begin{bmatrix} 2 & 1 \\ -1 & 3 \\ 2 & 0 \end{bmatrix}$

b. $\begin{bmatrix} 3 & 1 & -1 \\ 0 & -1 & 2 \end{bmatrix} \cdot \begin{bmatrix} 1 & -1 \\ 0 & 2 \\ 1 & 0 \end{bmatrix}$

Solutions. a. $\begin{bmatrix} 6 & 3 \\ -3 & 9 \\ 6 & 0 \end{bmatrix}$

b. $\begin{bmatrix} 3+0-1 & -3+2+0 \\ 0+0+2 & 0-2+0 \end{bmatrix} = \begin{bmatrix} 2 & -1 \\ 2 & -2 \end{bmatrix}$

1. $-5 \begin{bmatrix} 0 & 1 & -1 \\ 3 & -1 & 2 \end{bmatrix}$

2. $2 \begin{bmatrix} 2 & 1 & 3 & -2 \\ 4 & 2 & 0 & -1 \\ 0 & 0 & -1 & 2 \end{bmatrix}$

3. $[1 \quad -2] \cdot \begin{bmatrix} 3 \\ 2 \end{bmatrix}$

4. $[3 \quad -2 \quad 2] \cdot \begin{bmatrix} 1 \\ 0 \\ -2 \end{bmatrix}$

5. $\begin{bmatrix} -3 & 1 & 0 \\ 2 & 1 & 1 \end{bmatrix} \cdot \begin{bmatrix} 2 & 0 \\ 1 & -1 \\ 3 & 0 \end{bmatrix}$

6. $\begin{bmatrix} 2 & -3 & 1 \\ 0 & 1 & -1 \\ 2 & 0 & 0 \end{bmatrix} \cdot \begin{bmatrix} 1 & 0 & 0 \\ 0 & 1 & 0 \\ 0 & 0 & 1 \end{bmatrix}$

7. $\begin{bmatrix} 2 & -2 & -1 \\ 1 & 1 & -2 \\ 1 & 0 & -1 \end{bmatrix} \cdot \begin{bmatrix} -1 & -2 & 5 \\ -1 & -1 & 3 \\ -1 & -2 & 4 \end{bmatrix}$

8. $\begin{bmatrix} -1 & -2 & 5 \\ -1 & -1 & 3 \\ -1 & -2 & 4 \end{bmatrix} \cdot \begin{bmatrix} 2 & -2 & -1 \\ 1 & 1 & -2 \\ 1 & 0 & -1 \end{bmatrix}$

Let $A = \begin{bmatrix} 1 & -2 \\ 1 & 0 \end{bmatrix}$ and $B = \begin{bmatrix} -1 & 2 \\ -1 & 1 \end{bmatrix}$. Compute each of the following.

9. AB 10. BA 11. $(AB)A$

12. $(BA)B$ 13. A^2 14. B^2

15. A^tB 16. AB^t

Find a matrix X satisfying each matrix equation.

17. $3X + \begin{bmatrix} 1 & 0 \\ 2 & 1 \end{bmatrix} = \begin{bmatrix} -2 & 3 \\ -1 & -2 \end{bmatrix}$ 18. $2X + 3\begin{bmatrix} 1 & 1 \\ 0 & 1 \end{bmatrix} = \begin{bmatrix} 7 & -1 \\ 3 & -5 \end{bmatrix}$

19. $X + 2I = \begin{bmatrix} 3 & -1 \\ 1 & 2 \end{bmatrix}$ Hint: $2I = \begin{bmatrix} 2 & 0 \\ 0 & 2 \end{bmatrix}$.

20. $3X - 2I = \begin{bmatrix} 7 & 3 \\ 6 & 4 \end{bmatrix}$

21. Show that if $A = \begin{bmatrix} -1 & 2 \\ 0 & 1 \end{bmatrix}$ and $B = \begin{bmatrix} 1 & 0 \\ -1 & 2 \end{bmatrix}$, then

     a. $(A + B)(A + B) \neq A^2 + 2AB + B^2$,
     b. $(A + B)(A - B) \neq A^2 - B^2$.

22. a. Show that for each matrix $A_{2 \times 2}$,
$$A_{2 \times 2} \cdot I_{2 \times 2} = I_{2 \times 2} \cdot A_{2 \times 2} = A_{2 \times 2}.$$

     b. Show that if, for a given matrix $B_{2 \times 2}$ and for *all* $A_{2 \times 2}$,
$$A_{2 \times 2} \cdot B_{2 \times 2} = B_{2 \times 2} \cdot A_{2 \times 2} = A_{2 \times 2},$$

     then $B_{2 \times 2} = I_{2 \times 2}$.

23. Show that
$$\left(\begin{bmatrix} a_{11} & a_{12} \\ a_{21} & a_{22} \end{bmatrix} \cdot \begin{bmatrix} b_{11} & b_{12} \\ b_{21} & b_{22} \end{bmatrix} \right) \cdot \begin{bmatrix} c_{11} & c_{12} \\ c_{21} & c_{22} \end{bmatrix} =$$
$$\begin{bmatrix} a_{11} & a_{12} \\ a_{21} & a_{22} \end{bmatrix} \cdot \left(\begin{bmatrix} b_{11} & b_{12} \\ b_{21} & b_{22} \end{bmatrix} \cdot \begin{bmatrix} c_{11} & c_{12} \\ c_{21} & c_{22} \end{bmatrix} \right).$$

24. Show that
$$\begin{bmatrix} a_{11} & a_{12} \\ a_{21} & a_{22} \end{bmatrix} \cdot \left(\begin{bmatrix} b_{11} & b_{12} \\ b_{21} & b_{22} \end{bmatrix} + \begin{bmatrix} c_{11} & c_{12} \\ c_{21} & c_{22} \end{bmatrix} \right) =$$
$$\begin{bmatrix} a_{11} & a_{12} \\ a_{21} & a_{22} \end{bmatrix} \cdot \begin{bmatrix} b_{11} & b_{12} \\ b_{21} & b_{22} \end{bmatrix} + \begin{bmatrix} a_{11} & a_{12} \\ a_{21} & a_{22} \end{bmatrix} \cdot \begin{bmatrix} c_{11} & c_{12} \\ c_{21} & c_{22} \end{bmatrix}.$$

25. Show that
$$\left(\begin{bmatrix} b_{11} & b_{12} \\ b_{21} & b_{22} \end{bmatrix} + \begin{bmatrix} c_{11} & c_{12} \\ c_{21} & c_{22} \end{bmatrix} \right) \cdot \begin{bmatrix} a_{11} & a_{12} \\ a_{21} & a_{22} \end{bmatrix} =$$
$$\begin{bmatrix} b_{11} & b_{12} \\ b_{21} & b_{22} \end{bmatrix} \cdot \begin{bmatrix} a_{11} & a_{12} \\ a_{21} & a_{22} \end{bmatrix} + \begin{bmatrix} c_{11} & c_{12} \\ c_{21} & c_{22} \end{bmatrix} \cdot \begin{bmatrix} a_{11} & a_{12} \\ a_{21} & a_{22} \end{bmatrix}.$$

26. Show that $\begin{bmatrix} 0 & a \\ a & 0 \end{bmatrix}^2 = a^2 I.$

27. Show that $(A_{2 \times 2} \cdot B_{2 \times 2})^t = B^t_{2 \times 2} \cdot A^t_{2 \times 2}.$

28. Show that $A^2_{2 \times 2} = (-A_{2 \times 2})^2.$

In Problems 29–35, prove the specified part of Theorem 10.2 for 2×2 matrices.

29. Part I   30. Part II   31. Part III   32. Part V

33. Part VI   34. Part VII   35. Part VIII

36. Prove that if A and B are 2×2 matrices and a is a real number, then $a(AB) = (aA)B = A(aB).$

10.3 THE DETERMINANT FUNCTION

Associated with each square matrix A having real-number entries is a real number called the **determinant** of A and denoted by δA or $\delta(A)$ (read "the determinant of A"). Thus δ (delta) is a function with domain the set of all square matrices having real-number entries and with range the set of all real numbers. We say that $\delta(A_{n \times n})$ is a determinant of **order** n.

Let us begin by examining δ over the set $S_{2 \times 2}$ of 2×2 matrices.

DEFINITION 10.11 *The **determinant** of the matrix*

$$\begin{bmatrix} a_{11} & a_{12} \\ a_{21} & a_{22} \end{bmatrix}$$

is the number $a_{11}a_{22} - a_{12}a_{21}.$

Determinant notation	The determinant of a matrix is customarily displayed in the same form as a matrix, but with vertical bars in lieu of brackets. Thus,

$$\delta \begin{bmatrix} a_{11} & a_{12} \\ a_{21} & a_{22} \end{bmatrix} = \begin{vmatrix} a_{11} & a_{12} \\ a_{21} & a_{22} \end{vmatrix} = a_{11}a_{22} - a_{12}a_{21}.$$

Example. If $A = \begin{bmatrix} 3 & 1 \\ -2 & 3 \end{bmatrix}$, find $\delta A.$

Solution.

$$\delta A = \delta \begin{bmatrix} 3 & 1 \\ -2 & 3 \end{bmatrix} = \begin{vmatrix} 3 & 1 \\ -2 & 3 \end{vmatrix} = 3 \cdot 3 - (1)(-2) = 9 + 2 = 11.$$

Turning next to 3×3 matrices, we have the following.

DEFINITION 10.12 *The **determinant** of the matrix*

$$\begin{bmatrix} a_{11} & a_{12} & a_{13} \\ a_{21} & a_{22} & a_{23} \\ a_{31} & a_{32} & a_{33} \end{bmatrix}, \quad denoted\ by \quad \begin{vmatrix} a_{11} & a_{12} & a_{13} \\ a_{21} & a_{22} & a_{23} \\ a_{31} & a_{32} & a_{33} \end{vmatrix},$$

is given by the expression

$$a_{11}a_{22}a_{33} - a_{11}a_{23}a_{32} + a_{12}a_{23}a_{31} - a_{12}a_{21}a_{33} + a_{13}a_{21}a_{32} - a_{13}a_{22}a_{31}.$$

An inspection of the subscripts of the factors of the products involved in this determinant (as well as those of the determinant of a 2×2 matrix) will show that each product is formed by taking one entry from each row and one entry from each column, with the restriction that no two factors be entries in the same row or column. The determinant consists of the sum of all such $\pm$ products as are possible.

Sign of a term in the expression of a determinant

Whether a product or its negative is used in computing the sum of the terms in a determinant depends on the number of **inversions** in the second subscripts in the product when the first subscripts are in natural order, 1 2 3 $\cdots$. An inversion occurs in a sequence of natural numbers each time a natural number is preceded by a greater natural number. For example, in the sequence 1 4 3 2, there are three inversions, because 4 precedes 3, 4 precedes 2, and 3 precedes 2. Now, if there is an odd number of inversions in the sequence formed by the *second subscripts of the factors in a product* when the first subscripts are in natural order, then the negative of the product is used; otherwise, the product itself is used.

With this means of distinguishing the signs associated with products, we can generalize our definition of the determinant of a matrix.

DEFINITION 10.13 *The **determinant** of the square matrix*

$$\begin{bmatrix} a_{11} & a_{12} & \cdots & a_{1n} \\ a_{21} & a_{22} & \cdots & a_{2n} \\ \vdots & \vdots & & \vdots \\ a_{n1} & a_{n2} & \cdots & a_{nn} \end{bmatrix}, \quad denoted\ by \quad \begin{vmatrix} a_{11} & a_{12} & \cdots & a_{1n} \\ a_{21} & a_{22} & \cdots & a_{2n} \\ \vdots & \vdots & & \vdots \\ a_{n1} & a_{n2} & \cdots & a_{nn} \end{vmatrix},$$

is equal to the sum of all products, $\pm a_{1j_1}a_{2j_2}a_{3j_3}\cdots a_{nj_n}$, where each j takes on all values from 1 to n, and no j's in the same product have the same subscript. For each term in the sum, the negative sign is used if the number of inversions in the sequence formed by the j's is odd; otherwise, the positive sign is used.

It is evident from this definition that the determinant of a matrix with real entries is a real number. We shall refer to this real number as the **value** of the determinant; the process of computing the number is called **expanding** the determinant. In particular, the value of the determinant of the matrix $[a_{11}]$ is a_{11}.

Example. In expanding the determinant of a 4×4 square matrix, one of the products is $a_{11}a_{23}a_{32}a_{44}$. Is this product a term in the expansion or is its negative a term in the expansion?

Solution. The first subscripts are in natural order, 1 2 3 4, and the second subscripts are in the order 1 3 2 4. Since the only inversion is that 3 appears before 2, the negative of $a_{11}a_{23}a_{32}a_{44}$ is in the expansion of the determinant.

DEFINITION 10.14 *The **minor** M_{ij} of the element a_{ij} in a given determinant is the determinant that remains after the ith row and jth column in the given determinant have been deleted.*

For example, in the determinant

$$\begin{vmatrix} a_{11} & a_{12} & a_{13} \\ a_{21} & a_{22} & a_{23} \\ a_{31} & a_{32} & a_{33} \end{vmatrix}, \tag{1}$$

the minor of the element a_{11} is $M_{11} - \begin{vmatrix} a_{22} & a_{23} \\ a_{32} & a_{33} \end{vmatrix}$,

the minor of the element a_{23} is $M_{23} = \begin{vmatrix} a_{11} & a_{12} \\ a_{31} & a_{32} \end{vmatrix}$,

the minor of the element a_{31} is $M_{31} = \begin{vmatrix} a_{12} & a_{13} \\ a_{22} & a_{23} \end{vmatrix}$.

DEFINITION 10.15 *The **cofactor** A_{ij} of the element a_{ij} is the minor of a_{ij} if $i + j$ is an even integer, and the negative of the minor of a_{ij} if $i + j$ is an odd integer.*

For example, in the determinant (1),

the cofactor of a_{11} is $\begin{vmatrix} a_{22} & a_{23} \\ a_{32} & a_{33} \end{vmatrix}$,

because $1 + 1$ is 2, an even integer;

the cofactor of a_{23} is $-\begin{vmatrix} a_{11} & a_{12} \\ a_{31} & a_{32} \end{vmatrix}$,

because $2 + 3$ is 5, an odd integer;

the cofactor of a_{31} is $\begin{vmatrix} a_{12} & a_{13} \\ a_{22} & a_{23} \end{vmatrix}$,

because $3 + 1$ is 4, an even integer.

Signs of the cofactors in a determinant

The following sign array is a convenient means of determining whether the cofactor of a given element equals the minor or whether it equals the negative of the minor.

$$
\begin{array}{cccccc}
+ & - & + & \cdot & \cdot & \cdot \quad (-)^{n+1} \\
- & + & - & \cdot & \cdot & \cdot \\
+ & - & + & \cdot & \cdot & \cdot \\
\cdot & \cdot & \cdot & \cdot & \cdot & \cdot \\
\cdot & \cdot & \cdot & \cdot & \cdot & \cdot \\
\cdot & \cdot & \cdot & \cdot & \cdot & \cdot \\
(-)^{n+1} & & \cdot & \cdot & \cdot & +
\end{array}
$$

Expansion by cofactors

With the definition of a cofactor in mind, let us look again at the definition on page 247 for the determinant of the matrix

$$
A = \begin{bmatrix} a_{11} & a_{12} & a_{13} \\ a_{21} & a_{22} & a_{23} \\ a_{31} & a_{32} & a_{33} \end{bmatrix}.
$$

By Definition 10.12, the value of this determinant is

$$
\delta(A) = a_{11}a_{22}a_{33} - a_{11}a_{23}a_{32} + a_{12}a_{23}a_{31} - a_{12}a_{21}a_{33} \\
+ a_{13}a_{21}a_{32} - a_{13}a_{22}a_{31}.
$$

By suitably factoring pairs of terms in the right-hand member, we obtain

$$
\delta(A) = a_{11}(a_{22}a_{33} - a_{23}a_{32}) + a_{12}(a_{23}a_{31} - a_{21}a_{33}) + a_{13}(a_{21}a_{32} - a_{22}a_{31}).
$$

If now the binomial factor in the middle term is rewritten $-(a_{21}a_{33} - a_{23}a_{31})$, we have

$$
\delta(A) = a_{11}(a_{22}a_{33} - a_{23}a_{32}) + a_{12}[-(a_{21}a_{33} - a_{23}a_{31})] + a_{13}(a_{21}a_{32} - a_{22}a_{31}),
$$

which is equal to

$$
a_{11}\begin{vmatrix} a_{22} & a_{23} \\ a_{32} & a_{33} \end{vmatrix} + a_{12}\left(-\begin{vmatrix} a_{21} & a_{23} \\ a_{31} & a_{33} \end{vmatrix}\right) + a_{13}\begin{vmatrix} a_{21} & a_{22} \\ a_{31} & a_{32} \end{vmatrix}.
$$

Accordingly, we have

$$
\delta(A) = a_{11}A_{11} + a_{12}A_{12} + a_{13}A_{13}.
$$

Thus, the determinant

$$
\delta(A) = \begin{vmatrix} a_{11} & a_{12} & a_{13} \\ a_{21} & a_{22} & a_{23} \\ a_{31} & a_{32} & a_{33} \end{vmatrix}
$$

is equal to the sum formed by multiplying each entry in the first row by its cofactor and then adding these products.

In the exercises at the end of this section, you will be asked to show that this determinant is also equal to the sum formed by multiplying each entry in *any* row (or column) by its cofactor and then adding the products.

Although we shall not show it here, Definition 10.13 on page 247 is logically equivalent to the following.

DEFINITION 10.16   *The **determinant** of the square matrix*

$$\begin{bmatrix} a_{11} & a_{12} & \cdots & a_{1n} \\ a_{21} & a_{22} & \cdots & a_{2n} \\ \vdots & & & \vdots \\ a_{n1} & a_{n2} & \cdots & a_{nn} \end{bmatrix}$$

is the sum of the n products formed by multiplying each entry in any single row (or any single column) by its cofactor.

When this latter definition is used to rewrite a determinant, the determinant is said to be **expanded** about whatever row (or column) is chosen.

Example.   If

$$A = \begin{bmatrix} 3 & 2 & 1 \\ 0 & 1 & -2 \\ 1 & 3 & 4 \end{bmatrix},$$

find $\delta(A)$ by expansion about the first column.

Solution.   Noting that $a_{11} = 3$, $a_{21} = 0$, and $a_{31} = 1$, we have

$$A = 3 \begin{vmatrix} 1 & -2 \\ 3 & 4 \end{vmatrix} + 0 \left(- \begin{vmatrix} 2 & 1 \\ 3 & 4 \end{vmatrix} \right) + 1 \begin{vmatrix} 2 & 1 \\ 1 & -2 \end{vmatrix}$$

$$= 3(10) + 0 + (-5) = 25.$$

EXERCISE 10.3

Let

$$A = \begin{bmatrix} 2 & 1 & -2 & 0 \\ 1 & 0 & 3 & -1 \\ -2 & 1 & 2 & 2 \\ 1 & -1 & 3 & 1 \end{bmatrix}.$$

Each of the following is a term in an expansion of $\delta(A)$. Determine the product, and write the product or its negative in accordance with the number of inversions in the second subscripts.

1. $a_{11}a_{22}a_{33}a_{44}$ 2. $a_{11}a_{23}a_{34}a_{42}$ 3. $a_{11}a_{24}a_{32}a_{43}$

4. $a_{12}a_{21}a_{33}a_{44}$ 5. $a_{13}a_{24}a_{32}a_{41}$ 6. $a_{14}a_{23}a_{32}a_{41}$

Let A be the matrix given above. Determine the minor M_{ij} and cofactor A_{ij} (in determinant form) of each of the following entries.

7. a_{11} 8. a_{13} 9. a_{23} 10. a_{41}

11. a_{31} 12. a_{33} 13. a_{44} 14. a_{14}

Evaluate each determinant.

Examples.   a. $\begin{vmatrix} 2 & -3 \\ 1 & 4 \end{vmatrix}$ b. $\begin{vmatrix} 1 & 2 & 0 \\ 3 & -1 & 4 \\ -2 & 1 & 3 \end{vmatrix}$

Solutions.   a. $\begin{vmatrix} 2 & -3 \\ 1 & 4 \end{vmatrix} = (2)(4) - (-3)(1) = 11.$

b. Expand about any row or column; the first row is used here:

$$\begin{vmatrix} 1 & 2 & 0 \\ 3 & -1 & 4 \\ -2 & 1 & 3 \end{vmatrix} = 1 \begin{vmatrix} -1 & 4 \\ 1 & 3 \end{vmatrix} - 2 \begin{vmatrix} 3 & 4 \\ -2 & 3 \end{vmatrix} + 0 \begin{vmatrix} 3 & -1 \\ -2 & 1 \end{vmatrix}$$

$$= 1[(-1)(3) - (4)(1)] - 2[(3)(3) - (4)(-2)] + 0$$
$$= -41.$$

15. $\begin{vmatrix} 1 & 0 \\ 2 & 1 \end{vmatrix}$ 16. $\begin{vmatrix} 3 & -2 \\ 4 & 1 \end{vmatrix}$ 17. $\begin{vmatrix} -5 & -1 \\ 3 & \dfrac{3}{5} \end{vmatrix}$ 18. $\begin{vmatrix} -1 & 6 \\ 0 & -2 \end{vmatrix}$

19. $\begin{vmatrix} 2 & 0 & 1 \\ 1 & 1 & 2 \\ -1 & 0 & 1 \end{vmatrix}$ 20. $\begin{vmatrix} 1 & 3 & 1 \\ -1 & 2 & 1 \\ 0 & 2 & 0 \end{vmatrix}$ 21. $\begin{vmatrix} 1 & 2 & 3 \\ 3 & -1 & 2 \\ 2 & 0 & 2 \end{vmatrix}$

22. $\begin{vmatrix} 1 & 0 & 0 \\ 0 & 1 & 2 \\ 0 & 3 & 4 \end{vmatrix}$ 23. $\begin{vmatrix} -1 & 0 & 2 \\ -2 & 1 & 0 \\ 0 & 1 & -3 \end{vmatrix}$ 24. $\begin{vmatrix} 2 & 1 & 4 \\ 3 & 2 & 6 \\ 5 & -3 & 10 \end{vmatrix}$

25. $\begin{vmatrix} a & b & 1 \\ a & b & 1 \\ 1 & 1 & 1 \end{vmatrix}$ 26. $\begin{vmatrix} a & a & a \\ 1 & 2 & 3 \\ 4 & 5 & 6 \end{vmatrix}$ 27. $\begin{vmatrix} x & 0 & 0 \\ 0 & x & 0 \\ 0 & 0 & x \end{vmatrix}$ 28. $\begin{vmatrix} 0 & 0 & x \\ 0 & x & 0 \\ x & 0 & 0 \end{vmatrix}$

Solve for x.

29. $\begin{vmatrix} x & 0 & 0 \\ 2 & 1 & 3 \\ 0 & 1 & 4 \end{vmatrix} = 3$ 30. $\begin{vmatrix} x^2 & x & 1 \\ 0 & 2 & 1 \\ 3 & 1 & 4 \end{vmatrix} = 28$

Expand by cofactors and verify.

31. $\begin{vmatrix} 0 & 1 & 0 & 0 \\ 1 & 0 & 3 & 2 \\ 5 & -1 & 2 & 1 \\ 1 & 0 & 1 & 1 \end{vmatrix} = 5$ 32. $\begin{vmatrix} 1 & 2 & 0 & -1 \\ 1 & 0 & -1 & 2 \\ 0 & 1 & 1 & 1 \\ 2 & -1 & 0 & 1 \end{vmatrix} = 17$

33. In accordance with Definition 10.13, the determinant of an $n \times n$ matrix is the sum of a certain number of products. What is this number for $n = 2$? For $n = 3$? For $n = 4$?

34. Generalize the results of Problem 33, making a conjecture about the number of such products in the determinant of an $n \times n$ matrix.

In Problems 35–40, consider the determinant of

$$\begin{bmatrix} a_{11} & a_{12} & a_{13} \\ a_{21} & a_{22} & a_{23} \\ a_{31} & a_{32} & a_{33} \end{bmatrix}.$$

35. Show that $a_{11}A_{11} + a_{12}A_{12} + a_{13}A_{13} = a_{21}A_{21} + a_{22}A_{22} + a_{23}A_{23}$.

36. Show that $a_{11}A_{11} + a_{12}A_{12} + a_{13}A_{13} = a_{31}A_{31} + a_{32}A_{32} + a_{33}A_{33}$.

37. Show that $a_{11}A_{11} + a_{12}A_{12} + a_{13}A_{13} = a_{11}A_{11} + a_{21}A_{21} + a_{31}A_{31}$.

38. Show that $a_{11}A_{11} + a_{12}A_{12} + a_{13}A_{13} = a_{12}A_{12} + a_{22}A_{22} + a_{32}A_{32}$.

39. Show that $a_{11}A_{11} + a_{12}A_{12} + a_{13}A_{13} = a_{13}A_{13} + a_{23}A_{23} + a_{33}A_{33}$.

40. Summarize the results of Problems 35–39.

41. Show that for any 2×2 matrix A, $\delta(aA) = a^2\delta(A)$.

42. Show that for any 2×2 matrix A, $\delta(A^t) = \delta(A)$.

43. Show that for any 2×2 matrices A and B, $\delta(AB) = \delta(A) \cdot \delta(B)$.

10.4 PROPERTIES OF DETERMINANTS

Determinants have some properties that are useful by virtue of the fact that they permit us to generate equal determinants with different and simpler configurations of entries. This, in turn, helps us find values for determinants. We shall list these properties in the form of theorems, and leave the proofs for the case of 2×2 determinants as exercises.

THEOREM 10.8 *If each entry in any row, or each entry in any column, of a determinant is 0, then the determinant is equal to 0.*

Examples.

a. $\begin{vmatrix} 0 & 0 \\ 1 & 2 \end{vmatrix} = 0$ b. $\begin{vmatrix} 1 & 1 & 0 \\ 3 & 5 & 0 \\ 2 & 7 & 0 \end{vmatrix} = 0$ c. $\begin{vmatrix} 0 & 1 & 0 & 0 \\ 1 & 0 & 0 & 0 \\ 0 & 0 & 0 & 1 \\ 0 & 0 & 0 & 1 \end{vmatrix} = 0.$

THEOREM 10.9 *If any two rows (or columns) of a determinant are interchanged, the resulting determinant is the negative of the original determinant.*

Examples.

a. $\begin{vmatrix} 1 & 2 \\ 3 & 4 \end{vmatrix} = - \begin{vmatrix} 3 & 4 \\ 1 & 2 \end{vmatrix}$ b. $\begin{vmatrix} 1 & 2 & 3 \\ 4 & 5 & 6 \\ 7 & 8 & 9 \end{vmatrix} = - \begin{vmatrix} 3 & 2 & 1 \\ 6 & 5 & 4 \\ 9 & 8 & 7 \end{vmatrix}$

In the first example, rows 1 and 2 were interchanged. In the second example, columns 1 and 3 were interchanged.

THEOREM 10.10 *If two rows (or two columns) in a determinant have corresponding entries that are equal, the determinant is equal to 0.*

Examples.

a. $\begin{vmatrix} 1 & 1 \\ 3 & 3 \end{vmatrix} = 0$

b. $\begin{vmatrix} 1 & 2 & 1 \\ 3 & 1 & 0 \\ 1 & 2 & 1 \end{vmatrix} = 0$

c. $\begin{vmatrix} 1 & 2 & 3 & 4 \\ 5 & 6 & 7 & 8 \\ 0 & 0 & 1 & 0 \\ 1 & 2 & 3 & 4 \end{vmatrix} = 0$

THEOREM 10.11 *If each of the entries of one row (or column) of a determinant is multiplied by k, then the determinant is multiplied by k.*

Examples.

a. $\begin{vmatrix} 1 & 0 & 0 \\ 2 & 1 & 3 \\ 1 \times 2 & 3 \times 2 & 4 \times 2 \end{vmatrix} = 2\begin{vmatrix} 1 & 0 & 0 \\ 2 & 1 & 3 \\ 1 & 3 & 4 \end{vmatrix}$

b. $\begin{vmatrix} 4 & 5 & 8 \\ 1 & 1 & 2 \\ 3 & 1 & 6 \end{vmatrix} = 2\begin{vmatrix} 4 & 5 & 4 \\ 1 & 1 & 1 \\ 3 & 1 & 3 \end{vmatrix}$

Note that this process is different from that of the scalar multiplication of a matrix. In scalar multiplication, each entry in the matrix is multiplied by a real number, rather than, as here, only the entries in a single row or column being so multiplied.

THEOREM 10.12 *If each entry in a row (or column) of a determinant is written as the sum of two terms, then the determinant can be written as the sum of two determinants as follows: If*

$$D = \begin{vmatrix} a_{11} & a_{12} & \cdots & a_{1n} \\ \vdots & \vdots & & \vdots \\ b_{i1} + c_{i1} & b_{i2} + c_{i2} & \cdots & b_{in} + c_{in} \\ \vdots & \vdots & & \vdots \\ a_{n1} & a_{n2} & \cdots & a_{nn} \end{vmatrix},$$

then

$$D = \begin{vmatrix} a_{11} & a_{12} & \cdots & a_{1n} \\ \vdots & \vdots & & \vdots \\ b_{i1} & b_{i2} & \cdots & b_{in} \\ \vdots & \vdots & & \vdots \\ a_{n1} & a_{n2} & \cdots & a_{nn} \end{vmatrix} + \begin{vmatrix} a_{11} & a_{12} & \cdots & a_{1n} \\ \vdots & \vdots & & \vdots \\ c_{i1} & c_{i2} & \cdots & c_{in} \\ \vdots & \vdots & & \vdots \\ a_{n1} & a_{n2} & \cdots & a_{nn} \end{vmatrix};$$

and if

$$D = \begin{vmatrix} a_{11} & \cdots & b_{1j} + c_{1j} & \cdots & a_{1n} \\ a_{21} & \cdots & b_{2j} + c_{2j} & \cdots & a_{2n} \\ \vdots & & \vdots & & \vdots \\ a_{n1} & \cdots & b_{nj} + c_{nj} & \cdots & a_{nn} \end{vmatrix},$$

then

$$
D = \begin{vmatrix} a_{11} & \cdots & b_{1j} & \cdots & a_{1n} \\ a_{21} & \cdots & b_{2j} & \cdots & a_{2n} \\ \vdots & & \vdots & & \vdots \\ a_{n1} & \cdots & b_{nj} & \cdots & a_{nn} \end{vmatrix} + \begin{vmatrix} a_{11} & \cdots & c_{1j} & \cdots & a_{1n} \\ a_{21} & \cdots & c_{2j} & \cdots & a_{2n} \\ \vdots & & \vdots & & \vdots \\ a_{n1} & \cdots & c_{nj} & \cdots & a_{nn} \end{vmatrix}.
$$

Examples. a. $\begin{vmatrix} 1 & 3 \\ 2 & 5 \end{vmatrix} = \begin{vmatrix} 1 & 1 \\ 2 & 4 \end{vmatrix} + \begin{vmatrix} 1 & 2 \\ 2 & 1 \end{vmatrix}$

  b. $\begin{vmatrix} 4 & 0 & 0 \\ 0 & 4 & 0 \\ 0 & 0 & 4 \end{vmatrix} = \begin{vmatrix} 2 & 0 & 0 \\ 0 & 4 & 0 \\ 0 & 0 & 4 \end{vmatrix} + \begin{vmatrix} 2 & 0 & 0 \\ 0 & 4 & 0 \\ 0 & 0 & 4 \end{vmatrix}$

THEOREM 10.13 *If each entry of one row (or column) of a determinant is multiplied by a real number k and the resulting product is added to the corresponding entry in another row (or column, respectively) in the determinant, then the resulting determinant is equal to the original determinant.*

Examples. a. $\begin{vmatrix} 1 & 1 \\ 2 & 1 \end{vmatrix} = \begin{vmatrix} 1 & 1 \\ 2+3(1) & 1+3(1) \end{vmatrix} = \begin{vmatrix} 1 & 1 \\ 5 & 4 \end{vmatrix}$

  b. $\begin{vmatrix} 1 & 2 & 3 \\ 4 & 5 & 6 \\ 7 & 8 & 9 \end{vmatrix} = \begin{vmatrix} 1+2(3) & 2 & 3 \\ 4+2(6) & 5 & 6 \\ 7+2(9) & 8 & 9 \end{vmatrix} = \begin{vmatrix} 7 & 2 & 3 \\ 16 & 5 & 6 \\ 25 & 8 & 9 \end{vmatrix}$

The preceding theorems can be used to write sequences of equal determinants, leading from one form of a determinant to another and more useful form.

Example. Expand

$$
D = \begin{vmatrix} 2 & -1 & 1 & -3 \\ 1 & 3 & -4 & 2 \\ 1 & 0 & -2 & 1 \\ 3 & -1 & 5 & 2 \end{vmatrix}.
$$

Solution. As a step toward expanding the determinant, we shall use Theorem 10.13 to produce an equal determinant with a row or a column containing zero entries in all but one place. Let us arbitrarily select the second column for this role, because one entry is already zero. Multiplying a_{1j} by 3 and adding the result to a_{2j}, we obtain

$$
D = \begin{vmatrix} 2 & -1 & 1 & -3 \\ 1+3(2) & 3+3(-1) & -4+3(1) & 2+3(-3) \\ 1 & 0 & -2 & 1 \\ 3 & -1 & 5 & 2 \end{vmatrix} = \begin{vmatrix} 2 & -1 & 1 & -3 \\ 7 & 0 & -1 & -7 \\ 1 & 0 & -2 & 1 \\ 3 & -1 & 5 & 2 \end{vmatrix}.
$$

Next, multiplying a_{1j} by -1 and adding the result to a_{4j}, we find that

$$
D = \begin{vmatrix} 2 & -1 & 1 & -3 \\ 7 & 0 & -1 & -7 \\ 1 & 0 & -2 & 1 \\ 3-1(2) & -1-1(-1) & 5-1(1) & 2-1(-3) \end{vmatrix} = \begin{vmatrix} 2 & -1 & 1 & -3 \\ 7 & 0 & -1 & -7 \\ 1 & 0 & -2 & 1 \\ 1 & 0 & 4 & 5 \end{vmatrix}.
$$

If we now expand the determinant about the second column, we have

$$D = \begin{vmatrix} 2 & -1 & 1 & -3 \\ 7 & 0 & -1 & -7 \\ 1 & 0 & -2 & 1 \\ 1 & 0 & 4 & 5 \end{vmatrix} = -(-1) \begin{vmatrix} 7 & -1 & -7 \\ 1 & -2 & 1 \\ 1 & 4 & 5 \end{vmatrix} + 0A_{22} - 0A_{32} + 0A_{42}.$$

From this point, we can reduce the third-order determinant to a second-order determinant by a similar procedure or, alternatively, expand directly about the elements in any row or column. Expanding about the elements of the first row, we obtain

$$D = \begin{vmatrix} 7 & -1 & -7 \\ 1 & -2 & 1 \\ 1 & 4 & 5 \end{vmatrix} = 7 \begin{vmatrix} -2 & 1 \\ 4 & 5 \end{vmatrix} - (-1) \begin{vmatrix} 1 & 1 \\ 1 & 5 \end{vmatrix} + (-7) \begin{vmatrix} 1 & -2 \\ 1 & 4 \end{vmatrix},$$

from which

$$D = 7(-14) + (4) - 7(6) = -98 + 4 - 42 = -136.$$

EXERCISE 10.4

Without evaluating, state why each statement is true. Verify selected examples by expansion.

1. $\begin{vmatrix} 2 & 3 & 1 \\ 0 & 0 & 0 \\ -1 & 2 & 0 \end{vmatrix} = 0$

2. $\begin{vmatrix} 3 & 1 & 3 \\ 0 & 1 & 0 \\ 1 & 2 & 1 \end{vmatrix} = 0$

3. $\begin{vmatrix} -2 & 1 & 0 \\ 3 & 4 & 1 \\ -4 & 2 & 0 \end{vmatrix} = 0$

4. $\begin{vmatrix} 7 & 3 & 2 & 0 \\ 2 & 1 & 2 & 0 \\ 4 & 1 & 1 & 0 \\ 0 & 2 & 1 & 0 \end{vmatrix} = 0$

5. $\begin{vmatrix} 2 & 3 & 1 & 1 \\ 2 & 0 & 1 & 2 \\ 2 & 3 & 1 & 1 \\ 0 & 1 & 2 & 0 \end{vmatrix} = 0$

6. $\begin{vmatrix} 6 & 1 & 3 & 2 \\ -2 & 0 & 1 & 4 \\ 3 & 6 & 1 & 2 \\ -4 & 0 & 2 & 8 \end{vmatrix} = 0$

7. $\begin{vmatrix} 2 & 3 \\ 1 & -1 \end{vmatrix} = - \begin{vmatrix} 3 & 2 \\ -1 & 1 \end{vmatrix}$

8. $\begin{vmatrix} -2 & 3 & 1 \\ -1 & 0 & 1 \\ -2 & 1 & 0 \end{vmatrix} = - \begin{vmatrix} 2 & 3 & 1 \\ 1 & 0 & 1 \\ 2 & 1 & 0 \end{vmatrix}$

9. $\begin{vmatrix} 4 & 2 & 1 \\ 0 & -1 & -2 \\ 1 & 0 & 2 \end{vmatrix} = - \begin{vmatrix} 4 & 2 & 1 \\ 0 & 1 & 2 \\ 1 & 0 & 2 \end{vmatrix}$

10. $\begin{vmatrix} 3 & 1 & 0 \\ -2 & 1 & 1 \\ 0 & 2 & -1 \end{vmatrix} = - \begin{vmatrix} 0 & 1 & 3 \\ 1 & 1 & -2 \\ -1 & 2 & 0 \end{vmatrix}$

11. $2 \begin{vmatrix} 1 & 0 & 2 \\ -1 & 2 & 0 \\ 1 & 1 & 1 \end{vmatrix} = \begin{vmatrix} 1 & 0 & 2 \\ -1 & 2 & 0 \\ 2 & 2 & 2 \end{vmatrix}$

12. $\begin{vmatrix} 3 & -4 & 2 \\ 1 & -2 & 0 \\ 0 & 8 & 1 \end{vmatrix} = - 2 \begin{vmatrix} 3 & 2 & 2 \\ 1 & 1 & 0 \\ 0 & -4 & 1 \end{vmatrix}$

13. $\begin{vmatrix} 3 & 0 & 6 \\ -2 & 1 & 2 \\ 0 & 1 & 2 \end{vmatrix} = 6 \begin{vmatrix} 1 & 0 & 1 \\ -2 & 1 & 1 \\ 0 & 1 & 1 \end{vmatrix}$

14. $\begin{vmatrix} 1 & 2 & 1 \\ -1 & 0 & -2 \\ 2 & 4 & 1 \end{vmatrix} = -2 \begin{vmatrix} 1 & 1 & 1 \\ 1 & 0 & 2 \\ 2 & 2 & 1 \end{vmatrix}$

15. $\begin{vmatrix} 1 & 2 \\ 3 & 4 \end{vmatrix} = \begin{vmatrix} 1+2 & 2 \\ 3+4 & 4 \end{vmatrix}$

16. $\begin{vmatrix} 1 & 2 \\ 3 & 4 \end{vmatrix} = \begin{vmatrix} 1+4 & 2 \\ 3+8 & 4 \end{vmatrix}$

17. $\begin{vmatrix} 1 & 2 \\ 3 & 4 \end{vmatrix} = \begin{vmatrix} 1 & 2 \\ 3-3 & 4-6 \end{vmatrix}$

18. $\begin{vmatrix} 1 & 2 \\ 3 & 4 \end{vmatrix} = \begin{vmatrix} 1 & 0 \\ 3 & 4-6 \end{vmatrix}$

19. $\begin{vmatrix} 1 & 2 & 1 \\ 0 & 2 & 3 \\ 2 & -1 & 2 \end{vmatrix} = \begin{vmatrix} 1 & 2 & 1 \\ 0 & 2 & 3 \\ 0 & -5 & 0 \end{vmatrix}$

20. $\begin{vmatrix} -1 & 1 & 0 \\ 2 & 3 & -1 \\ 2 & 1 & 2 \end{vmatrix} = \begin{vmatrix} 0 & 1 & 0 \\ 5 & 3 & -1 \\ 3 & 1 & 2 \end{vmatrix}$

Theorem 10.13 was used on the left-hand member of each of the following equalities to produce the elements in the right-hand member. Complete the entries.

21. $\begin{vmatrix} 1 & 3 \\ 2 & 2 \end{vmatrix} = \begin{vmatrix} 1 & 3 \\ 0 & \end{vmatrix}$

22. $\begin{vmatrix} 2 & -1 \\ 3 & 1 \end{vmatrix} = \begin{vmatrix} & 0 \\ 3 & 1 \end{vmatrix}$

23. $\begin{vmatrix} 1 & -2 & 1 \\ 3 & 1 & 4 \\ 0 & 2 & 1 \end{vmatrix} = \begin{vmatrix} 1 & -2 & 1 \\ 0 & 7 & \\ 0 & 2 & 1 \end{vmatrix}$

24. $\begin{vmatrix} 3 & -1 & 0 \\ 1 & 2 & 1 \\ 2 & 3 & 1 \end{vmatrix} = \begin{vmatrix} 3 & -1 & 0 \\ 1 & 2 & 1 \\ 1 & & 0 \end{vmatrix}$

25. $\begin{vmatrix} 2 & 3 & 1 & 4 \\ 0 & 2 & 1 & 2 \\ 1 & 1 & 2 & 3 \\ 0 & 1 & 1 & 1 \end{vmatrix} = \begin{vmatrix} 0 & 1 & & -2 \\ 0 & 2 & 1 & 2 \\ 1 & 1 & 2 & 3 \\ 0 & 1 & 1 & 1 \end{vmatrix}$

26. $\begin{vmatrix} 2 & 1 & 1 & 0 \\ 1 & 2 & 0 & 2 \\ 3 & 1 & 0 & 3 \\ 2 & 1 & 4 & 2 \end{vmatrix} = \begin{vmatrix} 2 & 1 & 1 & 0 \\ 1 & 2 & 0 & 2 \\ 3 & 1 & 0 & 3 \\ & -3 & 0 & 2 \end{vmatrix}$

27. $\begin{vmatrix} 1 & 2 & 3 & 1 \\ 2 & 0 & 1 & 2 \\ 3 & 1 & 2 & 1 \\ 0 & 1 & 1 & 1 \end{vmatrix} = \begin{vmatrix} 1 & 1 & 2 & 1 \\ 2 & -2 & -1 & 2 \\ 3 & & 1 & 1 \\ 0 & 0 & 0 & 1 \end{vmatrix}$

28. $\begin{vmatrix} 1 & 2 & 1 & 3 \\ 2 & 1 & 2 & 1 \\ 4 & 2 & 3 & 4 \\ 2 & 1 & 2 & 1 \end{vmatrix} = \begin{vmatrix} & 2 & 0 & 1 \\ 0 & 1 & 0 & 0 \\ 0 & 2 & -1 & 2 \\ 0 & 1 & 0 & 0 \end{vmatrix}$

First reduce each determinant to an equal 2×2 determinant and then evaluate.

29. $\begin{vmatrix} 2 & 1 & 0 \\ 3 & 2 & 1 \\ -1 & 2 & 0 \end{vmatrix}$

30. $\begin{vmatrix} 1 & 2 & 1 \\ 2 & -1 & 2 \\ 0 & 1 & 0 \end{vmatrix}$

31. $\begin{vmatrix} 1 & 0 & 3 \\ 2 & -1 & 1 \\ 1 & 2 & 1 \end{vmatrix}$

32. $\begin{vmatrix} 1 & 2 & -1 \\ 2 & 1 & 3 \\ 0 & 1 & 2 \end{vmatrix}$

33. $\begin{vmatrix} 1 & 2 & 1 \\ -1 & 2 & 3 \\ 2 & -1 & 1 \end{vmatrix}$

34. $\begin{vmatrix} 3 & -1 & 2 \\ 1 & 2 & 1 \\ -2 & 1 & 3 \end{vmatrix}$

35. $\begin{vmatrix} 0 & 0 & 1 & 2 \\ 6 & 0 & 0 & 1 \\ 6 & 1 & 0 & -1 \\ 6 & 1 & 0 & 2 \end{vmatrix}$

36. $\begin{vmatrix} 4 & 2 & 0 & 2 \\ -1 & 0 & 2 & 1 \\ 3 & 0 & -1 & 1 \\ 0 & 0 & 2 & 1 \end{vmatrix}$

37. $\begin{vmatrix} 0 & 1 & 0 & 2 \\ 0 & 2 & 0 & 3 \\ 2 & -1 & 1 & 0 \\ 0 & 0 & 8 & 8 \end{vmatrix}$

38. $\begin{vmatrix} 0 & 2 & -1 & 3 \\ 0 & 0 & 2 & 1 \\ 3 & 0 & 1 & 0 \\ -6 & 6 & 0 & 0 \end{vmatrix}$

39. $\begin{vmatrix} 1 & 2 & 3 & -1 \\ 0 & 4 & 8 & 4 \\ -2 & 0 & 1 & 1 \\ 2 & 1 & 0 & 1 \end{vmatrix}$

40. $\begin{vmatrix} 1 & 2 & 1 & 1 \\ 2 & -1 & 0 & 1 \\ 0 & 6 & 3 & 9 \\ 2 & 0 & -1 & 1 \end{vmatrix}$

41. Show that

$$\begin{vmatrix} x & y & 1 \\ x_1 & y_1 & 1 \\ x_2 & y_2 & 1 \end{vmatrix} = 0$$

represents an equation of the straight line through the points (x_1, y_1) and (x_2, y_2).

42. Use the results in Problem 41 to find an equation of the line through the points $(3, -1)$ and $(-2, 5)$.

43. Show that

$$\begin{vmatrix} 1 & a & a^2 \\ 1 & b & b^2 \\ 1 & c & c^2 \end{vmatrix} = (b - c)(c - a)(a - b).$$

44. Show that

$$\begin{vmatrix} a_{11} & a_{12} & a_{13} & a_{14} \\ a_{21} & a_{22} & a_{23} & a_{24} \\ 0 & 0 & a_{33} & a_{34} \\ 0 & 0 & a_{43} & a_{44} \end{vmatrix} = \begin{vmatrix} a_{11} & a_{12} \\ a_{21} & a_{22} \end{vmatrix} \cdot \begin{vmatrix} a_{33} & a_{34} \\ a_{43} & a_{44} \end{vmatrix}.$$

Prove each theorem in the case of 2×2 matrices.

45. Theorem 10.7   46. Theorem 10.8   47. Theorem 10.9

48. Theorem 10.10   49. Theorem 10.11   50. Theorem 10.12

10.5 THE INVERSE OF A SQUARE MATRIX

In the field of real numbers, every element a except 0 has a multiplicative inverse $1/a$, with the property that $a \cdot (1/a) = 1$. The question should (and does) arise, "Does every square matrix A have a multiplicative inverse A^{-1}?"

DEFINITION 10.17 *For a given square matrix A of order n, if there is a square matrix A^{-1} of order n such that*

$$AA^{-1} = I \quad and \quad A^{-1}A = I,$$

*where I is the multiplicative identity matrix of order n, then A^{-1} is the **multiplicative inverse** of A.*

To answer the question about the existence of a multiplicative inverse for a matrix, we shall begin by considering the simple case of 2×2 matrices. If we let

$$A = \begin{bmatrix} a_{11} & a_{12} \\ a_{21} & a_{22} \end{bmatrix},$$

then we must see whether there exists a 2×2 matrix A^{-1} such that $AA^{-1} = I$. If so, let $A^{-1} = \begin{bmatrix} b & c \\ d & e \end{bmatrix}$. We wish to have

$$\begin{bmatrix} a_{11} & a_{12} \\ a_{21} & a_{22} \end{bmatrix} \begin{bmatrix} b & c \\ d & e \end{bmatrix} = \begin{bmatrix} 1 & 0 \\ 0 & 1 \end{bmatrix}.$$

This leads to

$$\begin{bmatrix} a_{11}b + a_{12}d & a_{11}c + a_{12}e \\ a_{21}b + a_{22}d & a_{21}c + a_{22}e \end{bmatrix} = \begin{bmatrix} 1 & 0 \\ 0 & 1 \end{bmatrix},$$

which is true if and only if

$$a_{11}b + a_{12}d = 1, \quad a_{11}c + a_{12}e = 0,$$
$$a_{21}b + a_{22}d = 0, \quad a_{21}c + a_{22}e = 1.$$

Solving these equations for b, c, d, and e, we have

$$(a_{11}a_{22} - a_{12}a_{21})b = a_{22}, \quad (a_{11}a_{22} - a_{12}a_{21})c = -a_{12},$$
$$(a_{11}a_{22} - a_{12}a_{21})d = -a_{21}, \quad (a_{11}a_{22} - a_{12}a_{21})e = a_{11}, \tag{1}$$

from which

$$b = \frac{a_{22}}{a_{11}a_{22} - a_{12}a_{21}}, \quad c = \frac{-a_{12}}{a_{11}a_{22} - a_{12}a_{21}},$$

$$d = \frac{-a_{21}}{a_{11}a_{22} - a_{12}a_{21}}, \quad e = \frac{a_{11}}{a_{11}a_{22} - a_{12}a_{21}},$$

provided that $a_{11}a_{22} - a_{12}a_{21} \neq 0$. Now the denominator of each of these fractions is just $\delta(A)$, so that

$$A^{-1} = \begin{bmatrix} \dfrac{a_{22}}{\delta(A)} & \dfrac{-a_{12}}{\delta(A)} \\ \dfrac{-a_{21}}{\delta(A)} & \dfrac{a_{11}}{\delta(A)} \end{bmatrix} = \frac{1}{\delta(A)} \begin{bmatrix} a_{22} & -a_{12} \\ -a_{21} & a_{11} \end{bmatrix}.$$

By direct multiplication, it can be verified not only that

$$AA^{-1} = I,$$

but also (surprisingly, since matrix multiplication is not always commutative) that

$$A^{-1}A = I.$$

The inverse of a 2×2 matrix   Thus, to write the inverse of a 2×2 square matrix A for which $\delta(A) \neq 0$, we interchange the entries on the principal diagonal, replace each of the other two entries with its negative, and multiply the result by $1/\delta(A)$.

Example. If $A = \begin{bmatrix} 1 & 3 \\ 2 & -1 \end{bmatrix}$, find A^{-1}.

Solution. We first observe that $\delta(A) = -7$. Hence,

$$A^{-1} = -\frac{1}{7}\begin{bmatrix} -1 & -3 \\ -2 & 1 \end{bmatrix} = \begin{bmatrix} \dfrac{1}{7} & \dfrac{3}{7} \\ \dfrac{2}{7} & -\dfrac{1}{7} \end{bmatrix}.$$

It is a good idea always to check the result when finding A^{-1}, because there is much room for blundering in the process of determining the inverse. In the above example, we have

$$A^{-1}A = -\frac{1}{7}\begin{bmatrix} -1 & -3 \\ -2 & 1 \end{bmatrix}\begin{bmatrix} 1 & 3 \\ 2 & -1 \end{bmatrix} = -\frac{1}{7}\begin{bmatrix} -7 & 0 \\ 0 & -7 \end{bmatrix} = \begin{bmatrix} 1 & 0 \\ 0 & 1 \end{bmatrix}.$$

Matrices that have no inverse   Moreover, from the above analysis we can now answer the question, "Does every 2×2 square matrix A have an inverse?" The answer is "No," for if $\delta(A)$ is 0, then the foregoing equations for b, c, d, e would have no solution. Square matrices A for which $\delta(A) = 0$ are called **singular matrices**.

Example. Show that $\begin{bmatrix} 3 & 5 \\ 6 & 10 \end{bmatrix}$ is singular, and hence has no inverse.

Solution. Since $\delta(A) = 3(10) - 6(5) = 0$, no inverse exists.

The inverse of an $n \times n$ matrix   More generally, and without proving it, we have the following.

THEOREM 10.14 *If*

$$A = \begin{bmatrix} a_{11} & a_{12} & \cdots & a_{1n} \\ a_{21} & a_{22} & \cdots & a_{2n} \\ \vdots & \vdots & & \vdots \\ a_{n1} & a_{n2} & \cdots & a_{nn} \end{bmatrix}$$

and if $\delta(A) \neq 0$, then

$$A^{-1} = \frac{1}{\delta(A)}\begin{bmatrix} A_{11} & A_{21} & \cdots & A_{n1} \\ A_{12} & A_{22} & \cdots & A_{n2} \\ \vdots & \vdots & & \vdots \\ A_{1n} & A_{2n} & \cdots & A_{nn} \end{bmatrix},$$

where A_{ij} is the cofactor of a_{ij} in A. If $\delta(A) = 0$, then A has no inverse.

Observe that A^{-1} is the matrix having as its entries the cofactors of the entries in A multiplied by $1/\delta(A)$, but that the cofactors of the *row* entries in A are the *column* entries in A^{-1}. One way to obtain A^{-1} is to replace each entry in A with its cofactor, and multiply the *transpose* of the resulting matrix by $1/\delta(A)$.

Example. If $A = \begin{bmatrix} 1 & 0 & 1 \\ 2 & 1 & 0 \\ 1 & -1 & 1 \end{bmatrix}$, find A^{-1}.

Solution. We first observe that $\delta(A) = -2$. Therefore, since $\delta(A)$ is not zero, A has an inverse. Next, replacing each entry in A with its cofactor, we obtain the matrix

$$\begin{bmatrix} 1 & -2 & -3 \\ -1 & 0 & 1 \\ -1 & 2 & 1 \end{bmatrix} \text{ whose transpose is } \begin{bmatrix} 1 & -1 & -1 \\ -2 & 0 & 2 \\ -3 & 1 & 1 \end{bmatrix},$$

so that

$$A^{-1} = -\frac{1}{2}\begin{bmatrix} 1 & -1 & -1 \\ -2 & 0 & 2 \\ -3 & 1 & 1 \end{bmatrix}.$$

As a check, we have

$$A^{-1}A = -\frac{1}{2}\begin{bmatrix} 1 & -1 & -1 \\ -2 & 0 & 2 \\ -3 & 1 & 1 \end{bmatrix}\begin{bmatrix} 1 & 0 & 1 \\ 2 & 1 & 0 \\ 1 & -1 & 1 \end{bmatrix}$$

$$= -\frac{1}{2}\begin{bmatrix} -2 & 0 & 0 \\ 0 & -2 & 0 \\ 0 & 0 & -2 \end{bmatrix} = \begin{bmatrix} 1 & 0 & 0 \\ 0 & 1 & 0 \\ 0 & 0 & 1 \end{bmatrix}.$$

Theorem 10.14 is applicable to $n \times n$ square matrices, although, clearly, the process of actually determining A^{-1} becomes very laborious for matrices much larger than 3×3.

Properties of matrices and their inverses   There are a number of useful properties associated with matrices and their inverses. For example, we have the following.

THEOREM 10.15   *If A and B are $n \times n$ nonsingular square matrices, then AB has an inverse, namely*

$$(AB)^{-1} = B^{-1}A^{-1}.$$

Proof. If we right-multiply AB by $B^{-1}A^{-1}$ and apply the associative law for the multiplication of matrices, we have

$$AB \cdot B^{-1}A^{-1} = A \cdot I \cdot A^{-1} = A \cdot A^{-1} = I.$$

Moreover, if we left-multiply AB by $B^{-1}A^{-1}$, we have

$$B^{-1}A^{-1} \cdot AB = B^{-1} \cdot I \cdot B = B^{-1} \cdot B = I.$$

Thus, since $(AB)(B^{-1}A^{-1}) = (B^{-1}A^{-1})(AB) = I$, by the definition of the inverse of a matrix we have

$$(AB)^{-1} = B^{-1}A^{-1}.$$

This theorem can be used to find the inverse of products of any number of nonsingular matrices. For example, if there are three factors A, B, and C in such a product, then

$$(ABC)^{-1} = [(AB)C]^{-1} = C^{-1}(AB)^{-1} = C^{-1}B^{-1}A^{-1}.$$

EXERCISE 10.5

Find the inverse of each matrix if the inverse exists.

Example.

$$B = \begin{bmatrix} 1 & 0 & -1 \\ 1 & 3 & 1 \\ 0 & 1 & 2 \end{bmatrix}$$

Solution. The determinant $\delta(B)$ is given by

$$\delta \begin{bmatrix} 1 & 0 & -1 \\ 1 & 3 & 1 \\ 0 & 1 & 2 \end{bmatrix} = 1(5) - 0 - 1(1) = 4.$$

Replacing each entry of B with its cofactor gives

$$\begin{bmatrix} 5 & -2 & 1 \\ -1 & 2 & -1 \\ 3 & -2 & 3 \end{bmatrix}; \quad \begin{bmatrix} 5 & -2 & 1 \\ -1 & 2 & -1 \\ 3 & -2 & 3 \end{bmatrix}^t = \begin{bmatrix} 5 & -1 & 3 \\ -2 & 2 & -2 \\ 1 & -1 & 3 \end{bmatrix};$$

$$B^{-1} = \frac{1}{\delta(B)} \begin{bmatrix} \text{each } b_{ij} \text{ of} \\ B \text{ replaced} \\ \text{by } B_{ij} \end{bmatrix}^t = \frac{1}{4} \begin{bmatrix} 5 & -1 & 3 \\ -2 & 2 & -2 \\ 1 & -1 & 3 \end{bmatrix} = \begin{bmatrix} \dfrac{5}{4} & -\dfrac{1}{4} & \dfrac{3}{4} \\ -\dfrac{2}{4} & \dfrac{2}{4} & -\dfrac{2}{4} \\ \dfrac{1}{4} & -\dfrac{1}{4} & \dfrac{3}{4} \end{bmatrix}.$$

1. $\begin{bmatrix} 1 & 2 \\ 1 & 3 \end{bmatrix}$
2. $\begin{bmatrix} 3 & 1 \\ 2 & -1 \end{bmatrix}$
3. $\begin{bmatrix} 2 & -3 \\ 1 & 1 \end{bmatrix}$

4. $\begin{bmatrix} 3 & -2 \\ 2 & 1 \end{bmatrix}$
5. $\begin{bmatrix} -2 & -1 \\ 4 & 2 \end{bmatrix}$
6. $\begin{bmatrix} 3 & 1 \\ 9 & 3 \end{bmatrix}$

7. $\begin{bmatrix} 1 & -1 & 2 \\ 2 & 1 & 3 \\ 0 & 0 & 2 \end{bmatrix}$
8. $\begin{bmatrix} 0 & 4 & 2 \\ 1 & 0 & 2 \\ 0 & -1 & 1 \end{bmatrix}$
9. $\begin{bmatrix} 2 & -1 & 1 \\ 3 & 0 & 1 \\ 2 & 2 & 1 \end{bmatrix}$

10. $\begin{bmatrix} 1 & 2 & 1 \\ 0 & 2 & 1 \\ -2 & 2 & 3 \end{bmatrix}$
11. $\begin{bmatrix} 2 & 1 & 1 \\ 1 & 0 & 2 \\ 4 & 2 & 2 \end{bmatrix}$
12. $\begin{bmatrix} -3 & 1 & -6 \\ 2 & 1 & 4 \\ 2 & 0 & 4 \end{bmatrix}$

13. Verify that

$$\left(\begin{bmatrix} 2 & 3 \\ 1 & -1 \end{bmatrix} \cdot \begin{bmatrix} 0 & 1 \\ 3 & 1 \end{bmatrix} \right)^{-1} = \begin{bmatrix} 0 & 1 \\ 3 & 1 \end{bmatrix}^{-1} \cdot \begin{bmatrix} 2 & 3 \\ 1 & -1 \end{bmatrix}^{-1}.$$

14. Verify that

$$\left(\begin{bmatrix} 1 & 2 \\ -1 & 0 \end{bmatrix} \cdot \begin{bmatrix} 1 & 1 \\ 2 & 0 \end{bmatrix} \cdot \begin{bmatrix} 2 & -1 \\ 0 & 1 \end{bmatrix} \right)^{-1} = \begin{bmatrix} 2 & -1 \\ 0 & 1 \end{bmatrix}^{-1} \cdot \begin{bmatrix} 1 & 1 \\ 2 & 0 \end{bmatrix}^{-1} \cdot \begin{bmatrix} 1 & 2 \\ -1 & 0 \end{bmatrix}^{-1}.$$

15. Verify that

$$\left(\begin{bmatrix} 3 & 0 & 1 \\ 2 & 1 & 0 \\ 0 & 1 & 2 \end{bmatrix} \cdot \begin{bmatrix} 2 & 1 & 0 \\ 1 & 1 & 2 \\ 0 & 1 & 0 \end{bmatrix} \right)^{-1} = \begin{bmatrix} 2 & 1 & 0 \\ 1 & 1 & 2 \\ 0 & 1 & 0 \end{bmatrix}^{-1} \cdot \begin{bmatrix} 3 & 0 & 1 \\ 2 & 1 & 0 \\ 0 & 1 & 2 \end{bmatrix}^{-1}.$$

16. Show that $[A^t]^{-1} = [A^{-1}]^t$ for each nonsingular 2×2 matrix.

17. Show that $\delta(A^{-1}) = 1/\delta(A)$ for each nonsingular 2×2 matrix.

18. Prove that if a and b are any real numbers, then $\delta(aA^2 + bA) = \delta(aA + bI)\delta(A)$ for all 2×2 matrices A.

19. Prove that $\delta(B^{-1}AB) = \delta(A)$ for all nonsingular 2×2 matrices A and B.

20. Prove that if A is a 2×2 matrix and a, b, and c are real numbers with $c \neq 0$, and if $aA^2 + bA + cI = \mathbf{0}$, then A has an inverse.

11 LINEAR SYSTEMS

11.1 SOLUTION OF LINEAR SYSTEMS BY SUBSTITUTION AND LINEAR COMBINATIONS

Solution by substitution

You should recall from earlier studies of algebra that systems of linear equations can be solved in a variety of ways. One elementary way to solve a system is by *substitution*.

Example. Solve

$$2x + 3y = 1 \tag{1}$$

$$3x - y = 7 \tag{2}$$

in R^2, that is, in $R \times R$.

Solution. Solving equation (2) for y in terms of x produces $y = 3x - 7$. Then, replacing y in (1) with $3x - 7$, we have

$$2x + 3(3x - 7) = 1,$$

$$2x + 9x - 21 = 1,$$

$$11x = 22,$$

$$x = 2.$$

Upon replacing x in $y = 3x - 7$ with 2, we find that

$$y = 3(2) - 7 = -1.$$

Therefore, the solution set in R^2 of the given system is $\{(2, -1)\}$.

Solution by linear combinations

A second method commonly used to solve systems of equations and with which you should also be familiar is that of eliminating a variable by forming one or more *linear combinations* of the left-hand members of the equations in a system in which the right-hand members are zero. This technique is sometimes referred to as solution by *addition* (or *subtraction*).

Example. Solve

$$x + 2y - 3z + 4 = 0, \tag{3}$$

$$2x - y + z - 3 = 0, \tag{4}$$

$$3x + 2y + z - 10 = 0 \tag{5}$$

in R^3, that is, in $R \times R \times R$.

Solution. To eliminate x between Equations (3) and (4), we can multiply each member of Equation (3) by -2 and add the results to the corresponding members of Equation (4) to obtain

$$-2(x + 2y - 3z + 4) + (2x - y + z - 3) = 0,$$
$$-5y + 7z - 11 = 0. \tag{6}$$

We can next eliminate x between Equation (3) and Equation (5) by multiplying each member of (3) by -3 and adding the result to the corresponding member of (5) to produce

$$-3(x + 2y - 3z + 4) + (3x + 2y + z - 10) = 0,$$
$$-4y + 10z - 22 = 0. \tag{7}$$

Next, to solve the system consisting of (6) and (7), we add -4 times each member of (6) to 5 times the corresponding member of (7), obtaining

$$-4(-5y + 7z - 11) + 5(-4y + 10z - 22) = 0,$$
$$22z = 66,$$
$$z = 3.$$

By successive substitutions in, say, (6) and (3), we obtain $y = 2$ and $x = 1$, so that the solution set of the given system in R^3 is $\{(1, 2, 3)\}$.

Matrices also offer a means of finding solutions of systems of linear equations. We first verify the matrix-product equation

$$\begin{bmatrix} a_{11} & a_{12} & \cdots & a_{1n} \\ \vdots & \vdots & & \vdots \\ a_{n1} & a_{n2} & \cdots & a_{nn} \end{bmatrix} \begin{bmatrix} x_1 \\ \vdots \\ x_n \end{bmatrix} = \begin{bmatrix} a_{11}x_1 + a_{12}x_2 + \cdots + a_{1n}x_n \\ \vdots \\ a_{n1}x_1 + a_{n2}x_2 + \cdots + a_{nn}x_n \end{bmatrix},$$

and hence note that the linear system

$$a_{11}x_1 + a_{12}x_2 + \cdots + a_{1n}x_n = c_1$$
$$a_{21}x_1 + a_{22}x_2 + \cdots + a_{2n}x_n = c_2$$
$$\vdots \qquad \vdots \qquad \qquad \vdots \qquad \vdots$$
$$a_{n1}x_1 + a_{2n}x_2 + \cdots + a_{nn}x_n = c_n$$

Solution by matrices

can be written as the matrix equation

$$\begin{bmatrix} a_{11} & a_{12} & \cdots & a_{1n} \\ \vdots & \vdots & & \vdots \\ a_{n1} & a_{n2} & \cdots & a_{nn} \end{bmatrix} \begin{bmatrix} x_1 \\ \vdots \\ x_n \end{bmatrix} = \begin{bmatrix} c_1 \\ \vdots \\ c_n \end{bmatrix},$$

where the first factor in the left-hand member is called the **coefficient matrix** for the system. In more concise notation, this latter equation can be written

$$AX = B, \tag{8}$$

where A is an $n \times n$ square matrix, and X and B are $n \times 1$ column matrices. If now A is nonsingular, we can left-multiply both members of this equation by A^{-1} to obtain

$$A^{-1}AX = A^{-1}B,$$

$$IX = A^{-1}B,$$

$$X = A^{-1}B, \tag{9}$$

where $A^{-1}B$ is an $n \times 1$ column matrix. Since X and $A^{-1}B$ are equal, each entry in X is equal to the corresponding entry in $A^{-1}B$, and hence these latter entries constitute the components of the solution of the given linear system. Conversely, left-multiplying (9) by A shows that the X given by (9) satisfies (8). If A is a singular matrix, then of course it has no inverse, and either the system has no solution or the solution is not unique.

Example.   Use matrices to find the solution set of

$$2x + y + z = 1$$

$$x - 2y - 3z = 1$$

$$3x + 2y + 4z = 5$$

in R^3.

Solution.   We first write the system as a matrix equation of the form $AX = B$, thus:

$$\begin{bmatrix} 2 & 1 & 1 \\ 1 & -2 & -3 \\ 3 & 2 & 4 \end{bmatrix} \begin{bmatrix} x \\ y \\ z \end{bmatrix} = \begin{bmatrix} 1 \\ 1 \\ 5 \end{bmatrix}.$$

We next expand $\delta(A)$ about its first row, obtaining

$$\delta(A) = \delta \begin{bmatrix} 2 & 1 & 1 \\ 1 & -2 & -3 \\ 3 & 2 & 4 \end{bmatrix} = 2(-2) - 1(13) + 1(8) = -9,$$

and observe that A is nonsingular. Then

$$A^{-1} = \begin{bmatrix} 2 & 1 & 1 \\ 1 & -2 & -3 \\ 3 & 2 & 4 \end{bmatrix}^{-1} = -\frac{1}{9} \begin{bmatrix} -2 & -2 & -1 \\ -13 & 5 & 7 \\ 8 & -1 & -5 \end{bmatrix}.$$

Now, because $X = A^{-1}B$, we have

$$\begin{bmatrix} x \\ y \\ z \end{bmatrix} = -\frac{1}{9} \begin{bmatrix} -2 & -2 & -1 \\ -13 & 5 & 7 \\ 8 & -1 & -5 \end{bmatrix} \begin{bmatrix} 1 \\ 1 \\ 5 \end{bmatrix} = -\frac{1}{9} \begin{bmatrix} -9 \\ 27 \\ -18 \end{bmatrix} = \begin{bmatrix} 1 \\ -3 \\ 2 \end{bmatrix}.$$

Hence $x = 1$, $y = -3$, and $z = 2$, and the solution set of the system in R^3 is $\{(1, -3, 2)\}$.

The computation of A^{-1} is laborious when A is a square matrix containing many rows and columns. The foregoing method is not always the easiest to use in determining an inverse, particularly when an electronic digital computer is available, but it is most valuable for theoretical developments.

EXERCISE 11.1

Solve each system by (a) substitution and/or linear combinations and (b) matrices. If the system has no solution, so state.

1. $2x - 3y = -1$
   $x + 4y = 5$

2. $3x - 4y = -2$
   $x - 2y = 0$

3. $3x - 4y = -2$
   $6x + 12y = 36$

4. $2x - 4y = 7$
   $x - 2y = 1$

5. $2x - 3y = 0$
   $2x + y = 16$

6. $2x + 3y = 3$
   $3x - 4y = 0$

7. $x + y = 2$
   $2x - z = 1$
   $2y - 3z = -1$

8. $2x - 6y + 3z = -12$
   $3x - 2y + 5z = -4$
   $4x + 5y - 2z = 10$

9. $x - 2y + z = -1$
   $3x + y - 2z = 4$
   $y - z = 1$

10. $2x + 5z = 9$
    $4x + 3y = -1$
    $3y - 4z = -13$

11. $2x + 2y + z = 1$
    $x - y + 6z = 21$
    $3x + 2y - z = -4$

12. $4x + 8y + z = -6$
    $2x - 3y + 2z = 0$
    $x + 7y - 3z = -8$

13. $x + y + z = 0$
    $2x - y - 4z = 15$
    $x - 2y - z = 7$

14. $x + y - 2z = 3$
    $3x - y + z = 5$
    $3x + 3y - 6z = 9$

11.2 CRAMER'S RULE

If the matrix technique for solving linear systems discussed in the preceding

Solution by means of determinants

section is viewed in terms of determinants, we arrive at a general solution for such systems. This, however, is of more theoretical than computational value.

If the coefficient matrix A in the matrix equation $AX = B$ is nonsingular, then its inverse, A^{-1}, is

$$A^{-1} = \frac{1}{\delta(A)} \begin{bmatrix} A_{11} & A_{21} & \cdots & A_{n1} \\ \vdots & \vdots & & \vdots \\ A_{1n} & A_{2n} & \cdots & A_{nn} \end{bmatrix}.$$

Now, let $B = \begin{bmatrix} c_1 \\ c_2 \\ \vdots \\ c_n \end{bmatrix}$, so that

$$A^{-1}B = \frac{1}{\delta(A)} \begin{bmatrix} c_1A_{11} + c_2A_{21} + \cdots + c_nA_{n1} \\ c_1A_{12} + c_2A_{22} + \cdots + c_nA_{n2} \\ \vdots \quad \vdots \quad\quad \vdots \\ c_1A_{1n} + c_2A_{2n} + \cdots + c_nA_{nn} \end{bmatrix}.$$

Each entry in $A^{-1}B$ can be seen to be of the form

$$\frac{c_1A_{1j} + c_2A_{2j} + \cdots + c_nA_{nj}}{\delta(A)}.$$

But $c_1A_{1j} + c_2A_{2j} + \cdots + c_nA_{nj}$ is just the expansion of the determinant

$$\begin{array}{c} j\text{th} \\ \text{column} \\ \downarrow \end{array}$$

$$\begin{vmatrix} a_{11} & a_{12} & \cdots & c_1 & \cdots & a_{1n} \\ a_{21} & a_{22} & \cdots & c_2 & \cdots & a_{2n} \\ \vdots & \vdots & & \vdots & & \vdots \\ a_{n1} & a_{n2} & \cdots & c_n & \cdots & a_{nn} \end{vmatrix}$$

about the jth column, which has entries, $c_1, c_2, c_3, \cdots c_n$. Thus, if the variables in a linear system are denoted by $x_1, x_2, \cdots x_n$, then each entry x_j in $A^{-1}B$ is given by

$$\begin{array}{c} j\text{th} \\ \text{column} \\ \downarrow \end{array}$$

$$x_j = \frac{\delta(A_j)}{\delta(A)} = \frac{\begin{vmatrix} a_{11} & a_{12} & \cdots & c_1 & \cdots & a_{1n} \\ a_{21} & a_{22} & \cdots & c_2 & \cdots & a_{2n} \\ \vdots & \vdots & & \vdots & & \vdots \\ a_{n1} & a_{n2} & \cdots & c_n & \cdots & a_{nn} \end{vmatrix}}{\begin{vmatrix} a_{11} & a_{12} & & \cdots & & a_{1n} \\ a_{21} & a_{22} & & \cdots & & a_{2n} \\ \vdots & \vdots & & & & \vdots \\ a_{n1} & a_{n2} & & \cdots & & a_{nn} \end{vmatrix}}.$$

This relationship expresses **Cramer's rule.** Cramer's rule is the assertion that if the determinant of the coefficient matrix of an $n \times n$ linear system *is not* 0, then the equations are consistent (the system has a solution), and the unique solution in R^n can be found for each variable in the system as follows:

Application of Cramer's rule

1 Write the determinant of the coefficient matrix for the system.
2 Replace each entry in the jth column of the coefficient matrix A with the corresponding entry from the column matrix B, and find the determinant of the resulting matrix.
3 Divide the result in Step 2 by the result in Step 1. The quotient is x_j.

Example. Use Cramer's rule to solve the system

$$-4x + 2y - 9z = 2$$
$$3x + 4y + z = 5$$
$$x - 3y + 2z = 8$$

in R^3.

Solution. By inspection, the coefficient matrix is

$$A = \begin{bmatrix} -4 & 2 & -9 \\ 3 & 4 & 1 \\ 1 & -3 & 2 \end{bmatrix},$$

so that

$$\delta(A) = -4(11) - 2(5) - 9(-13) = -44 - 10 + 117 = 63.$$

Replacing the entries in the first column of A with corresponding constants 2, 5, and 8, we have

$$A_x = \begin{bmatrix} 2 & 2 & -9 \\ 5 & 4 & 1 \\ 8 & -3 & 2 \end{bmatrix},$$

$$\delta(A_x) = 2(11) - 2(2) - 9(-47) = 22 - 4 + 423 = 441.$$

Hence

$$x = \frac{\delta(A_x)}{\delta(A)} = \frac{441}{63} = 7.$$

Similarly, by replacing, in turn, the entries of the second and third columns of A with the corresponding constants 2, 5, and 8, we have

$$A_y = \begin{bmatrix} -4 & 2 & -9 \\ 3 & 5 & 1 \\ 1 & 8 & 2 \end{bmatrix} \quad \text{and} \quad A_z = \begin{bmatrix} -4 & 2 & 2 \\ 3 & 4 & 5 \\ 1 & -3 & 8 \end{bmatrix}.$$

Now,

$$\delta(A_y) = -4(2) - 2(5) - 9(19) = -8 - 10 - 171 = -189,$$
$$\delta(A_z) = -4(47) - 2(19) + 2(-13) = -188 - 38 - 26 = -252,$$

so that

$$y = \frac{\delta(A_y)}{\delta(A)} = \frac{-189}{63} = -3,$$

$$z = \frac{\delta(A_z)}{\delta(A)} = \frac{-252}{63} = -4.$$

Hence the solution set in R^3 of the system is $\{(7, -3, -4)\}$.

Singular systems   If $\delta(A) = 0$ for a linear system, then the system either has infinitely many members in its solution set (the equations are consistent, and one of them can be obtained from the others by linear combinations) or has an empty solution set (the equations are inconsistent). The distinction can be determined as follows: Consider the matrix of coefficients

$$\begin{bmatrix} a_{11} & \cdots & a_{1n} \\ \vdots & & \vdots \\ a_{n1} & \cdots & a_{nn} \end{bmatrix}$$

of a linear system (see page 264) and the **augmented matrix**

$$\begin{bmatrix} a_{11} & \cdots & a_{1n} & c_1 \\ \vdots & & \vdots & \vdots \\ a_{n1} & \cdots & a_{nn} & c_n \end{bmatrix},$$

and in each find a determinant (obtained by striking out certain rows and columns) of order as great as possible with value not 0. The order of such a nonvanishing determinant is called the **rank** of the matrix. The rank of the augmented matrix

Test for consistency   is either the same as, or 1 greater than, that of the matrix of coefficients. It can be shown that the equations are consistent if and only if the two ranks are the same.

For example, the coefficient matrix C and the augmented matrix C_A of the system

$$x + 2y + 3z = 2$$
$$2x + 4y + 2z = -1$$
$$x + 2y - 2z = 5$$

are given by

$$C = \begin{bmatrix} 1 & 2 & 3 \\ 2 & 4 & 2 \\ 1 & 2 & -2 \end{bmatrix} \quad \text{and} \quad C_A = \begin{bmatrix} 1 & 2 & 3 & 2 \\ 2 & 4 & 2 & -1 \\ 1 & 2 & -2 & 5 \end{bmatrix}.$$

Since $\delta(C) = 0$ (check this), the system does not have a unique solution. If the first column and third row are deleted, the remaining determinant,

$$\begin{vmatrix} 2 & 3 \\ 4 & 2 \end{vmatrix},$$

is not zero, so C has rank 2 (check this). Now, if the first column of C_A is deleted, the remaining entries form the determinant

$$\delta \begin{bmatrix} 2 & 3 & 2 \\ 4 & 2 & -1 \\ 2 & -2 & 5 \end{bmatrix},$$

which is also not zero (check this), so C_A has rank 3. Therefore, the system of equations is inconsistent.

EXERCISE 11.2

Find the solution set of each of the following systems by Cramer's rule. If $\delta(A) = 0$ in any of the systems, use the ranks of the coefficient matrix and the augmented matrix to determine whether or not the equations in the system are consistent.

1. $x - y = 2$
   $x + 4y = 5$

2. $x + y = 4$
   $x - 2y = 0$

3. $3x - 4y = -2$
   $x + y = 6$

4. $\dfrac{2}{3}x + y = 1$

   $x - \dfrac{4}{3}y = 0$

5. $x - 2y = 5$

   $\dfrac{2}{3}x - \dfrac{4}{3}y = 6$

6. $2x - 3y = 12$

   $x = 4$

7. $ax + by = 1$
   $bx + ay = 1$

8. $x + y = a$
   $x - y = b$

9. $x - 2y + z = -1$
   $3x + y - 2z = 4$
   $y - z = 1$

10. $2x + 5z = 9$
    $4x + 3y = -1$
    $3y - 4z = -13$

11. $2x + 2y + z = 1$
    $x - y + 6z = 21$
    $3x + 2y - z = -4$

12. $4x + 8y + z = -6$
    $2x - 3y + 2z = 0$
    $x + 7y - 3z = -8$

13. $x + y + z = 0$
    $2x - y - 4z = 15$
    $x - 2y - z = 7$

14. $x + y - 2z = 2$
    $3x - y + z = 5$
    $3x + 3y - 6z = 6$

15. $x - 2y - 2z = 3$
    $2x - 4y + 4z = 1$
    $3x - 3y - 3z = 4$

16. $3x - 2y + 5z = 6$
    $4x - 4y + 3z = 0$
    $5x - 4y + z = -5$

17. $x + y + z = 0$
    $w + 2y - z = 4$
    $2w - y + 2z = 3$
    $-2w + 2y - z = -2$

18. $x + y + z = 0$
    $x + z + w = 0$
    $x + y + w = 0$
    $y + z + w = 0$

19. Show that if both $\delta(A_y) = 0$ and $\delta(A_x) = 0$, and if c_1 and c_2 are not both 0, then $\delta(A) = 0$, and the equations in the linear system (a_1 and b_1 not both 0, a_2 and b_2 not both 0)

$$a_1 x + b_1 y + c_1 = 0$$
$$a_2 x + b_2 y + c_2 = 0$$

are consistent. *Hint:* Show that the first two determinant equations imply that $a_1 c_2 = a_2 c_1$ and $b_1 c_2 = b_2 c_1$ and that the rest follows from the formation of a proportion with these equations.

20. Show that if $\delta(A) = 0$ and $\delta(A_x) = 0$, and if a_1 and a_2 are not both 0, then $\delta(A_y) = 0$, where $\delta(A)$ is the determinant of the coefficient matrix of the system in Problem 19.

11.3 LINEAR TRANSFORMATIONS OF THE PLANE

In Section 11.1, you saw how matrices can be used to solve systems of linear equations. It is possible to view the same procedure in the broader context of inverse functions. For simplicity, we shall confine this discussion to systems of two linear equations in two variables, although most of the ideas involved can be applied more generally.

Consider the system

$$a_1 x + b_1 y = u,$$

$$a_2 x + b_2 y = v,$$

which in matrix form can be written

$$AX = Y,$$

where

$$A = \begin{bmatrix} a_1 & b_1 \\ a_2 & b_2 \end{bmatrix}, \quad X = \begin{bmatrix} x \\ y \end{bmatrix}, \quad \text{and} \quad Y = \begin{bmatrix} u \\ v \end{bmatrix}.$$

For a specified matrix A, any ordered pair $\begin{bmatrix} x \\ y \end{bmatrix}$ in R^2 is associated with a unique ordered pair $\begin{bmatrix} u \\ v \end{bmatrix}$ by such an equation. For example, if $A = \begin{bmatrix} 2 & -1 \\ 1 & 3 \end{bmatrix}$ and $X = \begin{bmatrix} 1 \\ 2 \end{bmatrix}$, then

$$Y = \begin{bmatrix} u \\ v \end{bmatrix} = \begin{bmatrix} 2 & -1 \\ 1 & 3 \end{bmatrix} \begin{bmatrix} 1 \\ 2 \end{bmatrix} = \begin{bmatrix} 0 \\ 7 \end{bmatrix}.$$

Function determined by a matrix

Thus the matrix A might be considered as determining a function

$$f = \{(X, Y) \mid Y = AX\}, \quad \text{for} \quad X = \begin{bmatrix} x \\ y \end{bmatrix} \in R^2.$$

The domain of the function is the set of ordered pairs X in R^2, and each element Y in the range is related to an element in the domain by the equation $Y = AX$.

Functions are sometimes referred to as **mappings**. The elements in the domain are called the **preimages** of the elements in the range, and the elements in the range are called the **images** of the elements in the domain. This terminology arises from the fact that a function pairs the elements of one set (preimages) with those of another (images) in much the same way a map pairs a set of points, say on the surface of the earth, with a set of points on a piece of paper. Thus, in the example above, $\begin{bmatrix} 1 \\ 2 \end{bmatrix}$ is the preimage of $\begin{bmatrix} 0 \\ 7 \end{bmatrix}$, and $\begin{bmatrix} 0 \\ 7 \end{bmatrix}$ is the image of $\begin{bmatrix} 1 \\ 2 \end{bmatrix}$ for the matrix

$$A = \begin{bmatrix} 2 & -1 \\ 1 & 3 \end{bmatrix}.$$

The entire function f determined by the matrix can be considered a one-to-one mapping of the entire plane onto itself in a unique way.

Now if we left-multiply

$$Y = AX$$

by A^{-1}, we have

$$A^{-1} Y = A^{-1} AX,$$

$$A^{-1} Y = I \cdot X = X,$$

or

$$X = A^{-1} Y,$$

so that A^{-1} also determines a function, the inverse f^{-1} of the function f. Thus we have

$$f^{-1} = \{(Y, X) \mid X = A^{-1} Y\}, \quad \text{for} \quad Y \in R^2.$$

For example, if

$$A = \begin{bmatrix} 2 & -1 \\ 1 & 3 \end{bmatrix} \quad \text{and} \quad Y = \begin{bmatrix} 0 \\ 7 \end{bmatrix},$$

then

$$A^{-1} = \frac{1}{7}\begin{bmatrix} 3 & 1 \\ -1 & 2 \end{bmatrix} = \begin{bmatrix} \dfrac{3}{7} & \dfrac{1}{7} \\ -\dfrac{1}{7} & \dfrac{2}{7} \end{bmatrix},$$

and

$$X = A^{-1} Y = \begin{bmatrix} \dfrac{3}{7} & \dfrac{1}{7} \\ -\dfrac{1}{7} & \dfrac{2}{7} \end{bmatrix} \begin{bmatrix} 0 \\ 7 \end{bmatrix} = \begin{bmatrix} 1 \\ 2 \end{bmatrix}.$$

Any mapping f determined by a 2×2 matrix A has the **linearity properties** (see Exercise 11.3, Problems 25 and 26).

$$f(X_1 + X_2) = f(X_1) + f(X_2),$$
$$f(cX_1) = cf(X_1),$$

for all $X_1, X_2 \in R^2$ and all $c \in R$. The mapping determined by A is called a **linear transformation of the plane**. A linear transformation is said to be **nonsingular** if and only if the matrix A of the transformation is nonsingular, that is, if and only if $\delta(A) \neq 0$. If $\delta(A) = 0$, then the transformation is called **singular** and there is no inverse matrix A^{-1}.

Certain simple nonsingular linear transformations, called **elementary transformations**, are
important because all nonsingular linear transformations can be expressed in terms of them. Elementary

Classification
Classification of elementary transfor- mations

transformations can perhaps
most readily be visualized by
considering their effect on a
single figure such as that shown

Figure 11.1

in Figure 11.1. Elementary transformations are of
the three following kinds.

(1) **Horizontal and vertical multiplications**, determined respectively by matrices of
the form

$$\begin{bmatrix} k & 0 \\ 0 & 1 \end{bmatrix} \text{ and } \begin{bmatrix} 1 & 0 \\ 0 & k \end{bmatrix}, \quad k \neq 0.$$

For example, consider the mapping determined by

$$A = \begin{bmatrix} 2 & 0 \\ 0 & 1 \end{bmatrix}.$$

For this, we have

$$\begin{bmatrix} 2 & 0 \\ 0 & 1 \end{bmatrix} \begin{bmatrix} x \\ y \end{bmatrix} = \begin{bmatrix} 2x \\ y \end{bmatrix}.$$

Thus, we have the horizontal stretching shown in Figure 11.2. Transformations of
this kind are called **stretchings** if $k > 1$, or **shrinkings** if $0 < k < 1$.

Figure 11.2

Reflections in the coordinate axes are determined
by matrices of the form

$$\begin{bmatrix} -1 & 0 \\ 0 & 1 \end{bmatrix} \text{ and } \begin{bmatrix} 1 & 0 \\ 0 & -1 \end{bmatrix}.$$

For example, the mapping determined by

$$\begin{bmatrix} 1 & 0 \\ 0 & -1 \end{bmatrix}$$

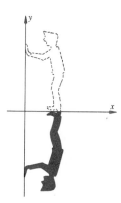

Figure 11.3

maps the ordered pair $\begin{bmatrix} x \\ y \end{bmatrix}$ into $\begin{bmatrix} x \\ -y \end{bmatrix}$ and has the effect shown in Figure 11.3.

In general, for $k < 0$ a horizontal or vertical multiplication amounts to a reflection in the respective axis combined with a stretching or shrinking by the factor $|k|$.

(2) **Reflections in the line with equation** $y = x$ are determined by the matrix $\begin{bmatrix} 0 & 1 \\ 1 & 0 \end{bmatrix}$. This matrix maps each ordered pair $\begin{bmatrix} x \\ y \end{bmatrix}$ into $\begin{bmatrix} y \\ x \end{bmatrix}$. It has the effect shown in Figure 11.4.

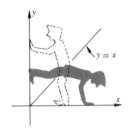

Figure 11.4

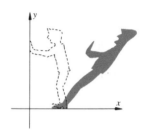

Figure 11.5

TABLE 11.1

ELEMENTARY TRANSFORMATIONS

Transformation	Matrix	Inverse Transformation	Inverse Matrix
Horizontal multiplication with factor $k \neq 0$ Horizontal stretch, $\|k\| > 1$	$\begin{bmatrix} k & 0 \\ 0 & 1 \end{bmatrix}$	Horizontal multiplication with factor $\dfrac{1}{k} \neq 0$ Horizontal shrink, $\|k\| > 1$	$\begin{bmatrix} \dfrac{1}{k} & 0 \\ 0 & 1 \end{bmatrix}$
		(includes reflection in the y-axis if $k < 0$)	
Vertical multiplication with factor $k \neq 0$ Vertical stretch, $\|k\| > 1$	$\begin{bmatrix} 1 & 0 \\ 0 & k \end{bmatrix}$	Vertical multiplication with factor $\dfrac{1}{k} \neq 0$ Vertical shrink, $\|k\| > 1$	$\begin{bmatrix} 1 & 0 \\ 0 & \dfrac{1}{k} \end{bmatrix}$
		(includes reflection in the x-axis if $k < 0$)	
Reflection in the line with equation $y = x$	$\begin{bmatrix} 0 & 1 \\ 1 & 0 \end{bmatrix}$	Reflection in the line with equation $y = x$	$\begin{bmatrix} 0 & 1 \\ 1 & 0 \end{bmatrix}$
Horizontal shear with constant k	$\begin{bmatrix} 1 & k \\ 0 & 1 \end{bmatrix}$	Horizontal shear with constant $-k$	$\begin{bmatrix} 1 & -k \\ 0 & 1 \end{bmatrix}$
Vertical shear with constant k	$\begin{bmatrix} 1 & 0 \\ k & 1 \end{bmatrix}$	Vertical shear with constant $-k$	$\begin{bmatrix} 1 & 0 \\ -k & 1 \end{bmatrix}$

(3) **Horizontal and vertical shears of the plane** are determined by matrices of the form

$$\begin{bmatrix} 1 & k \\ 0 & 1 \end{bmatrix} \text{ and } \begin{bmatrix} 1 & 0 \\ k & 1 \end{bmatrix}.$$

These matrices map the ordered pair $\begin{bmatrix} x \\ y \end{bmatrix}$ into

$$\begin{bmatrix} x + ky \\ y \end{bmatrix} \text{ and } \begin{bmatrix} x \\ kx + y \end{bmatrix},$$

respectively. For example, $\begin{bmatrix} 1 & 1 \\ 0 & 1 \end{bmatrix}$ has the effect shown in Figure 11.5.

Matrices determining elementary transformations are called **elementary matrices.** The elementary plane transformations and their matrices are listed, along with their inverses, in Table 11.1.

Inverses of elementary matrices

You can readily check, of course, that the inverse matrices actually are as given, and that the inverse transformations "undo" what the matrices "do."

The results of left-multiplying an arbitrary 2×2 matrix

$$M = \begin{bmatrix} a & b \\ c & d \end{bmatrix}$$

by an elementary matrix are shown in Table 11.2.

TABLE 11.2

LEFT MULTIPLICATION OF MATRICES

Multiplication	Result
$\begin{bmatrix} k & 0 \\ 0 & 1 \end{bmatrix} \begin{bmatrix} a & b \\ c & d \end{bmatrix} = \begin{bmatrix} ka & kb \\ c & d \end{bmatrix}$	Entries of first row multiplied by $k \neq 0$
$\begin{bmatrix} 1 & 0 \\ 0 & k \end{bmatrix} \begin{bmatrix} a & b \\ c & d \end{bmatrix} = \begin{bmatrix} a & b \\ kc & kd \end{bmatrix}$	Entries of second row multiplied by $k \neq 0$
$\begin{bmatrix} 0 & 1 \\ 1 & 0 \end{bmatrix} \begin{bmatrix} a & b \\ c & d \end{bmatrix} = \begin{bmatrix} c & d \\ a & b \end{bmatrix}$	First and second rows interchanged
$\begin{bmatrix} 1 & k \\ 0 & 1 \end{bmatrix} \begin{bmatrix} a & b \\ c & d \end{bmatrix} = \begin{bmatrix} a + kc & b + kd \\ c & d \end{bmatrix}$	Entries of second row multiplied by k and added to corresponding entries of first row
$\begin{bmatrix} 1 & 0 \\ k & 1 \end{bmatrix} \begin{bmatrix} a & b \\ c & d \end{bmatrix} = \begin{bmatrix} a & b \\ ka + c & kb + d \end{bmatrix}$	Entries of first row multiplied by k and added to corresponding entries of second row

Note, in each case, that the premultiplication factor, or elementary matrix, bears the same relationship to the identity matrix $I = \begin{bmatrix} 1 & 0 \\ 0 & 1 \end{bmatrix}$ as the product matrix bears to the matrix $M = \begin{bmatrix} a & b \\ c & d \end{bmatrix}$.

Products of elementary matrices   You can use products of elementary matrices to perform a combination of two or more elementary transformations at the same time.

Example. Find a matrix that multiples the entries in the second row of a 2×2 matrix by 3 and interchanges the first and second rows.

Solution. We seek a matrix A such that

$$A \cdot \begin{bmatrix} a & b \\ c & d \end{bmatrix} = \begin{bmatrix} 3c & 3d \\ a & b \end{bmatrix}.$$

From Table 11.2, we see that multiplication by $\begin{bmatrix} 1 & 0 \\ 0 & 3 \end{bmatrix}$ multiplies elements c and d by 3, and multiplication by $\begin{bmatrix} 0 & 1 \\ 1 & 0 \end{bmatrix}$ interchanges the first and second rows. Thus the matrix we seek is

$$A = \begin{bmatrix} 0 & 1 \\ 1 & 0 \end{bmatrix} \begin{bmatrix} 1 & 0 \\ 0 & 3 \end{bmatrix} = \begin{bmatrix} 0 & 3 \\ 1 & 0 \end{bmatrix}.$$

As a check we observe that

$$\begin{bmatrix} 0 & 3 \\ 1 & 0 \end{bmatrix} \begin{bmatrix} a & b \\ c & d \end{bmatrix} = \begin{bmatrix} 3c & 3d \\ a & b \end{bmatrix}.$$

EXERCISE 11.3

Determine the image of the given ordered pair under the mapping with matrix as given.

1. $\begin{bmatrix} 2 \\ 0 \end{bmatrix} ; \begin{bmatrix} 3 & 1 \\ 0 & 2 \end{bmatrix}$ 2. $\begin{bmatrix} 1 \\ 3 \end{bmatrix} ; \begin{bmatrix} 1 & 0 \\ 3 & -1 \end{bmatrix}$ 3. $\begin{bmatrix} -3 \\ 2 \end{bmatrix} ; \begin{bmatrix} 2 & 4 \\ 1 & 0 \end{bmatrix}$

4. $\begin{bmatrix} -1 \\ -5 \end{bmatrix} ; \begin{bmatrix} 5 & -1 \\ 2 & -2 \end{bmatrix}$ 5. $\begin{bmatrix} x \\ y \end{bmatrix} ; \begin{bmatrix} 1 & -3 \\ -2 & -1 \end{bmatrix}$ 6. $\begin{bmatrix} x \\ y \end{bmatrix} ; \begin{bmatrix} 4 & 1 \\ -2 & -3 \end{bmatrix}$

Determine the preimage of the given ordered pair under the mapping with matrix as given.

Example. $\begin{bmatrix} 0 \\ 1 \end{bmatrix} ; \begin{bmatrix} 1 & 2 \\ 0 & 3 \end{bmatrix}$.

Solution. If

$$\begin{bmatrix} 1 & 2 \\ 0 & 3 \end{bmatrix}\begin{bmatrix} x \\ y \end{bmatrix} = \begin{bmatrix} 0 \\ 1 \end{bmatrix},$$

then

$$\begin{bmatrix} x \\ y \end{bmatrix} = \begin{bmatrix} 1 & 2 \\ 0 & 3 \end{bmatrix}^{-1}\begin{bmatrix} 0 \\ 1 \end{bmatrix} = \begin{bmatrix} 1 & -\dfrac{2}{3} \\ 0 & \dfrac{1}{3} \end{bmatrix}\begin{bmatrix} 0 \\ 1 \end{bmatrix} = \begin{bmatrix} -\dfrac{2}{3} \\ \dfrac{1}{3} \end{bmatrix}.$$

7. $\begin{bmatrix} 2 \\ 0 \end{bmatrix} ; \begin{bmatrix} 1 & 1 \\ 3 & 1 \end{bmatrix}$ 8. $\begin{bmatrix} 1 \\ 3 \end{bmatrix} ; \begin{bmatrix} 0 & 3 \\ 2 & 1 \end{bmatrix}$ 9. $\begin{bmatrix} 1 \\ -1 \end{bmatrix} ; \begin{bmatrix} 2 & -1 \\ 3 & 4 \end{bmatrix}$

10. $\begin{bmatrix} -2 \\ 3 \end{bmatrix} ; \begin{bmatrix} 4 & -2 \\ 1 & 0 \end{bmatrix}$ 11. $\begin{bmatrix} a \\ b \end{bmatrix} ; \begin{bmatrix} 0 & 1 \\ 2 & 3 \end{bmatrix}$ 12. $\begin{bmatrix} a \\ b \end{bmatrix} ; \begin{bmatrix} 2 & 4 \\ 1 & -2 \end{bmatrix}$

Find a product of elementary matrices equal to the given matrix.

13. $\begin{bmatrix} 0 & 2 \\ 1 & 0 \end{bmatrix}$ 14. $\begin{bmatrix} 1 & 0 \\ 4 & 3 \end{bmatrix}$ 15. $\begin{bmatrix} 1 & 3 \\ 0 & 2 \end{bmatrix}$ 16. $\begin{bmatrix} 2 & 0 \\ \dfrac{1}{2} & 3 \end{bmatrix}$

17. Identify the kind or kinds of elementary transformations of the plane associated with the matrix in Problem 13.

18. Identify the kind or kinds of elementary transformations of the plane associated with the matrix in Problem 16.

In the plane, consider the square with vertices $(0, 0)$, $(1, 0)$, $(1, 1)$, and $(0, 1)$. Into what figure is the square mapped by the given matrix?

19. $\begin{bmatrix} 3 & 0 \\ 0 & 1 \end{bmatrix}$ 20. $\begin{bmatrix} 0 & 1 \\ 1 & 0 \end{bmatrix}$ 21. $\begin{bmatrix} 1 & 0 \\ 0 & \dfrac{1}{2} \end{bmatrix}$

22. $\begin{bmatrix} 1 & 1 \\ 0 & 1 \end{bmatrix}$ 23. $\begin{bmatrix} 1 & 0 \\ 1 & 1 \end{bmatrix}$ 24. $\begin{bmatrix} 1 & 2 \\ 0 & 1 \end{bmatrix}$

25. Prove that if

$$f = \{(X, f(X)) \mid f(X) = AX\},$$

for $X \in R^2$, $f(X) \in R^2$, and A a 2×2 matrix, then

$$f(X_1 + X_2) = f(X_1) + f(X_2)$$

for each $X_1 \in R^2$ and $X_2 \in R^2$.

26. Prove that if f is the function defined in Exercise 25, then for each $c \in R$,

$$f(cX_1) = cf(X_1)$$

for each $X_1 \in R^2$.

11.4 ROW-EQUIVALENT MATRICES

The left-multiplication of a 2×2 matrix A by an elementary matrix as summarized in Table 11.2 on page 275 results in a new matrix B which differs from A in one or more rows. We say that the matrix B is *row-equivalent* to A. More generally, we have the following.

DEFINITION 11.1 *If B is a matrix resulting from a finite number of elementary transformations on a matrix A, then A and B are **row-equivalent** matrices. This is expressed by writing $A \sim B$ or $B \sim A$.*

The effects of an elementary transformation on a 2×2 matrix as detailed in the right-hand column of Table 11.2 can be extended to $n \times n$ square matrices. Row-equivalent matrices can be obtained in a routine way by observing the results in this table. Some of these results are analogous to statements for determinants given in Section 10.4.

Elementary transformations of $n \times n$ matrices

Example. Show that $\begin{bmatrix} 1 & 2 & 1 \\ -1 & 1 & 0 \\ 1 & 0 & 1 \end{bmatrix} \sim \begin{bmatrix} 1 & 0 & 0 \\ 0 & 1 & 0 \\ 0 & 0 & 1 \end{bmatrix}$.

Solution. We first make appropriate transformations to obtain "0" elements in each entry (except for the principal diagonal) in columns 1, 2, and 3. Each reference to a row indicates the row of the preceding matrix.

$$\begin{bmatrix} 1 & 2 & 1 \\ -1 & 1 & 0 \\ 1 & 0 & 1 \end{bmatrix} \sim \begin{bmatrix} 1 & 2 & 1 \\ 0 & 3 & 1 \\ 0 & -2 & 0 \end{bmatrix} \begin{array}{l} \\ \text{Row 2} + \text{Row 1} \\ \text{Row 3} + [(-1) \times \text{Row 1}] \end{array}$$

$$\sim \begin{bmatrix} 1 & 0 & 1 \\ 0 & 3 & 1 \\ 0 & 0 & \frac{2}{3} \end{bmatrix} \begin{array}{l} \text{Row 1} + \text{Row 3} \\ \\ \text{Row 3} + \left[\left(\frac{2}{3} \right) \times \text{Row 2} \right] \end{array}$$

Row equivalence of a nonsingular $n \times n$ matrix and $I_{n \times n}$

$$\sim \begin{bmatrix} 1 & 0 & 0 \\ 0 & 3 & 0 \\ 0 & 0 & \frac{2}{3} \end{bmatrix} \begin{array}{l} \text{Row 1} + \left[\left(-\frac{3}{2} \right) \times \text{Row 3} \right] \\ \text{Row 2} + \left[\left(-\frac{3}{2} \right) \times \text{Row 3} \right] \\ \\ \end{array}$$

$$\sim \begin{bmatrix} 1 & 0 & 0 \\ 0 & 1 & 0 \\ 0 & 0 & 1 \end{bmatrix} \begin{array}{l} \\ \left(\frac{1}{3} \right) \times \text{Row 2} \\ \\ \left(\frac{3}{2} \right) \times \text{Row 3} \end{array}$$

The foregoing example is a special case of a more general result, which we state here without proof.

THEOREM 11.1   *If A is a nonsingular $n \times n$ square matrix, then A is row-equivalent to $I_{n \times n}$.*

Now, for any $n \times n$ nonsingular matrix A, we know from Theorem 11.1 that there are a finite number of elementary matrices, E_1, E_2, E_3, $\cdots$, E_i such that

$$E_1\, E_2\, E_3 \cdots E_i A = I. \tag{1}$$

We can use this relationship to provide us with another means of obtaining A^{-1} from A. We begin with the fact that, since A is nonsingular, there is a matrix A^{-1} such that

$$A A^{-1} = I.$$

Determination of the inverse of a nonsingular matrix by elementary transformations   Left-multiplying each member of this equation by the product $E_1\, E_2\, E_3 \cdots E_i$, we obtain

$$E_1\, E_2\, E_3 \cdots E_i A A^{-1} = E_1\, E_2\, E_3 \cdots E_i I. \tag{2}$$

From (1), we can replace $E_1\, E_2\, E_3 \cdots E_i A$ in the left-hand member of (2) by I to obtain

$$I A^{-1} = E_1\, E_2\, E_3 \cdots E_i I,$$

from which

$$A^{-1} = E_1\, E_2\, E_3 \cdots E_i I.$$

The implication of the foregoing argument is that *if A is row-transformed to I by a sequence of elementary row transformations, then the same sequence will transform I to A^{-1}.*

This provides us with another means of obtaining A^{-1} from A. In using this procedure, it is convenient to use a single matrix combining A and I as illustrated in the following example.

Example.   Find A^{-1} if $A = \begin{bmatrix} 1 & 0 & 1 \\ 2 & 1 & 0 \\ 1 & -1 & 1 \end{bmatrix}$.

Solution.   List the rows of A and those of I side-by-side, as shown below.

$$\begin{array}{ccc|ccc} \multicolumn{3}{c}{A} & \multicolumn{3}{c}{I} \\ 1 & 0 & 1 & 1 & 0 & 0 \\ 2 & 1 & 0 & 0 & 1 & 0 \\ 1 & -1 & 1 & 0 & 0 & 1 \end{array}$$

(Solution continued overleaf.)

Apply row-transformations to this matrix to reduce the first three columns to I.

$$\left[\begin{array}{ccc|ccc}
1 & 0 & 1 & 1 & 0 & 0 \\
0 & 1 & -2 & -2 & 1 & 0 \\
0 & -1 & 0 & -1 & 0 & 1
\end{array}\right] \begin{array}{l} \\ \text{Row } 2 + [(-2) \times \text{Row } 1] \\ \text{Row } 3 + [(-1) \times \text{Row } 1] \end{array}$$

$$\left[\begin{array}{ccc|ccc}
1 & 0 & 1 & 1 & 0 & 0 \\
0 & 1 & -2 & -2 & 1 & 0 \\
0 & 0 & -2 & -3 & 1 & 1
\end{array}\right] \begin{array}{l} \\ \\ \text{Row } 3 + \text{Row } 2 \end{array}$$

$$\left[\begin{array}{ccc|ccc}
1 & 0 & 0 & -\dfrac{1}{2} & \dfrac{1}{2} & \dfrac{1}{2} \\
0 & 1 & 0 & 1 & 0 & -1 \\
0 & 0 & -2 & -3 & 1 & 1
\end{array}\right] \begin{array}{l} \text{Row } 1 + \left[\left(\dfrac{1}{2}\right) \times \text{Row } 3\right] \\ \text{Row } 2 + [(-1) \times \text{Row } 3] \\ \end{array}$$

$$\underset{\displaystyle I}{\underbrace{\phantom{\left[\begin{array}{ccc}1&0&0\\0&1&0\\0&0&1\end{array}\right]}}} \quad \underset{\displaystyle A^{-1}}{\underbrace{}}$$

$$\left[\begin{array}{ccc|ccc}
1 & 0 & 0 & -\dfrac{1}{2} & \dfrac{1}{2} & \dfrac{1}{2} \\
0 & 1 & 0 & 1 & 0 & -1 \\
0 & 0 & 1 & \dfrac{3}{2} & -\dfrac{1}{2} & -\dfrac{1}{2}
\end{array}\right] \left(-\dfrac{1}{2}\right) \times \text{Row } 3$$

At this point, the original matrix A has been transformed to $I_{3 \times 3}$, and the matrix $I_{3 \times 3}$ has been simultaneously transformed to A^{-1}. To verify this, you can compare the last three columns of the final matrix with the result obtained on page 260, where A^{-1} for the same matrix A is obtained in another way.

EXERCISE 11.4

Row-reduce each matrix to an identity matrix of the same dimensions.

1. $\begin{bmatrix} 1 & 2 \\ 1 & 1 \end{bmatrix}$ 2. $\begin{bmatrix} 1 & 3 \\ 2 & 1 \end{bmatrix}$ 3. $\begin{bmatrix} 2 & 3 \\ 1 & -4 \end{bmatrix}$

4. $\begin{bmatrix} -3 & 1 \\ 2 & 6 \end{bmatrix}$ 5. $\begin{bmatrix} 1 & 3 & 1 \\ 1 & 2 & 0 \\ -1 & 2 & 0 \end{bmatrix}$ 6. $\begin{bmatrix} 1 & -2 & 4 \\ 2 & -3 & 1 \\ 1 & 2 & -1 \end{bmatrix}$

7. $\begin{bmatrix} 2 & -1 & 3 \\ 1 & 5 & 7 \\ 1 & -1 & 0 \end{bmatrix}$ 8. $\begin{bmatrix} -2 & 2 & 4 \\ 3 & 1 & 0 \\ 4 & 2 & 0 \end{bmatrix}$

9–16. Use row-transformations to find the inverse of each matrix in Problems 1–8.

17. Show that if $a \neq 0$ and $ad - bc \neq 0$, then

$$\begin{bmatrix} 1 & 0 \\ \dfrac{c}{a} & 1 \end{bmatrix}\begin{bmatrix} 1 & \dfrac{ab}{ad-bc} \\ 0 & 1 \end{bmatrix}\begin{bmatrix} \dfrac{a}{ad-bc} & 0 \\ 0 & 1 \end{bmatrix}\begin{bmatrix} ad-bc & 0 \\ 0 & 1 \end{bmatrix}\begin{bmatrix} 1 & 0 \\ 0 & \dfrac{ad-bc}{a} \end{bmatrix} = \begin{bmatrix} a & b \\ c & d \end{bmatrix},$$

so that $\begin{bmatrix} a & b \\ c & d \end{bmatrix}$ can be expressed as the product of elementary matrices.

18. Show that if $a = 0$ but $ad - bc \neq 0$, then $\begin{bmatrix} a & b \\ c & d \end{bmatrix}$ can be expressed as the product of elementary matrices. *Hint:* Show that $c \neq 0$, premultiply $\begin{bmatrix} a & b \\ c & d \end{bmatrix}$ by $\begin{bmatrix} 0 & 1 \\ 1 & 0 \end{bmatrix}$, and apply the result of Problem 17.

19. Use the results of Problem 18 or some other means to express

$$\begin{bmatrix} 0 & 1 \\ 2 & 3 \end{bmatrix}$$

as a product of elementary matrices.

20. Use the results of Problem 17 or some other means to express

$$\begin{bmatrix} 1 & 4 \\ 3 & 2 \end{bmatrix}$$

as a product of elementary matrices.

11.5 SOLVING LINEAR SYSTEMS BY USING EQUIVALENT SYSTEMS

In previous sections of this chapter, you solved linear systems by various methods. Yet another method involves using row-equivalent matrices starting with the augmented matrix of the system. The validity of the method, which is illustrated by example below, follows from the fact that performing elementary row-transformations on the augmented matrix of a system corresponds in this context to forming equivalent systems of equations.

Solution by elementary transformations

Example.   Solve $x + 2y - 3z = -4$
$2x - y + z = 3$
$3x + 2y + z = 10$

Solution.   The augmented matrix of the system is given by

$$\begin{bmatrix} 1 & 2 & -3 & | & -4 \\ 2 & -1 & 1 & | & 3 \\ 3 & 2 & 1 & | & 10 \end{bmatrix}.$$

The system of equations corresponding to each successive matrix is shown on the right of the matrix in the following solution.

$$\begin{matrix} & \begin{bmatrix} 1 & 2 & -3 & | & -4 \\ 0 & -5 & 7 & | & 11 \\ 0 & -4 & 10 & | & 22 \end{bmatrix} \end{matrix}$$

Row 2 + [−2 × Row 1]
Row 3 + [−3 × Row 1]

$x + 2y - 3z = -4$
$0x - 5y + 7z = 11$
$0x - 4y + 10z = 22$

$$\text{Row } 1 + \left[\frac{2}{5} \times \text{Row } 2\right] \begin{bmatrix} 1 & 0 & -\frac{1}{5} & \bigg| & \frac{2}{5} \\ 0 & -5 & 7 & \bigg| & 11 \\ 0 & 0 & \frac{22}{5} & \bigg| & \frac{66}{5} \end{bmatrix} \qquad \begin{aligned} x + 0y - \frac{1}{5}z &= \frac{2}{5} \\ 0x - 5y + 7z &= 11 \\ 0x + 0y + \frac{22}{5}z &= \frac{66}{5} \end{aligned}$$

$$\text{Row } 3 + \left[-\frac{4}{5} \times \text{Row } 2\right]$$

$$5 \times \text{Row } 1 \begin{bmatrix} 5 & 0 & -1 & \bigg| & 2 \\ 0 & -5 & 7 & \bigg| & 11 \\ 0 & 0 & 1 & \bigg| & 3 \end{bmatrix} \qquad \begin{aligned} 5x + 0y - z &= 2 \\ 0x - 5y + 7z &= 11 \\ 0x - 0y + z &= 3 \end{aligned}$$

$$\frac{5}{22} \times \text{Row } 3$$

$$\begin{aligned} \text{Row } 1 + \text{Row } 3 \\ \text{Row } 2 + [-7 \times \text{Row } 3] \end{aligned} \begin{bmatrix} 5 & 0 & 0 & \bigg| & 5 \\ 0 & -5 & 0 & \bigg| & -10 \\ 0 & 0 & 1 & \bigg| & 3 \end{bmatrix} \qquad \begin{aligned} 5x + 0y - 0z &= 5 \\ 0x - 5y + 0z &= -10 \\ 0x - 0y + z &= 3 \end{aligned}$$

$$\frac{1}{5} \times \text{Row } 1$$
$$-\frac{1}{5} \times \text{Row } 2 \begin{bmatrix} 1 & 0 & 0 & \bigg| & 1 \\ 0 & 1 & 0 & \bigg| & 2 \\ 0 & 0 & 1 & \bigg| & 3 \end{bmatrix} \qquad \begin{aligned} x + 0y - 0z &= 1 \\ 0x + y + 0z &= 2 \\ 0x + 0y + z &= 3 \end{aligned}$$

The last system is equivalent to

$$x = 1$$
$$y = 2$$
$$z = 3$$

From this the solution set, $\{(1, 2, 3)\}$, for the given system is evident by inspection.

For any given $n \times n$ linear system, there are many sequences of row operations which will transform the augmented matrix of a system equivalently to one of the form

$$\begin{bmatrix} 1 & 0 & 0 & \cdots & 0 & \bigg| & x_1 \\ 0 & 1 & 0 & & 0 & \bigg| & \cdot \\ 0 & 0 & 1 & & 0 & \bigg| & \cdot \\ \vdots & & & & \vdots & \bigg| & \cdot \\ 0 & 0 & 0 & \cdots & 1 & \bigg| & x_n \end{bmatrix},$$

from which the solution set, $\{(x_1, \cdots x_n)\}$, of the original system is evident by inspection. Finding the most efficient such sequence depends on experience and insight.

EXERCISE 11.5

Use row-transformations on an augmented matrix to solve each system of equations.

1. $x - 2y = 4$
   $x + 3y = -1$

2. $x + y = -1$
   $x - 4y = -14$

3. $3x - 2y = 13$
   $4x - y = 19$

4. $4x - 3y = 16$
   $2x + y = 8$

5. $x - 2y = 6$
   $3x + y = 25$

6. $x - y = -8$
   $x + 2y = 9$

7. $x + y - z = 2$
   $2x - y + z = 4$
   $x + 2y - 2z = 2$

8. $2x - y + 3z = 1$
   $x + 2y - z = -1$
   $3x + y + z = 2$

9. $2x - y = 0$
   $3y + z = 7$
   $2x + 3z = 1$

10. $3x - z = 7$
    $2x + y = 6$
    $3y - z = 7$

11. $2x - 5y + 3z = -1$
    $-3x - y + 2z = 11$
    $-2x + 7y + 5z = 9$

12. $2x + y + z = 4$
    $3x - z = 3$
    $2x + 3z = 13$

12 COMPLEX NUMBERS AND VECTORS

12.1 DEFINITIONS AND THEIR CONSEQUENCES

In Chapter 1, we observed that the system of real numbers constitutes a complete ordered field; that is, the real numbers satisfy the field postulates F-1 through F-11, the order postulates O-1 through O-3, and the completeness postulate.

We wish now to consider another mathematical system, one in which the elements consist of ordered pairs of real numbers (a, b), that is, a system involving the members of $R \times R$, or R^2. By suitably defining operations on the members of R^2, we can exhibit a system that is a field, but not an ordered field. While we shall not, for the moment, relate the ordered pairs (a, b) in R^2 to anything in particular, later in this chapter we shall examine various aspects of the systems we develop. We shall, to begin with, use z to denote an ordered pair of real numbers (a, b), and C to denote the set of all such numbers.

> A field having the members of R^2 as elements

DEFINITION 12.1 $C = R \times R = R^2 = \{(a, b) \mid a \in R \text{ and } b \in R\}$.

This simply establishes the set of numbers with which we shall be working.

DEFINITION 12.2 *Let* $z_1 = (a_1, b_1) \in C$ *and* $z_2 = (a_2, b_2) \in C$. *Then* $z_1 = z_2$ *if and only if* $a_1 = a_2$ *and* $b_1 = b_2$.

> Equality properties in the set C

This gives meaning to **equality** in C. Since the equality postulates E-1 through E-4 hold in the set R of real numbers, it follows from Definition 12.2 that they hold also in the set C. Formal verification is left as an exercise.

DEFINITION 12.3 *If* $z_1 = (a_1, b_1) \in C$ *and* $z_2 = (a_2, b_2) \in C$, *then*

I $z_1 + z_2 = (a_1, b_1) + (a_2, b_2) = (a_1 + a_2, b_1 + b_2)$,

II $z_1 z_2 = (a_1, b_1) \cdot (a_2, b_2) = (a_1 a_2 - b_1 b_2, a_1 b_2 + a_2 b_1)$.

This establishes two operations, addition and multiplication, for the numbers in our set.

Examples.   a. $(3, 5) + (7, 9) = (3 + 7, 5 + 9) = (10, 14)$

   b. $(3, 5) \cdot (7, 9) = (3 \cdot 7 - 5 \cdot 9, \, 3 \cdot 9 + 5 \cdot 7)$

$$= (21 - 45, \, 27 + 35)$$

$$= (-24, 62)$$

> **Addition properties in the set C**

Relative to the operations of addition and multiplication, as thus defined, we can now prove that the set C constitutes a field. The proof is divided into two theorems to provide an opportunity to discuss some related ideas.

THEOREM 12.1   *If $z_1 = (a_1, b_1) \in C$, $z_2 = (a_2, b_2) \in C$, and $z_3 = (a_3, b_3) \in C$, then*:

F-1 $z_1 + z_2 \in C$.   *Closure law for addition.*

F-2 $(z_1 + z_2) + z_3 = z_1 + (z_2 + z_3)$.   *Associative law for addition.*

F-3   *There exists an element*   *Additive-identity law.*
     $z_0 = (0, 0) \in C$ such that

     $z + z_0 = z$ *and* $z_0 + z = z$

     for all z in C.

F-4   *For each $z \in C$ there exists an ele-*   *Additive-inverse law.*
     ment $-z \in C$ such that

     $z + (-z) = z_0$ *and* $(-z) + z = z_0$.

F-5 $z_1 + z_2 = z_2 + z_1$.   *Commutative law for addition.*

Proof of F-1.   Let $z_1 = (a_1, b_1)$ and $z_2 = (a_2, b_2)$. By Definition 12.3-I,

$$z_1 + z_2 = (a_1, b_1) + (a_2, b_2) = (a_1 + a_2, b_1 + b_2),$$

and since the operation of addition is closed in the field R of real numbers, we have $(a_1 + a_2) \in R$ and $(b_1 + b_2) \in R$. Hence, by Definition 12.1, we see that $(a_1 + a_2, b_1 + b_2) \in C$; that is, $z_1 + z_2 \in C$.

The proof of F-2 is left as an exercise. It depends on Definition 12.3-I and the fact that addition is associative in the field R of real numbers.

To give meaning to the expressions $z_1 + z_2 + z_3$ and $z_1 z_2 z_3$, let us agree to the following:

DEFINITION 12.4   *If $z_1 \in C$, $z_2 \in C$, and $z_3 \in C$, then*

$$z_1 + z_2 + z_3 = (z_1 + z_2) + z_3 \quad and \quad z_1 z_2 z_3 = (z_1 z_2) z_3.$$

This definition can be extended to cover $z_1 + z_2 + z_3 + z_4$, etc. According to Property F-2, it is immaterial whether $z_1 + z_2 + z_3$ is considered in accordance with Definition 12.4 or as $z_1 + (z_2 + z_3)$.

Proof of F-3. Let $z = (a, b)$, and consider the element $z_0 = (0, 0) \in C$. By Definition 12.3-I,

$$z + z_0 = (a, b) + (0, 0) = (a + 0, b + 0) = (a, b) = z$$

and

$$z_0 + z = (0, 0) + (a, b) = (0 + a, 0 + b) = (a, b) = z.$$

Here, of course, we have used the fact that 0 is the identity element for addition in the field R of real numbers. We say that $z_0 = (0, 0)$ is the **identity element for addition**, or the **zero element**, in the set C.

Proof of F-4. Let $z = (a, b)$, and consider the element $-z = (-a, -b) \in C$. We have

$$z + (-z) = (a, b) + (-a, -b) = (a + (-a), b + (-b)) = (0, 0),$$

and similarly

$$(-z) + z = (-a, -b) + (a, b) = ((-a) + a, (-b) + b) = (0, 0).$$

We say that $-z = (-a, -b)$ is the **additive inverse**, or the **negative**, of $z = (a, b)$.

Multiplication properties in the set C   Turning now to properties of multiplication, we have the following result.

THEOREM 12.2 *If $z_1 = (a_1, b_1) \in C$, $z_2 = (a_2, b_2) \in C$, and $z_3 = (a_3, b_3) \in C$, then:*

F-6 $z_1 z_2 \in C$.   *Closure law for multiplication.*

F-7 $(z_1 z_2)z_3 = z_1(z_2 z_3)$.   *Associative law for multiplication.*

F-8 $z_1(z_2 + z_3) = z_1 z_2 + z_1 z_3$ *Distributive law.*

    and

    $(z_2 + z_3)z_1 = z_2 z_1 + z_3 z_1$.

F-9 *There exists an element*   *Multiplicative-identity law.*
    $z_I = (1, 0) \in C$ *such that*

    $z z_I = z$ *and* $z_I z = z$

    for all $z \in C$.

F-10 $z_1 z_2 = z_2 z_1$.   *Commutative law for multiplication.*

F-11 *For each $z \in C$ other*   *Multiplicative-inverse law.*
      than the zero element z_0 there
      exists an element $z^{-1} \in C$ such that

$$zz^{-1} = z_I \text{ and } z^{-1}z = z_I.$$

The proof of F-6 is analogous to that of F-1, with multiplication in place of addition. It is left as an exercise, as is the proof of F-7.

For efficiency, let us prove F-10 before turning to F-8, F-9, and F-11.

Proof of F-10. Let $z_1 = (a_1, b_1)$ and $z_2 = (a_2, b_2)$; then by Definition 12.3-II,

$$z_1 z_2 = (a_1, b_1)(a_2, b_2) = (a_1 a_2 - b_1 b_2, a_1 b_2 + a_2 b_1)$$

and

$$z_2 z_1 = (a_2, b_2)(a_1, b_1) = (a_2 a_1 - b_2 b_1, a_2 b_1 + a_1 b_2).$$

But since multiplication and addition are commutative in the field R of real numbers, we have

$$a_1 a_2 - b_1 b_2 = a_2 a_1 - b_2 b_1 \quad \text{and} \quad a_1 b_2 + a_2 b_1 = a_2 b_1 + a_1 b_2,$$

from which

$$z_1 z_2 = z_2 z_1.$$

Since we now know that the commutative law holds for both addition and multiplication in C, we see that the validity of the second equation in F-8 follows from that of the first. The proof of the first consists of writing each member as an ordered pair and showing that these ordered pairs are equal. This is left as an exercise.

Proof of F-9. Let $z = (a, b)$, and consider the element $z_I = (1, 0) \in C$. We have

$$zz_I = (a, b)(1, 0) = (a \cdot 1 - b \cdot 0, a \cdot 0 + 1 \cdot b) = (a, b) = z.$$

Similarly,

$$z_I z = (1, 0)(a, b) = (1 \cdot a - 0 \cdot b, 1 \cdot b + a \cdot 0) = (a, b) = z,$$

though this follows equally well from the former result together with F-10.

We say that $(1, 0)$ is the **identity element for multiplication** in the set C.

Proof of F-11. Let $z = (a, b)$. Since $a \in R$ and $b \in R$, and $(a, b) \neq (0, 0)$, we have $a^2 + b^2 \neq 0$. Now consider the element

$$z^{-1} = \left(\frac{a}{a^2 + b^2}, \frac{-b}{a^2 + b^2} \right) \in C. \tag{1}$$

By direct computation, we obtain

$$zz^{-1} = (a, b)\left(\frac{a}{a^2 + b^2}, \frac{-b}{a^2 + b^2} \right) = \left(\frac{a^2 + b^2}{a^2 + b^2}, \frac{-ab + ab}{a^2 + b^2} \right) = (1, 0),$$

as desired. By F-10, we observe also that

$$z^{-1}z = (1, 0),$$

thus completing the proof of F-11. We say that z^{-1}, given by (1), is the **multiplicative inverse** of $z = (a, b)$.

You might wonder how the expression (1) entered the picture. Actually, it can be found by solving the equation

$$(a, b)(x, y) = (1, 0)$$

for (x, y), a task that is left as an exercise.

Let us recapitulate. We started with the set C of ordered pairs of real numbers, defined equality and the operations of addition and multiplica-

The field properties for C

tion on the elements of this set, and then, one-by-one, established as theorems the properties F-1 through F-11 that characterize a field. Thus we have shown that the elements of R^2, when viewed in this way, are the elements of a field.

EXERCISE 12.1

Write each sum as an ordered pair (a, b).

1. $(3, 6) + (2, 1)$ 2. $(7, 1) + (3, -5)$ 3. $(-6, -2) + (0, 1)$

4. $(3, -2) + (-2, 0)$ 5. $(0, 7) + (3, 0)$ 6. $(-2, -1) + (2, 1)$

7. $(2, 3) + (1, 1)$ 8. $(4, 5) + (0, 0)$

Write each product as an ordered pair (a, b).

9. $(1, 1) \cdot (1, 1)$ 10. $(1, 0) \cdot (2, 1)$ 11. $(2, 3) \cdot (4, 1)$

12. $(3, 1) \cdot (0, 2)$ 13. $(2, 2) \cdot (3, 4)$ 14. $(-2, 1) \cdot (1, 3)$

15. $(3, -2) \cdot (1, -1)$ 16. $(0, 1) \cdot (1, 0)$ 17. $(3, 4) \cdot (1, 1)$

18. $(0, 1) \cdot (0, 2)$

19. Write the sum $(a_1, 0) + (a_2, 0)$ as an ordered pair. Write the product $(a_1, 0) \cdot (a_2, 0)$ as an ordered pair.

20. Use Definition 12.1 to show that since the equality postulates E-1 through E-4 of Chapter 1 hold in the set R of real numbers, they hold also in the set C.

21. Make a chart showing F-1 through F-11 for the set R of real numbers compared with the corresponding properties of the set C of ordered pairs (a, b). Start the chart thus:

     If $a, b \in R$, then: If $(a, b), (c, d) \in C$, then:

         F-1 $a + b \in R$ $(a, b) + (c, d) \in C$ *Closure law for addition.*

Let $z_1, z_2, z_3 \in C$.

22. Show that $(z_1 + z_2) + z_3 = z_1 + (z_2 + z_3)$.

23. Show that $z_1 + z_2 = z_2 + z_1$.

24. Show that $z_1 z_2 \in C$.

25. Show that $(z_1 \cdot z_2) \cdot z_3 = z_1 \cdot (z_2 \cdot z_3)$.

26. Show that $z_1 \cdot (z_2 + z_3) = z_1 \cdot z_2 + z_1 \cdot z_3$.

27. Solve the equation $(a, b)(x, y) = (1, 0)$ for (x, y), given that $(a, b) \neq (0, 0)$.

28. Show that if $z_1 \cdot z_2 = (0, 0)$, then either $z_1 = (0, 0)$, $z_2 = (0, 0)$, or both.

12.2 SOME ALGEBRA OF ORDERED PAIRS

We can extend the work of the preceding section to explore a few of the proper-

Subtraction and division in C

ties of the field of ordered pairs in C. First, let us define two more operations, subtraction and division, for the field C, in terms of addition and multiplication, respectively.

DEFINITION 12.5 *If $z_1 \in C$ and $z_2 \in C$, then*

$$z_1 - z_2 = z_1 + (-z_2).$$

You will recall that if $z_2 = (a, b)$ then $-z_2 = (-a, -b)$. The number $z_1 - z_2$ is called the **difference** of z_1 and z_2, and is viewed as the result of **subtracting** z_2 from z_1.

DEFINITION 12.6 *If $z_1 \in C$ and $z_2 \in C$, and $z_2 \neq (0, 0)$, then*

$$\frac{z_1}{z_2} = z_1 \cdot z_2^{-1}.$$

You will recall from Equation (1) in Section 12.1 that if $z_2 = (a, b)$, then

$$z_2^{-1} = \left(\frac{a}{a^2 + b^2}, \frac{-b}{a^2 + b^2} \right).$$

The number z_1/z_2 is called the **quotient** of z_1 and z_2, and is viewed as the result of **dividing** z_1 by z_2.

Examples.

a. $(2, 3) - (5, 6) = (2, 3) + (-5, -6) = (-3, -3)$

b. $\dfrac{(2, 3)}{(5, 6)} = (2, 3)\left(\dfrac{5}{25 + 36}, \dfrac{-6}{25 + 36} \right) = \left(\dfrac{2 \cdot 5 + 3 \cdot 6}{61}, \dfrac{-2 \cdot 6 + 5 \cdot 3}{61} \right) = \left(\dfrac{28}{61}, \dfrac{3}{61} \right)$

It might be noted that the foregoing eefinitions of subtraction and division in the field C are analogous to the respective definitions given in Chapter 1 for subtraction and division in the field R of real numbers. Indeed, these definitions might be extended to *any* field, since in any field each element has an additive inverse, and each element other than the zero element has a multiplicative inverse.

We can now obtain a considerable advantage from our structural study of algebraic systems. In Section 1.5, many properties of the field **The structure** R of real numbers were established. Since, however, the **of algebraic** theorems stated there were derived exclusively from the field **systems** postulates along with the equality postulates, and did not otherwise depend on the fact that we were dealing with real numbers, it follows that the results are valid in any field—in particular, in the field C. Thus from Theorem 1.3 and Problem 22 of Exercise 1.4, we conclude that for $z \in C$, the additive inverse and (except for the zero element z_0) the multiplicative inverse are unique.

The remaining results of Section 1.5 also extend, of course, to the field C. As an example, let us consider the analogue of Theorem 1.10, the *fundamental principle of fractions*, for elements of C.

THEOREM 12.3 *If z_1, z_2, and z_3 are elements of C, and z_2 and z_3 are not the zero element z_0 then*

$$\frac{z_1}{z_2} = \frac{z_1 z_3}{z_2 z_3}.$$

To show an application of this theorem, let us adopt the following definition.

DEFINITION 12.7 *The **conjugate** of $z = (a, b) \in C$, denoted by $\bar{z}$, is*

$$\bar{z} = (a, -b).$$

Thus, the conjugate of $(2, 5)$ is $(2, -5)$, and if $z = (-2, -7)$, then $\bar{z} = (-2, 7)$.

Now, for $(c, d) \neq (0, 0)$, the quotient $(a, b)/(c, d)$, which **Determination** we already know is an element of C, can be written as an ordered **of a quotient** pair by multiplying the numerator and the denominator of **in** C $(a, b)/(c, d)$ by the conjugate of the denominator $(c, -d)$. The following theorem is helpful.

THEOREM 12.4 *If $(a, b) \in C$ and $c \neq 0$, then*

$$\frac{(a, b)}{(c, 0)} = \left(\frac{a}{c}, \frac{b}{c}\right).$$

Proof. From Definition 12.6 and Equation (1) in Section 12.1,

$$\frac{(a, b)}{(c, 0)} = (a, b)(c, 0)^{-1} = (a, b)\left(\frac{c}{c^2 + 0^2}, \frac{0}{c^2 + 0^2}\right) = (a, b)\left(\frac{1}{c}, 0\right),$$

from which, by Definition 12.3, we obtain

$$\frac{(a, b)}{(c, 0)} = \left(\frac{a}{c}, \frac{b}{c}\right).$$

Example. Write the quotient $\dfrac{(3, -2)}{(5, 1)}$ as an ordered pair, by first using Theorem 12.3 and then using Theorem 12.4.

Solution. By Theorem 12.3 and Definition 12.3, we have

$$\frac{(3, -2)}{(5, 1)} = \frac{(3, -2)(5, -1)}{(5, 1)(5, -1)} = \frac{(15 - 2, -3 - 10)}{(25 + 1, 0)} = \frac{(13, -13)}{(26, 0)},$$

from which we obtain, by Theorem 12.4,

$$\frac{(13, -13)}{(26, 0)} = \left(\frac{13}{26}, \frac{-13}{26}\right) = \left(\frac{1}{2}, -\frac{1}{2}\right).$$

EXERCISE 12.2

Write each difference as an ordered pair.

1. $(4, 2) - (1, 1)$ 2. $(-3, 4) - (0, 5)$ 3. $(-6, 1) - (3, 0)$

4. $(0, 1) - (6, 6)$ 5. $(4, -4) - (-4, 4)$ 6. $(0, 0) - (2, -3)$

Write each quotient as an ordered pair. Use Definition 12.6,

$$\frac{(a, b)}{(c, d)} = (a, b) \cdot (c, d)^{-1}.$$

7. $\dfrac{(4, 3)}{(2, 2)}$ 8. $\dfrac{(6, 1)}{(1, 3)}$ 9. $\dfrac{(2, 1)}{(-1, 3)}$

10. $\dfrac{(6, -3)}{(4, 1)}$ 11. $\dfrac{(-2, -2)}{(1, 1)}$ 12. $\dfrac{(0, 0)}{(3, 3)}$

13. Write the product $\dfrac{(4, 1)}{(1, 2)} \cdot \dfrac{(-1, 3)}{(6, 1)}$ as an ordered pair. *Hint*: Use any of the field properties.

14. Write the product $\dfrac{(0, 1)}{(3, -1)} \cdot \dfrac{(2, 0)}{(2, 1)}$ as an ordered pair.

Write each quotient as an ordered pair by first multiplying the numerator and denominator by the conjugate of the denominator.

15. $\dfrac{(4, 1)}{(-1, 2)}$ 16. $\dfrac{(6, -1)}{(0, 4)}$ 17. $\dfrac{(2, 3)}{(-1, -1)}$

18. $\dfrac{(0, 1)}{(2, -3)}$ 19. $\dfrac{(4, -4)}{(2, -2)}$ 20. $\dfrac{(0, 0)}{(-2, 3)}$

21. Show that $\dfrac{(a, b)}{(a, b)} = (1, 0)$ for every nonzero ordered pair (a, b).

22. Show that if z_1, z_2, and z_3 are elements of C, and z_2 and z_3 are not $(0, 0)$, then

$$\frac{z_1}{z_2} = \frac{z_1 z_3}{z_2 z_3}.$$

23. Show that $\overline{z_1 + z_2} = \overline{z_1} + \overline{z_2}$.   24. Show that $\overline{z_1 \cdot z_2} = \overline{z_1} \cdot \overline{z_2}$.

25. Show that the set of ordered pairs of the form $(a, 0)$, $a \in R$, with the operations of addition and multiplication in C, constitutes a field. (Show that the field postulates are all satisfied in this set.)

12.3 COMPLEX NUMBERS

Let us turn next to a practical interpretation of the set C when this set is subject to the properties discussed in Sections 12.1 and 12.2. First recall that, graphically, the set of ordered pairs of real numbers (a, b) is in one-to-one correspondence with the points in the geometric (x, y)-plane, just as the set R of real numbers a is in one-to-one correspondence with the points on the x-axis. Thus, the subset $\{(a, 0) \,|\, a \in R\}$ of C can be considered as corresponding in a one-to-one way to the set R.

The set R of real numbers as a subset of C

Moreover, from Definitions 12.3, 12.5, 12.6, and Equation (1), page 287, we have the following:

$$\left.\begin{aligned}
(a_1, 0) + (a_2, 0) &= (a_1 + a_2, 0), \\
(a_1, 0) \cdot (a_2, 0) &= (a_1 a_2, 0), \\
(a_1, 0) - (a_2, 0) &= (a_1 - a_2, 0), \\
\frac{(a_1, 0)}{(a_2, 0)} &= \left(\frac{a_1}{a_2}, 0\right), \quad a_2 \neq 0.
\end{aligned}\right\} \quad (1)$$

The behavior exhibited under the four basic operations by the first components a of the numbers, $(a, 0) \in C$, and by the numbers $a \in R$, is identical. Let us, then, identify $(a, 0)$ and a by means of the following.

DEFINITION 12.8 *The element $(a, 0)$ in the set C is **identified** with the element a in the set R, and we write*

$$a = (a, 0).$$

By virtue of the identical behavior under the basic operations, as exhibited in (1), this one-to-one correspondence is an isomorphism. It should be noted, of course, that a and $(a, 0)$ actually are *conceptually* different, but the identification is useful and should not be confusing. Under this convention, we consider that $R \subset C$.

Now, consider the subset of C consisting of all ordered pairs of the form $(0, b)$, with $b \neq 0$. In particular, observe that if we square $(0, b)$, we obtain

$$(0, b)^2 = (0, b) \cdot (0, b) = (-b^2, 0).$$

Since we have agreed to identify $(-b^2, 0)$ with the real number $-b^2$, and since

Elements of
C that have
negative
squares

$b^2 > 0$ for every real number $b \neq 0$, we have $-b^2 < 0$ for every such number. Thus we see that the set C provides us with a square root, $(0, b)$, for each negative real number $-b^2$! Moreover, since

$$(0, -b)^2 = (0, -b)\cdot(0, -b) = (-b^2, 0),$$

C provides us with *two* such square roots. That is, $(0, b)$ and $(0, -b)$ are square roots of $(-b^2, 0)$, or $-b^2$. The square roots of nonnegative real numbers are in $\{(a, 0) \mid a \in R\}$, and those of negative real numbers are in $\{(0, b) \mid b \in R, b \neq 0\}$. As a special case, the square roots of $(-1, 0)$, or -1, are $(0, 1)$ and $(0, -1)$. Let us adopt the following convention.

DEFINITION 12.9   *In the set C,*

$$i = (0, 1).$$

With this definition, and with the convention $b = (b, 0)$ of Definition 12.8,

$$bi = (b, 0)(0, 1) = (0, b).$$

The numbers bi, with $b \in R$, $b \neq 0$, are the numbers that, in Chapter 1, we called **pure imaginary.**

In accordance with this definition, we can extend our symbolism $\sqrt{b^2} = |b|$, which was first introduced on page 59.

DEFINITION 12.10   *In the set C, for $b \in R$,*

$$\sqrt{-b^2} = |b|i.$$

In particular,

$$\sqrt{-1} = 1\cdot i = i.$$

Representation
of (a, b) in the
form a+bi

Any ordered pair (a, b) can now be represented by the sum $(a, 0) + (0, b)$, so that, in our new notation, for $a, b \in R$,

$$(a, b) = a + bi = a + b\sqrt{-1}.$$

If $b \neq 0$, then as in Chapter 1 we say that $a + bi$ is an **imaginary number.**

When the foregoing viewpoint is taken of C, then C is called the set of **complex numbers.** The number i is called the **imaginary unit,** a is called the **real part** of $a + bi$, and b is called its **imaginary part.** We write

$$a = \text{Re } (a + bi), \quad b = \text{Im } (a + bi).$$

Definitons 12.2, 12.3, 12.5, and 12.6 can now be expressed using $a + bi$.

DEFINITION 12.11 *If $a_1, b_1, a_2, b_2 \in R$ and $i = (0, 1) = \sqrt{-1}$, then*

I $a_1 + b_1 i = a_2 + b_2 i$ *if and only if $a_1 = a_2$ and $b_1 = b_2$,*

II $(a_1 + b_1 i) + (a_2 + b_2 i) = (a_1 + a_2) + (b_1 + b_2)i,$

III $(a_1 + b_1 i) \cdot (a_2 + b_2 i) = (a_1 a_2 - b_1 b_2) + (a_1 b_2 + a_2 b_1)i,$

IV $(a_1 + b_1 i) - (a_2 + b_2 i) = (a_1 - a_2) + (b_1 - b_2)i,$

V $\dfrac{a_1 + b_1 i}{a_2 + b_2 i} = \dfrac{a_1 a_2 + b_1 b_2}{a_2^2 + b_2^2} + \dfrac{b_1 a_2 - a_1 b_2}{a_2^2 + b_2^2} i$ *(a_2, b_2 not both 0).*

It can be shown that Definition 12.11-V is consistent with Theorem 12.3. Thus we may rewrite expressions involving complex numbers in the form $a + bi$ in the same way that we rewrote real polynomial expressions, except that i^2 is replaced with -1.

Examples.

a. $(2 + 3i) + (6 - 2i) = (2 + 6) + (3 - 2)i = 8 + i$

b. $(2 - i)(1 + 3i) = 2 + 6i - i - 3i^2 = 5 + 5i$

c. $i - (2 + 3i) = (0 - 2) + (1 - 3)i = -2 - 2i$

d. $\dfrac{4 - i}{1 + i} = \dfrac{(4 - i)(1 - i)}{(1 + i)(1 - i)} = \dfrac{4 - 5i + i^2}{1 - i^2} = \dfrac{3}{2} - \dfrac{5}{2}i$

Observe that, in example (d) above, Theorem 12.3 was applied to multiply both $4 - i$ and $1 + i$ by $1 - i$, the conjugate of $1 + i$.

In accordance with Definition 12.10, $\sqrt{-b} = i\sqrt{b}$, $b > 0$. The symbol
$\sqrt{-b}$, $b > 0$, should be used with care since certain relation-

| The symbol |
| $\sqrt{-b}$, $b>0$ |

ships involving the square root symbol that are valid for real numbers are not valid when the symbol does not represent a real number. For instance,

$$\sqrt{2}\,\sqrt{3} = \sqrt{6} = \sqrt{(2)(3)},$$

but

$$\sqrt{-2}\,\sqrt{-3} = (i\sqrt{2})(i\sqrt{3}) = i^2\sqrt{6} = -\sqrt{6} \neq \sqrt{(-2)(-3)}.$$

To avoid difficulty with this point, you should rewrite all expressions of the form $\sqrt{-b}$, $b > 0$, in the form $i\sqrt{b}$ before rewriting expressions involving complex numbers.

Examples.

a. $3 + \sqrt{-5} = 3 + \sqrt{5}\,i$

b. $(2 + \sqrt{-3})(2 - \sqrt{-3}) = (2 + \sqrt{3}i)(2 - \sqrt{3}i) = 4 - 3i^2 = 7$

c. $\dfrac{1}{1 + \sqrt{-4}} = \dfrac{1(1 - 2i)}{(1 + 2i)(1 - 2i)} = \dfrac{1 - 2i}{1 - 4i^2} = \dfrac{1}{5} - \dfrac{2}{5}i$

The number of zeros of a polynomial over C

In Section 5.2, it was observed that every polynomial function of degree $n \geq 1$ over the field of complex numbers has exactly n zeros. This is a consequence of the following, which is called the **fundamental theorem of algebra.**

THEOREM 12.5 *Every polynomial function of degree $n \geq 1$ over the field C of complex numbers has at least one complex zero.*

The proof of this theorem involves concepts beyond those available to us and is omitted.

As an extension of Theorem 12.5, we have the following consequent result.

THEOREM 12.6 *Every polynomial, of degree $n \geq 1$, over the field C of complex numbers can be expressed as a product of n linear factors.*

Proof. Let $P(x) = a_0 x^n + a_1 x^{n-1} + \cdots + a_n$, where $a_i \in C$, $a_0 \neq 0$, $x \in C$, and $n \in N$, $n \geq 1$. Then, since this equation defines a polynomial function, by the fundamental theorem of algebra there is at least one real or complex x, say x_1, such that

$$P(x_1) = a_0 x_1^n + a_1 x_1^{n-1} + \cdots + a_n = 0.$$

By the factor theorem, which by the field properties holds in C as well as in P,

$$P(x) = (x - x_1)Q_{n-1}(x),$$

where $Q_{n-1}(x)$ is of degree $n - 1$. Again, by the fundamental theorem, if $n - 1 \geq 1$, there must exist an $x_2 \in C$ such that $Q_{n-1}(x_2) = 0$. Hence we can write

$$P(x) = (x - x_1)(x - x_2)Q_{n-2}(x),$$

where $Q_{n-2}(x)$ is a polynomial of degree $n - 2$. If this factoring process is performed n times, the result is

$$P(x) = (x - x_1)(x - x_2) \cdots (x - x_n)Q_0(x),$$

where $Q_0(x)$ consists solely of a_0, and the theorem is proved.

If a factor $(x - x_i)$ occurs k times in such a linear factorization, then x_i is said to be a zero of $P(x)$ of **multiplicity** k. With this agreement, Theorem 12.6 shows that every polynomial function defined by a polynomial $P(x)$ of degree n with complex coefficients has exactly n zeros.

Zeros and roots

Note that, as observed in Section 4.4, any theorem stated in terms of zeros of polynomial functions applies to roots (solutions) of polynomial equations, and vice versa; a *zero* of

$$\{(x, P(x)) \mid P(x) = a_0 x^n + a_1 x^{n-1} + \cdots + a_n\}$$

is a *solution* or *root* of $P(x) = 0$.

|Imaginary zeros of real polynomials in conjugate pairs| We can use Theorem 12.6, the fact that if $a + bi$ is a zero of a polynomial P with real coefficients then so is $a - bi$ (Problem 17, Exercise 13.1), and the theorems in Chapter 5 applicable to real zeros to help us study zeros of polynomial functions over R.|

Example. Find the zeros of $\{(x, P(x)) \mid P(x) = x^3 - 2x^2 + 3x - 6\}$.

Solution. The only possible rational zeros of $P(x)$ are $1, -1, 2, -2, 3, -3, 6,$ and -6. Using synthetic division, we obtain:

	1	−2	3	−6
1	1	−1	2	−4
−1	1	−3	6	−12
2	1	0	3	0

From the entries in the last row, we note that $x - 2$ is a factor of $P(x)$, and so is $x^2 + 3$. Hence we can conclude that

$$P(x) = (x - 2)(x^2 + 3)$$
$$= (x - 2)(x - 3i)(x + 3i).$$

For zeros of P, then, we have solutions of $(x - 2)(x - 3i)(x + 3i) = 0$, which are $2, 3i,$ and $-3i$.

EXERCISE   12.3

Write each ordered pair (complex number) in the form $a + bi$.

1. (2, 6)   2. (−3, 4)   3. (5, −2)   4. (0, 6)

5. (−7, −3)   6. (−3, 2)   7. (4, 0)   8. (0, 0)

Write each complex number as an ordered pair.

9. $2 + 3i$ 10. $4 - 2i$ 11. $-3 + i$ 12. $-6 - 3i$

13. $4i$ 14. 0   15. 7   16. $-i$

17–24. Write the conjugate of each complex number in 9–16 in the form $a + bi$.

Find real numbers x and y for which the following are true.

Example. $(x - 2i)^2 = yi$

Solution. Write each member in the form $a + bi$.

$$x^2 - 4xi + 4i^2 = yi$$
$$(x^2 - 4) - 4xi = yi$$

For equality,

$$x^2 - 4 = 0 \quad \text{and} \quad -4x = y.$$

Therefore, $x = 2$ or -2. If $x = 2$, then $y = -8$; and if $x = -2$, then $y = 8$. The desired real numbers are 2 and -8, and -2 and 8.

25. $2x - yi = 3 + 2i$ 26. $-2i = 3x + yi$ 27. $4 + xi = x^2 - yi$

28. $x + 9i = y + y^2 i$ 29. $(x + 3i)^2 = 2yi$ 30. $(x - 2i)^2 = 3x + yi$

Write each of the following in the form $a + bi$.

31. $(2 + 4i) + (3 + i)$ 32. $(4 - i) - (6 - 2i)$ 33. $(2 - i) + (3 - 2i)$

34. $(2 + i) - (4 - 2i)$ 35. $3 - (4 + 2i)$ 36. $(2 - 6i) - 3$

37. $\dfrac{2}{1 - i}$ 38. $\dfrac{6}{3 + 2i}$ 39. $\dfrac{2 + i}{1 - 3i}$

40. $\dfrac{3 - i}{2i}$ 41. $(1 - 3i)^2$ 42. $(2 + i)^2$

43. $(1 - i)^2(1 + i)$ 44. $(3 - 4i)^2(1 - i)^2$ 45. $4 - \sqrt{-7}$

46. $2 + \sqrt{-1}$ 47. $5 - \sqrt{-4}$ 48. $\sqrt{-9}$

49. $\sqrt{-7}\,\sqrt{-1}$ 50. $\sqrt{-4}\,\sqrt{-5}$ 51. $\dfrac{2}{1 + \sqrt{-1}}$

52. $\dfrac{3}{1 - \sqrt{-4}}$ 53. $\dfrac{2 + \sqrt{-1}}{3 - \sqrt{-4}}$ 54. $\dfrac{\sqrt{-3}}{1 - \sqrt{-7}}$

In Problems 55–62, find all complex zeros.

Example. $\{(x, P(x)) \mid P(x) = x^2 - 2x + 4\}$

Solution.   Using the quadratic formula on the defining equation for $P(x) = 0$, we have

$$x = \frac{-(-2) \pm \sqrt{(-2)^2 - 4(1)(4)}}{2}$$

$$= \frac{2 \pm 2i\sqrt{3}}{2} = 1 \pm i\sqrt{3}.$$

Thus, zeros of the function are $1 + i\sqrt{3}$ and $1 - i\sqrt{3}$.

55. $\{(x, P(x)) \mid P(x) = x^2 + 1\}$ 56. $\{(x, P(x)) \mid P(x) = x^2 + x + 1\}$

57. $\{(x, P(x)) \mid P(x) = 2x^2 - 3x + 1\}$ 58. $\{(x, P(x)) \mid P(x) = 3x^2 - 2x + 4\}$

59. $\{(x, P(x)) \mid P(x) = 3x^3 - 5x^2 - 14x - 4\}$ *Hint:* First find all rational zeros.

60. $\{(x, P(x)) \mid P(x) = x^3 - 4x^2 - 5x + 14\}$

61. $\{(x, P(x)) \mid P(x) = 2x^4 + 3x^3 + 2x^2 - 1\}$

62. $\{(x, P(x)) \mid P(x) = 8x^4 - 22x^3 + 29x^2 - 66x + 15\}$

63. Factor the polynomial $2x^3 + 3x^2 + 2x + 3$ over C.

64. Factor the polynomial $x^4 - 6x^3 - 3x^2 - 24x - 28$ over C.

65. Show that $\sqrt{3}$ is irrational. *Hint:* Consider the equation $x^2 - 3 = 0$.

66. Show that $\sqrt[3]{2}$ is irrational.

12.4 TRIGONOMETRIC FORM OF COMPLEX NUMBERS

> **Complex numbers and points in the plane**

In Chapter 4, we used Cartesian coordinates to establish a one-to-one correspondence between the set of ordered pairs (a, b) in R^2 and the set of points $P(a, b)$ in the geometric plane. Since a complex number can also be represented by an ordered pair (a, b), each point in the plane can be viewed as the graph of a complex number. Thus, the graph of the complex number (a, b), or $a + bi$, is as shown in Figure 12.1 Since the real part of $a + bi$, $a = \text{Re } (a + bi)$, is taken as the abscissa, or x-coordinate, of P, in this context the x-axis is called the **real axis.** Similarly, since the imaginary part, $b = \text{Im } (a + bi)$, is taken as the ordinate or y-coordinate of P, the y-axis is called the **imaginary axis.**

Just as we sometimes speak, for instance, of the point $(2, 3)$, meaning of course the point having coordinates 2 and 3, we likewise speak of the point $2 + 3i$, meaning the point representing the complex number $2 + 3i$.

A plane on which complex numbers are thus represented is often called a **complex plane.** It is also sometimes called an **Argand plane**, after the French mathematician Jean Robert Argand (1768–1822) who systematically used it, or a **Gauss plane**, after the great German mathematician Carl Friedrich Gauss (1777–1855).

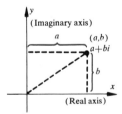

Figure 12.1

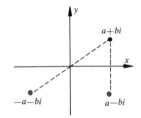

Figure 12.2

> **Graph of the conjugate and of the negative of a complex number**

A complex number $z = a + bi$, its conjugate $\bar{z} = a - bi$, and its negative $-z = -a - bi$ are represented in Figure 12.2. It is evident that $\bar{z}$ is the reflection of z in the real axis, that $-z$ is the reflection of z in the origin, and that $-z$ is the reflection of $\bar{z}$ in the imaginary axis.

Since each nonzero complex number $z = a + bi$ lies on a ray with the origin as endpoint (Figure 12.3), we can associate with each z two useful concepts.

DEFINITION 12.12 *The **absolute value** or **modulus** of the complex number* $z = a + bi$ *is denoted by* r, $|z|$, *or* $|a + bi|$, *and is given by*

$$r = |z| = |a + bi| = \sqrt{a^2 + b^2}.$$

Thus the modulus $|a + bi|$ is just the distance from the origin to the point $a + bi$.

DEFINITION 12.13 *An **argument**, or **amplitude**, of the complex number* $z = a + bi$, *denoted by* $\arg (a + bi)$, *is an angle* θ *with initial side the positive x-axis and terminal side the ray from the origin containing* $a + bi$.

Note that if θ is an argument of $a + bi$, then so is $\theta + 2k\pi^R$, or $\theta + k360°$, for each $k \in J$. For $a + bi = 0$, that is, for $a^2 + b^2 = 0$, any angle θ might be used as $\arg (a + bi)$. Also if θ is an argument of $a + bi$, then $b/a = \tan \theta$ when $a \neq 0$.

Because any ordered pair (a, b) can be written in the form $(r \cos \theta, r \sin \theta)$, where r is the modulus $\sqrt{a^2 + b^2}$ of $a + bi$ and θ is an argument of $a + bi$, it follows that any complex number $a + bi$ can be written in the form

$$r \cos \theta + ir \sin \theta, \quad \text{or} \quad r(\cos \theta + i \sin \theta),$$

General trigonometric form for a complex number

which is called the **trigonometric form** or **polar form** for a complex number (see Figure 12.4). More generally, using degree measure for angles, we have

$$a + bi = r[\cos (\theta + k360°) + i \sin (\theta + k360°)], \quad k \in J.$$

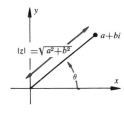

Figure 12.3

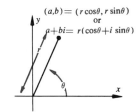

Figure 12.4

A convenient abbreviation that is used for the expression $\cos \theta + i \sin \theta$ is **cis** θ (read " cosine θ plus i sine θ "), so that we can write

$$a + bi = r \text{ cis } (\theta + k360°), \quad k \in J.$$

We ordinarily use for θ the angle of smallest nonnegative measure that is a solution of $a + bi = r$ cis θ.

Example. Represent $1 + \sqrt{3}i$ in trigonometric form.

Solution. $r = |1 + \sqrt{3}i| = \sqrt{1 + 3} = 2$; $\tan \theta = \sqrt{3}/1$, and $\theta = 60°$. Therefore,

$$1 + \sqrt{3}i = 2(\cos 60° + i \sin 60°) = 2\text{cis } 60°.$$

Example.   Represent 4 cis 225° graphically, and write the number in rectangular form.

Solution.

$$a = r \cos \theta = 4 \left(-\frac{\sqrt{2}}{2} \right) = -2\sqrt{2},$$

$$b = r \sin \theta = 4 \left(-\frac{\sqrt{2}}{2} \right) = -2\sqrt{2},$$

and

$$a + bi = -2\sqrt{2} - 2\sqrt{2}i.$$

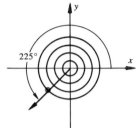

| **Products and quotients in trigonometric form** | Products and quotients of complex numbers can be found quite easily when the complex numbers are given in trigonometric form, as shown by the following results. |

THEOREM 12.7   *If z_1, $z_2 \in C$, with $z_1 = r_1$ cis θ_1 and $z_2 = r_2$ cis θ_2, then*

I $z_1 \cdot z_2 = r_1 r_2$ cis $(\theta_1 + \theta_2)$,

II $\dfrac{z_1}{z_2} = \dfrac{r_1}{r_2}$ cis $(\theta_1 - \theta_2)$ $(z_2 \neq 0 + 0i)$.

We shall prove only Part I here and leave the proof of Part II as an exercise.

Proof of Theorem 12.7-I   We have

$$z_1 = r_1 (\cos \theta_1 + i \sin \theta_1) \quad \text{and} \quad z_2 = r_2 (\cos \theta_2 + i \sin \theta_2),$$

from which

$$z_1 \cdot z_2 = r_1(\cos \theta_1 + i \sin \theta_1) \cdot r_2(\cos \theta_2 + i \sin \theta_2)$$
$$= r_1 \cdot r_2 \cdot [\cos \theta_1 \cos \theta_2 + i \cos \theta_1 \sin \theta_2 + i \sin \theta_1 \cos \theta_2 + i^2 \sin \theta_1 \sin \theta_2]$$
$$= r_1 \cdot r_2 \cdot [(\cos \theta_1 \cos \theta_2 - \sin \theta_1 \sin \theta_2) + i(\cos \theta_1 \sin \theta_2 + \sin \theta_1 \cos \theta_2)].$$

By Theorems 7.3 and 7.6, the right-hand member can be written

$$r_1 r_2 [\cos (\theta_1 + \theta_2) + i \sin (\theta_1 + \theta_2)],$$

so that

$$z_1 \cdot z_2 = r_1 r_2 \text{ cis } (\theta_1 + \theta_2),$$

as was to be shown.

Example.   Write the product 3 cis 80° · 5 cis 40° as a complex number in the form $a + bi$.

Solution.   By Theorem 12.7-I,

$$3 \text{ cis } 80° \cdot 5 \text{ cis } 40° = 15 \text{ cis } 120° = 15(\cos 120° + i \sin 120°).$$

Since $\cos 120° = -\dfrac{1}{2}$ and $\sin 120° = \dfrac{\sqrt{3}}{2}$, we have

$$15 (\cos 120° + i \sin 120°) = 15 \left(-\frac{1}{2} + \frac{\sqrt{3}}{2} i \right) = -\frac{15}{2} + \frac{15\sqrt{3}}{2} i.$$

Example.   Write the quotient $\dfrac{8 \text{ cis } 540°}{2 \text{ cis } 225°}$ as a complex number in the form $a + bi$.

Solution.   By Theorem 12.7-II,

$$\frac{8 \text{ cis } 540°}{2 \text{ cis } 225°} = \frac{8}{2} \text{ cis } (540° - 225°) = 4 \text{ cis } 315°$$

$$= 4 (\cos 315° + i \sin 315°).$$

Since $\cos 315° = 1/\sqrt{2}$ and $\sin 315° = -1/\sqrt{2}$, we have

$$4 (\cos 315° + i \sin 315°) = 4 \left(\frac{1}{\sqrt{2}} - \frac{1}{\sqrt{2}} i \right) = 2\sqrt{2} - 2\sqrt{2} i.$$

EXERCISE   12.4

Graph each complex number, its conjugate, its negative, and the negative of its conjugate. Draw line segments joining each pair of these four points.

1. $2 + 3i$ 2. $-3 + 4i$ 3. $4 - i$

4. $-2 - i$ 5. $4i$ 6. $-3i$

Write without absolute-value notation.

Examples.

a. $|-3|$ b. $|2 + 5i|$ c. $|(-3, 2)|$

Solutions.   By Definition 12.12,

a. $\sqrt{(-3)^2} = 3$ b. $\sqrt{2^2 + 5^2} = \sqrt{29}$ c. $\sqrt{(-3)^2 + (2)^2} = \sqrt{13}$

7. $|4|$ 8. $|-2|$ 9. $|3 + 2i|$

10. $|4 - i|$ 11. $|(2, 0)|$ 12. $|(3, -5)|$

13. $|(-2, -1)|$ 14. $|(-7, -1)|$

Write each complex number in the form $r \text{ cis } \theta$.

15. $3 + 3i$ 16. $2 - 2i$ 17. 5

18. $-7i$ 19. $2\sqrt{3} - 2i$ 20. $-3\sqrt{3} - 3i$

Write each complex number in the form $a + bi$.

21. $4 \text{ cis } 240°$ 22. $3 \text{ cis } 300°$ 23. $6 \text{ cis } (-30°)$

24. $5 \text{ cis } 180°$ 25. $12 \text{ cis } 420°$ 26. $10 \text{ cis } (-480°)$

For each given pair of complex numbers z_1 and z_2, find (a) $z_1 \cdot z_2$ and (b) z_1/z_2. Express each result in the form $a + bi$. Use Table VI as needed.

27. $z_1 = 3$ cis $90°$ and $z_2 = \sqrt{2}$ cis $45°$

28. $z_1 = 4$ cis $30°$ and $z_2 = 2$ cis $60°$

29. $z_1 = 6$ cis $150°$ and $z_2 = 18$ cis $570°$

30. $z_1 = 14$ cis $210°$ and $z_2 = 2$ cis $120°$

31. $z_1 = -3 + i$ and $z_2 = -2 - 4i$

32. $z_1 = 2 + 3i$ and $z_2 = 2 + 3i$

33. Write $\left(-\dfrac{1}{2} - \dfrac{i\sqrt{3}}{2}\right)^3$ in the form $a + bi$.

34. Write $\left(-\dfrac{1}{2} + \dfrac{i\sqrt{3}}{2}\right)^3$ in the form $a + bi$.

35. Prove that the sum and product of two conjugate complex numbers are both real.

36. Prove that $|z_1 \cdot z_2| = |z_1| \cdot |z_2|$.

37. Show that the conjugate of the complex number r cis θ is r cis $(-\theta)$.

38. Show that if $a + bi = r$ cis θ, then $(a + bi)^2 = r^2$ cis 2θ.

39. Use the result of Problem 38 to show that if $a + bi = r$ cis θ, then

$$(a + bi)^3 = r^3 \text{ cis } 3\theta.$$

40. Show that if z_1 and z_2 are complex numbers, then $z_1 \cdot z_2 = 0 + 0i$ if and only if either z_1 or z_2 or both are equal to $0 + 0i$.

12.5 DE MOIVRE'S THEOREM—POWERS AND ROOTS

Since $a + bi = r$ cis θ, an application of Theorem 12.7-I to $(a + bi)^2$ results in

$$(a + bi)^2 = (r \text{ cis } \theta)(r \text{ cis } \theta) = r^2 \text{ cis } 2\theta. \tag{1}$$

Powers of complex numbers

Because

$$(a + bi)^3 = (a + bi)^2(a + bi),$$

from (1) we have

$$(a + bi)^3 = (r^2 \text{ cis } 2\theta)(r \text{ cis } \theta) = r^3 \text{ cis } 3\theta.$$

In a similar way, we can show that

$$(a + bi)^4 = (r^3 \text{ cis } 3\theta)(r \text{ cis } \theta) = r^4 \text{ cis } 4\theta,$$

and it seems plausible to assert the following.

THEOREM 12.8　*If $z \in C$, $z = r$ cis θ and $n \in N$, then*

$$z^n = r^n \text{ cis } n\theta.$$

The proof of this result, called **De Moivre's theorem,** is omitted.

Example.　Write $(\sqrt{3} + i)^7$ in the form $a + bi$.

Solution.　For the modulus, we have $r = \sqrt{(\sqrt{3})^2 + 1^2} = 2$. For the argument, from $\tan \theta = 1/\sqrt{3}$, we obtain $\theta = 30°$. Thus, $(\sqrt{3} + i)^7 = (2 \text{ cis } 30°)^7$. Then, by De Moivre's theorem,

$$(2 \text{ cis } 30°)^7 = 2^7 \text{ cis } (7 \cdot 30)° = 128 \text{ cis } 210°.$$

Converting to the form $a + bi$, we find

$$128 (\cos 210° + i \sin 210°) = 128 \left(-\frac{\sqrt{3}}{2} - \frac{1}{2} i \right) = -64\sqrt{3} - 64i,$$

so

$$(\sqrt{3} + i)^7 = -64\sqrt{3} - 64i.$$

By appropriately defining z^0 and z^{-n}, we can extend De Moivre's theorem to include as exponents all $n \in J$.

DEFINITION 12.14　*If $z \neq 0 + 0i$, then*

$$\text{I}\quad z^0 = 1 + 0i,$$

$$\text{II}\quad z^{-n} = \frac{1}{z^n}, \quad \text{for} \quad n \in J.$$

With these definitions, we can assert the following result.

THEOREM 12.9　*If $z \in C$, $z \neq 0 + 0i$, $z = r$ cis θ and $n \in J$, then*

$$z^n = r^n \text{ cis } n\theta.$$

Example.　Write $(1 + i)^{-6}$ in the form $a + bi$.

Solution.　Since $r = \sqrt{1^2 + 1^2} = \sqrt{2}$ and $\tan \theta = 1/1$, we have $\theta = 45°$, and

$$(1 + i)^{-6} = (\sqrt{2} \text{ cis } 45°)^{-6}.$$

By Theorem 12.9,

$$(\sqrt{2} \text{ cis } 45°)^{-6} = (\sqrt{2})^{-6} \text{ cis } (-6 \cdot 45)°$$

$$= \frac{1}{8} \text{ cis } (-270°)$$

$$= \frac{1}{8} [\cos (-270°) + i \sin (-270°)].$$

(Solution continued overleaf.)

Since $\cos(-270°) = 0$ and $\sin(-270°) = 1$, we obtain

$$(1 + i)^{-6} = \frac{1}{8}(0 + i) = \frac{1}{8}i.$$

Roots of complex numbers   Yet another extension of De Moivre's theorem is possible if we make the following definition.

DEFINITION 12.15   *For $z \in C$, $n \in N$, w is an **nth root of** z provided*

$$w^n = z.$$

THEOREM 12.10   *If $z \in C$, $z = r$ cis θ and $n \in N$, then*

$$w = r^{1/n} \text{ cis} \left(\frac{\theta}{n}\right)$$

is an nth root of z.

This theorem follows directly from Theorem 12.8. The fact that

$$\text{cis } \theta = \text{cis } (\theta + k360°)$$

for $k \in J$ enables us to find n distinct complex nth roots for each $z \in C$, $z \neq 0 + 0i$, as illustrated in the following example.

Example.   Write each of the four fourth roots of $z = 2 + 2\sqrt{3}i$ in the form r cis θ.

Solution.   Since $r = \sqrt{2^2 + (2\sqrt{3})^2} = 4$ and $\theta = \text{Tan}^{-1} \, 2\sqrt{3}/2 = 60°$, we can write

$$z = 2 + 2\sqrt{3}i = 4 \text{ cis } 60°.$$

From Theorem 12.10 and the periodic property of cosine and sine, each number

$$4^{1/4} \text{ cis} \left(\frac{60° + k360°}{4}\right),$$

for $k \in J$, is a fourth root of z. Taking $k = 0, 1, 2$, and 3, in turn, gives the roots

$$w_0 = \sqrt{2} \text{ cis } 15°, \quad w_1 = \sqrt{2} \text{ cis } 105°, \quad w_2 = \sqrt{2} \text{ cis } 195°, \quad \text{and} \quad w_3 = \sqrt{2} \text{ cis } 285°.$$

The substitution of any other integer for k will produce one of these four complex numbers.

EXERCISE 12.5

Use Theorem 12.6 or 12.7 as appropriate to write each of the given expressions as a complex number of the form $a + bi$. Use Table VI as necessary.

1. $[2 \text{ cis } (-30°)]^7$
2. $(4 \text{ cis } 36°)^5$
3. $(-\frac{1}{2} + \frac{1}{2}\sqrt{3}i)^3$

4. $(1 + i)^{12}$
5. $(\sqrt{3} \text{ cis } 5°)^{12}$
6. $(\sqrt{2} \text{ cis } 30°)^{-7}$

7. $(\sqrt{3} - i)^{-5}$ 8. $(1 - i)^{-6}$ 9. $\dfrac{(1 + i)^3}{(1 + i\sqrt{3})^5(1 - i)^2}$

10. $\dfrac{4(\sqrt{3} + i)^3}{(1 - i)^3}$ 11. $\dfrac{(1 - i)^5}{(1 + i)^6}$ 12. $\dfrac{(1 + \sqrt{3}i)^{-4}}{(\sqrt{3} + i)^{-6}}$

Find the nth roots of z by applying Theorem 12.10. Leave the results in trigonometric form, and list all n of the nth roots.

13. $z = 32 \text{ cis } 45°, \quad n = 5$ 14. $z = 27, \quad n = 3$ 15. $z = -16\sqrt{3} + 16i, \quad n = 5$

16. $z = 1 - i, \quad n = 4$ 17. $z = -i, \quad n = 6$ 18. $z = 2 + 2\sqrt{3}i, \quad n = 3$

Solve each of the following equations over C.

19. $x^5 = 16 - 16\sqrt{3}i$ 20. $x^3 + 4i = 4\sqrt{3}$

21. $x^7 + 1 = 0$ 22. $x^7 - 1 = 0$

23. Factor $x^4 + 16$ into linear factors.   24. Factor $x^5 - 1$ into linear factors.

25. Show that the sum of the four fourth roots of 1 is $0 + 0i$.

26. Explain why the sum of the nth roots of any complex number is zero for all $n > 1$.

27. Use De Moivre's theorem to prove that

$$\cos 3\theta = 4 \cos^3 \theta - 3 \cos \theta \quad \text{and} \quad \sin 3\theta = 3 \sin \theta - 4 \sin^3 \theta.$$

12.6 ORDERED PAIRS AS VECTORS

Let us now turn to another interpretation of the ordered pairs (a, b) in R^2 under some of the properties developed in Sections 12.1 and 12.2.

In Chapter 10, we considered the set of $m \times n$ matrices, for m and n fixed, as a vector space over the field of real numbers (page 240). In particular, we referred to a $1 \times n$ matrix $[a_1 \, a_2 \cdots a_n]$ as a row vector, and its transpose $[a_1 \, a_2 \cdots a_n]^t$ as a column vector. The two operations involved in a vector space S, it will be recalled,

Ordered pairs of real numbers as vectors are (i) the addition of vectors in S and (ii) the multiplication of vectors in S by elements of R. We can develop a similar vector space using ordered pairs of real numbers as vectors, and we begin by making another definition.

DEFINITION 12.16   *A **two-dimensional vector** v is an ordered pair of real numbers. That is, if $a, b \in R$, then*

$$\mathbf{v} = (a, b),$$

and the set of all such vectors is the set

$$V = \{(a, b) \mid a \in R \text{ and } b \in R\}.$$

Vector
notation Note that we are using **boldface** type to denote vectors. In handwritten form, vectors are frequently identified by arrows drawn above symbols. Thus, $\vec{v}$ denotes a vector.

Since we shall be dealing only with two-dimensional vectors, that is, vectors with only two components, we shall refer to these simply as *vectors*. Most of the concepts developed here, however, extend to sets of ordered triples, ordered quadruples, or, indeed, to ordered *n*-tuples of real numbers. These, in turn, can be considered as sets of vectors of three, four, or *n* dimensions.

There is a geometric interpretation that can be made of the vector-space algebra of ordered pairs, because every ordered pair (a, b) can be associated with a directed line segment, or **geometric vector**, originating **Geometric representation of vectors** (having **initial point**) at the origin and terminating (having **terminal point**) at the point in the plane corresponding to (a, b) (Figure 12.5).

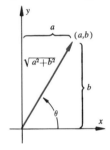

Figure 12.5

DEFINITION 12.17 *For each vector* $\mathbf{v} = (a, b)$, *the **norm**, or **magnitude**, of* $\mathbf{v}$ *is the real number*

$$\|\mathbf{v}\| = \sqrt{a^2 + b^2}.$$

It is evident from the Pythagorean theorem that the norm of a vector is just the length of the associated geometric vector.

DEFINITION 12.18 *For each vector* $\mathbf{v} = (a, b)$, *with* $\|\mathbf{v}\| \neq 0$, ***the direction angle** of* $\mathbf{v}$ *is the angle* θ *satisfying*

$$\cos \theta = \frac{a}{\|\mathbf{v}\|}, \qquad \sin \theta = \frac{b}{\|\mathbf{v}\|}, \qquad -180° < \theta \leq 180°.$$

Thus the direction angle of $\mathbf{v}$ is the angle θ, $-180° < \theta \leq 180°$, from the positive *x*-axis to the geometric vector associated with $\mathbf{v}$. If θ is *the* direction angle of $\mathbf{v}$, then of course any angle $\theta + k360°$, $k \in J$, might also be taken as *a* direction angle of $\mathbf{v}$.

Example. Find the norm and direction angle, to the nearest 10′, of $\mathbf{v} = (4, -5)$.

Solution. $\|\mathbf{v}\| = \sqrt{4^2 + (-5)^2} = \sqrt{41}$. Since $P(4, -5)$ is in the fourth quadrant,

$$\theta = \mathrm{Sin}^{-1} \frac{-5}{\sqrt{41}} \approx -51° \, 20′.$$

DEFINITION 12.19 *If* $\mathbf{v}_1 = (a_1, b_1)$ *and* $\mathbf{v}_2 = (a_2, b_2)$, *then* $\mathbf{v}_1 = \mathbf{v}_2$ *if and only if* $a_1 = a_2$ *and* $b_1 = b_2$.

Accordingly, vectors are equal if and only if they correspond to the same geometric vector.

Now, let us define two operations, as follows.

DEFINITION 12.20 *If* $v_1 = (a_1, b_1)$, $v_2 = (a_2, b_2)$, *and c is any real number,*

$$\text{I} \quad v_1 + v_2 = (a_1, b_1) + (a_2, b_2) = (a_1 + a_2, b_1 + b_2),$$

$$\text{II} \quad cv_1 = c(a_1, b_1) = (ca_1, cb_1).$$

From the vector viewpoint of ordered pairs, real numbers, such as c in the foregoing definition, are called **scalars**, and the operation defined in Definition 12.20-II is called the multiplication of a vector by a scalar.

Geometric representation   Graphically, the two operations defined above can be interpreted in terms of geometric vectors, as shown in Figures 12.6 and 12.7.

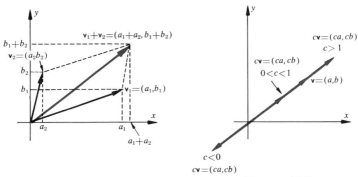

Figure 12.6   **Figure 12.7**

In Figure 12.6, the vectors v_1 and v_2 are said to be **noncollinear** because they correspond to noncollinear geometric vectors. It is evident that the sum of two such noncollinear vectors v_1 and v_2 corresponds to the diagonal of the parallelogram with adjacent sides corresponding to v_1 and v_2. This statement can be considered valid, in a limiting way, even if the geometric vectors corresponding to v_1 and v_2 are collinear. Accordingly, we say that vectors are added according to the **parallelogram law.**

Geometric representation of the product of a scalar and a vector   In Figure 12.7, the vectors v_1 and cv_1 are said to be collinear, since they correspond to geometric vectors on the same line. For $c > 0$, the product cv corresponds to a geometric vector with the *same direction* as the one corresponding to v. If $0 < c < 1$, then $\|cv\| < \|v\|$. If $c < 0$, then cv corresponds to a geometric vector of *direction opposite* to the geometric vector corresponding to v.

DEFINITION 12.21 *The zero vector,* **0**, *or identity vector for addition, is given*

$$0 = (0, 0).$$

The zero vector has the property that $\mathbf{v} + \mathbf{0} = \mathbf{0} + \mathbf{v} = \mathbf{v}$ for each vector $\mathbf{v}$. The norm of $\mathbf{0}$ is, of course, 0. No particular direction is assigned to the geometric vector corresponding to $\mathbf{0}$; for this reason, *any and every direction might be assigned to it,* as suits our convenience.

> **Properties of the zero vector**

DEFINITION 12.22 *If $\mathbf{v} = (a, b)$ is a vector, then the **negative of** $\mathbf{v}$ is given by*

$$-\mathbf{v} = (-a, -b).$$

In accord with Definition 12.22, we can also define the *difference* of two vectors.

DEFINITION 12.23 *If $\mathbf{v}_1$ and $\mathbf{v}_2$ are vectors, then the **difference**, $\mathbf{v}_1 - \mathbf{v}_2$ is defined by*

$$\mathbf{v}_1 - \mathbf{v}_2 = \mathbf{v}_1 + (-\mathbf{v}_2),$$

and is viewed as the result of subtracting $\mathbf{v}_2$ from $\mathbf{v}_1$.

The geometric vector associated with $\mathbf{v}_1 - \mathbf{v}_2$ is shown in Figure 12.8.

With Definitions 12.19–12.23, we now have exactly the same algebra, as regards addition and the multiplication by a real-number scalar, for the set of real-number pairs (a, b), whether they are regarded as 1×2 matrices, as 2×1 matrices, or as vectors. Since we have shown that

$$\{(a, b) \mid a \in R, b \in R\}$$

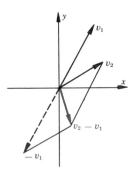

Figure 12.8

> **The set of vectors (a, b) as a vector space over R**

is a vector space when viewed as the set of 1×2 matrices, it follows that the set is also a vector space when viewed as a set of vectors. We can state the result for vectors $\mathbf{v} = (a, b)$ as follows:

THEOREM 12.11 *The set V of vectors $\mathbf{v} = (a, b)$, $a \in R$, $b \in R$, with the set R of real numbers as scalar multipliers, is a vector space over the field R of real numbers. That is, if $\mathbf{v}_1$, $\mathbf{v}_2$, and $\mathbf{v}_3$ are vectors, and c and d are real scalars, then*

I $\quad \mathbf{v}_1 + \mathbf{v}_2 \in V$,

II $\quad \mathbf{v}_1 + \mathbf{v}_2 = \mathbf{v}_2 + \mathbf{v}_1$,

III $\quad (\mathbf{v}_1 + \mathbf{v}_2) + \mathbf{v}_3 = \mathbf{v}_1 + (\mathbf{v}_2 + \mathbf{v}_3)$,

IV $\quad \mathbf{v}_1 + \mathbf{0} = \mathbf{v}_1$,

V $\quad \mathbf{v}_1 + (-\mathbf{v}_1) = \mathbf{0}$,

VI $\quad c\mathbf{v}_1 \in V$,

VII $\quad c(d\mathbf{v}_1) = (cd)\mathbf{v}_1$,

VIII $\quad (c + d)\mathbf{v}_1 = c\mathbf{v}_1 + d\mathbf{v}_1$,

IX $\quad c(\mathbf{v}_1 + \mathbf{v}_2) = c\mathbf{v}_1 + c\mathbf{v}_2$,

X $\quad 1 \cdot \mathbf{v}_1 = \mathbf{v}_1$,

XI $\quad (-1)\mathbf{v}_1 = -\mathbf{v}_1$,

XII $\quad 0 \cdot \mathbf{v}_1 = \mathbf{0}$,

XIII $\quad c \cdot \mathbf{0} = \mathbf{0}$.

The proofs of the various parts of this theorem are omitted since they were considered in Chapter 10. Actually, properties XI, XII, and XIII are logical consequences of the first ten properties, and could therefore be omitted as fundamental properties of a vector space. We have included them for ready reference here since they are often used in vector computations.

As mentioned earlier, the set of vectors (a, b) comprises a **two-dimensional vector space**, since each vector has two components. It can be shown that if v_1 and v_2 are two noncollinear vectors in a two-dimensional vector space, then for each v in the vector space there exist scalars c_1 and c_2 such that

$$v = c_1 v_1 + c_2 v_2.$$

Figure 12.9 shows two geometric examples of such combinations. Since linear combinations of any two noncollinear vectors v_1 and v_2 can be used to represent any vector in a two-dimensional vector space, two such vectors are said to form a **basis** for the space.

Basis for a vector space

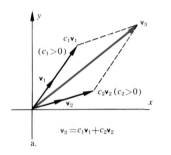 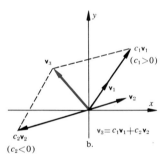

Figure   12.9

Any two vectors corresponding to geometric vectors that are perpendicular to each other are said to be **orthogonal**, and in general such vectors, neither of which is $(0, 0)$, form the most useful basis for a vector space.

DEFINITION 12.24   *A unit vector is any vector v such that $\|v\| = 1$.*

If we let $x = (1, 0)$ and $y = (0, 1)$ be the unit vectors whose corresponding geometric vectors are in the direction of the positive x- and y-axes, respectively, then x and y form an orthogonal basis for our two-dimensional vector space, and for each vector $v = (x, y)$ in the space we have

The standard coordinate basis

$$v = xx + yy.$$

Several graphical examples of linear combinations of x and y are shown in Figure 12.10.

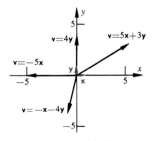

Figure   12.10

If $\mathbf{v} \neq (0, 0)$, and if $\|\mathbf{v}\|$ is factored from the right-hand member of the vector equation $\mathbf{v} = x\mathbf{x} + y\mathbf{y}$, we have

$$\mathbf{v} = \sqrt{x^2 + y^2}\left(\frac{x}{\sqrt{x^2 + y^2}}\,\mathbf{x} + \frac{y}{\sqrt{x^2 + y^2}}\,\mathbf{y}\right),$$

Unit vector in the direction of a given vector

and it can be shown that the vector in the parentheses in the right-hand member here is a unit vector in the same direction as $\mathbf{v}$. In other words, we have the following.

THEOREM 12.12 *If $\mathbf{v}$ is any nonzero vector in $\mathbf{v}$ then the vector $\mathbf{v}^*$, given by*

$$\mathbf{v}^* = \frac{1}{\|\mathbf{v}\|}\cdot\mathbf{v},$$

is a unit vector in the same direction as $\mathbf{v}$.

Example.   Find a unit vector $\mathbf{v}^*$ in the same direction as $\mathbf{v} = (3, 7)$.

Solution. $\|(3, 7)\| = \sqrt{9 + 49} = \sqrt{58}$. Hence,

$$\mathbf{v}^* = \frac{1}{\sqrt{58}}(3, 7) = \left(\frac{3}{\sqrt{58}}, \frac{7}{\sqrt{58}}\right).$$

EXERCISE 12.6

Write each of the following in the form (a, b), represent the vector operation(s) graphically, and find the norm and direction angle of (a, b).

Example. $(5, 3) - (2, -1)$

Solution. $(5, 3) - (2, -1) = (5, 3) + (-2, 1)$

$$= (3, 4),$$

$$\|(3, 4)\| = \sqrt{3^2 + 4^2} = 5,$$

$$\theta = \mathrm{Cos}^{-1}\frac{3}{5} \approx 53°\ 10'.$$

1. $(2, 4) + (6, 1)$

2. $(3, -1) + (4, 2)$

3. $(-3, 4) + (2, -1)$

4. $(-2, -4) + (7, -2)$

5. $(0, 3) + (5, 6)$

6. $(5, 2) + (3, 0)$

7. $(2, 0) + (3, 5) + (3, 1)$

8. $(-2, 4) + (3, 0) + (4, 3)$

9. $(6, -1) + (2, 0) + (0, 2)$

10. $(0, 4) + (2, -1) + (5, 4)$

11. $(5, 3) - (2, 2)$

12. $(7, 8) - (3, 4)$

13. $(-2, 4) - (2, -1)$

14. $(8, -3) - (2, -1)$

15. $(2, 4) + (0, 3) - (2, -1)$

16. $(-3, 0) + (2, 1) - (-1, 0)$

17. $(0, 2) - (3, 1) + (2, 0)$

18. $(4, 2) - (0, -2) + (4, 4)$

Example. $2(3, 5) + 3(1, -2)$

Solution.

$2(3, 5) + 3(1, -2) = (6, 10) + (3, -6)$

$$= (9, 4),$$

$$\|(9, 4)\| = \sqrt{9^2 + 4^2}$$

$$= \sqrt{97},$$

$$\theta = \text{Cos}^{-1} \frac{9}{\sqrt{97}} \approx \text{Cos}^{-1} 0.914 \approx 24°.$$

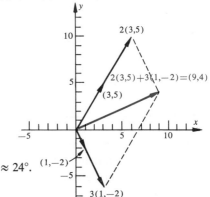

19. $3(1, 1) + 4(2, 2)$

20. $3(1, -4) + 2(3, 5)$

21. $5(0, 2) + 3(-2, -3)$

22. $2(3, 1) + 5(-6, 0)$

23. $(5, 6) - 2(1, -2)$

24. $(6, 2) - 3(-1, 2)$

25. $3(0, 4) - 4(2, 0)$

26. $7(5, 0) - 2(-3, 0)$

27. $2(1, 3) - 4(-2, 1) + 2(0, 1)$

28. $3(0, 2) + 5(1, -2) - 3(0, 1)$

Represent each vector graphically, find the norm and direction angle of each vector, and find the unit vector $\mathbf{v}^*$ in the same direction as the given vector $\mathbf{v}$.

Example. $\mathbf{v} = 3\mathbf{x} + 4\mathbf{y}$

Solution.

$$\|\mathbf{v}\| = \|3\mathbf{x} + 4\mathbf{y}\| = \sqrt{3^2 + 4^2} = 5, \; \theta = \text{Cos}^{-1} \frac{3}{5} \approx 53° \; 10'.$$

$$\mathbf{v}^* = \frac{\|\mathbf{v}\|}{\mathbf{v}} = \frac{3\mathbf{x} + 4\mathbf{y}}{5}$$

$$= \frac{3}{5}\mathbf{x} + \frac{3}{8}\mathbf{y}.$$

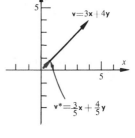

29. $\mathbf{v} = 2\mathbf{x} + 7\mathbf{y}$

30. $\mathbf{v} = 5\mathbf{x} + 2\mathbf{y}$

31. $\mathbf{v} = 3\mathbf{x} - \mathbf{y}$

32. $\mathbf{v} = -4\mathbf{x} + 3\mathbf{y}$

33. $\mathbf{v} = -6\mathbf{x} - 7\mathbf{y}$

34. $\mathbf{v} = -5\mathbf{x} - \mathbf{y}$

35. $\mathbf{v} = 3\mathbf{y}$

36. $\mathbf{v} = -7\mathbf{x}$

37. Show that if $\mathbf{v} = x\mathbf{x} + y\mathbf{y}$, then $\dfrac{x}{\|\mathbf{v}\|}\mathbf{x} + \dfrac{y}{\|\mathbf{v}\|}\mathbf{y}$ is the unit vector in the same direction as $\mathbf{v}$.

12.7 APPLICATIONS OF VECTORS

Geometric vectors with arbitrary initial points   In applications, it is convenient to consider all directed line segments—or geometric vectors—in the plane, not just those with initial point at the origin.

DEFINITION 12.25 *Two geometric vectors are **equivalent** if they have the same length (magnitude) and the same direction.*

Thus the geometric vector from (0, 0) to (2, 3) and the geometric vector from (4, 2) to (6, 5) are equivalent. See Figure 12.11, where these and other geometric vectors equivalent to them are pictured.

Of course, every geometric vector in the plane is equivalent to infinitely many other such vectors, and, in particular, every geometric vector is equivalent to one in **standard position**, that is, with initial point at the origin.

If you imagine a geometric vector as free to "slide"

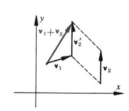

Figure 12.11

"Free" geometric vectors   (parallel to its initial position) in the plane, then you can always "slide" any geometric vector in the plane onto any vector equivalent to it, as shown in Figure 12.12.

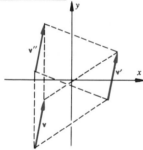

Figure 12.12   **Figure 12.13**

Using this notion, you can visualize the sum of two geometric vectors v_1 and v_2 as being determined by sliding one vector, say v_2, onto an equivalent vector v_2', the initial point of which lies on the terminal point of v_1. The sum $v_1 + v_2$ is then the vector with initial point the initial point of v_1 and terminal point the terminal point of v_2', as shown in Figure 12.13. Since the opposite sides of a parallelogram can be viewed as equivalent geometric vectors, it is evident that this viewpoint of the sum of two vectors (Figure 12.14) is just another way to visualize the sum of geometric vectors mentioned on page 307.

The sum of free geometric vectors

Test for equivalence of geometric vectors   To express analytically the conditions for the equivalence of two geometric vectors in the plane, we have the following result.

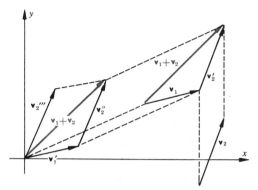

Figure 12.14

THEOREM 12.13 *The geometric vector from* (a_1, b_1) *to* (c_1, d_1) *and the geometric vector from* (a_2, b_2) *to* (c_2, d_2) *are equivalent if and only if*

$$c_1 - a_1 = c_2 - a_2 \text{ and } d_1 - b_1 = d_2 - b_2.$$

If they are equivalent, then both are geometric representations of the vector

$$(c_1 - a_1, d_1 - b_1).$$

The proof is left as an exercise.

Physical quantities as vector quantities   Many physical quantities, such as displacement, force, velocity, and acceleration, are specified by a magnitude and a direction. Accordingly, vector methods are extensively used in treating these quantities.

Example. An airplane flies 340 miles per hour in a direction 60° clockwise from north for two hours and then flies due north at the same speed for one hour. How far from the starting point is the airplane at the end of this time?

Solution. The conditions can be represented with geometric vectors as illustrated in Figure 12.15-a or -b. *(Solution continued overleaf.)*

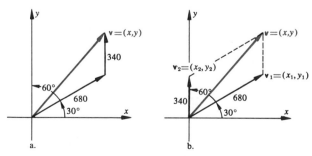

Figure 12.15

Since $\sin 30° = \dfrac{1}{2} = \dfrac{y_1}{680}$, we have $y_1 = 340$; since $\cos 30° = \dfrac{\sqrt{3}}{2} = \dfrac{x_1}{680}$, we have $x_1 = 340\sqrt{3}$; hence $\mathbf{v_1} = (340\sqrt{3},\ 340)$. Since $\mathbf{v_2} = (x_2,\ y_2) = (0,\ 340)$, we have

$$\mathbf{v_3} = \mathbf{v_1} + \mathbf{v_2} = (340\sqrt{3},\ 340) + (0,\ 340)$$
$$= (340\sqrt{3},\ 680),$$
$$\|\mathbf{v_3}\| = \sqrt{340^2 \cdot 3 + 680^2} = \sqrt{809{,}200}.$$

Hence, the airplane is $\sqrt{809{,}200}$, or about 900, miles from its starting point.

Consider next an application of a different sort.

Example.   A force of magnitude 10 lbs is applied to an iron ring in a direction making an angle of $30°$ with the positive x-direction, and a second force, of magnitude 18 lbs, is applied to the ring in a direction making' an angle of $45°$ with the positive x-direction. Determine the magnitude and direction of the force on the ring that will just balance these two forces.

Solution.   Since $\sin 30° = \dfrac{1}{2} = \dfrac{b}{10}$ and $\cos 30° = \dfrac{\sqrt{3}}{2} = \dfrac{a}{10}$, the first force can be represented by the vector $(a,\ b) = (5\sqrt{3},\ 5)$. Since $\sin 45° = \cos 45° = \dfrac{1}{\sqrt{2}} = \dfrac{c}{18} = \dfrac{d}{18}$, the second force can be represented by the vector $(c,\ d) = (9\sqrt{2},\ 9\sqrt{2})$. If the force $F(x,\ y)$ is to balance these, then the sum of the three forces must vanish:

$$(5\sqrt{3},\ 5) + (9\sqrt{2},\ 9\sqrt{2}) + (x,\ y) = (0,\ 0),$$
$$(x,\ y) = (-5\sqrt{3} - 9\sqrt{2},\ -5 - 9\sqrt{2})$$
$$\approx (-21.4,\ -17.7).$$

The magnitude of the force F therefore is

$$\|F\| = \sqrt{x^2 + y^2}$$
$$\approx \sqrt{(-21.4)^2 + (-17.7)^2} \approx 27.8.$$

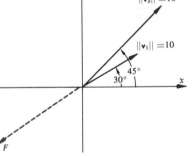

Since $x < 0$ and $y < 0$, F must be directed into the third quadrant; its angle θ from the positive x-direction is given by

$$\sin \theta = \frac{y}{\sqrt{x^2 + y^2}} \approx \frac{-17.7}{27.8} \approx -0.637, \text{ with } -180° < \theta < 180°,$$

so that $\theta \approx -140°\ 30'$.

EXERCISE 12.7

Specify each vector as an equivalent vector with initial point at the origin.

Example. $\mathbf{v}$: $(4,\ -1)$ to $(5,\ 3)$

Solution. By Theorem 12.13, this vector is equivalent to

$$[5 - 4, 3 - (-1)] \quad \text{or} \quad (1, 4).$$

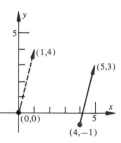

1. $\mathbf{v}$: (2, 3) to (6, 7)   2. $\mathbf{v}$: (4, −3) to (6, 2)

3. $\mathbf{v}$: (−2, 5) to (7, −1)   4. $\mathbf{v}$: (4, −2) to (−3, 0)

5. $\mathbf{v}$: (−5, −3) to (0, 0)   6. $\mathbf{v}$: (−5, 0) to (0, −3)

The figure shows several geometric vectors. Express each of the following combinations of the associated vectors as an ordered pair (a, b).

Example. $\mathbf{v}_2 + \mathbf{v}_7$

Solution.

$\mathbf{v}_2$ is equivalent to

$$(5 - 8, 14 - 9) = (-3, 5),$$

$\mathbf{v}_7$ is equivalent to

$$(11 - 3, -6 - (-6)) = (8, 0),$$

$$\mathbf{v}_2 + \mathbf{v}_7 = (-3, 5) + (8, 0)$$

$$= (-3 + 8, 5 + 0)$$

$$= (5, 5).$$

7. $\mathbf{v}_1 + \mathbf{v}_5$ 8. $\mathbf{v}_3 + \mathbf{v}_7$ 9. $\mathbf{v}_6 - \mathbf{v}_2$

10. $\mathbf{v}_3 - \mathbf{v}_4$ 11. $\mathbf{v}_2 + \mathbf{v}_3 + \mathbf{v}_4$ 12. $\mathbf{v}_6 + \mathbf{v}_1 + \mathbf{v}_5$

13. $\mathbf{v}_2 + \mathbf{v}_4 - \mathbf{v}_1$ 14. $\mathbf{v}_4 - \mathbf{v}_7 + \mathbf{v}_2$

15. An airplane flies 800 miles due south and then flies 600 miles 60° clockwise from north. How far from the starting point is the airplane at the end of this time?

16. An airplane is flying at 20,000 ft on a heading of 300° clockwise from north at 450 mph. The wind velocity at this level is 90 mph from 240° clockwise from north. Find the ground speed and the direction of the flight over the ground.

17. A weight of 160 lbs is placed on a smooth plane inclined at an angle of 30° with the horizontal (see figure). What is the minimum force that must be exerted against the weight and parallel to the plane to prevent the weight from slipping? *Hint:* Resolve the vertical force into components in the direction of the plane and perpendicular to it.

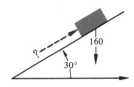

18. A force of 40 lbs is directed to the right. What vertical force must be applied so that the magnitude of the resultant force is 80 lbs? What angle does the resultant force make with the horizontal?

19. Forces having magnitudes of 12 and 18 lbs are applied to an iron ring in directions making clockwise angles measuring 30° and 120°, respectively, with the positive *x*-direction. Determine the magnitude and direction of the force on the ring that will just balance these two forces.

20. Determine the magnitude and direction of the force required for equilibrium in Problem 19 if the force making an angle of 30° has a magnitude of 18 lbs and the force making an angle of 120° has a magnitude of 10 lbs.

13 SEQUENCES AND SERIES

13.1 MATHEMATICAL INDUCTION

The material in the present section depends on a special property of the set

$$N = \{1, 2, 3, \cdots\}$$

of natural numbers, or positive integers.

A set S is called an **inductive set** if it has the following properties:

a. $1 \in S$.

b. If $k \in S$, then $k + 1 \in S$.

These two properties might be illustrated, for example, with the set Q_+ of the positive elements of the set Q of rational numbers, or the set R_+ of positive elements of the set R of real numbers, and with $k = \frac{1}{2}$.

Characteriz-ation of N   What makes the set N of positive integers stand apart from other inductive sets is that N *contains no elements not implied by properties a and b.* In this sense, the set N is the least extensive of all inductive sets. We state this property (which we shall not prove) as follows:

c. Let M be a set of positive integers. If $1 \in M$ and if the assumption that $k \in M$ implies that $k + 1 \in M$, then $M = N$.

This property underlies the following theorem, which is called the **principle of mathematical induction.**

THEOREM 13.1   *If a given open sentence involving n is true for n = 1, and if its truth for n = k implies its truth for n = k + 1, then it is true for every natural number n.*

Proof.   Let M be the set of positive integers for which the open sentence is true. An application of the foregoing property (c) shows that the sentence is true for all natural numbers.

Series is a sum of numbers

Requirements of a proof by mathematical induction   We can exploit Theorem 13.1 to prove a number of assertions. Although the technique we shall use is called **proof by mathematical induction**, the argument we shall employ is deductive, as have been all of the other arguments in this book. Proofs by mathematical induction require two things:

a. A demonstration that the assertion to be proved is true for the natural number 1.
b. A demonstration that the truth of the assertion for a natural number k implies its truth for $k + 1$.

When these two demonstrations have been made, the principle of mathematical induction assures us that the assertion is true for every natural number.

Example. Prove that the sum of the first n natural numbers is $n(n + 1)/2$.

Solution. In symbols, we wish to show that

$$1 + 2 + 3 + \cdots + n = \frac{n(n + 1)}{2}.$$

As always in proofs by mathematical induction, we must do two things:

1. We must first show that the assertion is true for $n = 1$, i.e., that

$$1 = \frac{1(1 + 1)}{2},$$

which is true.

2. We must next show that the truth of

$$1 + 2 + 3 + \cdots + k = \frac{k(k + 1)}{2}$$

implies the truth of

$$1 + 2 + 3 + \cdots + k + (k + 1) = \frac{(k + 1)[(k + 1) + 1]}{2}.$$

That is, we must show that the truth of the assertion for $n = k$ implies its truth for $n = k + 1$. Now, assume the truth of

$$1 + 2 + 3 + \cdots + k = \frac{k(k + 1)}{2}.$$

Then, by adding $k + 1$ to each member of this equation, we obtain

$$1 + 2 + 3 + \cdots + k + (k + 1) = \frac{k(k + 1)}{2} + (k + 1)$$

$$= (k + 1)\left(\frac{k}{2} + 1\right)$$

$$= (k + 1)\left(\frac{k + 2}{2}\right)$$

$$= \frac{(k + 1)[(k + 1) + 1]}{2}.$$

$\dfrac{k(1(+1) + 2(k+1))}{2} = \dfrac{(k+1)(k+2)}{2}$

Thus the second fact necessary for our proof is established. By the principle of mathematical induction, the assertion is true for every natural number n.

An alternative means is available to us for accomplishing the second part of the proof. We assume that

$$1 + 2 + 3 + \cdots + k = \frac{k(k+1)}{2}$$

is true, and then consider the desired consequence,

$$1 + 2 + 3 + \cdots + k + (k+1) = \frac{(k+1)[(k+1)+1]}{2}.$$

We can establish the truth of the latter statement by replacing $1 + 2 + 3 + \cdots + k$ in the left-hand member by its equal, $k(k+1)/2$, to give us

$$\frac{k(k+1)}{2} + (k+1) = \frac{(k+1)[(k+1)+1]}{2},$$

and then show that this is an identity.

Analogy with row of dominoes

This method of proof is often compared to lining up a row of dominoes, with the assumption that whenever one domino is toppled, the one following will topple. One then needs only to topple the first domino ($n=1$) and the whole row following will topple, as indicated in Figure 13.1.

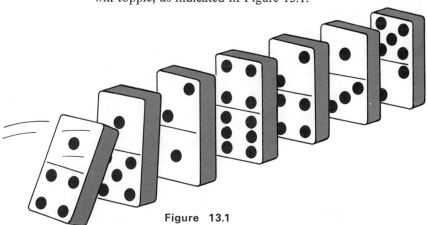

Figure 13.1

Here is another example of a proof by mathematical induction:

Example. Prove that $2^n > n$ for every natural number n.

Solution. The proof consists of two parts.

1. We must first show that $2^n > n$ for $n = 1$. We have

$$2^1 = 2 > 1,$$

so that the assertion is true for $n = 1$. (This topples the first domino.)

(Solution continued overleaf.)

Handwritten top: $2 \cdot 4 \cdot 6 + 2n = 2(2 \cdot 4 \cdot 6 \cdots n) = n(n+1)$

Even : $n(n+1)$

Odd : $(En + On) - En$

2. We must next show that if $2^k > k$, then $2^{k+1} > k + 1$. (Compare this with "If any domino is toppled, then its successor will be toppled.") We begin by assuming that $2^k > k$. Then, by Theorem 1.15-III,

$$2 \cdot 2^k > 2 \cdot k.$$

Furthermore, for each natural number k, it is true that $2k \geq k + 1$, because, $2k = k + k$, and $k + k \geq k + 1$ for every $k \geq 1$. Therefore, we have

$$2 \cdot 2^k > 2k \geq k + 1,$$

$$2^{k+1} > k + 1.$$

Hence the assumption that $2^k > k$ implies that $2^{k+1} > k + 1$. This completes our demonstration of the two facts required in a proof by mathematical induction. We have shown that:

1. $2^n > n$ for $n = 1$;

2. $2^k > k$ implies that $2^{k+1} > k + 1$.

Thus the principle of mathematical induction assures us that $2^n > n$ for every natural number n.

Handwritten: Be sure to factor out

EXERCISE 13.1

By mathematical induction, prove the validity of the formulas in Problems 1–10 for all positive integral values of n.

Handwritten left: formula for odd, no

1. $\dfrac{1}{2} + \dfrac{2}{2} + \dfrac{3}{2} + \cdots + \dfrac{n}{2} = \dfrac{n(n+1)}{4}$

Handwritten right: $1 + 3 + 5 \cdots (2k-1) = k^2$; $k^2 + (2(k+1)-1)$

$1, 3, 5 \cdots (2k+1) + (2(k+1)-1) =$ $k^2 + 2k + 1$ $(k+1)^2$

2. $1 + 3 + 5 + \cdots + (2n - 1) = n^2$

3. $2 + 4 + 6 + \cdots + 2n = n(n + 1)$

4. $2 + 6 + 10 + \cdots + (4n - 2) = 2n^2$

Handwritten: $2 + 2^2 \cdots + 2^k + 2^{k+1} = 2^{k+1} - 2 + 2^k$ $= 2^{k+1} - 2 + 2^{k+1}$

5. $1^2 + 2^2 + 3^2 + \cdots + n^2 = \dfrac{n(n + 1)(2n + 1)}{6}$

6. $2 + 2^2 + 2^3 + \cdots + 2^n = 2^{n+1} - 2$

7. $1^3 + 3^3 + 5^3 + \cdots + (2n - 1)^3 = n^2(2n^2 - 1)$

8. $\dfrac{1}{1 \cdot 2} + \dfrac{1}{2 \cdot 3} + \dfrac{1}{3 \cdot 4} + \cdots + \dfrac{1}{n(n + 1)} = \dfrac{n}{n + 1}$

9. $1 \cdot 2 + 2 \cdot 3 + 3 \cdot 4 + \cdots + n(n + 1) = \dfrac{n(n + 1)(n + 2)}{3}$

10. $1 \cdot 4 + 2 \cdot 9 + 3 \cdot 16 + \cdots + n(n + 1)^2 = \dfrac{1}{12} n(n + 1)(n + 2)(3n + 5)$

11. Show that if $2 + 4 + 6 + \cdots + 2n = n(n + 1) + 2$ is true for $n = k$, then it is true for $n = k + 1$. Is it true for every $n \in N$?

12. Show that $n^3 + 11n = 6(n^2 + 1)$ is true for $n = 1$, 2, and 3. Is it true for every $n \in N$?

13. Prove that $1 + 2 + 3 + \cdots + n < \frac{1}{8}(2n + 1)^2$ for every $n \in N$.

14. Prove that $\bar{z}_1 + \bar{z}_2 + \cdots + \bar{z}_n = \overline{z_1 + z_2 + \cdots z_n}$ for all $z_j \in C$ and every $n \in N$. *Hint:* Use the result of Problem 23, Exercise 12.2.

15. Prove that $\bar{z}_1 \cdot \bar{z}_2 \cdots \bar{z}_n = \overline{z_1 \cdot z_2 \cdots z_n}$ for all $z_j \in C$ and every $n \in N$. *Hint:* Use the result of Problem 24, Exercise 12.2.

16. Prove that if $P(z)$ is a polynomial with real coefficients, then $P(\bar{z}) = \overline{P(z)}$. *Hint:* Use the results of Problems 14 and 15 above.

17. Prove that if $P(z)$ is a polynomial with real coefficients, and $P(z_0) = 0$, then $P(\bar{z}_0) = 0$. *Hint:* Use the result of Problem 16 above.

13.2 SEQUENCES

Let us consider a class of functions in which each function has as its domain either the set N of positive integers or a subset of N.

DEFINITION 13.1 *A sequence function is a function having as its domain the set N of positive integers 1, 2, 3, $\cdots$. A finite-sequence function has as its domain the set of positive integers 1, 2, 3, $\cdots$, n, for some fixed n.*

For example, the function defined by

$$s(n) = n + 3, \quad n \in \{1, 2, 3, \cdots\}, \tag{1}$$

is a sequence function. The elements in the range of such a function, considered in the order

$$s(1), s(2), s(3), s(4), \cdots,$$

are said to form a **sequence**. Similarly, the elements of a finite-sequence function, considered in order, constitute a **finite sequence**.

For example, the sequence associated with (1) is found by successively substituting the numbers 1, 2, 3, $\cdots$, for n:

$$s(1) = 1 + 3 = 4,$$

$$s(2) = 2 + 3 = 5,$$

$$s(3) = 3 + 3 = 6,$$

$$s(4) = 4 + 3 = 7,$$

etc. Thus the first four terms of (1) are 4, 5, 6, and 7. The nth term, or general term, is $n + 3$. As another example, the first five terms of the sequence defined by the equation

$$s(n) = \frac{3}{2n - 1}, \quad n \in \{1, 2, 3, \cdots\},$$

are 3/1, 3/3, 3/5, 3/7, and 3/9, and the twenty-fifty term is

$$s(25) = \frac{3}{2(25) - 1} = \frac{3}{49}.$$

Given several terms in a sequence, we are often able to construct an expression for the general term of a sequence to which they belong. Thus, if the first three terms in a sequence are

$$2, 4, 6, \cdots,$$

we may *surmise* that the general term is

$$s(n) = 2n.$$

Note, however, that the sequences for both

$$s(n) = 2n$$

and

$$t(n) = 2n + (n - 1)(n - 2)(n - 3)$$

start with 2, 4, 6, but that the two sequences differ for terms following the third.

The notation ordinarily used for the terms in a sequence is not function notation as such. It is customary to denote the *j*th term in a sequence by

Sequence notation

means of a subscript. Thus, we would use s_j rather than $s(j)$, and the sequence $s(1), s(2), s(3), s(4), \cdots$ would appear as

$$s_1, s_2, s_3, s_4, \cdots.$$

Let us next consider two special kinds of sequences that have many applications. The first kind can be defined as follows.

DEFINITION 13.2   *An **arithmetic progression** is a sequence defined by equations of the form*

$$s_1 = a,$$

$$s_{n+1} = s_n + d,$$

where $a \in R$, $d \in R$, and $n \in N$.

Determination of a given term of an arithmetic progression

Since each term in such a sequence is obtained from the preceding term by adding d, d is called the **common difference**. Thus 3, 7, 11, 15, $\cdots$ is an arithmetic progression, in which $s_1 = 3$, $d = 4$. For each such sequence, the general term is established by the following result.

THEOREM 13.2   *The nth term in the sequence defined by*

$$s_1 = a,$$

$$s_{n+1} = s_n + d,$$

where $a \in R$, $d \in R$, and $n \in N$, is

$$s_n = a + (n - 1)d. \tag{2}$$

Proof. We shall use mathematical induction. That (2) is true for the natural number 1 is evident by direct substitution of 1 in (2):

$$s_1 = a + (1-1)d = a.$$

If now we assume that (2) is true for the natural number k, then we have

$$s_k = a + (k-1)d.$$

By the defining equation, we accordingly have

$$s_{k+1} = s_k + d.$$

Replacing s_k in this expression with $a+(k-1)d$, we obtain

$$s_{k+1} = a + (k-1)d + d$$

$$= a + kd$$

$$= a + [(k+1)-1]d,$$

and the principle of mathematical induction assures us that the relationship (2) is valid for all natural numbers.

The second kind of sequence we shall consider can be defined as follows:

DEFINITION 13.3 *A **geometric progression** is a sequence defined by equations of the form*

$$s_1 = a,$$

$$s_{n+1} = rs_n,$$

where $a \in R$, $r \in R$, $a \neq 0$, $r \neq 0$, and $n \in N$.

Thus, 3, 9, 27, 81, $\cdots$ is a geometric progression in which each term except the first is obtained by multiplying the preceding term by 3. Since the effect of multiplying the terms in this way is to produce a fixed ratio between any two successive terms, the multiplier, r, is called the **common ratio**. The general term for a geometric progression is that established by the following theorem. The proof by induction is left as an exercise.

> **Determination of a given term of a geometric progression**

THEOREM 13.3 *The nth term in the sequence defined by*

$$s_1 = a,$$

$$s_{n+1} = rs_n,$$

where $a, r \in R$, $a \neq 0$, $r \neq 0$, and $n \in N$, is

$$s_n = ar^{n-1}.$$

EXERCISE 13.2

Find the first four terms in the sequence with the general term as given.

Examples.

a. $s_n = \dfrac{n(n+1)}{2}$

b. $s_n = (-1)^n 2^n$

Solutions.

a. $s_1 = \dfrac{1(1+1)}{2} = 1$

b. $s_1 = (-1)^1 2^1 = -2$

$s_2 = \dfrac{2(2+1)}{2} = 3$

$s_2 = (-1)^2 2^2 = 4$

$s_3 = \dfrac{3(3+1)}{2} = 6$

$s_3 = (-1)^3 2^3 = -8$

$s_4 = \dfrac{4(4+1)}{2} = 10;$

$s_4 = (-1)^4 2^4 = 16;$

1, 3, 6, 10

$-2, 4, -8, 16$

1. $s_n = n - 5$

2. $s_n = 2n - 3$

3. $s_n = \dfrac{n^2 - 2}{2}$

4. $s_n = \dfrac{3}{n^2 + 1}$

5. $s_n = 1 + \dfrac{1}{n}$

6. $s_n = \dfrac{n}{2n - 1}$

7. $s_n = \dfrac{n(n-1)}{2}$

8. $s_n = \dfrac{5}{n(n+1)}$

9. $s_n = (-1)^n$

10. $s_n = (-1)^{n+1}$

11. $s_n = \dfrac{(-1)^n (n-2)}{n}$

12. $s_n = (-1)^{n-1} 3^{n+1}$

Write the next three terms in each of the following arithmetic progressions.

Examples.

a. $5, 9, \cdots$

b. $x, x - a, \cdots$

Solutions. Find the common difference and then continue the sequence.

a. $d = 9 - 5 = 4;$

b. $d = (x - a) - x = -a;$

13, 17, 21

$x - 2a, x - 3a, x - 4a$

13. $3, 7, \cdots$

14. $-6, -1, \cdots$

15. $x, x + 1, \cdots$

16. $a, a + 5, \cdots$

17. $2x + 1, 2x + 4, \cdots$

18. $3a, 5a, \cdots$

Write the next four terms in each of the following geometric progressions.

Examples.

a. $3, 6, \cdots$ b. $x, 2, \cdots$

Solutions.   Find the common ratio, and then continue the sequence.

a. $r = \dfrac{6}{3} = 2;$ b. $r = \dfrac{2}{x}$ $(x \neq 0);$

     $12, 24, 48, 96$ $\dfrac{4}{4}, \dfrac{8}{x^2}, \dfrac{16}{x^3}, \dfrac{32}{x^4}$

19. $2, 8, \cdots$ 20. $4, 8, \cdots$ 21. $\dfrac{2}{3}, \dfrac{4}{3}, \cdots$

22. $\dfrac{1}{2}, -\dfrac{3}{2}, \cdots$ 23. $\dfrac{a}{x}, -1, \cdots$ 24. $\dfrac{a}{b}, \dfrac{a}{bc}, \cdots$

Example.   Find the general term and the fourteenth term of the arithmetic progression $-6, -1, \cdots$.

Solution.   Find the common difference.

$$d = -1 - (-6) = 5$$

Use $s_n = a + (n-1)d$.

$$s_n = -6 + (n-1)5 = 5n - 11$$

$$s_{14} = 5(14) - 11 = 59$$

25. Find the general term and the seventh term in the arithmetic progression $7, 11, \cdots$.

26. Find the twelfth term in the arithmetic progression $2, \dfrac{5}{2}, \cdots$.

27. Find the twentieth term in the arithmetic progression $3, -2, \cdots$.

28. Find the general term in the arithmetic progression $\dfrac{3}{4}, 2, \cdots$.

Example.   Find the general term and also the ninth term of the geometric progression $-24, 12, \cdots$.

Solution.   Find the common ratio.

$$r = \frac{12}{-24} = -\frac{1}{2}$$

Use $s_n = ar^{n-1}$.

$$s_n = -24\left(-\frac{1}{2}\right)^{n-1}$$

$$s_9 = -24\left(-\frac{1}{2}\right)^8 = -\frac{3}{32}$$

29. Find the sixth term in the geometric progression 48, 96, $\cdots$.

30. Find the eighth term in the geometric progression $-3, \dfrac{3}{2}, \cdots$.

31. Find the general term in the geometric progression $-\dfrac{1}{3} a^2, a^5, \cdots$.

32. Find the ninth term in the geometric progression $-81, -27, \cdots$.

33. If the third term in an arithmetic progression is 7 and the eighth term is 17, find the common difference. What are the first and the twentieth terms?

34. If the fifth term of an arithmetic progression is -16 and the twentieth term is -46, what is the twelfth term?

35. Which term in the arithmetic progression 4, 1, $\cdots$ is -77?

36. What is the twelfth term in an arithmetic progression in which the second term is x and the third term is y?

37. Find the first term of a geometric progression with fifth term 48 and ratio 2.

38. Find two different values for x so that $-\dfrac{3}{2}, x, -\dfrac{8}{27}$ will be in geometric progression.

39. By mathematical induction, prove Theorem 13.3.

13.3 SERIES

Associated with any sequence is a *series*.

DEFINITION 13.4   *A series is the indicated sum of the terms in a sequence.*

For example, with the finite sequence

$$4, 7, 10, \cdots, 3n + 1,$$

for a given counting number n, there is associated the finite series

$$S_n = 4 + 7 + 10 + \cdots + (3n + 1);$$

similarly, with the finite sequence

$$x, x^2, x^3, x^4, \cdots, x^n,$$

there is associated the finite series

$$S_n = x + x^2 + x^3 + x^4 + \cdots + x^n.$$

Sequences and their associated series   Since the terms in the series are the same as those in the sequence, we can refer to the first term or the second term or the general term of a series in the same manner as we do for a sequence.

Consider the series S_n of the first n terms of the general arithmetic progression,

$$S_n = a + (a + d) + (a + 2d) + \cdots + [a + (n - 1)d], \tag{1}$$

and then consider the same series written as

$$S_n = s_n + (s_n - d) + (s_n - 2d) + \cdots + [s_n - (n - 1)d], \tag{2}$$

where the terms are displayed in reverse order. Adding (1) and (2) term by term, we have

$$S_n + S_n = (a + s_n) + (a + s_n) + (a + s_n) + \cdots + (a + s_n),$$

where the term $(a + s_n)$ occurs n times. Then

Sum of the first n terms of an arithmetic progression

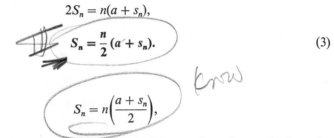

$$2S_n = n(a + s_n),$$

$$S_n = \frac{n}{2}(a + s_n). \tag{3}$$

If (3) is rewritten

$$S_n = n\left(\frac{a + s_n}{2}\right),$$

know

we observe that the sum is given by the product of the number of terms in the series and the average of the first and last terms. The validity of (3) can be established by mathematical induction and is left as an exercise.

An alternative form for (3) is obtained by substituting $a + (n - 1)d$ for s_n in (3) to obtain

$$S_n = \frac{n}{2}(a + [a + (n - 1)d]),$$

An alternative form

$$S_n = \frac{n}{2}[2a + (n - 1)d], \qquad \text{this one}$$

where the sum is now expressed in terms of a, n, and d.

To find an explicit representation for the sum of a given number of terms in a geometric progression in terms of a, r, and n, we employ a device somewhat similar to the one used in finding the sum in an arithmetic progression. Consider the geometric series (4) containing n terms, and the series (5) obtained by multiplying both members of (4) by r:

$$S_n = a + ar + ar^2 + ar^3 + \cdots + ar^{n-2} + ar^{n-1}, \tag{4}$$

$$rS_n = ar + ar^2 + ar^3 + ar^4 + \cdots + ar^{n-1} + ar^n. \tag{5}$$

When we subtract (5) from (4), all terms in the right-hand members except the first term in (4) and the last term in (5) vanish, yielding

$$S_n - rS_n = a - ar^n.$$

4, 12, 36 ... ₐₘ   ① ar^{n-1} $4(3)^{n-1}$
           ② add 1ˢᵗ 12 terms

Factoring S_n from the left-hand member gives

Sum of the first n terms of a geometric progression

$$(1 - r)S_n = a - ar^n,$$

$$S_n = \frac{a - ar^n}{1 - r}, \tag{6}$$

if $r \neq 1$, and we have a formula for the sum of the first n terms of a geometric progression. The validity of Equation (6) can be established by mathematical induction and is left as an exercise.

An alternative expression for (6) can be obtained by first writing

$$S_n = \frac{a - r(ar^{n-1})}{1 - r},$$

and then, since $s_n = ar^{n-1}$, expressing this as

An alternative form

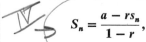

$$S_n = \frac{a - rs_n}{1 - r}, \tag{7}$$

Know

where the sum is now given in terms of a, s_n, and r.

Know

A series for which the general term is known can be represented in a very convenient, compact way by means of what is called **sigma**, or **summation, notation**. The Greek letter $\sum$ (sigma) is used to denote a sum. For example,

$$S_n = 4 + 7 + 10 + \cdots + (3n + 1)$$

can be written

$$S_n = \sum_{j=1}^{n} (3j + 1),$$

where we understand that S_n is the series having terms obtained by replacing j in the expression $3j + 1$ with the numbers $1, 2, 3, \cdots, n$, successively. Similarly,

$$S = \sum_{j=3}^{6} j^2$$

appears in expanded form as

$$S = 3^2 + 4^2 + 5^2 + 6^2,$$

where the first value for j is 3 and the last is 6.

The variable used in conjunction with summation notation is called the **index of summation**, and the set of integers over which we sum (in this case, $\{3, 4, 5, 6\}$) is called the **range of summation**.

Notation for an infinite sum

To indicate that a series has an infinite number of terms, we cannot use the notation S_n for the sum, because there is no value to substitute for n. We therefore adopt notation such as

$$S_\infty \sim \sum_{j=1}^{\infty} \frac{1}{2^j} \tag{8}$$

to indicate that there is no last term in a series. In expanded form, the infinite sequence (8) is given by

$$S_\infty \sim \frac{1}{2} + \frac{1}{4} + \frac{1}{8} + \cdots.$$

The meaning, if any, of such an infinite sum will be discussed in Section 13.4.

EXERCISE 13.3

Write each series in expanded form.

Examples.

a. $\displaystyle\sum_{j=2}^{5}(j^2 + 1)$

b. $\displaystyle\sum_{k=1}^{\infty}(-1)^k 2^{k+1}$

Solutions.

a. $j = 2,\quad 2^2 + 1 = 5;$
   $j = 3,\quad 3^2 + 1 = 10;$
   $j = 4,\quad 4^2 + 1 = 17;$
   $j = 5,\quad 5^2 + 1 = 26.$

b. $k = 1,\quad (-1)^1 2^{1+1} = (-1)(4) = -4;$
   $k = 2,\quad (-1)^2 2^{2+1} = (1)(8) = 8;$
   $k = 3,\quad (-1)^3 2^{3+1} = (-1)(16) = -16.$

$\displaystyle\sum_{j=2}^{5}(j^2 + 1) = 5 + 10 + 17 + 26$

$\displaystyle\sum_{k=1}^{\infty}(-1)^k 2^{k+1} = -4 + 8 - 16 + \cdots$

1. $\displaystyle\sum_{j=1}^{4} j^2$

2. $\displaystyle\sum_{j=1}^{3}(3j - 2)$

3. $\displaystyle\sum_{j=1}^{4}\frac{(-1)^j}{2^j}$

4. $\displaystyle\sum_{i=3}^{5}\frac{(-1)^{i+1}}{i-2}$

5. $\displaystyle\sum_{k=0}^{\infty}\frac{1}{2^k}$

6. $\displaystyle\sum_{k=0}^{\infty}\frac{k}{1+k}$

Write each series in sigma notation.

Examples.

a. $5 + 8 + 11 + 14$

b. $x^2 + x^4 + x^6 + \cdots + x^{2n}$

c. $\dfrac{3}{5} + \dfrac{5}{7} + \dfrac{7}{9} + \cdots$

Solutions. Find an expression for the general term and write in sigma notation.

a. $3j + 2$

b. x^{2j}

c. $\dfrac{2j+1}{2j+3}$

$\displaystyle\sum_{j=1}^{4}(3j + 2)$

$\displaystyle\sum_{j=1}^{n} x^{2j}$

$\displaystyle\sum_{j=1}^{\infty}\frac{2j+1}{2j+3}$

7. $x + x^3 + x^5 + x^7$

8. $x^3 + x^5 + x^7 + x^9 + x^{11}$

9. $1 + 4 + 9 + 16 + 25$

10. $\dfrac{1}{3} + \dfrac{1}{9} + \dfrac{1}{27} + \dfrac{1}{81}$

11. $1 \cdot 2 + 2 \cdot 3 + 3 \cdot 4 + 4 \cdot 5 + \cdots$

12. $\dfrac{1}{2} + \dfrac{2}{3} + \dfrac{3}{4} + \dfrac{4}{5} + \cdots$

13. $\dfrac{2}{1} + \dfrac{3}{2} + \dfrac{4}{3} + \dfrac{5}{4} + \cdots$

14. $\dfrac{1}{1} + \dfrac{2}{3} + \dfrac{3}{5} + \dfrac{4}{7} + \cdots$

$$\sum_{j=1}^{\infty} \frac{1}{2i+1}$$

Find each of the following sums.

Example. $\displaystyle\sum_{j=1}^{12} (4j + 1)$

$$\sum_{j=1}^{\infty} \frac{1}{j+1}$$

Solution. Write the first two or three terms in expanded form:

$$5 + 9 + 13 + \cdots .$$

This is an arithmetic series. The first term is 5 and the common difference is 4. Therefore we can use

$$S_n = \frac{n}{2}[2a + (n-1)d] \qquad a = \text{1st term}$$

to obtain

$$S_{12} = \frac{12}{2}[2(5) + (12-1)4] = 324.$$

$S_n = \dfrac{7}{2}\left[2(3) + (7-1)2\right]$
$\quad \dfrac{6 + 12}{+8 \; 9 = 63}$

$3, 5$

15. $\displaystyle\sum_{j=1}^{7} (2j+1)$

16. $\displaystyle\sum_{j=1}^{21} (3j-2)$

17. $\displaystyle\sum_{j=3}^{15} (7j-1)$

18. $\displaystyle\sum_{j=10}^{20} (2j-3)$

19. $\displaystyle\sum_{k=1}^{8} \left(\frac{1}{2}k - 3\right)$

20. $\displaystyle\sum_{k-1}^{100} k$

Example. $\displaystyle\sum_{j=2}^{5} \left(\frac{1}{3}\right)^{j}$

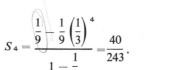

Solution. Write the first two terms in expanded form:

$$\left(\frac{1}{3}\right)^{2} + \left(\frac{1}{3}\right)^{3} + \cdots .$$

This is a geometric series in which the first term is $\dfrac{1}{9}$, the ratio is $\dfrac{1}{3}$, and $n = 4$. Therefore we can use $S_n = \dfrac{a - ar^n}{1 - r}$ to obtain

$$S_4 = \frac{\dfrac{1}{9} - \dfrac{1}{9}\left(\dfrac{1}{3}\right)^{4}}{1 - \dfrac{1}{3}} = \frac{40}{243}.$$

$S_n = a r^{(n-1)}$

$S_n = \dfrac{a - r a^n}{1 - r}$

21. $\displaystyle\sum_{j=1}^{6} 3^{j}$

22. $\displaystyle\sum_{j=1}^{4} (-2)^{j}$

23. $\displaystyle\sum_{k=3}^{7} \left(\frac{1}{2}\right)^{k-2}$

24. $\displaystyle\sum_{j=3}^{12} 2^{j-5}$

25. $\displaystyle\sum_{j=1}^{6} \left(\frac{1}{3}\right)^{j}$

26. $\displaystyle\sum_{j=1}^{4} (3 + 2^{j})$

27. Find the sum of all even integers n, for $13 < n < 29$.

28. Find the sum of all integral multiples of 7 between 8 and 110.

29. How many bricks will there be in a pile one brick in thickness if there are 27 bricks in the bottom row, 25 in the second row, etc., and one in the top row?

30. If there are a total of 256 bricks in a pile arranged in the manner of those in Problem 29, how many bricks are there in the third row from the bottom of the pile?

31. Find $\sum_{j=1}^{n} \left(\frac{1}{2}\right)^{j}$ for $n = 2, 3, 4$, and 5. What value do you think $\sum_{j=1}^{n} \left(\frac{1}{2}\right)^{j}$ approximates as n becomes larger and larger?

32. Find a if $\sum_{j=1}^{5} aj = 14$.

33. Find p and q if $\sum_{j=1}^{4} (pj + q) = 28$ and $\sum_{j=2}^{5} (pj + q) = 44$.

34. Consider

$$S_n = \sum_{i=1}^{n} f(i).$$

Explain why this equation defines a sequence function. What is the variable denoting an element in the domain? The range?

35. By mathematical induction, prove that for an arithmetic progression, $S_n = \frac{n}{2}(a + s_n)$ for all positive integral values of n.

36. Show that the sequence formed by adding the corresponding terms in two arithmetic progressions is an arithmetic progression.

37. Show that the sum of the terms in two series with terms in arithmetic progression can be written as a series with terms in arithmetic progression.

38. By mathematical induction, prove that, for a geometric progression, $S_n = \frac{a - ar^n}{1 - r}$ for all positive integral values of n, provided $r \neq 1$.

13.4 LIMITS OF SEQUENCES AND SERIES

A sequence that is strictly increasing but bounded

Consider the sequence function defined by

$$S_n = \frac{n}{n + 1}, n \in N. \tag{1}$$

If we write the range of (1) in the form

$$\frac{1}{2}, \frac{2}{3}, \frac{3}{4}, \frac{4}{5}, \cdots, \frac{n}{n + 1}, \cdots,$$

then it is clear that each of the terms is greater than the preceding term; indeed, the difference of consecutive terms is

$$\frac{n+1}{n+2} - \frac{n}{n+1} = \frac{(n^2+2n+1)-(n^2+2n)}{(n+1)(n+2)} = \frac{1}{(n+1)(n+2)} > 0.$$

Such a sequence is said to be **strictly increasing**. On the other hand, it is also clear that, no matter how large a value is assigned to n, we have

$$\frac{n}{n+1} < 1,$$

because the denominator is one larger than the numerator; in fact, we have

$$1 - \frac{n}{n+1} = \frac{(n+1)-n}{n+1} = \frac{1}{n+1} > 0.$$

Thus we have a sequence in which each term is greater than the preceding term and yet no term is equal to or greater than 1.

We note, however—and this is a very basic consideration—that the value of $n/(n+1)$ is as close to 1 as we please if n is large enough. For example, the difference satisfies

$$1 - \frac{n}{n+1} = \frac{1}{n+1}, \quad \text{and we have} \quad \frac{1}{n+1} < \frac{1}{1000}$$

provided $n + 1 > 1000$—that is, $n > 999$. If it is true that the nth term in a sequence differs from the number L by as little as we please for all sufficiently large n, we say that **the sequence approaches the number L as a limit**. The symbolism

Notation for the limit of a sequence

$$\lim_{n \to \infty} s_n = L$$

(read "the limit, as n increases without bound, of s_n is L") is used to denote this situation. A thorough discussion of the notion of a limit is included in courses in calculus, and will not be attempted here. A few elementary ideas, however, are in order.

A sequence in which the nth term approaches a number L as $n \to \infty$ is said to be a **convergent sequence**, and the sequence is said to **converge** to L.

It is not necessary for convergence that a sequence be strictly increasing. For example,

$$1, \frac{1}{2}, \frac{1}{3}, \frac{1}{4}, \cdots, \frac{1}{n}, \cdots$$

converges to 0, but each term in the sequence is less than, instead of greater than, the term that precedes it. Again, the sequence

$$-1, \frac{1}{2}, -\frac{1}{3}, \frac{1}{4}, \cdots, \frac{(-1)^n}{n}, \cdots$$

converges to 0 but is neither increasing nor decreasing.

We can rephrase the definition of convergence of a sequence as follows:

DEFINITION 13.5   *A sequence $s_1, s_2, \cdots, s_n, \cdots$ converges to the number L,*

$$\lim_{n \to \infty} s_n = L,$$

if and only if the absolute value of the difference between the nth term in the sequence and the number L is as small as we please for all sufficiently large n. Thus the sequence converges to the number L if and only if

$$\lim_{n \to \infty} |L - s_n| = 0.$$

For example, the **alternating** (because the signs alternate) **sequence**

$$\frac{-2}{3}, \frac{4}{9}, \frac{-8}{27}, \cdots, \left(\frac{-2}{3}\right)^n, \cdots$$

converges to 0 since the absolute value of the difference between $(-2/3)^n$ and 0, i.e., $|0 - (-2/3)^n|$, is as small as we please for n large enough. We express this by writing

$$\lim_{n \to \infty} \left(\frac{-2}{3}\right)^n = 0.$$

On the other hand, the alternating sequence

$$\frac{1}{2}, -\frac{2}{3}, \frac{3}{4}, -\frac{4}{5}, \cdots, (-1)^{n+1}\frac{n}{n+1}, \cdots$$

does not converge. As n increases, the nth term oscillates back and forth from the neighborhood of $+1$ to the neighborhood of -1, and we cannot find a number L such that $\lim_{n \to \infty} |L - s_n| = 0$. Such a sequence is said to **diverge**. A sequence such as

$$1, 2, 3, \cdots, n, \cdots$$

also is said to diverge. An answer to the logical question of what we mean by "enough" when we say "n large enough" requires a more precise definition of limit than we have given here. As remarked earlier, a course in the calculus will treat this in detail.

For an infinite series,

$$S_\infty \sim \sum_{j=1}^{\infty} s_j,$$

we can consider the infinite sequence of **partial sums**:

$$S_1 = s_1,$$

$$S_2 = s_1 + s_2,$$

| The associated |
| sequence of |
| partial sums |
| of a series |

$$. \quad . \quad . \quad .$$

$$S_n = s_1 + s_2 + \cdots + s_n,$$

$$. \quad . \quad . \quad . \quad . \quad . \quad . \quad .$$

DEFINITION 13.6 *An infinite series*

$$S_\infty \sim \sum_{j=1}^{\infty} s_j$$

converges *if and only if* $S_1, S_2, \cdots, S_n, \cdots$, *the corresponding sequence of partial sums, converges.*

If the sequence of partial sums converges to the number L,

$$\lim_{n \to \infty} S_n = L,$$

then L is said to be the **sum** of the infinite series, and we write

$$S_\infty = \sum_{j=1}^{\infty} s_j = L.$$

If the sequence of partial sums diverges, then the series is said to **diverge**.

We recall from Section 13.3 that the sum of n terms (the nth partial sum) of a geometric progression is given, for $r \neq 1$, by

$$S_n = \frac{a - ar^n}{1 - r}. \tag{2}$$

If $|r| < 1$, that is, if $-1 < r < 1$, then $|r|^n$ becomes smaller and smaller for increasingly large n. For example, if $r = \frac{1}{2}$, then

$$r^2 = \frac{1}{4}, \quad r^3 = \frac{1}{8}, \quad r^4 = \frac{1}{16},$$

etc., and $(1/2)^n$ is as small as we please if n is sufficiently large. Writing (2) as

$$S_n = \frac{a}{1 - r}(1 - r^n), \tag{3}$$

we see that the value of the factor $(1 - r^n)$ is as close as we please to 1 provided $|r| < 1$ and n is taken large enough. Since this argument shows that the sequence of partial sums (3) converges to

$$\frac{a}{1 - r},$$

we have the following result.

THEOREM 13.4 *The sum of an infinite geometric progression, $a + ar + ar^2 + \cdots + ar^n + \cdots$, with $|r| < 1$, is*

$$S_\infty = \lim_{n \to \infty} S_n = \frac{a}{1 - r}.$$

An interesting application of this sum arises in connection with repeating decimals—that is, decimal numerals that, after a finite number of decimal places, have endlessly repeating groups of digits. For example,

Repeating decimals as infinite geometric progressions

$$0.2121\overline{21},$$

$$0.138512512\overline{512}$$

are repeating decimals. The bar denotes that the numerals appearing under it are repeated endlessly. Consider the problem of expressing such a decimal fraction as an arithmetic fraction. We illustrate the process involved with the first example above. The decimal $0.21212\overline{1}$ can be written as

$$0.21 + 0.0021 + 0.000021 + \cdots, \qquad (4)$$

which is a geometric progression with ratio $r = 0.01$. Since the ratio is less than 1 in absolute value, we can use Theorem 13.4 to find the sum of the infinite series (4). Thus

$$S_\infty = \frac{a}{1-r} = \frac{0.21}{1-0.01} = \frac{21}{99} = \frac{7}{33},$$

and the given decimal fraction is equivalent to 7/33.

The function values in the ranges of some important nonalgebraic functions are not easily evaluated for all x in the domain. Fortunately, though, infinite **power series** in x, or series of the form

Power series for circular functions

$$a_0 + a_1 x + \cdots a_n x^n + \cdots,$$

for these functions can be determined by means of calculus.

For example, by means of calculus, it can be shown that, for all $x \in R$,

$$\cos x = 1 - \frac{x^2}{2!} + \frac{x^4}{4!} - \frac{x^6}{6!} + \cdots + (-1)^{n-1} \frac{x^{2n-2}}{(2n-2)!} + \cdots, \qquad (5)$$

$$\sin x = x - \frac{x^3}{3!} + \frac{x^5}{5!} - \frac{x^7}{7!} + \cdots + (-1)^{n-1} \frac{x^{2n-1}}{(2n-1)!} + \cdots. \qquad (6)$$

Example. Find an approximation for cos 0.1, using the first two terms in the series (5), above.

Solution. $\cos(0.1) \approx 1 - \dfrac{(0.1)^2}{2!} = 1.00000 - 0.00500$

$$= 0.99500.$$

Power series for e^x

We shall consider one more series, namely the power series for e^x. It can be shown that, for all $x \in R$,

$$e^x = 1 + x + \frac{x^2}{2!} + \frac{x^3}{3!} + \cdots + \frac{x^{n-1}}{(n-1)!} + \cdots, \qquad (7)$$

and for all $z \in C$,

$$e^z = 1 + z + \frac{z^2}{2!} + \frac{z^3}{3!} + \cdots + \frac{z^{n-1}}{(n-1)!} + \cdots.$$

In particular, for $z = ix$, we have

$$e^{ix} = 1 + ix - \frac{x^2}{2!} - i\frac{x^3}{3!} + \cdots + \frac{(ix)^{n-1}}{(n-1)!} + \cdots.$$

Now the terms in the series for e^{ix} are alternately the terms in the series for $\cos x$ and i times the terms in the series for $\sin x$. Accordingly, we have the celebrated identity

$$e^{ix} = \cos x + i \sin x,$$

which is known as **Euler's formula** in honor of its discoverer, the prolific Swiss mathematician Leonhard Euler (1701–1783).

EXERCISE 13.4

Discuss the limiting behavior of each expression as $n \to \infty$.

Example. $\dfrac{n^2 + 3}{n^2}$

Solution. By writing $\dfrac{n^2 + 3}{n^2}$ as $\dfrac{n^2}{n^2} + \dfrac{3}{n^2}$ and then as $1 + \dfrac{3}{n^2}$, we observe that

$$\lim_{n \to \infty} \frac{n^2 + 3}{n^2} = \lim \left(1 + \frac{3}{n^2}\right) = 1 + 0 = 1.$$

1. $\dfrac{1}{n}$ 2. $1 + \dfrac{1}{n^2}$ 3. $\dfrac{n+1}{n}$ 4. $\dfrac{n+3}{n^2}$

5. $2n$ 6. $(-1)^n$ 7. $\dfrac{1}{2^n}$ 8. $(-1)^n\dfrac{1}{n}$

State which of the following sequences are convergent.

Example. $1, \dfrac{3}{2}, \dfrac{7}{4}, \dfrac{15}{8}, \cdots, \dfrac{2^n - 1}{2^{n-1}}$

Solution. Writing the general term as $\dfrac{2^n}{2^{n-1}} - \dfrac{1}{2^{n-1}}$, or $2 - \dfrac{1}{2^{n-1}}$, we observe that

$$\lim_{n \to \infty} \frac{2^n - 1}{2^{n-1}} = \lim_{n \to \infty} \left(2 - \frac{1}{2^{n-1}}\right) = 2 - 0 = 2.$$

The sequence is convergent.

9. $\dfrac{1}{2}, \dfrac{1}{4}, \dfrac{1}{8}, \dfrac{1}{16}, \cdots, \dfrac{1}{2^n}$

10. $2, \dfrac{3}{2}, \dfrac{4}{3}, \dfrac{5}{4}, \cdots, \dfrac{n+1}{n}$

11. $1, 2, 3, 4, 5, \cdots, n$

12. $2, 4, 6, 8, \cdots, 2n$

13. $1, -\dfrac{1}{2}, \dfrac{1}{4}, -\dfrac{1}{8}, \cdots, (-1)^{n+1}\dfrac{1}{2^{n-1}}$

14. $1, -1, 1, -1, \cdots, (-1)^{n+1}$

Find the sum of each of the following infinite geometric series. If the series has no sum, so state.

Examples.

a. $3 + 2 + \cdots$

b. $\dfrac{1}{81} - \dfrac{1}{54} + \cdots$

Solutions.

a. $r = \dfrac{2}{3}$; series has a sum since $|r| < 1$.

$$S_\infty = \dfrac{a}{1-r} = \dfrac{3}{1-\dfrac{2}{3}} = 9$$

b. $r = -\dfrac{1}{54} \div \dfrac{1}{81} = -\dfrac{3}{2}$; series does not have a sum since $|r| > 1$.

15. $12 + 6 + \cdots$

16. $2 + 1 + \cdots$

17. $\dfrac{1}{36} + \dfrac{1}{30} + \cdots$

18. $\dfrac{1}{16} - \dfrac{1}{8} + \cdots$

19. $\displaystyle\sum_{j=1}^{\infty} \left(\dfrac{2}{3}\right)^j$

20. $\displaystyle\sum_{j=1}^{\infty} \left(-\dfrac{1}{4}\right)^j$

Find an arithmetic fraction equal to each of the given decimal numerals.

Example. $0.81\overline{81}$

Solution. Rewrite as a series: $0.81 + 0.0081 + 0.000081 + \cdots$.

Find the common ratio: $r = 0.01$. Use $S_\infty = \dfrac{a}{1-r}$.

$$S_\infty = \dfrac{0.81}{1 - 0.01} = \dfrac{81}{99} = \dfrac{9}{11}.$$

21. $0.3131\overline{31}$

22. $0.4545\overline{45}$

23. $2.4104\overline{10}$

24. $3.027\overline{027}$

25. $0.12888\overline{8}$

26. $0.8333\overline{3}$

27. A force is applied to a particle moving in a straight line in such a fashion that each second it moves only one half of the distance it moved the preceding second. If the particle moves ten centimeters the first second, approximately how far will it move before coming to rest?

28. The arc length through which the bob on a pendulum moves is nine-tenths of its preceding arc length. Approximately how far will the bob move before coming to rest if the first arc length is 12 inches?

In Problems 29–36, use the first two terms of equation (5), (6), or (7), in this section to find an approximation for the given expression.

29. cos 0.2   30. cos 0.3   31. cos 0.4   32. sin 0.1

33. sin 0.3   34. sin 0.4   35. e^0 36. $e^{0.1}$

37. Use Euler's formula to find a value for $e^{i\pi}$.

38. Use Euler's formula to show that $e^{-ix} = \cos x - i \sin x$.

13.5 THE BINOMIAL THEOREM

There are situations, as in the binomial expansion given below, in which it is

Factorial notation

necessary to write the product of consecutive positive integers. To facilitate writing products of this type, we use a special symbol, $n!$ (read "n factorial" or "factorial n"), which is defined recursively by

$$0! = 1,$$

$$n! = n \cdot (n-1)!, \quad n \in N.$$

It follows from this definition that

$$n! = n(n-1)(n-2) \cdots (1),$$

for every $n \in N$ (see Problem 43, Exercise 13.5).

Examples.   a. $4! = 4 \cdot 3 \cdot 2 \cdot 1$ b. $27! = 27 \cdot 26!$ c. $(n+2)! = (n+2)(n+1)!$

The series obtained by expanding a binomial of the form

$$(a + b)^n$$

is particularly useful in certain branches of mathematics. Starting with familiar examples, in which n has the value 1, 2, 3, 4, and 5 in turn, we can show by direct multiplication that

$$(a + b)^1 = a + b,$$
$$(a + b)^2 = a^2 + 2ab + b^2,$$
$$(a + b)^3 = a^3 + 3a^2b + 3ab^2 + b^3,$$
$$(a + b)^4 = a^4 + 4a^3b + 6a^2b^2 + 4ab^3 + b^4,$$
$$(a + b)^5 = a^5 + 5a^4b + 10a^3b^2 + 10a^2b^3 + 5ab^4 + b^5.$$

$(a+b)^4 = a^4 + 4a^3b + 6a^2b^2 + 4ab^3 + b^4$

$(a+b)^5 = a^5 + 5a^4b + 10a^3b^2 + 10a^2b^3 + 5ab^4 + b^5$

The coefficients of the terms form the following pattern, known as **Pascal's triangle**:

$$
\begin{array}{ll}
(a+b)^0 & \quad\quad\quad\quad 1 \\
(a+b)^1 & \quad\quad\quad 1 \quad 1 \\
(a+b)^2 & \quad\quad 1 \quad 2 \quad 1 \\
(a+b)^3 & \quad 1 \quad 3 \quad 3 \quad 1 \\
(a+b)^4 & 1 \quad 4 \quad 6 \quad 4 \quad 1 \\
(a+b)^5 & 1 \quad 5 \quad 10 \quad 10 \quad 5 \quad 1
\end{array}
$$

Here each entry other than the 1's is obtained by addition from the two nearest entries in the immediately preceding row, as suggested by the red arrows.

The foregoing expansions suggest the following result, which is called the **binomial theorem**.

$$\frac{n}{k} = \frac{n!}{(n-k)!\,k!}$$

$$\sum_{k=0}^{n} \binom{n}{k} a^{n-k} \cdot b^{k}$$

THEOREM 13.5 *For each natural number n,*

$$(a+b)^n = a^n + \frac{n!}{(n-1)!\,1!}\,a^{n-1}b + \frac{n!}{(n-2)!\,2!}\,a^{n-2}b^2$$

$$+ \frac{n!}{(n-3)!\,3!}\,a^{n-3}b^3 + \cdots + \frac{n!}{1!(n-1)!}\,ab^{n-1} + b^n,$$

in which the coefficient of $a^{n-r}b^r$ is

$$\frac{n!}{(n-r)!\,r!}.$$

learn ↑

$$\binom{5}{2}$$

$$\frac{r}{s} = \frac{r}{s(r-s)}$$

$$= \frac{5 \cdot 4 \cdot 3 \cdot 2 \cdot 1}{1 \cdot 2} \frac{1 \cdot 2 \cdot 3}{}$$

The proof, which is not given, can be accomplished by using mathematical induction.

Note that the *t*-th term in Theorem 13.5 is given by

General term in a geometric progression	$\dfrac{n!}{(n-r)!\,r!}\,a^{n-r}b^r,$	(1)

where $r = t - 1$.

An alternative and useful form of (1) is given by

$$\frac{n\cdot(n-1)\cdot(n-2)\cdots(n-t+2)}{(t-1)!}\,a^{n-t+1}b^{t-1},\qquad(2)$$

where r has been replaced by $t - 1$.

$$\binom{r}{0} + \binom{r}{1} + \binom{r}{2} \cdots \quad \frac{r}{r-2} + \frac{r}{r-1} + \frac{r}{r} = 2^r$$

number of subsets in a set is 2^r

EXERCISE 13.5

Simplify each expression.

Examples. a. $\dfrac{4!6!}{8!}$ b. $\dfrac{(n-1)!}{(n-3)!}$

Solutions. a. $\dfrac{4\cdot3\cdot2\cdot1\cdot6!}{8\cdot7\cdot6!} = \dfrac{3}{7}$ b. $\dfrac{(n-1)(n-2)(n-3)!}{(n-3)!} = (n-1)(n-2)$

1. $4!$ 2. $6!$ 3. $\dfrac{9!}{8!}$

4. $\dfrac{13!}{10!}$ 5. $\dfrac{5!7!}{8!}$ 6. $\dfrac{(12!)(8!)}{16!}$

7. $\dfrac{(8-2)!}{(4+1)!}$ 8. $\dfrac{(10+3)!}{(12-1)!}$ 9. $\dfrac{6!}{7!-6!}$

10. $\dfrac{3!+4!}{4!}$ 11. $\dfrac{3!+5!}{5!-3!}$ 12. $\dfrac{n!}{(n-1)!}$

13. $\dfrac{(n+2)!}{n!}$ 14. $\dfrac{(n+2)!}{(n-1)!}$ 15. $\dfrac{(n+1)(n+2)!}{(n+3)!}$

Write each binomial power in expanded form and simplify.

Example. $(a-3b)^4$

Solution. $a^4 + 4a^3(-3b) + \dfrac{12}{2!}a^2(-3b)^2 + \dfrac{24}{3!}a(-3b)^3 + \dfrac{24}{4!}(-3b)^4$

$$= a^4 - 12a^3b + 54a^2b^2 - 108ab^3 + 81b^4$$

16. $(x-y)^5$ 17. $(x+y)^5$ 18. $(x+y)^4$

19. $(x-3)^4$ 20. $(2x-1)^5$ 21. $\left(2x-\dfrac{y}{2}\right)^3$

22. $\left(\dfrac{x}{3}+3\right)^5$ 23. $\left(\dfrac{x}{2}+2\right)^6$ 24. $\left(\dfrac{2}{3}-a^2\right)^4$

Write the first four terms in the expansion of each binomial power. Do not simplify.

Example. $(x+2y)^{15}$

Solution. $x^{15} + 15x^{14}(2y) + \dfrac{15\cdot14}{2!}x^{13}(2y)^2 + \dfrac{15\cdot14\cdot13}{3!}x^{12}(2y)^3 + \cdots$

25. $(x+y)^{20}$ 26. $(x-y)^{15}$ 27. $(a-2b)^{12}$

28. $(2a-b)^{12}$ 29. $(x-\sqrt{2})^{10}$ 30. $\left(\dfrac{x}{2}+2\right)^8$

Find to the nearest hundredth.

31. $(1.02)^{10}$ *Hint:* $1.02 = (1 + 0.02)$.

32. $(1.01)^{15}$ 33. $(0.99)^8$ 34. $(0.98)^8$

35. If an amount A of money is invested at 4% compounded annually, the amount P present at the end of n years is given by $P = A(1 + 0.04)^n$. Find the amount present, to the nearest cent, if $1000 is invested for 5 years.

36. In Problem 35, find the amount present at the end of 20 years.

Find the specified term in the expansion of each binomial power.

Example. $(x - 2y)^{12}$, the seventh term.

Solution. In Formula (2), page 339, use $n = 12$ and $t = 7$.

The seventh term is $\dfrac{12 \cdot 11 \cdot 10 \cdot 9 \cdot 8 \cdot 7}{6!} \; x^6 \, (-2y)^6 = 59{,}136 x^6 y^6.$

37. $(a - b)^{15}$, the sixth term.   38. $(x + 2)^{12}$, the fifth term.

39. $(x - 2y)^{10}$, the fifth term.   40. $(a^3 - b)^9$, the seventh term.

41. Given that the binomial formula holds as an infinite "sum" for $(1 + x)^n$, where n is a negative integer and $|x| < 1$,

   (a) write the first four terms of $(1 + x)^{-1}$;

   (b) find the first four terms of the quotient $1/(1 + x)$ by dividing $(1 + x)$ into 1.

   Compare the results of (a) and (b).

42. Given that the binomial formula holds as an infinite "sum" for $(1 + x)^n$, where n is a rational number and $|x| < 1$, find to two decimal places:

   (a) $\sqrt{1.02}$;   (b) $\sqrt{0.99}$. *Hint:* Make the reasonable assumption that all terms after the third can be neglected.

43. Prove from the recursive definition $0! = 1$, $n! = n(n - 1)!$, $n \in N$, that

$$n! = n(n - 1)(n - 2) \cdots (1) \quad \text{for every } n \in N.$$

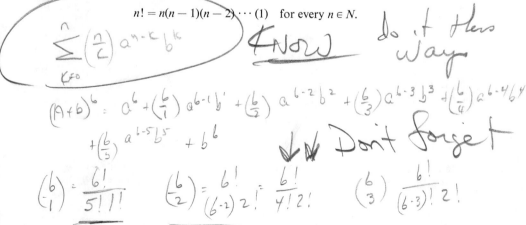

14 PROBABILITY

14.1 BASIC COUNTING PRINCIPLES; PERMUTATIONS

Associated with each finite set A is a nonnegative integer n, namely the number of elements in A. Hence, we have a function from the set of all finite sets to the set of nonnegative integers. The symbolism $n(A)$ is used to denote elements in the range of this set function n. For example, if

$$A = \{5, 7, 9\}, \quad B = \{1/2, 0, 3, -5, 7\}, \quad C = \emptyset,$$

then

$$n(A) = 3, \quad n(B) = 5, \quad \text{and} \quad n(C) = 0.$$

All the sets with which we shall hereafter be concerned are assumed to be finite sets. We then have the following properties, called **counting properties**, for the function n.

I $n(A \cup B) = n(A) + n(B)$, if $A \cap B = \emptyset$.

Thus, if A and B are disjoint sets, then the number of elements in their union is the sum of the number of elements in A and the number of elements in B. Set functions with Property I are said to be **finitely additive**; that is, a set function f is finitely additive provided that, for all A, B satisfying $A \cap B = \emptyset$, we have $f(A \cup B) = f(A) + f(B)$.

The number of elements in the union of two sets

For example, suppose there are five roads from town R to town S, and two railroads from town R to town S. If A is the set of roads and B the set of railroads from R to S, then $n(A) = 5$, $n(B) = 2$, and $n(A \cup B) = 5 + 2 = 7$; thus there are seven ways one can go from town R to town S by driving or riding on a train.

II $n(A \cup B) = n(A) + n(B) - n(A \cap B)$, if $A \cap B \neq \emptyset$.

That is, if A and B overlap, then to count the number of elements in $A \cup B$, we might add the number of elements in A to the number of elements in B. But since any elements in the intersection of A and B are counted twice in this process (once in A and once in B), we must subtract the number of such elements from the sum $n(A) + n(B)$ to obtain the number of elements in $A \cup B$, as suggested in Figure 14.1.

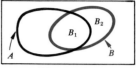

Figure 14.1

For example, suppose there are fifteen unrelated girls and seventeen unrelated boys in a mathematics class, and suppose that there are precisely two brother-sister pairs in the class. If A denotes the set of different families represented by the girls and if B denotes the set of different families represented by the boys, then the number of different families represented by the members of the class is $n(A) + n(B) - n(A \cap B) = 15 + 17 - 2 = 30$.

Actually, it can be shown that Property II is a consequence of Property I.

III $n(A \times B) = n(A) \cdot n(B)$.

> **The number of elements in the Cartesian product of two sets**

This asserts that the number of elements in the Cartesian product of sets A and B is the product of the number of elements in A and the number of elements in B.

For example, suppose again that there are five roads from town R to town S (set A), and further suppose that there are three roads from town S to town T (set B). Then for each element of A there are three elements of B, and the total possible ways one can drive from R to T via S is

$$n(A \times B) = n(A) \cdot n(B) = 5 \cdot 3 = 15.$$

Given the set of digits $A = \{1, 2, 3\}$, how many different three-digit numerals can be constructed from the members of A if no member is used more than once? The answer to this question can be obtained by simply listing the different three-digit numerals, $123, 132, 213, 231, 312, 321$, and counting them. Such a procedure would be quite impracticable, however, if the number of members of the given set of numerals were very large. Another way to arrive at the same conclusion is by applying the third counting property. If we let A denote the set of possible first digits in the foregoing numerals, then $n(A) = 3$. Since no numeral may be used more than once, and since one numeral has already been used for a first digit, there remain but two possibilities for the second digit. If B denotes the set of possible second digits after the first digit has been chosen, then $n(B) = 2$. By similar reasoning, if C is the set of possible third digits after the first two have been chosen, then $n(C) = 1$. By the third counting property (applied twice), we find that

$$n(A \times B \times C) = [n(A) \cdot n(B)] \cdot n(C) = 3 \cdot 2 \cdot 1 = 6.$$

We can generalize from this example. First, however, let us make the following definition.

DEFINITION 14.1 *A **permutation** of a set A is an ordering (first, second, etc.) of the members of A.*

The number of permutations of a set For example, each of the three-digit numerals discussed above was a permutation of the elements of the set of numerals $\{1, 2, 3\}$. With Definition 14.1, we can state the following result.

THEOREM 14.1 *Let $P_{n,n}$ denote the number of distinct permutations of a set A, where $n(A) = n$. Then*

$$P_{n,n} = n!. \tag{1}$$

The symbol $P_{n,n}$ [or sometimes $_nP_n$ or $P\binom{n}{n}$] is read "the number of permutations of n things taken n at a time."

Proof. Let A_1 denote the set of possible selections for the first member. Then $A_1 = A$, and $n(A_1) = n(A) = n$. Having made a first selection, let A_2 denote the set of possible second selections. Then $A_2 \subset A$, and $n(A_2) = n(A_1) - 1 = n - 1$. A continuation of this procedure, together with successive application of the third counting principle, leads to

$$P_{n,n} = n(A_1) \cdot n(A_2) \cdot \cdots \cdot n(A_n) = n \cdot (n - 1)(n - 2) \cdots 1 = n!,$$

as was to be proved.

Example. In how many ways can nine men be assigned positions to form distinct baseball teams?

Solution. Let A denote the set of men, so that $n(A) = 9$. The total number of ways in which 9 men can be assigned 9 positions on a team, or, in other words, the number of possible permutations of the members of a 9-element set, is, by (1) above,

$$P_{9,9} = 9! = 9 \cdot 8 \cdot 7 \cdots 1 = 362{,}880.$$

THEOREM 14.2 *Let $P_{n,r}$ denote the number of permutations of the elements of a set A [$n(A) = n$] taken r at a time; that is, let $P_{n,r}$ be the number of distinct orderings of r elements when there is a set A of n elements from which to choose. Then*

$$P_{n,r} = n(n - 1)(n - 2) \cdots [n - (r - 1)]$$

$$= n(n - 1)(n - 2) \cdots (n - r + 1). \tag{2}$$

The proof follows the proof of Theorem 14.1, except that the last subset considered is such that $n(A_r) = n - r + 1$.

Example. In how many ways can a basketball team be formed by choosing players for the five positions from a set of ten players?

Solution. Let A denote the set of players, so that $n(A) = 10$. Then from (2) and the fact that a basketball team consists of 5 players, we have

$$P_{10,5} = 10 \cdot 9 \cdot 8 \cdots (10 - 5 + 1) = 10 \cdot 9 \cdot 8 \cdot 7 \cdot 6 = 30{,}240.$$

An alternative form for $P_{n,r}$ An alternative expression for $P_{n,r}$ can be obtained by observing that

$$P_{n,r} = n(n-1)(n-2) \cdots (n-r+1)$$
$$= \frac{n(n-1)(n-2) \cdots (n-r+1) \cdot (n-r)!}{(n-r)!},$$

so that

$$P_{n,r} = \frac{n!}{(n-r)!}. \tag{3}$$

The problem of finding the number of distinguishable permutations of n objects taken n at a time, if some of the objects are identical, requires a little more careful analysis. As an example, consider the number of permutations of the letters of the word *DIVISIBLE*.

Distinguishable permutations

We can make a distinction between the three I's by assigning subscripts to each so that we have nine distinct letters,

$$D, I_1, V, I_2, S, I_3, B, L, E.$$

The number of permutations of these nine letters is of course $9!$. If the letters other than I_1, I_2, and I_3 are retained in the position they occupy in the permutation above, I_1, I_2, and I_3 can be permuted among themselves $3!$ ways. Thus, if P is the number of distinguishable permutations of the letters

$$D, I, V, I, S, I, B, L, E,$$

then since for each of these there are $3!$ ways in which the I's can be permuted without otherwise changing the order of the other letters, it follows that

$$3! \cdot P = 9!,$$

from which

$$P = \frac{9!}{3!}.$$

As another example, consider the letters of the word *MISSISSIPPI*. There would exist $11!$ distinguishable permutations of the letters in this word if each letter were distinct. Note, however, that the letters S and I each appear four times and the letter P appears twice. Reasoning as we did in the previous example, we see that the number of distinguishable permutations of the letters in *MISSISSIPPI* is given by

$$4!4!2!P = 11!,$$

from which

$$P = \frac{11!}{4!4!2!}.$$

EXERCISE   14.1

Consider the following sets. Find $n(A \cap B)$, $n(A \cup B)$, and $n(A \times B)$.

Example. $A = \{a, b, c\}$, $B = \{c, d\}$

Solution.

$$A \cap B = \{c\}.   \text{Therefore } n(A \cap B) = 1.$$

$$A \cup B = \{a, b, c, d\}.   \text{Therefore } n(A \cup B) = 4.$$

$$A \times B = \{(a, c), (a, d), (b, c), (b, d), (c, c), (c, d)\}.   \text{Therefore } n(A \times B) = 6.$$

1. $A = \{d, e\}$, $B = \{e, f, g, h\}$ 2. $A = \{e\}$, $B = \{a, b, c, d\}$

3. $A = \{1, 2, 3, 4\}$, $B = \{3, 4, 5, 6\}$ 4. $A = \{1, 2\}$, $B = \{3, 4, 5\}$

5. $A = \{1, 2\}$, $B = \{1, 2\}$ 6. $A = \emptyset$, $B = \{2, 3, 4\}$

Example.   In how many different ways can three members of a class be assigned a grade of A, B, C, or D so that no two members receive the same grade?

Solution.   Sometimes a simple diagram, such as ____, ____, ____, designating a sequence, is a helpful preliminary device. Since the first student may receive any one of four different grades, the second student may then receive any one of three different grades, and the third student may then receive any one of two different grades, the sequence would appear as 4, 3, 2. From counting property III, there are $4 \cdot 3 \cdot 2$, or 24, possible ways the grades may be assigned. We could have obtained the same result directly from Theorem 14.2, since $P_{4,3} = 4 \cdot 3 \cdot 2 = 24$.

In the following problems, a digit or letter may be used more than once unless stated otherwise.

7. How many different two-digit numerals can be formed from the digits 5 and 6?

8. How many different two-digit numerals can be formed from the digits 7, 8, 9?

9. In how many different ways can four students be seated in a row?

10. In how many different ways can five students be seated in a row?

11. In how many different ways can four questions on a true-false test be answered?

12. In how many different ways can five questions on a true-false test be answered?

13. In how many ways can you write different three-digit numerals, using $\{2, 3, 4, 5\}$?

14. In how many ways can you write different three-digit numerals, using $\{2, 3, 4, 5\}$, if no digit is to be used more than once in each numeral?

15. How many different seven-digit telephone numbers can be formed from $\{1, 2, 3, 4, 5, 6, 7, 8, 9, 0\}$?

16. How many different seven-digit telephone numbers can be formed from $\{1, 2, 3, 4, 5, 6, 7, 8, 9, 0\}$ if no digit is to be used more than once in any number?

17. How many three-letter arrangements can be formed from $\{A, N, S, W, E, R\}$?

18. How many different three-letter arrangements can be formed from $\{A, N, S, W, E, R\}$ if no letter is to be used more than once in any arrangement?

19. How many four-digit numerals for positive odd integers can be formed from $\{1, 2, 3, 4, 5\}$?

20. How many positive even integers with numerals containing four digits can be formed from $\{1, 2, 3, 4, 5\}$?

21. How many numerals for positive integers less than 500 can be formed from $\{3, 4, 5\}$?

22. How many numerals for positive odd integers less than 500 can be formed from $\{3, 4, 5\}$?

23. How many numerals for positive even integers less than 500 can be formed from $\{3, 4, 5\}$?

24. How many numerals for positive even integers between 400 and 500, inclusive, can be formed from $\{3, 4, 5\}$?

25. How many permutations of the elements of $\{P, R, I, M, E\}$ end in a vowel?

26. How many permutations of the elements of $\{P, R, O, D, U, C, T\}$ end in a vowel?

27. Find the number of distinguishable permutations of the letters in the word *LIMIT*.

28. Find the number of distinguishable permutations of the letters in the word

COMBINATION.

29. Find the number of distinguishable permutations of the letters in the word

COLORADO.

30. Find the number of distinguishable permutations of the letters in the word

TALLAHASSEE.

31. Show that $P_{5,3} = 5(P_{4,2})$.   32. Show that $P_{5,r} = 5(P_{4,r-1})$.

33. Show that $P_{n,3} = n(P_{n-1,2})$.   34. Show that $P_{n,3} - P_{n,2} = (n-3)(P_{n,2})$.

35. Solve for n: $P_{n,5} = 5(P_{n,4})$.   36. Solve for n: $P_{n,5} = 9(P_{n-1,4})$.

Example. In how many ways can four students be seated around a circular table?

Solution. In any such arrangement (which is called a **circular permutation**), there is no first position. Each person can take four different initial positions without affecting the arrangement. Thus, there are $4!/4 = 6$ arrangements. In general, there are $\dfrac{n!}{n} = (n-$ circular permutations of n things taken n at a time.

37. In how many ways can five students be seated around a circular table?

38. In how many ways can six students be seated around a circular table?

39. In how many ways can six students be seated around a circular table if a certain two must be seated together?

40. In how many ways can three different keys be arranged on a key ring? *Hint:* Arrangements should be considered identical if one can be obtained from the other by turning the ring over. In general, there are only $(1/2)(n-1)!$ distinct arrangements of n keys on a ring $(n \geq 3)$.

14.2 COMBINATIONS

An additional counting concept is needed before we turn our attention to probability—namely, finding the number of distinct r-element subsets of an n-element set.

To begin with, we make the following definition.

DEFINITION 14.2 *An r-element subset of an n-element set is called a* **combination**.

Thus, a combination is simply a subset of a set of objects with no reference to relative order of the elements in the subset. For example, five different playing cards can be arranged in 5! permutations, but to a poker player they represent the same hand. There is only one *combination* here.

The counting of combinations is related to the counting of permutations. From Theorem 14.2, we know that the number of distinct permutations of n elements of a set A taken r at a time is given by

$$P_{n,r} = \frac{n!}{(n-r)!}.$$

With this in mind, consider the following.

THEOREM 14.3 *Let $\binom{n}{r}$ denote the number of distinct combinations of the elements of a set A of n objects $[n(A) = n]$, taken r at a time. Then*

$$\binom{n}{r} = \frac{P_{n,r}}{r!}. \tag{1}$$

Proof. There are, by definition, $\binom{n}{r}$ r-element subsets of the set A, where $n(A) = n$.

Also, from Theorem 14.1, each of these subsets has $r!$ permutations of its members. There are therefore $\binom{n}{r}r!$ permutations of n elements of A taken r at a time. That is, we have

$$P_{n,r} = \binom{n}{r}r!,$$

from which we obtain

$$\binom{n}{r} = \frac{P_{n,r}}{r!},$$

as was to be shown.

Thus, to find the number of r-element subsets of an n-element set A, we count the number of permutations of the elements of A taken r at a time, and then divide by the number of possible permutations of an r-element set. This seems very much like counting a set of people by counting the number of arms and legs and dividing the result by 4, but this approach gives us a very useful expression for the number we seek, $\binom{n}{r}$. Since

$$P_{n,r} = n(n-1)(n-2) \cdots (n-r+1) = \frac{n!}{(n-r)!},$$

it follows that

$$\binom{n}{r} = \frac{P_{n,r}}{r!} = \frac{n(n-1)(n-2)\cdots(n-r+1)}{r!}, \tag{2}$$

or, equivalently,

$$\binom{n}{r} = \frac{P_{n,r}}{r!} = \frac{n!}{r!(n-r)!} \tag{3}$$

Combinations and the binomial coefficients   Observe that the right-hand member of (3) is the same as the coefficient of the $(r+1)$st term in the binomial expansion on page 339.

Example. In how many ways can a committee of five be selected from a set of twelve persons?

Solution. What we wish here is the number of 5-element subsets of a 12-element set. From (3), we have

$$\binom{12}{5} = \frac{12!}{5!7!} = \frac{12 \cdot 11 \cdot 10 \cdot 9 \cdot 8 \cdot 7!}{5!7!}$$

$$= \frac{12 \cdot 11 \cdot 10 \cdot 9 \cdot 8}{5 \cdot 4 \cdot 3 \cdot 2 \cdot 1} = 792.$$

Since the numbers $\binom{n}{r}$ are the coefficients in the binomial expansion, and since these coefficients are symmetric, we have the following plausible assertion.

THEOREM 14.4 $\left(\begin{array}{c}n\\r\end{array}\right) = \left(\begin{array}{c}n\\n-r\end{array}\right)$.

Proof. From (3), we have

$$\left(\begin{array}{c}n\\r\end{array}\right) = \frac{n!}{r!(n-r)!}$$

and

$$\left(\begin{array}{c}n\\n-r\end{array}\right) = \frac{n!}{(n-r)!\,[n-(n-r)]!} = \frac{n!}{(n-r)!\,r!},$$

and the theorem is proved.

Theorem 14.4 is plausible also since each time a distinct set of r objects is chosen, a distinct set of $n-r$ objects remains unchosen.

EXERCISE 14.2

Example. How many different amounts of money can be formed from a penny, a nickel, a dime, and a quarter?

Solution. We want to find the total number of combinations that can be formed by taking the coins 1, 2, 3, and 4 at a time. By (3) we have,

$$\left(\begin{array}{c}4\\1\end{array}\right) = \frac{4!}{1!3!} = 4, \quad \left(\begin{array}{c}4\\2\end{array}\right) = \frac{4!}{2!2!} = 6, \quad \left(\begin{array}{c}4\\3\end{array}\right) = \frac{4!}{3!1!} = 4, \quad \left(\begin{array}{c}4\\4\end{array}\right) = \frac{4!}{4!0!} = 1,$$

and the total number of combinations is 15. Clearly each gives a different amount.

1. How many different amounts of money can be formed from a penny, a nickel, and a dime?

2. How many different amounts of money can be formed from a penny, a nickel, a dime, a quarter, and a half-dollar?

3. How many different committees of four persons each can be chosen from a group of six persons?

4. How many different committees of four persons each can be chosen from a group of ten persons?

5. In how many different ways can a set of five cards be selected from a deck containing 52 cards?

6. In how many different ways can a set of 13 cards be selected from a deck of 52 cards?

7. In how many different ways can a hand consisting of five spades, five hearts, and three diamonds be selected from a standard bridge deck?

8. In how many different ways can a hand consisting of ten spades, one heart, one diamond, and one club be selected from a standard bridge deck?

9. In how many different ways can a hand consisting of either five spades, five hearts, five diamonds, or five clubs be selected from a standard bridge deck?

10. In how many different ways can a hand consisting of three aces and two cards that are not aces be selected from a standard bridge deck?

11. A combination of three balls is picked at random from a box containing five red, four white, and three blue balls. In how many ways can the set chosen contain at least one white ball?

12. In Problem 11, in how many ways can the set chosen contain at least one white and one blue ball?

13. A set of five distinct points lies on a circle. How many inscribed triangles can be drawn having all their vertices in this set?

14. A set of ten distinct points lies on a circle. How many inscribed quadrilaterals can be drawn having all their vertices in this set?

15. A set of ten distinct points lies on a circle. How many inscribed hexagons can be drawn having all their vertices in this set?

16. Given $\binom{n}{3} = \binom{50}{47}$, find n.

17. Given $\binom{n}{7} = \binom{n}{5}$, find n.

18. Expand $(a + b)^5$. Write the coefficient of each term in the form $\binom{n}{r}$.

19. Write the first four terms of the expansion of $(a + b)^{10}$. Write the coefficient of each term in the form $\binom{n}{r}$.

20. Write the first eight terms of the expansion of $(a + b)^{12}$. Write the coefficient of each term in the form $\binom{n}{r}$.

14.3 SAMPLE SPACES AND EVENTS

Sample spaces and their outcomes   When an experiment of some kind is undertaken, associated with the experiment is a set of possible results. For example, when a die is rolled, let us assume that it will come to a stop with one of the numerals 1, 2, 3, 4, 5, or 6 on its upper face—that is, a number of spots corresponding to one of these numerals. This exhausts all possibilities.

DEFINITION 14.3 *The set of all possible results of an experiment is called a **sample space** for the experiment.*

DEFINITION 14.4 *Each element of a sample space is called an **outcome** or **sample point**.*

There may be more than one possible sample space for an experiment. Consider a bag in which there are some small balls. A certain number of the balls are made of glass, say, and the rest of plastic. Some of each kind are blue and some are red. If we now conduct an experiment in which a ball is drawn from the bag, we might be interested in one of the following:

a. We might be concerned with whether a glass or a plastic ball is drawn. If g denotes the drawing of a glass and p a plastic ball, then our sample space is $\{g, p\}$.

b. We might be concerned with whether a red or a blue ball is drawn. Then we have $\{r, b\}$ for a sample space, where r denotes the outcome of a red and b of a blue ball.

c. We might be concerned with both the color of the ball and the material of which it is made. With g, p, r, and b as before, our sample space consists of

$$\{(g, r), (g, b), (p, r), (p, b)\},$$

where the elements of the sample space are ordered pairs.

There are numerous other possibilities. The point to be made here is that in setting up a sample space, one must do so with a particular kind of outcome in mind.

DEFINITION 14.5 *Any subset of a sample space is called an **event**, and is commonly denoted by the letter E.*

Sets of outcomes

The reason for this terminology is that, in conducting an experiment, one may be interested in sets of outcomes rather than in individual outcomes. In the tossing of a die, for example, if the sample space is taken as $\{1, 2, 3, 4, 5, 6\}$, then the event that an outcome (a numeral) denotes an even integer is the set $\{2, 4, 6\}$, which is a subset of the sample space. The event that an outcome denotes an odd integer is the set $\{1, 3, 5\}$. These two events are complements of each other, and are examples of **complementary events**, that is, two events whose intersection is $\emptyset$ and whose union is the entire sample space.

The number of possible events in an n-element sample space is the number of possible subsets of an n-element set, namely 2^n, where both the null set (impossible event) and the entire sample space (certain event) are included. That is,

$$\binom{n}{0} + \binom{n}{1} + \binom{n}{2} + \cdots + \binom{n}{n} = 2^n, \tag{1}$$

where $\binom{n}{0}$ represents the single event that is contributed by the null set.

EXERCISE   14.3

1. A die is cast. List the sample space. List the event that the number on the upper face of the die is greater than 2.

2. A coin is tossed. List the sample space. List the event that a head appears.

3. Two coins are tossed. List the sample space. List the event that either two heads or two tails appear.

4. A die is cast and a coin is tossed. List the sample space. List the event that a head is tossed.

5. Two numbers are chosen at random from the integers 3, 4, 5, and 6. List the sample space. List the event that the sum of the numbers is an odd integer.

6. Two bags contain marbles. The first bag contains red and white marbles, and the second bag contains blue and white marbles. One marble is drawn from each bag. List the sample space. List the event that at least one white marble is drawn.

7. Consider the data in the preceding problem and list the event that only one white marble is drawn

8. How many events are there in the sample space $\{1, 2, 3\}$ if $\varnothing$ is considered as an event?

9. How many events are there in the sample space $\{1, 2, 3, 4, 5, 6\}$ if each event must contain at least one outcome?

10. Two cards are drawn from a standard deck of 52. Describe the sample space. Describe the event that one card is a face card. Describe the event that one card is a face card and one is not.

11. Verify Equation (1) in this section for the sample space $\{1, 2, 3, 4, 5, 6\}$.

14.4 PROBABILITY FUNCTIONS

Random outcomes   The word "random" as used in mathematics is generally taken to be an undefined term, but it is ordinarily employed to discuss phenomena in which seemingly identical processes produce diverse data. If we roll a die, for example, and if the die or other factors are not "loaded," then any one of the outcomes 1, 2, 3, 4, 5, 6 can be considered to be equally likely, and the actual outcome is termed "random." We shall use the word "random" herein in this sense, and we shall consider outcomes in an experiment as random unless otherwise specified.

We define a function P on a sample space S as follows.

DEFINITION 14.6 *Let S denote a sample space of random outcomes, and let P be a real-valued function with domain the set of all events $E \subseteq S$. Then P is a* **probability function** *if and only if the following conditions are satisfied:*

   a. *$P(E) \geq 0$ for each $E \subseteq S$.*
   b. *$P(S) = 1$.*
   c. *$P(E)$ is finitely additive; that is, if $E_1 \cap E_2 = \varnothing$, then*

$$P(E_1 \cup E_2) = P(E_1) + P(E_2).$$

By definition, then, any real-valued function having as domain the events E in a sample space may be called a probability function, provided it satisfies the above

Choice of a probability function

conditions a, b, and c. In practice, however, the probability functions ordinarily considered are somehow connected with our intuitive notions of likelihood of occurrence. These notions usually are based on considerations of the types discussed below.

A priori considerations involve physical, geometrical, and other inherent properties of the experiment in question. They involve no sampling of outcomes. Thus, when a die that appears to be cubical and to have a uniform distribution of mass is cast from a distance onto a flat table, and we admit as outcomes the die's stopping with any of its six different faces uppermost, then without making any trial throws we would assign the value $1/6$ as the probability of each of the six possible outcomes.

Thus we are led to the probability function defined by

$$P(E) = \frac{n(E)}{n(S)} \tag{1}$$

for a sample space of seemingly "equally likely" occurrences. Here $n(E)$ is the number of distinct ways in which the event E can occur, and $n(S)$ is the number of distinct outcomes in the sample space. In solving the problems in Exercises 14.4 and 14.5, (1) defines the probability function that should be employed unless another function is given.

It is easy to check that the function P defined by (1) is a probability function. Since, in (1), $n(E)$ is a nonnegative integer and $n(S)$ is a positive integer, it follows that $P(E)$ is a nonnegative rational number for each $E \subseteq S$. Further, we have

$$P(S) = \frac{n(S)}{n(S)} = 1.$$

Finally, since $n(E)$ is finitely additive, so is $P(E)$.

A posteriori considerations involve testing the experiment a certain number of times. Mortality tables give probability functions of this sort. Actually, (1) can still be used in defining such probability functions, provided we interpret the function $n(E)$ as being the number of times the event E occurred in the test, and $n(S)$ as being the total number of times the experiment was performed in the test.

Example. If two dice are cast, what is the (a priori) probability that the sum of the digits showing on the top faces of the dice is less than 6?

Solution. For our sample spaces, let us consider A the set of possible outcomes for one die and B the set for the other. Then $n(A) = 6$ and $n(B) = 6$. The possible outcomes for both would be $S = A \times B$, the Cartesian product of A and B, and $n(A \times B) = n(S) = 36$. Each outcome here is an ordered pair (a, b), where a is the numeral on the upper face of the first die, and b on that of the second die. The event we seek is the event $\{(a, b) \mid a + b < 6\}$. The lattice in Figure 14.2 shows the situation schematically.

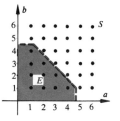

Figure 14.2

Since $E = \{(1, 1), (1, 2), (1, 3), (1, 4), (2, 1), (2, 2), (2, 3), (3, 1), (3, 2), (4, 1)\}$, we have $n(E) = 10$, and

$$P(E) = \frac{n(E)}{n(S)} = \frac{10}{36} = \frac{5}{18}.$$

Interpretation of the probability of an event   Care must be taken in interpreting the meaning of "the probability of an event." In the foregoing example, $5/18$ does not assure us, for instance, that E will occur 5 times out of 18 casts, or, indeed, that even one cast out of 18 will produce the event described. What it does imply, however, is that if you cast the dice a very great number of times, then you can *expect* the sum on the exposed faces to be less than 6 about $5/18$ of the time.

If we denote the complement of an event E in a sample space S by E', then $P(E')$ denotes the probability of the occurrence of E'. Since an outcome in S must lie in either E or E', but not both, and since $P(S) = 1$, it follows that

$$P(E) + P(E') = 1,$$

or

$$P(E') = 1 - P(E).$$

Thus, in the example above, the probability that a single cast of two dice will produce a sum on the exposed faces greater than or equal to 6 is

$$P(E') = 1 - P(E) = 1 - \frac{5}{18} = \frac{13}{18}.$$

DEFINITION 14.7   *The **odds** that an experiment with sample space S will result in an event E are given by*

$$\frac{P(E)}{P(E')} = \frac{P(E)}{1 - P(E)}, \quad P(E') \neq 0.$$

Thus, the odds that the sum of the numbers determined by the exposed faces of two dice will be less than 6 are 5 to 13, and that they will be greater than or equal to 6 are 13 to 5.

By the definition of the probability function, this function is finitely additive. Consequently, if the sample space S is partitioned into n mutually disjoint events $E_1, E_2, \cdots, E_n$, then

$$P(S) = P(E_1) + P(E_2) + \cdots + P(E_n) = 1.$$

Further, since for any event E we have $E \cup \varnothing = E$ and $E \cap \varnothing = \varnothing$, it follows that

Probability of the empty event
$$P(E) = P(E \cap \varnothing) = P(E) + P(\varnothing),$$

from which

$$P(\varnothing) = 0.$$

Moreover, we have the following result.

THEOREM 14.5 *If S is a sample space, and E_1 and E_2 are any events in S, then*

$$P(E_1 \text{ or } E_2) = P(E_1 \cup E_2) = P(E_1) + P(E_2) - P(E_1 \cap E_2).$$

Proof. If $E_2 = E_3 \cup E_4$, where $E_3 = E_1 \cap E_2$ and $E_3 \cap E_4 = \varnothing$, then

$$P(E_1 \cup E_2) = P(E_1 \cup E_4) = P(E_1) + P(E_4) = P(E_1) + P(E_2) - P(E_3),$$

by Definition 14.6, as desired.

Example. If two cards are drawn from a standard deck of playing cards, what is the probability that either both are red or both are Jacks?

Solution. A deck of cards contains 52 cards, and an outcome here consists of two cards. Hence, the number of elements of the sample space is the number of ways (combinations) one can draw two cards from 52, which is $\binom{52}{2}$. Let E_1 be the event that both are red. Since there are 26 red cards in a deck, the number of outcomes (combinations) in the event E_1 is $n(E_1) = \binom{26}{2}$. Let E_2 be the event that both cards are Jacks. Then, because there are four Jacks in a deck, $n(E_2) = \binom{4}{2}$. Since there is only one pair of red Jacks, $n(E_1 \cap E_2) = 1$. We then have

$$P(E_1 \cup E_2) = P(E_1) + P(E_2) - P(E_1 \cap E_2)$$

$$= \frac{\binom{26}{2}}{\binom{52}{2}} + \frac{\binom{4}{2}}{\binom{52}{2}} - \frac{1}{\binom{52}{2}} = \frac{\binom{26}{2} + \binom{4}{2} - 1}{\binom{52}{2}}$$

$$= \frac{\frac{26 \cdot 25}{1 \cdot 2} + \frac{4 \cdot 3}{1 \cdot 2} - 1}{\frac{52 \cdot 51}{1 \cdot 2}} = \frac{325 + 6 - 1}{1326} = \frac{330}{1326} = \frac{165}{668}.$$

Probability of the union of disjoint events   Of course, if E_1 and E_2 are *disjoint*, then $E_1 \cap E_2 = \varnothing$, so that $P(E_1 \cap E_2) = 0$, and the equation in Theorem 14.5 reduces to the equation in Definition 14.6, namely,

$$P(E_1 \cup E_2) = P(E_1) + P(E_2).$$

Disjoint events are said to be **mutually exclusive**.

Example. A card is drawn at random from a standard deck of 52 cards. What is the probability that the card is either a face card (Jack, Queen, or King) or a four?

Solution. Let E_1 be the event that the card is a four. There are four such cards in a deck, so that $n(E_1) = 4$ Let E_2 be the event that the card is a Jack, Queen, or King. There are twelve such cards in a deck, so that $n(E_2) = 12$. Since the sample space is just the entire deck, $n(S) = 52$, and since E_1 and E_2 are mutually exclusive,

$$P(E_1 \text{ or } E_2) = P(E_1) + P(E_2)$$

$$= \frac{4}{52} + \frac{12}{52} = \frac{16}{52} = \frac{4}{13}.$$

EXERCISE 14.4

Two dice are cast. Let E be the event that both dice show the same numeral. Let F be the event that the sum of the numbers thrown is greater than eight. Find the following.

1. $P(E)$ 2. $P(F)$ 3. $P(E \cup F)$

4. $P(E')$ 5. $P(F')$ 6. $P(E' \cup F')$

A box contains five red, four white, and three blue marbles. Two marbles are drawn from the box. Let RR be the event that both marbles are red, WW that both marbles are white, BB that both marbles are blue, and RW, RB, BW that a red and a white, a red and a blue, and a blue and a white are drawn, respectively. Find the following.

7. $P(RR)$ 8. $P(BB)$ 9. $P(WW)$

10. $P(RW)$ 11. $P(RB)$ 12. $P(BW)$

13. What is the probability that neither is white?

14. What is the probability that neither is blue?

15. What is the probability that at least one is red?

16. What is the probability that either one is red or else both are white?

17. What is the probability that by drawing a single card from a standard deck of 52 cards, one will get a 2, 3, or 4?

18. What is the probability that if two cards are drawn from a standard deck of 52 cards they will be of the same suit? Different suits?

19. One box contains three red and eight white marbles, and a second box contains five red and two white marbles. If one marble is drawn from each box, what is the probability of drawing:
    a. Two red marbles?
    b. Two white marbles?
    c. One red and one white marble?

20. In Problem 19, what are the odds of drawing:
    a. Two red marbles?
    b. Two white marbles?
    c. One red and one white marble?

If the probability of the event E that a person will receive k dollars is $P(E)$, then the person's **mathematical expectation** relative to this event is $kP(E)$.

21. A lottery offers a prize of $50, and 70 tickets are sold. What is the mathematical expectation of a person who buys three tickets? If each ticket costs $1, is the person's expectation greater or less than his outlay?

22. The odds that a certain horse will win the Irish Sweepstakes are 2 to 7. If you hold a ticket on this horse to pay $100,000 if he wins, what is your mathematical expectation?

If E_1, E_2, E_3, etc., are mutually exclusive events, and the return to you is k_1 if E_1 occurs, is k_2 if E_2 occurs, etc., then your mathematical expectation is $\sum_{i=1}^{n} k_i P(E_i)$.

23. One coin is selected at random from a collection containing a penny, a nickel, and a dime. What is the expectation?

24. One coin is selected at random from a collection containing a dime, a quarter, and a half-dollar. What is the expectation?

25. Three $1 bills and four $5 bills are hidden from view. What is the expectation on a single selection?

26. Three $1 bills, four $5 bills, and one $10 bill are hidden from view. What is the expectation on a single draw?

14.5 INDEPENDENT AND DEPENDENT EVENTS

In some experiments, we may be interested in events that are not dependent on each other, in the sense that the occurrence of one may have no effect on the probability of the occurrence or nonoccurrence of the other.

Consider an experiment in which two cards are drawn at random, one after the other, from a deck of ten cards, six of which are red and four blue. We can inquire into the probability that the first card drawn is red and the second blue. The simplest such situation would be one in which the first card is drawn, observed, and returned to the deck, which is then shuffled thoroughly before the second card is drawn. In this case, the sample space would consist of a set of ordered pairs (x, y), where x is the result of the first draw and y the result of the second draw. Since there are ten possibilities in each case, the sample space would consist of $10 \times 10 = 100$ ordered pairs. The horizontal axis in Figure 14.3 is labeled x and the vertical y, and r_i and b_i are used to designate the drawing of red and blue cards, respectively.

The events E_1 that the first card drawn is a red card and E_2 that the second card drawn is a blue card are outlined in the figure. The event

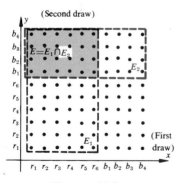

Figure 14.3

E that both E_1 and E_2 occur is the intersection of E_1 and E_2; that is, $E = E_1 \cap E_2$. By inspection,

$$P(E_1) = \frac{60}{100} = \frac{3}{5}, \qquad P(E_2) = \frac{40}{100} = \frac{2}{5},$$

and

$$P(E) = P(E_1 \cap E_2) = \frac{24}{100} = \frac{6}{25}.$$

Moreover, in this example, it is evident that

$$P(E) = P(E_1 \cap E_2) = P(E_1) \cdot P(E_2).$$

DEFINITION   14.8 *If E_1 and E_2 are events in a sample space, and if*

$$P(E_1 \cap E_2) = P(E_1) \cdot P(E_2),$$

*then E_1 and E_2 are **independent events**. If two events are not independent, then they are said to be **dependent**.*

Now consider the same experiment, except that this time the first card is not returned to the deck before the second is taken. Then there will be ten possible first draws, but only nine possible second draws. The sample space will therefore contain 10×9 ordered pairs, such that no ordered pair with first and second components the same remains in the set.

Dependent events

Figure 14.4 shows a graph of the sample space, which is the same as that in the preceding figure except that one diagonal is missing. Sets with graphs that have a missing diagonal are called **deleted Cartesian sets**. Again, the figure shows E_1 and E_2, the events that a red and a blue are obtained on the first and second draw, respectively. The event that both occur is $E = E_1 \cap E_2$, which is also shown in the figure. By inspection,

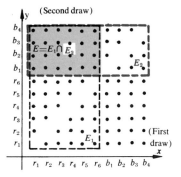

Figure   14.4

$$P(E_1) = \frac{54}{90} = \frac{3}{5}, \qquad P(E_2) = \frac{36}{90} = \frac{2}{5},$$

and

$$P(E) = P(E_1 \cap E_2) = \frac{24}{90} = \frac{4}{15}.$$

This time,

$$P(E_1 \cap E_2) \neq P(E_1) \cdot P(E_2),$$

so that the events are dependent.

If, however, we write 4/15 as

$$\frac{4}{15} = \frac{3}{5} \cdot \frac{4}{9},$$

then we have

$$P(E_1 \cap E_2) = P(E_1) \cdot \frac{4}{9},$$

Conditional probability   where 4/9 can be interpreted as the probability of the occurrence of E_2, *given the occurrence of E_1*. This probability is denoted by the symbol $P(E_2 \mid E_1)$.

DEFINITION 14.9   *If E_1 and E_2 are events in a sample space, and $P(E_1) \neq 0$, then the **conditional probability** $P(E_2 \mid E_1)$ of E_2 given E_1 is*

$$P(E_2 \mid E_1) = \frac{P(E_1 \cap E_2)}{P(E_1)}.$$

If E_1 and E_2 are independent events and $P(E_1) \neq 0$, then by Definitions 14.8 and 14.9,

$$P(E_2 \mid E_1) = \frac{P(E_1 \cap E_2)}{P(E_1)} = \frac{P(E_1) \cdot P(E_2)}{P(E_1)} = P(E_2).$$

Example.   A die is cast and a coin is tossed. What is the probability that a number less than five is thrown and a head is tossed? Are these events independent?

Solution.   The sample space is a set of ordered pairs (x, y), where x is the result of casting the die and y is the result of tossing the coin. Since there are six results x and two results y, there are 6×2, or 12, ordered pairs in S. Of these, there will be 4×1, or 4, outcomes in E, so

$$P(E) = \frac{4}{12} = \frac{1}{3}.$$

Now, let E_1 be the event of casting a 1, 2, 3, or 4, and let E_2 be the event of tossing a head. Then

$$P(E_1) = \frac{8}{12} = \frac{2}{3} \quad \text{and} \quad P(E_2) = \frac{6}{12} = \frac{1}{2},$$

Since

$$\frac{1}{3} = \frac{2}{3} \cdot \frac{1}{2}.$$

E_1 and E_2 are independent.

EXERCISE 14.5

1. A bag contains four red marbles and ten blue marbles. If two marbles are drawn in succession, and if the first is not replaced, what is the probability that the first is red and the second is blue? Are the two draws independent events?

2. A red die and a green die are cast. What is the probability of obtaining a sum greater than 9, given that the green die shows 4?

3. A bag contains four white and six red marbles. Two marbles are drawn from the bag and replaced, and two more marbles are then drawn from the bag. What is the probability of drawing:
   a. Two red marbles on the first draw and two white ones on the second draw?
   b. A total of two white marbles?
   c. Four white marbles?
   d. Four red marbles?

4. In Problem 3, what is the probability of drawing:
   a. Exactly three white marbles in the two draws?
   b. At least three white marbles in the two draws?
   c. Exactly two red marbles in the two draws?
   d. At least two red marbles in the two draws?

5. A red and a green die are cast. Let E_1 be the event that at least one die shows 3, and E_2 be the event that the sum of the two numbers thrown is 8.
   a. Find $P(E_1)$.   b. Find $P(E_2)$.
   c. Find $P(E_2 \mid E_1)$.   d. Are E_1 and E_2 independent?

6. In Problem 5, let E_1 be the event that neither die shows a result larger than 4, and let E_2 be the event that the dice do not show the same number.
   a. Find $P(E_1)$.   b. Find $P(E_2)$.
   c. Find $P(E_2 \mid E_1)$.   d. Are E_1 and E_2 independent?

7. A coin is tossed three consecutive times. What is the probability that:
   a. The second toss is a head?
   b. The third toss is a head?
   c. Both the second and third tosses are heads?
   d. The first and third tosses are heads?
   e. The first and third tosses are heads but the second is not?

8. In Problem 7, state whether each of the following pairs of events is independent.
   a. *a* and *b*   b. *a* and *c*   c. *a* and *d*
   d. *a* and *e*   e. *d* and *e*

9. The probability that *A* will pass a course in college algebra is 5/6, that *B* will pass, 3/4, and that *C* will pass, 2/3. What is the probability that:
   a. At least one of the three will pass?
   b. At least *A* and *C* will pass?
   c. *A* and *C* will pass but *B* will not?
   d. At least two of the three will pass?

10. In Problem 9, what is the probability of c, given the occurrence of a— that is, assuming that at least one of the three will pass? Are the events a and c independent?

11. A day is selected at random in some fashion such that any day of the week is an equally likely choice. Let the probability be 1/30 that a day selected at random will be a rainy day.
    a. What is the probability that a rainy Wednesday will be selected?
    b. What is the probability that a dry Thursday will be selected?
    c. What is the probability that either Monday, Tuesday, or Wednesday will be selected, and that it will not rain that day?
    d. Let E_1 be the selection of Sunday, and let E_2 be the event that it does not rain on the day selected. What is the conditional probability of E_2, given the occurrence of E_1? Are E_1 and E_2 independent?

12. Argue that if E_1 and E_2 are mutually exclusive events with nonzero probabilities, then E_1 and E_2 are not independent.

APPENDIX

TABLE I

COMMON LOGARITHMS

x	0	1	2	3	4	5	6	7	8	9
1.0	.0000	.0043	.0086	.0128	.0170	.0212	.0253	.0294	.0334	.0374
1.1	.0414	.0453	.0492	.0531	.0569	.0607	.0645	.0682	.0719	.0755
1.2	.0792	.0828	.0864	.0899	.0934	.0969	.1004	.1038	.1072	.1106
1.3	.1139	.1173	.1206	.1239	.1271	.1303	.1335	.1367	.1399	.1430
1.4	.1461	.1492	.1523	.1553	.1584	.1614	.1644	.1673	.1703	.1732
1.5	.1761	.1790	.1818	.1847	.1875	.1903	.1931	.1959	.1987	.2014
1.6	.2041	.2068	.2095	.2122	.2148	.2175	.2201	.2227	.2253	.2279
1.7	.2304	.2330	.2355	.2380	.2405	.2430	.2455	.2480	.2504	.2529
1.8	.2553	.2577	.2601	.2625	.2648	.2672	.2695	.2718	.2742	.2765
1.9	.2788	.2810	.2833	.2856	.2878	.2900	.2923	.2945	.2967	.2989
2.0	.3010	.3032	.3054	.3075	.3096	.3118	.3139	.3160	.3181	.3201
2.1	.3222	.3243	.3263	.3284	.3304	.3324	.3345	.3365	.3385	.3404
2.2	.3424	.3444	.3464	.3483	.3502	.3522	.3541	.3560	.3579	.3598
2.3	.3617	.3636	.3655	.3674	.3692	.3711	.3729	.3747	.3766	.3784
2.4	.3802	.3820	.3838	.3856	.3874	.3892	.3909	.3927	.3945	.3962
2.5	.3979	.3997	.4014	.4031	.4048	.4065	.4082	.4099	.4116	.4133
2.6	.4150	.4166	.4183	.4200	.4216	.4232	.4249	.4265	.4281	.4298
2.7	.4314	.4330	.4346	.4362	.4378	.4393	.4409	.4425	.4440	.4456
2.8	.4472	.4487	.4502	.4518	.4533	.4548	.4564	.4579	.4594	.4609
2.9	.4624	.4639	.4654	.4669	.4683	.4698	.4713	.4728	.4742	.4757
3.0	.4771	.4786	.4800	.4814	.4829	.4843	.4857	.4871	.4886	.4900
3.1	.4914	.4928	.4942	.4955	.4969	.4983	.4997	.5011	.5024	.5038
3.2	.5051	.5065	.5079	.5092	.5105	.5119	.5132	.5145	.5159	.5172
3.3	.5185	.5198	.5211	.5224	.5237	.5250	.5263	.5276	.5289	.5302
3.4	.5315	.5328	.5340	.5353	.5366	.5378	.5391	.5403	.5416	.5428
3.5	.5441	.5453	.5465	.5478	.5490	.5502	.5514	.5527	.5539	.5551
3.6	.5563	.5575	.5587	.5599	.5611	.5623	.5635	.5647	.5658	.5670
3.7	.5682	.5694	.5705	.5717	.5729	.5740	.5752	.5763	.5775	.5786
3.8	.5798	.5809	.5821	.5832	.5843	.5855	.5866	.5877	.5888	.5899
3.9	.5911	.5922	.5933	.5944	.5955	.5966	.5977	.5988	.5999	.6010
4.0	.6021	.6031	.6042	.6053	.6064	.6075	.6085	.6096	.6107	.6117
4.1	.6128	.6138	.6149	.6160	.6170	.6180	.6191	.6201	.6212	.6222
4.2	.6232	.6243	.6253	.6263	.6274	.6284	.6294	.6304	.6314	.6325
4.3	.6335	.6345	.6355	.6365	.6375	.6385	.6395	.6405	.6415	.6425
4.4	.6435	.6444	.6454	.6464	.6474	.6484	.6493	.6503	.6513	.6522
4.5	.6532	.6542	.6551	.6561	.6571	.6580	.6590	.6599	.6609	.6618
4.6	.6628	.6637	.6646	.6656	.6665	.6675	.6684	.6693	.6702	.6712
4.7	.6721	.6730	.6739	.6749	.6758	.6767	.6776	.6785	.6794	.6803
4.8	.6812	.6821	.6830	.6839	.6848	.6857	.6866	.6875	.6884	.6893
4.9	.6902	.6911	.6920	.6928	.6937	.6946	.6955	.6964	.6972	.6981
5.0	.6990	.6998	.7007	.7016	.7024	.7033	.7042	.7050	.7059	.7067
5.1	.7076	.7084	.7093	.7101	.7110	.7118	.7126	.7135	.7143	.7152
5.2	.7160	.7168	.7177	.7185	.7193	.7202	.7210	.7218	.7226	.7235
5.3	.7243	.7251	.7259	.7267	.7275	.7284	.7292	.7300	.7308	.7316
5.4	.7324	.7332	.7340	.7348	.7356	.7364	.7372	.7380	.7388	.7396
x	0	1	2	3	4	5	6	7	8	9

TABLE I (*continued*)

x	0	1	2	3	4	5	6	7	8	9
5.5	.7404	.7412	.7419	.7427	.7435	.7443	.7451	.7459	.7466	.7474
5.6	.7482	.7490	.7497	.7505	.7513	.7520	.7528	.7536	.7543	.7551
5.7	.7559	.7566	.7574	.7582	.7589	.7597	.7604	.7612	.7619	.7627
5.8	.7634	.7642	.7649	.7657	.7664	.7672	.7679	.7686	.7694	.7701
5.9	.7709	.7716	.7723	.7731	.7738	.7745	.7752	.7760	.7767	.7774
6.0	.7782	.7789	.7796	.7803	.7810	.7818	.7825	.7832	.7839	.7846
6.1	.7853	.7860	.7868	.7875	.7882	.7889	.7896	.7903	.7910	.7917
6.2	.7924	.7931	.7938	.7945	.7952	.7959	.7966	.7973	.7980	.7987
6.3	.7993	.8000	.8007	.8014	.8021	.8028	.8035	.8041	.8048	.8055
6.4	.8062	.8069	.8075	.8082	.8089	.8096	.8102	.8109	.8116	.8122
6.5	.8129	.8136	.8142	.8149	.8156	.8162	.8169	.8176	.8182	.8189
6.6	.8195	.8202	.8209	.8215	.8222	.8228	.8235	.8241	.8248	.8254
6.7	.8261	.8267	.8274	.8280	.8287	.8293	.8299	.8306	.8312	.8319
6.8	.8325	.8331	.8338	.8344	.8351	.8357	.8363	.8370	.8376	.8382
6.9	.8388	.8395	.8401	.8407	.8414	.8420	.8426	.8432	.8439	.8445
7.0	.8451	.8457	.8463	.8470	.8476	.8482	.8488	.8494	.8500	.8506
7.1	.8513	.8519	.8525	.8531	.8537	.8543	.8549	.8555	.8561	.8567
7.2	.8573	.8579	.8585	.8591	.8597	.8603	.8609	.8615	.8621	.8627
7.3	.8633	.8639	.8645	.8651	.8657	.8663	.8669	.8675	.8681	.8686
7.4	.8692	.8698	.8704	.8710	.8716	.8722	.8727	.8733	.8739	.8745
7.5	.8751	.8756	.8762	.8768	.8774	.8779	.8785	.8791	.8797	.8802
7.6	.8808	.8814	.8820	.8825	.8831	.8837	.8842	.8848	.8854	.8859
7.7	.8865	.8871	.8876	.8882	.8887	.8893	.8899	.8904	.8910	.8915
7.8	.8921	.8927	.8932	.8938	.8943	.8949	.8954	.8960	.8965	.8971
7.9	.8976	.8982	.8987	.8993	.8998	.9004	.9009	.9015	.9020	.9025
8.0	.9031	.9036	.9042	.9047	.9053	.9058	.9063	.9069	.9074	.9079
8.1	.9085	.9090	.9096	.9101	.9106	.9112	.9117	.9122	.9128	.9133
8.2	.9138	.9143	.9149	.9154	.9159	.9165	.9170	.9175	.9180	.9186
8.3	.9191	.9196	.9201	.9206	.9212	.9217	.9222	.9227	.9232	.9238
8.4	.9243	.9248	.9253	.9258	.9263	.9269	.9274	.9279	.9284	.9289
8.5	.9294	.9299	.9304	.9309	.9315	.9320	.9325	.9330	.9335	.9340
8.6	.9345	.9350	.9355	.9360	.9365	.9370	.9375	.9380	.9385	.9390
8.7	.9395	.9400	.9405	.9410	.9415	.9420	.9425	.9430	.9435	.9440
8.8	.9445	.9450	.9455	.9460	.9465	.9469	.9474	.9479	.9484	.9489
8.9	.9494	.9499	.9504	.9509	.9513	.9518	.9523	.9528	.9533	.9538
9.0	.9542	.9547	.9552	.9557	.9562	.9566	.9571	.9576	.9581	.9586
9.1	.9590	.9595	.9600	.9605	.9609	.9614	.9619	.9624	.9628	.9633
9.2	.9638	.9643	.9647	.9652	.9657	.9661	.9666	.9671	.9675	.9680
9.3	.9685	.9689	.9694	.9699	.9703	.9708	.9713	.9717	.9722	.9727
9.4	.9731	.9736	.9741	.9745	.9750	.9754	.9759	.9763	.9768	.9773
9.5	.9777	.9782	.9786	.9791	.9795	.9800	.9805	.9809	.9814	.9818
9.6	.9823	.9827	.9832	.9836	.9841	.9845	.9850	.9854	.9859	.9863
9.7	.9868	.9872	.9877	.9881	.9886	.9890	.9894	.9899	.9903	.9908
9.8	.9912	.9917	.9921	.9926	.9930	.9934	.9939	.9943	.9948	.9952
9.9	.9956	.9961	.9965	.9969	.9974	.9978	.9983	.9987	.9991	.9996
x	0	1	2	3	4	5	6	7	8	9

TABLE II

EXPONENTIAL FUNCTIONS

x	e^x	e^{-x}	x	e^x	e^{-x}
0.00	1.0000	1.0000	1.5	4.4817	0.2231
0.01	1.0101	0.9901	1.6	4.9530	0.2019
0.02	1.0202	0.9802	1.7	5.4739	0.1827
0.03	1.0305	0.9705	1.8	6.0496	0.1653
0.04	1.0408	0.9608	1.9	6.6859	0.1496
0.05	1.0513	0.9512	2.0	7.3891	0.1353
0.06	1.0618	0.9418	2.1	8.1662	0.1225
0.07	1.0725	0.9324	2.2	9.0250	0.1108
0.08	1.0833	0.9331	2.3	9.9742	0.1003
0.09	1.0942	0.9139	2.4	11.023	0.0907
0.10	1.1052	0.9048	2.5	12.182	0.0821
0.11	1.1163	0.8958	2.6	13.464	0.0743
0.12	1.1275	0.8869	2.7	14.880	0.0672
0.13	1.1388	0.8781	2.8	16.445	0.0608
0.14	1.1503	0.8694	2.9	18.174	0.0550
0.15	1.1618	0.8607	3.0	20.086	0.0498
0.16	1.1735	0.8521	3.1	22.198	0.0450
0.17	1.1853	0.8437	3.2	24.533	0.0408
0.18	1.1972	0.8353	3.3	27.113	0.0369
0.19	1.2092	0.8270	3.4	29.964	0.0334
0.20	1.2214	0.8187	3.5	33.115	0.0302
0.21	1.2337	0.8106	3.6	36.598	0.0273
0.22	1.2461	0.8025	3.7	40.447	0.0247
0.23	1.2586	0.7945	3.8	44.701	0.0224
0.24	1.2712	0.7866	3.9	49.402	0.0202
0.25	1.2840	0.7788	4.0	54.598	0.0183
0.30	1.3499	0.7408	4.1	60.340	0.0166
0.35	1.4191	0.7047	4.2	66.686	0.0150
0.40	1.4918	0.6703	4.3	73.700	0.0136
0.45	1.5683	0.6376	4.4	81.451	0.0123
0.50	1.6487	0.6065	4.5	90.017	0.0111
0.55	1.7333	0.5769	4.6	99.484	0.0101
0.60	1.8221	0.5488	4.7	109.95	0.0091
0.65	1.9155	0.5220	4.8	121.51	0.0082
0.70	2.0138	0.4966	4.9	134.29	0.0074
0.75	2.1170	0.4724	5.0	148.41	0.0067
0.80	2.2255	0.4493	5.5	244.69	0.0041
0.85	2.3396	0.4274	6.0	403.43	0.0025
0.90	2.4596	0.4066	6.5	665.14	0.0015
0.95	2.5857	0.3867	7.0	1096.6	0.0009
1.0	2.7183	0.3679	7.5	1808.0	0.0006
1.1	3.0042	0.3329	8.0	2981.0	0.0003
1.2	3.3201	0.3012	8.5	4914.8	0.0002
1.3	3.6693	0.2725	9.0	8103.1	0.0001
1.4	4.0552	0.2466	10.0	22026	0.00005

TABLE III

NATURAL LOGARITHMS OF NUMBERS

n	$\log_e n$	n	$\log_e n$	n	$\log_e n$
	*	4.5	1.5041	9.0	2.1972
0.1	7.6974	4.6	1.5261	9.1	2.2083
0.2	8.3906	4.7	1.5476	9.2	2.2192
0.3	8.7960	4.8	1.5686	9.3	2.2300
0.4	9.0837	4.9	1.5892	9.4	2.2407
0.5	9.3069	5.0	1.6094	9.5	2.2513
0.6	9.4892	5.1	1.6292	9.6	2.2618
0.7	9.6433	5.2	1.6487	9.7	2.2721
0.8	9.7769	5.3	1.6677	9.8	2.2824
0.9	9.8946	5.4	1.6864	9.9	2.2925
1.0	0.0000	5.5	1.7047	10	2.3026
1.1	0.0953	5.6	1.7228	11	2.3979
1.2	0.1823	5.7	1.7405	12	2.4849
1.3	0.2624	5.8	1.7579	13	2.5649
1.4	0.3365	5.9	1.7750	14	2.6391
1.5	0.4055	6.0	1.7918	15	2.7081
1.6	0.4700	6.1	1.8083	16	2.7726
1.7	0.5306	6.2	1.8245	17	2.8332
1.8	0.5878	6.3	1.8405	18	2.8904
1.9	0.6419	6.4	1.8563	19	2.9444
2.0	0.6931	6.5	1.8718	20	2.9957
2.1	0.7419	6.6	1.8871	25	3.2189
2.2	0.7885	6.7	1.9021	30	3.4012
2.3	0.8329	6.8	1.9169	35	3.5553
2.4	0.8755	6.9	1.9315	40	3.6889
2.5	0.9163	7.0	1.9459	45	3.8067
2.6	0.9555	7.1	1.9601	50	3.9120
2.7	0.9933	7.2	1.9741	55	4.0073
2.8	1.0296	7.3	1.9879	60	4.0943
2.9	1.0647	7.4	2.0015	65	4.1744
3.0	1.0986	7.5	2.0149	70	4.2485
3.1	1.1314	7.6	2.0281	75	4.3175
3.2	1.1632	7.7	2.0412	80	4.3820
3.3	1.1939	7.8	2.0541	85	4.4427
3.4	1.2238	7.9	2.0669	90	4.4998
3.5	1.2528	8.0	2.0794	100	4.6052
3.6	1.2809	8.1	2.0919	110	4.7005
3.7	1.3083	8.2	2.1041	120	4.7875
3.8	1.3350	8.3	2.1163	130	4.8676
3.9	1.3610	8.4	2.1282	140	4.9416
4.0	1.3863	8.5	2.1401	150	5.0106
4.1	1.4110	8.6	2.1518	160	5.0752
4.2	1.4351	8.7	2.1633	170	5.1358
4.3	1.4586	8.8	2.1748	180	5.1930
4.4	1.4816	8.9	2.1861	190	5.2470

* Subtract 10 for $n < 1$. Thus $\log_e 0.1 = 7.6974 - 10 = -2.3026$.

TABLE IV

SQUARES, SQUARE ROOTS, AND PRIME FACTORS

No.	Sq.	Sq. Rt.	Factors	No.	Sq.	Sq. Rt.	Factors
1	1	1.000		51	2,601	7.141	$3 \cdot 17$
2	4	1.414	2	52	2,704	7.211	$2^2 \cdot 13$
3	9	1.732	3	53	2,809	7.280	53
4	16	2.000	2^2	54	2,916	7.348	$2 \cdot 3^3$
5	25	2.236	5	55	3,025	7.416	$5 \cdot 11$
6	36	2.449	$2 \cdot 3$	56	3,136	7.483	$2^3 \cdot 7$
7	49	2.646	7	57	3,249	7.550	$3 \cdot 19$
8	64	2.828	2^3	58	3,364	7.616	$2 \cdot 29$
9	81	3.000	3^2	59	3,481	7.681	59
10	100	3.162	$2 \cdot 5$	60	3,600	7.746	$2^2 \cdot 3 \cdot 5$
11	121	3.317	11	61	3,721	7.810	61
12	144	3.464	$2^2 \cdot 3$	62	3,844	7.874	$2 \cdot 31$
13	169	3.606	13	63	3,969	7.937	$3^2 \cdot 7$
14	196	3.742	$2 \cdot 7$	64	4,096	8.000	2^6
15	225	3.873	$3 \cdot 5$	65	4,225	8.062	$5 \cdot 13$
16	256	4.000	2^4	66	4,356	8.124	$2 \cdot 3 \cdot 11$
17	289	4.123	17	67	4,489	8.185	67
18	324	4.243	$2 \cdot 3^2$	68	4,624	8.246	$2^2 \cdot 17$
19	361	4.359	19	69	4,761	8.307	$3 \cdot 23$
20	400	4.472	$2^2 \cdot 5$	70	4,900	8.367	$2 \cdot 5 \cdot 7$
21	441	4.583	$3 \cdot 7$	71	5,041	8.426	71
22	484	4.690	$2 \cdot 11$	72	5,184	8.485	$2^3 \cdot 3^2$
23	529	4.796	23	73	5,329	8.544	73
24	576	4.899	$2^3 \cdot 3$	74	5,476	8.602	$2 \cdot 37$
25	625	5.000	5^2	75	5,625	8.660	$3 \cdot 5^2$
26	676	5.099	$2 \cdot 13$	76	5,776	8.718	$2^2 \cdot 19$
27	729	5.196	3^3	77	5,929	8.775	$7 \cdot 11$
28	784	5.292	$2^2 \cdot 7$	78	6,084	8.832	$2 \cdot 3 \cdot 13$
29	841	5.385	29	79	6,241	8.888	79
30	900	5.477	$2 \cdot 3 \cdot 5$	80	6,400	8.944	$2^4 \cdot 5$
31	961	5.568	31	81	6,561	9.000	3^4
32	1,024	5.657	2^5	82	6,724	9.055	$2 \cdot 41$
33	1,089	5.745	$3 \cdot 11$	83	6,889	9.110	83
34	1,156	5.831	$2 \cdot 17$	84	7,056	9.165	$2^2 \cdot 3 \cdot 7$
35	1,225	5.916	$5 \cdot 7$	85	7,225	9.220	$5 \cdot 17$
36	1,296	6.000	$2^2 \cdot 3^2$	86	7,396	9.274	$2 \cdot 43$
37	1,369	6.083	37	87	7,569	9.327	$3 \cdot 29$
38	1,444	6.164	$2 \cdot 19$	88	7,744	9.381	$2^3 \cdot 11$
39	1,521	6.245	$3 \cdot 13$	89	7,921	9.434	89
40	1,600	6.325	$2^3 \cdot 5$	90	8,100	9.487	$2 \cdot 3^2 \cdot 5$
41	1,681	6.403	41	91	8,281	9.539	$7 \cdot 13$
42	1,764	6.481	$2 \cdot 3 \cdot 7$	92	8,464	9.592	$2^2 \cdot 23$
43	1,849	6.557	43	93	8,649	9.644	$3 \cdot 31$
44	1,936	6.633	$2^2 \cdot 11$	94	8,836	9.695	$2 \cdot 47$
45	2,025	6.708	$3^2 \cdot 5$	95	9,025	9.747	$5 \cdot 19$
46	2,116	6.782	$2 \cdot 23$	96	9,216	9.798	$2^5 \cdot 3$
47	2,209	6.856	47	97	9,409	9.849	97
48	2,304	6.928	$2^4 \cdot 3$	98	9,604	9.899	$2 \cdot 7^2$
49	2,401	7.000	7^2	99	9,801	9.950	$3^2 \cdot 11$
50	2,500	7.071	$2 \cdot 5^2$	100	10,000	10.000	$2^2 \cdot 5^2$

TABLE V

VALUES OF CIRCULAR FUNCTIONS

Real Number x or θ radians	θ/degrees	sin x or sin θ	csc x or csc θ	tan x or tan θ	cot x or cot θ	sec x or sec θ	cos x or cos θ
0.00	0° 00′	0.0000	No value	0.0000	No value	1.000	1.000
.01	0° 34′	.0100	100.0	.0100	100.0	1.000	1.000
.02	1° 09′	.0200	50.00	.0200	49.99	1.000	0.9998
.03	1° 43′	.0300	33.34	.0300	33.32	1.000	0.9996
.04	2° 18′	.0400	25.01	.0400	24.99	1.001	0.9992
0.05	2° 52′	0.0500	20.01	0.0500	19.98	1.001	0.9988
.06	3° 26′	.0600	16.68	.0601	16.65	1.002	.9982
.07	4° 01′	.0699	14.30	.0701	14.26	1.002	.9976
.08	4° 35′	.0799	12.51	.0802	12.47	1.003	.9968
.09	5° 09′	.0899	11.13	.0902	11.08	1.004	.9960
0.10	5° 44′	0.0998	10.02	0.1003	9.967	1.005	0.9950
.11	6° 18′	.1098	9.109	.1104	9.054	1.006	.9940
.12	6° 53′	.1197	8.353	.1206	8.293	1.007	.9928
.13	7° 27′	.1296	7.714	.1307	7.649	1.009	.9916
.14	8° 01′	.1395	7.166	.1409	7.096	1.010	.9902
0.15	8° 36′	0.1494	6.692	0.1511	6.617	1.011	0.9888
.16	9° 10′	.1593	6.277	.1614	6.197	1.013	.9872
.17	9° 44′	.1692	5.911	.1717	5.826	1.015	.9856
.18	10° 19′	.1790	5.586	.1820	5.495	1.016	.9838
.19	10° 53′	.1889	5.295	.1923	5.200	1.018	.9820
0.20	11° 28′	0.1987	5.033	0.2027	4.933	1.020	0.9801
.21	12° 02′	.2085	4.797	.2131	4.692	1.022	.9780
.22	12° 36′	.2182	4.582	.2236	4.472	1.025	.9759
.23	13° 11′	.2280	4.386	.2341	4.271	1.027	.9737
.24	13° 45′	.2377	4.207	.2447	4.086	1.030	.9713
0.25	14° 19′	0.2474	4.042	0.2553	3.916	1.032	0.9689
.26	14° 54′	.2571	3.890	.2660	3.759	1.035	.9664
.27	15° 28′	.2667	3.749	.2768	3.613	1.038	.9638
.28	16° 03′	.2764	3.619	.2876	3.478	1.041	.9611
.29	16° 37′	.2860	3.497	.2984	3.351	1.044	.9582
0.30	17° 11′	0.2955	3.384	0.3093	3.233	1.047	0.9553
.31	17° 46′	.3051	3.278	.3203	3.122	1.050	.9523
.32	18° 20′	.3146	3.179	.3314	3.018	1.053	.9492
.33	18° 54′	.3240	3.086	.3425	2.920	1.057	.9460
.34	19° 29′	.3335	2.999	.3537	2.827	1.061	.9428
0.35	20° 03′	0.3429	2.916	0.3650	2.740	1.065	0.9394
.36	20° 38′	.3523	2.839	.3764	2.657	1.068	.9359
.37	21° 12′	.3616	2.765	.3879	2.578	1.073	.9323
.38	21° 46′	.3709	2.696	.3994	2.504	1.077	.9287
.39	22° 21′	.3802	2.630	.4111	2.433	1.081	.9249
0.40	22° 55′	0.3894	2.568	0.4228	2.365	1.086	0.9211
.41	23° 29′	.3986	2.509	.4346	2.301	1.090	.9171
.42	24° 04′	.4078	2.452	.4466	2.239	1.095	.9131
.43	24° 38′	.4169	2.399	.4586	2.180	1.100	.9090
.44	25° 13′	.4259	2.348	.4708	2.124	1.105	.9048
0.45	25° 47′	0.4350	2.299	0.4831	2.070	1.111	0.9004

TABLE V (*continued*)

Real Number x or θ radians	θ degrees	$\sin x$ or $\sin \theta$	$\csc x$ or $\csc \theta$	$\tan x$ or $\tan \theta$	$\cot x$ or $\cot \theta$	$\sec x$ or $\sec \theta$	$\cos x$ or $\cos \theta$
0.45	25° 47′	0.4350	2.299	0.4831	2.070	1.111	0.9004
.46	26° 21′	.4439	2.253	.4954	2.018	1.116	.8961
.47	26° 56′	.4529	2.208	.5080	1.969	1.122	.8916
.48	27° 30′	.4618	2.166	.5206	1.921	1.127	.8870
.49	28° 04′	.4706	2.125	.5334	1.875	1.133	.8823
0.50	28° 39′	0.4794	2.086	0.5463	1.830	1.139	0.8776
.51	29° 13′	.4882	2.048	.5594	1.788	1.146	.8727
.52	29° 48′	.4969	2.013	.5726	1.747	1.152	.8678
.53	30° 22′	.5055	1.978	.5859	1.707	1.159	.8628
.54	30° 56′	.5141	1.945	.5994	1.668	1.166	.8577
0.55	31° 31′	0.5227	1.913	0.6131	1.631	1.173	0.8525
.56	32° 05′	.5312	1.883	.6269	1.595	1.180	.8473
.57	32° 40′	.5396	1.853	.6410	1.560	1.188	.8419
.58	33° 14′	.5480	1.825	.6552	1.526	1.196	.8365
.59	33° 48′	.5564	1.797	.6696	1.494	1.203	.8309
0.60	34° 23′	0.5646	1.771	0.6841	1.462	1.212	0.8253
.61	34° 57′	.5729	1.746	.6989	1.431	1.220	.8196
.62	35° 31′	.5810	1.721	.7139	1.401	1.229	.8139
.63	36° 06′	.5891	1.697	.7291	1.372	1.238	.8080
.64	36° 40′	.5972	1.674	.7445	1.343	1.247	.8021
0.65	37° 15′	0.6052	1.652	0.7602	1.315	1.256	0.7961
.66	37° 49′	.6131	1.631	.7761	1.288	1.266	.7900
.67	38° 23′	.6210	1.610	.7923	1.262	1.276	.7838
.68	38° 58′	.6288	1.590	.8087	1.237	1.286	.7776
.69	39° 32′	.6365	1.571	.8253	1.212	1.297	.7712
0.70	40° 06′	0.6442	1.552	0.8423	1.187	1.307	0.7648
.71	40° 41′	.6518	1.534	.8595	1.163	1.319	.7584
.72	41° 15′	.6594	1.517	.8771	1.140	1.330	.7518
.73	41° 50′	.6669	1.500	.8949	1.117	1.342	.7452
.74	42° 24′	.6743	1.483	.9131	1.095	1.354	.7385
0.75	42° 58′	0.6816	1.467	0.9316	1.073	1.367	0.7317
.76	43° 33′	.6889	1.452	.9505	1.052	1.380	.7248
.77	44° 07′	.6961	1.436	.9697	1.031	1.393	.7179
.78	44° 41′	.7033	1.422	.9893	1.011	1.407	.7109
.79	45° 16′	.7104	1.408	1.009	.9908	1.421	.7038
0.80	45° 50′	0.7174	1.394	1.030	0.9712	1.435	0.6967
.81	46° 25′	.7243	1.381	1.050	.9520	1.450	.6895
.82	46° 59′	.7311	1.368	1.072	.9331	1.466	.6822
.83	47° 33′	.7379	1.355	1.093	.9146	1.482	.6749
.84	48° 08′	.7446	1.343	1.116	.8964	1.498	.6675
0.85	48° 42′	0.7513	1.331	1.138	0.8785	1.515	0.6600
.86	49° 16′	.7578	1.320	1.162	.8609	1.533	.6524
.87	49° 51′	.7643	1.308	1.185	.8437	1.551	.6448
.88	50° 25′	.7707	1.297	1.210	.8267	1.569	.6372
.89	51° 00′	.7771	1.287	1.235	.8100	1.589	.6294
0.90	51° 34′	0.7833	1.277	1.260	0.7936	1.609	0.6216
.91	52° 08′	.7895	1.267	1.286	.7774	1.629	.6137
.92	52° 43′	.7956	1.257	1.313	.7615	1.651	.6058
.93	53° 17′	.8016	1.247	1.341	.7458	1.673	.5978
.94	53° 51′	.8076	1.238	1.369	.7303	1.696	.5898
0.95	54° 26′	0.8134	1.229	1.398	0.7151	1.719	0.5817

TABLE V (*continued*)

Real Number x or θ radians	θ degrees	$\sin x$ or $\sin \theta$	$\csc x$ or $\csc \theta$	$\tan x$ or $\tan \theta$	$\cot x$ or $\cot \theta$	$\sec x$ or $\sec \theta$	$\cos x$ or $\cos \theta$
0.95	54° 26′	0.8134	1.229	1.398	0.7151	1.719	0.5817
.96	55° 00′	.8192	1.221	1.428	.7001	1.744	.5735
.97	55° 35′	.8249	1.212	1.459	.6853	1.769	.5653
.98	56° 09′	.8305	1.204	1.491	.6707	1.795	.5570
.99	56° 43′	.8360	1.196	1.524	.6563	1.823	.5487
1.00	57° 18′	0.8415	1.188	1.557	0.6421	1.851	0.5403
1.01	57° 52′	.8468	1.181	1.592	.6281	1.880	.5319
1.02	58° 27′	.8521	1.174	1.628	.6142	1.911	.5234
1.03	59° 01′	.8573	1.166	1.665	.6005	1.942	.5148
1.04	59° 35′	.8624	1.160	1.704	.5870	1.975	.5062
1.05	60° 10′	0.8674	1.153	1.743	0.5736	2.010	0.4976
1.06	60° 44′	.8724	1.146	1.784	.5604	2.046	.4889
1.07	61° 18′	.8772	1.140	1.827	.5473	2.083	.4801
1.08	61° 53′	.8820	1.134	1.871	.5344	2.122	.4713
1.09	62° 27′	.8866	1.128	1.917	.5216	2.162	.4625
1.10	63° 02′	0.8912	1.122	1.965	0.5090	2.205	0.4536
1.11	63° 36′	.8957	1.116	2.014	.4964	2.249	.4447
1.12	64° 10′	.9001	1.111	2.066	.4840	2.295	.4357
1.13	64° 45′	.9044	1.106	2.120	.4718	2.344	.4267
1.14	65° 19′	.9086	1.101	2.176	.4596	2.395	.4176
1.15	65° 53′	0.9128	1.096	2.234	0.4475	2.448	0.4085
1.16	66° 28′	.9168	1.091	2.296	.4356	2.504	.3993
1.17	67° 02′	.9208	1.086	2.360	.4237	2.563	.3902
1.18	67° 37′	.9246	1.082	2.247	.4120	2.625	.3809
1.19	68° 11′	.9284	1.077	2.498	.4003	2.691	.3717
1.20	68° 45′	0.9320	1.073	2.572	0.3888	2.760	0.3624
1.21	69° 20′	.9356	1.069	2.650	.3773	2.833	.3530
1.22	69° 54′	.9391	1.065	2.733	.3659	2.910	.3436
1.23	70° 28′	.9425	1.061	2.820	.3546	2.992	.3342
1.24	71° 03′	.9458	1.057	2.912	.3434	3.079	.3248
1.25	71° 37′	0.9490	1.054	3.010	0.3323	3.171	0.3153
1.26	72° 12′	.9521	1.050	3.113	.3212	3.270	.3058
1.27	72° 46′	.9551	1.047	3.224	.3102	3.375	.2963
1.28	72° 20′	.9580	1.044	3.341	.2993	3.488	.2867
1.29	73° 55′	.9608	1.041	3.467	.2884	3.609	.2771
1.30	74° 29′	0.9636	1.038	3.602	0.2776	3.738	0.2675
1.31	75° 03′	.9662	1.035	3.747	.2669	3.878	.2579
1.32	75° 38′	.9687	1.032	3.903	.2562	4.029	.2482
1.33	76° 12′	.9711	1.030	4.072	.2456	4.193	.2385
1.34	76° 47′	.9735	1.027	4.256	.2350	4.372	.2288
1.35	77° 21′	0.9757	1.025	4.455	0.2245	4.566	0.2190
1.36	77° 55′	.9779	1.023	4.673	.2140	4.779	.2092
1.37	78° 30′	.9799	1.021	4.913	.2035	5.014	.1994
1.38	79° 04′	.9819	1.018	5.177	.1931	5.273	.1896
1.39	79° 38′	.9837	1.017	5.471	.1828	5.561	.1798
1.40	80° 13′	0.9854	1.015	5.798	0.1725	5.883	0.1700
1.41	80° 47′	.9871	1.013	6.165	.1622	6.246	.1601
1.42	81° 22′	.9887	1.011	6.581	.1519	6.657	.1502
1.43	81° 56′	.9901	1.010	7.055	.1417	7.126	.1403
1.44	82° 30′	.9915	1.009	7.602	.1315	7.667	.1304
1.45	83° 05′	0.9927	1.007	8.238	0.1214	8.299	0.1205

TABLE V (*continued*)

Real Number x or θ radians	θ degrees	sin x or sin θ	csc x or csc θ	tan x or tan θ	cot x or cot θ	sec x or sec θ	cos x or cos θ
1.45	83° 05′	0.9927	1.007	8.238	0.1214	8.299	0.1205
1.46	83° 39′	.9939	1.006	8.989	.1113	9.044	.1106
1.47	84° 13′	.9949	1.005	9.887	.1011	9.938	.1006
1.48	84° 48′	.9959	1.004	10.98	.0910	11.03	.0907
1.49	85° 22′	.9967	1.003	12.35	.0810	12.39	.0807
1.50	85° 57′	0.9975	1.003	14.10	0.0709	14.14	0.0707
1.51	86° 31′	.9982	1.002	16.43	.0609	16.46	.0608
1.52	87° 05′	.9987	1.001	19.67	.0508	19.69	.0508
1.53	87° 40′	.9992	1.001	24.50	.0408	24.52	.0408
1.54	88° 14′	.9995	1.000	32.46	.0308	32.48	.0308
1.55	88° 49′	0.9998	1.000	48.08	0.0208	48.09	0.0208
1.56	89° 23′	.9999	1.000	92.62	.0108	92.63	.0108
1.57	89° 57′	1.000	1.000	1256	.0008	1256	.0008

TABLE VI

VALUES OF TRIGONOMETRIC FUNCTIONS

Angle θ									
Degrees	Radians	sin θ	csc θ	tan θ	cot θ	sec θ	cos θ		
0° 00′	.0000	.0000	No value	.0000	No value	1.000	1.0000	1.5708	90° 00′
10	029	029	343.8	029	343.8	000	000	679	50
20	058	058	171.9	058	171.9	000	000	650	40
30	087	087	114.6	087	114.6	000	1.0000	621	30
40	116	116	85.95	116	85.94	000	.9999	592	20
50	145	145	68.76	145	68.75	000	999	563	10
1° 00′	.0175	.0175	57.30	.0175	57.29	1.000	.9998	1.5533	89° 00′
10	204	204	49.11	204	49.10	000	998	504	50
20	233	233	42.98	233	42.96	000	997	475	40
30	262	262	38.20	262	38.19	000	997	446	30
40	291	291	34.38	291	34.37	000	996	417	20
50	320	320	31.26	320	31.24	001	995	388	10
2° 00′	.0349	.0349	28.65	.0349	28.64	1.001	.9994	1.5359	88° 00′
10	378	378	26.45	378	26.43	001	993	330	50
20	407	407	24.56	407	24.54	001	992	301	40
30	436	436	22.93	437	22.90	001	990	272	30
40	465	465	21.49	466	21.47	001	989	243	20
50	495	494	20.23	495	20.21	001	988	213	10
3° 00′	.0524	.0523	19.11	.0524	19.08	1.001	.9986	1.5184	87° 00′
10	553	552	18.10	553	18.07	002	985	155	50
20	582	581	17.20	582	17.17	002	983	126	40
30	611	610	16.38	612	16.35	002	981	097	30
40	640	640	15.64	641	15.60	002	980	068	20
50	669	669	14.96	670	14.92	002	978	039	10
4° 00′	.0698	.0698	14.34	.0699	14.30	1.002	.9976	1.5010	86° 00′
10	727	727	13.76	729	13.73	003	974	981	50
20	756	765	13.23	758	13.20	003	971	952	40
30	785	785	12.75	787	12.71	003	969	923	30
40	814	814	12.29	816	12.25	003	967	893	20
50	844	843	11.87	846	11.83	004	964	864	10
5° 00′	.0873	.0872	11.47	0.875	11.43	1.004	.9962	1.4835	85° 00′
10	902	901	11.10	904	11.06	004	959	806	50
20	931	929	10.76	934	10.71	004	957	777	40
30	960	958	10.43	963	10.39	005	954	748	30
40	.0989	.0987	10.13	.0992	10.08	005	951	719	20
50	.1018	.1016	9.839	.1022	9.788	005	948	690	10
6° 00′	.1047	.1045	9.567	.1051	9.514	1.006	.9945	1.4661	84° 00′
10	076	074	9.309	080	9.255	006	942	632	50
20	105	103	9.065	110	9.010	006	939	603	40
30	134	132	8.834	139	8.777	006	936	573	30
40	164	161	8.614	169	8.556	007	932	544	20
50	193	190	8.405	198	8.345	007	929	515	10
7° 00′	.1222	.1219	8.206	.1228	8.144	1.008	.9925	1.4486	83° 00′
10	251	248	8.016	257	7.953	008	922	457	50
20	280	276	7.834	287	7.770	008	918	428	40
30	309	305	7.661	317	7.596	009	914	399	30
40	338	334	7.496	346	7.429	009	911	370	20
50	367	363	7.337	376	7.269	009	907	341	10
8° 00′	.1396	.1392	7.185	.1405	7.115	1.010	.9903	1.4312	82° 00′
		cos θ	sec θ	cot θ	tan θ	csc θ	sin θ	Radians	Degrees
								Angle θ	

TABLE VI (continued)

Angle θ		sin θ	csc θ	tan θ	cot θ	sec θ	cos θ		
Degrees	Radians								
8° 00′	.1396	.1392	7.185	.1405	7.115	1.010	.9903	1.4312	82° 00′
10	425	421	7.040	435	6.968	010	899	283	50
20	454	449	6.900	465	827	011	894	254	40
30	484	478	765	495	691	011	890	224	30
40	513	507	636	524	561	012	886	195	20
50	542	536	512	554	435	012	881	166	10
9° 00′	.1571	.1564	6.392	.1584	6.314	1.012	.9877	1.4137	81° 00′
10	600	593	277	614	197	013	872	108	50
20	629	622	166	644	6.084	013	868	079	40
30	658	650	6.059	673	5.976	014	863	050	30
40	687	679	5.955	703	871	014	858	1.4021	20
50	716	708	855	733	769	015	853	1.3992	10
10° 00′	.1745	.1736	5.759	.1763	5.671	1.015	.9848	1.3963	80° 00′
10	774	765	665	793	576	016	843	934	50
20	804	794	575	823	485	016	838	904	40
30	833	822	487	853	396	017	833	875	30
40	862	851	403	883	309	018	827	846	20
50	891	880	320	914	226	018	822	817	10
11° 00′	.1920	.1908	5.241	.1944	5.145	1.019	.9816	1.3788	79° 00′
10	949	937	164	.1974	5.066	019	811	759	50
20	.1978	965	089	.2004	4.989	020	805	730	40
30	.2007	.1994	5.016	035	915	020	799	701	30
40	036	.2022	4.945	065	843	021	793	672	20
50	065	051	876	095	773	022	787	643	10
12° 00′	.2094	.2079	4.810	.2126	4.705	1.022	.9781	1.3614	78° 00′
10	123	108	745	156	638	023	775	584	50
20	153	136	682	186	574	024	769	555	40
30	182	164	620	217	511	024	763	526	30
40	211	193	560	247	449	025	757	497	20
50	240	221	502	278	390	026	750	468	10
13° 00′	.2269	.2250	4.445	.2309	4.331	1.026	.9744	1.3439	77° 00′
10	298	278	390	339	275	027	737	410	50
20	327	306	336	370	219	028	730	381	40
30	356	334	284	401	165	028	724	352	30
40	385	363	232	432	113	029	717	323	20
50	414	391	182	462	061	030	710	294	10
14° 00′	.2443	.2419	4.134	.2493	4.011	1.031	.9703	1.3265	76° 00′
10	473	447	086	524	3.962	031	696	235	50
20	502	476	4.039	555	914	032	689	206	40
30	531	504	3.994	586	867	033	681	177	30
40	560	532	950	617	821	034	674	148	20
50	589	560	906	648	776	034	667	119	10
15° 00′	.2618	.2588	3.864	.2679	3.732	1.035	.9659	1.3090	75° 00′
10	647	616	822	711	689	036	652	061	50
20	676	644	782	742	647	037	644	032	40
30	705	672	742	773	606	038	636	1.3003	30
40	734	700	703	805	566	039	628	1.2974	20
50	763	728	665	836	526	039	621	945	10
16° 00′	.2793	.2756	3.628	.2867	3.487	1.040	.9613	1.2915	74° 00′
		cos θ	sec θ	cot θ	tan θ	csc θ	sin θ	Radians	Degrees
									Angle θ

TABLE VI (continued)

Angle θ									
Degrees	Radians	sin θ	csc θ	tan θ	cot θ	sec θ	cos θ		
16° 00′	.2793	.2756	3.628	.2867	3.487	1.040	.9613	1.2915	74° 00′
10	822	784	592	899	450	041	605	886	50
20	851	812	556	931	412	042	596	857	40
30	880	840	521	962	376	043	588	828	30
40	909	868	487	.2944	340	044	580	799	20
50	938	896	453	.3026	305	045	572	770	10
17° 00′	.2967	.2924	3.420	.3057	3.271	1.046	.9563	1.2741	73° 00′
10	.2996	952	388	089	237	047	555	712	50
20	.3025	.2979	357	121	204	048	546	683	40
30	054	.3007	326	153	172	048	537	654	30
40	083	035	295	185	140	049	528	625	20
50	113	062	265	217	108	050	520	595	10
18° 00′	.3142	.3090	3.236	.3249	3.078	1.051	.9511	1.2566	72° 00′
10	171	118	207	281	047	052	502	537	50
20	200	145	179	314	3.018	053	492	508	40
30	229	173	152	346	2.989	054	483	479	30
40	258	201	124	378	960	056	474	450	20
50	287	228	098	411	932	057	465	421	10
19° 00′	.3316	.3256	3.072	.3443	2.904	1.058	.9455	1.2392	71° 00′
10	345	283	046	476	877	059	446	363	50
20	374	311	3.021	508	850	060	436	334	40
30	403	338	2.996	541	824	061	426	305	30
40	432	365	971	574	798	062	417	275	20
50	462	393	947	607	773	063	407	246	10
20° 00′	.3491	.3420	2.924	.3640	2.747	1.064	.9397	1.2217	70° 00′
10	520	448	901	673	723	065	387	188	50
20	549	475	878	706	699	066	377	159	40
30	578	502	855	739	675	068	367	130	30
40	607	529	833	772	651	069	356	101	20
50	636	557	812	805	628	070	346	072	10
21° 00′	.3665	.3584	2.790	.3839	2.605	1.071	.9336	1.2043	69° 00′
10	694	611	769	872	583	072	325	1.2014	50
20	723	638	749	906	560	074	315	985	40
30	752	665	729	939	539	075	304	956	30
40	782	692	709	.3973	517	076	293	926	20
50	811	719	689	.4006	496	077	283	897	10
22° 00′	.3840	.3746	2.669	.4040	2.475	1.079	.9272	1.1868	68° 00′
10	869	773	650	074	455	080	261	839	50
20	898	800	632	108	434	081	250	810	40
30	927	827	613	142	414	082	239	781	30
40	956	854	595	176	394	084	228	752	20
50	985	881	577	210	375	085	216	723	10
23° 00′	.4014	.3907	2.559	.4245	2.356	1.086	.9205	1.1694	67° 00′
10	043	934	542	279	337	088	194	665	50
20	072	961	525	314	318	089	182	636	40
30	102	.3987	508	348	300	090	171	606	30
40	131	.4014	491	383	282	092	159	577	20
50	160	041	475	417	264	093	147	548	10
24° 00′	.4189	.4067	2.459	.4452	2.246	1.095	.9135	1.1519	66° 00′
		cos θ	sec θ	cot θ	tan θ	csc θ	sin θ	Radians	Degrees
								Angle θ	

TABLE VI (*continued*)

Angle θ		sin θ	csc θ	tan θ	cot θ	sec θ	cos θ		
Degrees	Radians	sin θ	csc θ	tan θ	cot θ	sec θ	cos θ		
24° 00′	.4189	.4067	2.459	.4452	2.246	1.095	.9135	1.1519	66° 00′
10	218	094	443	487	229	096	124	490	50
20	247	120	427	522	211	097	112	461	40
30	276	147	411	557	194	099	100	432	30
40	305	173	396	592	177	100	088	403	20
50	334	200	381	628	161	102	075	374	10
25° 00′	.4363	.4226	2.366	.4663	2.145	1.103	.9063	1.1345	65° 00′
10	392	253	352	699	128	105	051	316	50
20	422	279	337	734	112	106	038	286	40
30	451	305	323	770	097	108	026	257	30
40	480	331	309	806	081	109	013	228	20
50	509	358	295	841	066	111	.9001	199	10
26° 00′	.4538	.4384	2.281	.4877	2.050	1.113	.8988	1.1170	64° 00′
10	567	410	268	913	035	114	975	141	50
20	596	436	254	950	020	116	962	112	40
30	625	462	241	.4986	2.006	117	949	083	30
40	654	488	228	.5022	1.991	119	936	054	20
50	683	514	215	059	977	121	923	1.1025	10
27° 00′	.4712	.4540	2.203	.5095	1.963	1.122	.8910	1.0996	63° 00′
10	741	566	190	132	949	124	897	966	50
20	771	592	178	169	935	126	884	937	40
30	800	617	166	206	921	127	870	908	30
40	829	643	154	243	907	129	857	879	20
50	858	669	142	280	894	131	843	850	10
28° 00′	.4887	.4695	2.130	.5317	1.881	1.133	.8829	1.0821	62° 00′
10	916	720	118	354	868	134	816	792	50
20	945	746	107	392	855	136	802	763	40
30	.4974	772	096	430	842	138	788	734	30
40	.5003	797	085	467	829	140	774	705	20
50	032	823	074	505	816	142	760	676	10
29° 00′	.5061	.4848	2.063	.5543	1.804	1.143	.8746	1.0647	61° 00′
10	091	874	052	581	792	145	732	617	50
20	120	899	041	619	780	147	718	588	40
30	149	924	031	658	767	149	704	559	30
40	178	950	020	696	756	151	689	530	20
50	207	.4975	010	735	744	153	675	501	10
30° 00′	.5236	.5000	2.000	.5774	1.732	1.155	.8660	1.0472	60° 00′
10	265	025	1.990	812	720	157	646	443	50
20	294	050	980	851	709	159	631	414	40
30	323	075	970	890	698	161	616	385	30
40	352	100	961	930	686	163	601	356	20
50	381	125	951	.5969	675	165	587	327	10
31° 00′	.5411	.5150	1.942	.6009	1.664	1.167	.8572	1.0297	59° 00′
10	440	175	932	048	653	169	557	268	50
20	469	200	923	088	643	171	542	239	40
30	498	225	914	128	632	173	526	210	30
40	527	250	905	168	621	175	511	181	20
50	556	275	896	208	611	177	496	152	10
32° 00′	.5585	.5299	1.887	.6249	1.600	1.179	.8480	1.0123	58° 00′
		cos θ	sec θ	cot θ	tan θ	csc θ	sin θ	Radians	Degrees
								Angle θ	

TABLE VI (*continued*)

Angle θ									
Degrees	Radians	sin θ	csc θ	tan θ	cot θ	sec θ	cos θ		
32° 00′	.5585	.5299	1.887	.6249	1.600	1.179	.8480	1.0123	58° 00′
10	614	324	878	289	590	181	465	094	50
20	643	348	870	330	580	184	450	065	40
30	672	373	861	371	570	186	434	036	30
40	701	398	853	412	560	188	418	1.0007	20
50	730	422	844	453	550	190	403	.9977	10
33° 00′	.5760	.5446	1.836	.6494	1.540	1.192	.8387	.9948	57° 00′
10	789	471	828	536	530	195	371	919	50
20	818	495	820	577	520	197	355	890	40
30	847	519	812	619	511	199	339	861	30
40	876	544	804	661	501	202	323	832	20
50	905	568	796	703	492	204	307	803	10
34° 00′	.5934	.5592	1.788	.6745	1.483	1.206	.8290	.9774	56° 00′
10	963	616	781	787	473	209	274	745	50
20	.5992	640	773	830	464	211	258	716	40
30	.6021	664	766	873	455	213	241	687	30
40	050	688	758	916	446	216	225	657	20
50	080	712	751	.6959	437	218	208	628	10
35° 00′	.6109	.5736	1.743	.7002	1.428	1.221	.8192	.9599	55° 00′
10	138	760	736	046	419	223	175	570	50
20	167	783	729	089	411	226	158	541	40
30	196	807	722	133	402	228	141	512	30
40	225	831	715	177	393	231	124	483	20
50	254	854	708	221	385	233	107	454	10
36° 00′	.6283	.5878	1.701	.7265	1.376	1.236	.8090	.9425	54° 00′
10	312	901	695	310	368	239	073	396	50
20	341	925	688	355	360	241	056	367	40
30	370	948	681	400	351	244	039	338	30
40	400	972	675	445	343	247	021	308	20
50	429	.5995	668	490	335	249	.8004	279	10
37° 00′	.6458	.6018	1.662	.7536	1.327	1.252	.7986	.9250	53° 00′
10	487	041	655	581	319	255	696	221	50
20	516	065	649	627	311	258	951	192	40
30	545	088	643	673	303	260	934	163	30
40	574	111	636	720	295	263	916	134	20
50	603	134	630	766	288	266	898	105	10
38° 00′	.6632	.6157	1.624	.7813	1.280	1.269	.7880	.9076	52° 00′
10	661	180	618	860	272	272	862	047	50
20	690	202	612	907	265	275	844	.9018	40
30	720	225	606	.7954	257	278	826	.8988	30
40	749	248	601	.8002	250	281	808	959	20
50	778	271	595	050	242	284	790	930	10
39° 00′	.6807	.6293	1.589	.8098	1.235	1.287	.7771	.8901	51° 00′
10	836	316	583	146	228	290	753	872	50
20	865	338	578	195	220	293	735	843	40
30	894	361	572	243	213	296	716	814	30
40	923	383	567	292	206	299	698	785	20
50	952	406	561	342	199	302	679	756	10
40° 00′	.6981	.6428	1.556	.8391	1.192	1.305	.7660	.8727	50° 00′
		cos θ	sec θ	cot θ	tan θ	csc θ	sin θ	Radians	Degrees
								Angle θ	

TABLE VI (*continued*)

Angle θ									
Degrees	Radians	sin θ	csc θ	tan θ	cot θ	sec θ	cos θ		
40° 00′	.6981	.6428	1.556	.8391	1.192	1.305	.7660	.8727	50° 00′
10	.7010	450	550	441	185	309	642	698	50
20	039	472	545	491	178	312	623	668	40
30	069	494	540	541	171	315	604	639	30
40	098	517	535	591	164	318	585	610	20
50	127	539	529	642	157	322	566	581	10
41° 00′	.7156	.6561	1.524	.8693	1.150	1.325	.7547	.8552	49° 00′
10	185	583	519	744	144	328	528	523	50
20	214	604	514	796	137	332	509	494	40
30	243	626	509	847	130	335	490	465	30
40	272	648	504	899	124	339	470	436	20
50	301	670	499	.8952	117	342	451	407	10
42° 00′	.7330	.6691	1.494	.9004	1.111	1.346	.7431	.8378	48° 00′
10	359	713	490	057	104	349	412	348	50
20	389	734	485	110	098	353	392	319	40
30	418	756	480	163	091	356	373	290	30
40	447	777	476	217	085	360	353	261	20
50	476	799	471	271	079	364	333	232	10
43° 00′	.7505	.6820	1.466	.9325	1.072	1.367	.7314	.8203	47° 00′
10	534	841	462	380	066	371	294	174	50
20	563	862	457	435	060	375	274	145	40
30	592	884	453	490	054	379	254	116	30
40	621	905	448	545	048	382	234	087	20
50	650	926	444	601	042	386	214	058	10
44° 00′	.7679	.6947	1.440	.9657	1.036	1.390	.7193	.8029	46° 00′
10	709	967	435	713	030	394	173	.7999	50
20	738	.6988	431	770	024	398	153	970	40
30	767	.7009	427	827	018	402	133	941	30
40	796	030	423	884	012	406	112	912	20
50	825	050	418	.9942	006	410	092	883	10
45° 00′	.7854	.7071	1.414	1.000	1.000	1.414	.7071	.7854	45° 00′
		cos θ	sec θ	cot θ	tan θ	csc θ	sin θ	Radians	Degrees
								Angle θ	

379

ANSWERS

Exercise 1.1 (Page 4)   **1.** {4, 5, 6, 7, 8, 9}   **3.** {Sunday, Monday, Tuesday, Wednesday, Thursday, Friday, Saturday}   **7.** $\{x \mid x$ is an odd natural number$\}$ **9.** $\{x \mid 2^x = 5\}$
11. $\{x \mid x \notin A\}$ **13.** No   **15.** No   **17.** {natural numbers less than three} = {1, 2}
19. $\varnothing \neq \{0\}$ **21.** $3 \in \{2, 3, 4\}$ **23.** $\{2\} \notin \{2, 3, 4\}$ **25.** $5 \notin \{4, 5, 6\}$ **27.** $\varnothing \subset \{4, 5, 6\}$
29. a. {5, 6, 7} **b.** {5, 6}, {5, 7}, {6, 7} **c.** {5}, {6}, {7} **d.** $\varnothing$ **31. a.** $A \subset U$ **b.** $C \notin A$
c. $A \notin B$ **d.** $C \subset B$

Exercise 1.2 (Page 7)   **1.** $A' = \{1, 3, 5, 7, 9\} = C$ **3.** $C' = \{2, 4, 6, 8, 10\} = A$ **5.** $A \cup B =$
$\{1, 2, 3, 4, 5, 6, 8, 10\}$ **7.** $A \cap C = \varnothing$ **9.** $A' \cup C' = U$ or $\{1, 2, 3, 4, 5, 6, 7, 8, 9, 10\}$
11. $A' \cup C = C$ or $\{1, 3, 5, 7, 9\}$

13. 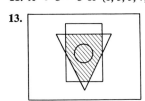   **15.** 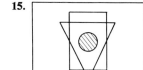   **17.**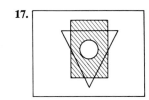

19. 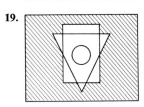   **21.** 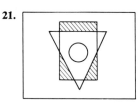   **23.**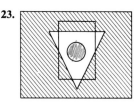

25. $(A')' = A$ **27.** $A \cap U = A$ **29.** $A \cup U = U$ **31.** $A \cup \varnothing = A$ **33.** $\varnothing' \cap \varnothing = \varnothing$
35. $\varnothing \cup \varnothing = \varnothing$ **37. a.** $A \cup B = \varnothing$ if $A = B = \varnothing$ **b.** $A \cup \varnothing = \varnothing$ if $A = \varnothing$ **c.** $A \cap U =$
U if $A = U$ **d.** $A \cup B = A$ if $B \subseteq A$ **e.** $A \cup \varnothing = U$ if $A = U$ **f.** $A' \cap U = U$ if $A = \varnothing$
g. $A \cap B = A$ if $A \subseteq B$ **h.** $A' \cup \varnothing = \varnothing$ if $A = U$ **i.** $A \cup B = A \cap B$ if $A = B$

Exercise 1.3 (Page 12)   **1.** False   **3.** True   **5.** True   **7.** False   **9.** True   **11.** True
13. {1, 2, 3, 4, 5}   **15.** {1, 2, 3, 4, 5, 6}   **17.** {−9, −8, −7, −6}   **19.** $\{x \mid x \in N\}$
21. $\{x \mid x \in R\}$ **23.** $\{x \mid x \in R, -4 < x < 3\}$ **25. a.** {4} **b.** {4, −2, 0} **c.** $\{4, -2, \frac{2}{5}, 0, -\frac{3}{4}\}$
d. $\{4, -2, \frac{2}{5}, 0, -\frac{3}{4}, \sqrt{2}, \sqrt{7}\}$ **27.** Substitution law for equality, E-4   **29.** Symmetric
law for equality, E-2   **31.** Transitive law for equality, E-3   **33.** Closure law for multiplication, F-6   **35.** Associative law for multiplication, F-7   **37.** Additive-law inverse, F-4
39. Commutative law for multiplication, F-10   **41.** Commutative law for addition, F-5
43. Distributive law, F-8   **45.** Commutative law for addition, F-5   **47.** Commutative law
for multiplication, F-10   **49.** Distributive Law, F-8   **51.** Closed   **53.** Closed   **55.** Closed
57. Not closed

Exercise 1.4 (Page 19)   **1.** 1.1   **3.** 1.8-V   **5.** 1.11-III   **7.** 1.7   **9.** 1.9   **11.** 1.11-VII
13. 1.8-III   **15.** 1.11-IV   **17.** 1.2   **19.** 1.5

For Problems 21–43, the proofs given are not unique.

21.
1. $a, b, c \in R$ and $a = b$ 1. Hyp.
2. $ac, bc \in R$ 2. F-6

3. $ac = ac$ and $ca = ca$ 3. E-1
4. $ac = bc$ and $ca = cb$ 4. E-4

23.
1. Let $a + b = a$ and
    $a + b' = a$ 1. Hyp.
2. $a + b = a + b'$ 2. E-3
3. $b = b'$ 3. Th. 1.4
4. $a + 0 = a$ 4. F-3
5. $a + 0 = a + b$ 5. E-4
6. $0 = b$ 6. Th. 1.4
7. $b' = 0$ 7. E-4

25.
1. $ac = bc$ and $c \neq 0$ 1. Hyp.
2. $ac\left(\dfrac{1}{c}\right) = bc\left(\dfrac{1}{c}\right)$ 2. Th. 1.2
3. $a\left(c \cdot \dfrac{1}{c}\right) = b\left(c \cdot \dfrac{1}{c}\right)$ 3. F-7
4. $a \cdot 1 = b \cdot 1$ 4. F-11
5. $a = b$ 5. F-9

27.
1. $ab = 0$ and $a \neq 0$ 1. Hyp.
2. $\dfrac{1}{a}(ab) = \dfrac{1}{a}(0)$ 2. Th. 1.2
3. $\left(\dfrac{1}{a} \cdot a\right)b = \dfrac{1}{a}(0)$ 3. F-7
4. $1 \cdot b = 0$ 4. F-11; Th. 1.6
5. $b = 0$ 5. F-9
Similarly, if $ab = 0$ and $b \neq 0$, then $a = 0$.

29.
1. $(-a)(b) + [-(-a)(b)] = 0$ and
    $(ab) + [-(ab)] = 0$ 1. F-4
2. $-(-a)(b) = ab$ 2. Th. 1.8-I
3. $(-a)(b) + ab = ab + [-(ab)]$ 3. E-4
4. $(-a)(b) + ab = [-(ab)] + ab$ 4. F-5
5. $(-a)(b) = -(ab)$ 5. Th. 1.1

31.
1. $\dfrac{-a}{b}$ and $b \neq 0$ 1. Hyp.

2. $\dfrac{-a}{b} = (-a)\left(\dfrac{1}{b}\right) = -\left(a \cdot \dfrac{1}{b}\right)$ 2. Def. 1.3; Th. 1.8-III

3. $\dfrac{-a}{b} = -\dfrac{a}{b}$ 3. Def. 1.3

4. $-\dfrac{a}{b} = 1 \cdot \left(-\dfrac{a}{b}\right) = -\left(1 \cdot \dfrac{a}{b}\right)$ 4. F-9; Th. 1.8-III

5. $-\left[1 \cdot \dfrac{a}{b}\right] = -\left[1 \cdot \left(a \cdot \dfrac{1}{b}\right)\right]$

    $= -\left[\dfrac{1}{b} \cdot a\right]$ 5. Def. 1.3; F-10, F-7, and F-9

6. $-\left[\dfrac{1}{b} \cdot a\right] = \left[a \cdot \left(-\dfrac{1}{b}\right)\right] = \dfrac{a}{-b}$ 6. Th. 1.8-III; F-10; Def. 1.3

7. $\dfrac{-a}{b} = \dfrac{a}{-b} = \dfrac{a}{b}$ 7. E-4

33. (A)
1. $\dfrac{a}{b} = \dfrac{c}{d}$ and $b, d \neq 0$ 1. Hyp.

2. $\left(a \cdot \dfrac{1}{b}\right) = \left(c \cdot \dfrac{1}{d}\right)$ 2. Def. 1.3

3. $\left(a \cdot \dfrac{1}{b}\right)(bd) = \left(c \cdot \dfrac{1}{d}\right)(bd)$ 3. Th. 1.2

4. $(ad)\left(\dfrac{1}{b} \cdot b\right) = (bc)\left(\dfrac{1}{d} \cdot d\right)$ 4. F-7; F-10

5. $ad = bc$ 5. F-11; F-9

(B) 1. $ad = bc$ and $b, d \neq 0$ 1. Hyp.

2. $(ad)\left(\dfrac{1}{b} \cdot \dfrac{1}{d}\right) = (bc)\left(\dfrac{1}{b} \cdot \dfrac{1}{d}\right)$ 2. Th. 1.2

3. $\left(a \cdot \dfrac{1}{b}\right)\left(d \cdot \dfrac{1}{d}\right) = \left(b \cdot \dfrac{1}{b}\right)\left(c \cdot \dfrac{1}{d}\right)$ 3. F-7; F-10

4. $\dfrac{a}{b} = \dfrac{c}{d}$ 4. F-11; F-9; Def. 1.3

35. 1. $a \cdot b = ab$ 1. Alternative method of writing a product

2. $(a \cdot b) \cdot \left(\dfrac{1}{a \cdot b}\right) = 1$ 2. F-11

3. $(ab) \cdot \dfrac{1}{a \cdot b} = 1$ 3. E-4

4. $\dfrac{1}{ab}\left[(ab) \cdot \dfrac{1}{a \cdot b}\right] = \dfrac{1}{ab}$ [1]   4. Th. 1.2

5. $\dfrac{1}{a \cdot b} = \dfrac{1}{ab}$ 5. F-7; F-11; F-9

37. 1 $a + b = a + b$ 1. E-1

2. $(a + b)\dfrac{1}{c} = (a + b)\dfrac{1}{c}$ 2. Th. 1.2

3. $a \cdot \dfrac{1}{c} + b \cdot \dfrac{1}{c} = (a + b)\dfrac{1}{c}$ 3. F-8

4. $\dfrac{a}{c} + \dfrac{b}{c} = \dfrac{a + b}{c}$ 4. Def. 1.3

39. 1. $\dfrac{a}{b} - \dfrac{c}{d} = \dfrac{a}{b} + \dfrac{-c}{d}$ 1. Def. 1.2

2. $\dfrac{a}{b} + \dfrac{-c}{d} = \dfrac{ad + (-c)b}{bd} = \dfrac{ad - bc}{bd}$ 2. Th. 1.11-IV; F-10; Th. 1.8-III

41. 1. $\dfrac{\frac{a}{b}}{\frac{c}{d}} = \dfrac{a}{b}\left(\dfrac{1}{\frac{c}{d}}\right) = \dfrac{a}{b}\left(\dfrac{d}{c}\right)$ 1. Def. 1.3; Th. 1.1I-VI

2. $\dfrac{a}{b}\left(\dfrac{d}{c}\right) = \dfrac{ad}{bc}$ 2. Th. 1.11-II

43. 1. $a(b + c) = ab + ac$ 1. F-8

2. $(b + c)a = ba + ca$ 2. F-10

Exercise 1.5 (Page 25)   **1.** I   **3.** III   **5.** II   **7.** IV   **9.** $7 > 3$ **11.** $-4 < -3$
13. $-1 \leq x \leq 1$ **15.** $x > 0$ **17.** $x \geq 0$ **19.** $-2 < 5$ **21.** $-7 < -1$ **23.** $|-3| = |3|$
25. $2 < 5$ **27.** $7 < 8$ **29.** $|x| < 3$ **31.** 0   **33.** $\sqrt{7}$

Exercise 2.1 (Page 30)   **1.** 3 in y **3.** 4 in x, y; 3 in x; 2 in y **5.** Not a polynomial
7. $-1,\ 1,\ -2, 20$ **9.** 1, 1, 0, 1, 0   **11.** 1, 1, 5   **13.** 39, 6, 39   **15.** $2x + 1, 4x - 5$
17. $3x^2 - 4x + 2, -x^2 + 4$ **19.** $3x^2 - 5x + 5$ **21.** $3x^2 - 4x + 4$ **23.** $x^2 - 2x + 6$
25. n, n

Exercise 2.2 (Page 33)   **1.** $-6x^3y^4$ **3.** a^{2n} **5.** $a^2bc - ab^2c + 2abc^2$ **7.** $x^2 + 7x + 10$
9. $x^2 - 4xy + 4y^2$ **11.** $10x^2 + 17x + 3$ **13.** $9a^2 - 4b^2$ **15.** $x^3 + 6x^2 + 7x - 4$
17. $2x^2 + 8x + 6$ **19.** $-2ac + 6ad + bc - 3bd$ **21.** $a^4 - ab^3$ **23.** $4a + 4$ **25.** $20x^2 + 4x$
27. $x^2 - 5x + 11,\ x^2 - x + 5$ **29.** $x^4 + 6x^3 + 9x^2,\ a^8 - 6a^6 + 8a^4 + 3a^2,\ 9x^4 - 18x^3 + 9x^2$
31. $2ab;\ 0 > 2ab;\ 0 < 2ab$

Exercise 2.3 (Page 36)   **1.** $3x^3y(3x^2 - x + 2)$ **3.** $x^n(x^{2n} + 1)$ **5.** $x^n(x^2 - x + 2)$
7. $(x - 6)(x - 2)$ **9.** $(x - 5)(x + 5)$ **11.** $3(x + 2)(x + 2)$ **13.** $(y^2 + 2)(y^2 + 1)$
15. $(2a^2 + 1)(a + 1)(a - 1)$ **17.** $[x^2 - (y - 2x)^2][x^2 + (y - 2x)^2]$ **19.** $(x + y)(x + a)$
21. $(a - 2b)(a^2 + 2b^2)$ **23.** $(y - 3x)(y^2 + 3xy + 9x^2)$ **25.** $(2x - y)(x^2 - xy + y^2)$
27. $(a^n - 2)(a^n + 2)$ **29.** $(x^n - y^n)(x^n + y^n)(x^{2n} + y^{2n})$ **31.** $(3x^{2n} - 1)(x^{2n} - 3)$
33. $2(y^n - 30)(y^n + 24)$ **35.** $ac - ad + bd - bc = a(c - d) - b(c - d) = (a - b)(c - d)$;
$ac - ad + bd - bc = bd - ad - bc + ac = d(b - a) - c(b - a) = (b - a)(d - c)$
37. $(x^2 + xy + y^2)(x^2 - xy + y^2)$

Exercise 2.4 (Page 43)   **1.** $4ay^2(a, y \neq 0)$ **3.** $x^{n+3}(x \neq 0)$ **5.** $x^ny^n(x, y \neq 0)$

7. $4a^2 + 2a + 2$ **9.** $x^2 - 4x - 3(x \neq 0)$ **11.** $3x^2 - 2x + \dfrac{3}{5x}\ (x, y \neq 0)$ **13.** $2y^2 - y + \frac{13}{2}$,

$R = -\frac{3}{2}(y \neq -\frac{1}{2})$ **15.** $2y^3 - y^2 - \dfrac{1}{2}y - \dfrac{5}{4} + \dfrac{-13y/4 + 9/4}{2y^2 + y + 1}$ **17.** $x^3 - x^2 - \dfrac{1}{x - 2}\ (x \neq 2)$

19. $2x^2 - 2x + 3 + \dfrac{-8}{x + 1}\ (x \neq -1)$ **21.** $2x^3 + 10x^2 + 50x + 249 + \dfrac{1251}{x - 5}\ (x \neq 5)$

23. $x^2 + 2x - 3 + \dfrac{4}{x + 2}\ (y \neq -2)$ **25.** $x^5 + x^4 + 2x^3 + 2x^2 + 2x + 1 + \dfrac{1}{x - 1}\ (x \neq 1)$

27. $x^4 + x^3 + x^2 + x + 1\ (x \neq 1)$ **29.** $x^5 + x^4 + x^3 + x^2 + x + 1\ (x \neq 1)$
31. 3, 17, 47   **33.** 56, 12, 326   **35.** $-685, 95, 719$ **37.** Calculations produce
only $+1$'s for successive sums, hence always produce 0 when combined with -1 of $x^n - 1$

Exercise 2.5 (Page 47)   **1.** $\dfrac{a}{b}, a, b, c \neq 0$ **3.** $2, x + y \neq 0$ **5.** $-1, b - a \neq 0$

7. $-(x + 1), x \neq 1$ **9.** $x^2 - 2x - \frac{3}{2}, x \neq 0$ **11.** $y + 7, y \neq 2$ **13.** $-(2y + 5), y \neq \frac{1}{2}$
15. $\dfrac{x^2 + xy + y^2}{x + y}, x^2 + y^2 \neq 0$ **17.** $\dfrac{y^2 + 4}{y^2 + 3}, y^2 - 4 \neq 0$ **19.** $\dfrac{x - y + 1}{-(x + y)}, x \neq y, x \neq -y$

21. $\dfrac{9}{12}$ **23.** $\dfrac{ab^2}{a^2b}, a, b \neq 0$ **25.** $\dfrac{3(y - 3)}{y^2 - y - 6}, y \neq -2, 3$ **27.** $\dfrac{3(a^2 - 3a + 9)}{a^3 + 27}, a \neq -3$
29. No, $x = 1, 2$ **31.** For $N > 0, a - b < 0$ or $a < b$; for $N < 0, a - b > 0$ or $a > b$

Exercise 2.6 (Page 50)   **1.** $\dfrac{2x - 1}{2y}$ **3.** 1   **5.** $\dfrac{2a + 9}{9}$ **7.** $\dfrac{5}{2a + 2b}$ **9.** $\dfrac{3}{3 - x}$

11. $\dfrac{-1}{(a + 2)(a + 3)}$ **13.** $\dfrac{-3x^2 - 3y^2}{(2x - y)(x - 2y)}$ **15.** $\dfrac{y(y - 11)}{(y - 4)(y + 4)(y - 1)}$ **17.** $\dfrac{x^3 - 2x^2 + 2x - 2}{(x - 1)^2}$

19. $\dfrac{4x^3 - 4x^2 + 4x + 4}{(2x + 1)(2x - 1)}$ **21.** $\dfrac{4}{(y + 1)(y + 3)}$ **23.** $\dfrac{y^2 + xz}{(y - x)(y - z)}$

Exercise 2.7 (Page 52)   **1.** $\dfrac{-b^2}{a}$ **3.** $\dfrac{1}{ax^2y}$ **5.** $\dfrac{x - 5}{x + 3}$ **7.** $(5ab - 4)(4ab + 3)$ **9.** $x - y$

11. $\dfrac{x^2 - 1}{x^2}$ **13.** $\dfrac{x + 5}{x(x + 1)}$ **15.** $\dfrac{2y^2 - 6y + 3}{3}$ **17.** $\dfrac{7}{10a + 2}$ **19.** $\dfrac{4a^2 - 3a}{4a + 1}$ **21.** $\dfrac{-1}{y - 3}$

23. $\dfrac{a - 2b}{a + 2b}$

Exercise 2.8 (Page 57)   **1.** 2   **3.** $\frac{1}{27}$ **5.** 32   **7.** $\frac{8}{27}$ **9.** x^2 **11.** $a^{17/12}$ **13.** $x^{1/3}$

15. $\dfrac{1}{x^{16/15}}$ **17.** $\dfrac{y^2}{x}$ **19.** $\left(\dfrac{x}{y}\right)^{5/4}$ **21.** $x^n \cdot y^4$ **23.** $x^{3n/2}$ **25.** $x^{5n/2} \cdot y^{3m/2 - 1}$

27. $x - x^{2/3}$ **29.** $x - 2x^{1/2}y^{-1/2} + y^{-1}$ **31.** $x + y - (x + y)^{3/2}$ **33.** $x + y$
35. $x(x^{1/2} + 1)$ **37.** $x^{-1/2}(x^{-1} + 1)$ **39.** $(x + 1)^{-1/2}(x)$ **41.** $x^{n/2}(x^{3n/2} + 1)$

43. $(x^{1/2} - y^{1/2})(x^{1/2} + y^{1/2})$ **45.** 5   **47.** $2|x|$ **49.** $\dfrac{2}{|x|\,(x + 1)^{1/2}}$

Exercise 2.9 (Page 61)   **1.** $\sqrt[3]{a^2}$ **3.** $3\sqrt[3]{x}$ **5.** $-6\sqrt[3]{(xy)^2}$ **7.** $\sqrt[7]{(x - y)^4}$ **9.** $x^{2/3}$
11. $(2xy^2)^{1/5}$ **13.** $-3(a^3b)^{1/4}$ **15.** $3(x^2 - y)^{1/3}$ **17.** 12   **19.** -3 **21.** x^2y **23.** $\frac{2}{3}x^3y^5$

25. $2x^2\sqrt{x}$ **27.** $xy\sqrt[4]{3xy}$ **29.** $3\sqrt[4]{3}$ **31.** $\dfrac{\sqrt{3y}}{y}$ **33.** $\sqrt[3]{2b}$ **35.** xy **37.** b **39.** $\dfrac{1}{\sqrt{7}}$

41. $\dfrac{2y}{\sqrt[3]{xy^2}}$ **43.** $\sqrt[3]{9}$ **45.** $2\sqrt{x}$ **47.** $\sqrt{2x}$ **49.** $\sqrt[3]{x - 1}$ **51.** $\sqrt[4]{8}$ **53.** $\sqrt[8]{32a^4b^6}$

55. $\sqrt{2}$ **57.** $3\sqrt{3}$ **59.** $-4\sqrt{2}$ **61.** $5\sqrt[3]{2}$ **63.** $3\sqrt{2} + \sqrt{6}$ **65.** $1 - \sqrt{5}$

67. $x - \sqrt{3x} - 6$ **69.** $2(1 - \sqrt{3})$ **71.** $\dfrac{x(\sqrt{x} + 3)}{x - 9}$ **73.** $\dfrac{37 - 8\sqrt{10}}{27}$ **75.** $\dfrac{-1}{2(1 + \sqrt{2})}$

77. $-3\sqrt{2} + 3$ **79.** $\dfrac{\sqrt[3]{a^2} + \sqrt[3]{ab} + \sqrt[3]{b^2}}{a - b}$ **81.** $2|x|$ **83.** $3|x|\sqrt{x - 1}$

Exercise 3.1 (Page 67)   **1.** $\{-2\}$ **3.** $\{1\}$ **5.** $\{-7\}$ **7.** $\{15\}$ **9.** $\emptyset$ **11.** $\{-\frac{14}{5}\}$

13. $k = v - gt$ **15.** $c = \dfrac{2A - bh}{h}$ **17.** $n = \dfrac{l - a + d}{d}$ **19.** $y' = \dfrac{3x + 1}{x^2 - 2y^3}$ **21.** $x_1 = \dfrac{x_4}{x_2 - 2x_3}$

23. $y = 6(x - x_1) + y_1$ **25.** $-\frac{3}{5}$ **27.** 6 in.   **29.** \$600 at 4%, \$1400 at 3%   **31.** 32 and 64 mph

Exercise 3.2 (Page 71)   **1.** $\{0, -2\}$ **3.** $\{2, -7\}$ **5.** $\{\frac{1}{2}, 1\}$ **7.** $\{1, -\frac{10}{3}\}$ **9.** $\{2, -2\}$
11. $\{\sqrt{5}, -\sqrt{5}\}$ **13.** $\{6 + \sqrt{5}, 6 - \sqrt{5}\}$ **15.** $\{2, -6\}$ **17.** $\{-4, -5\}$
19. $\{\frac{1}{2}, -2\}$ **21.** $(x - 2)^2 + (y - 2)^2 = 5^2$ **23.** $[x - (-3)]^2 + (y - 1)^2 = 2^2$

25. $\left(x - \dfrac{1}{2}\right)^2 + [y - (-1)]^2 = 2^2$ **27.** $\{1, 2\}$ **29.** $\{2, \frac{3}{2}\}$ **31.** $\{3, -\frac{3}{2}\}$

33. $\{\sqrt{5}\}$ **35.** $\left\{\sqrt{3}, -\dfrac{\sqrt{3}}{2}\right\}$ **37.** $\{2k, -k\}$ **39.** $\left\{\dfrac{1 + \sqrt{1 - 4ac}}{2a}, \dfrac{1 - \sqrt{1 - 4ac}}{2a}\right\}$

41. 4   **43.** $k \le -2$ **45.** 6, 7   **47.** 12 in.   **49.** $2\frac{1}{2}$ sec, $\frac{5}{4}\sqrt{6}$ sec

Exercise 3.3 (Page 76)   **1.** $\{64\}$ **3.** $\{-25\}$ **5.** $\{4\}$ **7.** $\{5\}$ **9.** $\{16\}$ **11.** $\{4\}$

13. $\{1, 3\}$ **15.** $A = \pi r^2$ **17.** $y = \dfrac{1}{x^3}$ **19.** $y = \sqrt{a^2 - x^2}$ **21.** $\{25\}$ **23.** $\left\{\dfrac{\sqrt{2}}{2}, -\dfrac{\sqrt{2}}{2}\right\}$

25. $\{2, -7, -3, -2\}$ **27.** $\{64, -8\}$ **29.** $\{\frac{1}{4}, -\frac{1}{3}\}$

Exercise 3.4 (Page 81)

1. $\{x \mid x > 1\}$

3. $\{x \mid x > 3\}$

5. $\{x \mid x \leq \frac{13}{2}\}$

7. $\{x \mid -2 < x < 5\}$

9. $\{x \mid x \geq 13\}$

11. $\{x \mid x < -1 \text{ or } x > 2\}$

13. $\{x \mid x < -1 \text{ or } x > 4\}$

15. $\{x \mid -\sqrt{5} < x < \sqrt{5}\}$

17. $\{x \mid x < 0 \text{ or } x \geq \frac{1}{2}\}$

19. $\{x \mid -\frac{8}{3} < x < -2\}$

21. $\{x \mid x < 0 \text{ or } 2 < x \leq 4\}$

23. $\{x \mid -3 < x < 0 \text{ or } x > 2\}$

Exercise 3.5 (Page 84)   **1.** $\{6, -6\}$ **3.** $\{-3, 5\}$ **5.** $\{1, \frac{2}{3}\}$

7. $\{x \mid -2 < x < 2\}$

9. $\{x \mid x \leq -7 \text{ or } x \geq 1\}$

11. $\{x \mid x \leq 1 \text{ or } x \geq 4\}$

13. $|x - 2| < 1$ **15.** $|x + 8| \leq 1$ **17.** $|4x - 5| \leq 19$ **19.** At least 48% but less than 98%
21. (I) if $a \geq 0$, by Def. 1.15, $|-a| = |-(+a)| = |-a| = a$; also $|a| = a$; hence $|-a| = |a|$.
(II) if $a < 0$, by Def. 1.15 $|-a| = |-(-a)| = |a| = a$; also $|a| = |+(-a)| = |-a| = a$; hence
$|-a| = |a|$ **23.** $|a|^2 = a^2$ (Def. 1.15); $|a|^2 = |a| \cdot |a| = a \cdot a = a^2$; hence $|a^2| = |a|^2 = a^2$ **25.** Since,
by Def. 1.15, $\left|\frac{1}{b}\right| = \frac{1}{b}$ and $\frac{1}{|b|} = \frac{1}{b}$, then $\left|\frac{1}{b}\right| = \frac{1}{|b|}$ $(b \neq 0)$. Then, by Def. 1.3 and Ex. 24,
$\left|\frac{a}{b}\right| = \left|a \cdot \frac{1}{b}\right| = |a| \cdot \left|\frac{1}{b}\right|$; hence $|a| \cdot \left|\frac{1}{b}\right| = |a| \cdot \frac{1}{|b|} = \frac{|a|}{|b|}$.

Exercise 4.1 (Page 87)   **1.** $\{(1, -1), (1, -2)\}$ **3.** $\{(-1, 0), (-1, 1), (0, 0), (0, 1), (1, 0), 1, 1)\}$
5. $\{(a, c), (a, d), (b, c), (b, d)\}$ **7.** $\{(0, 6), (1, 4), (2, 2), (-3, 12), (\frac{2}{3}, \frac{14}{3})\}$ **9.** $\{(0, 0), (1, -3),$
$(2, 3), (-3, -\frac{9}{2}), (\frac{2}{3}, -\frac{9}{7})\}$ **11.** $\{(0, \sqrt{11}), (1, \sqrt{14}), (2, \sqrt{17}), (-3, \sqrt{2}), (\frac{2}{3}, \sqrt{13})\}$
13. a. $n \cdot m$ **b.** $m \cdot n$ **c.** $n(2m - n)$ **d.** n^2 **15. a.** $\{(1, 2), (1, 3), (1, 4), (2, 1), (2, 3), (2, 4),$
$(3, 1), (3, 2), (3, 4), (4, 1), (4, 2), (4, 3)\}$ **b.** 12 **c.** $n^2 - n$

Exercise 4.2 (Page 91)   **1.** Domain: $\{x \mid x \in R\}$ **3.** Domain: $\{x \mid x \in R\}$ **5.** Domain:
$\{x \mid x \in R, x \neq 2\}$ **7.** Domain: $\{x \mid x \in R, x \geq 0\}$ **9.** Domain: $\{x \mid x \in R, -2 \leq x \leq 2\}$
11. Domain: $\{x \mid x \in R, x \neq 0, 1\}$ **13.** Yes   **15.** Yes   **17.** No   **19.** No   **21.** 2
23. -1 **25.** 9   **27.** a^2 **29.** 1   **31.** $a - 2$ **33.** ± 1 **35.** ± 3 **37. a.** 2 **b.** 0
c. 2   **d.** x **39.** No   **41.** $x = y + 2$ or $y = x - 2$; yes   **43.** $2y - 3x = 6$ or $y = \frac{3}{2}x + 3$;
yes   **45.** $x = y^2 + 3$ or $y = \pm\sqrt{x + 3}$; no

Exercise 4.3 (Page 97)   **1.** Distance, 5; slope, $\frac{4}{3}$ **3.** Distance, 13; slope $\frac{12}{5}$
5. Distance, $\sqrt{2}$; slope, 1   **7.** 7, $\sqrt{68}$, $\sqrt{89}$ **9.** 10, 21, 17
11. $x - 2y - 1 = 0$ **13.** $x - y + 1 = 0$ **15.** $y - 2 = 0$

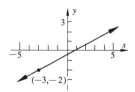

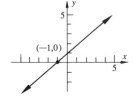

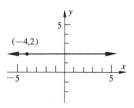

17. $y = -\frac{3}{2}x + \frac{1}{2}$; slope, $-\frac{3}{2}$; intercept, $\frac{1}{2}$ **19.** $y = \frac{1}{3}x - \frac{2}{3}$; slope, $\frac{1}{3}$; intercept, $-\frac{2}{3}$

     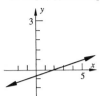

21. $y = \frac{8}{3}x$; slope, $\frac{8}{3}$; intercept, 0   **23.** $x - 2y = 0$

25. Since $m = \dfrac{y_2 - y_1}{x_2 - x_1}$ and $y - y_1 = m(x - x_1)$ we have by substitution $y - y_1 = \left(\dfrac{y_2 - y_1}{x_2 - x_1}\right)(x - x_1)$

27. $F(x) = \dfrac{-x + 11}{3}$ **29. a.** $x - 3y - 3 = 0$
      b. $x - y + 2 = 0$

31. Let $M(x, y)$ be midpoint of P_1P_2, then from triangles P_1AM and P_1BP_2 $\dfrac{x - x_1}{x_2 - x_1} = \dfrac{P_1M}{P_1P_2} = \dfrac{1}{2}$

and $x = \dfrac{x_1 + x_2}{2}$; similarly, $\dfrac{y - y_1}{y_2 - y_1} = \dfrac{1}{2}$ and $y = \dfrac{y_1 + y_2}{2}$

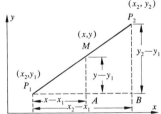

33. $y = -\dfrac{B}{A}x - \dfrac{C}{A}$; $A \neq 0$

Exercise 4.4 (Page 102)

1. $(4, 0); (1, 0); (\frac{5}{2}, -\frac{9}{4})$, minimum   **3.** $(7, 0); (-1, 0); (3, -16)$, minimum

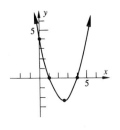   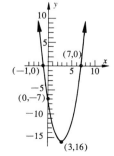

5. $(4, 0)$; $(1, 0)$; $(\frac{5}{2}, \frac{9}{4})$, maximum   **7.** No intercepts; $(0, 2)$, minimum   **9.**

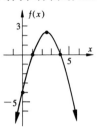

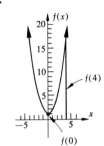

11. $4; 4$
13. Parabola; no, not a function   **15.**   **17.**

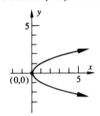

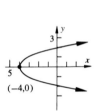

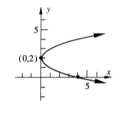

Exercise 4.5 (Page 105)

1. Circle   **3.** Ellipse   **5.** Pair of straight lines through origin

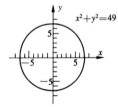

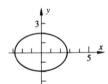

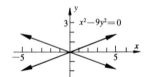

7. Circle   **9.** Parabola   **11.** Moves the minimum point upward

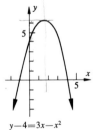

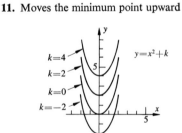

13. Pair of straight lines
through the origin

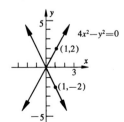

Exercise 4.6   (Page 108)

1.

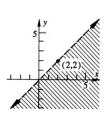

3.

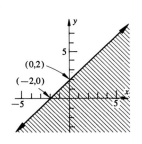

5.

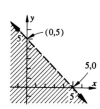

7.

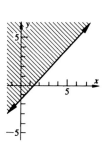

9.

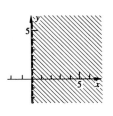

11.

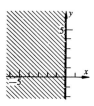

13.

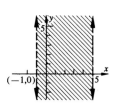

15.

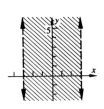

17.

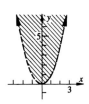

19.

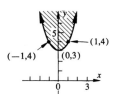

21.

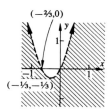

23.

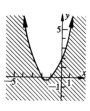

25.

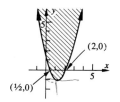

27.

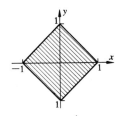

29.

Exercises 4.7 (Page 111)   **1. a.** $(2, 1, 1)$ **b.** $(-1, 0, 3)$ **c.** $(6, 2, -2)$ **3. a.** $(4, 0, -16)$
b. $(0, \sqrt{2}, -4,), (0, -\sqrt{2}, -4)$ **c.** No point exists   **5. a.** $(-1, 2, 8)$ **b.** No point exists
c. No point exists   **7. a.** $(0, 0, 2)$ **b.** $(0, 3, 0)$ **c.** $(6, 0, 0)$ **9. a.** $(0, 0, 2), (0, 0, -2)$
b. $(0, 2, 0), (0, -2, 0)$ **c.** $(\sqrt{2}, 0, 0), (-\sqrt{2}, 0, 0)$ **11. a.** No point exists   **b.** $(0, -9, 0)$
c. $(3, 0, 0), (-3, 0, 0)$ **13. a.** $(0, 0, 0)$ **b.** $(0, 0, 0)$ **c.** $(0, 0, 0)$ **15.** $(2, -2, z)$
17. $(\sqrt{13}, y, 2), (-\sqrt{13}, y, 2)$ **19.** $(x, 3, z)$ **21.** $(-2, y, z)$

23.

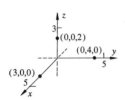

25.

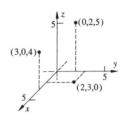

27.

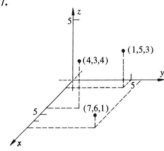

29.

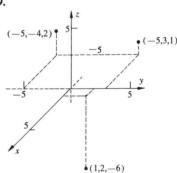

31. $\sqrt{19}$ **33.** $\sqrt{14}$ **35.** $\sqrt{22}$

Exercise 4.8 (Page 117)

1.

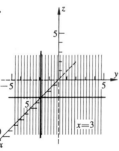

3.

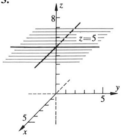

5.

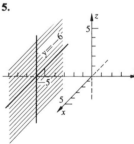

7.

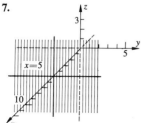

9.

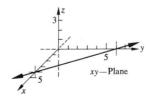

11.

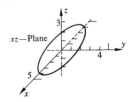

13.

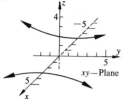

15. No trace exists

17.

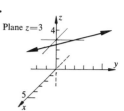

19.

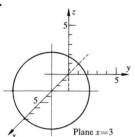

21.

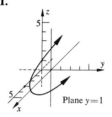

23.

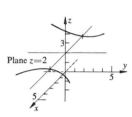

25.

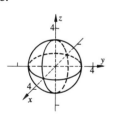

27.

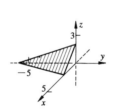

29.

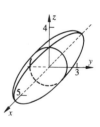

31.

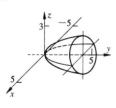

33.

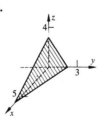

35.

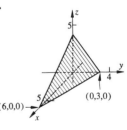

37.

39.

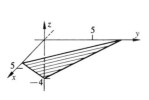

41.

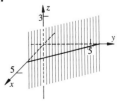

43.

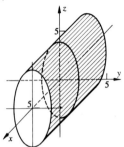

45.

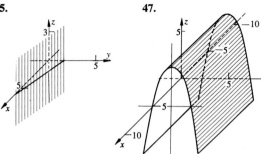

47.

Exercise 5.1 (Page 121)

1.

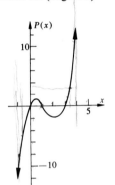

3.

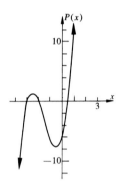

5.

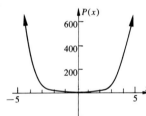

7.

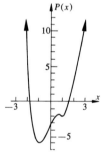

Exercise 5.2 (Page 125)   **1.** 2 positive; 2 negative   **3.** No positive; 1 negative   **5.** No positive; no negative   **7.** Upper bound 3; lower bound −4   **9.** Upper bound 4; lower bound −3   **11.** Upper bound 2; lower bound −3   **13.** Upper bound 1; lower bound −2

21.

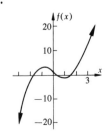

23.

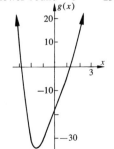

25.

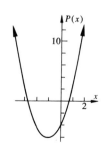

Exercise 5.3 (Page 127) **1.** $\{4)\}$ **3.** $\{1, -2\}$ **5.** None **7.** $\{-\frac{3}{2}\}$ **9.** $\{2, -\frac{7}{4}\}$
11. $\{\frac{3}{2}\}$

13.

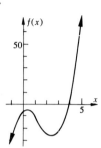

15.

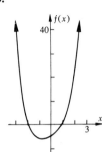

17.

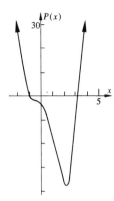

Exercise 5.4 (Page 130) **1.** 1.53 **3.** 2.1 **5.** 1.67 **7.** 0.68 **9.** 1.71

Exercise 5.5 (Page 134) **1.** $x = 3$ **3.** $x = 3; x = -2$ **5.** $x = -1; x = -4$ **7.** $x = -1$

9.

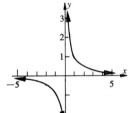

11.

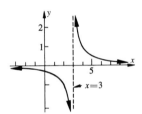

13.

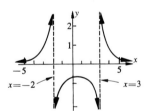

15.

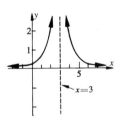

17. $x = 2; x = -2; y = 0$ **19.** $x = 4; y = x + 4$ **21.** $x = 4; x = -1; y = 1$

23.

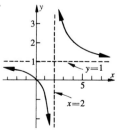

25.

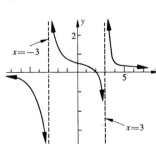

27.

29.

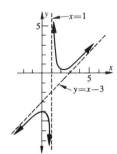

31.

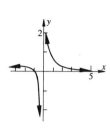

Exercise 6.1 (Page 139)   **1.** (0, 1), (1, 3), (2, 9)   **3.** (0, −1), (1, −5), (2, −25)   **5.** (−3, 8),
(0, 1), (3, $\frac{1}{8}$)   **7.** (−2, $\frac{1}{100}$), (1, 10), (0, 1)

9.

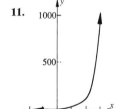

11.

13.

15.

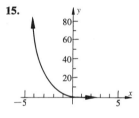

17.

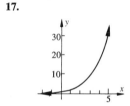

19.

No; a constant function

21. a. {−2}   **b.** {−4}   **c.** {$\frac{3}{4}$}

Exercise 6.2 (Page 142)   **1.** $\log_4 16 = 2$ **3.** $\log_3 27 = 3$ **5.** $\log_{1/2} \frac{1}{4} = 2$ **7.** $\log_8 \frac{1}{2} = -\frac{1}{3}$
9. $\log_{10} 100 = 2$ **11.** $\log_{10}(0.1) = -1$ **13.** $2^6 = 64$ **15.** $3^2 = 9$ **17.** $(\frac{1}{3})^{-2} = 9$
19. $10^3 = 1000$ **21.** $10^{-2} = 0.01$ **23.** 2   **25.** 3   **27.** $\frac{1}{2}$ **29.** −1   **31.** 1   **33.** 2
35. −1   **37.** {2}   **39.** {2}   **41.** {64}   **43.** {−3}   **45.** {100}   **47.** {4}   **49.** By
definition, $\log_b 1$ is a number such that $b^{\log_b 1} = 1$; therefore $\log_b 1 = 0$ **51.** $\text{Log}_b b^x = x$
implies $b^x = b^x$, which is true for all $x \in R$ **53.** $\log_b x + \log_b y$ **55.** $\log_b x - \log_b y$
57. $5 \log_b x$ **59.** $\frac{1}{3} \log_b x$ **61.** $\frac{1}{2}(\log_b x - \log_b z)$ **63.** $\frac{1}{3}(\log_{10} x + 2 \log_{10} y - \log_{10} z)$

65. $\log_{10} 2 + \log_{10} \pi + \frac{1}{2} \log_{10} l - \frac{1}{2} \log_{10} g$ **67.** $\log_b xy$ **69.** $\log_b x^2 y^3$ **71.** $\log_b \dfrac{x^3 y}{z^2}$

73. $\log_{10} \dfrac{x(x-2)}{z^2}$ **75.** By Th. 6.3-III, $\frac{1}{4} \log_{10} 8 = \frac{1}{4} \log_{10} 2^3 = \frac{3}{4} \log_{10} 2$; hence, $\frac{1}{4} \log_{10} 8$
$+ \frac{1}{4} \log_{10} 2 = \frac{3}{4} \log_{10} 2 + \frac{1}{4} \log_{10} 2 = \log_{10} 2$ **77.** By Th. 6.3-III, $10^{2 \log_{10} x} = 10^{\log_{10} x^2} = x^2$
79. Since $\log_5 5 = 1$ and $\log_3 3 = 1$, $\log_{10}[\log_3(\log_5 125)] = \log_{10}[\log_3(\log_5 5^3)] =$
$\log_{10}[\log_3(3 \log_5 5)] = \log_{10}[\log_3 3] = \log_{10} 1 = 0$

Exercise 6.3 (Page 149)   **1.** 0.8280   **3.** 9.9101 − 10   **5.** 2.3945   **7.** 4.10   **9.** 3.67
11. 0.0642   **13.** 0.6246   **15.** 3.1824   **17.** 9.7095 − 10   **19.** 3.225   **21.** 10.52

23. 0.05075   **25.** 4.014   **27.** 64.34   **29.** 3.436 × 10⁻¹⁰   **31.** 3.208   **33.** $\left(\dfrac{\log_{10} 8}{\log_{10} 3} - 1\right)$

35. $\left\{\dfrac{1}{\log_{10} 3} - 2\right\}$　**37.** $\left\{\sqrt{\dfrac{\log_{10} 21}{\log_{10} 8}},\ -\sqrt{\dfrac{\log_{10} 21}{\log_{10} 8}}\right\}$　**39.** $n = \dfrac{\log_{10} y}{\log_{10} x}$　**41.** $t = \dfrac{\log_{10} y}{k \log_{10} e}$

43. 2.66　**45.** 1.11 sec　**47.** 2, 5, 2, 1

Exercise 6.4 (Page 153)　**1.** 3.32　**3.** 3.41　**5.** 1.08　**7.** 0.79　**9.** 1.0986　**11.** 2.8332
13. 5.7900　**15.** 6.1093　**17.** 1.6487　**19.** 29.964　**21.** 1.260　**23.** 0.8607　**25.** 0.0821
27. 0.7600　**29.** $\frac{1}{3}$　**31.** 2.10　**33.** 2.86　**35.** Since $\log_{10} 4 = \log_{10} 2^2 = 2 \log_{10} 2$ and

$\log_2 10 = \dfrac{\log_{10} 10}{\log_{10} 2}$ and $\log_{10} 10 = 1$, $(\log_{10} 4 - \log_{10} 2)(\log_2 10) = (2 \log_{10} 2 - \log_{10} 2)\left(\dfrac{1}{\log_{10} 2}\right)$

$= (\log_{10} 2)\left(\dfrac{1}{\log_{10} 2}\right) = 1$　**37.** 12.048 gr

Exercise 7.1 (Page 162)　**1.** $\dfrac{1}{\sqrt{2}}$　**3.** $-\frac{1}{2}$　**5.** 1　**7.** 1　**9.** 0　**11.** 0　**13.** $\dfrac{1}{\sqrt{2}}$

15. $-\frac{1}{2}$　**17.** $\frac{3}{2}\sqrt{2}$　**19.** $-\frac{12}{13}$　**21.** $\frac{1}{4}\sqrt{15}$　**23.** $\dfrac{\pi}{4}$　**25.** $\dfrac{5\pi}{6}$　**27.** $\frac{2}{3}\pi$　**29.** $\dfrac{\pi}{4} < s \le \pi$

31. $\cos(\pi - s) = -\cos s$　**33.** $\sin\left(\dfrac{\pi}{2} + s\right) = \cos s$

35.

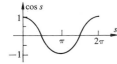

37. Since $\sin(s + 2\pi) = \sin s$, then 2π is a period of $\sin s$. To show 2π is the fundamental period, suppose there exists a such that $0 < a < 2\pi$ and $\sin(s + a) = \sin a$. Then, $\sin(0 + a) = \sin 0 = 0$. But this is impossible for $0 < a < 2\pi$ since $(0, 1)$ is the only point on the unit circle with second coordinate 1

Exercise 7.2 (Page 167)　**1.** 0.8309　**3.** 0.2482　**5.** 0.9780　**7.** 0.9249　**9.** 0.9725
11. 0.5045　**13.** 0.3086　**15.** 0.6234　**17.** -0.4267　**19.** 0.4801　**21.** -0.3530
23. 0.8916　**25.** -0.5312　**27.** -0.9950　**29.** 0.26　**31.** 0.79　**33.** 0.537　**35.** Use
$\cos(s_1 - s_2) = \cos[s_1 + (-s_2)]$ and Th. 7.4 followed by Th. 7.3; then $\cos(s_1 - s_2) = \cos[s_1 + (-s_2)] = \cos s_1 \cos(-s_2) - \sin s_1 \sin(-s_2) = \cos s_1 \cos s_2 + \sin s_1 \sin s_2$　**37.** Use Th. 7.4

and substitution since $\cos \dfrac{\pi}{2} = 0$ and $\sin \dfrac{\pi}{2} = 1$; then $\cos\left(\dfrac{\pi}{2} - s\right) = \cos \dfrac{\pi}{2} \cos s + \sin \dfrac{\pi}{2} \sin s =$

$(0) \cos s + (1) \sin s = \sin s$　**39.** Use Th. 7.4 and substitution since $\cos \dfrac{3\pi}{2} = 0$ and

$\sin \dfrac{\pi}{2} = -1$; then $\cos\left(\dfrac{3\pi}{2} - s\right) = \cos \dfrac{3\pi}{2} \cos s + \sin \dfrac{3\pi}{2} \sin s = (0) \cos s + (-1) \sin s = -\sin s$

41. Use Th. 7.4 and substitution since $\cos 2\pi = 1$ and $\sin 2\pi = 0$; then $\cos(2\pi - s) = \cos 2\pi \cos s + \sin^2 \pi \sin s = (1) \cos s + 0(\sin s) = \cos s$　**43.** Use Th. 7.4 and let $s = x - \pi$; then $-\cos s = \cos(\pi - s)$; $\cos s = -\cos(\pi - s)$; substitution gives $\cos(x - \pi) = -\cos[\pi - (x - \pi)] = -\cos(-x) = -\cos x$ (Th. 7.3)　**45.** Use Th. 7.5-III and let $s = \dfrac{\pi}{2} - x$;

then $\sin s = \cos\left(\dfrac{\pi}{2} - s\right)$, and substitution gives $\sin\left(\dfrac{\pi}{2} - x\right) = \cos\left[\dfrac{\pi}{2} - \left(\dfrac{\pi}{2} - x\right)\right] = \cos x$

Exercise 7.3 (Page 170)　**1.** 0.3051　**3.** 0.9356　**5.** 0.8468　**7.** 0.7578　**9.** 0.9783
11. 0.6845　**13.** 0.9753　**15.** 0.9512　**17.** 0.8016　**19.** -0.7243　**21.** 0.9551

23. -0.3051 **25.** 0.9711 **27.** 0.1889 **29.** 1.50 **31.** 1.03 **33.** 0.413
35. Use $\sin(x_1 - x_2) = \sin[x_1 + (-x_2)]$ and Th. 7.6 followed by Th. 7.3; then $\sin(x_1 - x_2) =$
$\sin[x_1 + (-x_2)] = \sin x_1 \cos(-x_2) + \cos x_1 \sin(-x_2) = \sin x_1 \cos x_2 - \cos x_1 \sin x_2$ **37.** Use
Th. 7.6 and substitution since $\sin \pi = 0$ and $\cos \pi = -1$; $\sin(\pi + x) = \sin \pi \cos x + \cos \pi \sin x$

$= (0) \cos x + (-1) \sin x = -\sin x$ **39.** Use Th. 7.6 and substitution since $\sin \dfrac{\pi}{2} = 1$ and

$\cos \dfrac{\pi}{2} = 0$; then $\sin\left(\dfrac{\pi}{2} + x\right) = \sin \dfrac{\pi}{2} \cos x + \cos \dfrac{\pi}{2} \sin x = (1) \cos x + (0) \sin x = \cos x$ **41.** Use

Th. 7.6 and substitution since $\sin \dfrac{3\pi}{2} = -1$ and $\cos \dfrac{3\pi}{2} = 0$; then $\sin\left(\dfrac{3\pi}{2} + x\right) = \sin \dfrac{3\pi}{2} \cos x$

$+ \cos \dfrac{3\pi}{2} \sin x = (-1) \cos x + (0) \sin x = -\cos x$ **43.** Use Th. 7.8-II with $x = (x - \pi)$; then

$\sin(x - \pi) = -\sin[(x + \pi) - \pi] = -\sin x$ **45.** Use Th. 7.5-III with $s = x$; then $\cos\left(\dfrac{\pi}{2} - x\right) =$

x; then use Th. 7.8-I and $\sin(\pi - x) = \sin x$; hence $\cos\left(\dfrac{\pi}{2} - x\right) = \sin(\pi - x)$ **47.** Use 7.5-V

with $s = x$; then $\cos\left(\dfrac{3\pi}{2} + x\right) = \sin x$; then use Th. 7.8-II and $\sin(\pi - x) = -\sin x$, hence

$-\sin(\pi - x) = -(-\sin x) = \sin x$; hence, $\cos\left(\dfrac{3\pi}{2} + x\right) = -\sin(\pi - x)$

Exercise 7.4 (Page 176)

1.
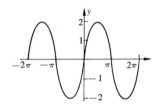

3.
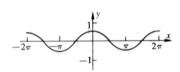

5.
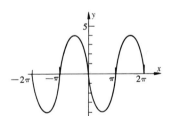

7.
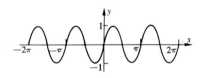

9.
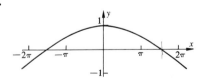

11.
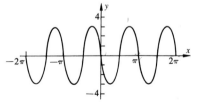

13.
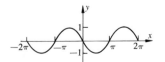

15.
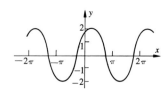

17.

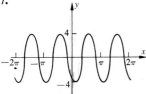

19.

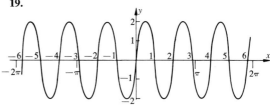

NOTE: LONG MARKS π UNITS; SHORT MARKS INTEGERS

21.

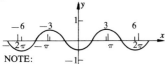

NOTE:
LONG MARKS π UNITS;
SHORT MARKS INTEGERS

23. $\left\{ -2\pi, -\dfrac{3\pi}{2}, -\pi, -\dfrac{\pi}{2}, 0, \dfrac{\pi}{2}, \pi, \dfrac{3\pi}{2}, 2\pi \right\}$

25. $\left\{ -\dfrac{3\pi}{2}, \dfrac{3\pi}{2} \right\}$

27. $\{-6, -5, -4, -3, -2, -1, 0, 1, 2, 3, 4, 5, 6\}$

29.

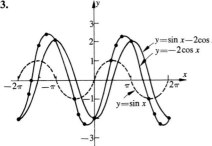

31.

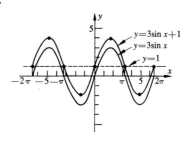

33.

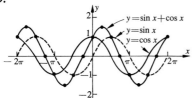

35.

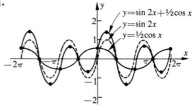

37.

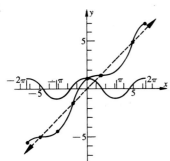

Exercise 7.5 (Page 179)   **1.** $\sqrt{\dfrac{\sqrt{2}-1}{2\sqrt{2}}}$ **3.** $\sqrt{\dfrac{\sqrt{2}+1}{2\sqrt{2}}}$ **5.** $\sqrt{\dfrac{2+\sqrt{3}}{4}}$ **7. a.** -0.71

b. -0.02 **c.** -0.99 **d.** -0.92 **e.** 0.39 **9. a.** -0.95 **b.** 0.82 **c.** 0.57 **d.** -0.16 **e.** 0.99

11. $\frac{1}{2}$ **13.** $-\dfrac{\sqrt{3}}{2}$ **15.** Let $x = x + \pi$, then use Th. 7.6 and substitution $\cos 2\pi = 1$, $\sin 2\pi = 0$; then $\sin 2x = \sin[2(x + \pi)] = \sin(2x + 2\pi) = \sin 2x$; hence, π is a period of $\sin 2x$. To show π is fundamental period: suppose there exists a, $0 < a < \pi$, such that $\sin 2(x + a) = \sin 2x$. Then, $\sin 2(x + a) = \sin(2x + 2a) = \sin 2x$ implies $a = 0$, but assumption was $0 < a < \pi$, hence no a exists; hence π is the fundamental period of $\sin 2x$ **17.** Let $x = x + 4\pi$, then use substitution $\cos 2\pi = 1$ and $\sin 2\pi = 0$; then $\sin \dfrac{x}{2} = \sin\left[\dfrac{1}{2}(x + 4\pi)\right] = \sin\left[\dfrac{x}{2} + 2\pi\right] = \sin \dfrac{x}{2}$; hence 4π is a period for $\sin \dfrac{x}{2}$. To show π is fundamental period, use procedure of problem 15 above assuming $0 < a < 4\pi$ **19.** By formula (3), $\cos 2x = 1 - 2 \sin^2 x$, hence $\sin^2 x = \frac{1}{2}(1 - \cos 2x)$ **21.** Use $\cos^3 x = \cos(2x + x)$, Th. 7.3, Th. 7.9; then $\cos^3 x = \cos(2x + x) = \cos^2 x \cos x - \sin^2 x \sin x = (\cos^2 x - \sin^2 x) \cos x - (2 \sin x \cos x) \sin x = \cos^3 x - \sin^2 x \cos x - 2 \sin^2 x \cos x = \cos^3 x - 3 \sin^2 x \cos x$ From Th. 7.1, with $s = x$, $\cos^2 x + \sin^2 = 1$ and $\sin^2 x = 1 - \cos^2 x$; hence $\cos^3 x - 3 \sin^2 \cos x = \cos^3 x - 3(1 - \cos^2 x) \cos x = \cos^3 x - 3 \cos x + 3 \cos^3 x = 4 \cos^3 x - 3 \cos x$ **23.** By formula (4) with $x = \dfrac{x}{2}$, $\cos 2\left(\dfrac{x}{2}\right) = 2 \cos^2\left(\dfrac{x}{2}\right) - 1$ Then $\cos x = 2 \cos^2\left(\dfrac{x}{2}\right) - 1$ and $\cos^2\left(\dfrac{x}{2}\right) = \dfrac{1 + \cos x}{2}$; hence $\cos \dfrac{x}{2} = \pm\sqrt{\dfrac{1 + \cos x}{2}}$

Exercise 7.6 (Page 186)

1.

x	$\tan x$	$\sec x$	$\csc x$	$\cot x$
0	0	1	not defined	not defined
$\dfrac{\pi}{6}$	$\dfrac{1}{\sqrt{3}}$	$\dfrac{2}{\sqrt{3}}$	2	$\sqrt{3}$
$\dfrac{\pi}{4}$	1	$\sqrt{2}$	$\sqrt{2}$	1
$\dfrac{\pi}{3}$	$\sqrt{3}$	2	$\dfrac{2}{\sqrt{3}}$	$\dfrac{1}{\sqrt{3}}$
$\dfrac{\pi}{2}$	not defined	not defined	1	0
$\dfrac{2\pi}{3}$	$-\sqrt{3}$	-2	$\dfrac{2}{\sqrt{3}}$	$-\dfrac{1}{\sqrt{3}}$
$\dfrac{3\pi}{4}$	-1	$-\sqrt{2}$	$\sqrt{2}$	-1
$\dfrac{5\pi}{6}$	$-\dfrac{1}{\sqrt{3}}$	$-\dfrac{2}{\sqrt{3}}$	2	$-\sqrt{3}$
π	0	-1	not defined	not defined

3. $\sin x = \frac{5}{13}, = \cos x = \frac{12}{13}, \sec x = \frac{13}{12}, \csc x = \frac{13}{5}, \cot x = \frac{12}{5}$ **5.** $\cos x = -\frac{15}{17}, \sec x = -\frac{17}{15},$

$\csc x = -\frac{17}{8}, \tan x = \frac{8}{15}, \cot x = \frac{15}{8}$ **7.** $\sin x = -\dfrac{1}{\sqrt{10}}, \cos x = \dfrac{3}{\sqrt{10}}, \sec x = \dfrac{\sqrt{10}}{3},$

$\csc x = -\sqrt{10}$, $\tan x = -\frac{1}{3}$ **9.** Use Def. 7.4-I with $x = \left(\dfrac{\pi}{2} + x\right)$; Th. 7.8-IV and Th. 7.5-IV and

Def. 7.4-IV; then $\tan\left(\dfrac{\pi}{2} + x\right) = \dfrac{\sin\left(\dfrac{\pi}{2} + x\right)}{\cos\left(\dfrac{\pi}{2} + x\right)} = \dfrac{\cos x}{-\sin x} = -\dfrac{\cos x}{\sin x} = -\cot x;\ x \in R, x \neq 0, \pi$

11. Use Th. 7.11 and substitution $\tan \pi = 0$; then $\tan(\pi + x) = \dfrac{\tan \pi + \tan x}{1 - \tan \pi \tan x} = \tan x;\ x \in R,$

$x \neq \dfrac{\pi}{2}, \dfrac{3\pi}{2}$ **13.** Use Def. 7.4-I with $x = \left(\dfrac{3\pi}{2} + x\right)$; Th. 7.8-VI and Th. 7.5-VI followed by

Def. 7.4-IV; then $\tan\left(\dfrac{3\pi}{2} + x\right) = \dfrac{\sin\left(\dfrac{3\pi}{2} + x\right)}{\cos\left(\dfrac{3\pi}{2} + x\right)} = \dfrac{-\cos x}{\sin x} = \dfrac{-\cos x}{\sin x} = -\cot x$ **15.** Use

Def. 7.4-IV with $x = x_1 + x_2$ and procedure similar to proof of Th. 7.11; then $\cot(x_1 + x_2) =$

$\dfrac{\cos(x_1 + x_2)}{\sin(x_1 + x_2)} = \dfrac{\cos x_1 \cos x_2 - \sin x_1 \sin x_2}{\sin x_1 \cos x_2 + \cos x_1 \sin x_2} = \dfrac{\dfrac{\cos x_1 \cos x_2}{\sin x_1 \sin x_2} - \dfrac{\sin x_1 \sin x_2}{\sin x_1 \sin x_2}}{\dfrac{\sin x_1 \cos x_2}{\sin x_1 \sin x_2} + \dfrac{\cos x_1 \sin x_2}{\sin x_1 \sin x_2}} = \dfrac{\cot x_1 \cot x_2 - 1}{\cot x_2 \cot x_1}$

$= \dfrac{\cot x_1 \cot x_2 - 1}{\cot x_1 + \cot x_2};\ x \in R,\ \cot x_1 + \cot x_2 \neq 0$ **17.** Use result of Problem 15 above with

$x = x_1 = x_2$; then $\cot 2x = \cot(x + x) = \dfrac{\cot x \cot x - 1}{\cot x + \cot x} = \dfrac{\cot^2 x - 1}{2 \cot x};\ x \in R;\ \cot x \neq 0$ **19.** By

Th. 7.1, $\sin^2 x + \cos^2 x = 1$ and $\dfrac{\sin^2 x}{\cos^2 x} + \dfrac{\cos^2 x}{\cos^2 x} = \dfrac{1}{\cos^2 x}$, $\cos^2 x \neq 0$; then $\tan^2 x + 1 = \sec^2 x$

or $\tan^2 x = \sec^2 x - 1$; now use this result and result of Problem 18 above; then $\sec 2x =$

$\sec(x + x) = \dfrac{\sec x \sec x}{1 - \tan x \tan x} = \dfrac{\sec^2 x}{1 - \tan^2 x} = \dfrac{\sec^2 x}{1 - (\sec^2 x - 1)} = \dfrac{\sec^2 x}{2 - \sec^2 x};\ x \in R,\ \sec^2 x \neq 2$

21. 5.177   **23.** 1.116   **25.** -0.0601 **27.** 0.97   **29.** 1.15   **31.** 1.55

33.

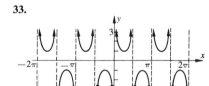

35.

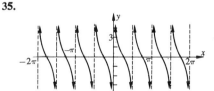

37.

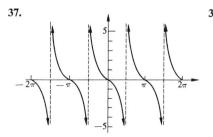

39.

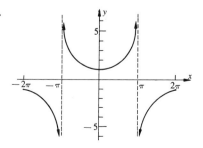

41.

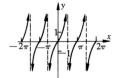

NOTE:

$y = \tan x$ and $y = \cot\left(\dfrac{\pi}{2} - x\right)$ have same graph

Exercise 7.7 (Page 191)   **1.** $-\tan x$ **3.** $\tan x$ **5.** $\tan(x_1 + x_2)$ **7.** $\cos 2x$
9. $\sin(x_1 - x_2)$ **11.** $\tan 6x$ **13.** $\sin^2 x$ **15.** $\cos 2x_1$ **17.** By Identity 12, $\tan x =$

$\dfrac{\sin x}{\cos x}$; hence $\cos x \tan x = \cos x \left(\dfrac{\sin x}{\cos x}\right) = \sin x$ **19.** By Identity 17, $\cot x = \dfrac{\cos x}{\sin x}$, then

$\cot^2 x = \dfrac{\cos^2 x}{\sin^2 x}$; hence $\sin^2 x \cot^2 x = \sin^2 x \left(\dfrac{\cos^2 x}{\sin^2 x}\right) = 1$ **21.** By Th. 7.15, $1 + \tan^2 x = \sec^2 x$;

and by Identity (14), $\sec x = \dfrac{1}{\cos x}$, then $\sec^2 x = \dfrac{1}{\cos^2 x}$; hence $\cos^2 x (1 + \tan^2 x) = \cos^2 x (\sec^2 x) =$

$\cos^2 x \left(\dfrac{1}{\cos^2 x}\right) = 1$ **23.** By Identity 1, $\sin^2 x + \cos^2 x = 1$, hence $1 - \cos^2 x = \sin^2 x$. Using

Identities (14), (15), and (17) with this result, $\sec x \csc x - \cot x = \left(\dfrac{1}{\cos x}\right)\left(\dfrac{1}{\sin x}\right) - \dfrac{\cos x}{\sin x} =$

$\dfrac{1 - \cos^2 x}{\cos x \sin x} = \dfrac{\sin^2 x}{\cos x \sin x} = \dfrac{\sin x}{\cos x} = \tan x$ **25.** By Identities (14) and (12), $\dfrac{\sin x \sec x}{\tan x} =$

$\dfrac{(\sin x)\left(\dfrac{1}{\cos x}\right)}{\left(\dfrac{\sin x}{\cos x}\right)} = \dfrac{\sin x}{\sin x} = 1$ **27.** By Th. 7.15, $\tan^2 x + 1 = \sec^2 x$, hence $\sec^2 x - 1 = \tan^2 x$;

also, by Identity 1, $\sin^2 x + \cos^2 x = 1$, and if $\sin^2 x \neq 0$, then $\dfrac{\sin^2 x}{\sin^2 x} + \dfrac{\cos^2 x}{\sin^2 x} = \dfrac{1}{\sin^2 x}$ or $1 + \cot^2 x$

$= \csc^2 x$; hence $\csc^2 x - 1 = \cot^2 x$. Using these results with Identity 16 yields $(\sec^2 x - 1)$

$(\csc^2 x - 1) = (\tan^2 x)(\cot^2 x) = (\tan^2 x)\left(\dfrac{1}{\tan^2 x}\right) = 1$ **29.** From Identity 1, since $\sin^2 x$

$+ \cos^2 x = 1$, then $1 - \sin^2 x = \cos^2 x$. From this result and Identity 14, $\dfrac{1}{1 + \sin x} + \dfrac{1}{1 - \sin x} =$

$\dfrac{1 - \sin x + 1 + \sin x}{(1 + \sin x)(1 - \sin x)} = \dfrac{2}{1 - \sin^2 x} = \dfrac{2}{\cos^2 x} = 2\left(\dfrac{1}{\cos x}\right)^2 = 2 \sec^2 x$ **31.** From Identity 17,

$\sin x \cot x = \sin x \left(\dfrac{\cos x}{\sin x}\right) = \cos x$ **33.** From Identities 14 and 12, $\sec x - \cos x = \dfrac{1}{\cos x}$

$- \cos x = \dfrac{1 - \cos^2 x}{\cos x} = \dfrac{\sin^2 x}{\cos x} = \sin x \left(\dfrac{\sin x}{\cos x}\right) = \sin x \tan x$ **35.** From Problem 27 above,

$1 + \cot^2 x = \csc^2 x$; also, from Identity 16, $\cot x = \dfrac{1}{\tan x}$; hence $\tan x \cot x = 1$ and $\tan x =$

$\dfrac{1}{\cot x}$, $x \neq 0$. Then $\dfrac{1 + \tan^2 x}{\tan^2 x} = \dfrac{1}{\tan^2 x} + 1 = \cot^2 x + 1 = 1 + \cot^2 x = \csc^2 x$ **37.** From

Identity 12 and the fact that $1 - \cos^2 x = \sin^2 x$ (from Problem 23 above) $\tan^2 x - \sin^2 x =$

$$\frac{\sin^2 x}{\cos^2 x} - \sin^2 x = \frac{\sin^2 x - \sin^2 x \cos^2 x}{\cos^2 x} = \frac{\sin^2 x(1 - \cos^2 x)}{\cos^2 x} = \left(\frac{\sin x}{\cos x}\right)^2 (1 - \cos^2 x) =$$

$$\tan^2 x \sin^2 x = \sin^2 x \tan^2 x \qquad\qquad \textbf{39.} \text{ Using Th. 7.15, } \frac{1}{\sec x - \tan x} \cdot \frac{\sec x + \tan x}{\sec x + \tan x}$$

$$= \frac{\sec x + \tan x}{\sec^2 x - \tan^2 x} = \frac{\sec x + \tan x}{(\tan^2 x + 1) - \tan^2 x} = \sec x + \tan x \qquad\qquad \textbf{41.} \text{ From Th. 7.15}$$

and Identities 12, 14, and 9, $\dfrac{2 \tan x}{1 + \tan^2 x} = \dfrac{2\left(\dfrac{\sin x}{\cos x}\right)}{\sec^2 x} = \dfrac{2\left(\dfrac{\sin x}{\cos x}\right)}{\left(\dfrac{1}{\cos x}\right)^2} = 2 \sin x \cos x = \sin 2x$

43. From Problem 27 above, $1 + \cot^2 x = \csc^2 x$, and from Problem 17, Exercise 7.6, $\cot 2x = \dfrac{\cot^2 x - 1}{2 \cot x}$. From these results and Identities 15 and 17, $\cot x - \cot 2x = \cot x - \dfrac{\cot x^2 - 1}{2 \cot x} =$

$$\frac{2 \cot^2 x - \cot^2 x + 1}{2 \cot x} = \frac{\cot^2 x + 1}{2 \cot x} = \frac{\csc^2 x}{2 \cot x} = \frac{\csc x}{2}\left(\frac{\csc x}{\cot x}\right) = \frac{\csc x}{2}\left(\frac{\dfrac{1}{\sin x}}{\dfrac{\cos x}{\sin x}}\right) = \frac{\csc x}{2 \cos x}$$

45. From Identities 8c, 9, and the fact that $1 - \sin^2 x = \cos^2 x$ derived from Identity 1, followed by Identity 17, then $\dfrac{1 + \cos^{\cdot \cdot} x}{\sin 2x} = \dfrac{1 + (1 - 2 \sin^2 x)}{2\sin x \cos x} = \dfrac{2(1 - \sin^2 x)}{2\sin x \cos x} = \dfrac{2 \cos^2 x}{2 \sin x \cos x} = \dfrac{\cos x}{\sin x} =$

$\cot x$ **47.** $\sin^2 x = \dfrac{1 - \cos 2x}{2}$; $\cos^2 x = \dfrac{1 + \cos 2x}{2}$ **49.** Adding Identities 4 and 5 and

solving for $\cos x_1 \cos x_2$ yields $\cos(x_1 + x_2) = \cos x_1 \cos x_2 - \sin x_1 \sin x_2$, $\cos(x_1 - x_2) = \cos x_1 \cos x_2 + \sin x_1 \sin x_2$;   then $\cos(x_1 + x_2) + \cos(x_1 - x_2) = 2 \cos x_1 \cos x_2$,   or $2 \cos x_1 \cos x_2 = \cos(x_1 + x_2) + \cos(x_1 - x_2)$; then $\cos x_1 \cos x_2 = \frac{1}{2}[\cos(x_1 + x_2) + \cos(x_1 - x_2)]$

Exercise 8.1 (Page 196)   **1. a.** $0°$ **b.** $90°$ **c.** $180°$ **d.** $270°$ **e.** $360°$ **3.** $40°$ **5.** $252°$
7. $17.2°$ **9.** $207.5°$ **11.** 0.35 **13.** 2.27 **15.** 7.33 **17.** 13.09 **19.** $57.3°$ **21.** $390°$,
$-330°$; $30° + 360°k, k \in J$ **23.** $120°, 480°; -240° + 360°k, k \in J$ **25.** $60°, -300°$;
$420° + 360°k, k \in J$ **27.** $30°, 390°; -330° + 360°k, k \in J$ **29.** $\approx 2.09''$ **31.** $\approx 0.72'$
33. $\approx 4.71''$

Exercise 8.2 (Page 203)   **1.** 0.5299 **3.** 0.6494 **5.** 1.046 **7.** 0.808 **9.** 0.152
11. 1.015 **13.** Since $\sin(\alpha - \beta) = \sin \alpha \cos \beta - \cos \alpha \sin \beta$, $\sin(90° - \theta) = \sin 90° \cos \theta$
$- \cos 90° \sin \theta = (1) \cos \theta - (0) \sin \theta = \cos \theta$ **15.** $\sin(180° - \theta) = \sin 180° \cos \theta -$
$\cos 180° \sin \theta = (0) \cos \theta - (-1) \sin \theta = \sin \theta$ **17.** $\sin(270° \mid \theta) = \sin 270° \cos \theta +$
$\cos 270° \sin \theta = (-1) \cos \theta + (0) \sin \theta = -\cos \theta$ **19.** $\tan(180° - \theta) = \dfrac{\tan 180° - \tan \theta}{1 + \tan 180° \tan \theta}$
$= \dfrac{0 - \tan \theta}{1 + (0) \tan \theta} = -\tan \theta$ **21.** $\sin(360° - \theta) = \sin 360° \cos \theta - \cos 360° \sin \theta =$
$(0) \cos \theta - (1) \sin \theta = -\sin \theta$ **23.** $\frac{1}{2}$ **25.** $-\dfrac{1}{\sqrt{3}}$ **27.** $-\dfrac{1}{\sqrt{2}}$ **29,** $-\frac{1}{2}$ **31.** $-\frac{1}{2}$

33. $\dfrac{\sqrt{3}}{2}$ **35.** $\sqrt{3}$ **37.** 0.7431 **39.** -0.8391 **41.** -0.6428 **43.** 0.8772 **45.** 1.827

47. -0.0610 **49.** IV   **51.** I   **53.** IV   **55.** $\tan(90° - \theta) = \dfrac{\sin(90° - \theta)}{\cos(90° - \theta)} = \dfrac{\cos \theta}{\sin \theta} = \cot \theta$

57. $\csc(90° - \theta) = \dfrac{1}{\sin(90° - \theta)} = \dfrac{1}{\cos \theta} = \sec \theta$ **59.** $(1 - \cos^2 \theta) \sec^2 \theta = \sin^2 \theta \left(\dfrac{1}{\cos^2 \theta}\right) =$

$$\left(\frac{\sin \theta}{\cos \theta}\right)^2 = \tan^2 \theta \quad \textbf{61.} \quad \frac{1 + \cot \theta}{\csc \theta} = \frac{1 + \dfrac{\cos \theta}{\sin \theta}}{\dfrac{1}{\sin \theta}} = \sin \theta + \cos \theta; \text{ also, } \frac{1 + \tan \theta}{\sec \theta} = \frac{1 + \dfrac{\sin \theta}{\cos \theta}}{\dfrac{1}{\cos \theta}} =$$

$\cos \theta + \sin \theta = \sin \theta + \cos \theta$; hence the identity is proved $\textbf{63.} \tan(\theta + 45°) = \dfrac{\tan \theta + \tan 45°}{1 - \tan \theta \tan 45°} =$

$\dfrac{\tan \theta + 1}{1 - (\tan \theta)(1)} = \dfrac{1 + \tan \theta}{1 - \tan \theta}$ $\textbf{65.} \cos^4 \theta - \sin^4 \theta = (\cos^2 \theta - \sin^2 \theta)(\cos^2 \theta + \sin^2 \theta) =$

$(\cos 2\theta)(1) = \cos 2\theta$

67. If the coordinates are associated with lengths of line segments as indicated in the figure, then

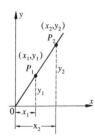

by the Pythagorean Th., $OP_1 = \sqrt{x_1{}^2 + y_1{}^2}$ and $OP_2 = \sqrt{x_2{}^2 + y_2{}^2}$. Since $\triangle OAP$ and $\triangle OBP_2$ are similar, their corresponding sides are proportional and the desired results follow by substituting

in the following ratios: $\dfrac{OA}{AP_1} = \dfrac{OB}{BP_2}; \dfrac{OA}{OP_1} = \dfrac{OB}{OP_2};$ and $\dfrac{AP_1}{OP_1} = \dfrac{BP_2}{OP_2}.$

Exercise 8.3 (Page 207)   **1.** $A = 36°\ 50', B = 53°\ 10', \mathcal{A} = 24.0$ **3.** $A = 36°, a = 87.2,$

$c = 148.3, \mathcal{A} = 5231$ **5.** $B = 68°, a = 6.0, b = 14.8, \mathcal{A} = 44.4$ **7.** 16   **9.** $\cos = \dfrac{-\sqrt{3}}{2},$

$\tan \theta = \dfrac{1}{\sqrt{3}}, \cot \theta = \sqrt{3}, \csc \theta = -2, \sec \theta = \dfrac{-2}{\sqrt{3}}$ **11.** 18.4 inches   **13.** $\cos \theta = \dfrac{4}{5}, \tan \theta = \dfrac{3}{4},$

$\cot \theta = \dfrac{4}{3}, \csc \theta = \dfrac{5}{3}, \sec \theta = \dfrac{5}{4};$ or $\cos \theta = \dfrac{-4}{5}, \tan \theta = \dfrac{-3}{4}, \cot \theta = \dfrac{-4}{3}, \csc \theta = \dfrac{5}{3}, \sec \theta = \dfrac{-5}{4}$

15. $\sin \theta = \dfrac{5}{13}, \cos \theta = \dfrac{12}{13}, \cot \theta = \dfrac{12}{5}, \csc \theta = \dfrac{13}{5}, \sec \theta = \dfrac{13}{12};$ or $\sin \theta = \dfrac{-5}{13}, \cos \theta = \dfrac{-12}{13},$

$\cot \theta = \dfrac{12}{5}, \csc \theta = \dfrac{-13}{5}, \sec \theta = \dfrac{-13}{12}$ **17.** $\sin \theta = \dfrac{\sqrt{3}}{2}, \cos \theta = \dfrac{1}{-2}, \tan \theta = -\sqrt{3},$

$\cot \theta = \dfrac{1}{-\sqrt{3}}, \csc \theta = \dfrac{2}{\sqrt{3}};$ or $\sin \theta = \dfrac{-\sqrt{3}}{2}, \cos \theta = \dfrac{-1}{2}, \tan \theta = \sqrt{3}, \cot \theta = \dfrac{1}{\sqrt{3}}, \csc \theta = \dfrac{-2}{\sqrt{3}}$

19. 2.2   **21.** 20.6   **23.** Altitude, 14.1; $\mathcal{A} = 394.8$ **25.** $38°\ 40', 51°\ 20'$ **27.** 82.6 feet.

29.

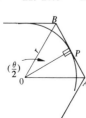

In the figure, O is center of inscribed circle with radius r and AB is side of regular polygon. Since $OP \perp AB$, $PB = \frac{1}{2}s$. Now if θ is central angle of circle, $\theta = \dfrac{360°}{n}$ where n is number of sides of the regular polygon. From right triangle OPB it follows that $\cot\left(\dfrac{\theta}{2}\right) = \dfrac{OB}{BP}$ and $\cot\left(\dfrac{360°}{n/2}\right) = \dfrac{r}{s/2}$; hence $r = \dfrac{1}{2}s \cot\left(\dfrac{180°}{n}\right)$.

Exercise 8.4 (Page 212)   **1.** $C = 70°$, $a = 19.7$, $c = 18.8$ **3.** $B = 58°$, $a = 74.9$, $b = 74.2$
5. $B = 47° \, 40'$, $b = 66.2$, $c = 34.0$ **7.** One triangle possible   **9.** One triangle possible
11. Two triangles possible   **13.** A right triangle   **15.** $B = 18° \, 40'$, $C = 48° \, 20'$, $b = 1.7$
17. $A = 108° \, 40'$, $C = 28° \, 40'$, $a = 8.7$ **19.** $A = 107° \, 20'$, $B = 40° \, 10'$, $a = 2.7$; or $A = 7°, 40'$, $B = 139° \, 50'$, $a = 0.4$ **21.** No possible solution   **23.** $B = 25° \, 40'$, $C = 94° \, 20'$, $c = 15.9$
25. $A = 93° \, 40'$, $C = 53° \, 00'$, $a = 763$ or $A = 19° \, 40'$, $C = 127° \, 00'$, $a = 257$ **27.** $\mathscr{A} = 21$
29. $\mathscr{A} = 3.8$ **31.** $\mathscr{A} = 2.6$ **33.** $\dfrac{23.1}{\sin 34° \, 20'} = \dfrac{b}{\sin 55° \, 40'} = \dfrac{c}{\sin 90°}$ **35.** $\dfrac{a}{\sin 48° \, 30'} =$
$\dfrac{0.497}{\sin 41° \, 30'} = \dfrac{c}{\sin 90°}$ **37.** From the law of sines, $\dfrac{a}{\sin \alpha} = \dfrac{c}{\sin \gamma}$ and $\alpha = 2\gamma$; then $\dfrac{a}{\sin 2\gamma} =$
$\dfrac{c}{\sin \gamma}$; $\dfrac{c \sin \gamma}{\sin^2 \gamma} = \dfrac{c}{a}$; $\dfrac{a \sin 2\gamma}{\sin \gamma} = \dfrac{c}{c}$; $\dfrac{a \cdot 2 \sin \gamma \cos \gamma}{\sin \gamma} = \dfrac{a}{c}$; $2 \cos \gamma = \dfrac{a}{c}$; $\cos \gamma = \dfrac{a}{2c}$ **41.** From the law of
sines and the properties of proportion, $\dfrac{a}{\sin \alpha} = \dfrac{b}{\sin \beta}$; $\dfrac{a}{b} = \dfrac{\sin \alpha}{\sin \beta}$; $\dfrac{a}{b} + 1 = \dfrac{\sin \alpha}{\sin \beta} + 1$; then $\dfrac{a+b}{b} =$
$\dfrac{\sin \alpha + \sin \beta}{\sin \beta}$ **43.** Dividing result from Problem 42 above by the result of Problem 41 gives
$\dfrac{a-b}{a+b} = \dfrac{\sin \alpha - \sin \beta}{\sin \alpha + \sin \beta}$; from Exercise 7.7, Problem 48, $\sin x_1 \cos x_1 = \frac{1}{2}[\sin(x_1 + x_2) + \sin(x_1 - x_2)]$;
hence $\sin(x_1 + x_2) + \sin(x_1 - x_2) = 2 \sin x_1 \cos x_2$. Let $\alpha = x_1 + x_2$ and $\beta = x_1 - x_2$; then
$2x_1 = \alpha + \beta$, $x_1 = \frac{1}{2}(\alpha + \beta)$; $2x_2 = \alpha - \beta$, $x_2 = \frac{1}{2}(\alpha - \beta)$;   so $\sin \alpha + \sin \beta =$
$2 \sin \frac{1}{2}(\alpha + \beta) \cos \frac{1}{2}(\alpha - \beta)$. Using this result and replacing β by $-\beta$ yields $\sin \alpha - \sin \beta =$
$2 \sin \frac{1}{2}(\alpha - \beta) \cos \frac{1}{2}(\alpha + \beta)$. Then $\dfrac{a-b}{a+b} = \dfrac{\sin \alpha - \sin \beta}{\sin \alpha + \sin \beta} = \dfrac{2 \sin \frac{1}{2}(\alpha - \beta) \cos \frac{1}{2}(\alpha + \beta)}{2 \sin \frac{1}{2}(\alpha + \beta) \cos \frac{1}{2}(\alpha - \beta)} =$
$\left[\dfrac{\sin \frac{1}{2}(\alpha - \beta)}{\cos \frac{1}{2}(\alpha - \beta)}\right] \cdot \left[\dfrac{\cos \frac{1}{2}(\alpha + \beta)}{\sin \frac{1}{2}(\alpha + \beta)}\right] = \tan \frac{1}{2}(\alpha - \beta) \cdot \cot \frac{1}{2}(\alpha + \beta) = \dfrac{\tan \frac{1}{2}(\alpha - \beta)}{\tan \frac{1}{2}(\alpha + \beta)}$

Exercise 8.5 (Page 216)   **1.** $c = 6.8$, $\alpha = 132° \, 50'$, $\beta = 17° \, 10'$ **3.** $b = 10.3$, $\alpha = 23° \, 40'$,
$\gamma = 34°$ **5.** $a = 14.9$, $\beta = 75° \, 10'$, $\gamma = 24° \, 10'$ **7.** $\alpha = 38° \, 10'$, $\beta = 81° \, 50'$, $\gamma = 60°$
9. $71° \, 40'$ **11.** $\mathscr{A} = 9.8$ **13.** From the law of cosines, $a^2 = b^2 + c^2 - 2bc \cos \alpha$; $\cos \alpha =$
$\dfrac{b^2 + c^2 - a^2}{2bc}$; then $1 + \cos \alpha = 1 + \dfrac{b^2 + c^2 - a^2}{2bc} = \dfrac{(b^2 + 2bc + c^2) - a^2}{2bc} = \dfrac{(b + c)^2 - a^2}{2bc} =$
$\dfrac{(b + c + a)(b + c - a)}{2bc}$ **15.** Since $s = \dfrac{a + b + c}{2}$, $s - a = \dfrac{a + b + c}{2} - a = \dfrac{b + c - a}{2}$. From
Problem 13 above, $1 + \cos \alpha = \dfrac{(b + c + a)(b + c - a)}{2bc}$; $\dfrac{1 + \cos \alpha}{2} = \left(\dfrac{b + c + a}{2}\right)\left(\dfrac{b + c - a}{2}\right) \cdot$
$\left(\dfrac{1}{bc}\right) = \dfrac{s(s - a)}{bc}$; hence $\cos \frac{1}{2}\alpha = \sqrt{\dfrac{1 + \cos \alpha}{2}} = \sqrt{\dfrac{s(s - a)}{bc}}$ **17.** $87° \, 30'$ **19.** Multiplying the
results of Problems 13 and 14 gives $1 - \cos^2 \alpha = \dfrac{(b + c + a)(b + c - a)(a - b + c)(a + b - c)}{4b^2c^2}$;
since $s = \dfrac{a + b + c}{2}$, $s - a = \dfrac{b + c - a}{2}$, $s - b = \dfrac{a - b + c}{2}$, and $s - c = \dfrac{a + b - c}{2}$. Using the

above results with the fact that $\mathcal{A} = \tfrac{1}{2}bc \sin \alpha$ and $\sin \alpha = \sqrt{1 - \cos^2 \alpha}$ yields

$$\mathcal{A} = \tfrac{1}{2}bc \sqrt{\frac{(b + c + a)(b + c - a)(a - b + c)(a + b - c)}{4b^2c^2}} =$$

$$\sqrt{\left(\frac{b + c + a}{2}\right)\left(\frac{b + c - a}{2}\right)\left(\frac{a - b + c}{2}\right)\left(\frac{a + b - c}{2}\right)} = \sqrt{s(s - a)(s - b)(s - c)}$$ **21.** Let α be

the right angle. Then a is the length of the hypotenuse in the right triangle; from the law
of cosines and the fact that $\cos 90° = 0$, $a^2 = b^2 + c^2 - 2bc \cos \alpha = b^2 + c^2 - 2bc \cos 90° = b^2 + c^2$
23. ≈ 16

Exercise 8.6 (Page 221)   **1.** $(6, 125°), (6, -235°), (-6, 305°), (-6, -55°)$ **3.** $(-2, -90°)$,
$(-2, 270°), (2, 90°), (2, -270°)$ **5.** $(6, -240°), (6, 120°), (-6, -60°), (-6, 300°)$ **7.** $\left(\dfrac{5}{\sqrt{2}}, \dfrac{5}{\sqrt{2}}\right)$

9. $\left(\dfrac{\sqrt{3}}{4}, -\dfrac{1}{4}\right)$ **11.** $\left(\dfrac{-10}{\sqrt{2}}, \dfrac{-10}{\sqrt{2}}\right)$ **13.** $(6, 45°), (6, -315°)$ **15.** $(2, 240°), (2, -120°)$

17. $(0, \theta°), (0, -\theta°)$, for any $\theta > 0$ **19.** $r = 5$ **21.** $r \sin \theta = -4$ **23.** $r^2(\cos^2 \theta + 9 \sin^2 \theta) = 9$

25. $x^2 + y^2 = 25$ **27.** $x^2 + y^2 - 9x = 0$ **29.** $y^2 = 4x + 4$ **31.** $\sec \theta/2 = \dfrac{1}{\cos(\theta/2)}$ and $\cos^2(\theta/2) =$

$\dfrac{1 + \cos \theta}{2}$; hence $r = \sec^2(\theta/2) = \dfrac{1}{\cos^2(\theta/2)} = \dfrac{2}{1 + \cos \theta}$. Now $\cos \theta = \dfrac{x}{r}$ and $r^2 = x^2 + y^2$, so $r =$

$\dfrac{2}{1 + \dfrac{x}{r}}$ and $r\left(1 + \dfrac{x}{r}\right) = 2$; hence $r + x = 2$ or $r = 2 - x$. Squaring both sides $r^2 = 4 - 4x + x^2$ and

substituting for r^2 gives $x = 1 - \tfrac{1}{4}y^2$, whose graph is a parabola

33.

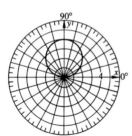

Exercise 9.1 (Page 226)   **1.** $\dfrac{\pi}{6}$ **3.** $\dfrac{\pi}{4}$ **5.** Does not exist   **7.** $\dfrac{-\pi}{6}$ **9.** 0.10 **11.** 0.39

13. -1.04 **15.** 1.29 **17.** $\dfrac{\pi}{4}$ **19.** $\dfrac{\pi}{3}$ **21.** $\dfrac{\sqrt{3}}{2}$ **23.** $\dfrac{-\sqrt{3}}{2}$ **25.** $\dfrac{\sqrt{3}}{2}$ **27.** $\dfrac{2}{3}$

29. $\dfrac{3 + 4\sqrt{3}}{10}$ **31.** $\dfrac{3\pi}{4}$ **33.** $\sqrt{1 - x^2}$ **35.** $\dfrac{y}{\sqrt{1 - y^2}}$ **37.** $\pm\sqrt{\dfrac{1 + x}{2}}$ **39.** $x = \dfrac{1}{2}\cos\dfrac{y}{3}$

41. $x = \tan 2y - \pi$ **43.** Since $-\dfrac{\pi}{2} \leq \text{Arc} \sin \dfrac{2}{5} \leq \dfrac{\pi}{2}$, $\tan\left(\text{Arc} \sin \dfrac{2}{5}\right) = \dfrac{2}{\sqrt{21}}$; hence Arc $\sin \dfrac{2}{5} =$

Arc $\tan \dfrac{2}{\sqrt{21}}$ **45.** Yes. Let Arc $\cos(\cos x) = \alpha$. Then $\cos \alpha = \cos x$; then $\alpha = x$, $0 \leq \alpha \leq \pi$

Exercise 9.2 (Page 230)

1. $\left\{ p \mid p = \dfrac{\pi}{6} + 2k\pi, \, k \in J \right\} \cup \left\{ p \mid p = \dfrac{5\pi}{6} + 2k\pi, \, k \in J \right\}$ **3.** $\varnothing$

5. $\left\{ r \mid r = \dfrac{\pi}{4} + 2k\pi, \, k \in J \right\} \cup \left\{ r \mid r = \dfrac{7\pi}{4} + 2k\pi, \, k \in J \right\}$

7. $\left\{ x \mid x = \dfrac{4\pi}{3} + 2k\pi, \, k \in J \right\} \cup \left\{ x \mid x = \dfrac{5\pi}{3} + 2k\pi, \, k \in J \right\}$

9. a. $\left\{ \dfrac{\pi}{3} + 2k\pi \right\} \cup \left\{ \dfrac{5\pi}{3} + 2k\pi \right\}, \, k \in J$ **b.** $\left\{ \left(\dfrac{\pi}{3} + 2k\pi \right)^R \right\} \cup \left\{ \left(\dfrac{5\pi}{3} + 2k\pi \right)^R \right\}, \, k \in J;$
$\{(60 + 360k)°\} \cup \{(300 + 360k)°\}, \, k \in J$

11. a. $\left\{ \dfrac{\pi}{3} + k\pi \right\}, \, k \in J$ **b.** $\left\{ \left(\dfrac{\pi}{3} + k\pi \right)^R \right\}, \, k \in J; \, \{(60 + 180k°)\}, \, k \in J$

13. a. $\left\{ \dfrac{\pi}{4} + 2k\pi \right\} \cup \left\{ \dfrac{7\pi}{4} + 2k\pi \right\}, \, k \in J$ **b.** $\left\{ \left(\dfrac{\pi}{4} + 2k\pi \right)^R \right\} \cup \left\{ \left(\dfrac{7\pi}{4} + 2k\pi \right)^R \right\}, \, k \in J;$
$\{(45 + 360k)°\} \cup \{(315 + 360k)°\}, \, k \in J$

15. a. $\{0.25 + 2k\pi\} \cup \{2.89 + 2k\pi\}, \, k \in J$ **b.** $\{(0.25 + 2k\pi)^R\} \cup \{2.89 + 2k\pi)^R\}, \, k \in J;$
$\{14° \ 30' + 360°k\} \cup \{165° \ 30' + 360°k\}, \, k \in J$ **17. a.** $\{1.25 + k\pi\}, \, k \in J$ **b.** $\{(1.25 + k)^R\};$
$k \in J; \, \{(71° \ 30' + 180°k)\}, \, k \in J$ **19. a.** $\{1.16 + 2k\pi\} \cup \{5.12 + 2k\pi\}, \, k \in J$
b. $\{(1.16 + 2k\pi)^R\} \cup \{(5.12 + 2k\pi)^R\}, \, k \in J; \, \{66° \ 30' + 360°k\} \cup \{293° \ 30' + 360°k\}, \, k \in J$

21. $\left\{ \dfrac{\pi}{3} + k\pi \right\}, \, k \in J$ **23.** $\left\{ \dfrac{\pi}{4} + \dfrac{k\pi}{2} \right\}, \, k \in J$ **25.** $\left\{ \dfrac{\pi}{2} + 2k\pi \right\}, \, k \in J$

27. $\{30°, 45°, 135°, 150°, 225°, 315°\}$ **29.** $\{0°, 120°, 180°, 240°\}$ **31.** $\{30°, 150°, 180°\}$

33. $\left\{ \dfrac{\pi^R}{4}, \dfrac{5\pi^R}{4} \right\}$ **35.** $\{0^R, 2\pi^R\}$ **37.** $\{1.11^R, 1.77^R, 4.25^R, 4.91^R\}$ **39.** $\{0.67^R, 2.48^R\}$

41. $\{1.9, -1.9\}$ **43.** $\{1.1\}$

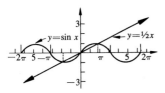

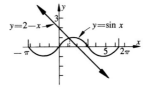

Exercise 9.3 (Page 233)   **1.** $\{22° \ 30', 157° \ 30', 202° \ 30', 337° \ 30'\}$ **3.** $\{60°, 300°\}$
5. $\{0°, 60°, 120°, 180°, 240°, 300°, 360°\}$ **7.** $\{45°, 225°\}$ **9.** $\{67° \ 30', 157° \ 30', 247°, 30',$
$337° \ 30'\}$ **11.** $\{30°, 90°, 150°, 210°, 270°, 330°\}$ **13.** $\left\{ \dfrac{\pi}{2} + k\pi, \dfrac{\pi}{6} + 2k\pi, \dfrac{5\pi}{6} + 2k\pi \right\}, \, k \in J$

15. $\left\{ \dfrac{\pi}{2} + k\pi, \dfrac{\pi}{3} + 2k\pi, \dfrac{5\pi}{3} + 2k\pi \right\}, \, k \in J$ **17.** $\left\{ k\pi, \dfrac{\pi}{2} + 2k\pi \right\}, \, k \in J$ **19.** $\left\{ \dfrac{k\pi}{2} \right\}, \, k \in J$

21. $\left\{ \dfrac{\pi}{6} + 2k\pi, \dfrac{5\pi}{6} + 2k\pi, \pi + 2k\pi \right\}, \, k \in J$

Exercise 10.1 (Page 238)   **1.** $2 \times 2, \begin{bmatrix} 6 & 2 \\ -1 & 3 \end{bmatrix}$ **3.** $2 \times 3, \begin{bmatrix} 2 & 1 \\ -7 & 4 \\ 3 & 0 \end{bmatrix}$

5. $3 \times 3, \begin{bmatrix} 2 & 4 & -2 \\ 3 & 0 & 3 \\ -1 & 1 & 1 \end{bmatrix}$ **7.** $2 \times 4, \begin{bmatrix} 4 & 2 \\ -3 & 1 \\ -1 & 1 \\ 0 & 6 \end{bmatrix}$ **9.** $1 \times 5, \begin{bmatrix} 0 \\ 0 \\ 0 \\ 0 \\ 0 \end{bmatrix}$

11. $\begin{bmatrix} 7 & -2 & 3 \\ 6 & 1 & -2 \end{bmatrix}$ **13.** [1 1 6 10] **15.** $\begin{bmatrix} 0 & 3 \\ -2 & 0 \\ 3 & 1 \end{bmatrix}$ **17.** $0_{3 \times 2}$

19. From the results of Problem 18 and Def. 10.3, $X + A = \begin{bmatrix} b_{11} - a_{11} & b_{12} - a_{12} \\ b_{21} - a_{21} & b_{22} - a_{22} \end{bmatrix}$

$+ \begin{bmatrix} a_{11} & a_{12} \\ a_{21} & a_{22} \end{bmatrix} = \begin{bmatrix} b_{11} & b_{12} \\ b_{21} & b_{22} \end{bmatrix} = B$; hence X is the solution for $X + A = B$. Since $B - A =$

$B + (-A)$, then by Def. 10.3, Def. 10.5, and the results of Problem 18, $B - A = B + (-A) =$

$\begin{bmatrix} b_{11} & b_{12} \\ b_{21} & b_{22} \end{bmatrix} + \begin{bmatrix} -a_{11} & -a_{12} \\ -a_{21} & -a_{22} \end{bmatrix} = \begin{bmatrix} b_{11} - a_{11} & b_{12} - a_{12} \\ b_{21} - a_{21} & b_{22} - a_{22} \end{bmatrix} = X$; hence X is also the solution for

$X = B - A$. Therefore $X + A = B$ and $X = B - A$ are equivalent matrix equations

21. $\begin{bmatrix} 2 & 2 \\ -1 & 1 \end{bmatrix}$ **23.** $\begin{bmatrix} 1 & 1 \\ 0 & 3 \end{bmatrix}$ **25.** Suppose $-A_{mxn}$ and B_{mxn} are both additive inverses of

A_{mxn}, and let entries of A_{mxn}, $-A_{mxn}$, and B_{mxn} be a_{ij}, $-a_{ij}$, and b_{ij} respectively; then, by Th. 10-IV, $A_{mxn} + B_{mxn} = 0_{mxn}$ and $a_{ij} + b_{ij} = 0_{ij}$; but this is true only if $b_{ij} = -a_{ij}$ (additive inverse for real numbers); therefore $B_{mxn} = -A_{mxn}$, since their corresponding entries are equal **27.** Let A_{mxn}, B_{mxn}, and C_{mxn} have entries a_{ij}, b_{ij}, and c_{ij} respectively; then, by Def. 10.3, each entry of $(A + B) + C$ is $a_{ij} + b_{ij} + c_{ij}$ and each entry of $A + (B + C)$ is $a_{ij} + b_{ij} + c_{ij}$; hence $(A + B) + C = A + (B + C)$

Exercise 10.2 (Page 244) **1.** $\begin{bmatrix} 0 & -5 & 5 \\ -15 & 5 & -10 \end{bmatrix}$ **3.** [−1] **5.** $\begin{bmatrix} -5 & -1 \\ 8 & -1 \end{bmatrix}$

7. $\begin{bmatrix} 1 & 0 & 0 \\ 0 & 1 & 0 \\ 0 & 0 & 1 \end{bmatrix}$ **9.** $\begin{bmatrix} 1 & 0 \\ -1 & 2 \end{bmatrix}$ **11.** $\begin{bmatrix} 1 & -2 \\ 1 & 2 \end{bmatrix}$ **13.** $\begin{bmatrix} -1 & -2 \\ 1 & -2 \end{bmatrix}$ **15.** $\begin{bmatrix} -2 & 3 \\ 2 & -4 \end{bmatrix}$

17. $\begin{bmatrix} -1 & 1 \\ -1 & -1 \end{bmatrix}$ **19.** $\begin{bmatrix} 1 & -1 \\ 1 & 0 \end{bmatrix}$ **21.** Since $A + B = \begin{bmatrix} 0 & 2 \\ -1 & 4 \end{bmatrix}$, $A - B = \begin{bmatrix} -2 & 2 \\ 1 & -1 \end{bmatrix}$,

$A^2 = \begin{bmatrix} 1 & 0 \\ 0 & 1 \end{bmatrix}$, $B^2 = \begin{bmatrix} 1 & 0 \\ -3 & 4 \end{bmatrix}$, and $AB = \begin{bmatrix} -3 & 4 \\ -1 & 2 \end{bmatrix}$, then **(a)** $(A + B)(A + B) =$

$\begin{bmatrix} 0 & 2 \\ -1 & 4 \end{bmatrix} \cdot \begin{bmatrix} 0 & 2 \\ -1 & 4 \end{bmatrix} = \begin{bmatrix} 2 & 8 \\ -4 & 14 \end{bmatrix}$ and $A^2 + 2AB + B^2 = \begin{bmatrix} 1 & 0 \\ 0 & 1 \end{bmatrix} + 2 \begin{bmatrix} -3 & 4 \\ -1 & 2 \end{bmatrix} + \begin{bmatrix} 1 & 0 \\ -3 & 4 \end{bmatrix}$

$= \begin{bmatrix} -4 & 8 \\ -5 & 9 \end{bmatrix}$; hence $(A + B)(A + B) \neq A^2 + 2AB + B^2$. **(b)** $(A + B)(A - B) =$

$\begin{bmatrix} 0 & 2 \\ -1 & 4 \end{bmatrix} \cdot \begin{bmatrix} -2 & 2 \\ 1 & -1 \end{bmatrix} = \begin{bmatrix} 2 & -2 \\ 6 & -6 \end{bmatrix}$ and $A^2 - B^2 = \begin{bmatrix} 1 & 0 \\ 0 & 1 \end{bmatrix} - \begin{bmatrix} 1 & 0 \\ -3 & 4 \end{bmatrix} = \begin{bmatrix} 0 & 0 \\ 3 & -3 \end{bmatrix}$;

hence $(A + B)(A - B) \neq A^2 - B^2$

For Problems 23 and 25, let $A = \begin{bmatrix} a_{11} & a_{12} \\ a_{21} & a_{22} \end{bmatrix}$, $B = \begin{bmatrix} b_{11} & b_{12} \\ b_{21} & b_{22} \end{bmatrix}$, and $C = \begin{bmatrix} c_{11} & c_{12} \\ c_{21} & c_{22} \end{bmatrix}$

23. Since $AB = \begin{bmatrix} a_{11}b_{11} + a_{12}b_{21} & a_{11}b_{12} + a_{12}b_{22} \\ a_{21}b_{11} + a_{22}b_{21} & a_{21}b_{12} + a_{22}b_{22} \end{bmatrix}$, $(AB)C =$

$\begin{bmatrix} (a_{11}b_{11} + a_{12}b_{21})c_{11} + (a_{11}b_{12} + a_{12}b_{22})c_{21} & (a_{11}b_{11} + a_{12}b_{21})c_{12} + (a_{11}b_{12} + a_{12}b_{22})c_{22} \\ (a_{21}b_{11} + a_{22}b_{21})c_{11} + (a_{21}b_{12} + a_{22}b_{22})c_{21} & (a_{21}b_{11} + a_{22}b_{21})c_{12} + (a_{21}b_{12} + a_{22}b_{22})c_{22} \end{bmatrix}$

The element in the first row, first column is given by $a_{11}b_{11}c_{11} + a_{12}b_{21}c_{11} + a_{11}b_{12}c_{21}$ $+ a_{12}b_{22}c_{21} = (a_{11}b_{11}c_{11} + a_{11}b_{12}c_{21}) + (a_{12}b_{21}c_{11} + a_{12}b_{22}c_{21}) = a_{11}(b_{11}c_{11} + b_{12}c_{21})$ $+ a_{12}(b_{21}c_{11} + b_{22}c_{21})$. When the remaining elements are treated in a similar manner, $(AB)C =$

$\begin{bmatrix} a_{11}(b_{11}c_{11} + b_{12}c_{21}) + a_{12}(b_{21}c_{11} + b_{22}c_{21}) & a_{11}(b_{11}c_{12} + b_{12}c_{22}) + a_{12}(b_{21}c_{12} + b_{22}c_{22}) \\ a_{21}(b_{11}c_{11} + b_{12}c_{21}) + a_{22}(b_{21}c_{11} + b_{22}c_{21}) & a_{21}(b_{11}c_{12} + b_{12}c_{22}) + a_{22}(b_{21}c_{12} + b_{22}c_{22}) \end{bmatrix} =$

$$\begin{bmatrix} a_{11} & a_{12} \\ a_{21} & a_{22} \end{bmatrix} \cdot \begin{bmatrix} b_{11}c_{11}+b_{12}c_{21} & b_{11}c_{12}+b_{12}c_{22} \\ b_{21}c_{11}+b_{22}c_{21} & b_{21}c_{12}+b_{22}c_{22} \end{bmatrix} = \begin{bmatrix} a_{11} & a_{12} \\ a_{21} & a_{22} \end{bmatrix} \cdot \left(\begin{bmatrix} b_{11} & b_{12} \\ b_{21} & b_{22} \end{bmatrix} \cdot \begin{bmatrix} c_{11} & c_{12} \\ c_{21} & c_{22} \end{bmatrix} \right)$$

$= A(BC)$ **25.** $B+C = \begin{bmatrix} b_{11}+c_{11} & b_{12}+c_{12} \\ b_{21}+c_{22} & b_{22}+c_{22} \end{bmatrix}$, hence $(B+C)A =$

$$\begin{bmatrix} (b_{11}+c_{11})a_{11}+(b_{12}+c_{12})a_{21} & (b_{11}+c_{11})a_{12}+(b_{12}+c_{12})a_{22} \\ (b_{21}+c_{22})a_{11}+(b_{22}+c_{22})a_{21} & (b_{21}+c_{22})a_{12}+(b_{22}+c_{22})a_{22} \end{bmatrix}.$$ The element in the first row,

first column is given by $b_{11}a_{11}+c_{11}a_{21}+b_{12}a_{21}+c_{12}a_{21} = (b_{11}a_{11}+b_{12}a_{21})+(c_{11}a_{11}+c_{12}a_{21})$. When the remaining elements are treated in a similar manner,

$$(B+C)A = \begin{bmatrix} (b_{11}a_{11}+b_{12}a_{21})+(c_{11}a_{11}+c_{12}a_{21}) & (b_{11}a_{12}+b_{12}a_{22})+(c_{11}a_{12}+c_{12}a_{22}) \\ (b_{21}a_{11}+b_{22}a_{21})+(c_{21}a_{11}+c_{22}a_{21}) & (b_{21}a_{12}+b_{22}a_{22})+(c_{21}a_{12}+c_{22}a_{22}) \end{bmatrix}$$

$$= \begin{bmatrix} b_{11}a_{11}+b_{12}a_{21} & b_{11}a_{12}+b_{12}a_{22} \\ b_{21}a_{11}+b_{22}a_{21} & b_{21}a_{12}+b_{22}a_{22} \end{bmatrix} + \begin{bmatrix} c_{11}a_{11}+c_{12}a_{21} & c_{11}a_{12}+c_{12}a_{22} \\ c_{21}a_{11}+c_{22}a_{21} & c_{21}a_{12}+c_{22}a_{22} \end{bmatrix} =$$

$$\begin{bmatrix} b_{11} & b_{12} \\ b_{21} & b_{22} \end{bmatrix} \cdot \begin{bmatrix} a_{11} & a_{12} \\ a_{21} & a_{22} \end{bmatrix} + \begin{bmatrix} c_{11} & c_{12} \\ c_{21} & c_{22} \end{bmatrix} \cdot \begin{bmatrix} a_{11} & a_{12} \\ a_{21} & a_{22} \end{bmatrix} = BC + CA$$

27. $(A_{2\times 2} \cdot B_{2\times 2}) = \begin{bmatrix} a_{11}b_{11}+a_{12}b_{21} & a_{11}b_{12}+a_{12}b_{22} \\ a_{21}b_{11}+a_{22}b_{21} & a_{21}b_{22}+a_{22}b_{22} \end{bmatrix}$.

Hence, $(A_{2\times 2} \cdot B_{2\times 2})^t = \begin{bmatrix} a_{11}b_{11}+a_{12}b_{21} & a_{21}b_{11}+a_{22}b_{21} \\ a_{11}b_{12}+a_{12}b_{22} & a_{21}b_{12}+a_{22}b_{22} \end{bmatrix}$.

By the commutative property of multiplication for real numbers, $(A_{2\times 2} \cdot B_{2\times 2})^t =$

$$\begin{bmatrix} b_{11}a_{11}+b_{21}a_{12} & b_{11}a_{21}+b_{21}a_{22} \\ b_{12}a_{11}+b_{22}a_{12} & b_{12}a_{21}+b_{22}a_{22} \end{bmatrix} = \begin{bmatrix} b_{11} & b_{21} \\ b_{12} & b_{22} \end{bmatrix} \cdot \begin{bmatrix} a_{11} & a_{21} \\ a_{12} & a_{22} \end{bmatrix} = B^t_{2\times 2} \cdot A^t_{2\times 2}$$

29. Let $A = \begin{bmatrix} a_{11} & a_{12} \\ a_{21} & a_{22} \end{bmatrix}$ and c be a scalar; then by Def. 10.6 and the closure property of

multiplication of real numbers, $c\begin{bmatrix} a_{11} & a_{12} \\ a_{21} & a_{22} \end{bmatrix} = \begin{bmatrix} ca_{11} & ca_{12} \\ ca_{21} & ca_{22} \end{bmatrix}$, which is an $m \times n$ matrix.

31. By Def. 10.6 and the distributive property for real numbers, and by Def. 10.3,

$$(c+d)\begin{bmatrix} a_{11} & a_{12} \\ a_{21} & a_{22} \end{bmatrix} = \begin{bmatrix} (c+d)a_{11} & (c+d)a_{12} \\ (c+d)a_{21} & (c+d)a_{22} \end{bmatrix} = \begin{bmatrix} ca_{11}+da_{11} & ca_{12}+da_{12} \\ ca_{21}+da_{21} & ca_{22}+da_{22} \end{bmatrix} =$$

$$\begin{bmatrix} ca_{11}+ca_{12} \\ ca_{21}+ca_{22} \end{bmatrix} + \begin{bmatrix} da_{11}+da_{12} \\ da_{21}+da_{22} \end{bmatrix} = c\begin{bmatrix} a_{11} & a_{12} \\ a_{21} & a_{22} \end{bmatrix} + d\begin{bmatrix} a_{11} & a_{12} \\ a_{21} & a_{22} \end{bmatrix} = cA + dA$$

33. By Def. 10.6 and 10.5, $(-1)A = -1\begin{bmatrix} a_{11} & a_{12} \\ a_{21} & a_{22} \end{bmatrix} = \begin{bmatrix} -a_{11} & -a_{12} \\ -a_{21} & -a_{22} \end{bmatrix} = -A$

35. $0_{2\times 2} = \begin{bmatrix} 0 & 0 \\ 0 & 0 \end{bmatrix}$; hence, by Def. 10.6, $c \cdot 0_{2\times 2} = c\begin{bmatrix} 0 & 0 \\ 0 & 0 \end{bmatrix} = \begin{bmatrix} c \cdot 0 & c \cdot 0 \\ c \cdot 0 & c \cdot 0 \end{bmatrix} = \begin{bmatrix} 0 & 0 \\ 0 & 0 \end{bmatrix} = 0_{2\times 2}$

Exercise 10.3 (Page 250)   **1.** 0   **3.** -6 **5.** -2

7. $M_{11} = \begin{vmatrix} 0 & 3 & -1 \\ 1 & 2 & 2 \\ -1 & 3 & 1 \end{vmatrix}, A_{11} = \begin{vmatrix} 0 & 3 & -1 \\ 1 & 2 & 2 \\ -1 & 3 & 1 \end{vmatrix}$

9. $M_{23} = \begin{vmatrix} 2 & 1 & 0 \\ -2 & 1 & 2 \\ 1 & -1 & 1 \end{vmatrix}, A_{23} = -\begin{vmatrix} 2 & 1 & 0 \\ -2 & 1 & 2 \\ 1 & -1 & 1 \end{vmatrix}$

11. $M_{31} = \begin{vmatrix} 1 & -2 & 0 \\ 0 & 3 & -1 \\ -1 & 3 & 1 \end{vmatrix}$, $A_{31} = \begin{vmatrix} 1 & -2 & 0 \\ 0 & 3 & -1 \\ -1 & 3 & 1 \end{vmatrix}$

13. $M_{44} = \begin{vmatrix} 2 & 1 & -2 \\ 1 & 0 & 3 \\ -2 & 1 & 2 \end{vmatrix}$, $A_{44} = \begin{vmatrix} 2 & 1 & -2 \\ 1 & 0 & 3 \\ -2 & 1 & 2 \end{vmatrix}$

15. 1   **17.** 0   **19.** 3   **21.** 0   **23.** -1 **25.** 0   **27.** x^3 **29.** $\{3\}$ **31.** Expanding by

elements in the first row yields $\begin{vmatrix} 0 & 1 & 0 & 0 \\ 1 & 0 & 3 & 2 \\ 5 & -1 & 2 & 1 \\ 1 & 0 & 1 & 1 \end{vmatrix} = -\begin{vmatrix} 1 & 3 & 2 \\ 5 & 2 & 1 \\ 1 & 1 & 1 \end{vmatrix}$; expanding by elements in the

third row yields $-\begin{vmatrix} 3 & 2 \\ 2 & 1 \end{vmatrix} + \begin{vmatrix} 1 & 2 \\ 2 & 1 \end{vmatrix} - \begin{vmatrix} 1 & 3 \\ 5 & 2 \end{vmatrix} = 1 - 9 + 13 = 5$ **33.** 2, 6, 24

35. By Def. 10.13, 14, 15, 16, and associative, commutative, and distributive properties of

real numbers, $a_{11}A_{11} + a_{12}A_{12} + a_{13}A_{13} = a_{11}\begin{vmatrix} a_{22} & a_{23} \\ a_{32} & a_{33} \end{vmatrix} - a_{12}\begin{vmatrix} a_{21} & a_{23} \\ a_{31} & a_{33} \end{vmatrix} + a_{13}\begin{vmatrix} a_{21} & a_{22} \\ a_{31} & a_{32} \end{vmatrix} =$

$a_{11}a_{22}a_{33} - a_{11}a_{23}a_{32} - a_{12}a_{21}a_{33} + a_{12}a_{23}a_{31} + a_{13}a_{21}a_{32} - a_{13}a_{22}a_{31} =$

$-a_{21}(a_{12}a_{33} - a_{13}a_{32}) + a_{22}(a_{11}a_{33} - a_{13}a_{31}) - a_{23}(a_{11}a_{32} - a_{12}a_{31}) = a_{21}\left(-\begin{vmatrix} a_{12} & a_{13} \\ a_{32} & a_{33} \end{vmatrix}\right)$

$+ a_{22}\begin{vmatrix} a_{11} & a_{13} \\ a_{31} & a_{33} \end{vmatrix} + a_{23}\left(-\begin{vmatrix} a_{11} & a_{12} \\ a_{31} & a_{32} \end{vmatrix}\right) = a_{21}A_{21} + a_{22}A_{22} + a_{23}A_{23}$ **37.** From Problem 35,

$a_{11}A_{11} + a_{12}A_{12} + a_{13}A_{13} = a_{11}a_{22}a_{33} - a_{11}a_{23}a_{23} - a_{12}a_{21}a_{33} + a_{12}a_{23}a_{31} + a_{13}a_{21}a_{32}$
$- a_{13}a_{22}a_{31} = a_{11}(a_{22}a_{33} - a_{23}a_{32}) - a_{21}(a_{12}a_{33} - a_{13}a_{32}) + a_{31}(a_{12}a_{23} - a_{13}a_{22}) =$

$a_{11}\begin{vmatrix} a_{22} & a_{23} \\ a_{32} & a_{33} \end{vmatrix} + a_{21}\left(-\begin{vmatrix} a_{12} & a_{13} \\ a_{32} & a_{33} \end{vmatrix}\right) + a_{31}\begin{vmatrix} a_{12} & a_{13} \\ a_{22} & a_{23} \end{vmatrix} = a_{11}A_{11} + a_{21}A_{21} + a_{31}A_{31}$

39. From Problem 35 above, $a_{11}A_{11} + a_{12}A_{12} + a_{13}A_{13} = a_{11}a_{22}a_{33} - a_{11}a_{23}a_{32} - a_{12}a_{21}a_{33}$
$+ a_{12}a_{23}a_{31} + a_{12}a_{23}a_{31} + a_{13}a_{21}a_{32} - a_{13}a_{22}a_{31} = a_{13}(a_{21}a_{32} - a_{22}a_{31}) - a_{23}(a_{11}a_{32}$

$- a_{12}a_{31}) + a_{33}(a_{11}a_{22} - a_{12}a_{21}) = a_{13}\begin{vmatrix} a_{21} & a_{22} \\ a_{31} & a_{32} \end{vmatrix} + a_{23}\left(-\begin{vmatrix} a_{11} & a_{12} \\ a_{31} & a_{32} \end{vmatrix}\right) + a_{33}\begin{vmatrix} a_{11} & a_{12} \\ a_{21} & a_{22} \end{vmatrix} =$

$a_{13}A_{13} + a_{23}A_{23} + a_{33}A_{33}$ **41.** Let $A = \begin{bmatrix} a_{11} & a_{12} \\ a_{21} & a_{22} \end{bmatrix}$; by Def. 10.6 and the fact that

$\delta(A) = a_{11}a_{22} - a_{12}a_{21}$, it follows that $aA = \begin{bmatrix} aa_{11} & aa_{12} \\ aa_{21} & aa_{22} \end{bmatrix}$ and $\delta(aA) = a^2a_{11}a_{22} - a^2a_{12}a_{21} =$

$a^2(a_{11}a_{22} - a_{12}a_{21}) = a^2\delta(A)$ **43.** Let $A = \begin{bmatrix} a_{11} & a_{12} \\ a_{21} & a_{22} \end{bmatrix}$ and $B = \begin{bmatrix} b_{11} & b_{12} \\ b_{21} & b_{22} \end{bmatrix}$; then

$\delta(A) = a_{11}a_{22} - a_{12}a_{21}$ and $\delta(B) = b_{11}b_{22} - b_{12}b_{21}$, $AB = \begin{bmatrix} a_{11}b_{11} + a_{12}b_{21} & a_{11}b_{12} + a_{12}b_{22} \\ a_{21}b_{11} + a_{22}b_{21} & a_{21}b_{12} + a_{22}b_{22} \end{bmatrix}$

and $\delta(AB) = (a_{11}b_{11} + a_{12}b_{21})(a_{21}b_{12} + a_{22}b_{22}) - (a_{11}b_{12} + a_{12}b_{22})(a_{21}b_{11} + a_{22}b_{21})$, which
simplifies to $a_{11}b_{11}a_{22}b_{22} - a_{11}b_{12}a_{22}b_{21} - a_{12}b_{22}a_{21}b_{11} + a_{12}b_{21}a_{21}b_{12} = a_{11}a_{22}(b_{11}b_{22}$
$- b_{12}b_{21}) - a_{12}a_{21}(b_{11}b_{22} - b_{12}b_{21}) = (a_{11}a_{22} - a_{12}a_{21})(b_{11}b_{22} - b_{12}b_{21}) = \delta(A) \cdot \delta(B)$

Exercise 10.4 (Page 255)   **1.** Theorem 10.8   **3.** Theorems 10.11 and 10.10   **5.** Theorem
10.10   **7.** Theorem 10.9   **9.** Theorem 10.11   **11.** Theorem 10.11   **13.** Theorem 10.11

15. Theorem 10.13   **17.** Theorem 10.13   **19.** Theorem 10.13   **21.** $\begin{vmatrix} 1 & 3 \\ 0 & -4 \end{vmatrix}$

23. $\begin{vmatrix} 1 & -2 & 1 \\ 0 & 7 & 1 \\ 0 & 2 & 1 \end{vmatrix}$ **25.** $\begin{vmatrix} 0 & 1 & -3 & -2 \\ 0 & 2 & 1 & 2 \\ 1 & 1 & 2 & 3 \\ 0 & 1 & 1 & 1 \end{vmatrix}$ **27.** $\begin{vmatrix} 1 & 1 & 2 & 1 \\ 2 & -2 & -1 & 2 \\ 3 & 0 & 1 & 1 \\ 0 & 0 & 0 & 1 \end{vmatrix}$

29. $-1\begin{vmatrix} 2 & 1 \\ -1 & 2 \end{vmatrix} = -5$ **31.** $\begin{vmatrix} -1 & -5 \\ 2 & -2 \end{vmatrix} = 12$ **33.** $\begin{vmatrix} 4 & 4 \\ 3 & 7 \end{vmatrix} = 16$ **35.** $\begin{vmatrix} 6 & 1 \\ 0 & 3 \end{vmatrix} = 18$

37. $-16\begin{vmatrix} 1 & 2 \\ 2 & 3 \end{vmatrix} = 16$ **39.** $\begin{vmatrix} 4 & -4 \\ 3 & -9 \end{vmatrix} = -24$ **41.** Let $A = \begin{vmatrix} x & y & 1 \\ x_1 & y_1 & 1 \\ x_2 & y_2 & 1 \end{vmatrix} = 0.$ Expanding

about the first row gives $\delta(A) = x\begin{vmatrix} y_1 & 1 \\ y_2 & 1 \end{vmatrix} - y\begin{vmatrix} x_1 & 1 \\ x_2 & 1 \end{vmatrix} + 1\begin{vmatrix} x_1 & y_1 \\ x_2 & y_2 \end{vmatrix} = 0;$ hence $(y_1 - y_2) x$

$+ (x_2 - x_1) y + (x_1 y_2 - y_1 x_2) = 0.$ Further, y_1, y_2, x_1, x_2 are real numbers; hence there exist real numbers a, b, c such that $(y_1 - y_2) = a, (x_2 - x_1) = b,$ and $(x_1 y_2 - y_1 x_2) = c.$ Substituting yields $ax + by + c = 0,$ which is the equation of a straight line   **43.** Multiply column 1 by $(-a)$ and add result to column 2; also, multiply column 1 by $(-a^2)$ and add result to column 3,

to obtain, $\begin{vmatrix} 1 & a & a^2 \\ 1 & b & b^2 \\ 1 & c & c^2 \end{vmatrix} = \begin{vmatrix} 1 & 0 & 0 \\ 1 & b-a & b^2-a^2 \\ 1 & c-a & c^2-a^2 \end{vmatrix}.$ Expand about the first row to obtain

$1\begin{vmatrix} b-a & b^2-a^2 \\ c-a & c^2-a^2 \end{vmatrix} = (b-a)[c^2-a^2] - (c-a)[b^2-a^2] = (b-a)[(c-a)(c+a)] - (c-a) \cdot$

$[(b-a)(b+a)] = -(a-b)[(c-a)(c+a)] + (c-a)[(a-b)(a+b)] = (a-b)(c-a)[-(c+a) \cdot$

$(a+b)] = (a-b)(c-a)(b-c) = (b-c)(c-a)(a-b)$ **45.** Let $A = \begin{bmatrix} a_{11} & a_{12} \\ a_{21} & a_{22} \end{bmatrix}$ and

$B = \begin{bmatrix} b_{11} & b_{12} \\ b_{21} & b_{22} \end{bmatrix}.$ Then, by Def. 10.7, $AB = \begin{bmatrix} a_{11}b_{11} + a_{12}b_{21} & a_{11}b_{12} + a_{12}b_{22} \\ a_{21}b_{11} + a_{22}b_{21} & a_{21}b_{12} + a_{21}b_{22} \end{bmatrix},$ and, by Def.

10.6, $a(AB) = \begin{bmatrix} a(a_{11}b_{11} + a_{12}b_{21}) & a(a_{11}b_{12} + a_{12}b_{22}) \\ a(a_{21}b_{11} + a_{22}b_{21}) & a(a_{21}b_{12} + a_{21}b_{22}) \end{bmatrix};$ also $aA = \begin{bmatrix} aa_{11} & aa_{12} \\ aa_{21} & aa_{22} \end{bmatrix}$ and $(aA)B =$

$\begin{bmatrix} aa_{11}b_{11} + aa_{12}b_{21} & aa_{11}b_{12} + aa_{12}b_{22} \\ aa_{21}b_{11} + aa_{22}b_{21} & aa_{21}b_{12} + aa_{22}b_{22} \end{bmatrix} = \begin{bmatrix} a(a_{11}b_{11} + a_{12}b_{21}) & a(a_{11}b_{12} + a_{12}b_{22}) \\ a(21b_{11} + a_{22}b_{21}) & a(a_{21}b_{12} + a_{21}b_{22}) \end{bmatrix} = a(AB);$

further, $aB = \begin{bmatrix} ab_{11} & ab_{12} \\ ab_{21} & ab_{22} \end{bmatrix}$ and $A(aB) = \begin{bmatrix} a_{11}ab_{11} + a_{12}ab_{21} & a_{11}ab_{12} + a_{12}ab_{22} \\ a_{21}ab_{11} + a_{22}ab_{21} & a_{21}ab_{12} + a_{21}ab_{22} \end{bmatrix} =$

$\begin{bmatrix} a(a_{11}b_{11} + a_{12}b_{21}) & a(a_{11}b_{12} + a_{12}b_{22}) \\ a(a_{21}b_{11} + a_{22}b_{21}) & a(a_{21}b_{12} + a_{21}b_{22}) \end{bmatrix} = a(AB)$ **47.** Let $A = \begin{vmatrix} a_{11} & a_{12} \\ a_{21} & a_{22} \end{vmatrix};$ $\delta(A) =$

$a_{11}a_{22} - a_{12}a_{21}.$ Interchange rows 1 and 2 and let $B = \begin{vmatrix} a_{21} & a_{22} \\ a_{11} & a_{12} \end{vmatrix};$ then $\delta(B) = a_{21}a_{12} - a_{22}a_{11} =$

$-(a_{11}a_{22} - a_{12}a_{21}) = -\delta(A).$ Interchange columns 1 and 2 and let $C = \begin{vmatrix} a_{12} & a_{11} \\ a_{22} & a_{22} \end{vmatrix};$ then

$\delta(C) = a_{12}a_{22} - a_{11}a_{22} = -(a_{11}a_{22} - a_{12}a_{22}) = -\delta(A)$ **49.** Let $A = \begin{vmatrix} a_{11} & a_{12} \\ a_{21} & a_{22} \end{vmatrix};$ then

$\delta(A) = a_{11}a_{22} - a_{12}a_{21}.$ Let $B = \begin{vmatrix} ka_{11} & ka_{12} \\ a_{21} & a_{22} \end{vmatrix};$ then $\delta(B) = ka_{11}a_{22} - ka_{12}a_{21} =$

$k(a_{11}a_{22} - a_{12}a_{21}) = k\delta(A);$ and similarly if $C = \begin{vmatrix} a_{11} & a_{12} \\ ka_{21} & ka_{22} \end{vmatrix}.$ Let $C = \begin{vmatrix} ka_{11} & ka_{12} \\ ka_{21} & a_{22} \end{vmatrix},$ then

$\delta(C) = ka_{11}a_{22} - a_{12}ka_{21} = k(a_{11}a_{22} - a_{12}a_{21}) = k\,\delta(A),$ and similarly if $D = \begin{vmatrix} a_{11} & ka_{12} \\ a_{21} & ka_{22} \end{vmatrix}$

Exercise 10.5 (Page 261)   **1.** $\begin{bmatrix} 3 & -2 \\ -1 & 1 \end{bmatrix}$ **3.** $\frac{1}{5}\begin{bmatrix} 1 & 3 \\ -1 & 2 \end{bmatrix}$ **5.** $|A| = 0;$ no inverse

7. $\dfrac{1}{6}\begin{bmatrix} 2 & 2 & -5 \\ -4 & 2 & 1 \\ 0 & 0 & 3 \end{bmatrix}$
  9. $\dfrac{1}{3}\begin{bmatrix} -2 & 3 & -1 \\ -1 & 0 & 1 \\ 6 & -6 & 3 \end{bmatrix}$
  11. $|A| = 0$; no inverse

13. Let $A \cdot B = \begin{bmatrix} 2 & 3 \\ 1 & -1 \end{bmatrix} \cdot \begin{bmatrix} 0 & 1 \\ 3 & 1 \end{bmatrix}$; $A \cdot B = \begin{bmatrix} 9 & 5 \\ -3 & 0 \end{bmatrix}$ and $\delta(AB) = 15$, so $(A \cdot B)^{-1} =$

$\dfrac{1}{15}\begin{bmatrix} 0 & -5 \\ 3 & 9 \end{bmatrix}$; also, since $\delta(A) = -5$ and $\delta(B) = -3$, $B^{-1} = -\dfrac{1}{3}\begin{bmatrix} 1 & -1 \\ -3 & 0 \end{bmatrix}$ and $\delta A^{-1} =$

$\dfrac{1}{5}\begin{bmatrix} -1 & -3 \\ -1 & 2 \end{bmatrix}$; $B^{-1} \cdot A^{-1} = \dfrac{1}{15}\begin{bmatrix} 0 & -5 \\ 3 & 9 \end{bmatrix}$; hence $(A \cdot B)^{-1} = B^{-1} \cdot A^{-1}$ **15.** Let $A =$

$\begin{bmatrix} 3 & 0 & 1 \\ 2 & 1 & 0 \\ 0 & 1 & 2 \end{bmatrix}$; then $\delta(A) = 8$ and $A^{-1} = \dfrac{1}{8}\begin{bmatrix} 2 & 1 & -1 \\ -4 & 6 & 2 \\ 2 & -3 & 3 \end{bmatrix}$. Let $B = \begin{bmatrix} 2 & 1 & 0 \\ 1 & 1 & 2 \\ 0 & 1 & 0 \end{bmatrix}$; then $\delta(B) =$

$-\dfrac{1}{4}$ and $B^{-1} = -\dfrac{1}{4}\begin{bmatrix} -2 & 0 & 2 \\ 0 & 0 & -4 \\ 1 & -2 & 1 \end{bmatrix}$; $A \cdot B = \begin{bmatrix} 6 & 4 & 0 \\ 5 & 3 & 2 \\ 1 & 3 & 2 \end{bmatrix}$, $\delta(A \cdot B) = -32$, and $(A \cdot B)^{-1} =$

$-\dfrac{1}{32}\begin{bmatrix} 0 & -8 & 8 \\ -8 & 12 & -12 \\ 12 & -14 & -2 \end{bmatrix}$; $B^{-1} \cdot A^{-1} = -\dfrac{1}{4}\begin{bmatrix} -2 & 0 & 2 \\ 0 & 0 & -4 \\ 1 & -2 & 1 \end{bmatrix} \cdot \dfrac{1}{8}\begin{bmatrix} 2 & 1 & -1 \\ -4 & 6 & 2 \\ 2 & -3 & 3 \end{bmatrix} =$

$-\dfrac{1}{32}\begin{bmatrix} 0 & -8 & 8 \\ -8 & 12 & -12 \\ 12 & -14 & -2 \end{bmatrix}$; hence $(A \cdot B)^{-1} = B^{-1} \cdot A^{-1}$ **17.** Let $A = \begin{bmatrix} a_{11} & a_{12} \\ a_{21} & a_{22} \end{bmatrix}$; then

$\delta(A) = (a_{11}a_{22} - a_{12}a_{21}) \neq 0$ since A is non-singular, and hence $\dfrac{1}{\delta(A)}$ is defined and A^{-1} exists.

$A^{-1} = \dfrac{1}{\delta(A)}\begin{bmatrix} a_{22} & -a_{12} \\ -a_{21} & a_{11} \end{bmatrix} = \begin{bmatrix} \dfrac{a_{22}}{\delta(A)} & \dfrac{-a_{12}}{\delta(A)} \\ \dfrac{-a_{21}}{\delta(A)} & \dfrac{a_{11}}{\delta(A)} \end{bmatrix}$ and $\delta(A^{-1}) = \dfrac{a_{22}a_{11}}{[\delta(A)]^2} - \dfrac{a_{12}a_{21}}{[\delta(A)]^2} = \dfrac{a_{22}a_{11} - a_{12}a_{21}}{[\delta(A)]^2}$

$= \dfrac{(\delta(A))}{[\delta(A)]^2} = \dfrac{1}{\delta(A)}$ **19.** From the results of Problem 43, Ex. 10.3, and Problem 17 above,

$\delta[B^{-1}AB] = \delta[B^{-1}(AB)] = \delta(B^{-1}) \cdot \delta(AB) = \delta(B^{-1}) \cdot \delta(A) \cdot \delta(B) = \dfrac{1}{\delta(B)} \cdot \delta(A) \cdot \delta(B) = \delta(A)$

Exercise 11.1 (Page 266)   **1.** $\{(1, 1)\}$ **3.** $\{(2, 2)\}$ **5.** $\{(6, 4)\}$ **7.** $\{(1, 1, 1)\}$
9. $\{(1, 1, 0)\}$ **11.** $\{(1, -2, 3)\}$ **13.** $\{(3, -1, -2)\}$

Exercise 11.2 Page 270)   **1.** $\{(\tfrac{13}{5}, \tfrac{3}{5})\}$ **3.** $\{(\tfrac{22}{7}, \tfrac{20}{7})\}$ **5.** Inconsistent

7. $\left\{\left(\dfrac{1}{a+b}, \dfrac{1}{a+b}\right)\right\}$ $(a \neq -b)$ **9.** $\{(1, 1, 0)\}$ **11.** $\{(1, -2, 3)\}$ **13.** $\{(3, -1, -2)\}$

15. $\{(-\tfrac{1}{3}, -\tfrac{25}{24}, -\tfrac{5}{8})\}$ **17.** $\{(-1, 1, 0, 2)\}$ **19.** $A = \begin{vmatrix} a_1 & b_1 \\ a_2 & b_2 \end{vmatrix}$ and $\delta(A) = a_1b_2 - a_2b_1$;

$Ay = \begin{vmatrix} a_1 & c_1 \\ a_2 & c_2 \end{vmatrix}$ and $\delta(Ay) = a_1c_2 - a_2c_1 = 0$, so $a_1c_2 = a_2c_1$; $Ax = \begin{vmatrix} c_1 & b_1 \\ c_2 & b_2 \end{vmatrix}$ and $\delta(Ax) =$

$b_2c_1 - b_1c_2 = 0$, so $b_1c_2 = b_2c_1$; hence $\dfrac{a_1c_2}{b_1c_2} = \dfrac{a_2c_1}{b_2c_1}$; $\dfrac{a_1}{b_1} = \dfrac{a_2}{b_2}$ and $a_1b_2 = a_2b_1$, so $a_1b_2 - a_2b_1 =$

0; therefore $\delta(A) = 0$

Exercise 11.3 (Page 276)   **1.** $\begin{bmatrix} 6 \\ 0 \end{bmatrix}$ **3.** $\begin{bmatrix} 2 \\ -3 \end{bmatrix}$ **5.** $\begin{bmatrix} x - 3y \\ -2x - y \end{bmatrix}$ **7.** $\begin{bmatrix} -1 \\ 3 \end{bmatrix}$

9. $\begin{bmatrix} \frac{3}{11} \\ \frac{-5}{11} \end{bmatrix}$ **11.** $\begin{bmatrix} b - 3a \\ 2 \\ a \end{bmatrix}$ **13.** $\begin{bmatrix} 0 & 1 \\ 1 & 0 \end{bmatrix} \cdot \begin{bmatrix} 1 & 0 \\ 0 & 2 \end{bmatrix}$ **15.** $\begin{bmatrix} 1 & 0 \\ 0 & 1 \end{bmatrix} \cdot \begin{bmatrix} 1 & 3 \\ 0 & 1 \end{bmatrix}$

17. Reflection in the line $y = x$; vertical multiplication with factor 2   **19.** New ordered pairs: (0,0), (3, 0), (3, 1), (0, 1); rectangle   **21.** New ordered pairs: (0, 0), (1, 0), (1, $\frac{1}{2}$), (0, $\frac{1}{2}$); rectangle   **23.** New ordered pairs: (0, 0), (1, 1), (1, 2), (0, 1); parallelogram   **25.** From $f = \{[X, f(X)] \mid f(X) = AX\}$ where A, X are 2×2 matrices, and Th. 10.4, $f(X_1 + X_2) = A(X_1 + X_2) = AX_1 + AX_2 = f(X_1) + f(X_2)$

Exercise 11.4 (Page 280)   **1.** $\begin{bmatrix} 1 & 0 & -1 & 2 \\ 0 & 1 & 1 & -1 \end{bmatrix}$ **3.** $\begin{bmatrix} 1 & 0 & \frac{4}{11} & \frac{3}{11} \\ 0 & 1 & \frac{1}{11} & -\frac{2}{11} \end{bmatrix}$

5. $\begin{bmatrix} 1 & 0 & 0 & 0 & \frac{1}{2} & -\frac{1}{2} \\ 0 & 1 & 0 & 0 & \frac{1}{4} & \frac{1}{4} \\ 0 & 0 & 1 & 1 & -\frac{5}{4} & -\frac{1}{4} \end{bmatrix}$ **7.** $\begin{bmatrix} 1 & 0 & 0 & -\frac{7}{11} & \frac{3}{11} & \frac{22}{11} \\ 0 & 1 & 0 & -\frac{7}{11} & \frac{3}{11} & \frac{11}{11} \\ 0 & 0 & 1 & \frac{16}{11} & -\frac{1}{11} & -\frac{11}{11} \end{bmatrix}$ **9.** $\begin{bmatrix} -1 & 2 \\ 1 & -1 \end{bmatrix}$

11. $\begin{bmatrix} \frac{4}{11} & \frac{3}{11} \\ \frac{1}{11} & -\frac{2}{11} \end{bmatrix}$ **13.** $\begin{bmatrix} 0 & \frac{1}{2} & -\frac{1}{2} \\ 0 & \frac{1}{4} & \frac{1}{4} \\ 1 & -\frac{5}{4} & -\frac{1}{4} \end{bmatrix}$ **15.** $\begin{bmatrix} -\frac{7}{11} & \frac{3}{11} & 2 \\ -\frac{7}{11} & \frac{3}{11} & 1 \\ \frac{16}{11} & -\frac{1}{11} & -1 \end{bmatrix}$

17. Let A, B, C, D, E be the respective matrices reading from left to right; then $DE = \begin{bmatrix} ad - bc & 0 \\ 0 & \frac{ad - bc}{a} \end{bmatrix}$; $C(DE) = \begin{bmatrix} a & 0 \\ 0 & \frac{ad - bc}{a} \end{bmatrix}$; $B(CDE) = \begin{bmatrix} a & b \\ 0 & \frac{ad - bc}{a} \end{bmatrix}$; and $A(BCDE) = \begin{bmatrix} a & b \\ c & d \end{bmatrix}$ **19.** $\begin{bmatrix} 0 & 1 \\ 1 & 0 \end{bmatrix}\begin{bmatrix} 1 & 0 \\ 0 & 1 \end{bmatrix}\begin{bmatrix} 1 & 3 \\ 0 & 1 \end{bmatrix}\begin{bmatrix} 1 & 0 \\ 0 & 1 \end{bmatrix}\begin{bmatrix} 2 & 0 \\ 0 & 1 \end{bmatrix}\begin{bmatrix} 1 & 0 \\ 0 & 1 \end{bmatrix} = \begin{bmatrix} 0 & 1 \\ 2 & 3 \end{bmatrix}$

Exercise 11.5 (Page 282)   **1.** $\{(2, -1)\}$ **3.** $\{(5, 1)\}$ **5.** $\{(8, 1)\}$ **7.** Since $y = z$ and $x = 2$, there are an infinite number of answers of the form $\{(2, a, a)\}$ where $a \in R$ **9.** $\{(\frac{5}{4}, \frac{5}{2}, -\frac{1}{2})\}$ **11.** $\{(-\frac{77}{27}, -\frac{8}{27}, \frac{29}{27})\}$

Exercise 12.1 (Page 288)   **1.** (5, 7)   **3.** (−6, −1)   **5.** (3, 7)   **7.** (3, 4)   **9.** (0, 2)   **11.** (5, 14)   **13.** (−2, 14)   **15.** (1, −5)   **17.** (−1, 7)   **19.** $(a_1 + a_2, 0)$; $(a_1 a_2, 0)$

21.

	If $a, b, c \in R$	If $(a, b), (c, d), (e, f) \in C$	
F-1	$a + b \in R$	$(a, b) + (c, d) \in C$	Closure law for addition
F-2	$(a + b) + c = a + (b + c)$	$[a, b) + (c, d)] + (e, f) = (a, b) + [(c, d) + (e, f)]$	Associative law for addition
F-3	There exists $0 \in R$ such that $a + 0 = 0 + a = a$	There exists $(0, 0) \in C$ such that $(a, b) + (0, 0) = (0, 0) + (a, b) = (a, b)$	Additive-identity law
F-4	For each $a \in R$, there exists $-a \in R$ such that $a + (-a) = 0$ and $(-a) + a = 0$	For each $(a, b) \in C$, there exists $-(a, b) \in C$ such that $(a, b) + [-(a, b)] = (0, 0)$ and $[-(a, b)] + (a, b) = (0, 0)$	Additive-inverse law

F-5	$a+b=b+a$	$(a,b)+(c,d)=(c,d)+(a,b)$	Commutative law for addition
F-6	$ab \in R$	$(a,b)\cdot(c,d) \in C$	Closure law for multiplication
F-7	$(ab)c=a(bc)$	$[(a,b)\cdot(c,d)]\cdot(e,f)=$ $(a,b)\cdot[(c,d)\cdot(e,f)]$	Associative law for multiplication
F-8	There exists $1 \in R$ such that $a \cdot 1 = a$ and $1 \cdot a = a$	There exists $(1,0) \in C$ such that $(a,b)\cdot(1,0)=(a,b)$ and $(1,0)\cdot(a,b)=(a,b)$	Multiplicative-identity law
F-9	For each $a \in R$, $a \neq 0$, there exists $a^{-1} \in R$, such that $aa^{-1}=1$ and $a^{-1}a=1$	For each $(a,b) \in C$, $(a,b) \neq (0,0)$, there exists $(a,b)^{-1} \in R$, such that $(a,b)\cdot(a,b)^{-1}=(1,0)$ and $(a,b)^{-1}\cdot(a,b)=(1,0)$	Multiplicative-inverse law
F-10	$ab=ba$	$(a,b)\cdot(c,d)=(c,d)\cdot(a,b)$	Commutative law for multiplication
F-11	$a(b+c)=ab+ac$ and $(b+c)a=ba+ca$	$(a,b)\cdot[(c,d)+(e,f)]=$ $(a,b)\cdot(c,d)+(a,b)\cdot(e,f)$ and $[(c,d)+(e,f)]\cdot(a,b) \doteq$ $(c,d)\cdot(a,b)+(e,f)\cdot(a,b)$	Distributive law

23. Let $z_1=(a_1,b_1)$ and $z_2=(a_2,b_2)$; then by Def. 12.3-I and F-5 for real numbers, $z_1+z_2=$ $(a_1,b_1)+(a_2,b_2)=(a_1+a_2,b_1+b_2)=(a_2+a_1,b_2+b_1)=z_2+z_1$ **25.** Let $z_1=(a_1,b_1)$, $z_2=(a_2,b_2)$, and $z_3=(a_3,b_3)$; then by Def. 12.13-II and F-11, F-2, F-5 for real numbers, $(z_1 \cdot z_2)z_3=[(a_1,b_1)\cdot(a_2,b_2)]\cdot(a_3,b_3)=[(a_1a_2-b_1b_2,\ a_1b_2+a_2b_1)]\cdot(a_3,b_3)=(a_1a_2-b_1b_2)\cdot$ $a_3-(a_1b_2+a_2b_1)b_3,\ (a_1a_2-b_1b_2)b_3+(a_1b_2+a_2b_1)a_3=a_1(a_2a_3-b_2b_3)-b_1(a_2b_3+b_2a_3),$ $a_1(a_2b_3+b_2a_3)+b_1(a_2a_3-b_2b_3)=(a_1,\ b_1)\cdot[a_2a_3-b_2b_3,\ a_2b_3+b_2a_3]=$ $(a_1,\ b_1)\cdot[(a_2,b_2)\cdot(a_3b_3)]$ **27.** $\left(\dfrac{a}{a^2+b_2},\dfrac{b}{a^2+b_2}\right)$, $(a^2+b^2) \neq 0$

Exercise 12.2 (Page 291)   **1.** $(3,1)$ **3.** $(-9,1)$ **5.** $(8,-8)$ **7.** $(\frac{7}{4},-\frac{1}{4})$ **9.** $(\frac{1}{10},-\frac{7}{10})$
11. $(-2,0)$ **13.** $(\frac{23}{37},\frac{27}{37})$ **15.** $(-\frac{2}{5},-\frac{9}{5})$ **17.** $(-\frac{5}{2},-\frac{1}{2})$ **19.** $(2,0)$ **21.** Let $z=(a,b)$; then $\bar{z}=(a,-b)$. From this result and Th. 12.3 and 12.4, $\dfrac{(a,b)}{(a,b)}=\dfrac{(a,b)\cdot(a,-b)}{(a,b)\cdot(a,-b)}=$ $\dfrac{(a^2+b^2,0)}{(a^2+b^2,0)}=\left(\dfrac{a^2+b^2}{a^2+b^2},\dfrac{0}{a^2+b^2}\right)=(1,0)$ **23.** Let $z_1=(a_1,b_1)$, $z_2=(a_2,b_2)$; then $\bar{z}_1=$ $(a_1,-b_1)$, $\bar{z}_2=(a_2,-b_2)$. $\bar{z}_1+\bar{z}_2=(a_1,-b)+(a_2,-b_2)=[(a_1+a_2),\ -(b_1+b_2)]=\overline{z_1+z_2}$ **25.** For F-1: $(a,0)+(b,0)=(a+b,0) \in C$. For F-2: $[(a,0)+(b,0)]+(c,0)=[a+b,0]$ $+(c,0)=[(a+b)+c,0]=[a+(b+c),0]=(a,0)+[b+c,0]=(a,0)+[(b,0)+(c,0)]$. For F-3: $(0,0)$ is the additive-identity law since $(a,0)+(0,0)=(a+0,0)=(a,0)$ and $(0,0)+(a,0)=$ $(0+a,0)=(a,0)$.   For F-4: $(-a,0)$ is the additive-inverse law since $(a,0)+(-a,0)=$ $(a-a,0)=(0,0)$ and $(-a,0)+(a,0)=(-a+a,0)=(0,0)$.   For F-5: $(a,0)+(b,0)=$ $(a+b,0)=(b+a,0)=(b,0)+(a,0)$.   For F-6: $(a,0)\cdot(b,0)=(ab-0,0+0)=(ab,0) \in C$. For F-7: $[(a,0)\cdot(b,0)]\cdot(c,0)=[ab,0]\cdot(c,0)=[(ab)c,0]=[a(bc),0]=(a,0)\cdot[bc,0]=$ $(a,0)\cdot[(b,0)\cdot(c,0)]$.   For F-8: $(1,0)$ is the multiplicative-identity law since $(a,0)\cdot(1,0)=$ $(a,0)$ and $(1,0)\cdot(a,0)=(a.0)$. For F-9: use $\left(\dfrac{1}{a},0\right)$ for multiplicative-inverse law since if

$a \neq 0$, $(a, 0) \cdot \left(\dfrac{1}{a}, 0\right) = (1, 0)$ and $\left(\dfrac{1}{a}, 0\right) \cdot (a, 0) = (1, 0)$. For F-10: $(a, 0) \cdot (b, 0) = (ab, 0) =$

$(ba, 0) = (b, 0) \cdot (a, 0)$. For F-11: $(a, 0) \cdot [(b, 0) + (c, 0)] = (a, 0) \cdot [b + c, 0] = [ab + ac, 0] =$
$(ab, 0) + (ac, 0) = (a, 0) \cdot (b, 0) + (a, 0) \cdot (c, 0)$; $[(b, 0) + (c, 0)] \cdot (a, 0) = [b + c, 0] \cdot (a, 0) =$
$[ba + ca, 0] = (ba, 0) + (ca, 0) = (b, 0) \cdot (a, 0) + (c, 0) + (a, 0)$

Exercise 12.3 (Page 296) **1.** $2 + 6i$ **3.** $5 - 2i$ **5.** $-7 - 3i$ **7.** $4 + 0i$ **9.** $(2, 3)$
11. $(-3, 1)$ **13.** $(0, 4)$ **15.** $(7, 0)$ **17.** $2 - 3i$ **19.** $-3 - i$ **21.** $0 - 4i$ **23.** $7 - 0i$
25. $x = \frac{3}{2}, y = -2$ **27.** $x = 2, y = -2; x = -2, y = 2$ **29.** $x = 3, y = 9; x = -3, y = -9$

31. $5 + 5i$ **33.** $5 - 3i$ **35.** $-1 - 2i$ **37.** $1 + i$ **39.** $-\dfrac{1}{10} + \dfrac{7}{10}i$ **41.** $-8 - 6i$

43. $2 - 2i$ **45.** $4 - i\sqrt{7}$ **47.** $5 - 2i$ **49.** $-\sqrt{7}$ **51.** $1 - i$ **53.** $\dfrac{4}{13} + \dfrac{7}{13}i$

55. $\{i, -i\}$ **57.** $\left\{1, \dfrac{1}{2}\right\}$ **59.** $\left\{-\dfrac{1}{3}, 1 + \sqrt{5}, 1 - \sqrt{5}\right\}$ **61.** $\left\{-1, \dfrac{1}{2}, -\dfrac{1}{2} + i\dfrac{\sqrt{3}}{2}, -\dfrac{1}{2} - i\dfrac{\sqrt{3}}{2}\right\}$

63. $(x - i)(x + i)(2x + 3)$ **65.** Let $x = \sqrt{3}$; then $x^2 = 3$, and $x^2 - 3 = 0$ is an equation with
real coefficients with $\sqrt{3}$ a root; the only possible rational roots are ± 1, ± 3, and substitution
shows none of these satisfies the equation and consequently cannot be roots. Since the equation
has no rational roots, but $\sqrt{3}$ is a root, it must be irrational

Exercise 12.4 (Page 301)

1.

3.

5.

7. 4 **9.** $\sqrt{13}$ **11.** 2 **13.** $\sqrt{5}$ **15.** $3\sqrt{2}$ cis $45°$ **17.** 5 cis $0°$ **19.** 4 cis$(-30°)$

21. $-2 - 2\sqrt{3}i$ **23.** $3\sqrt{3} - 3i$ **25.** $6 + 6\sqrt{3}i$ **27. a.** $-3 + 3i$ **b.** $\dfrac{3}{2} + \dfrac{3}{2}i$ **29. a.** 108

b. $\dfrac{1}{6} - \dfrac{\sqrt{3}}{6}i$ **31. a.** $10 + 10i$ **b.** $\dfrac{1}{10} - \dfrac{7}{10}i$ **33.** $1 + 0i$ **35.** Let $z = a + bi$; then
$\bar{z} = a - bi$. $(a + bi) + (a - bi) = (a + a) + (b - b)i = 2a + 0i = 2a \in R$; $(a + bi) \cdot (a - bi) =$
$(a^2 + b^2) + (ab - ab)i = (a^2 + b^2) + 0i = (a^2 + b^2) \in R$ **37.** r cis $\theta = r(\cos \theta + i \sin \theta) =$
$r \cos \theta + (r \sin \theta)i = a + bi$, where $a = r \cos \theta$ and $b = r \sin \theta$. For $(a + bi)$, $\bar{z} = a - bi =$
$a - bi = r \cos \theta - r \sin \theta i = r \cos(-\theta) + [r \sin(-\theta)]i = r$ cis$(-\theta)$ **39.** From the result of
Problem 38, and from Th. 12.7-I, $(a + bi)^3 = (a + bi)^2(a + bi) = (r^2$ cis $2\theta)(r$ cis $\theta) =$
r^3 cis $(2\theta + \theta) = r^3$ cis 3θ

Exercise 12.5 (Page 304)   **1.** $-64\sqrt{3} + 64i$ **3.** $1 + 0i$ **5.** $729\left(\dfrac{1}{2} + \dfrac{\sqrt{3}}{2}i\right)$

7. $\dfrac{1}{64}(-\sqrt{3} + i)$ **9.** $\dfrac{\sqrt{2}}{32}(0.2588 - 0.9659i)$ **11.** $-\dfrac{1}{\sqrt{2}} - \dfrac{1}{\sqrt{2}}i$

13. 2 cis 9°; 2 cis 81°; 2 cis 153°; 2 cis 225°; 2 cis 297°   **15.** 2 cis 30°; 2 cis 102°; 2 cis 174°; 2 cis 246°; 2 cis 318°   **17.** cis 45°; cis 105°; cis 165°; cis 225°; cis 285°; cis 345°   **19.** 2 cis 60°; 2 cis 132°; 2 cis 204°; 2 cis 276°; 2 cis 348°   **21.** cis $25\frac{5}{7}°$; cis $77\frac{1}{7}°$; cis $128\frac{4}{7}°$; cis 180°; cis $231\frac{3}{7}°$; cis $282\frac{6}{7}°$; cis $334\frac{2}{7}°$ **23.** $(x - 2 \text{ cis } 45°)(x - 2 \text{ cis } 135°)(x - 2 \text{ cis } 225°)(x - 2 \text{ cis } 315°)$ **25.** The four roots are $-1, 1, i, -i$; hence their sum is $0 + 0i$ **27.** By De Moivre's Theorem, $(\cos \theta + i \sin \theta)^3 = \cos 3\theta + i \sin 3\theta$. Since, $(\cos \theta + i \sin \theta)^3 = \cos^3 \theta + 3i \cos^2 \theta \sin \theta + 3i^2 \cos \theta \sin^2 \theta + i^3 \sin^3 \theta$, $i^2 = -1$, $i^3 = i$, $\cos^2 \theta = (1 - \sin^2 \theta)$, and $\sin^2 \theta = (1 - \cos^2 \theta)$, the left-hand member reduces to $(4 \cos^3 \theta - 3 \cos \theta) + (3 \sin \theta - 4 \sin^3 \theta) i$; Now, $(4 \cos^3 \theta - 3 \cos \theta) + (3 \sin \theta - 4 \sin^3 \theta) i = \cos 3\theta + (\sin 3\theta)i$. Hence by Definition of Equality of two complex numbers, $\cos 3\theta = 4 \cos^3 \theta - 3 \cos \theta$ and $\sin 3\theta = 3 \sin \theta - 4 \sin^3 \theta$

Exercise 12.6 (Page 310)

1. $(8, 5), \sqrt{89}, \approx 32°$ **3.** $(-1, 3), \sqrt{10}, \approx 108° 30'$ **5.** $(5, 9), \sqrt{106}, \approx 61°$

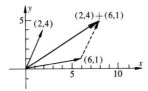

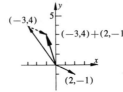

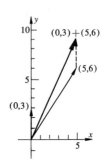

7. $(8, 6), 10, \approx 36° 50,$ **9.** $(8, 1), \sqrt{65}, \approx 7° 10'$ **11.** $(3, 1), \sqrt{10}, \approx 18° 20'$

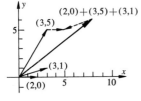

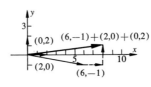

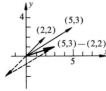

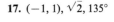

13. $(-4, 5), \sqrt{41}, \approx 128° 40'$ **15.** $(0, 8), 8, 90°$ **17.** $(-1, 1), \sqrt{2}, 135°$

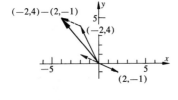

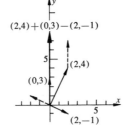

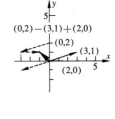

19. $(11, 11), 11\sqrt{2}, 45°$

21. $(-6, 1), \sqrt{37}, \approx 170° 30'$

23. $(3, 10), \sqrt{109}, \approx 73° 20,$

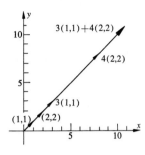

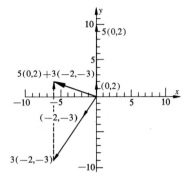

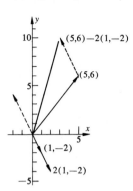

25. $(-8, 12), 4\sqrt{13}, \approx 123° 40'$

27. $(10, 4), 2\sqrt{29}, \approx 21° 50'$

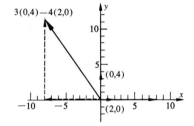

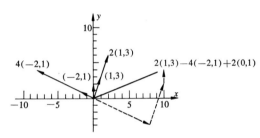

29. $\sqrt{53}, \approx 74°, \dfrac{2}{\sqrt{53}}\mathbf{x} + \dfrac{7}{\sqrt{53}}\mathbf{y}$

31. $\sqrt{10}, \approx -18° 30', \dfrac{3}{\sqrt{10}}\mathbf{x} - \dfrac{1}{\sqrt{10}}\mathbf{y}$

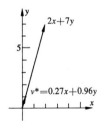

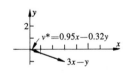

33. $\sqrt{85}, \approx -130° 40', -\dfrac{6}{\sqrt{85}}\mathbf{x} - \dfrac{7}{\sqrt{85}}\mathbf{y}$

35. $3, 90°, \mathbf{y}$

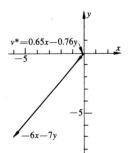

37. $\mathbf{v} = x\mathbf{x} + y\mathbf{y}$ and $\|\mathbf{v}\| = \sqrt{x^2 + y^2}$ and for $\mathbf{v}$, $\theta = \cos^{-1}\dfrac{x}{\sqrt{x^2 + y^2}}$; $\mathbf{v}^* = \dfrac{x}{\|\mathbf{v}\|}\mathbf{x} + \dfrac{y}{\|\mathbf{v}\|}\mathbf{y} =$

$\dfrac{x}{\sqrt{x^2 + y^2}}\mathbf{x} + \dfrac{y}{\sqrt{x^2 + y^2}}\mathbf{y}$ and $\|\mathbf{v}^*\| = \sqrt{\dfrac{x^2}{x^2 + y^2} + \dfrac{y^2}{x^2 + y^2}} = \sqrt{\dfrac{x^2 + y^2}{x^2 + y^2}} = \sqrt{1} = 1$; further, for

$\mathbf{v}^*$, $\theta = \cos^{-1}\left(\dfrac{x}{\sqrt{x^2 + y^2}/1}\right) = \cos^{-1}\dfrac{x}{\sqrt{x^2 + y^2}}$. Therefore $\mathbf{v}^*$ is unit vector with same direction

as $\mathbf{v}$.

Exercise 12.7 (Page 314)   **1.** $(4, 4)$ **3.** $(9, -6)$ **5.** $(5, 3)$ **7.** $(2, -10)$ **9.** $(5, -12)$
11. $(10, 15)$ **13.** $(-8, 14)$ **15.** $\sqrt{520,000}$ miles   **17.** 80 lbs   **19.** Magnitude, 21.6 lbs;
$\theta = -93°\ 40'$

Exercise 13.1 (Page 320)   **1. a.** For $n = 1$: $\dfrac{n}{2} = \dfrac{1}{2}$; $\dfrac{n(n+1)}{4} = \dfrac{1(1+1)}{4} = \dfrac{1}{2}$.   **b.** For $n = k$:

$\dfrac{1}{2} + \dfrac{2}{2} + \dfrac{3}{2} + \cdots + \dfrac{k}{2} = \dfrac{k(k+1)}{4}$ and $(k+1)$th term $= \dfrac{k+1}{2}$; hence $\dfrac{1}{2} + \dfrac{2}{2} + \dfrac{3}{2} + \cdots + \dfrac{k}{2} + \dfrac{k+1}{2}$

$= \dfrac{k(k+1)}{4} + \dfrac{k+1}{2} = \dfrac{k^2 + k + 2k + 2}{4} = \dfrac{k^2 + 3k + 2}{4} = \dfrac{(k+1)(k+2)}{4}$ **3. a.** For $n = 1$: $2n =$

$2(1) = 2$; $n(n+1) = 1(1+1) = 2$.   **b.** For $n = k$: $2 + 4 + 6 + \cdots + 2k = k(k+1)$ and $(k+1)$th
term is $2(k+1)$; hence $2 + 4 + 6 + \cdots + 2k + 2(k+1) = k(k+1) + 2(k+1) = (k+1)(k+2)$
5. a. For $n = 1$: $n^2 = 1^2 = 1$; $\dfrac{n(n+1)(2n+1)}{6} = \dfrac{1(2)(3)}{6} = 1$.   **b.** For $n = k$: $1^2 + 2^2 + 3^2$

$+ \cdots + k^2 = \dfrac{k(k+1)(2k+1)}{6}$ and $(k+1)$th term is $(k+1)^2$; hence $1^2 + 2^2 + 3^2 + \cdots + k^2$

$+ (k+1)^2 = \dfrac{k(k+1)(2k+1)}{6} + (k+1)^2 = \dfrac{k(k+1)(2k+1) + 6(k+1)^2}{6} =$

$\dfrac{(k+1)[k(2k+1) + 6(k+1)]}{6} = \dfrac{(k+1)(2k^2 + 7k + 6)}{6} = \dfrac{(k+1)(k+2)(2k+3)}{6} =$

$\dfrac{(k+1)[(k+1) + 1][2(k+1) + 1]}{6}$ **7. a.** For $n = 1$: $(2n - 1)^3 = (2 - 1)^3 = 1^3 = 1$; $n^2(2n^2 - 1)$

$= 1(2 - 1) = 1(1) = 1$.   **b.** For $n = k$: $1^3 + 3^3 + 5^3 + \cdots + (2k - 1)^3 = k^2(2k^2 - 1)$ and the
$(k+1)$th term is $[2(k+1) - 1]^3 = (2k+1)^3$; hence $1^3 + 3^3 + 5^3 + \cdots + (2k - 1)^3 + (2k+1)^3 =$
$k^2(2k^2 - 1) + (2k - 1)^3 = 2k^4 + 8k^3 + 11k^2 + 6k + 1$; by use of the Factor Theorem and synthetic division, $2k^4 + 8k^3 + 11k^2 + 6k + 1 = (k+1)(k+1)(2k^2 + 4k + 1)$; also, $2k^2 + 4k + 1 =$
$2(k^2 + 2k + 1) - 2 + 1 = 2(k+1)^2 - 1$; hence $2k^4 + 8k^3 + 11k^2 + 6k + 1 = (k+1)^2[2(k+1)^2$

$- 1]$ **9. a.** For $n = 1$: $n(n+1) = 1(2) = 2$; $\dfrac{n(n+1)(n+2)}{3} = \dfrac{1(2)(3)}{3} = 2$.   **b.** For $n = k$:

$1 \cdot 2 + 2 \cdot 3 + 3 \cdot 4 + \cdots + k(k+1) = \dfrac{k(k+1)(k+2)}{3}$ and the $(k+1)$th term is $(k+1)[(k+1)$

$+ 1] = (k+1)(k+2)$; hence $1 \cdot 2 + 2 \cdot 3 + 3 \cdot 4 + \cdots + k(k+1) + [(k+1)(k+2)] =$
$\dfrac{k(k+1)(k+2)}{3} + (k+1)(k+2) = \dfrac{[k(k+1)(k+2)] + [3(k+1)(k+2)]}{3} = \dfrac{(k+1)(k+2)(k+3)}{3}$

$= \dfrac{(k+1)[(k+1) + 1][(k+1) + 2]}{3}$ **11.** For $n = k$: $2 + 4 + 6 + \cdots + 2k = k(k+1) + 2$ and

$(k+1)$th term is $2(k+1)$; hence $2 + 4 + 6 + \cdots + 2k + 2(k+1) = k(k+1) + 2 + 2(k+1) =$
$(k^2 + 3k + 2) + 2 = (k+1)(k+2) + 2 = (k+1)[(k+1) + 1] + 2$. However, for $n = 1$: $2n =$
$2(1) = 2$; $n(n+1) + 2 = 1(2) + 2 = 4$. Hence not true for every $n \in N$ **13. a.** For $n = 1$:

$n = 1$; $\frac{1}{8}(2n + 1)^2 = \frac{9}{8}(3)^2 = \frac{9}{8}$; and $1 < \frac{9}{8}$. **b.** For $n = k$: $1 + 2 + 3 + \cdots + k < \frac{1}{8}(2k + 1)^2$ and $(k + 1)$th term is $(k + 1)$; hence $1 + 2 + 3 \cdots + k + (k + 1) < \frac{1}{8}(2k + 1)^2 + (k + 1)$ where the right-hand member reduces to $\dfrac{4k^2 + 12k + 9}{8} = \dfrac{(2k + 3)^2}{8} = \frac{1}{8}[2(k + 1) + 1]^2$ **15. a.** For $n = 1$,

$\bar{z}_1 = \bar{z}_1$; **b.** For $n = k$, $\overline{\bar{z}_1 + \bar{z}_2 + \cdots + \bar{z}_k} = \bar{z}_1 + \bar{z}_2 + \cdots \bar{z}_k + \bar{z}_{k+1}$; from Problem 23, Exercise 12.2, $\overline{z_1 + z_2 + \cdots z_k} + \bar{z}_{k+1} = \overline{z_1 + z_2 + \cdots + z_k + z_{k+1}}$ **17.** By Problem 16, $P(\bar{z}_0) = \overline{P(z_0)} = \bar{0} = 0$

Exercise 13.2 (Page 324)   **1.** $-4, -3, -2, -1$ **3.** $-\frac{1}{2}, 1, \frac{7}{2}, 7$ **5.** $2, \frac{3}{2}, \frac{4}{3}, \frac{5}{4}$ **7.** $0, 1, 3, 6$
9. $-1, 1, -1, 1$ **11.** $1, 0, -\frac{1}{3}, \frac{1}{2}$ **13.** $11, 15, 19$ **15.** $x + 2, x + 3, x + 4$ **17.** $2x + 7$,
$2x + 10, 2x + 13$ **19.** $32, 128, 512, 2048$ **21.** $\frac{8}{3}, \frac{16}{3}, \frac{32}{3}, \frac{64}{3}$ **23.** $\dfrac{x}{a}, -\dfrac{x^2}{a^2}, \dfrac{x^3}{a^3}, -\dfrac{x^4}{a^4}$ **25.** 31
27. -92 **29.** 1536   **31.** $(-3)^{n-2}a^{3n-1}$ **33.** $2; 3; 41$ **35.** 28th   **37.** 3   **39. a.** For $n = 1$: $s_n = s_1 = a$; $ar^{n-1} = a(r)^0 = a(1) = a$.   **b.** For $n = k$: $s_k = ar^{k-1}$; to obtain s_{k+1} multiply s_k by r; hence, multiplying both sides by r, $s_{k(r)} = s_{k+1} = (ar^{k-1})(r) = ar^{k-1+1} = ar^{(k+1)-1}$

Exercise 13.3 (Page 329)   **1.** $1 + 4 + 9 + 16$ **3.** $-\frac{1}{2} + \frac{1}{4} - \frac{1}{8} + \frac{1}{16}$ **5.** $1 + \frac{1}{2} + \frac{1}{4} + \cdots$
7. $\displaystyle\sum_{j=1}^{4} x^{2j-1}$ **9.** $\displaystyle\sum_{j=1}^{5} j^2$ **11.** $\displaystyle\sum_{j=1}^{\infty} j(j + 1)$ **13.** $\displaystyle\sum_{j=1}^{\infty} \dfrac{j + 1}{j}$ **15.** 63   **17.** 806   **19.** -6
21. 1092   **23.** $\frac{31}{32}$ **25.** $\frac{364}{729}$ **27.** 168   **29.** 196   **31.** $\frac{3}{4}, \frac{7}{8}, \frac{15}{16}, \frac{31}{32}; 1$ **33.** $p = 4$, $q = -3$ **35.** Since $s_n = a + (n - 1)d$ and $S_{n+1} = S_n + s_n$, it follows that **a.** For $n = 1$: $S_n = s_n = s_1 = a$; $\dfrac{n}{2}(a + s_n) = \dfrac{1}{2}(2a) = a$.   **b.** For $n = k$: $S_k = \dfrac{k}{2}(a + s_k)$, $s_k = a + (k - 1)d$; now $s_{k+1} = a + [(k + 1) - 1]d = a + kd$; adding to both sides produces $S_k + s_{k+1} = S_{k+1} = \dfrac{k}{2}(a + s_k) + (a + kd) = \dfrac{k}{2}[a + a + (k - 1)d] + \dfrac{2}{2}(a + kd) = \dfrac{2ka + k^2d - kd + 2a + 2kd}{2} = \dfrac{2ka + 2a + k^2d + kd}{2} = \dfrac{(k + 1)2a + k(k + 1)d}{2} = \dfrac{(k + 1)}{2}[2a + kd] = \dfrac{k + 1}{2}[a + (a + kd)] = \dfrac{k + 1}{2}[a + s_{n+1}]$ **37.** Let $s_1, s_2, s_3, \cdots, s_n$ and $t_1, t_2, t_3, \cdots, t_n$ be two sequences with terms in arithmetic progression; then, by Problem 36 above; $(s_1 + t_1), (s_2 + t_2), \cdots, (s_n + t_n)$ is also a sequence with terms in arithmetic progression. $S_1 = s_1 + s_2 + s_3 + \cdots + s_n = \displaystyle\sum_{j=1}^{n} s_j$, $S_2 = t_1 + t_2 + t_3 + \cdots + t_n = \displaystyle\sum_{j=1}^{n} t_j$, and $S_1 + S_2 = \displaystyle\sum_{j=1}^{n} s_j + \displaystyle\sum_{j=1}^{n} t_j$; however, $(S_1 + S_2) = (s_1 + t_1) + (s_2 + t_2) + \cdots + (s_n + t_n)$, and $S_1 + S_2 = \displaystyle\sum_{j=1}^{n} (sj + tj)$; hence $\displaystyle\sum_{j=1}^{n} sj + \displaystyle\sum_{j=1}^{n} tj = \displaystyle\sum_{j=1}^{n} (sj + tj)$

Exercise 13.4 (Page 336)   **1.** $\displaystyle\lim_{n \to \infty} s_n = 0$ **3.** $\displaystyle\lim_{n \to \infty} s_n = 1$ **5.** $\displaystyle\lim_{n \to \infty} s_n$ is undefined
7. $\displaystyle\lim_{n \to \infty} s_n = 0$ **9.** Convergent, $\displaystyle\lim_{n \to \infty} \left|0 - \dfrac{1}{2^n}\right| = 0$ **11.** Divergent, $\displaystyle\lim_{n \to \infty} n$ is undefined
13. Convergent, $\displaystyle\lim_{n \to \infty} \left|0 - (-1)^{n+1} \dfrac{1}{2^{n-1}}\right| = 0$ **15.** 24   **17.** No sum   **19.** 2   **21.** $\frac{31}{99}$
23. $2\frac{410}{999}$ **25.** $\frac{29}{225}$ **27.** 20 cm   **29.** 0.980   **31.** 0.920   **33.** 0.296   **35.** 1   **37.** -1

Exercise 13.5 (Page 340)   **1.** 24   **3.** 9   **5.** 15   **7.** 6   **9.** $\frac{1}{6}$ **11.** $\frac{21}{19}$ **13.** $(n + 1)(n + 2)$
15. $\dfrac{n + 1}{n + 3}$ **17.** $x^5 + 5x^4y + 10x^3y^2 + 10x^2y^3 + 5xy^4 + y^5$ **19.** $x^4 - 12x^3 + 54x^2 - 108x + 81$

21. $8x^3 - 6x^2y + \dfrac{3}{2}xy^2 - \dfrac{y^3}{8}$ **23.** $\dfrac{x^6}{64} + \dfrac{3x^5}{8} + \dfrac{15x^4}{4} + 20x^3 + 60x^2 + 96x + 64$

25. $x^{20} + \dfrac{20}{1}x^{19}y + \dfrac{20 \cdot 19}{1 \cdot 2}x^{18}y^2 + \dfrac{20 \cdot 19 \cdot 18}{1 \cdot 2 \cdot 3}x^{17}y^3 + \cdots$ **27.** $a^{12} + \dfrac{12}{1}a^{11}(-2b)$

$+ \dfrac{12 \cdot 11}{1 \cdot 2}a^{10}(-2b)^2 + \dfrac{12 \cdot 11 \cdot 10}{1 \cdot 2 \cdot 3}a^9(-2b)^3 + \cdots$ **29.** $x^{10} + \dfrac{10}{1}x^9(-\sqrt{2}) + \dfrac{10 \cdot 9}{1 \cdot 2}x^8(-\sqrt{2})^2$

$+ \dfrac{10 \cdot 9 \cdot 8}{1 \cdot 2 \cdot 3}x^7(-\sqrt{2})^3 + \cdots$ **31.** 1.22   **33.** 0.296   **35.** \$1,216.65   **37.** $-3003a^{10}b^5$

39. $3360x^6y^4$ **41.** $1 - x + x^2 - x^3$ **43. a.** For $n = 1$: $n! = 1! = 1$; $n(n-1)(n-2) \cdots 1 = 1$.
b. For $n = k$: by given definition, $(k+1)! = (k+1)\,k!$; using this fact and $k! = k(k-1)(k-2) \cdots 1$ and multiplying both members of the latter equation by $(k+1)$ yields $(k+1)\,k! = (k+1)(k)(k-1)(k-2) \cdots 1$;
$$(k+1)! = (k+1)[(k+1)-1][(k+1)-2][(k+1)-3] \cdots 1$$

Exercise 14.1 (Page 346)   **1.** 1, 5, 8   **3.** 2, 6, 16   **5.** 2, 2, 4   **7.** 4   **9.** 24   **11.** 16
13. 64   **15.** 10^7, or 10,000,000   **17.** 216   **19.** 375   **21.** 18   **23.** 6   **25.** 48

27. $\dfrac{5!}{2!}$ or 60   **29.** $\dfrac{8!}{3!}$, or 6720   **31.** $P_{5,3} = \dfrac{5!}{2!} = \dfrac{5 \cdot 4!}{2!} = 5\left(\dfrac{4!}{2!}\right) = 5(P_{4,2})$ **33.** $P_{n,3} =$

$\dfrac{n!}{(n-3)!} = \dfrac{n(n-1)!}{(n-3)!} = n\left[\dfrac{(n-1)!}{(n-3)!}\right] = n(P_{n-1,1})$ **35.** 9   **37.** 24   **39.** 48

Exercise 14.2 (Page 350)   **1.** 7   **3.** 15   **5.** $\dbinom{52}{5}$ **7.** $\dbinom{13}{5} \cdot \dbinom{13}{5} \cdot \dbinom{13}{3}$ **9.** $4 \cdot \dbinom{13}{5}$

11. 164   **13.** 10   **15.** 210   **17.** 12   **19.** $\dbinom{10}{10}a^{10} + \dbinom{10}{9}a^9b + \dbinom{10}{8}a^8b^2 + \dbinom{10}{7}a^7b^3 + \cdots$

Exercise 14.3 (Page 352)   **1.** $\{1, 2, 3, 4, 5, 6\}, \{3, 4, 5, 6\}$ **3.** $\{(h, h), (h, t), (t, h), (t, t)\}$,
$\{(h, h), (t, t)\}$ **5.** $\{(3, 4), (3, 5), (3, 6), (4, 5), (4, 6), (5, 6)\}, \{(3, 4), (3, 6), (4, 5), (5, 6)\}$
7. $\{(r, w), (w, b)\}$ **9.** 63   **11.** $\dbinom{6}{0} + \dbinom{6}{1} + \dbinom{6}{2} + \dbinom{6}{3} + \dbinom{6}{4} + \dbinom{6}{5} + \dbinom{6}{6} =$
$1 + 6 + 15 + 20 + 15 + 6 + 1 = 64 = 2^6$

Exercise 14.4 (Page 357)   **1.** $\frac{1}{6}$ **3.** $\frac{7}{18}$ **5.** $\frac{13}{18}$ **7.** $\frac{5}{33}$ **9.** $\frac{1}{11}$ **11.** $\frac{5}{22}$ **13.** $\frac{14}{33}$
15. $\frac{15}{22}$ **17.** $\frac{3}{13}$ **19.** $\frac{15}{77}, \frac{16}{77}, \frac{46}{77}$ **21.** \$2.14; less   **23.** 5.3 cents   **25.** \$3.29

Exercise 14.5 (Page 361)   **1.** $\frac{20}{91}$; no   **3. a.** $\frac{2}{45}$ **b.** $\frac{28}{75}$ **c.** $\frac{4}{225}$ **d.** $\frac{1}{9}$ **5. a.** $\frac{1}{3}$ **b.** $\frac{5}{36}$
c. $\frac{1}{6}$ **d.** No   **7. a.** $\frac{1}{2}$ **b.** $\frac{1}{2}$ **c.** $\frac{1}{4}$ **d.** $\frac{1}{4}$ **e.** $\frac{1}{8}$ **9. a.** $\frac{71}{72}$ **b.** $\frac{5}{9}$ **c.** $\frac{5}{36}$ **d.** $\frac{61}{72}$ **11. a.** $\frac{1}{210}$
b. $\frac{29}{210}$ **c.** $\frac{29}{70}$ **d.** $\frac{29}{30}$; yes

INDEX

INDEX

Division (*continued*)
  of real numbers, 12
  synthetic, 40
Domain:
  of an exponential function, 138
  of a logarithmic function, 141
  of a relation or function, 89
  of cosecant function, 182
  of cosine function, 157
  of cotangent function, 182
  of secant function, 182
  of sine function, 157
  of tangent function, 181
  of trigonometric functions, 200
Double-angle formula:
  for cosine function, 178, 202
  for sine function, 178, 202
  for tangent function, 183, 202
Double subscript notation, 236

E

e, 152
Element:
  of a matrix, 235
  of a set, 1
Elementary matrix:
  definition, 275
  inverse, 275
  products of, 276
Elementary transformation:
  in terms of matrices, 273
  of an equation, 66
  of an inequality, 79
Ellipsc, 104
Empty set, 2
Entry of a matrix, 235
Equality:
  addition law for, 15
  multiplication law for, 15
  of complex numbers, 284
  of like powers, 74
  of matrices, 236
  of ordered pairs, 284
  of quotients, 18

Equality (*continued*)
  of sets, 1
  of vectors, 306
  properties of, 9
Equation(s):
  conditional, 228, 232
  elementary transformation of an, 66
  equivalent, 65
  first-degree, in one variable, 65
  first-degree, in two variables, 87, 93
  graph of a linear, in two variables, 94
  inconsistent, 269
  in one variable, 65*ff*
  intercept form, 99
  in three variables, 108
  in two variables, 87
  linear, in one variable, 65
  linear, in two variables, 87, 93
  point-slope form, 96
  polar form, 220
  quadratic, in one variable, 68
  radical, 74*ff*
  second-degree, in one variable, 68
  slope-intercept form, 97
  solution of an, 65*ff*, 228
  solution set of an, 65
  two-point form, 99
Equivalence axioms, 10
Equivalence symbol, 2
Equivalent expressions, 27
Equivalent open sentences, 65
Equivalent rational expressions, 45
Euler's formula, 336
Even function, 162
Event(s):
  as a subset of a sample space, 352
  complementary, 352
  dependent, 359
  independent, 358, 359
  mutually exclusive, 356
  number of, possible in a sample space, 352
  probability of an, 353

ANALYTICAL GEOMETRY
SUPPLEMENTAL INDEX